C000255916

STRE 5

Dorset

Bournemouth and Poole

First published in 2002 by

Philip's, a division of
Octopus Publishing Group Ltd
2-4 Heron Quays, London E14 4JP

Second edition 2006
First impression 2006
DORBA

ISBN-10   0-540-08775-0 (pocket)
ISBN-13   978-0-540-08775-4 (pocket)

© Philip's 2006

Ordnance Survey®

This product includes mapping data licensed from
Ordnance Survey® with the permission of the
Controller of Her Majesty's Stationery Office.
© Crown copyright 2006. All rights reserved.
Licence number 100011710.

Printed by Toppan, China

Contents

III	**Key to map symbols**
IV	**Key to map pages**
VI	**Route planning**
X	**Administrative and Postcode boundaries**
1	**Street maps** at 2⅔ inches to 1 mile
188	**Street maps** at 1⅓ inches to 1 mile
212	**Street map** at 2⅔ inches to 1 mile
213	**Index** of towns and villages
216	**Index** of streets, hospitals, industrial estates, railway stations, schools, shopping centres, universities and places of interest

Digital Data

The exceptionally high-quality mapping found in this atlas is available as digital data in TIFF format, which is easily convertible to other bitmapped (raster) image formats.

The index is also available in digital form as a standard database table. It contains all the details found in the printed index together with the National Grid reference for the map square in which each entry is named.

For further information and to discuss your requirements, please contact Philip's on 020 7644 6932 or james.mann@philips-maps.co.uk

Motorway with junction number		◆	**Ambulance station**
Primary route – dual/single carriageway		◆	**Coastguard station**
A road – dual/single carriageway		◆	**Fire station**
B road – dual/single carriageway		◆	**Police station**
Minor road – dual/single carriageway		✚	**Accident and Emergency entrance to hospital**
Other minor road – dual/single carriageway		Ⓗ	**Hospital**
Road under construction		✛	**Place of worship**
Tunnel, covered road		🅸	**Information Centre** (open all year)
Rural track, private road or narrow road in urban area		🛒	**Shopping Centre**
Gate or obstruction to traffic (restrictions may not apply at all times or to all vehicles)		Ⓟ P&R	**Parking, Park and Ride**
Path, bridleway, byway open to all traffic, road used as a public path		PO	**Post Office**
		⋏	**Camping site**
Pedestrianised area		🚐	**Caravan site**
Postcode boundaries DY7		►	**Golf course**
County and unitary authority boundaries		⊠	**Picnic site**
Railway, tunnel, railway under construction		Prim Sch	**Important buildings, schools, colleges, universities and hospitals**
Tramway, tramway under construction			**Built up area**
Miniature railway			**Woods**
Railway station Walsall		River Ouse	**Tidal water, water name**
Private railway station			**Non-tidal water** – lake, river, canal or stream
Metro station South Shields			
Tram stop, tram stop under construction			**Lock, weir, tunnel**
Bus, coach station		Church	**Non-Roman antiquity**

Acad	**Academy**	Inst	**Institute**	Recn Gd	**Recreation Ground**
Allot Gdns	**Allotments**	Ct	**Law Court**		
Cemy	**Cemetery**	L Ctr	**Leisure Centre**	Resr	**Reservoir**
C Ctr	**Civic Centre**	LC	**Level Crossing**	Ret Pk	**Retail Park**
CH	**Club House**	Liby	**Library**	Sch	**School**
Coll	**College**	Mkt	**Market**	Sh Ctr	**Shopping Centre**
Crem	**Crematorium**	Meml	**Memorial**	TH	**Town Hall/House**
Ent	**Enterprise**	Mon	**Monument**	Trad Est	**Trading Estate**
Ex H	**Exhibition Hall**	Mus	**Museum**	Univ	**University**
Ind Est	**Industrial Estate**	Obsy	**Observatory**	W Twr	**Water Tower**
IRB Sta	**Inshore Rescue Boat Station**	Pal	**Royal Palace**	Wks	**Works**
		PH	**Public House**	YH	**Youth Hostel**

ROMAN FORT — **Roman antiquity**

67 — **Adjoining page indicators and overlap bands**

168 — The colour of the arrow and the band indicates the scale of the adjoining or overlapping page (see scales below)

■ The small numbers around the edges of the maps identify the 1 kilometre National Grid lines

■ The dark grey border on the inside edge of some pages indicates that the mapping does not continue onto the adjacent page

The scale of the maps on the pages numbered in blue is 4.2 cm to 1 km • 2⅔ inches to 1 mile • 1: 23810

0   ¼   ½   ¾   1 mile
0   250m   500m   750m   1 kilometre

The scale of the maps on pages numbered in green is 2.1 cm to 1 km • 1⅓ inches to 1 mile • 1: 47620

0   ¼   ½   ¾   1 mile
0 250m 500m 750m 1 kilometre

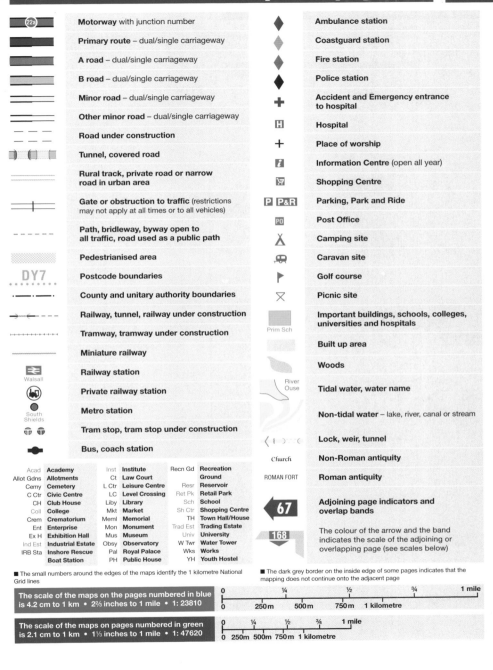

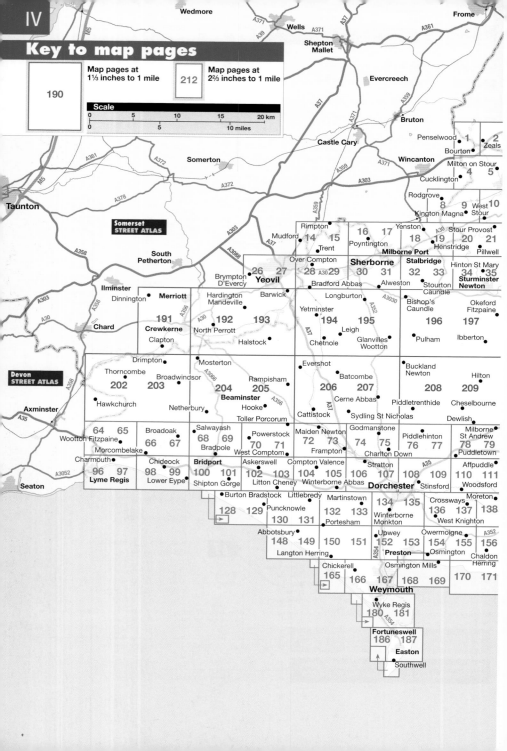

IV

Key to map pages

	Map pages at 1⅓ inches to 1 mile	212	Map pages at 2⅔ inches to 1 mile

190

Scale

0 — 5 — 10 — 15 — 20 km
0 — 5 — 10 miles

Wedmore

Wells A371

Frome

A361

Shepton Mallet

Evercreech

Bruton

Penselwood **1** **2** Zeals
Bourton

Castle Cary

Somerton

Wincanton

Milton on Stour
4 **5**

Cucklington

A372

A372

Rodgrove **8** **9** West **10**
Kington Magna Stour

Taunton

Somerset STREET ATLAS

Rimpton Yenston **16** **17** **18** **19** Stour Provost **20** **21**
Mudford **14** **15** Poyntington Henstridge Pillwell
Trent Milborne Port

South Petherton

Over Compton **28** A30 **29** **Sherborne** **Stalbridge** Hinton St Mary
Brympton D'Evercy **26** **27** **Yeovil** Bradford Abbas Alweston Stourton **30** **31** **32** **33** **34** **35** **Sturminster Newton**
Caundle

Ilminster

Hardington Mandeville Barwick Longburton A3030 Bishop's Caundle Okeford Fitzpaine
Dinnington **Merriott** **192** **193** Yetminster **194** **195** **196** **197**
Leigh
191 **Crewkerne** North Perrott Chetnole Glanvilles Wootton Pulham Ibberton
Chard Clapton Halstock

Drimpton Mosterton Evershot Buckland Newton Hilton
Devon STREET ATLAS Thorncombe Broadwindsor Rampisham Batcombe **208** **209**
202 **203** **204** **205** **206** **207**
Beaminster Cerne Abbas Piddletrenthide Cheselbourne
Axminster Hawkchurch Netherbury Hooke Cattistock Sydling St Nicholas Dewlish
Toller Porcorum

Wootton Fitzpaine **64** **65** Broadoak Salwayash Powerstock Maiden Newton Godmanstone Piddlehinton Milborne St Andrew
66 **67** **68** **69** **72** **73** **74** **75** **76** **77** **78** **79**
Morcombelake Bradpole **70** **71** Frampton Charlton Down Puddletown
West Compton

Charmouth Chideock Askerswell Compton Valence Stratton Affpuddle
96 **97** **98** **99** Bridport **100** **101** **102** **103** **104** **105** **106** **107** **108** **109** **110** **111**
Seaton **Lyme Regis** Lower Eype Shipton Gorge Litton Cheney Winterborne Abbas **Dorchester** Stinsford Woodsford

Burton Bradstock Littlebredy Martinstown **134** **135** Crossways Moreton
128 **129** Punknowle **132** **133** Winterborne Monkton **136** **137** **138**
130 **131** Portesham West Knighton

Abbotsbury Upwey Owermoigne A352
148 **149** **150** **151** **152** **153** **154** **155** **156**
Langton Herring **Preston** Osmington Chaldon Herring

Chickerell Osmington Mills
165 **166** **167** **168** **169** **170** **171**
Weymouth

Wyke Regis
180 **181**

Fortuneswell
186 **187**

Easton

Southwell

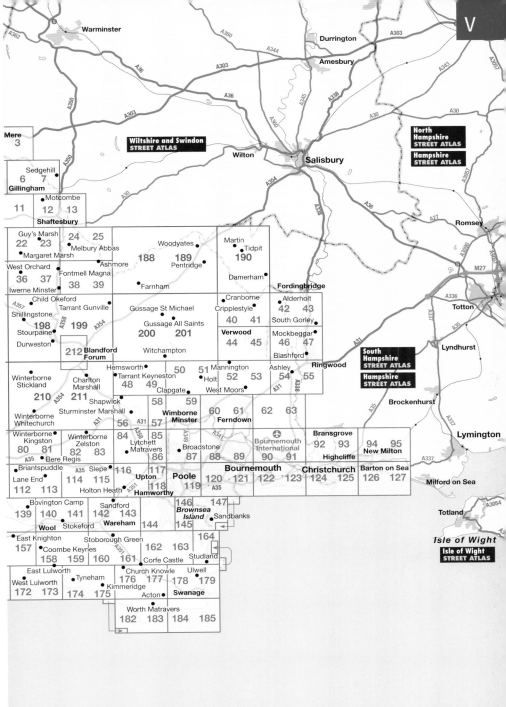

V

Warminster

Durrington

A303

Amesbury

Mere
3

Wiltshire and Swindon
STREET ATLAS

Wilton

Salisbury

North
Hampshire
STREET ATLAS

Hampshire
STREET ATLAS

Sedgehill
6   7
Gillingham

Motcombe
11   12   13
Shaftesbury

Romsey

M27

Totton

Guy's Marsh
22   23   24   25
Melbury Abbas
Margaret Marsh   Ashmore
West Orchard   Fontmell Magna
36   37   38   39
Iwerne Minster

Woodyates

188   189   190

Martin
Tidpit

Pentridge

Farnham

Damerham

Fordingbridge

Child Okeford
Shillingstone   Tarrant Gunville
198   199
Stourpaine
Durweston

212 Blandford
Forum

Gussage St Michael

Gussage All Saints
200   201

Witchampton

Cranborne   Alderholt
40   41   42   43
Cripplestyle   South Gorley
Verwood   Mockbeggar
44   45   46   47
Blashford

Lyndhurst

South
Hampshire
STREET ATLAS

Hampshire
STREET ATLAS

Winterborne
Stickland
210   211
Winterborne
Whitechurch

Charlton
Marshall
Shapwick
Sturminster Marshall
56   57

Hemsworth
Tarrant Keyneston
48   49
Clapgate

50   51 Mannington
Holt   52   53
West Moors

58   59

Ashley
54   55

Ringwood

Brockenhurst

Wimborne
Minster
60   61   62   63
Ferndown

Lymington

Winterborne
Kingston
80   81
Bere Regis

Winterborne
Zelston
82   83

84   85
Lytchett
Matravers
86

Broadstone
87   88   89

Bournemouth
International
90   91

Bransgrove
92   93
Highcliffe

94   95
New Milton

Briantspuddle
Lane End   Slepe
112   113   114   115
Holton Heath

116   117
Upton
118
Hamworthy

Poole
120   121
119

Bournemouth

Christchurch

94   95

Barton on Sea
126   127
Milford on Sea

122   123   124   125

Bovington Camp
139   140   141
Wool   Stokeford

Sandford
142   143
Wareham   144

146   147
Brownsea
Island   Sandbanks
145

Totland

Isle of Wight

Isle of Wight
STREET ATLAS

East Knighton
157   Coombe Keynes
158   159   160

162   163
161 Corfe Castle

164

Studland

East Lulworth   Church Knowle   Ulwell
West Lulworth   Tyneham   176   177   178   179
172   173   174   175
Kimmeridge   Acton   Swanage

Worth Matravers
182   183   184   185

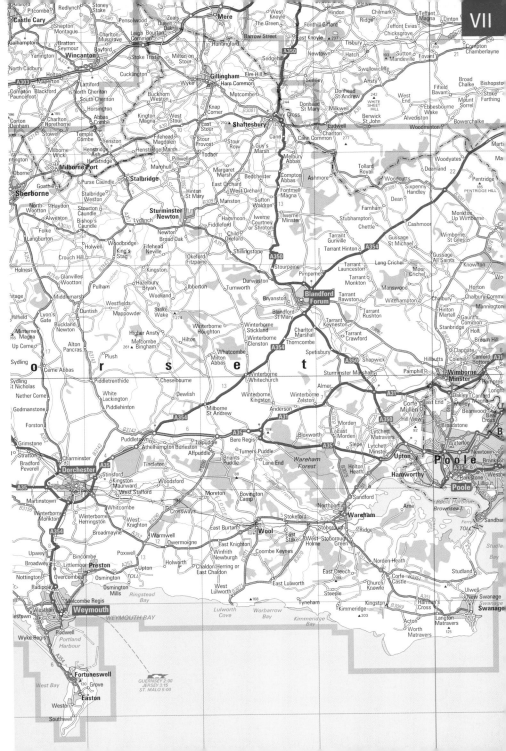

Administrative and Postcode boundaries

Legend:
- County and unitary authority boundaries
- District boundaries
- Postcode boundaries
- Area covered by this atlas

Key:
1. Bournemouth
2. Poole
3. Christchurch
4. Weymouth and Portland

Scale
0 5 10 15 20 25 30km
0 5 10 15 20 miles

Counties/Areas:
Somerset, Wiltshire, Hampshire, Devon, Dorset, West Dorset, North Dorset, East Dorset, Purbeck

Postcode areas: BA9, BA12, BA8, BA22, BA20, BA21, SP8, SP7, SP5, SP6, DT9, DT10, DT11, DT8, DT6, DT7, DT2, DT1, DT3, DT4, DT5, DT20, TA13, TA17, TA16, TA18, TA20, EX13, BH21, BH24, BH31, BH22, BH18, BH10, BH3, BH9, BH8, BH23, BH25, BH1, BH2, BH4, BH5, BH6, BH7, BH11, BH12, BH13, BH14, BH15, BH16, BH17, BH19, BH20

Place names: Stuckton, Damerham, Martin, Sixpenny Handley, Cranborne, Verwood, Ashley Heath, Ringwood, Blashford, Barton on Sea, New Milton, Bransgore, Christchurch, Bournemouth, Poole, Fernown, Wimborne Minster, Witchampton, Sturminster Marshall, Broadstone, Upton, Lytchett Matravers, Wareham, Sandbanks, Studland, Swanage, Corfe Castle, Langton Matravers, Harman's Cross, Bere Regis, Bovington Camp, Wool, West Lulworth, Owermoigne, Preston, Weymouth, Wyke Regis, Fortuneswell, Easton, Broadwey, Broadmayne, Martinstown, Dorchester, Puddletown, Piddlehinton, Milborne St Andrew, Winterborne Stickland, Blandford Forum, Pimperne, Tarrant Hinton, Iwerne Minster, Shillingstone, Stourpaine, Sturminster Newton, Mappowder, Kingston, Winterbourne Abbas, Maiden Newton, Cerne Abbas, Buckland Newton, Charminster, Abbotsbury, Swyre, Chickerell, Burton Bradstock, Chideock, Bridport, Powerstock, Netherbury, Beaminster, Broadwindsor, Chedington, Corscombe, Halstock, North Coker, Yeovil, Crewkerne, Haselbury Plucknett, Merriott, Thorncombe, Hawkchurch, Lyme Regis, Charmouth, Bishop's Caundle, Sherborne, Milborne Port, Sandford Orcas, Henstridge, Mere, Gillingham, Wyke, Cucklington, East Stour, Motcombe, Shaftesbury, Compton Abbas, Ashmore, Farnham, Wyke

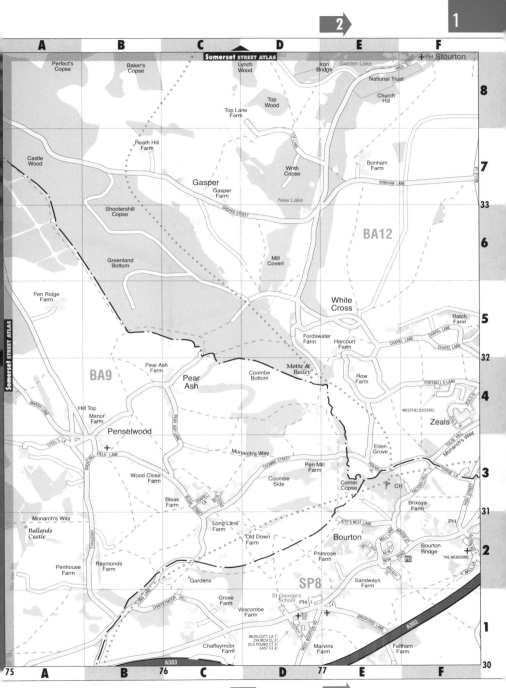

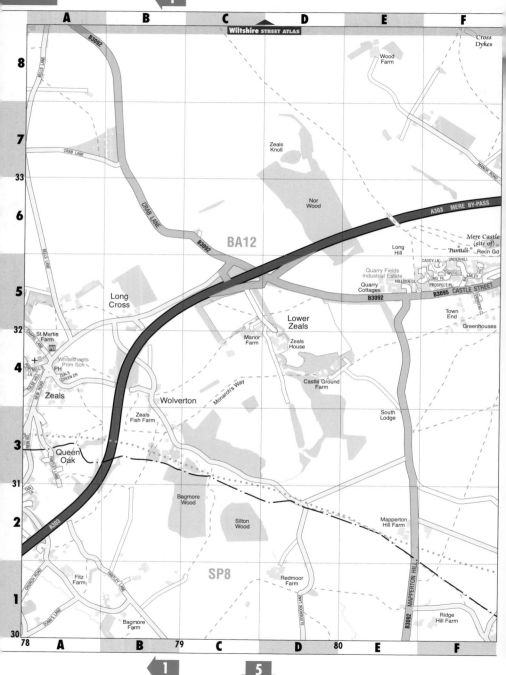

Wiltshire STREET ATLAS

A B C D E F

8

7

33

6

BA12

5

32

4

3

31

2

1

30

Cross
Dykes

Wood
Farm

Zeals
Knoll

Nor
Wood

A303 MERE BY-PASS

Mere Castle
(site of)
Tumuli Recn Gd

Long
Hill

Tumulus

CADDY LA
UNDERHILL
HOMEFIELD
LONG HL
Quarry Fields
Industrial Estate
HILLSIDE CL
Quarry
Cottages
PROSPECT PL
B3092
B3095 CASTLE STREET

CRAB LANE

B3092

BELLS LANE

BELLS LANE

CRAB LANE

B3092

Long
Cross

Lower
Zeals

Town
End

Greenhouses

St Martin
Farm
PO
Manor
Farm
Zeals
House

Whitesheets
Prim Sch
PH
CHAPEL LANE
ZEALS
GREEN DR

Castle Ground
Farm

PORTHILL
LA
TUDE HILL

Zeals
Wolverton

Monarch's Way

South
Lodge

NEW ROAD

Zeals
Fish Farm

Queen
Oak

FARLEY LANE

FAN LA

Bagmore
Wood

Mapperton
Hill Farm

A303

Silton
Wood

SP8

MAPPERTON HILL

CHURCH ROAD

Fitz
Farm

FARTLEY LANE

Redmoor
Farm

SOLDIERS LANE

B3092

Ridge
Hill Farm

Bagmore
Farm

DUNNS LANE

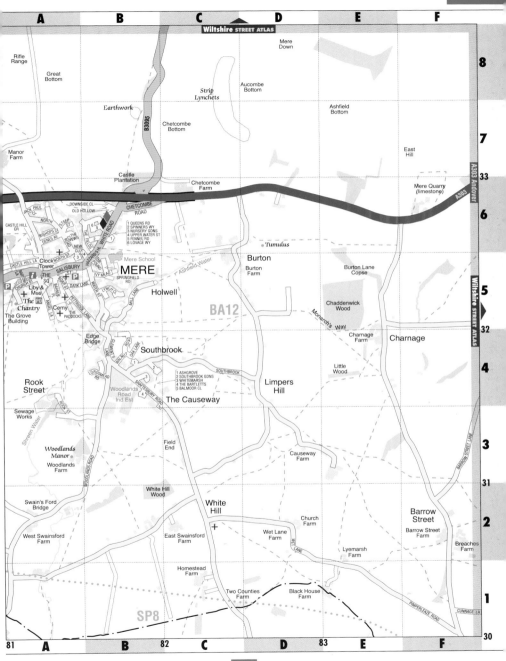

A **B** **C** **D** **E** **F**

8

Rifle
Range

Mere
Down

Great
Bottom

Aucombe
Bottom

Strip
Lynchets

Earthwork

Chetcombe
Bottom

Ashfield
Bottom

7

B3095

East
Hill

Manor
Farm

Castle
Plantation

Chetcombe
Farm

33

Mere Quarry
(limestone)

A303 Andover

A303

DOWNSIDE CL
OLD HOLLOW

CHETCOMBE
ROAD

6

JACK PAUL
CT

NORTH
ST

DOWNSIDE

1 QUEENS RD
2 SPINNERS WY
3 NURSERY GDNS
4 UPPER WATER ST
5 FENNEL RD
6 LOVAGE WY

CASTLE HILL
CR

BISHOPS CL

STEP
ST

WHITE ROAD

DENES RD

NEW
CUT

Tumulus

Wiltshire STREET ATLAS

CASTLE HILL LA

Clock
Tower

NORTH ST

Mere School

Ashfield Water

Burton

Burton
Farm

Burton Lane
Copse

5

SALISBURY

THE
SQ

SPRINGFIELD
RD

MERE

IVY MEAD

DARK LANE

Chaddenwick
Wood

CHURCH ST

Liby &
Mus

PETTRIDGE LANE

Holwell

BA12

Monarch's Way

32

The
Chantry

ANGEL LA

MILL LANE

Charnage
Farm

Charnage

The Grove
Building

Cemy

THE
PADDOCKS

4

Edge
Bridge

CLEMENTS LANE

WET LANE

Southbrook

SOUTHBROOK

Little
Wood

Rook
Street

LORDSMEAD
RD

1 ASHGROVE
2 SOUTHBROOK GDNS
3 WHITEMARSH
4 THE BARTLETTS
5 BALMOOR CL

Limpers
Hill

SHAFTESBURY ROAD

Woodlands
Road
Ind Est

The Causeway

3

Sewage
Works

Shreen Water

WOODLANDS ROAD

Field
End

Causeway
Farm

Woodlands
Manor

Woodlands
Farm

BARROW STREET LANE

31

White Hill
Wood

Swain's Ford
Bridge

White
Hill

Church
Farm

Barrow
Street

2

West Swainsford
Farm

East Swainsford
Farm

Wet Lane
Farm

WET LANE

Barrow Street
Farm

Breaches
Farm

Lyemarsh
Farm

Homestead
Farm

1

SP8

Two Counties
Farm

Black House
Farm

PIMPERLEAZE ROAD

CUNNAGE LA

81 **A** 82 **B** **C** 83 **D** **E** **F** 30

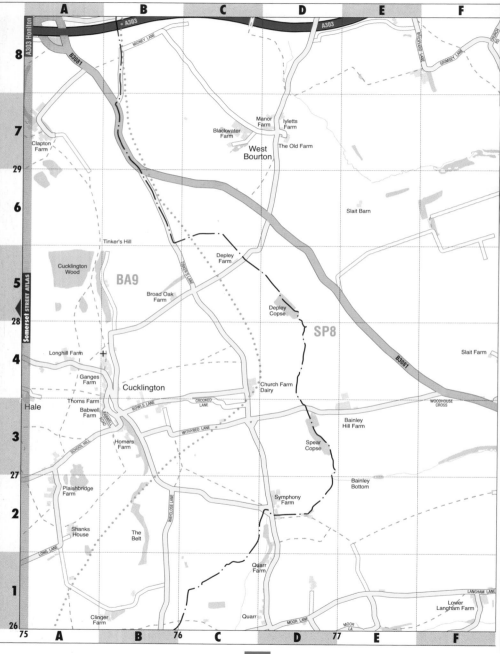

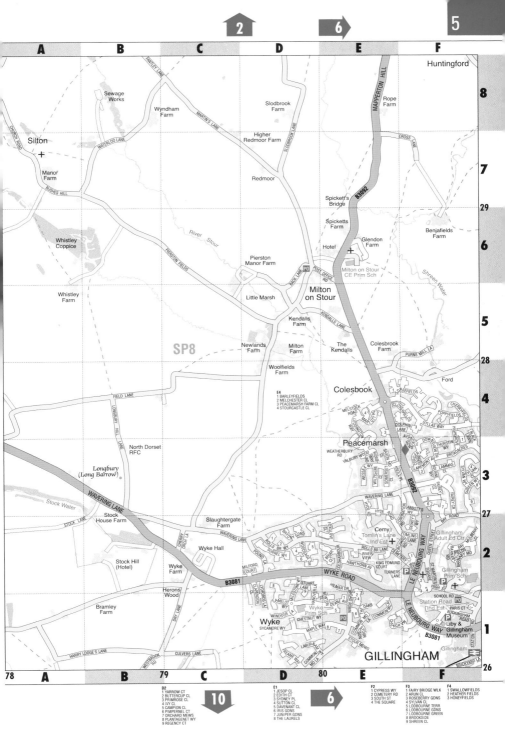

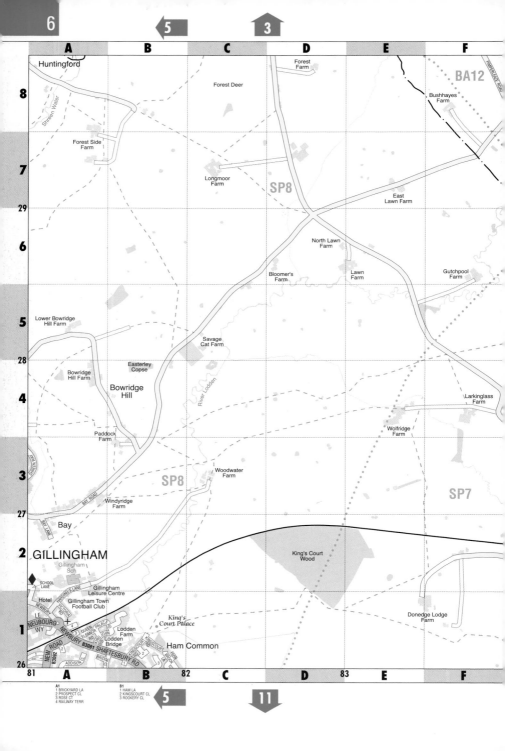

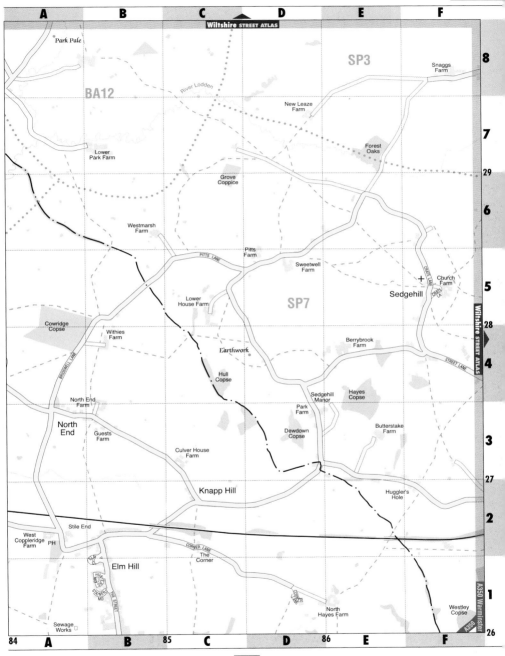

SP3

BA12

Park Pale

River Lodden

Snaggs
Farm

New Leaze
Farm

Lower
Park Farm

Forest
Oaks

Grove
Coppice

Westmarsh
Farm

PITTS LANE

Pitts
Farm

Sweetwell
Farm

Church
Farm

Sedgehill

Lower
House Farm

SP7

Cowridge
Copse

Withies
Farm

Earthwork

Berrybrook
Farm

STREET LANE

Hull
Copse

North End
Farm

Hayes
Copse

Sedgehill
Manor

Park
Farm

Butterstake
Farm

North
End

Guests
Farm

Culver House
Farm

Dewdown
Copse

Knapp Hill

Huggler's
Hole

West
Coppleridge
Farm

PH

Stile End

CORNER LANE

The
Corner

Elm Hill

North
Hayes Farm

Westley
Copse

Sewage
Works

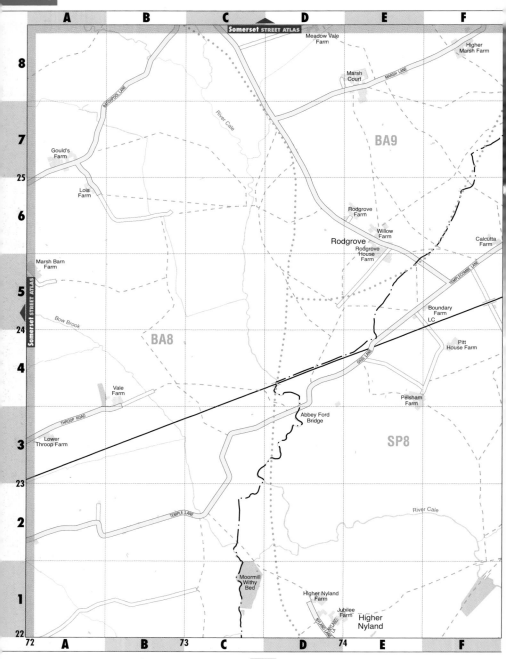

Meadow Vale Farm

Higher Marsh Farm

Marsh Court

MARSH LANE

River Cale

BA9

Gould's Farm

Lois Farm

Rodgrove Farm

Willow Farm

Rodgrove

Calcutta Farm

Rodgrove House Farm

Marsh Barn Farm

TEMPLECOMBE LANE

Bow Brook

Boundary Farm LC

BA8

Pitt House Farm

Vale Farm

GIBB LANE

THROOP ROAD

Pelsham Farm

Abbey Ford Bridge

Lower Throop Farm

SP8

River Cale

TEMPLE LANE

Moormill Withy Bed

Higher Nyland Farm

Jubilee Farm

Higher Nyland

NYLAND LANE

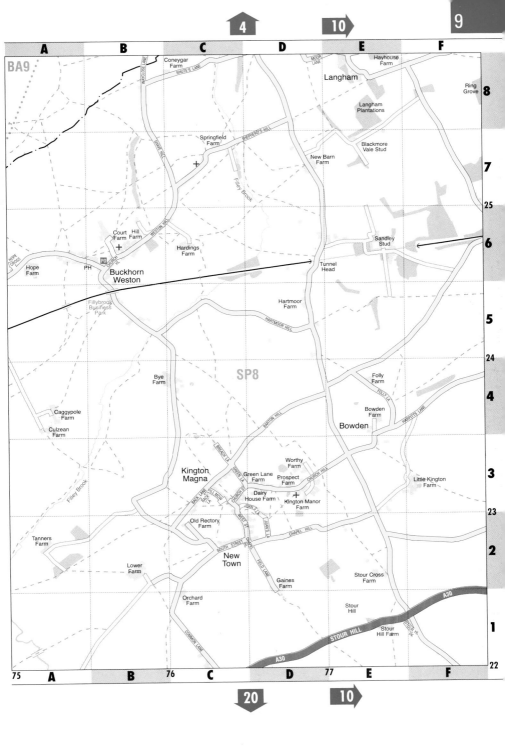

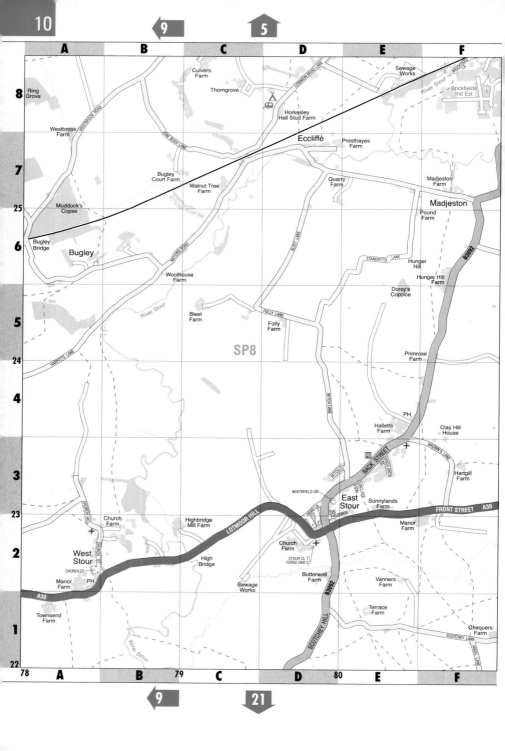

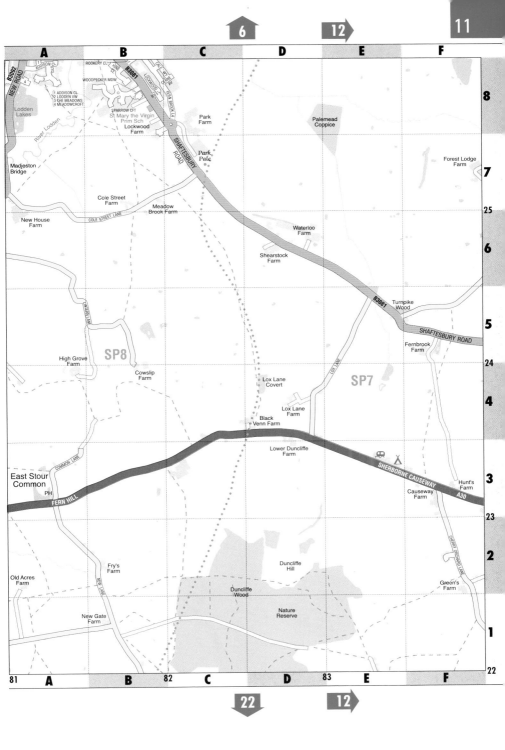

	A	B	C	D	E	F

PH
New Lane
Shorts Green Farm
Shorts Green Lane
Valencia
The Plantation
Motcombe
Mole End
Grant's Copse
Kingsettle Wood
Nature Reserve
Sheloes Copse

Motcombe CE VA Prim Sch
Avenue Farm
Church Farm
Little Grove
Bittles Green
Meaders Farm
Kingsettle Wood

Bittles Green Farm
Thanes Farm
North Heath

Manor Farm
Motcombe Park Sports Centre
Ryal's Plantation
Motcombe Road
The Cliff

Motcombe House Plantations
Motcombe Park
Port Regis Sch
Oates Plantation

B3081
Shaftesbury Road
Whitehouse Farm
SP7
Cowherd Shute Farm
HOMEFIELD
LITTLE DOWN
TOLLGATE

Hawkers Hill Farm
Old Brickyard Farm
GAVES LANE
Lady's Copse
Quoits Copse

SHAFTESBURY

GROSVENOR ROAD A350

B3081
New Road
NEW ROAD
LONG CROSS
NETTLEBED NURSERY
Longmead Ind Est

A30
Long Cross Farm
Enmore Green
BLEKE ST
NEW RD
CHRISTY'S LANE

SHERBORNE CAUSEWAY
Woolcotts Farm
CHURCH HILL
HORSEPONDS
SALLY KINGS LA
Gillingham L Adult Ed Ctr
Shaftesbury Arts Ctr
SALISBURY ST
HIGH ST

Grants Farm
BREACH LANE
UMBERS HL 1
LANGFORDS LA 2
LAUNDRY LA 3
Shaftesbury Abbey Mus & Gdn
Shaftesbury Town Mus
Shaftesbury L Ctr

BIMPORT
Westminster Meml
LOVE LANE
B3081 SALISBURY RD

Alcester
Abbots Vale
St James
Shaftesbury Sch

Church Farm
Abbey Prim Sch
FRENCH MILL RI

Cherry Orchard Farm
CHERRY DR LANE
FOYLE HILL
Edwards Farm
B3091
Brinscombe Farm
BRINSCOMBE LA

	A	85	B	C	D	86	E	F

E3
1 THE BEECHES
2 KINGS HL
3 PARSONS POOL
4 MUSTONS LA

F2
1 LOWER BLANDFORD RD

F3
1 ST EDWARDS
2 GRANVILLE GDNS
3 CHARLES GARRETT CL
4 JEANNEAU CL

F4
1 CRANBORNE DR
2 WESTMINSTER CL
3 FOUNTAIN MD
4 OXENCROFT

Lyefield's Copse

Oysters Coppice

Oysters Farm

Harthill Farm

Benett's Copse

Stib Acre Copse

Westwood Farm

Knipes Farm

Gutch Common

BINWAY LANE

Clift Farm

SP7

Froud's Copse

Hilldown Copse

Donhead Clift

Hatts Farm

Crates Wood

Tittle Path Hill

Aldermoor Copse

Castle Rings

Semley Hill

Lodge Wood

Bungalow Castle Farm

Lower Wincombe Farm

Nadder Head

Wincombe Business Park

Morgan's Copse

Wincombe Park

Ramshill Farm

Mullins' Copse

Step Cross Copse

Higher Wincombe Farm

Great Hanging

WINDWHISTLE CORNER

Ivy Cross

SP7

Eastleaze Farm

Langdale Farm

Mampits Farm

Dockham Bottom

St Marys Sch

Shaftesbury Prim Sch

Cemy

Long Bottom

Ten Acre Copse

Landsley Farm

Cave Copse

Coombe

Hotel

Long Copse

Knights Barn Farm

The Rising Sun (PH)

A30

Higher Blandford Rd

A30

White Close Farm

Mayo Farm

Hillside Farm

SALISBURY ROAD

CHARLTON LANE

Boyne Hollow

NEW LANE

A30 Salisbury

Wiltshire STREET ATLAS

A1
1 BUTTS MD
2 LWR BLANDFORD RD
3 BRINSCOMBE LA

A4
1 HAWTHORN CL
2 SPRINGFIELD CL

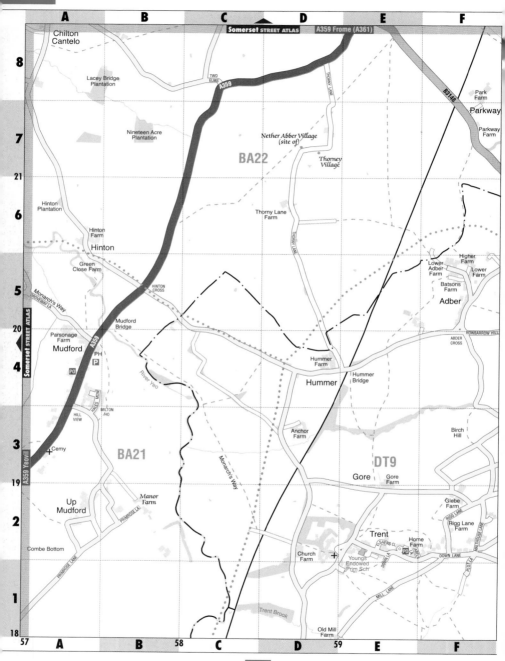

A359 Frome (A361)

Chilton
Cantelo

Lacey Bridge
Plantation

TWO
ELMS

A359

THORNY LANE

B3148

Park
Farm

Parkway

Parkway
Farm

Nineteen Acre
Plantation

BA22

Nether Abber Village
(site of)

Thorney
Village

Hinton
Plantation

Thorny Lane
Farm

THORNY LANE

Hinton
Farm

Hinton

Green
Close Farm

Higher
Farm

Lower
Adber
Farm

Lower
Farm

HINTON
CROSS

Batsons
Farm

Adber

Monarch's Way

GROVEHAY LA

A359

Mudford
Bridge

ABDER
CROSS

ROWBARROW HILL

Parsonage
Farm

Mudford

A359

PH

P

PO

HALL'S LANE

HILL
VIEW

MILTON
HO

River Yeo

Hummer
Farm

Hummer
Bridge

Hummer

Anchor
Farm

Birch
Hill

Cemy

BA21

Monarch's Way

DT9

Gore

Gore
Farm

Up
Mudford

Manor
Farm

Glebe
Farm

RIGG LANE

Rigg Lane
Farm

PRIMROSE LA

Trent

SHERS CL

Home
Farm

DOWN LANE

MALTHOUSE LANE

DORSET LA

Combe Bottom

Church
Farm

Youngs
Endowed
Prim Sch

MILL LANE

PLOTT LA

PRIMROSE LANE

Trent Brook

Old Mill
Farm

A359 Yeovil

Somerset STREET ATLAS

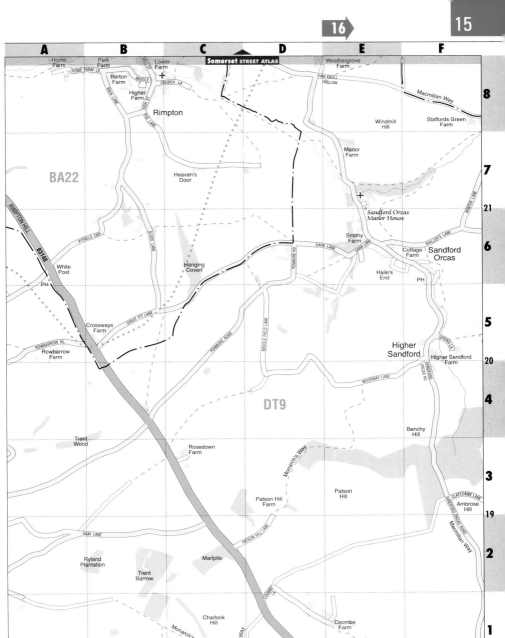

Somerset STREET ATLAS

A **B** **C** **D** **E** **F**

Home Farm
HOME FARM LA
Park Farm
Lower Farm
Weathergrove Farm
PARK KNOLL HOLLOW

Barton Farm
MIDDLE S
CHURCH LA
Macmillan Way
8

Higher Farm
HIGH POT LANE
BACK LANE
Rimpton
Windmill Hill
Staffords Green Farm

BA22
Heaven's Door
Manor Farm
7

RIMPTON HILL
Sandford Orcas Manor House
WHITER LANE
21

PITFIELD CMR
SLADE LANE
Smithy Farm
DARK LANE
DARK LANE
Cottage Farm
SHILLER'S LANE
Sandford Orcas
6

B3148
White Post
Hanging Covert
PENMORE RD
Haile's End
PH
5

PH
GREAT PIT LANE
PENMORE ROAD
MIDDLE FIELD LANE
Higher Sandford
SPRING LA
Higher Sandford Farm
20

Crossways Farm
ROWBARROW HL
Rowbarrow Farm
MOORWAY LANE
SANDFORD ORCAS RD
4

DT9
Benchy Hill

Trent Wood
Rosedown Farm
Monarch's Way
3

CLATCOMBE LANE
Ambrose Hill
19

Patson Hill Farm
Patson Hill
SANDFORD ORCAS ROAD
Macmillan Way

HAM LANE
PATSON HILL LANE
2

Ryland Plantation
Marlpits
Trent Barrow

Charlock Hill
COOMBE LA
Coombe Farm
1

Monarch's Way
Monarch's Way
B3148
18

60 **A** **B** 61 **C** **D** 62 **E** **F**

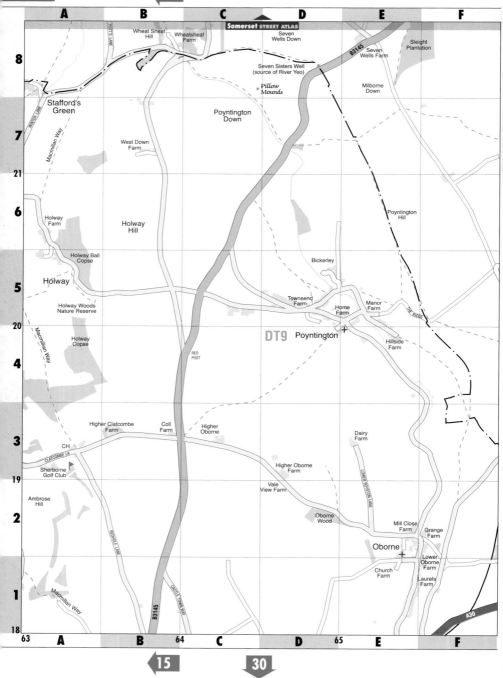

Somerset STREET ATLAS

Wheat Sheaf Hill
Wheatsheaf Farm
Seven Wells Down
B3145
Seven Wells Farm
Sleight Plantation

8

Seven Sisters Well (source of River Yeo)
Milborne Down

Stafford's Green

Pillow Mounds

Poyntington Down

7

Macmillan Way

West Down Farm

21

6

Holway Farm

Holway Hill

Poyntington Hill

Holway Ball Copse

Bickerley

5

Holway

Townsend Farm
Home Farm
Manor Farm
THE RIDGE

Holway Woods Nature Reserve

20

Holway Copse

DT9 Poyntington
Hillside Farm

4

RED POST

3

Higher Clatcombe Farm
Coll Farm
Higher Oborne
Dairy Farm

CH
CLATCOMBE LA

Sherborne Golf Club

Higher Oborne Farm

19

Vale View Farm

LOWER BOYSTON LANE

Ambrose Hill

2

Oborne Wood
Mill Close Farm
Grange Farm

Oborne
Lower Oborne Farm

Church Farm
Laurels Farm

1

Macmillan Way

B3145
CASTLE TOWN WAY

A30

18

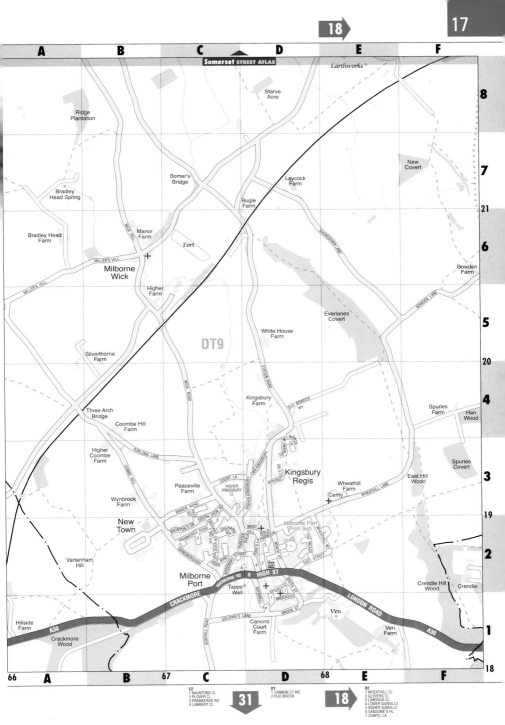

Somerset STREET ATLAS

31   18

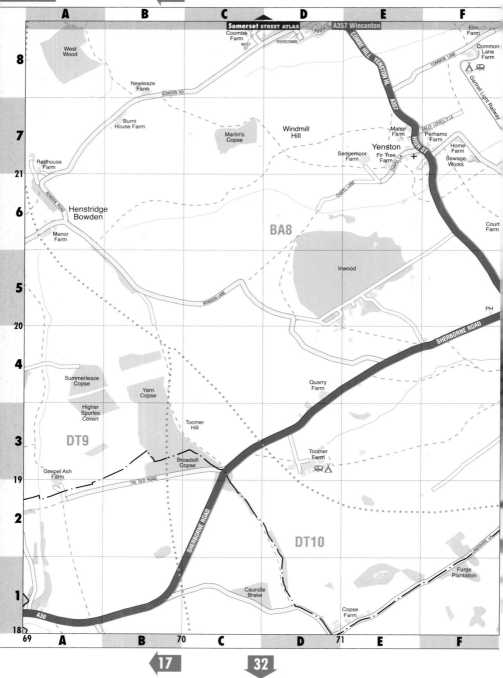

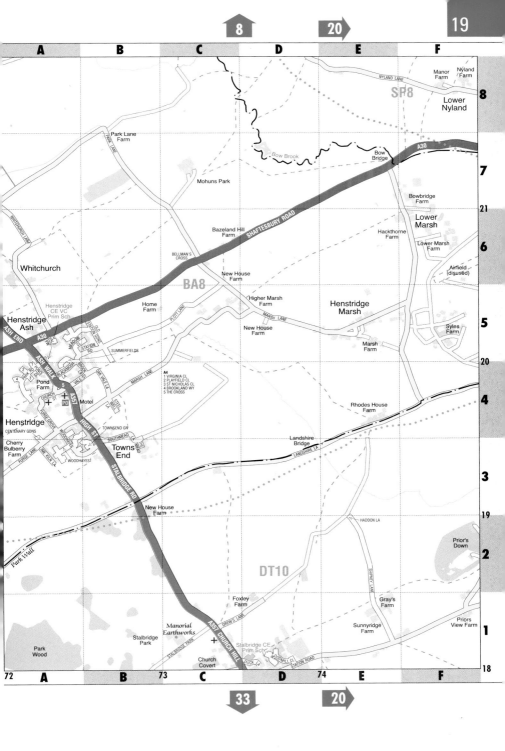

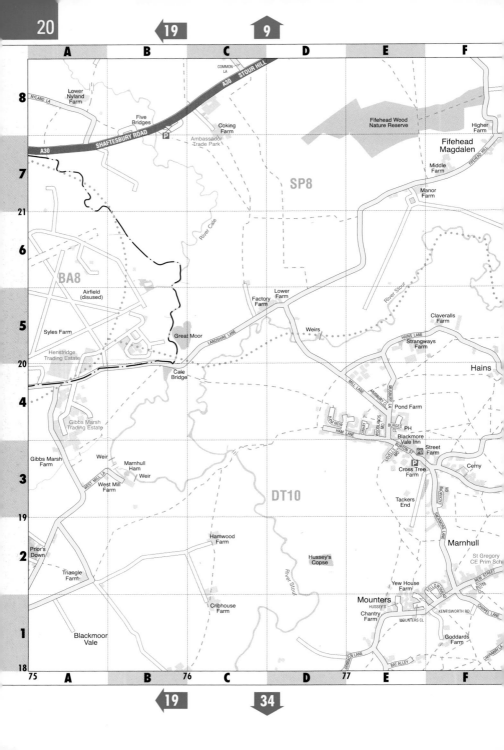

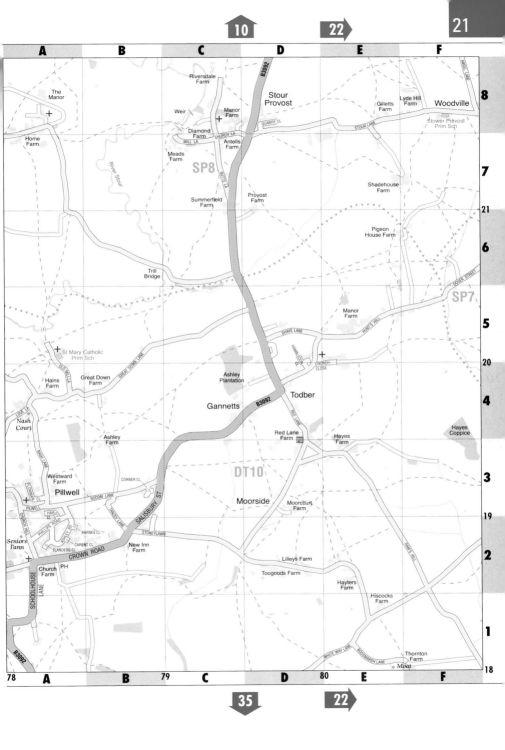

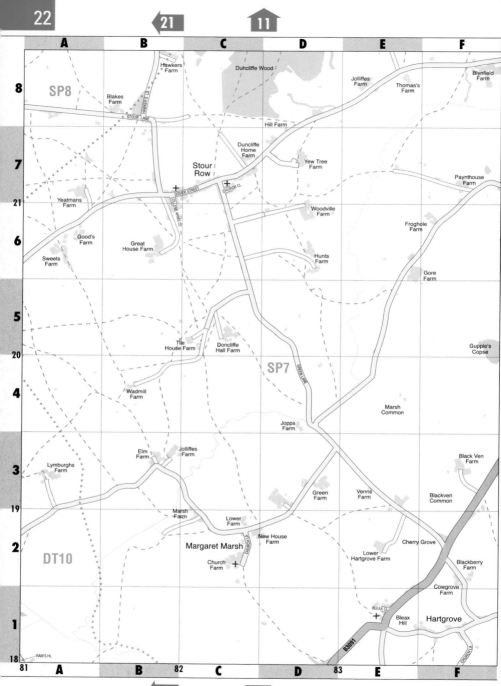

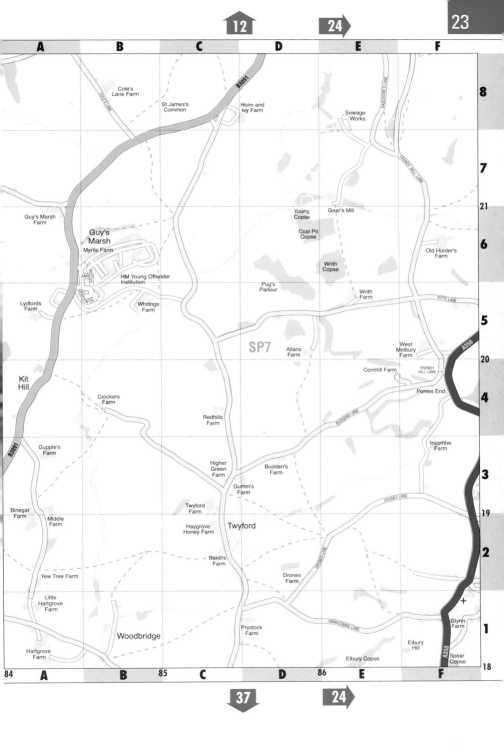

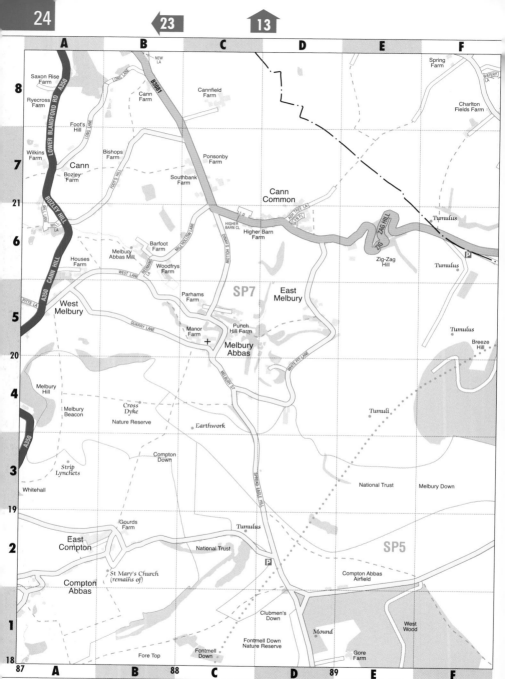

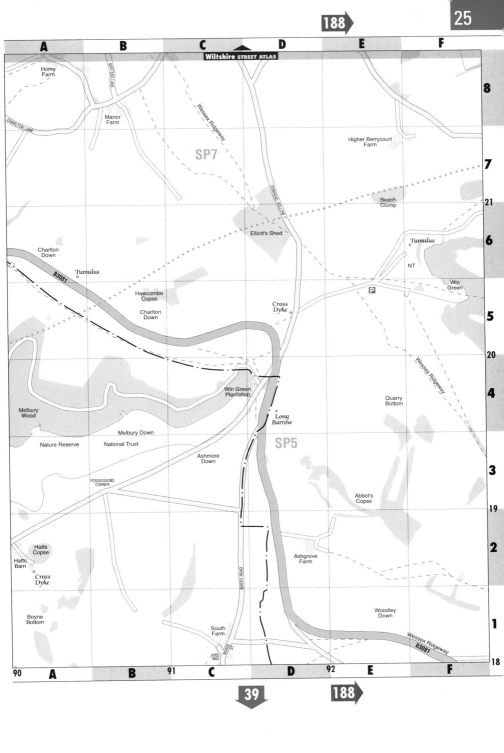

Wiltshire STREET ATLAS

8

7

21

6

5

20

4

3

19

2

1

18

A B C D E F

SP7

Home Farm

Manor Farm

CHARLTON LANE

BAXTERS LANE

Wessex Ridgeway

Higher Berrycourt Farm

DINHEAD HOLLOW

Beech Clump

Elliott's Shed

Tumulus

NT

Win Green

Charlton Down

B3081

Tumulus

Hawcombe Copse

Charlton Down

Cross Dyke

P

Wessex Ridgeway

Win Green Plantation

Quarry Bottom

Melbury Wood

Long Barrow

SP5

Melbury Down

Nature Reserve

National Trust

Ashmore Down

Abbot's Copse

POSSESSIONS CORNER

Hatts Copse

Hatts Barn

Cross Dyke

NORTH ROAD

Ashgrove Farm

Woodley Down

Boyne Bottom

South Farm

PO

BRIDGE ST

Wessex Ridgeway

B3081

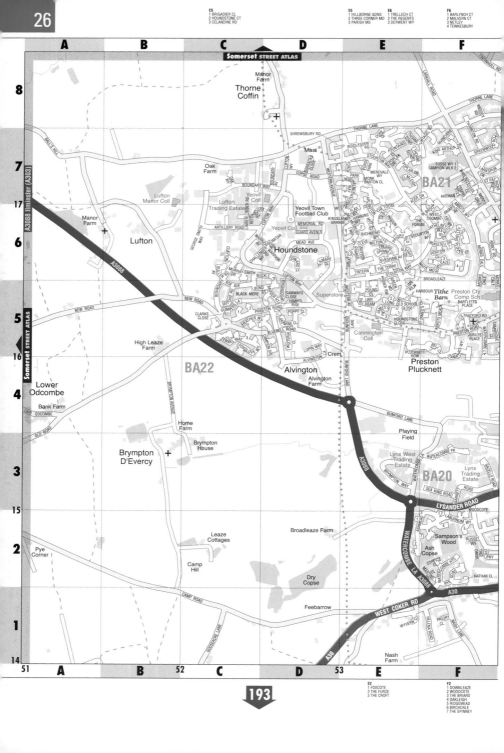

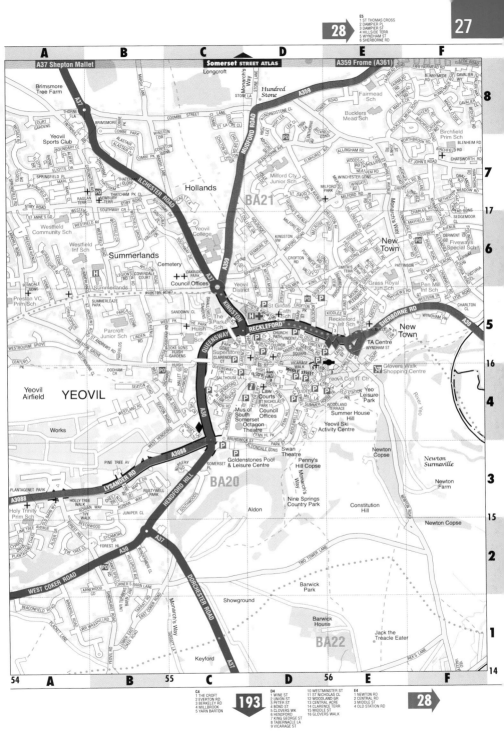

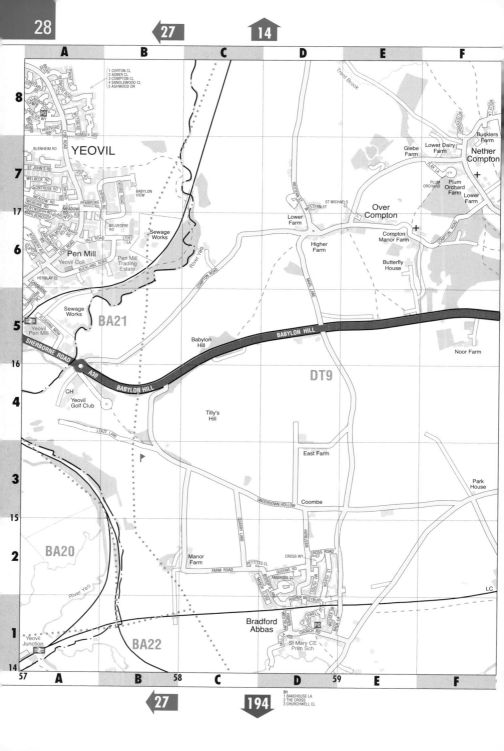

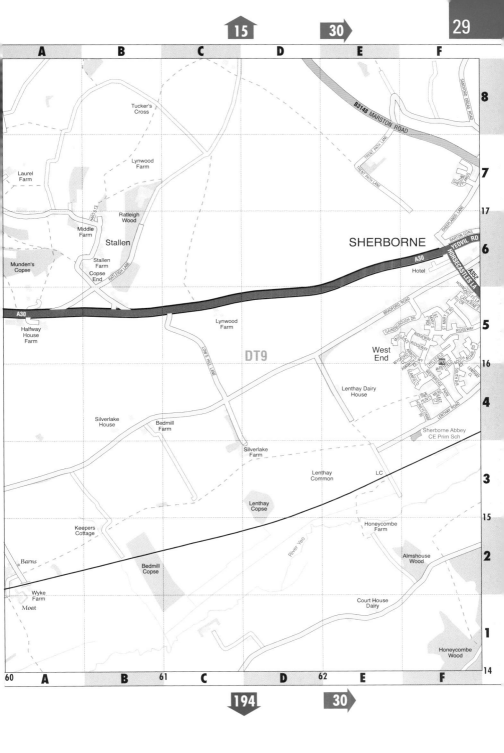

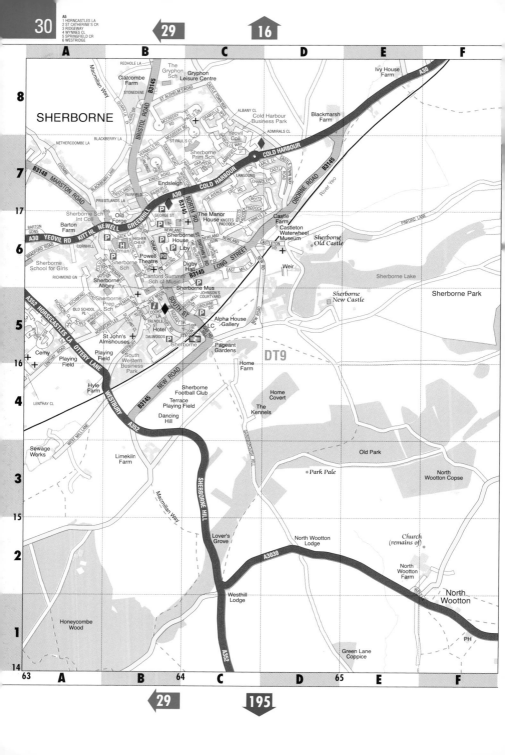

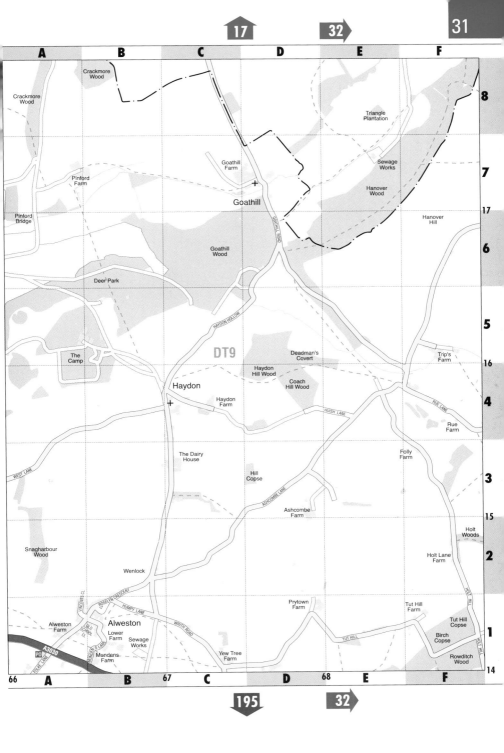

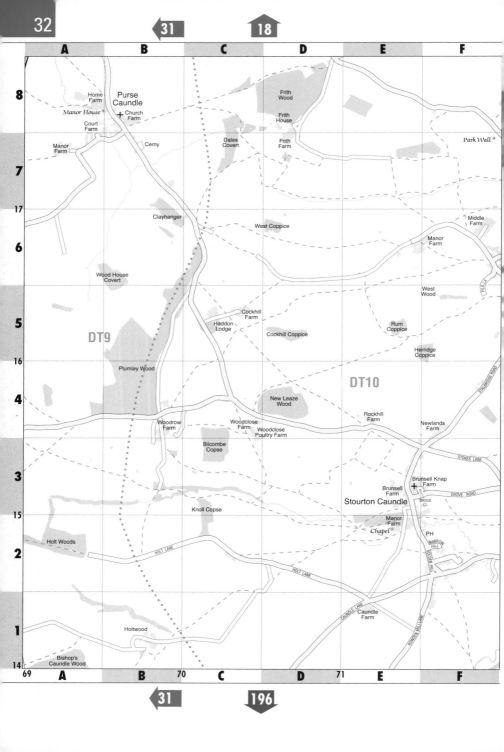

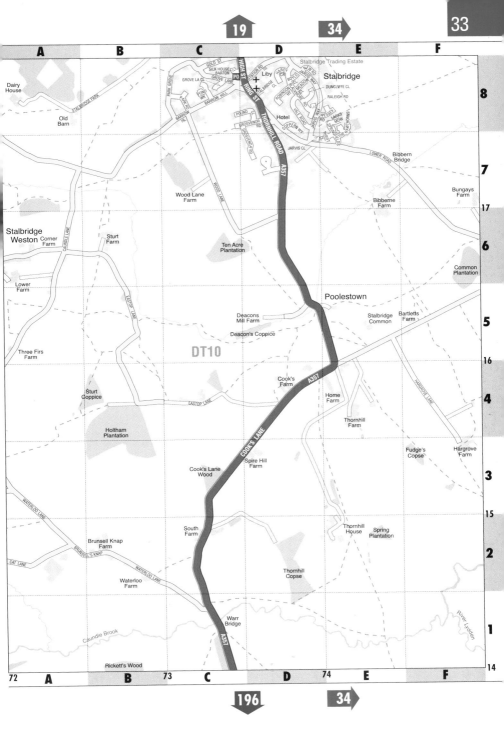

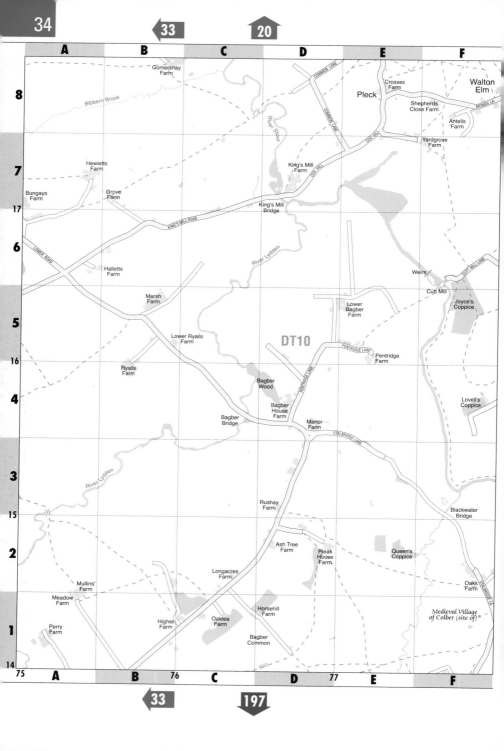

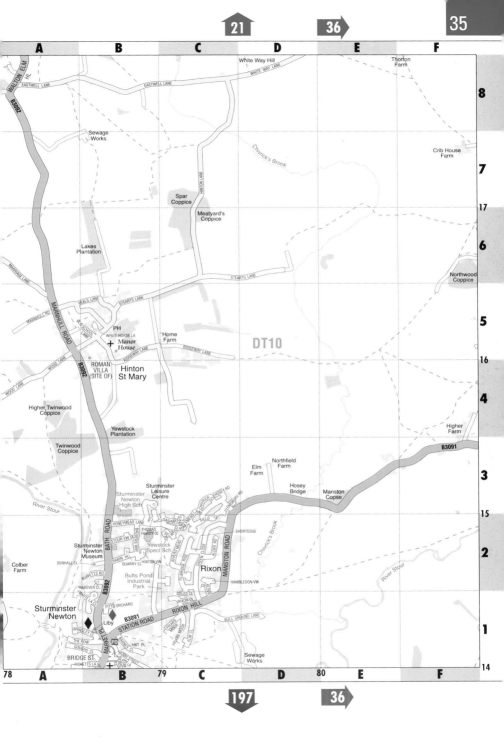

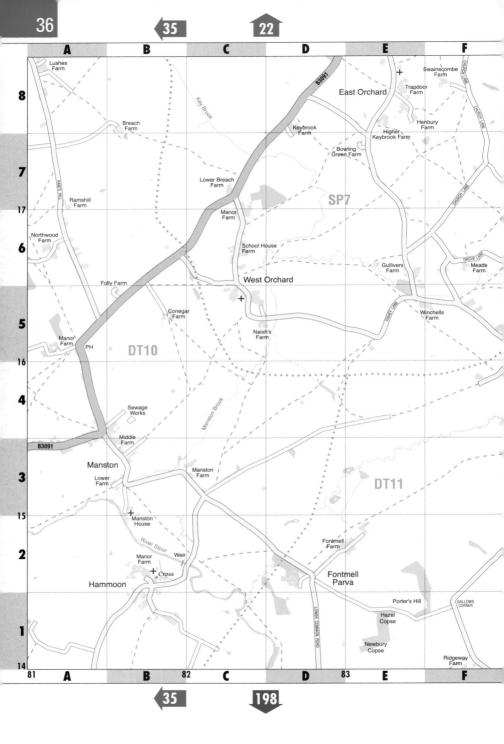

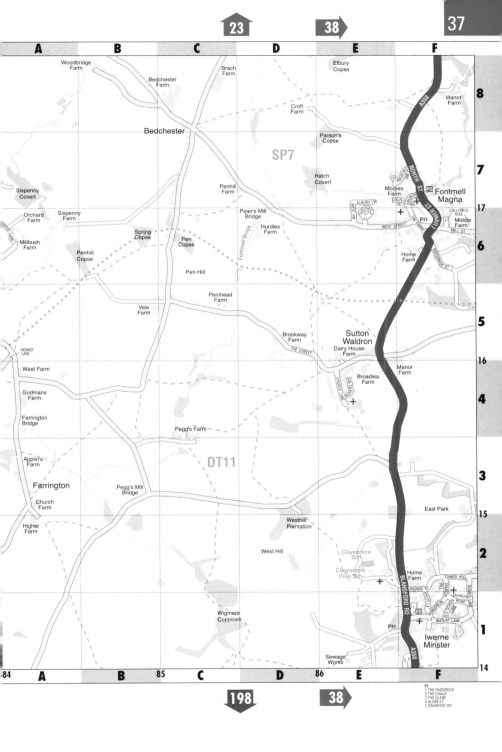

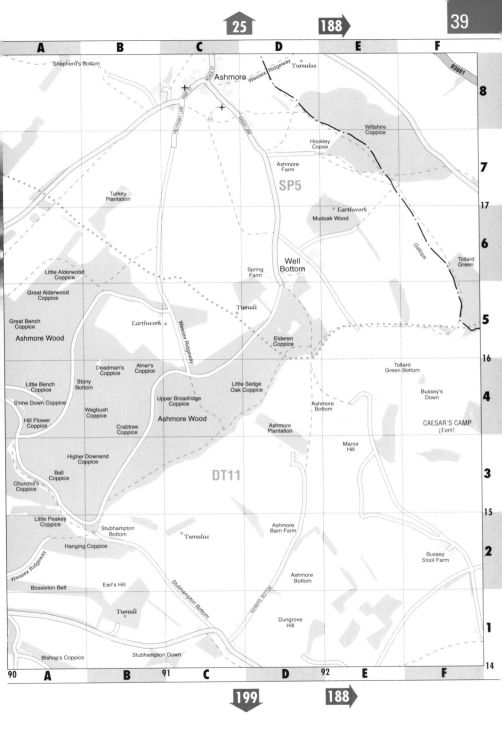

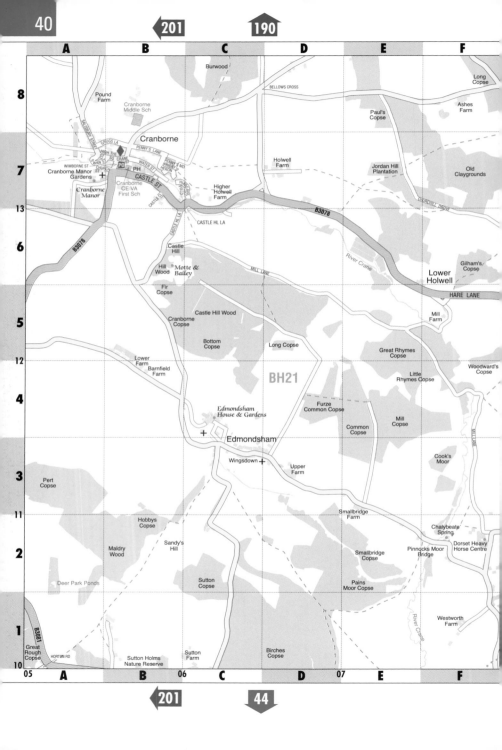

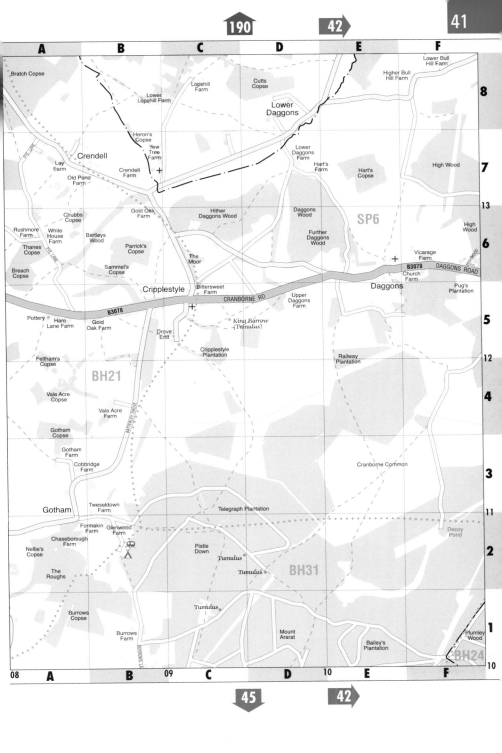

South Hampshire STREET ATLAS

42

A B C D E F

8

Lake Farm

Perry Copse

Hill Farm

Home Farm

Manor Farm

ASHFORD ROAD

BOWERWOOD ROAD

B3078

7

High Wood

Park Farm Alderholt Park

Hill Cottage Farm

FORDINGBRIDGE ROAD

New Farm

Midgham Wood

13

High Wood

CANE HEATH ROAD

Salisbury Arms Farm

Cross Farm

HILLBURY RD

Bonfire Hill

Wolvercroft Spinney

Wolvercrate Copse

Camel Green

Hilbury Wood

6

Alderholt

LIME TREE CL

ZUPPERS CL

HAYTERS WAY

CAMEL GREEN ROAD

1 GREEN DR
2 SILVERDALE CP
3 CAMEL GN RD

Midgham Farm

STATION ROAD

STATION RD

B3078

St James CE Fst Sch

ASTILE'S WAY

SOUTH RD

Hillbury Farm

Midgham Long Copse

DAGGONS ROAD

PH

STATION RD

CHURCHILL CL
BLACKWATER GR

SALTWOOD

APPLE TREE

ALDER DR

CARLSWOOD DR

TUDOR

HASTREL

Hillbury Farm

5

Charing Cross

CHARING CROSS

PINE ROAD

OAK ROAD

BROOMFIELD DR
BROOMFIELD DR

BIRCHWOOD DR

FERNS

HAZEL

SP6

RINGWOOD ROAD

12

Cross Roads Plantation

Sleepbrook Farm

Alderholt Sports Club

Marsh Lands

Oak Tree Farm

Drove End Farm

LOWER LANE

NORTH END LANE

4

Warren Park Farm

HARBRIDGE DROVE

LOWER LA

Lomer Copse

3

Alderholt Common

Whitefield Bottom

Plumley Wood

Braemoor

Bleak Hill Farm

Bleak Hill

Fern Hill Copse

11

Sleep Brook

Sleep Bottom

Whitefield Bottom

2

BH31

Plumley Wood

Cobley Wood

1

North Plumley Farm

Hamer Copse

BH24

10

Wiggs Copse

Kent Hill

Cootman's Copse

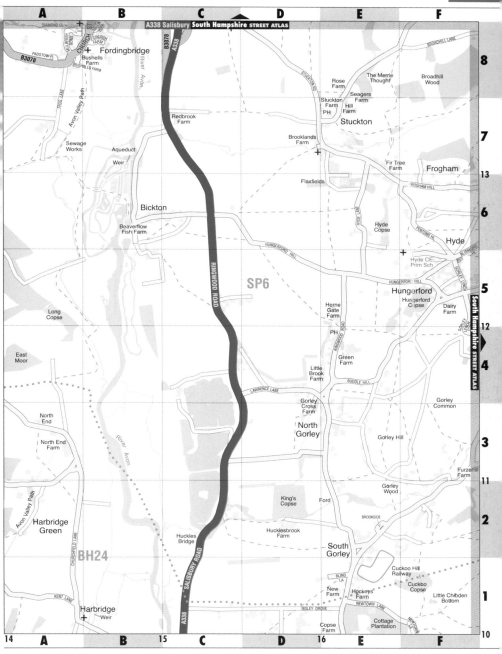

8

DIAMOND CL
PADSTOW PL
B3078

CHURCH ST
WILBERRY GDNS
CHURCH FARM
Bushells Farm
BUSHELLS FARM
Fordingbridge

B3078
A338

FROG LANE
River Avon

BROADHILL LANE

Rose Farm
The Merrie Thought
Broadhill Wood

STUCKTON RD

Redbrook Farm

Stuckton Farm PH
Seagers Farm
Hill Farm
Stuckton

7

Sewage Works
Aqueduct
Weir

Brooklands Farm

Fir Tree Farm

Frogham

13

Beaverflow Fish Farm

Bickton

Flaxfields

FROGHAM HILL

HYDE LANE

Hyde Copse

FENTONS HL

Hyde

6

Hungerford Hill

Hyde CE Prim Sch

BLISSFORD RD

GORLEY LYNCH

RINGWOOD ROAD

SP6

Hungerford Hill

Hungerford
Hungerford Copse
Dairy Farm

5

Long Copse

Herne Gate Farm

RINGWOOD ROAD

PH

GORLEY LYNCH

12

East Moor

Green Farm

Little Brook Farm

BUDDLE HILL

Gorley Common

4

LAWRENCE LANE

Gorley Cross Farm

North Gorley

Gorley Hill

Gorley Wood

3

River Avon

North End

North End Farm

CHURCHFIELD LANE

FurzeHill Farm

11

East Moor

King's Copse

Ford

BROOKSIDE

2

Harbridge Green

BH24

Huckles Bridge

Hucklesbrook Farm

South Gorley

Cuckoo Hill Railway
Cuckbo Copse
Little Chibden Bottom

Avon Valley Path

KENT LANE

SALISBURY ROAD

A338

BLIND LA

New Farm
Hockeys Farm

IBSLEY DROVE

NEWTOWN LANE

Copse Farm

Cottage Plantation

NEWTOWN

Harbridge
Weir

1

10

14   A   B   15   C   D   16   E   F

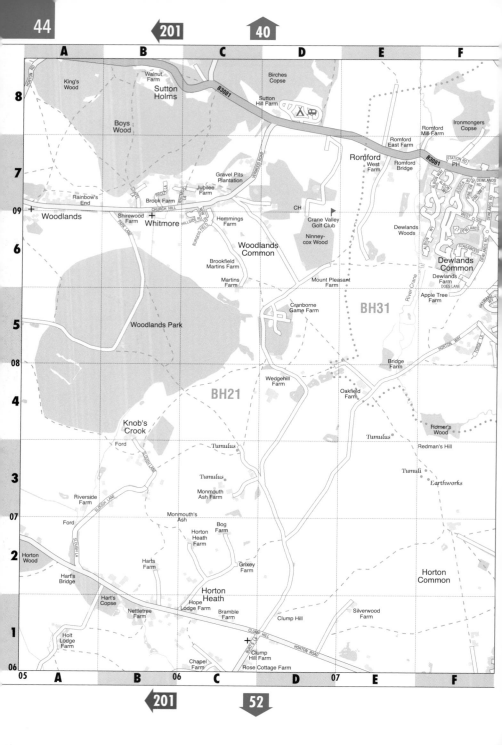

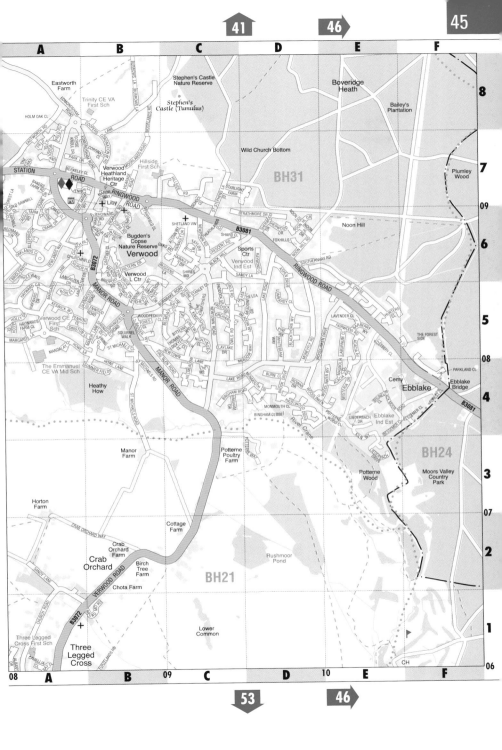

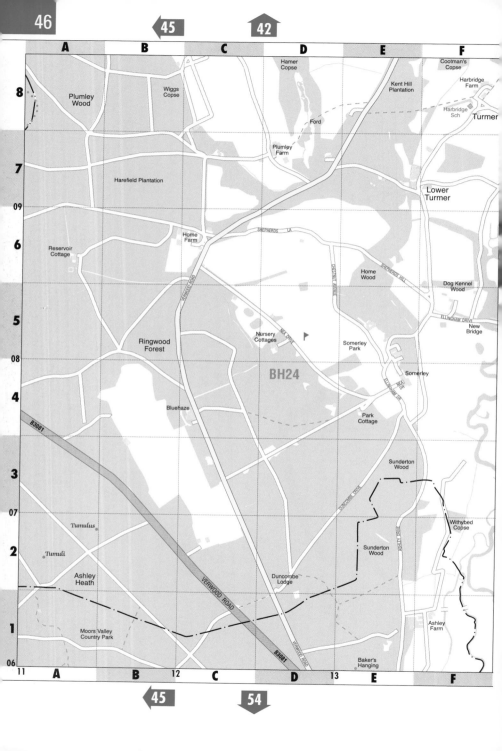

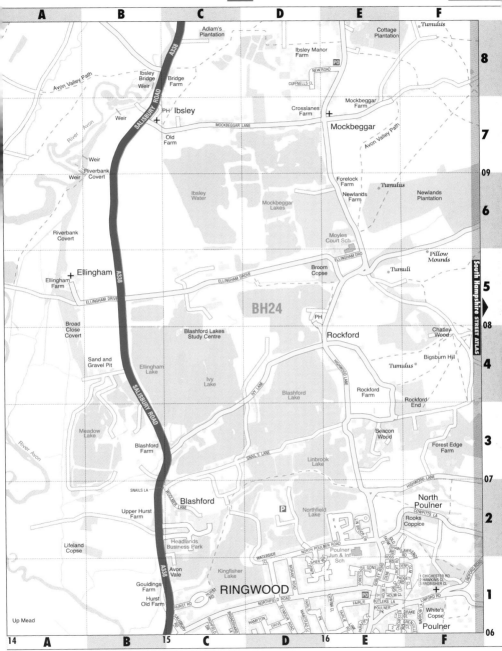

Adlam's Plantation

Cottage Plantation

Tumulus

Ibsley Manor Farm

PO

NEW ROAD

CUFFNELLS CL

8

Ibsley Bridge Weir

Bridge Farm

Ibsley

Avon Valley Path

Mockbeggar Farm

Crosslanes Farm

Mockbeggar

7

PH

Ibsley

SALISBURY ROAD

A338

Old Farm

MOCKBEGGAR LANE

Avon Valley Path

Weir

River Avon

Weir

Forelock Farm

Tumulus

Newlands Plantation

09

Weir

Riverbank Covert

Ibsley Water

Mockbeggar Lakes

Newlands Farm

6

Riverbank Covert

Moyles Court Sch

Pillow Mounds

Ellingham

A338

ELLINGHAM DRO

Broom Copse

Tumuli

South Hampshire STREET ATLAS

5

Ellingham Farm

ELLINGHAM DRIVE

ELLINGHAM DROVE

BH24

PH

08

Broad Close Covert

Blashford Lakes Study Centre

Rockford

Chatley Wood

Sand and Gravel Pit

Ellingham Lake

Ivy Lake

IVY LANE

Blashford Lake

Rockford Farm

Tumulus

Bigsburn Hill

Rockford End

4

HIGHWOOD LANE

Meadow Lake

Blashford Farm

SNAIL'S LANE

Beacon Wood

Forest Edge Farm

3

River Avon

SALISBURY ROAD

A338

Linbrook Lake

HIGHWOOD LANE

07

SNAILS LA

WOOLMER LANE

Blashford

Northfield Lake

North Poulner

2

Upper Hurst Farm

P

LINBROOK LA

COWPITTS LA

Rooks Coppice

Lifeland Copse

Headlands Business Park

WATERSIDE

NORTH POULNER ROAD

Poulner Jun & Inf Sch

LAWRENCE

1 CHICHESTER RD
2 HAWKINS CL
3 FROBISHER CL

Gouldings Farm

Avon Vale

Kingfisher Lake

RINGWOOD

NORTHFIELD ROAD

POULNER LA

White's Copse

1

Up Mead

Hurst Old Farm

HURST RD

BROADSHARD LA

HAMPTON

DRIVE

SEYMOUR ROAD

Poulner

06

14

A

B

15

C

D

16

E

F

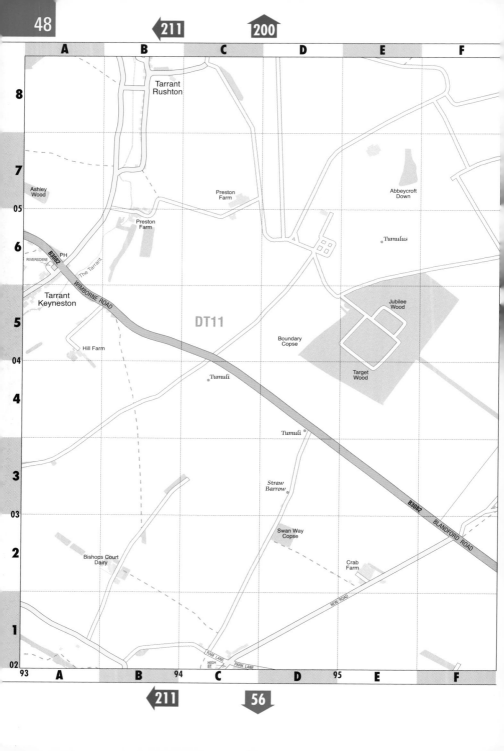

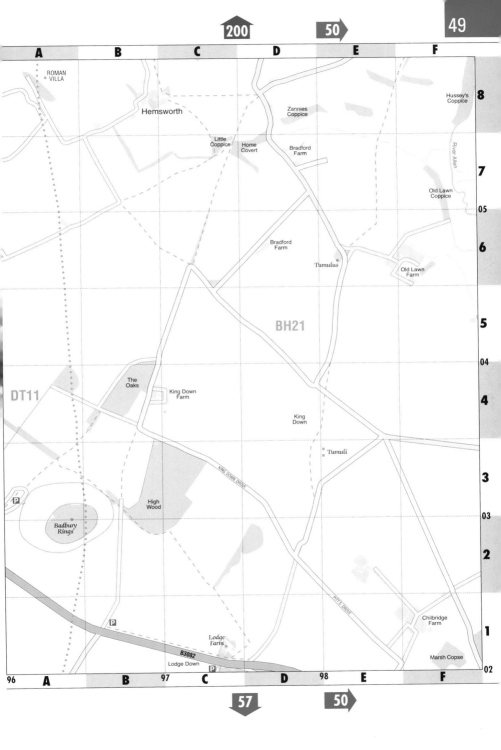

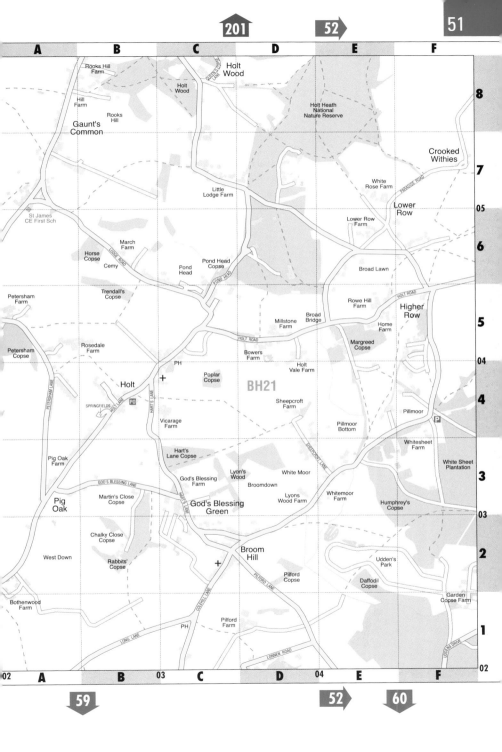

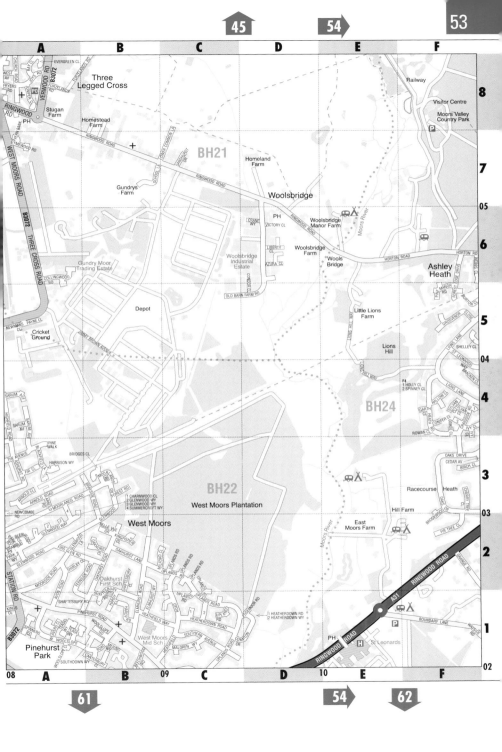

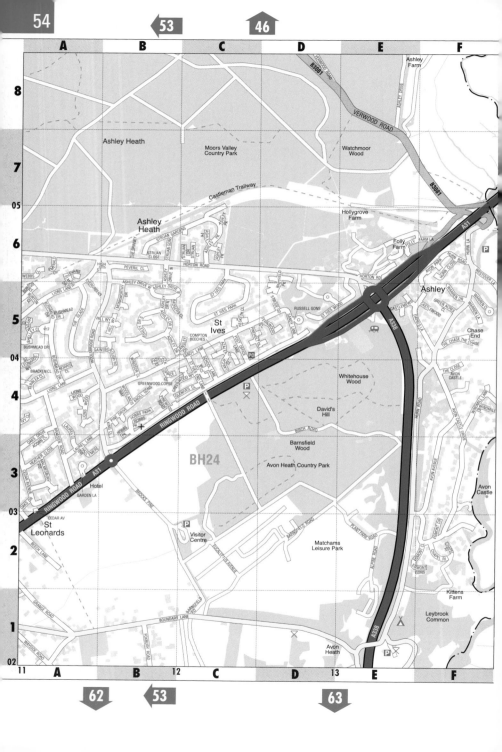

B7
1 THE SWEEP
2 STAR LA
3 FURLONG MEWS
4 PEDDLARS WK
5 COTTAGE MEWS
6 EBENEZER LA

7 GOOSEBERRY LA
8 DEWEYS LA

B8
1 LINDEN GDNS
2 MANOR GDNS
3 ORCHARD MD

C6
1 HARRY BARROW CL
2 CHARING CL
3 WATERLOO WY
4 SOUTHFIELD MS

D6
1 CROW ARCH LA
2 JOYCE DICKSON CL

D8
1 BEECHCROFT LA
2 BEECHCROFT MS
3 WANSTEAD CL
4 Lumby Dr
Mobile Home Pk

E6
1 OLD STACKS GDNS
2 THE CLOISTERS
3 SANDERLINGS

E8
1 WHITEHART FIELDS
2 PIPERS ASH
3 RALEIGH CL
4 CUNNINGHAM CL
5 MERRYWEATHER EST

F6
1 HOLMWOOD GARTH
2 ASHBURN GARTH
3 FOREST CT HILLS

47

55

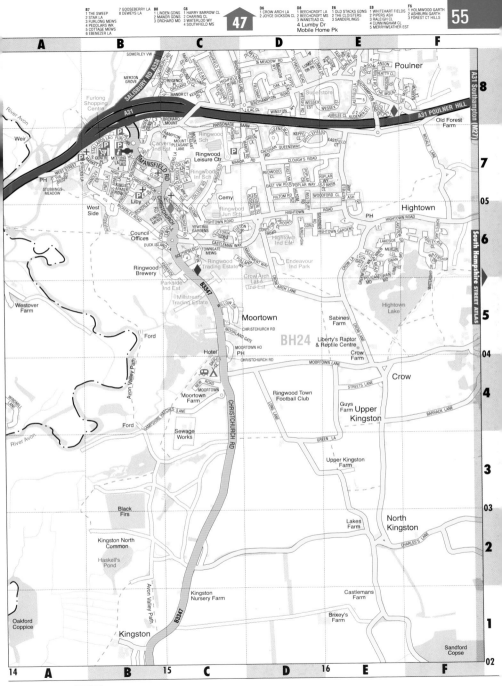

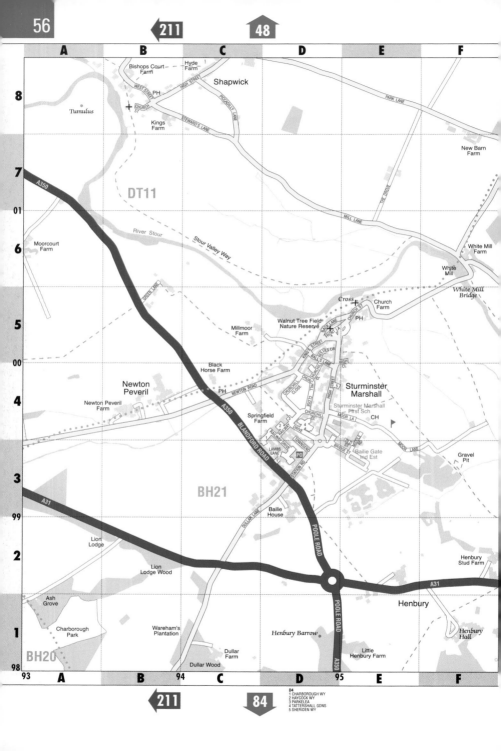

211

48

| | A | B | C | D | E | F |

8

Bishops Court Farm

Hyde Farm

Shapwick

PARK LANE

WEST STREET PH

HIGH STREET

PICCADILLY LANE

STEWARD'S LANE

CHURCH ST

Tumulus

Kings Farm

New Barn Farm

7

01

A350

DT11

THE DROVE

MILL LANE

6

Moorcourt Farm

River Stour

Stour Valley Way

White Mill Farm

White Mill

White Mill Bridge

Cross

Church Farm

PH

GREEN LANE

5

Millmoor Farm

Walnut Tree Field Nature Reserve

MILL LANE

CHURCH ST

00

Black Horse Farm

NEWTON ROAD

VINE STREET

JAMES DR

CROSS LANE

HIGH CL

4

Newton Peveril

Newton Peveril Farm

PH

A350

Springfield Farm

BLANDFORD ROAD

CHURCHILL CLOSE

CHURCHILL

CHURCHILL PL

MOOR LA

Sturminster Marshall

Sturminster Marshall Frst Sch

CH

MOOR LANE

3

BH21

A31

LAMBS LANE

PD

TOWNSEND

BRIDGE ST

NEWTON RD

Bailie Gate Ind Est

Gravel Pit

99

Baillie House

DULLAR LANE

POOLE ROAD

2

Lion Lodge

Lion Lodge Wood

Henbury Stud Farm

A31

1

Ash Grove

Charborough Park

Wareham's Plantation

Dullar Farm

Henbury Barrow

POOLE ROAD

Henbury

Little Henbury Farm

Henbury Hall

98

BH20

Dullar Wood

A350

| **93** | A | **94** B | C | **95** D | E | F |

211

84

D4
1 CHARBOROUGH WY
2 HAYCOCK WY
3 PARKELEA
4 TATTERSHALL GDNS
5 SHERIDEN WY

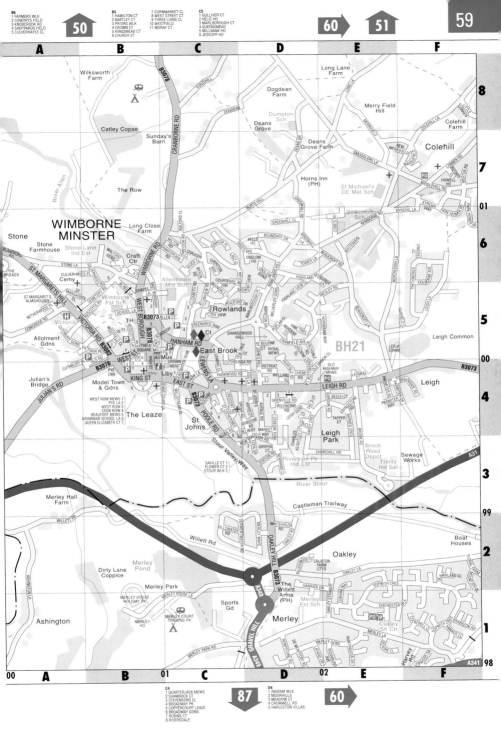

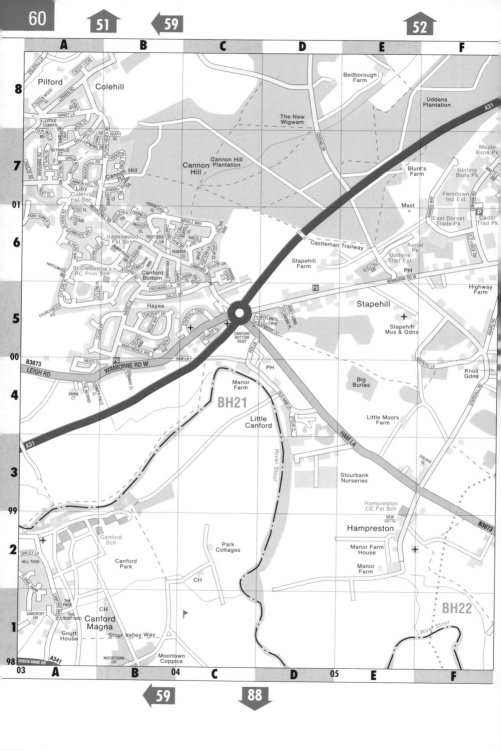

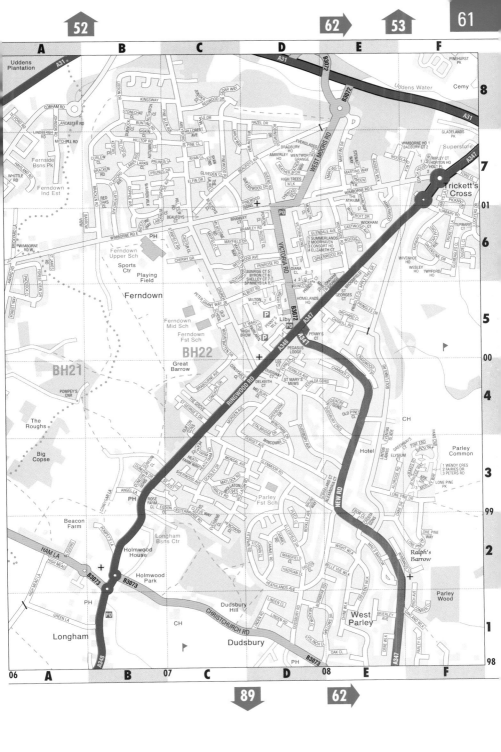

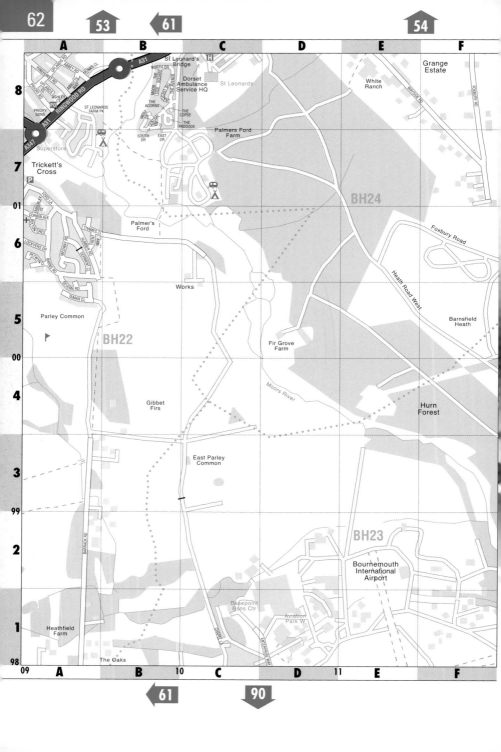

EX13

Wyld Warren

EX13

Skull Head Plantation

Higher Pound Farm

Ridge Plantations

Ridge Farm

Lower Pound Farm

Monarch's Way

Oak Coppice

Dodpen Farm

Newlands Farm

B3165

Laurel Covert

North Wootton Hill Plantation

Wootton Hill

Forest Farm

Ford

Wootton Hill Plantation

MONKTON WYLD CROSS

Champernhayes Marsh

Marsh Farm

Champernhayes Plantation

Champernhayes New Plantation

New Century Plantation

Airish Plantation

POUND LANE

Chestnut Plantation

B3165

Monarch's Way

Higher Wyld Farm

MONKTON WYLD LA

Higher Wyld Farm

Spence Farm

SPENCE LA

SCOTT'S LANE

Monkton Wyld

Stubb's Coppice

DT6

Champernhayes Farm

Spence Plantation

A35 Honiton

Monkton Wyld Wood

ELSDON'S LANE

Elsdons Farm

Liberty Trail

Bowshot Coppice

CHAMPERNHAYES LANE

MILL LA

SPENCE LANE

Harcombe Bottom

Hillside Farm

Penn Farm

Ford

Mill Plantation

Pit Coppice

MILL LANE

Devon STREET ATLAS

Harcombe Farm

HARCOMBE RD

Penn

Howland Coppice

Thorn Coppice

Ashcombe Wood

Smiths Farm

Ladder's Coppice

Tunnel Plantation

Westover Hill Plantation

Westover Farm

DT7

Fern Wood

ROCKET LA

Hole Common

Liberty Trail

Hogchester Plantation

WESTOVER HILL

Thistle Hill

Hogchester Farm

Hayfield Coppice

THE COACH ROAD

HARCOMBE ROAD

Rhode Hill Farm

Square Covert

Greenland Covert

Portymoor Coppice

Shorts Moor

RHODE LANE

ROCKET LANE

Lower Rhode Farm

Twenty Acre Coppice

PENN CROSS

A3052

Soggy Covert

Wood Covert

Rhode Hill

Sleech Wood

Rhode Barton Farm

Fern Hill

Fern Hill Coppice

A35

Cemy

Wood Farm

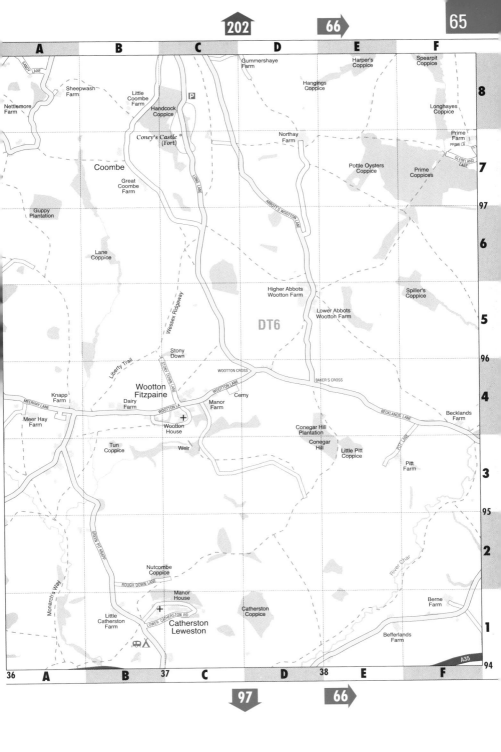

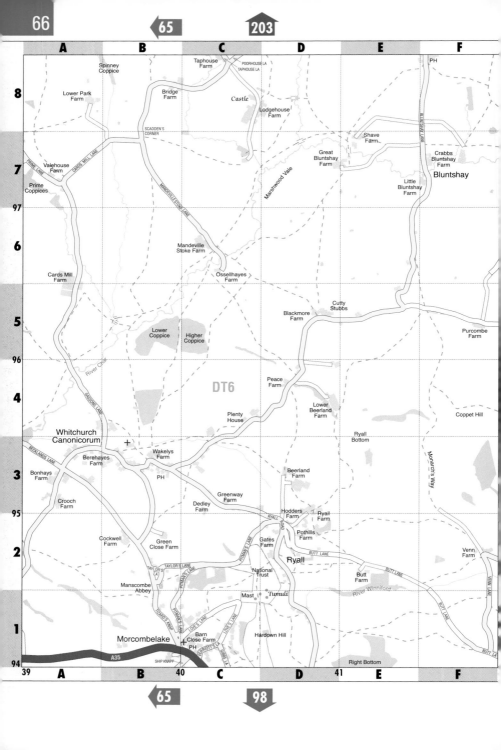

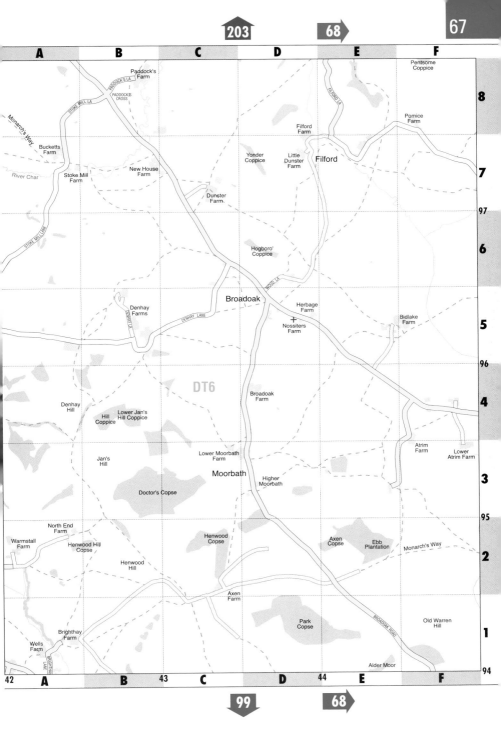

67
204

A B C D E F

Oxbridge

8

Higher
Kingsland Farm
Kershay
Farms
Nurserymead
Coppice
Long Bottom
Coppice
Salway Ash CE
Prim Sch
Perhay
Farm
Myrtle
Farm
Oxbridge
Farm

Shatcombe
Coppice
Waytown

B3162

Kingsland
White House
Farm
Way Farm

7

Higher Kershay
Farm
WHITHAY LA
Lower
Kershay Farm
Marlis
Farm
Camesworth

STRONGATE
LA
STRONGATE LA
Brinsham
Farm
Elwell
Lodge

97

Strongate
Farm
Ash
Farm
FIR TREE
CL
Elwell
Farms
Higher
Elwell
Farm
Foxmoor
Coppice

6

Church
Grounds
Pineapple
Farm
Higher Ford
Farm
Snailscroft
Farm

WHITHAY LANE
PINEAPPLE LANE
Pineapple
Business Park

Hill
Farm
PH
Salwayash
Lambrook

River Brit

5

B3162
Broadenham
Farm
Ash Lane
Farm
ASH LANE
Lambrook
Farm
Bingham's
Farm

96

Ash
Seaview
Farm

Limbury
Ashleigh
Farm
Higher
Ash Farm
Higher
Wooth Farm

DT6

4

Atrim
Sewage
Works

Colly Farm
Wooth Old
Farm

3

Dottery
Wooth
Farm
Wooth

Lower Ash
Farm
Watford
Farm

Higher
Pymore Farm
WATFORD LANE

95

PYMORE LANE

Bilshay
Farm
BILSHAY LANE
PH
Gore
Cross
BLIND LANE CL
GORE LANE

2

A3066
GORE CROSS
Monarch's Way
Middle
Pymore
Farm
Factory
Gore Cross
Business Park
TOWNSEND WY

New Close
Farm
THREAD MILL
LA
CORBIN WAY
RIDGEWAY
HILLVIEW

River Simene
Washingpool
Farm
Lower
Pymore
Farm
PYMORE ROAD
Pymore
The Sir John
Colfox Sch
QUEENWELL

1

DOTTERY ROAD
Seymour
Farm
BANTOM
SHARD
VILLAGE RD
COURT CL

B3162
River Brit
GIPSY LANE
ST ANDREW'S
ROAD
KNIGHTSTONE RI

94

45 A B 46 C D 47 E F

F1
1 FISHWEIR FIELDS
2 ACER AV
3 WHITE CL
4 SPRING CL
5 GORE CROSS WY
6 BATH ORCHARD

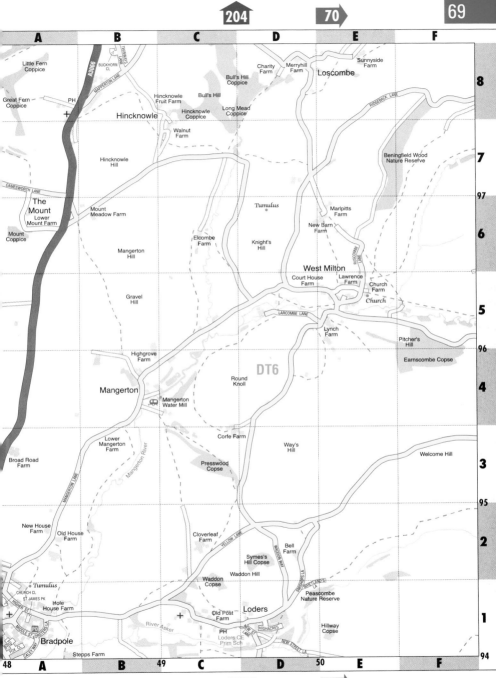

A B C D E F

Little Fern Coppice

Great Fern Coppice

PH

The Mount
Lower Mount Farm

Mount Coppice

BUCKHORN CL

TWINNERS LANE

MAPPERTON LANE

A3066

CAMESWORTH LANE

Hincknowle
Fruit Farm

Hincknowle

Hincknowle Coppice

Walnut Farm

Hincknowle Hill

Mount Meadow Farm

Mangerton Hill

Bull's Hill

Bull's Hill Coppice

Long Mead Coppice

Charity Farm

Merryhill Farm

Loscombe

Sunnyside Farm

RIDGEBACK LANE

Beningfield Wood
Nature Reserve

Tumulus

Elcombe Farm

Knight's Hill

Marlpitts Farm

New Barn Farm

West Milton

Court House Farm

Lawrence Farm

Church Farm

Church

RUSCOMBE LANE

Gravel Hill

LARCOMBE LANE

Lynch Farm

Pitcher's Hill

Earnscombe Copse

Highgrove Farm

DT6

Round Knoll

Mangerton

Mangerton Water Mill

Lower Mangerton Farm

Mangerton River

Corfe Farm

Way's Hill

Welcome Hill

Broad Road Farm

MANGERTON LANE

Presswood Copse

New House Farm

Old House Farm

Cloverleaf Farm

YELLOW LANE

Symes's Hill Copse

Waddon Copse

Waddon Hill

Bell Farm

WADDON WAY

UPLODERS LA

Peascombe Nature Reserve

Welcome Hill

Tumulus

CHURCH CL
ST JAMES PK

Hole House Farm

HIGHER ST

River Asker

Old Post Farm

PH

Loders CE Prim Sch

Loders

HIGHACRES

UPLODERS LANE

Hillway Copse

PO

MIDDLE ST
DORSET LA

CALES WAY

Bradpole

Stepps Farm

NEW STREET LA

8 7 97 6 5 96 4 3 95 2 1 94

	A	B	C	D	E	F

8

Regent's Coppice

RIDGEBACK LANE

South Poorton Farm

Spring Hill Farm

Leggland Farm

Bottom Farm

South Poorton

Strap's Coppice

Lower Long Hay Coppice

South Poorton Nature Reserve

Elmside Coppice

Caseley's Coppice

Poorton Hill Farm

7

Poorton Hill

LUKE HILL

Hungry Hill

Wytherston Wood

Strip Lynchets

Swyre Hill

97

Swyre Bottom

Swyre Coppice

Wytherston Farm

Quarry

DUGBERRY HILL

6

Strip Lynchets

Broadfield Coppice

Powerstock Common Nature Reserve

Strip Lynchets

Lower Townsend Farm

Townsend Farm

DT6

Whetley

5

Manor Farm

Glebe Farm

Powerstock CE Prim. Sch.

+Powerstock

PH

Eastwater Farm

KING'S LANE

Whetley Farm

96

Merriott

Motte & Bailey

Castle Mill Farm

King's Farm

4

PH

Southmead Farm

THE SQUARE

King's Farm

Mappercombe Manor Farm

Nettlecombe

3

Browns Farm

Marsh Farm

KING'S LANE

95

Mappercombe Manor

Bell Stone

Ridge Copse

Belstone Covert

Warren Plantation

Eggardor Hill

2

Sweed's Copse

Marsh Copse

Chaffins Coppice

Whinhill Copse

Knowle Hill

Knowle Plantation

1

Shedbush Copse

Knowle Copse

North Eggardon Farm

94

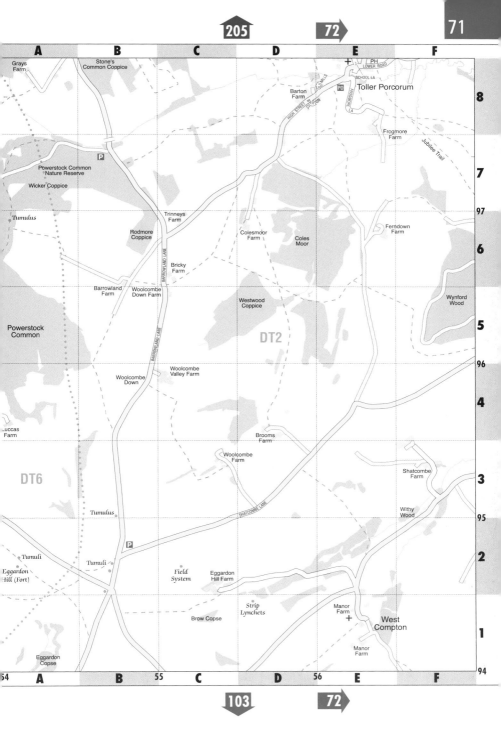

Grays Farm

Stone's Common Coppice

PH
LOWER ROAD
SCHOOL LA
Toller Porcorum

Barton Farm

HIGH STREET

PO

8

Frogmore Farm

Jubilee Trail

P
Powerstock Common
Nature Reserve

7

Wicker Coppice

Tumulus

Trinneys Farm

97

Rodmore Coppice

Colesmoor Farm

Coles Moor

Ferndown Farm

6

BARROWLAND LANE

Bricky Farm

Barrowland Farm

Woolcombe Down Farm

Westwood Coppice

Wynford Wood

Powerstock Common

DT2

5

BARROWLAND LANE

96

Woolcombe Down

Woolcombe Valley Farm

4

Luccas Farm

Brooms Farm

DT6

Woolcombe Farm

Shatcombe Farm

3

SHATCOMBE LANE

Tumulus

Withy Wood

95

P

Tumuli

2

Eggardon Hill (Fort)

Tumuli

Field System

Eggardon Hill Farm

Strip Lynchets

Manor Farm

West Compton

1

Brow Copse

Eggardon Copse

Manor Farm

94

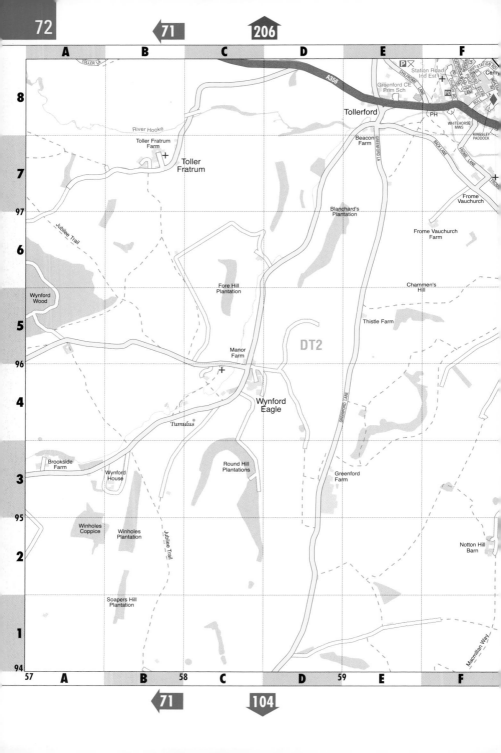

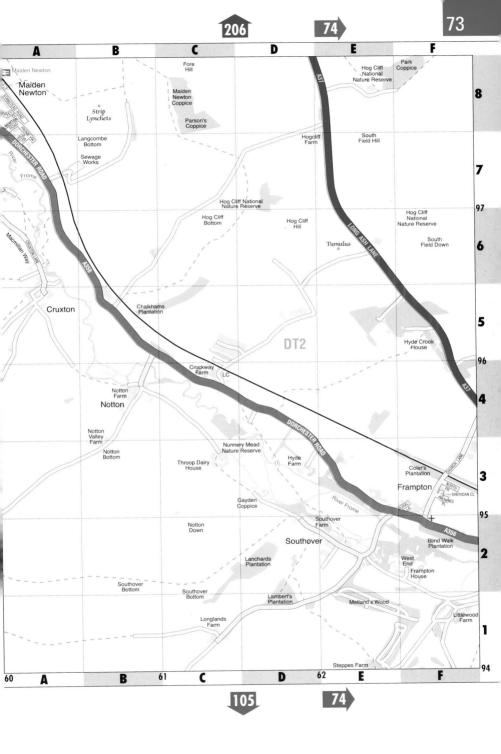

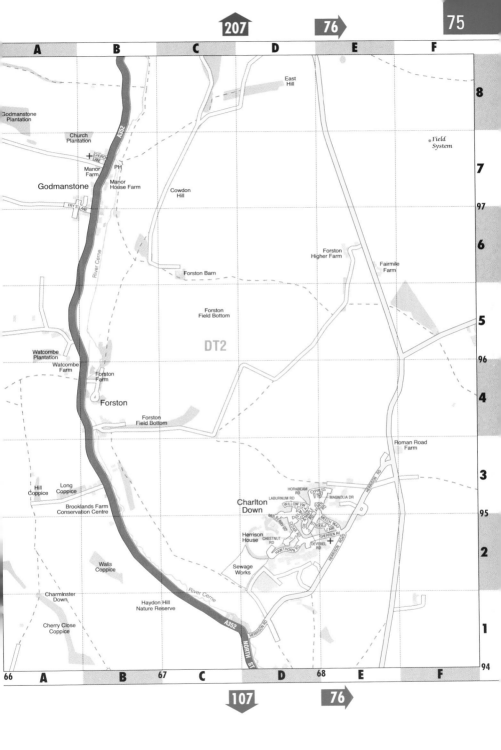

A B C D E F

8

East
Hill

Godmanstone
Plantation

Church
Plantation

7

Manor
Farm PH
Manor
House Farm

Godmanstone

Cowdon
Hill

FRY'S LANE

97

River Cerne

6

Forston
Higher Farm

Fairmile
Farm

Forston Barn

Forston
Field Bottom

5

DT2

96

Watcombe
Plantation
Watcombe
Farm
Forston
Farm

4

Forston

Forston
Field Bottom

Roman Road
Farm

3

Hill
Coppice
Long
Coppice

HERRISON RD

Brooklands Farm
Conservation Centre

Charlton
Down

HORNBEAM
RD
CYPRESS
RD
LABURNUM RD
WILLOW VW
MAGNOLIA DR

95

MULBERRY RD
CEDAR RD
BEECH WAY
LAUREL LANE

D

Herrison
House
CHESTNUT
RD

DEVENEL
RD

2

Walis
Coppice

HAWTHORN RD

SHERREN AV

HERRISON RD

Charminster
Down

River Cerne

Sewage
Works

Haydon Hill
Nature Reserve

A352

Cherry Close
Coppice

1

HERRISON RD

NORTH ST

94

66 A B 67 C 68 D E F

Field
System

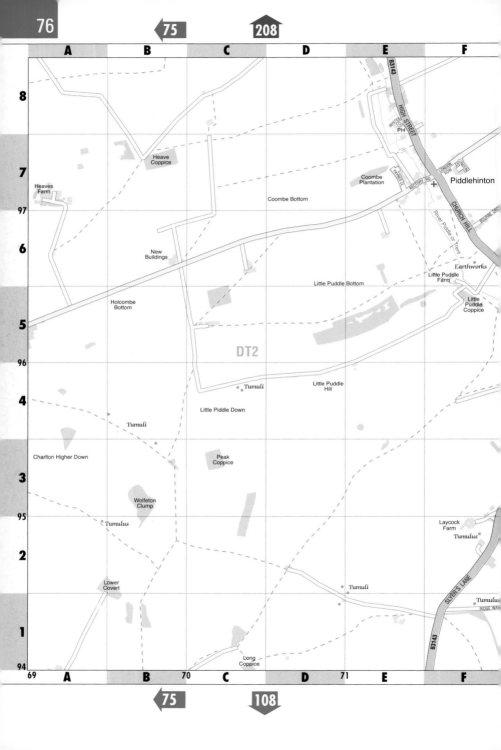

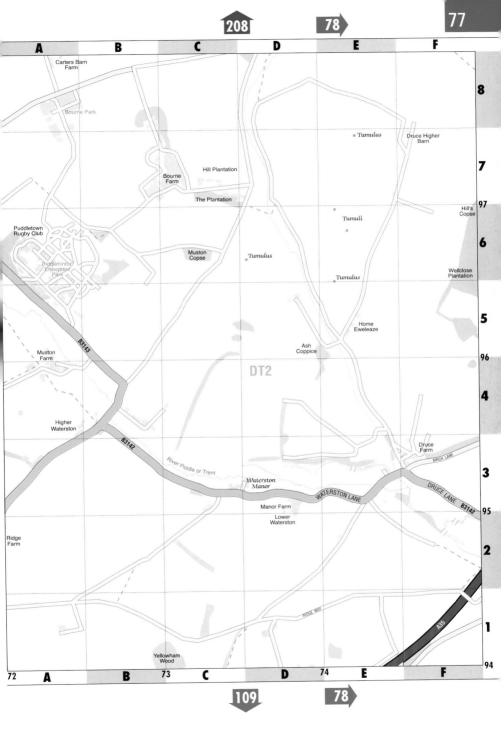

208
78

A   **B**   **C**   **D**   **E**   **F**

Carters Barn Farm

Bourne Park

• Tumulus

Druce Higher Barn

8

Bourne Farm

Hill Plantation

7

The Plantation

97

Hill's Copse

Puddletown Rugby Club

Tumuli

Piddlehinton Enterprise Park

Muston Copse

• Tumulus

6

Wellclose Plantation

• Tumulus

B3143

Home Eweleaze

5

Muston Farm

Ash Coppice

96

DT2

4

Higher Waterston

B3142

Druce Farm

River Piddle or Trent

BIRCH LANE

Waterston Manor

DRUCE LANE

3

WATERSTON LANE

Manor Farm

B3142

Lower Waterston

95

Ridge Farm

2

A35

RIDGE WAY

1

Yellowham Wood

94

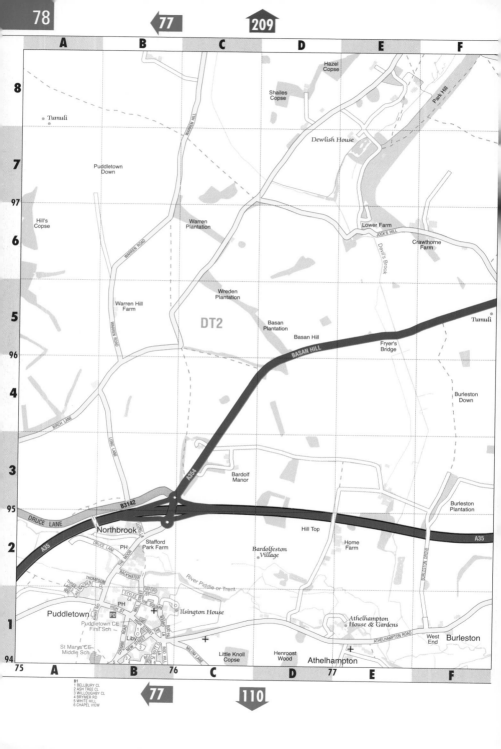

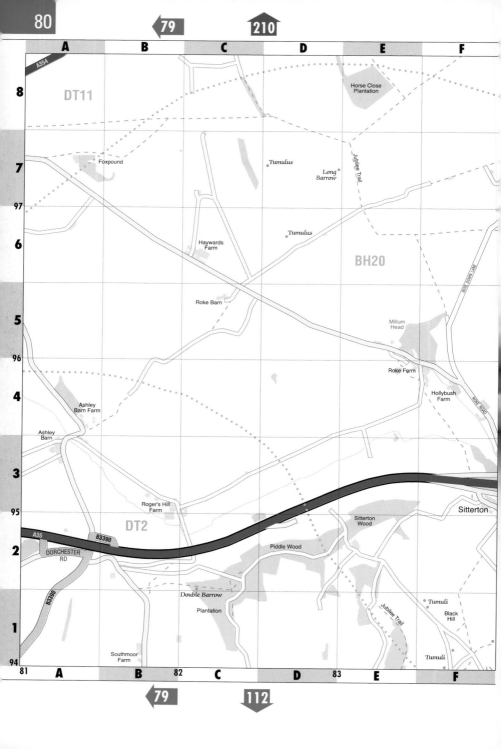

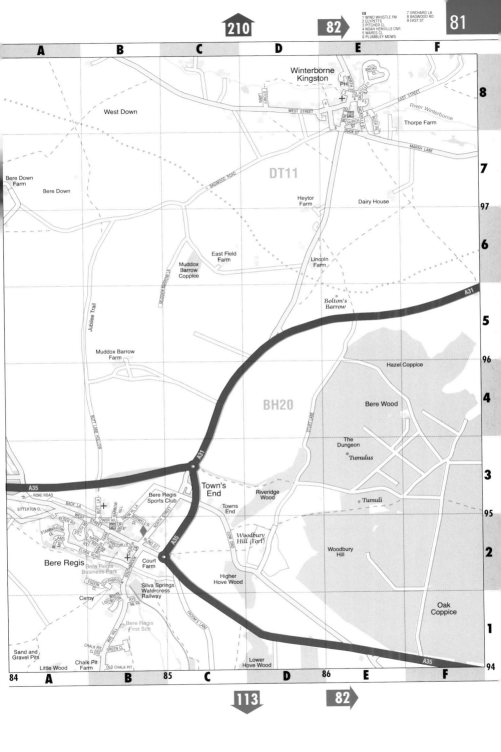

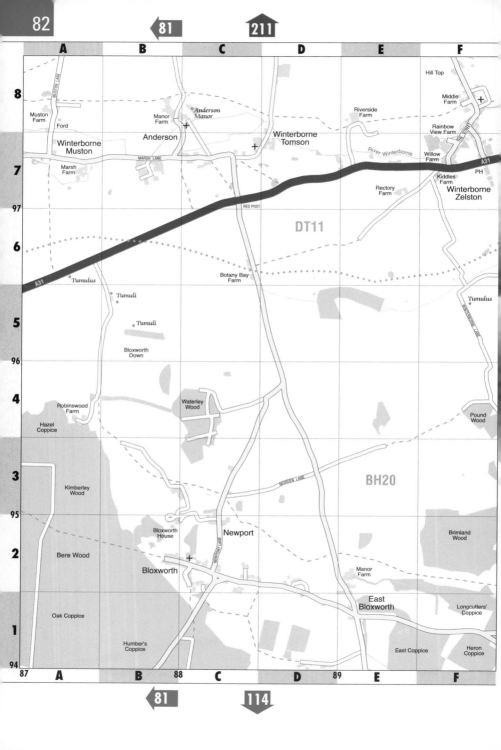

A **B** **C** **D** **E** **F**

8

Charborough Park

High Wood

Windmill Barrow Farm

West Wood

Dullar Wood

West Wood

Fox Holes Wood

Limekiln Coppice

BH21

Heron Grove

Windmill Barrow

Combe Almer

7

Higher Coombe Farm

BH20

97

Brock Hill

Notting Hill

DULLAR LANE

POOLE ROAD

A350

Village Earthworks

Loop Farm

Sandpits Farm

6

Bokers Farm

CASTLE FARM ROAD

Warmwell Farm

FLOWERS DROVE

COLDHILL ROAD

Winter's Coppice

Castle Hill

White Heather

POOLE ROAD

5

Lytchett House

Goat House Farm

BH16

Barrow Hill

CALCRAFTS LANE

96

Phillips's Coppice

Garden Wood

Dyett's Coppice

Allots

Sunnyside Farm

Dowdens Farm

PEATONS LANE

WIMBORNE ROAD

4

Bridge End

Peatons Farm

HIGH STREET

JENNYS LANE

HOPMANS CL

CASTLE FARM ROAD

TURBETTS CL

CHARBOROUGH CL

CHAPEL

RYE CL

LIME KILN ROAD

PUBLIC BILLARD

PURBECK DR

Lytchett Matravers

WIMBORNE RD

Ash Farm

CRUMPLER CL

PH

PUBLIC DR

ANNGOTT CL

ABBOTTS MEADOW

TIMS LANE

3

Druce Farm

Eddy Green Farm

CLAYLANE

Liby

High Street

Recn Gd

PH

HUNTICK ESTATE

North House Farm

Elder Moor

GREEN DROVE

VINEYARD CL

HANS LA

PROSPECT RD

SPDW ST RD

HUNTICK ROAD

95

Redbridge Farm

PALMERS OR

FLOWERS DROVE

CLAYERS

FOXHILLS DR

Foxhills Farm

BH20

Bartom's Hill

BRIDGE ROAD

BARTOM'S LANE

Lytchett Matravers Prim Sch

THE SPINNEY

BURBS CL

1 FOSTERS SPRING
2 PRYORS WK
3 LANDERS REACH

Huntick Farm

2

Holly Farm

DEANS DROVE

FOXHILLS LANE

Race Farm

DILLONS GDNS

PENROSE CL

BURBIDGE CL

DOLMANS HILL

QUARR LA

1

H Bulbury Farm

Quarr Farm

Quarr Hill Farm

HALLS CNR

GLEBE ROAD

CASTLE VW DR

BULBURY LA

HALLS ROAD

94

93 **A** **B** **94** **C** **D** **95** **E** **F**

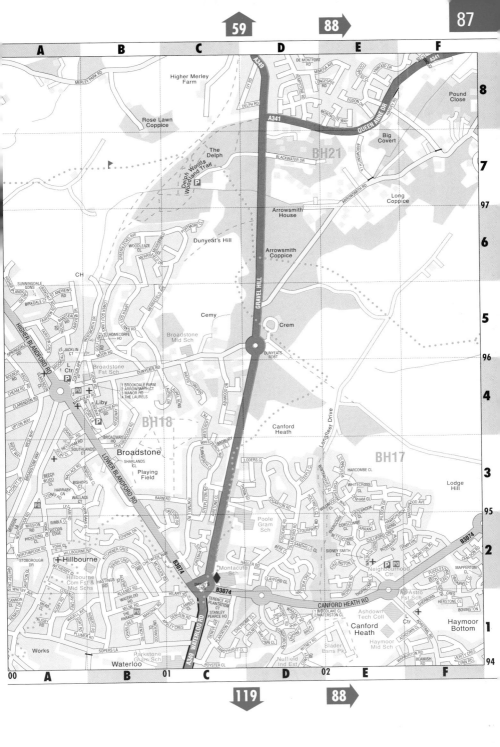

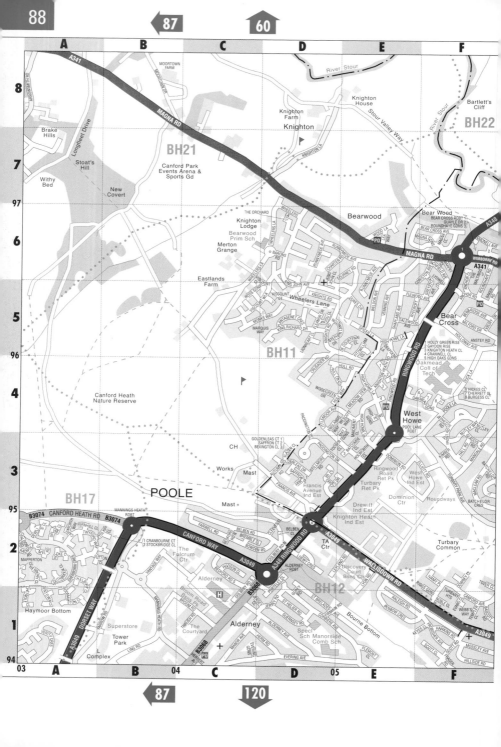

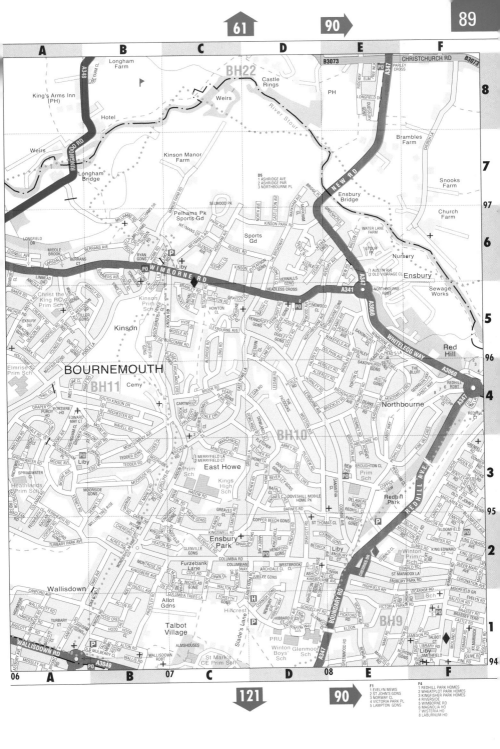

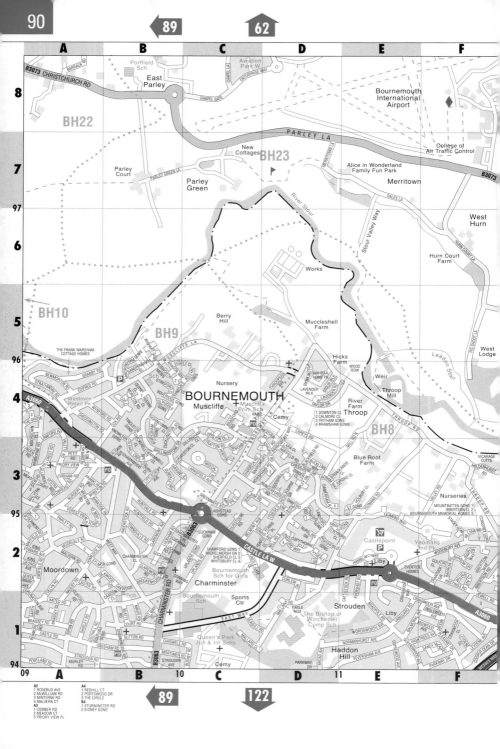

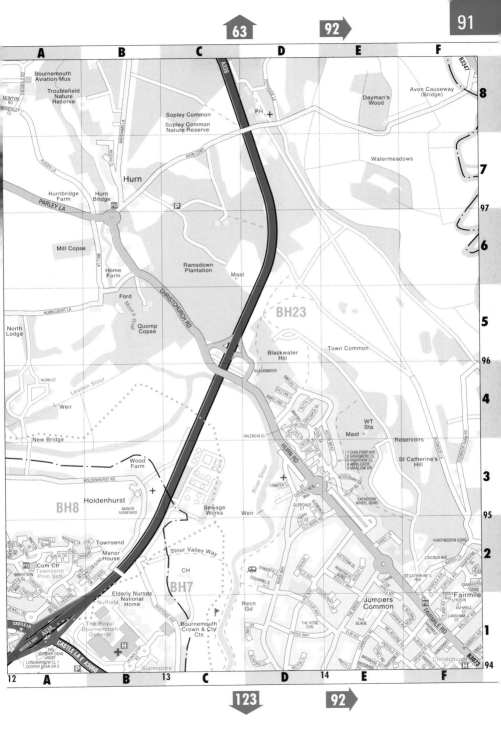

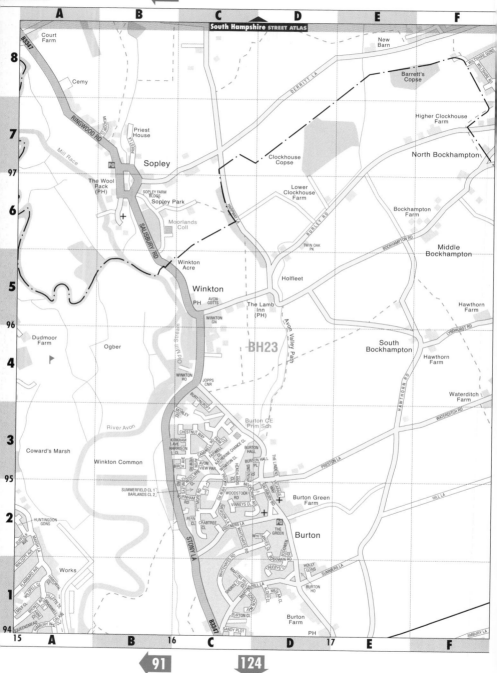

South Hampshire STREET ATLAS

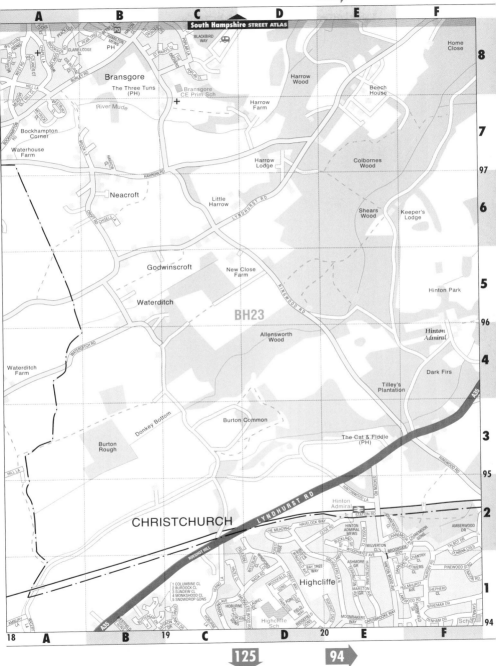

South Hampshire STREET ATLAS

BLACKBIRD WAY

Home Close

8

Bransgore

Harrow Wood

Beech House

The Three Tuns (PH)

Bransgore CE Prim Sch

Harrow Farm

Harrow Wood

River Mude

Bockhampton Corner

7

Waterhouse Farm

Harrow Lodge

Colbornes Wood

97

Neacroft

Little Harrow

6

Shears Wood

Keeper's Lodge

Godwinscroft

New Close Farm

Hinton Park

5

Waterditch

BH23

96

Allensworth Wood

Hinton Admiral

4

Waterditch Farm

Dark Firs

Tilley's Plantation

Donkey Bottom

Burton Common

The Cat & Fiddle (PH)

3

Burton Rough

95

HILL LA

HINTONWOOD LA

STATION RD

Hinton Admiral

2

CHRISTCHURCH

LYNDHURST RD

ROESHOT HILL

THE MEADWAY

HAVELOCK WAY

HINTON ADMIRAL MEWS

AMBERWOOD DR

TALBOT DR

Highcliffe

1 COLUMBINE CL
2 BURDOCK CL
3 SUNDEW CL
4 MONKSHOOD CL
5 SNOWDROP GDNS

Highcliffe Sch

MOONRAKERS WAY

CARISBROOKE WAY

SHEPHERD CL

BRAEMAR DR

DENHAM DR

1

A35

94

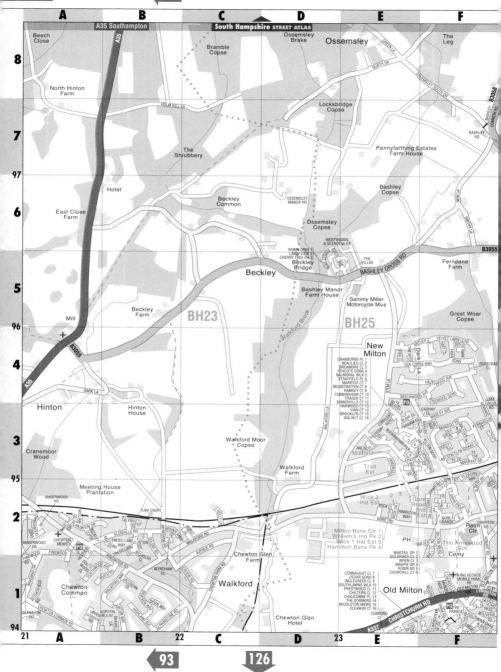

South Hampshire STREET ATLAS

A B C D E F

8

93

126

21 A B 22 C D 23 E F

Beech Close

North Hinton Farm

A35 Southampton

HOLM HILL LA

Bramble Copse

Ossemsley Brake

Ossemsley

The Leg

NORTH DR

GREEN LA

B3058

GREEMSLEY SOUTH DR

BASHLEY COMMON RD

Locksbridge Copse

BASHLEY RD

7

The Shrubbery

Pennyfarthing Estates Farm House

97

Hotel

Beckley Common

OSSEMSLEY MANOR HO

Bashley Copse

LA WK

SMITH LA

6

East Close Farm

Ossemsley Copse

WESTWOODS & GLENDENE PK

THE VILLAS

Ferndene Farm

B3055

Beckley Bridge

ROBIN CRES 1
LAWN VIEW 2
CHERRY TREE DR 3

BUSKETTS LA

Beckley

Beckley

BASHLEY CROSS RD

Bashley Manor Farm House

Sammy Miller Motorcycle Mus

5

Mill

Beckley Farm

BH23

Walkford Brook

BH25

Great Woar Copse

96

B3055

A35

DARK LA

Hinton House

CUTLER CL
VELVET LAWN RD
THE HILL
FERN CROFT
HART CL
PARK
GDNS
ROSECRAE CL

New Milton

Dark La

CRANBORNE PL 1
BEAULIEU CL 2
BREAMORE CL 3
FOXCOTE GDNS 4
BALMORAL WLK 5
STRATFIELD PL 6
MARRYAT CT 7
MOUNTBATTEN CT 8
RAMSEY CT 9
CUNNINGHAM CT 10
FRASER CT 11
SOMERVILLE CT 12
HARWOOD CT 13
VIAN CT 14
BROOKLYN CT 15
WALNUT CT 16.

DOE COPSE WAY
HAZELWOOD AVE
BEECHWOOD
PINEWOOD GDNS
CADHAY
MARLEY AVE
LAKE GROVE RD
KENNARD

4

Hinton

Hinton

DARK LA

Walkford Moor Copse

WALKFORD LA

Trad Est

ARUNDEL
Millfield

BLAIR PL
PANHAM CL

3

Cranemoor Wood

Walkford Farm

MARRYAT RD

NELSON CLO
DRAKE CL
COMPTON
MARRYAT RD

95

Meeting House Plantation

AMBERWOOD HO

TURF CROFT CT

Wick 2 Ind Est

WICK LA
GORE RD

Wick 1 Ind Est

HAMILTON WAY

GORE
GRANGE
Recn
Ctr

COMPTON CL

2

CHEWTON MEWS

GREENVIL

TRESILLIAN WAY

CLINTON
DOUGLAS CL

WALKFORD RD

BROADSTONE

CASTLE FARM RD

AVENUE RD

Milton Bsns Ctr 1
William's Ind Pk 2
Wick 1 Ind Est 3
Hamilton Bsns Pk 4

PH

The Arnewood Sch
Cemy

King George
MOBILE HOME
Arts
Ctr

WAGTAIL DR 1
GOLDFINCH CL 2
WREN CL 3
MAGPIE GR 4
ROBIN GR 5
CHURCHILL CT 6.

OLD MILTON RD

THE PARADE

BOUVERIE

AMBERWOOD DR

PINEWOOD RD

Chewton Common

WYNDHAM CL.

Chewton Glen Farm

Walkford

CONNAUGHT CL 7
CEDAR GDNS 8
INGLEGREEN CL 9
SOUTHAWWEL WLK 10
PRESTWOOD CL 11
CLEMENTS CL 12
CHAUCOMBE PL 13
THE DORMERS 14
MIDDLETON CL 15
ELEANOR CT 16.

Old Milton

CHILTERN DR

1

GLENAVON RD

CHEWTON COMMON RD

GORDON MOUNT

BRANKSOME

Chewton Glen Hotel

DUNFORD

CHRISTCHURCH RD

A337

94

21 A B 22 C D 23 E F

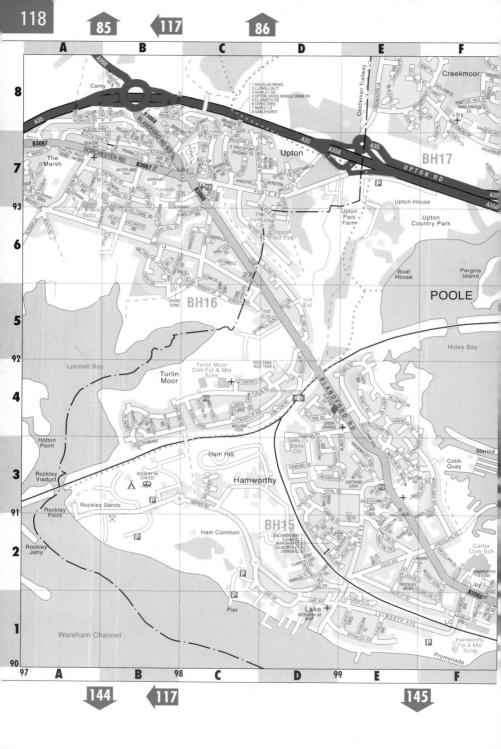

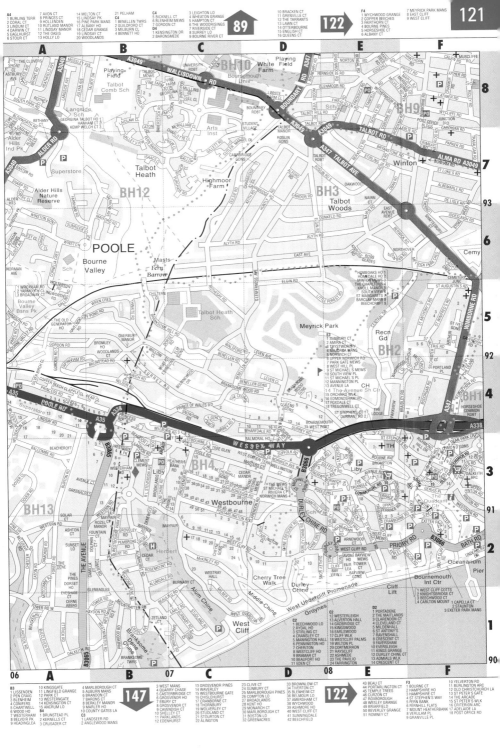

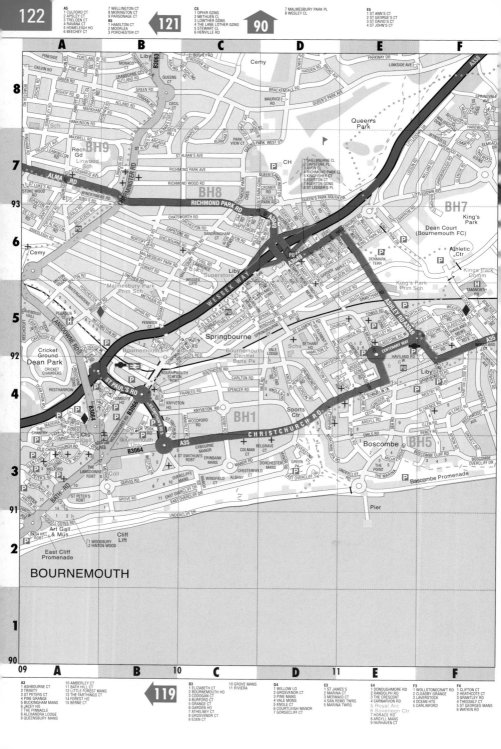

BOURNEMOUTH

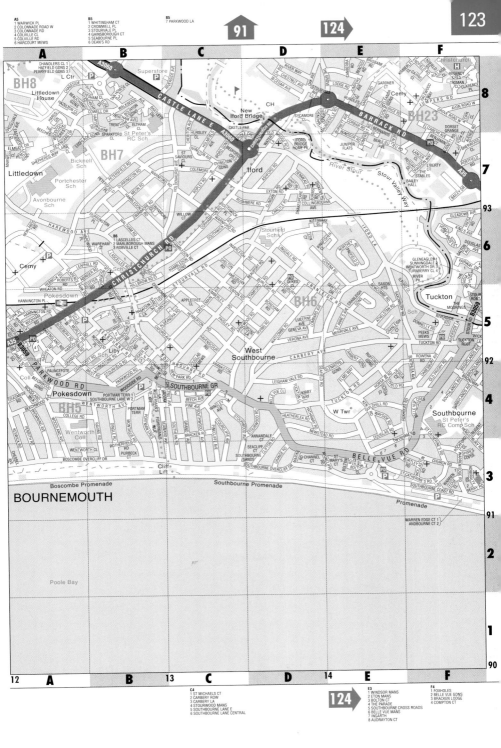

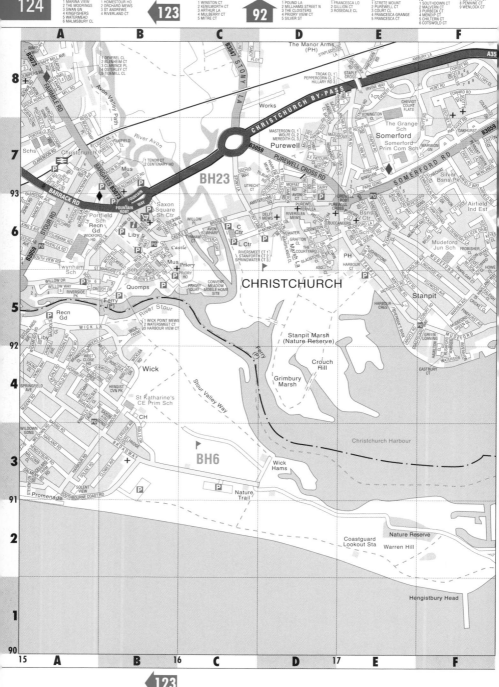

125
94

Groynes

A7
1 BUCKINGHAM CT
2 CASTLE CT
3 WINDSOR CT
4 HURST CT
5 BERMUDA CT
6 CLAIRE CT
7 DIANA CT
8 TRACEY CT

B7
1 CARISBROOKE CT
2 MERTON CT
3 BALMORAL CT
4 PEMBROKE CT
5 EXETER CT
6 HERTFORD CT
7 FRANCES CT
8 ROSEMARY CT
9 KENNETH CT
10 ALAN CT
11 WILLIAM CT
12 PENELOPE CT
13 STELLA CT

Groynes

WESTMINSTER CT 1
CRESCENT CT 2
MARINE PROSPECT 3
MARINE POINT 4
BARTON CHASE 5
BRACKLESHAM PL 6

Barton on Sea

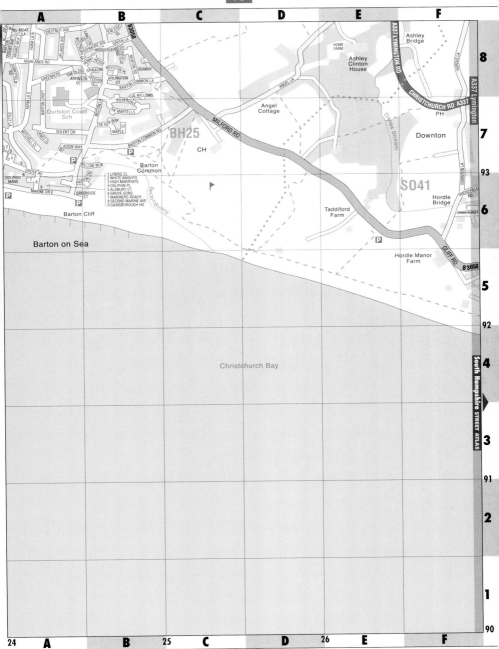

A B C D E F

8

CHESTNUT AVE
FARM LA
HIGHLANDS RD
GREENACRE
THE GLADE
ATKINSON
CT
ARLINGTON
CT
ROYSTON
SEAWAY
SPINACRE
HEDGERLEY
HE MARTELLS
SILVERDALE
THE WILLOWS
Durlston Court
Sch
MAPLE
SOLENT DR
THE FA WAY
MITCHELL CL

HOME
FARM

Ashley
Clinton
House

Ashley
Bridge

A337 LYMINGTON RD

A337 Lymington

CHRISTCHURCH RD A337

8

Angel
Cottage

ANGEL LA

MILFORD RD

PH

Downton

Daves Stream

7

BH25

CH

93

S041

Barton
Common

Hordle
Bridge

SHORFIELD RD

6

1 LYNRIC CL
2 WHITE KNIGHTS
3 HIGH MARRYATS
4 DOLPHIN PL
5 ALDBURY CT
6 GROVE GDNS
7 MARINERS REACH
8 SECOND MARINE AVE
9 GAINSBOROUGH HO

Taddiford
Farm

DANEHURST

MEADOW WAY

YELLOW WLK

GREENSIDE
CT

Becton Bunny

DOLPHIN
MANS

MARINE DR E

P

P

P

6

Barton Cliff

Hordle Manor
Farm

CLIFF RD

B 3058

Barton on Sea

5

92

Christchurch Bay

4

South Hampshire STREET ATLAS

3

91

2

1

90

24 A B 25 C D 26 E F

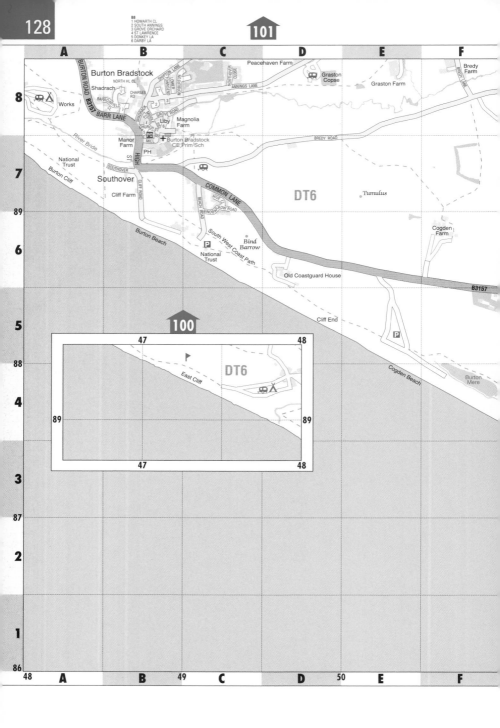

B8
1 HOWARTH CL
2 SOUTH ANNINGS
3 GROVE ORCHARD
4 ST LAWRENCE
5 DONKEY LA
6 DARBY LA

101

Peacehaven Farm

Burton Bradstock

Graston Copse

Graston Farm

Bredy Farm

BREDY LANE

Shadrach

NORTH HL DL

CHARLES RD

Magnolia Farm

BARR LANE

BURTON ROAD B3157

Works

River Bride

National Trust

Burton Cliff

Southover

SOUTHOVER

HIGH ST

CLIFF ROAD

Manor Farm

PH

Libry

Burton Bradstock CE Prim Sch

MILL

GROVE ROAD

CHURCH RD

BREDY ROAD

Cliff Farm

Burton Beach

COMMON LANE

BREDY ROAD

BARROW ROAD

DT6

Tumulus

Cogden Farm

8

89

7

6

5

88

4

89

3

87

2

1

86

Bind Barrow

National Trust

South West Coast Path

Old Coastguard House

B3157

Cliff End

100

47   48

East Cliff

DT6

89   89

47   48

Cogden Beach

Burton Mere

48   A   B   49   C   D   50   E   F

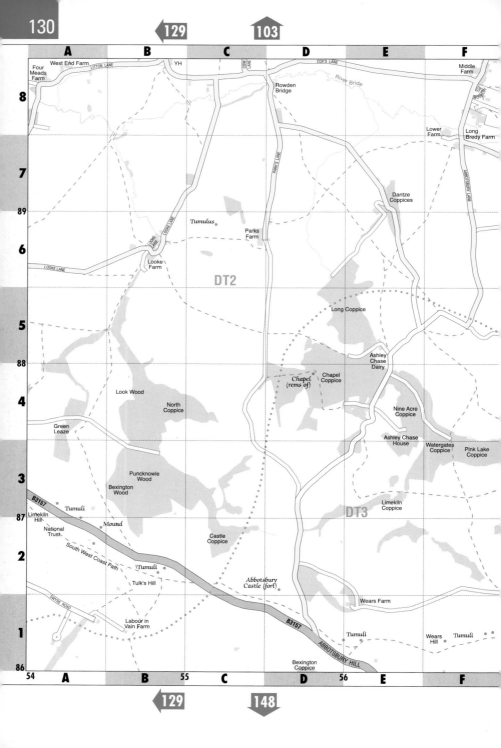

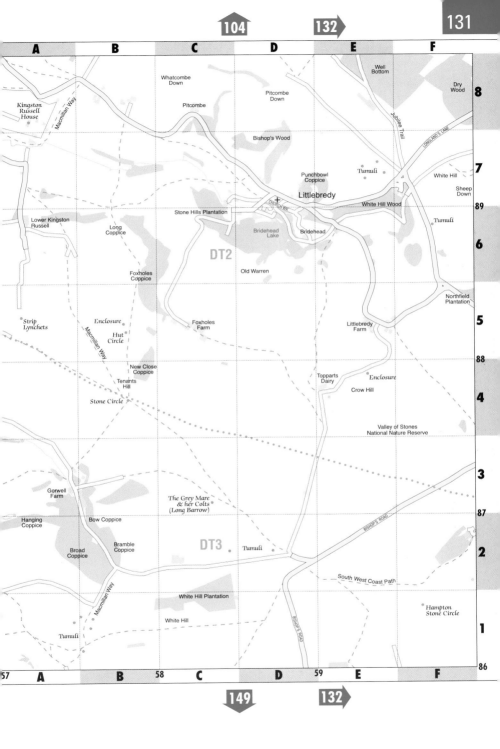

A   B   C   D   E   F

8

Well Bottom

Dry Wood

Kingston Russell House

Whatcombe Down

Pitcombe

Pitcombe Down

Macmillan Way

Bishop's Wood

Jubilee Trail

LONGLAND'S LANE

7

Punchbowl Coppice

Tumuli

White Hill

Littlebredy

Sheep Down

Church Wk

89

Lower Kingston Russell

Stone Hills Plantation

White Hill Wood

Tumuli

Long Coppice

Bridehead Lake

Bridehead

6

DT2

Foxholes Coppice

Old Warren

Northfield Plantation

5

Strip Lynchets

Enclosure

Foxholes Farm

Littlebredy Farm

Macmillan Way

Hut Circle

88

New Close Coppice

Topparts Dairy

Enclosure

Tenants Hill

Crow Hill

Stone Circle

4

Valley of Stones National Nature Reserve

3

Gorwell Farm

The Grey Mare & her Colts (Long Barrow)

87

Hanging Coppice

Bow Coppice

Bramble Coppice

DT3

Tumuli

BISHOP'S ROAD

2

Broad Coppice

Macmillan Way

South West Coast Path

Hampton Stone Circle

White Hill Plantation

BISHOP'S ROAD

White Hill

1

Tumuli

86

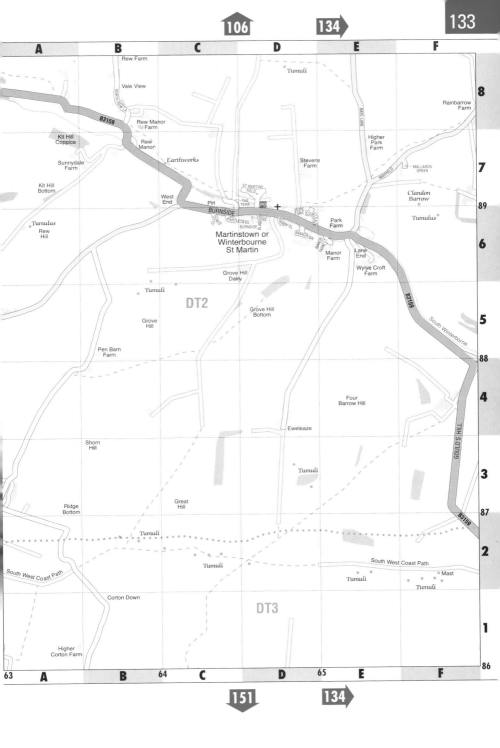

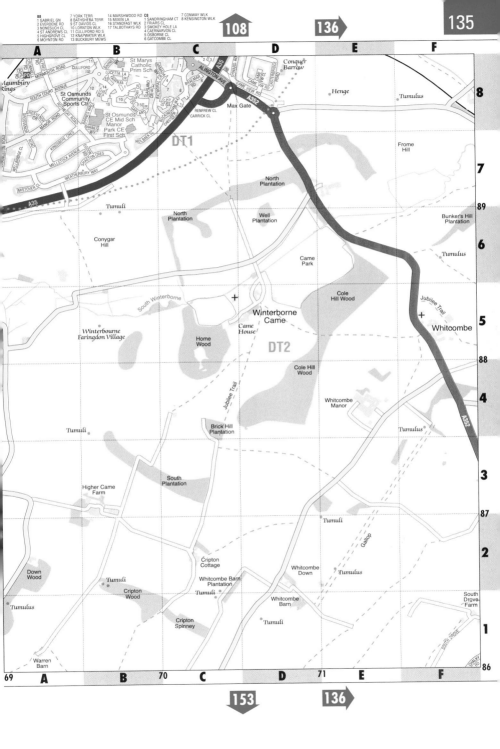

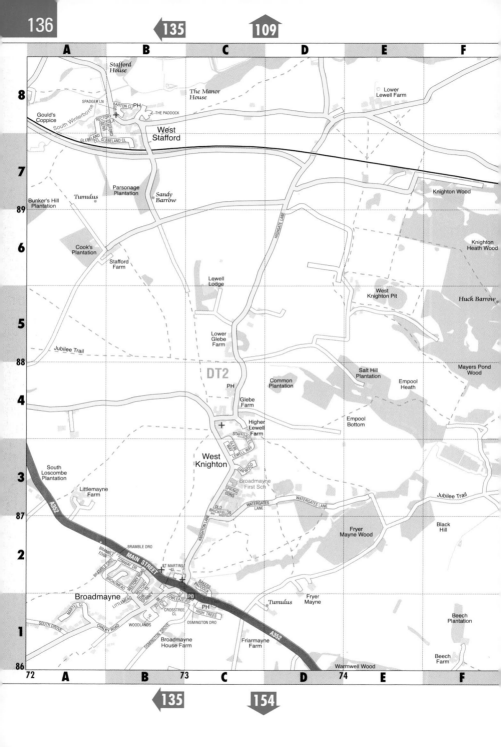

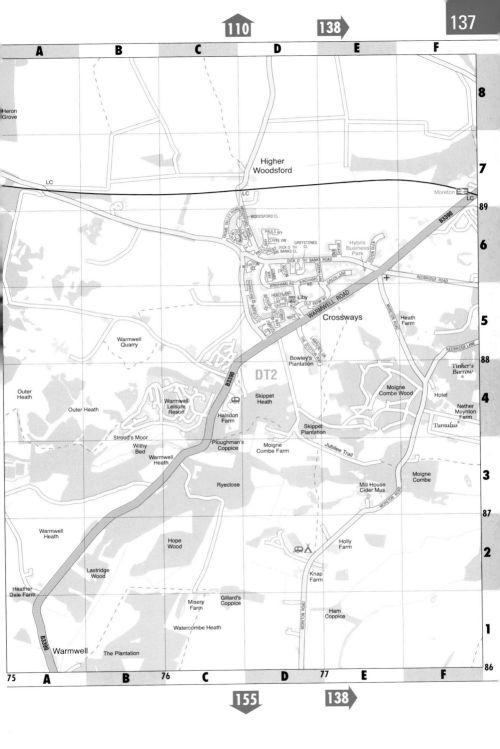

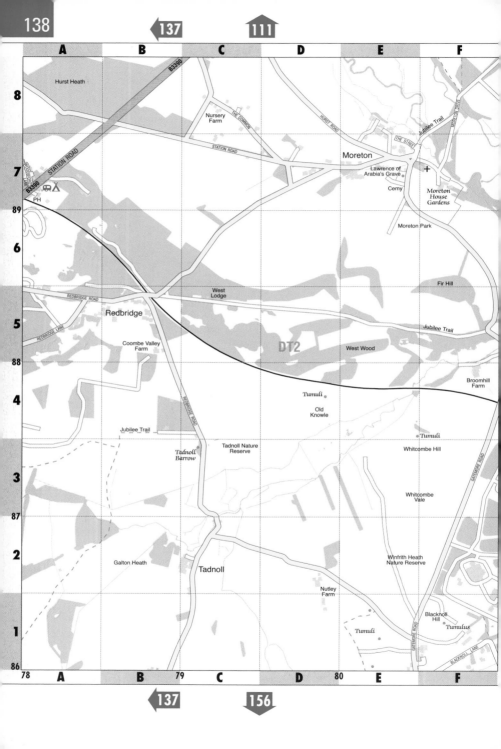

A   B   C   D   E   F

Hurst Heath

8

B3390

Nursery
Farm

THE COMMON

STATION ROAD

HURST ROAD

Moreton

THE STREET

Jubilee Trail

MORETON DRIVE

7

STATION ROAD

B3390

SPODDLE LANE

Lawrence of
Arabia's Grave

Cemy

+

Moreton
House
Gardens

PH

89

Moreton Park

6

West
Lodge

Fir Hill

REDBRIDGE ROAD

Redbridge

5

Jubilee Trail

REDBRIDGE LANE

Coombe Valley
Farm

DT2

West Wood

88

Broomhill
Farm

4

Tumuli

Old
Knowle

Tumuli

Jubilee Trail

REDBRIDGE ROAD

Tadnoll
Barrow

Tadnoll Nature
Reserve

Whitcombe Hill

3

Whitcombe
Vale

87

Galton Heath

2

Tadnoll

Winfrith Heath
Nature Reserve

GATEMORE ROAD

Nutley
Farm

Blacknoll
Hill

Tumulus

1

Tumuli

BLACKNOLL LANE

86

78   A   B   79   C   D   80   E   F

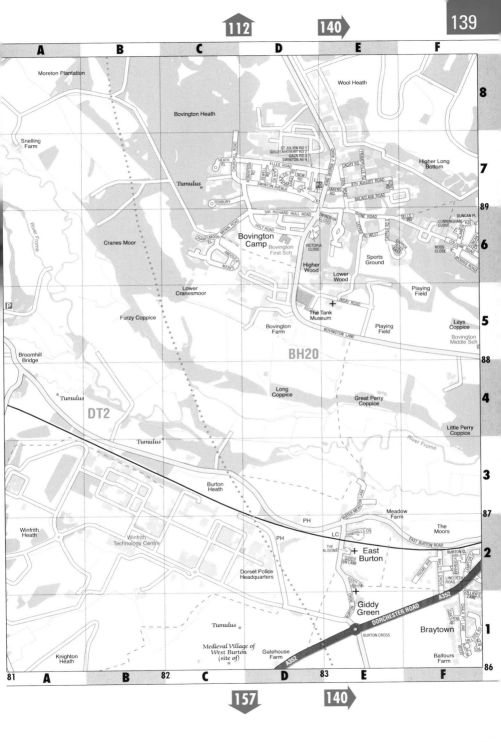

A   B   C   D   E   F

8

Moreton Plantation

Wool Heath

Bovington Heath

Snelling
Farm

Higher Long
Bottom

7

ST JULIEN RD 1
GOUZEAUCOURT RD 2
GAZA RD 3
SWINTON AV 4

HEATH
CL.

CHURCH ROAD

ELLES ROAD

ROBERTSON RD

SEWELL RD

NEW
RD

ARRAS RD

AMIENS RD

ANZIO RD

KING GEORGE V RD

CACHY RD

TREMATVILLE RD

8TH AUGUST ROAD

Tumulus

FOXBURY

SWINTON AVENUE

89

River Frome

SIR RICHARD HULL ROAD

WINDSOR
CLOSE

RHINE ROAD

BALACLAVA ROAD

SELLE
RD

DUNCAN RD

CUNNINGHAM
CLOSE

CULVER RD

COLGATE ROAD

DUNCAN RD

6

Cranes Moor

CRANES MOOR LANE

MENIN ROAD

HOLT ROAD

Bovington
Camp

Bovington
First Sch

VICTORIA
CLOSE

RD WEST

COPPER RD

ROSS
CLOSE

MORRIS ROAD

Lower
Cranesmoor

ANZIO GREEN

Higher
Wood

Lower
Wood

Sports
Ground

Playing
Field

P

Furzy Coppice

Bovington
Farm

LINDSAY ROAD

The Tank
Museum

Playing
Field

Lays
Coppice

Bovington
Middle Sch

5

Broomhill
Bridge

BH20

88

DT2

Tumulus

Long
Coppice

BOVINGTON LANE

Great Perry
Coppice

4

Tumulus

River Frome

Little Perry
Coppice

Burton
Heath

3

Winfrith
Heath

Winfrith
Technology Centre

PH

PATER MEADOW LANE

Meadow
Farm

The
Moors

87

LC

SANDHILLS CR

EAST BURTON ROAD

Dorset Police
Headquarters

PH

THE
ALISONS

East
Burton

GIDDY
GN LANE

GEORGE RD

BAILY'S DRIVE

STICKLAND RD

LINCLIETH
ROAD

BURTON CL

COLLIER'S LANE

2

GIDDY GN RD

CHURCH RD

Giddy
Green

DORCHESTER ROAD

A352

Braytown

GREYNE RD

CHALK PIT LANE

CHALKY RD

HILL CLOSE

NELSON RD

WOOLS LA.

CHALKY LANE

Tumulus

Medieval Village of
West Burton
(site of)

Gatehouse
Farm

BURTON CROSS

A352

Balfours
Farm

1

Knighton
Heath

A352

86

81   A   82   B   C   82   D   83   E   F

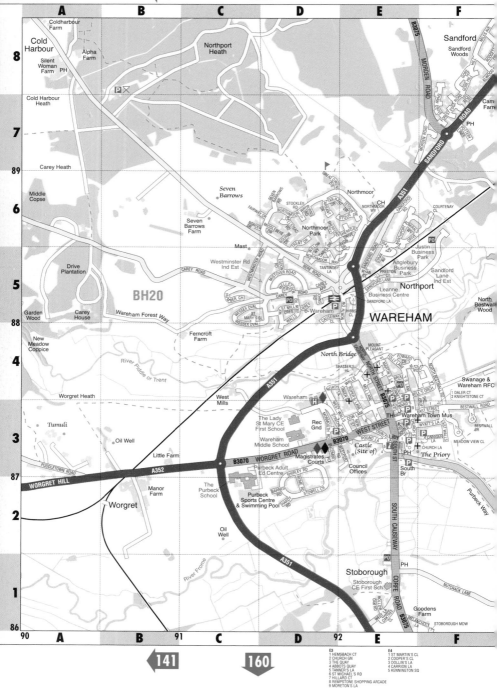

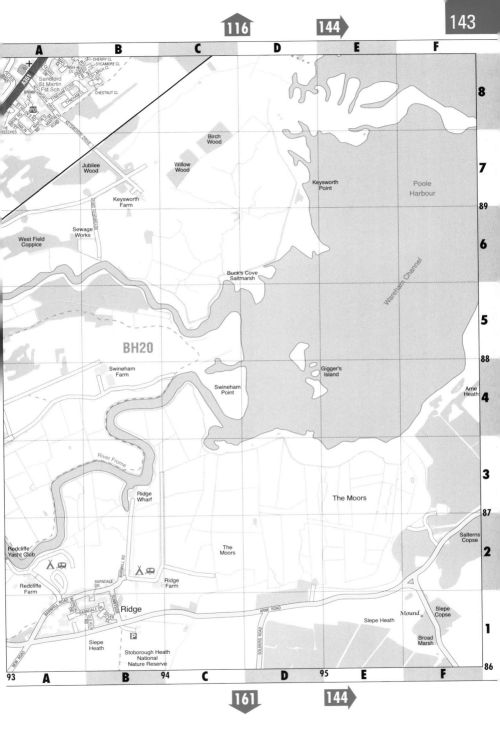

A B C D E F

8

7

89

6

5

88

4

3

87

2

1

86

Sandford
St Martin
Fst Sch
A351
CHERRY CL
SYCAMORE CL
CHESTNUT CL

Jubilee
Wood

Birch
Wood

Willow
Wood

Keysworth
Point

Poole
Harbour

Keysworth
Farm

Sewage
Works

West Field
Coppice

Buck's Cove
Saltmarsh

Wareham Channel

BH20

Swineham
Farm

Gigger's
Island

Swineham
Point

Arne
Heath

River Frome

Ridge
Wharf

The Moors

Salterns
Copse

Redcliffe
Yacht Club

The
Moors

Redcliffe
Farm

BARNDALE
DR

Ridge
Farm

Ridge

ARNE ROAD

Mound

Slepe
Copse

Slepe Heath

Broad
Marsh

Slepe
Heath

SOLDIERS ROAD

Stoborough Heath
National
Nature Reserve

NEW ROAD

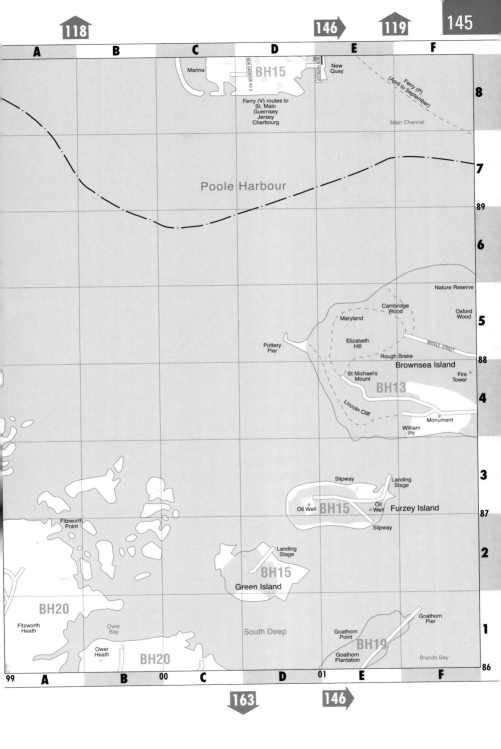

A   B   C   D   E   F

Marina

BH15

New Quay

NEW HARBOUR RD S

NEW HARBOUR RD

Ferry (P)
(April to September)

8

Ferry (V) routes to
St. Malo
Guernsey
Jersey
Cherbourg

Main Channel

Poole Harbour

7

89

6

Nature Reserve

Cambridge
Wood

Oxford
Wood

Maryland

5

Elizabeth
Hill

MIDDLE STREET

Pottery
Pier

Rough Brake

88

Brownsea Island

St Michael's
Mount

Fire
Tower

BH13

4

Lincoln Cliff

Monument

William
Pit

Slipway

3

Landing
Stage

Oil Well

BH15

Oil
Well

Furzey Island

87

Slipway

Landing
Stage

2

BH15

Green Island

BH20

Goathorn
Pier

Fitzworth
Point

1

Fitzworth
Heath

Ower
Bay

South Deep

Goathorn
Point

BH19

Brands Bay

Ower
Heath

BH20

Goathorn
Plantation

86

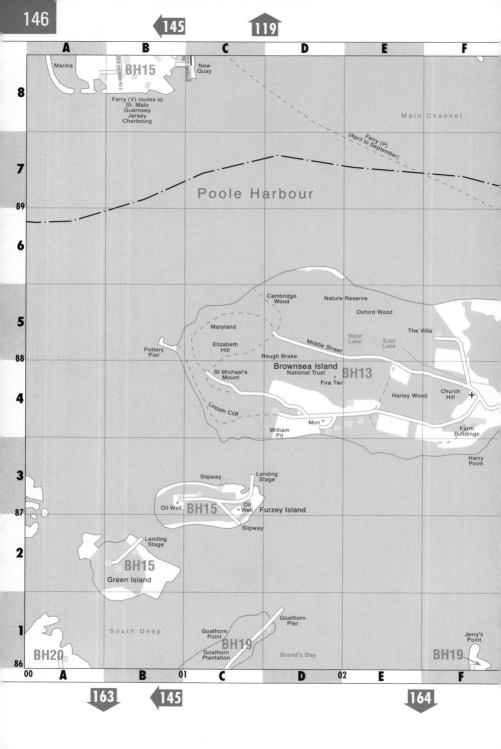

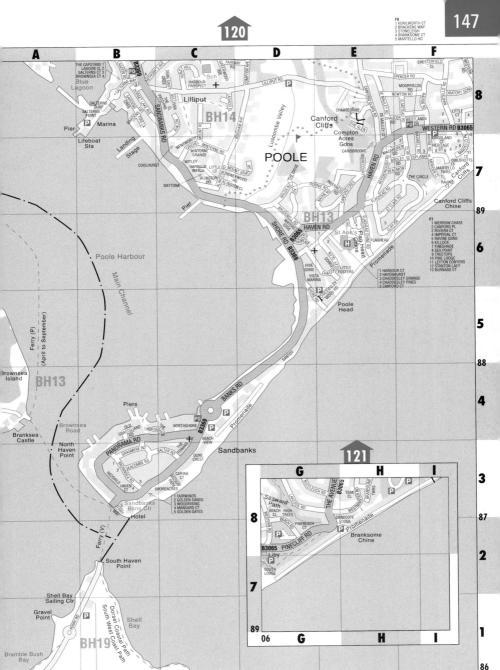

F8
1 KENILWORTH CT
2 BRACKENS WAY
3 STONELEIGH
4 BRANKSOME CT
5 MARTELLO HO

THE CAPSTANS 1
LAGOON CL 2
SALTERNS CT 3
BROWNSEA CT 4
Blue
Lagoon

SALTERNS
QUAY
SALTERNS
POINT

Pier

Marina

Lifeboat
Sta

Landing
Stage

Coolhurst

CHESTERFIELD

SPENCER RD

MOORFIELDS
RD
NEWTON RD

ORATORY GDNS

LITTLE
CL

8

WESTERN RD B3065

KINGSLAND
HERITAGE

THE ESPLANADE

OWLSHOTTS

MARTELLO
TWRS

Canford
Cliffs

THE CIRCLE

RAVINE
CT

7

Sch

FAIRWAY
RD

GREENWOOD
RD

Harbour
Prospect

Lilliput

BH14

LILLIPUT RD

Luscombe Valley

CHARTCOMBE

Canford
Cliffs

Compton
Acres
Gdns

CARISBROOKE

POOLE

WENTWORTH

MINTERNE
GRANGE

CRICHEL

MINTERNE RD

WITLEY

HONEYWOOD
HO

LITTLE
OAK
RD

MOUNT GRACE
DR

HARBOUR
WATCH

DAYTONA

ALINGTON
RD

ALINGTON CL

Pier

BH13

HAVEN RD

St Ann's
Hospl

Flag
Head
Chine

FLAGHEAD

Canford Cliffs
Chine

89

F7
1 MERROW CHASE
2 CANFORD PL
3 RIVIERA CT
4 IMPERIAL CT
5 RAVINE GDNS
6 KILLOCK
7 FINESHADE
8 SEA POINT
9 TREETOPS
10 PINE LODGE
11 LEYTON CONYERS
12 STANTON LACY
13 BURNAGE CT

SHORE RD
B3065

B3069

HAVEN RD

HIVE
GDNS

VISTA
MARINA

LITTLE
FOSTERS

6

H

Promenade

1 HARBOUR CT
2 HAVENHURST
3 CHADDESLEY GRANGE
4 CHADDESLEY PINES
5 CANFORD CT

Poole Harbour

Main Channel

Poole
Head

5

Ferry (P)
(April to September)

Brownsea
Island

BH13

88

BANKS RD

SANDY

4

Brownsea
Road

Branksea
Castle

North
Haven
Point

Piers

OLD
COASTGUARD
RD

HORSESHOE

Northshore

PANORAMA RD

GRASMERE RD

SEACOMBE RD

SALTER RD

THE TOWANS

B3065

Promenade

BEACH
VIEW

DUNE
CREST

Sandbanks

121

G

H

I

Ferry (V)

REGINALDS

HAVEN
CT

SHOREACRES

CARINA
CT

1 FAIRWINDS
2 GOLDEN SANDS
3 WOODRISING
4 MANSARD CT
5 GOLDEN GATES

Sandbanks
Bsns Ctr

Hotel

Seaward
Path

BUCCLEUCH RD

LAGGE RD

BEACH
CL

HIGH
TREES

THE AVENUE

TEAK CL

BRANKSOME
TWRS

B3065

8

PINEBEACH
CL

DENECOTE
LODGE

Promenade

Branksome
Chine

87

3

South Haven
Point

B3065

PINECLIFF RD

Liby

SOUTH
LODGE

2

Shell Bay
Sailing Ctr

Gravel
Point

FERRY RD

Dorset Coastal Path
South West Coast Path

Shell
Bay

BH19

89

06

G

H

I

1

86

Bramble Bush
Bay

03

A

04

B

C

05

D

E

F

7

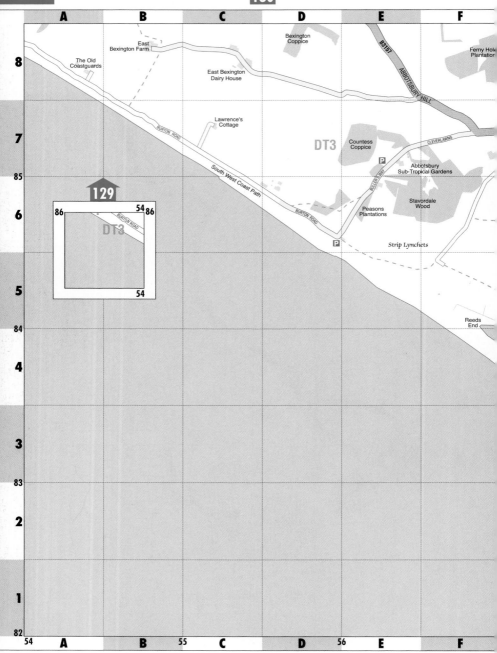

A B C D E F

8

Abbotsbury Plains

Oxlip Coppice

BISHOP'S ROAD

Jubilee Coppice

MALTHOUSE MD

Abbotsbury

ROSEMARY LA

BACK STREET

HANDS LANE

GLEBE CL.

GOOSE HILL

CONWAYS LANE

WEST STREET

B3157

MARKET ST

PH

PO

RODDEN ROW

B3157

7

P

Goose Hill

St Peter's Abbey

Tithe Barn Children's Farm

Abbey Barn

Sewage Works

85

Oddens Wood

West Elworth Farm

St Catherines Chapel

Nunnery Grove

Horsepool Farm

6

Chapel Hill

Chapel Coppice

GROVE LANE

P

Linton Hill

Linton Barn

West Elworth

South West Coast Path

DT3

Clayhanger Farm

Merry Hill

5

Abbotsbury Swannery

South West Coast Path

84

Hodder's Coppice

Tiny Coppice

NEW BARN ROAD

Warre Wood

4

Shipmoor Point

Cuckoo Coppice

Chesters Coppice

Walls Down

Chesters Hill

Wyke Wood

New Barn Farm

3

Berry Coppice

Higher Barn

83

Chesil Beach

West Fleet

South Sleight Coppice

2

Holywell Spring

1

82

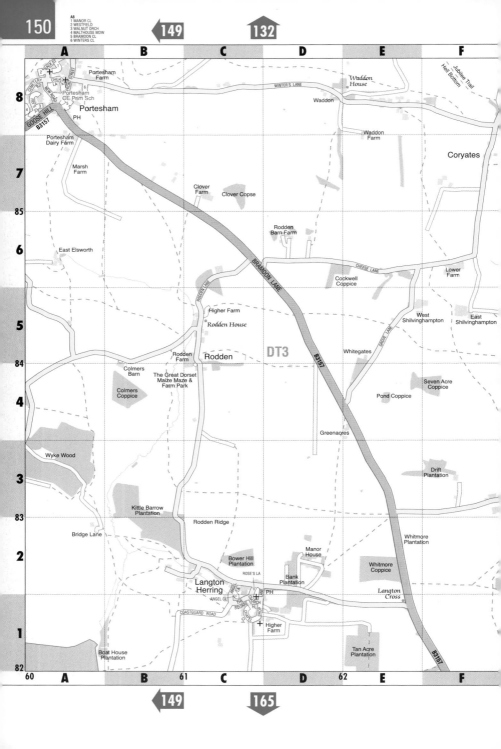

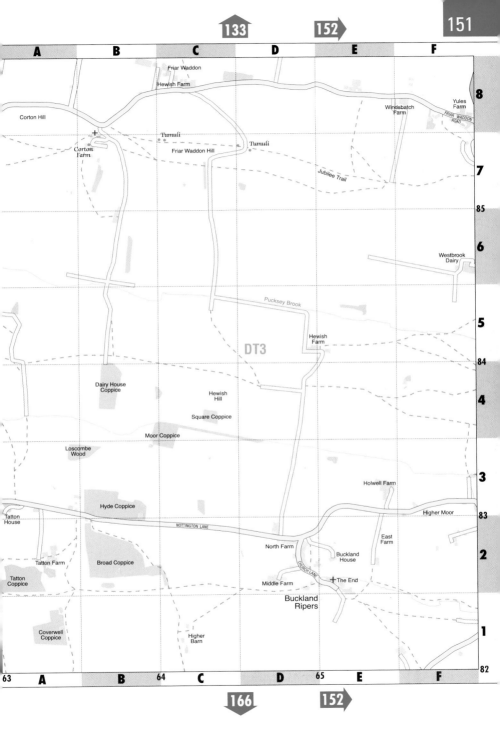

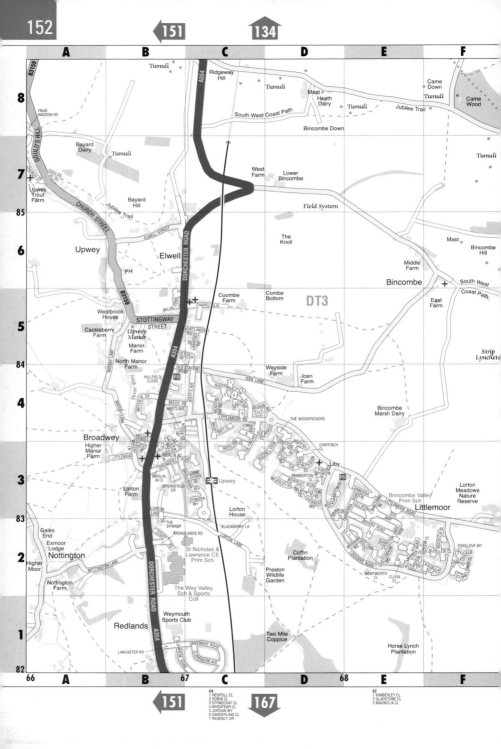

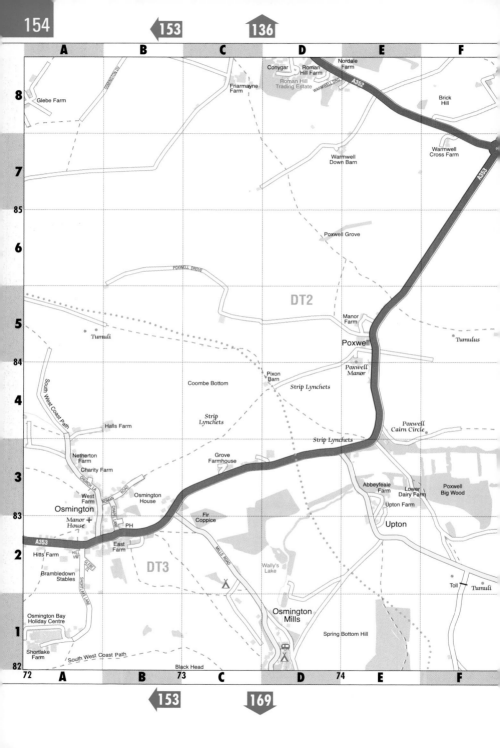

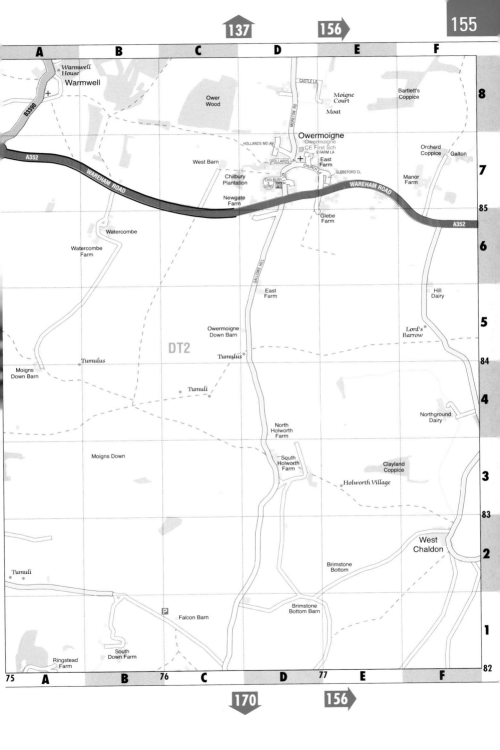

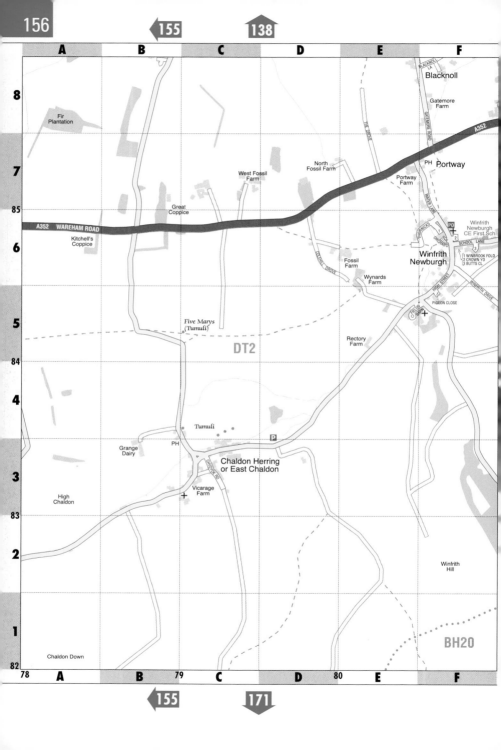

A   B   C   D   E   F

8

7

85

6

5

84

4

3

83

2

1

82

West Burton Farm

Home Farm

Longcutts Farm

PH

East Knighton

East Knighton Farm

Newburgh Farm

North Wood

Claypits Farm

Newburgh Dairy

Coombe Wood

DT2

Fields Farm

Drove Dairy

NEWTOWN HILL

B3071

Tumulus

BH20

Marley Bottom

Vine's Down Buildings

Lulworth Common

Tumulus

Marley Wood

Belhuish House

Burngate Wood

Marley Wood House

Belhuish Coppice

B3071

31   A   B   82   C   D   83   E   F

A	B	C	D	E	F

Chicks
Hill Farm

West Holme
Farm

East
Holme

8

Luckford
Lake Farm

French Grass
Coppice

West Holme

HOLME LANE

B3070

Heath
Range

DANGER AREA

New Barn
Farm

7

Highwood
Heath

Woodbury
Coppice

85

West Holme
Heath

6

Luckford Lake

DANGER
AREA

Tumuli

Five
Barrow Hill

5

Tumulus

Hurst
Mill

84

B3070

BH20

4

Lulworth
Heath

Tumuli

Pool
Pond

Mare
Pond

Povington
Heath

King's Standing

3

Tumuli

83

Earl's
Kitchen

North Hills
Plantation

2

DANGER AREA
(Tank Ranges)

West
Creech

West Creech
Farm

1

Povington
Barrow

Povington
Wood

Grey's
Coppice

82

87   A   **B**   88   **C**   D   89   **E**   F

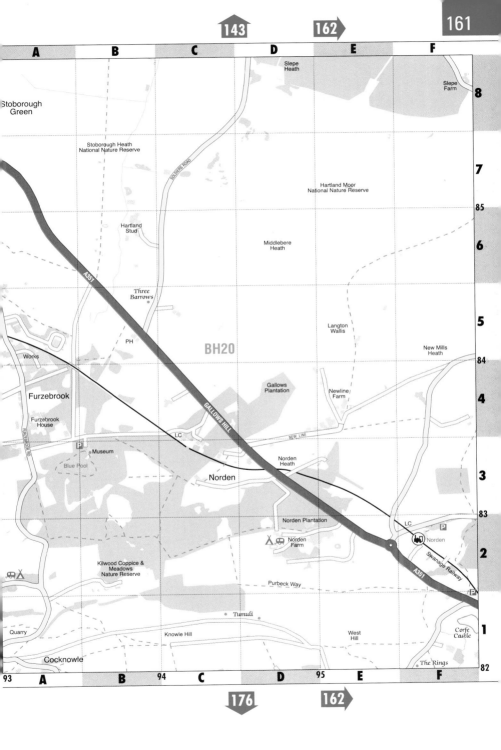

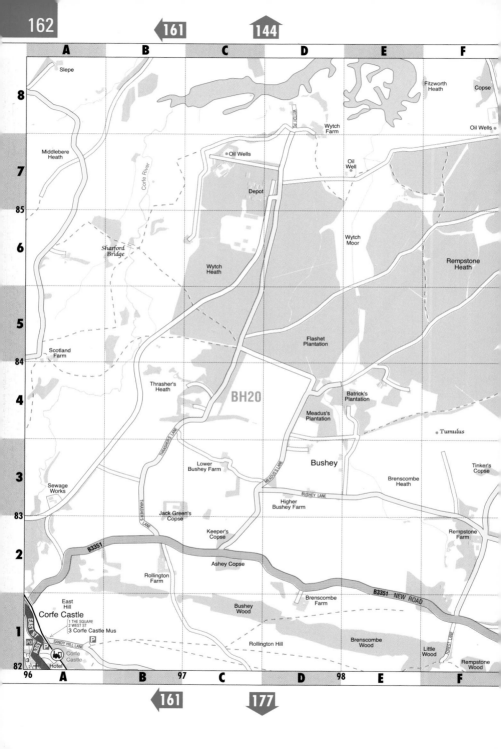

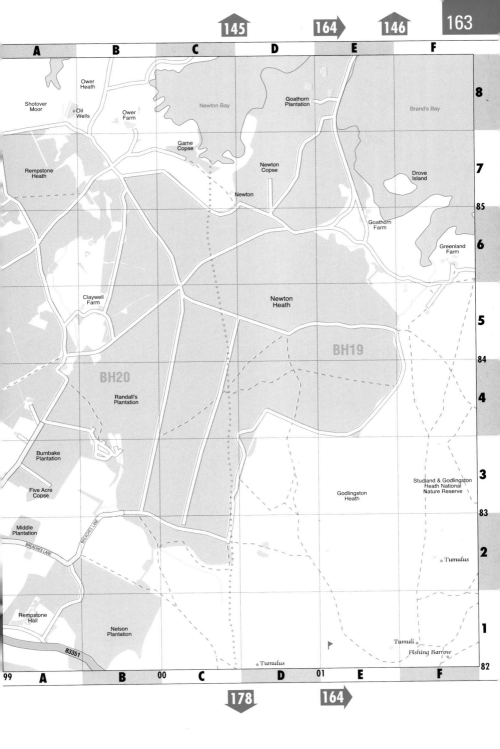

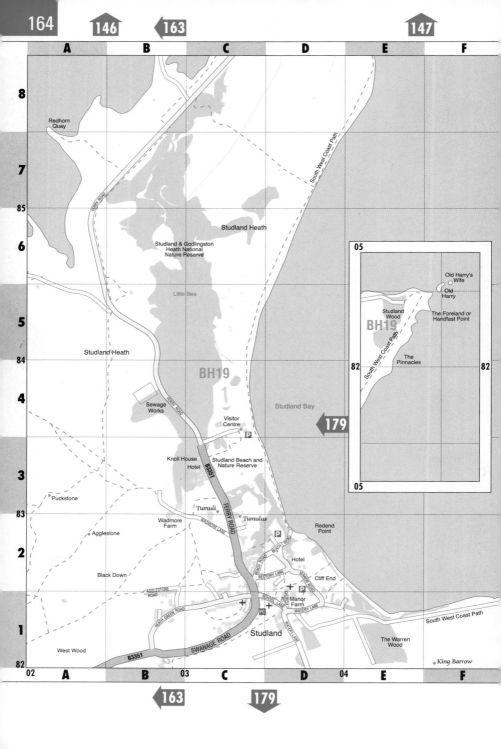

A B C D E F

8

7

85

6

5

84

4

83

3

2

1

82

Redhorn Quay

Studland Heath

Studland & Godlingston Heath National Nature Reserve

Little Sea

Studland Heath

BH19

Sewage Works

Visitor Centre
P

Knoll House Hotel

Studland Beach and Nature Reserve

FERRY ROAD

B3351

Puckstone

Tumuli

Wadmore Farm

WADMORE LANE

Tumulus

Agglestone

Black Down

AGGLESTONE ROAD

HEATH GREEN ROAD

West Wood

B3351

SWANAGE ROAD

BEACH ROAD

BEACH ROAD

RECTORY LANE

SCHOOL LANE

GLEBE LANE

Manor Farm

WATERY LANE

WATERY LANE

Studland

Redend Point

Hotel

Cliff End

The Warren Wood

King Barrow

Studland Bay

179

P

P

PC

South West Coast Path

South West Coast Path

05

82

05

82

Old Harry's Wife

Old Harry

Studland Wood

BH19

The Foreland or Handfast Point

The Pinnacles

South West Coast Path

02 A B 03 C D 04 E F

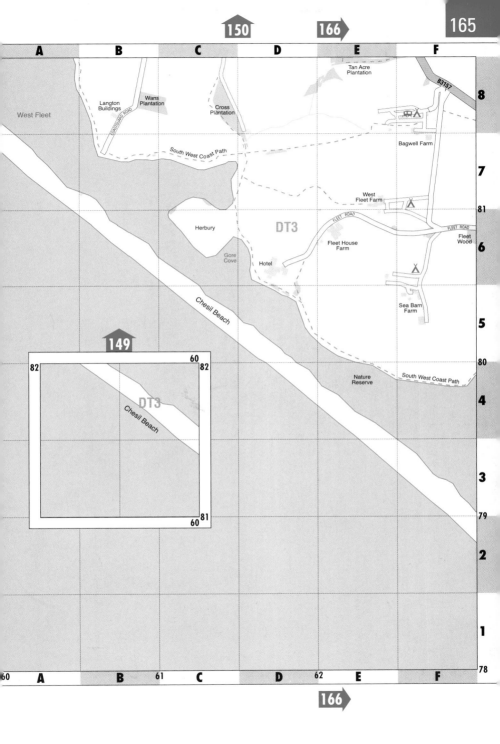

West Fleet

Tan Acre
Plantation

Langton
Buildings

Wans
Plantation

Cross
Plantation

South West Coast Path

Bagwell Farm

West
Fleet Farm

Herbury

DT3

FLEET ROAD

FLEET ROAD

Fleet
Wood

Gore
Cove

Hotel

Fleet House
Farm

Chesil Beach

Sea Barn
Farm

149

60
82

82

60
81

DT3

Chesil Beach

Nature
Reserve

South West Coast Path

B3157

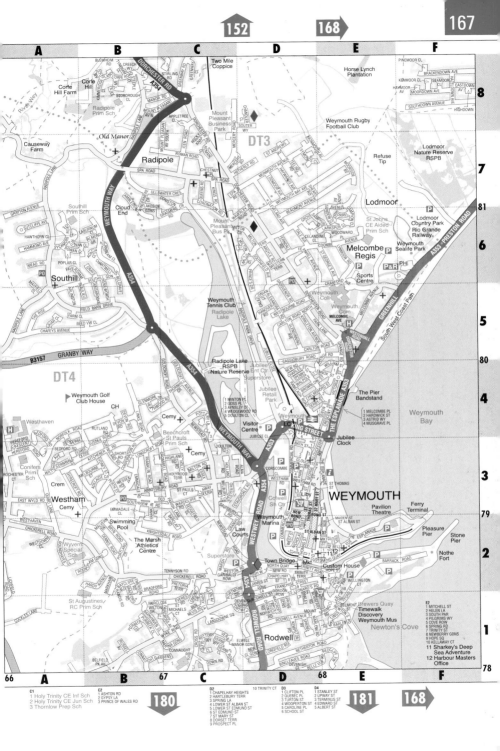

152

153

B8
1 MOORCOMBE DR
2 CHALBURY LODGE
3 HAZEL DR
4 WINGREEN CL
5 MAPLE CL
6 DEANSLEIGH CL

St Andrews CE Prim Sch

ALLBERRY GDNS

LITTLEMOOR ROAD

PRESTON ROAD

TELFORD CLOSE

Preston

FISHERBRIDGE ROAD

TALLIDGE CL

HOLCOMBE CL

Osmington Hill

CHALBURY CLOSE

Wyke Oliver Farm

CEDAR DRIVE

FORZHILL CLOSE

1 HALSTOCK CL
2 BROOKSIDE CL
3 HDRYFORD CL

ROMAN VILLA

River Jordan

A353

WYKE OLIVER ROAD

SAXONBURY RD

ORCHARD DR

TURZY CL

Overcombe

DUNFORTH DRIVE

JOHN CL

SUNNINGDALE RD

RINGSTEAD DR

OVERCOMBE DRIVE

JORDAN HILL ROMAN TEMPLE

New Barn

DT3

82

BOOKIN DR

BOURMOUTH AV

ELM CL

MELYN CL

BOWLEAZE COVEWAY

South West Coast Path

Hotel

1 BRACKENDOWN AV
2 EASTDOWN AV
3 EASTDOWN GDNS

Bowleaze Cove

HERON CL

PO

Furzy Cliff

PRESTON ROAD

Redcliff Point

Lodmoor Nature Reserve

A353

Weymouth Bay

169
155

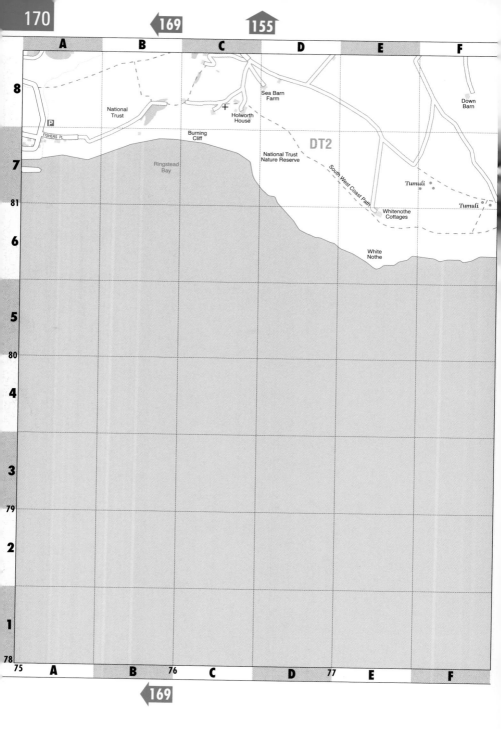

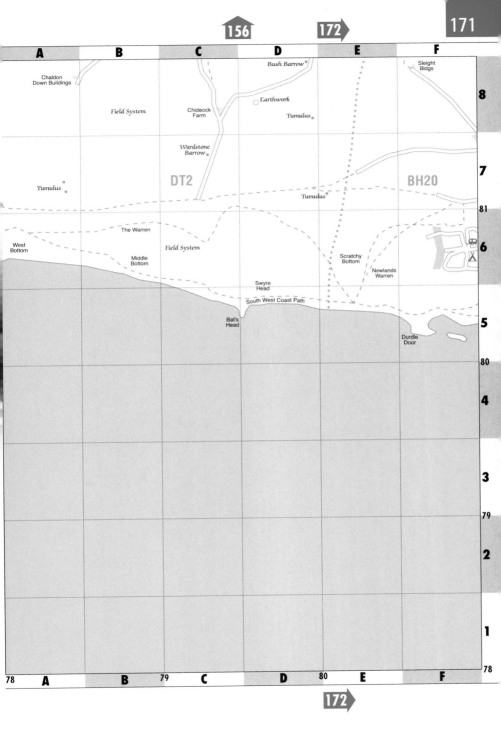

A B C D E F

Chaldon
Down Buildings

Field System

Chideock
Farm

Bush Barrow

○ Earthwork

Tumulus

Sleight
Bldgs

8

*Wardstone
Barrow*

DT2

BH20

7

Tumulus

Tumulus

81

The Warren

Field System

West
Bottom

Middle
Bottom

Scratchy
Bottom

Newlands
Warren

6

Swyre
Head

South West Coast Path

Bat's
Head

Durdle
Door

5

80

4

3

79

2

1

78

A **B** **C** **D** **E** **F**

Observation Tower

East Lulworth

B3070

P

B3070

Water Barrows

8

Milldown

PH

Ferny Barrows

DANGER AREA

DANGER AREA

Lulworth Camp

Broom's Plantation

Old Marl Plantation

Tumuli

Bower's Coppice

Tumulus

7

BH20

Monastery Farm

81

Bindon Range

Maiden Plantation

Rings Hill

6

Flower's Barrow (Hill Fort)

Tumuli

Tumuli

Halcombe Vale

DANGER AREA

5

Bindon Plantation

South West Coast Path

Arish Mell

Tumuli

Cockpit Head

Worbarrow Bay

80

Mupe Bay

4

Mupe Rocks

Worbarrow Tout

3

79

2

1

78

84 **A** **B** 85 **C** **D** 86 **E** **F**

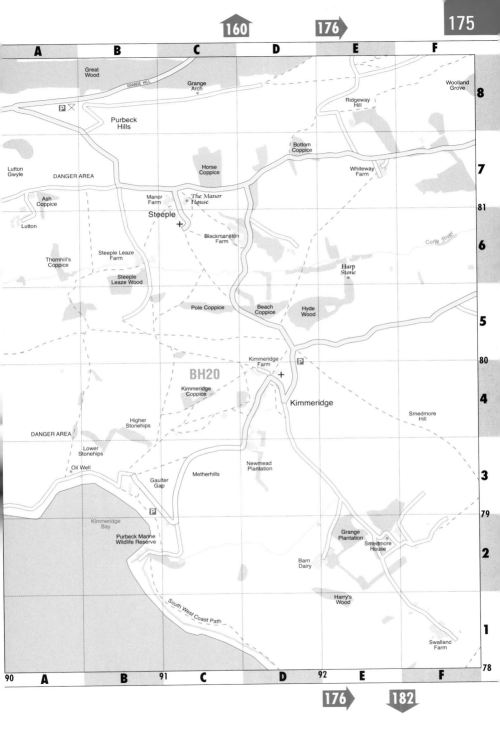

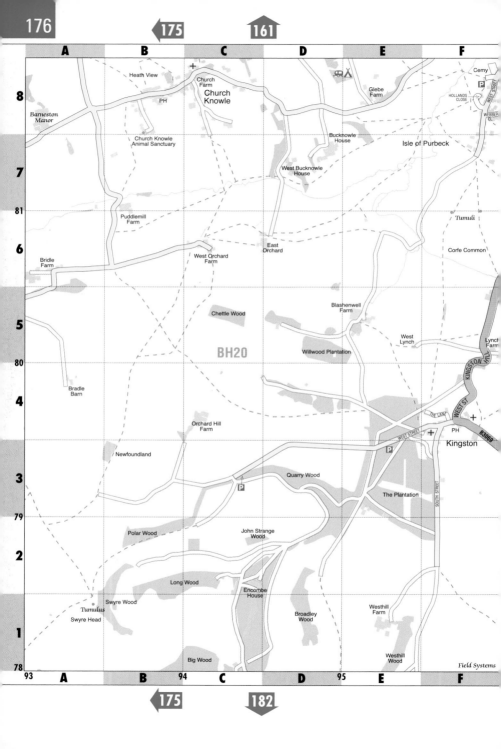

A **B** **C** **D** **E** **F**

8

Heath View

Church
Farm

Church
Knowle

PH

Barneston
Manor

Church Knowle
Animal Sanctuary

Glebe
Farm

Cemy

HOLLANDS
CLOSE

WEST STREET

WERBER
CL

Bucknowle
House

Isle of Purbeck

7

West Bucknowle
House

81

Puddlemill
Farm

Tumuli

6

Bridle
Farm

West Orchard
Farm

East
Orchard

Corfe Common

Chettle Wood

Blashenwell
Farm

West
Lynch

Lynch
Farm

5

BH20

Willwood Plantation

80

Bradle
Barn

KINGSTON LN

WEST ST

B3069

4

Orchard Hill
Farm

THE LANE

WEST STREET

PH

Kingston

Newfoundland

P

3

Quarry Wood

The Plantation

P

SOUTH STREET

79

Polar Wood

John Strange
Wood

2

Long Wood

Encombe
House

Broadley
Wood

Westhill
Farm

1

Tumulus

Swyre Wood

Swyre Head

Big Wood

Westhill
Wood

78

Field Systems

93 **A** **B** 94 **C** **D** 95 **E** **F**

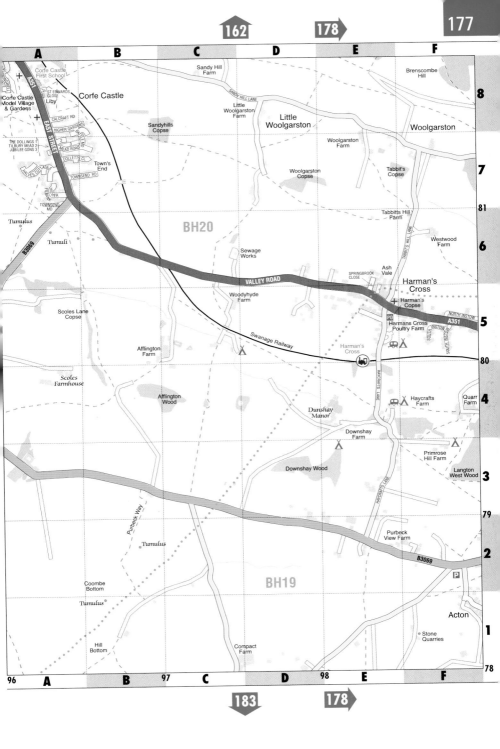

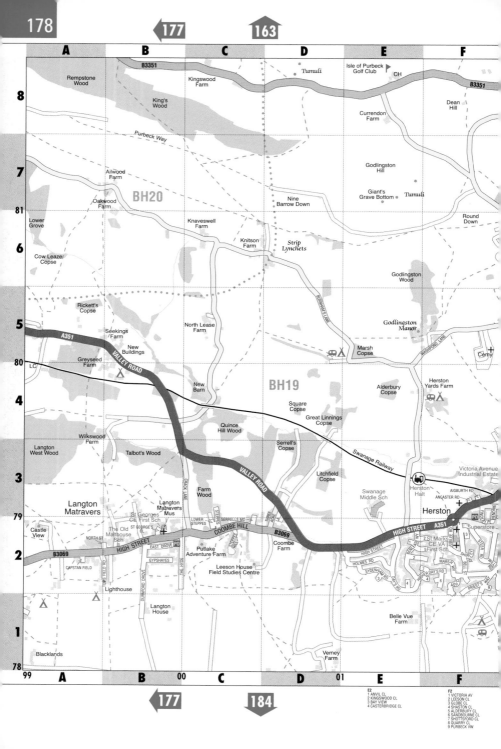

A B C D E F

B3351

Rempstone
Wood

Kingswood
Farm

Tumuli

Isle of Purbeck
Golf Club   CH

B3351

8

King's
Wood

Currendon
Farm

Dean
Hill

Purbeck Way

Godlingston
Hill

7

Ailwood
Farm

BH20

Oakwood
Farm

Giant's
Grave Bottom   Tumuli

81

Lower
Grove

Knaveswell
Farm

Nine
Barrow Down

Round
Down

6

Cow Leaze
Copse

Knitson
Farm

Strip
Lynchets

Godlingston
Wood

Rickett's
Copse

Godlingston
Manor

5

A351

Seekings
Farm

North Lease
Farm

Marsh
Copse

Carny

New
Buildings

VALLEY ROAD

80

LC

Greyseed
Farm

Herston
Yards Farm

BH19

Aiderbury
Copse

4

New Barn

Square
Copse

Great Linnings
Copse

Wilkswood
Farm

Quince
Hill Wood

Swanage Railway

Victoria Avenue
Industrial Estate

Langton
West Wood

Talbot's Wood

Serrell's
Copse

Litchfield
Copse

3

VALLEY ROAD

Farm
Wood

Swanage
Middle Sch

Herston
Halt

Langton
Matravers

Langton
Matravers
Mus

AIGBURTH RD

ANCASTER RD

79

Castle
View

St Georges
CE First Sch

The Old
Malthouse
Sch   ST GEORGE'S

LOWER
STEPPES

Serrells Rd

COOMBE HILL

B3069

HIGH STREET   A351

Herston

Superstore

2

B3069

HIGH STREET

EAST DROVE

Putlake
Adventure Farm

Coombe
Farm

St Marks
CE VA
First Sch

CAPSTAN FIELD

GYPSHAYES

Leeson House
Field Studies Centre

HOLMES RD

SYDENHAM RD   DAY'S RD

Lighthouse

Belle Vue
Farm

1

Langton
House

Blacklands

Verney
Farm

78

99   A   B   00   C   D   01   E   F

E2
1 ANVIL CL
2 KINGSWOOD CL
3 BAY VIEW
4 CASTERBRIDGE CL

F2
1 VICTORIA AV
2 LEESON CL
3 GLOBE CL
4 SHASTON CL
5 ALDERBURY CL
6 SANDBOURNE CL
7 SHOTTSFORD CL
8 QUARRY CL
9 PURBECK VW

A2	B2	C1	C2
1 COWLEASE	1 STATION PL	1 KNOLLSEA CL	1 COMMERCIAL RD
2 NEWTON MANOR CL	2 CHURCH HL	2 SALISBURY RD	2 CORNWALL RD
3 WEST DR	3 CHURCH RD	3 BELVEDERE RD	3 MOUNT PLEASANT LA
4 NEWTON RISE	4 SPRINGFIELD RD		4 EXETER RD
5 HOWARD RD	5 ELDON TERR		5 MARSHALL ROW
6 GORDON RD	6 MANWELL'S LA		6 BURT S PL
7 HANBURY RD	7 DUNFORD PL		
8 FOXHILL CL	8 QUEENS MD		
9 BISHOPS ROW			

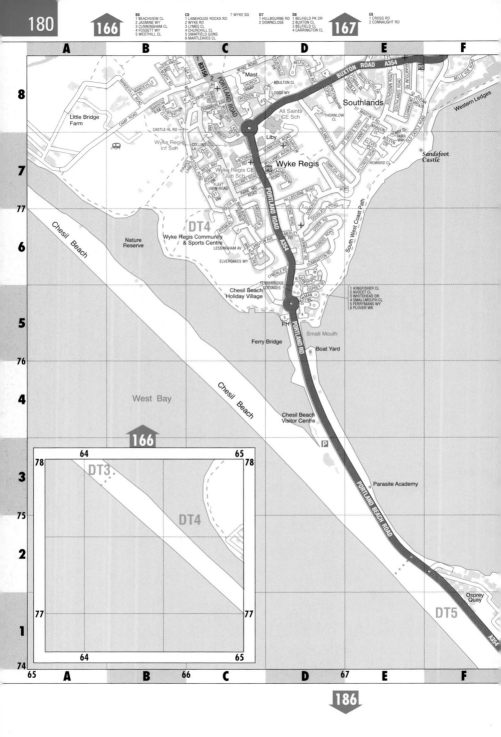

166

B6
1 BEACHVIEW CL
2 JASMINE WY
3 CUNNINGHAM CL
4 FOSSETT WY
5 WESTHILL CL

C6
1 LANEHOUSE ROCKS RD
2 WYKE RD
3 LYMES CL
4 CHURCHILL CL
5 SWAFFIELD GDNS
6 MARTLEAVES CL

7 WYKE SQ

D7
1 HILLBOURNE RD
2 DOWNCLOSE

D8
1 BELFIELD PK DR
2 BUXTON CL
3 BELFIELD CL
4 CARRINGTON CL

167

E8
1 CROSS RD
2 CONNAUGHT RD

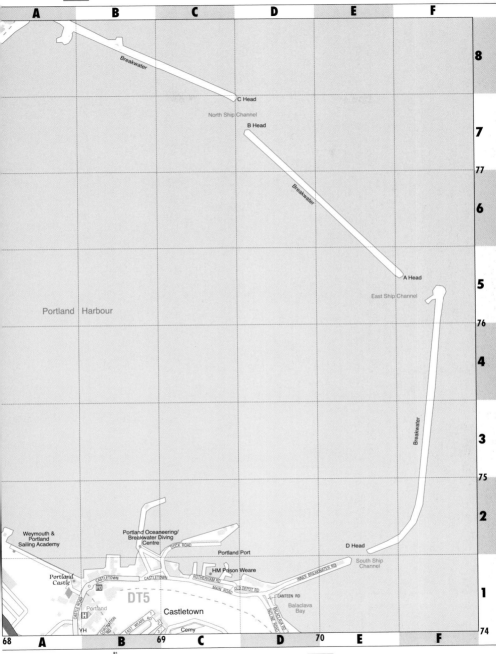

Breakwater

C Head

North Ship Channel

B Head

Breakwater

A Head

East Ship Channel

Portland Harbour

Breakwater

Weymouth & Portland Sailing Academy

Portland Oceaneering/ Breakwater Diving Centre

ROCK ROAD

Portland Port

HM Prison Weare

D Head

South Ship Channel

ROTHERHAM RD

CASTLETOWN

INNER BREAKWATER RD

OLD DEPOT RD

MAIN ROAD

Portland Castle

CASTLETOWN

CORONATION RD

CANTEEN RD

Balaclava Bay

PO

DT5

CASTLE ROAD

Portland

H

Castletown

Cemy

EAST WEARE RD

BEACHCROSS RD

INCLINE ROAD

YH

B1
1 LEET CL
2 BEEL CL
3 AMELIA CL

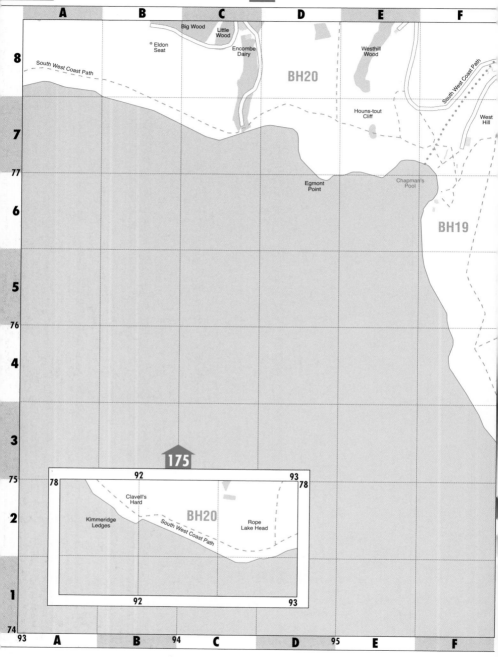

South West Coast Path

Big Wood

Little Wood

Eldon Seat

Encombe Dairy

BH20

Westhill Wood

South West Coast Path

Houns-tout Cliff

West Hill

Egmont Point

Chapman's Pool

BH19

175

Clavell's Hard

Kimmeridge Ledges

BH20

South West Coast Path

Rope Lake Head

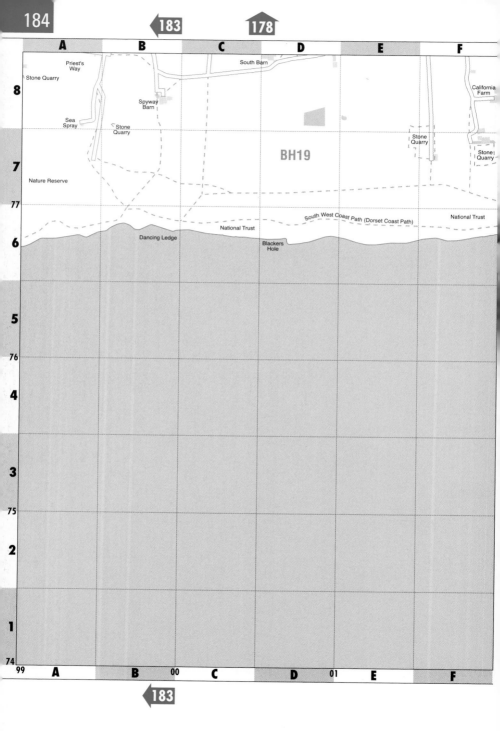

183
178

Priest's Way

Stone Quarry

South Barn

California Farm

Spyway Barn

Sea Spray

Stone Quarry

Stone Quarry

Stone Quarry

BH19

Nature Reserve

South West Coast Path (Dorset Coast Path)

National Trust

National Trust

Dancing Ledge

National Trust

Blackers Hole

179

BH19

Stone
Quarry

Durlston Country
Park

Round Down

Durlston
Bay

Visitor
Centre

Durlston
Head

Anvil Point
Lighthouse

Tilly Whim
Caves

Anvil
Point

DURLSTON
RD

SOUTH HILL RD

QUARRY RD

LIGHTHOUSE ROAD

DURLSTON RD

BOUNDARY
CL

SOLENT
RD

LIGHTHOUSE ROAD

ST CATHARINES ROAD

LIGHTHOUSE

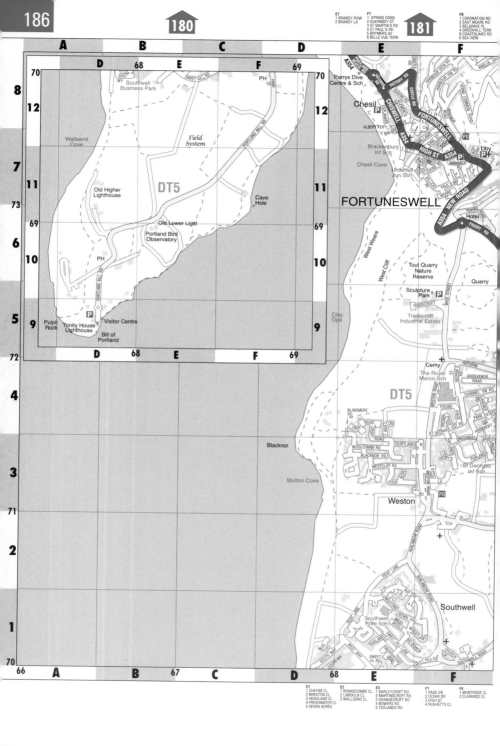

A354

Parrys Dive
Centre & Sch

Chesil

CHESIL

FORTUNESWELL

Libry
PH

Albert Terr

HIGH ST A354

Brackenbury
Inf Sch

Chesil Cove

Underhill
Jun Sch

FORTUNESWELL

Hotel

70

12

Southwell
Business Park

SWEET HILL RD

PH

SOUTH
WY

Wallsend
Cove

Field
System

DT5

70

12

PORTLAND BILL RD

73

7

11

Old Higher
Lighthouse

Cave
Hole

11

West Weare

West Weare

West Cliff

Tout Quarry
Nature
Reserve

Quarry

69

6

10

Old Lower Light

Portland Bird
Observatory

PH

PORTLAND BILL RD

69

10

Sculpture
Park

P

TRADECROFT

Tradecroft
Industrial Estate

5

9

Pulpit
Rock

P

Trinity House
Lighthouse

Visitor Centre

Bill of
Portland

9

Clay
Ope

72

D   68   E   F   69

Cemy

The Royal
Manor Sch

REFORNE

GROSVENOR
ROAD

DT5

4

BLINDMERE
RD

A354 NEW ROAD

CHANNEL VW RD

PARK LANE

Blacknor

WOOLCOMBE RD

COURTLANDS

COURTLANDS RD

ST GEORGES RD

GREENWAY

St Georges
Inf Sch

BLACKNOR RD

71

3

WESTCLIFF RD

Mutton Cove

Weston

FOUR

2

REAP LANE

Southwell

REAP LANE

1

Southwell
Prim Sch

SWEET
HL LA

SOUTHWELL ROAD

70

66   A   B   67   C   D   68

A **B** **C** **D** **E** **F**

8

Cemy

H.M. Prison

The Verne

7

ILLYCOMBE ROAD
VERNE HILL RD

Masts

King's Pier

73

King Barrow Quarry

Admiralty Quarries

Verne Yeates

East Weare

ISLE OF PORTLAND

6

A354

EASTON LANE

Grove

INCLINE RD

Grove Inf Sch

HM Young Offender Institution

Portland United Football Club

GROVE ROAD

AUGUSTA CL

WITHIES CFT

INMOSTHAY

DT5

VICTORIA RD

Mast

5

SHEPHERDS CROFT

SHEPHERDS CFT

CROWN FARM TERR

72

LONG ACRE

Quarry

Durdle Pier

Easton

MOORFIELD RD

STRAITS

4

Grove Cliff

Works

Tophill Jun Sch

Bottom Coombe Quarries

BUMPERS LA

3

Portland Mus

Church (rems of)

Rufus Castle

71

Hotel

WESTON STREET

Church Ope Cove

2

SOUTHWELL ROAD

P

1

Freshwater Bay

70

A 69 **B** 70 **C** **D** 71 **E** **F**

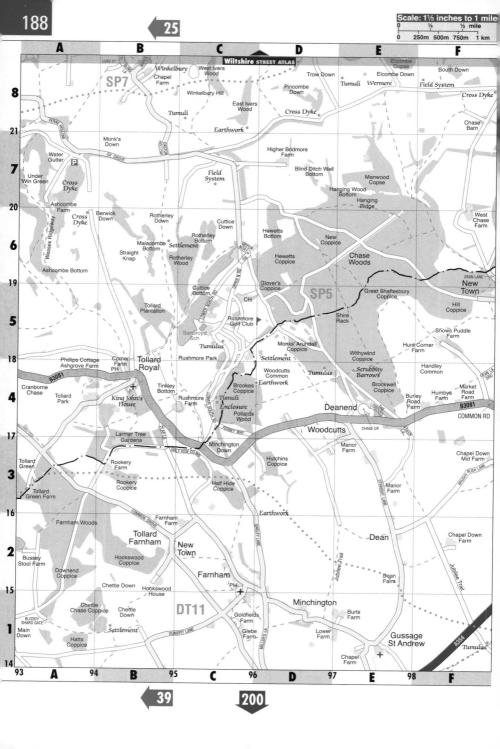

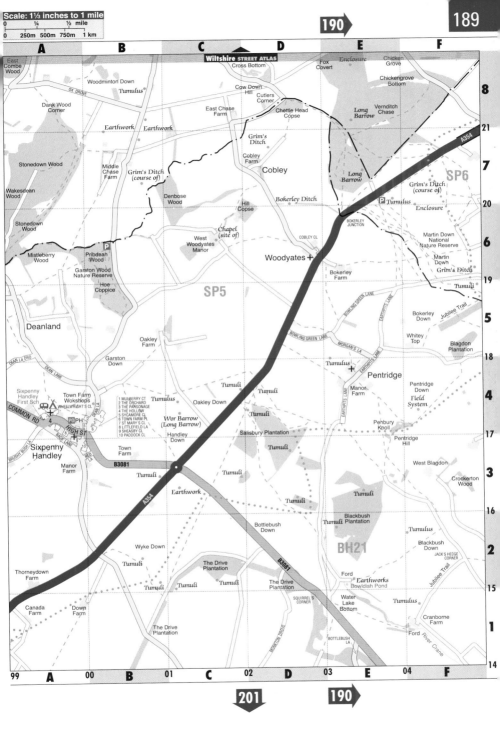

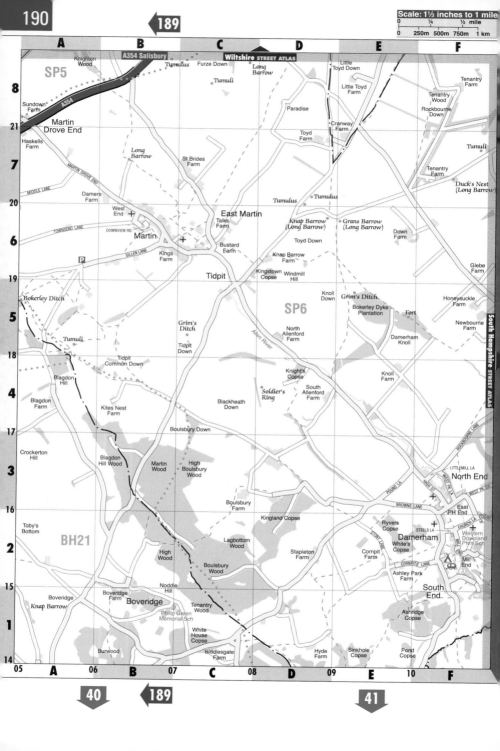

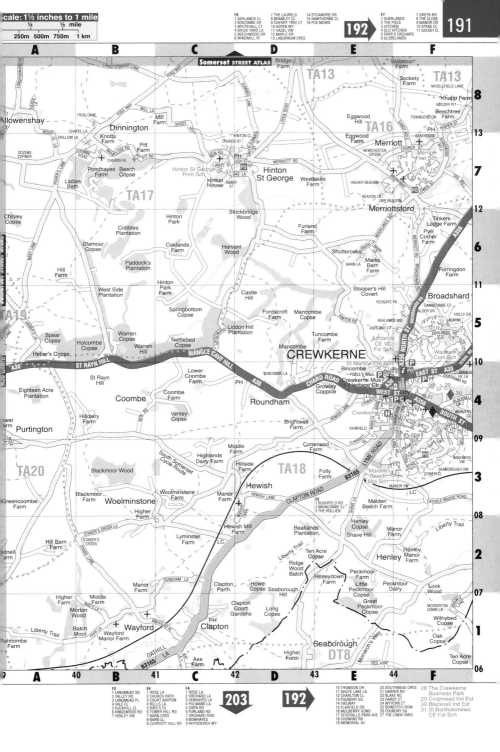

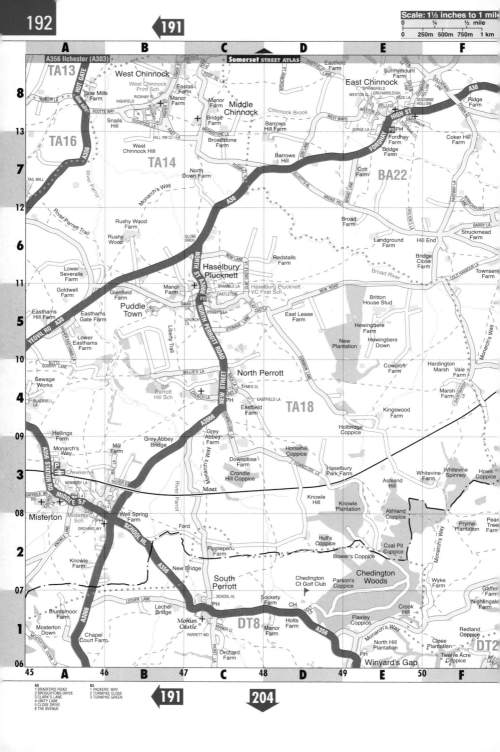

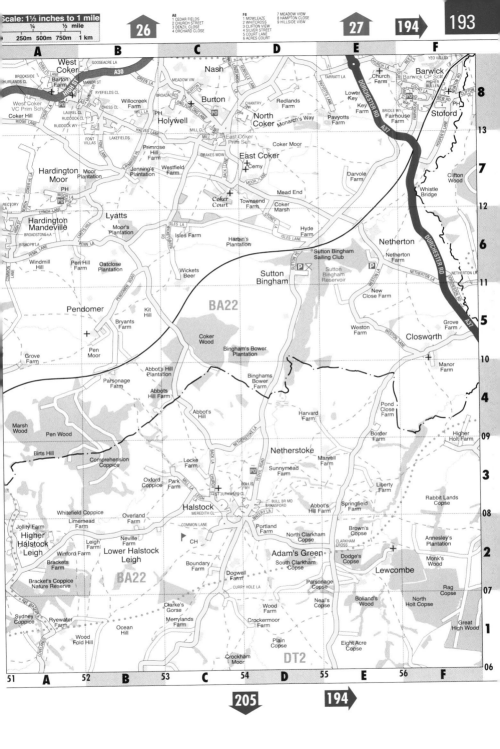

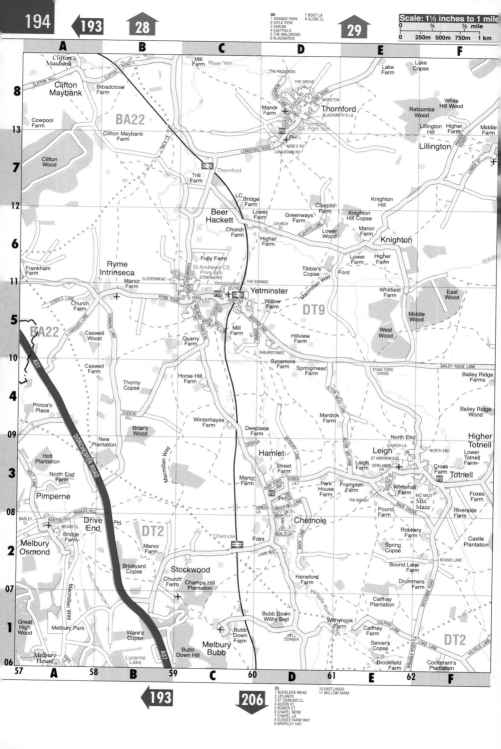

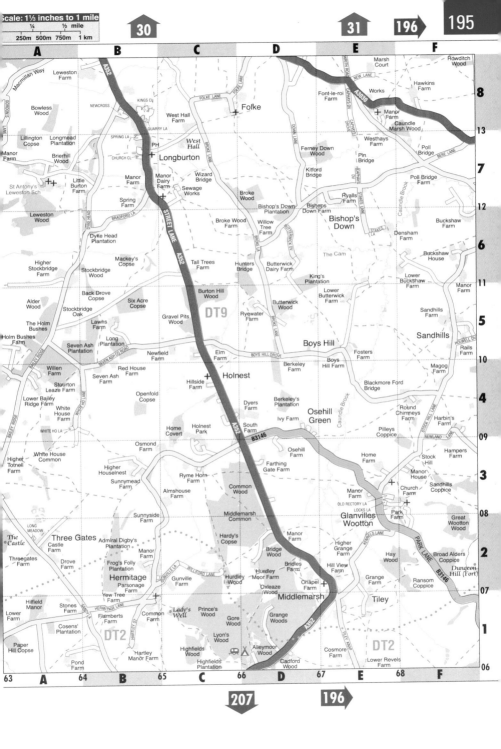

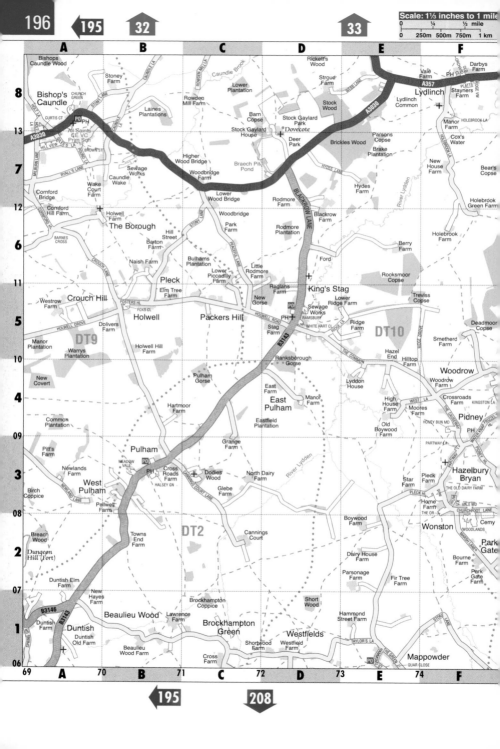

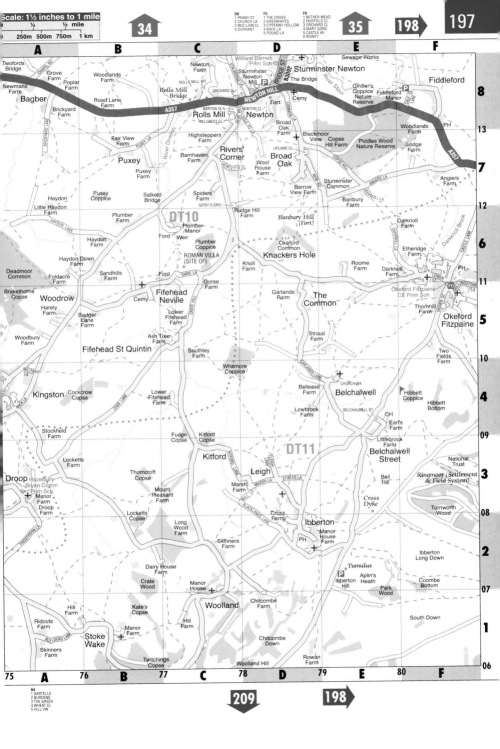

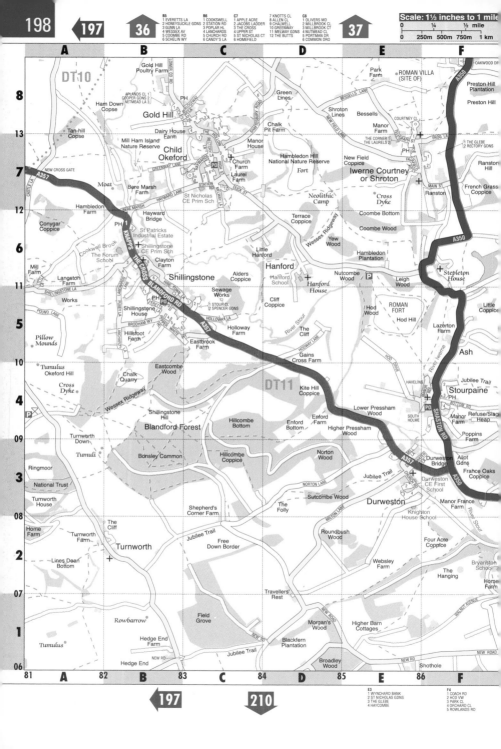

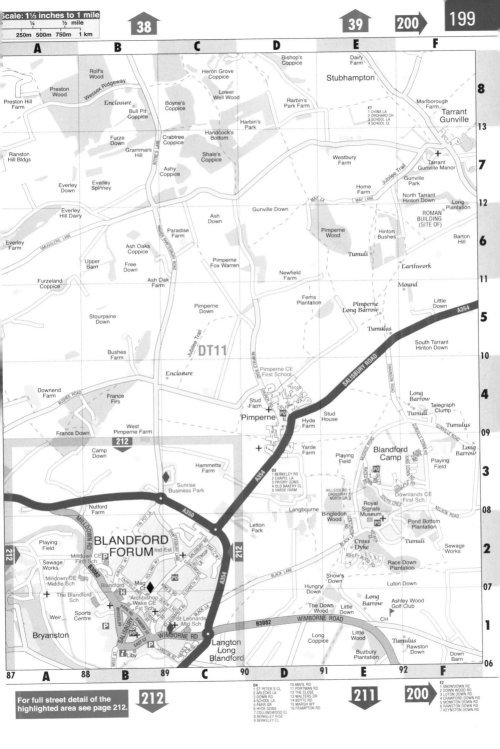

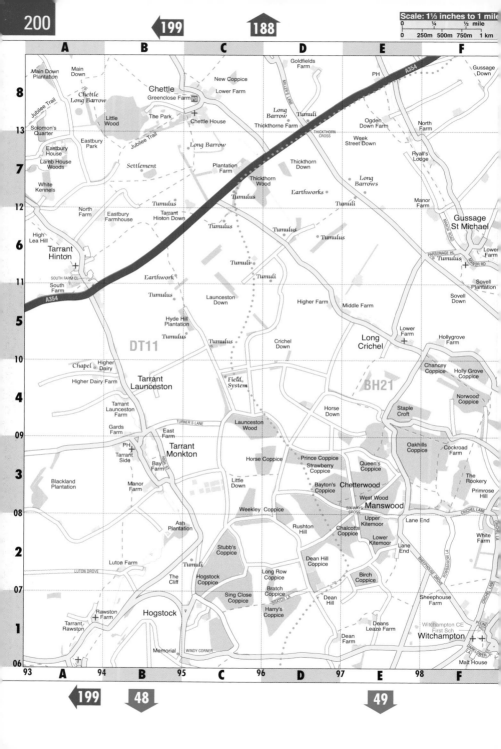

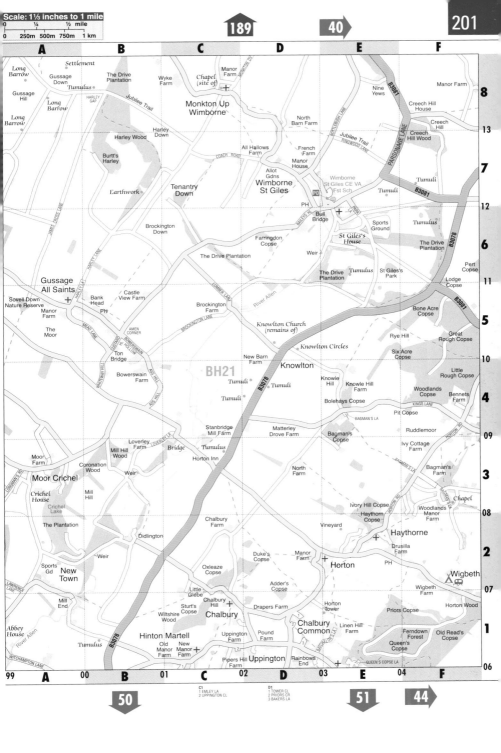

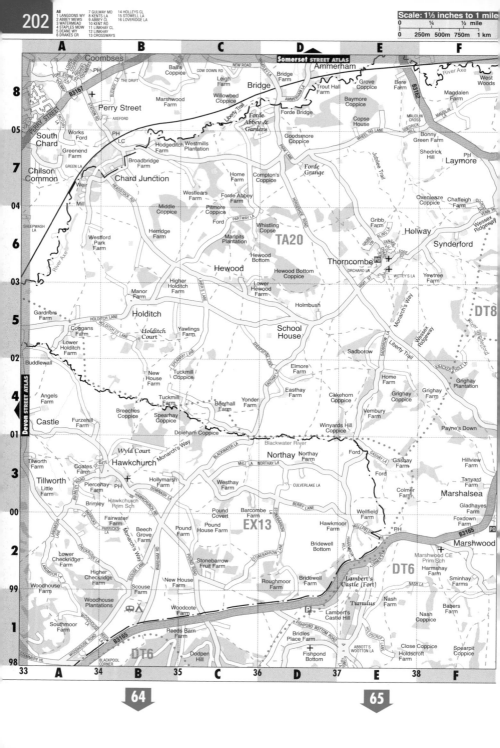

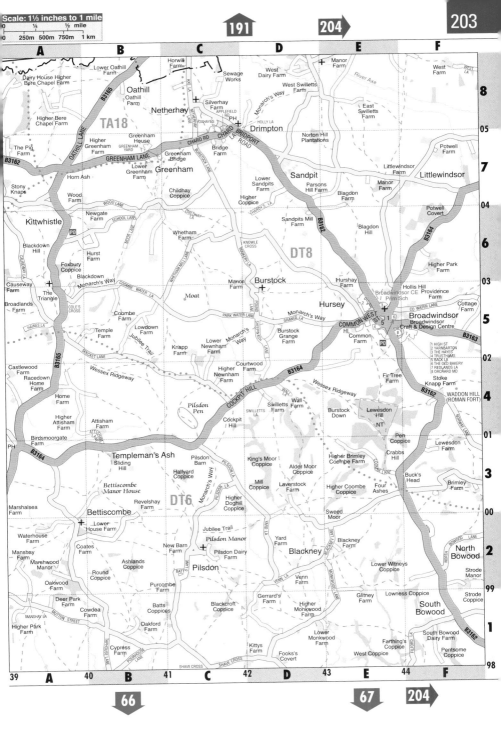

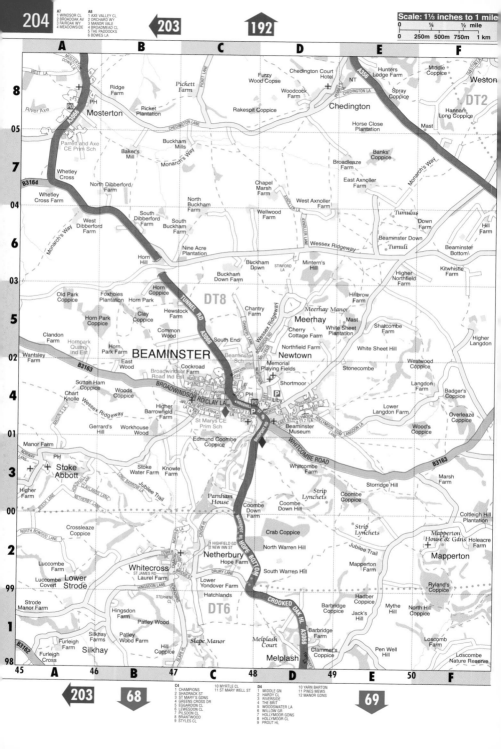

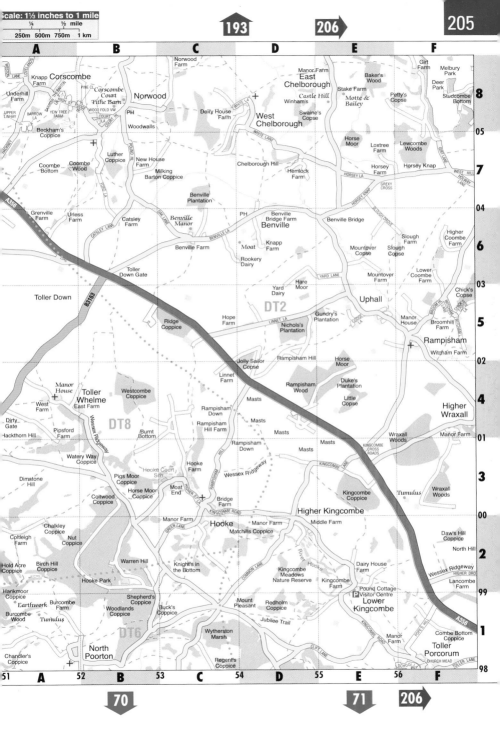

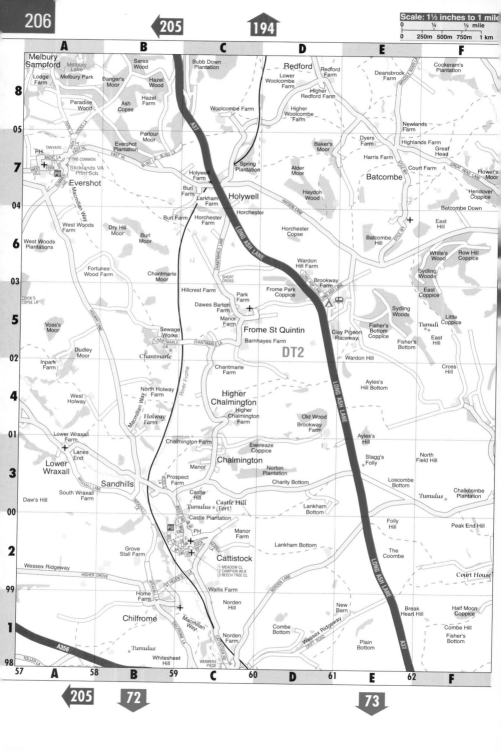

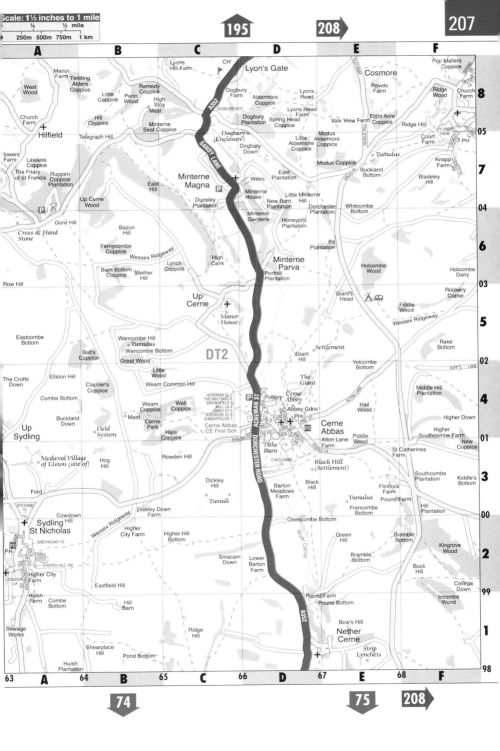

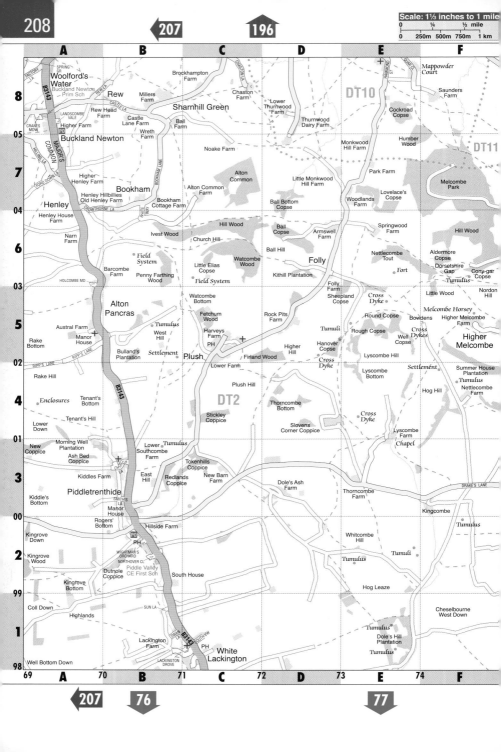

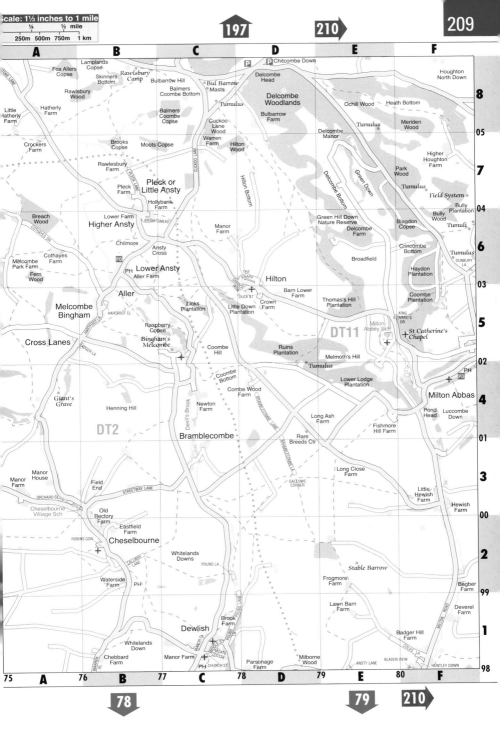

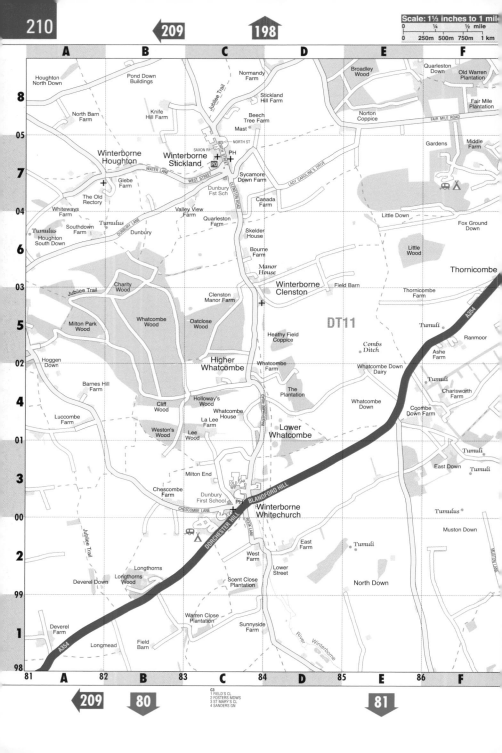

Scale: 1⅓ inches to 1 mile

¼ ½ mile

250m 500m 750m 1 km

212

199

48

211

D6
1 CHARLTON MANOR
2 RIVER LA
3 GREENFIELD RD
4 HOPEGOOD CL
5 MEADOW RD
6 CHARLTON MD

E5
1 BEECH CL
2 SLOPERS MD
3 PRIORY GDNS
4 ABBEY VW

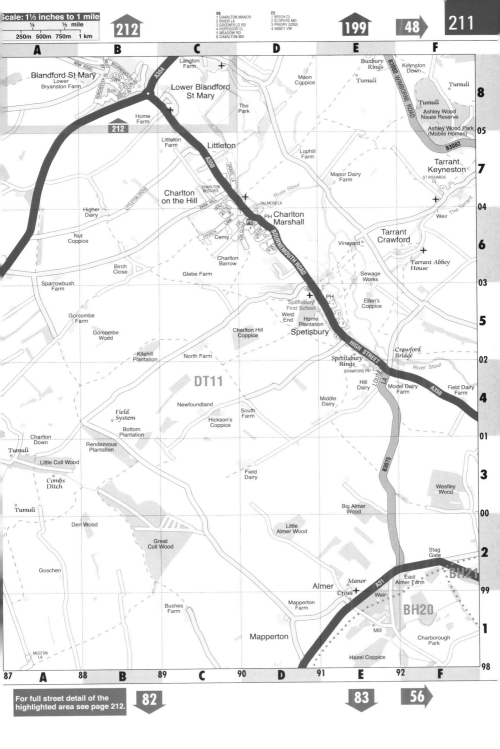

A B C D E F

NEW ROAD
Blandford St Mary
Lower
Bryanston Farm
Sch

DORCHESTER HL
BOURNEMOUTH RD
BIRCH AV

Langton
Farm

Lower Blandford
St Mary

Moon
Coppice

Buzbury
Rings

Keynston
Down

B3082 WIMBORNE ROAD

Tumuli

Tumuli

Tumuli

Ashley Wood
Naure Reserve

Ashley Wood Park
(Mobile Homes)

B3082

8

05

212

Home
Farm

A350

The
Park

Littleton
Farm

Littleton

Charlton
on the Hill

LITTLETON DRIVE

PARK HILL

GRAVEL LA

CHARLTON BEECHES

PALMERS LA

River Stour

Manor Dairy
Farm

Lophill
Farm

Tarrant
Keyneston

ST RICHARDS
CL

The Tarrant

Weir

7

04

Higher
Dairy

Nut
Coppice

PREST
CL
LANE

POST
CHURCH

PH
Charlton
Marshall
Cemy

GREEN LA

BOURNEMOUTH ROAD

Vineyard

Tarrant
Crawford

Tarrant Abbey
House

6

Birch
Close

Charlton
Barrow

Glebe Farm

Charlton Hill
Coppice

Sewage
Works

03

Sparrowbush
Farm

Gorcombe
Farm

Gorcombe
Wood

Kitehill
Plantation

North Farm

PH
Spetisbury
First School
West
End
Home
Plantation
Spetisbury

Ellen's
Coppice

Crawford
Bridge

River Stour

5

HIGH STREET

Spetisbury
Rings

CROWFORD PK

LOUDS LA

Model Dairy
Farm

A350

Field Dairy
Farm

02

DT11

Newfoundland

Hickson's
Coppice

South
Farm

Hill
Dairy

Middle
Dairy

4

Field
System

Bottom
Plantation

Charlton
Down

Rendezvous
Plantation

01

Tumuli

Little Coll Wood

Combs
Ditch

Field
Dairy

Westley
Wood

3

B3075

Tumuli

Den Wood

Great
Coll Wood

Little
Almer Wood

Big Almer
Wood

00

Goschen

Stag
Gate

East
Almer Farm

BH21

2

Almer

Manor
Cross

A31

Weir

BH20

99

Mapperton
Farm

Bushes
Farm

Mill

Charborough
Park

1

MUSTON
LA

Mapperton

Hazel Coppice

98

87 A 88 B 89 C 90 D 91 E 92 F

For full street detail of the
highlighted area see page 212.

82

83

56

Place name May be abbreviated on the map

Location number Present when a number indicates the place's position in a crowded area of mapping

Locality, town or village Shown when more than one place has the same name

Postcode district District for the indexed place

Page and grid square Page number and grid reference for the standard mapping

Church Rd 6 Beckenham BR2..........53 C6

Public and commercial buildings are highlighted in magenta. Places of interest are highlighted in blue with a star★

Abbreviations used in the index

Acad	**Academy**	Comm	**Common**	Gd	**Ground**	L	**Leisure**	Prom	**Promenade**
App	**Approach**	Cott	**Cottage**	Gdn	**Garden**	La	**Lane**	Rd	**Road**
Arc	**Arcade**	Cres	**Crescent**	Gn	**Green**	Liby	**Library**	Recn	**Recreation**
Ave	**Avenue**	Cswy	**Causeway**	Gr	**Grove**	Mdw	**Meadow**	Ret	**Retail**
Bglw	**Bungalow**	Ct	**Court**	H	**Hall**	Meml	**Memorial**	Sh	**Shopping**
Bldg	**Building**	Ctr	**Centre**	Ho	**House**	Mkt	**Market**	Sq	**Square**
Bsns, Bus	**Business**	Ctry	**Country**	Hospl	**Hospital**	Mus	**Museum**	St	**Street**
Bvd	**Boulevard**	Cty	**County**	HQ	**Headquarters**	Orch	**Orchard**	Sta	**Station**
Cath	**Cathedral**	Dr	**Drive**	Hts	**Heights**	Pal	**Palace**	Terr	**Terrace**
Cir	**Circus**	Dro	**Drove**	Ind	**Industrial**	Par	**Parade**	TH	**Town Hall**
Cl	**Close**	Ed	**Education**	Inst	**Institute**	Pas	**Passage**	Univ	**University**
Cnr	**Corner**	Emb	**Embankment**	Int	**International**	Pk	**Park**	Wk, Wlk	**Walk**
Coll	**College**	Est	**Estate**	Intc	**Interchange**	Pl	**Place**	Wr	**Water**
Com	**Community**	Ex	**Exhibition**	Junc	**Junction**	Prec	**Precinct**	Yd	**Yard**

Index of localities, towns and villages

A

Abbotsbury.....149 B8
Acton.....177 F1
Adam's Green.....193 D2
Adber.....14 F5
Affpuddle.....111 F7
Alcester.....12 D2
Alderholt.....42 B6
Alderney.....88 C1
Aller.....209 B5
Allington.....100 B7
Allowenshay.....191 A8
Almer.....211 E2
Alton Pancras.....208 B5
Alvington.....26 D4
Alweston.....31 B1
Ameysford.....52 E1
Ammerham.....202 D8
Anderson.....82 B7
Arne.....144 C5
Ash
  Blandford Forum.....198 F5
  Bridport.....68 C5
Ashington.....59 A1
Ashley
  New Milton.....95 D3
  Ringwood.....54 F5
Ashley Heath.....54 B6
Ashmore.....39 C8
Askerswell.....102 D6
Athelhampton.....78 E1
Atrim.....68 A4
Avon.....63 F2

B

Bagber.....197 A8
Barrow Hill.....84 F4
Barrow Street.....3 F2
Barton on Sea.....126 F6
Barwick.....193 F8
Bashley.....95 A7
Batcombe.....206 E7
Bay.....6 A2
Beacon Hill.....86 A2
Beaminster.....204 B5
Bear Cross.....88 F5
Bearwood.....88 E6
Beaulieu Wood.....196 B1
Beckley.....94 C5
Bedchester.....37 C7
Beer Hackett.....194 C6
Belchalwell.....197 E4
Belchalwell Street.....197 E3
Benville.....205 D6
Bere Regis.....81 A2
Bettiscombe.....203 B3
Bickton.....43 B6
Bincombe.....152 E6
Binnegar.....141 B3
Bishop's Caundle.....196 A8
Bishop's Down.....195 E6
Bisterne.....63 F6
Bittles Green.....12 D7
Blackney.....203 D2
Blacknoll.....156 F8
Blackwater.....91 D4
Blandford Camp.....199 E3
Blandford Forum.....212 C6
Blandford St Mary.....212 C2
Blashford.....47 C2
Bleak Hill.....42 E3
Bloxworth.....82 B2
Bluntshay.....66 F7
Bookham.....208 B7
Boscombe.....122 E3
Bothenhampton.....100 E3
Bournemouth.....122 A2
Bourne Valley.....121 B6
Bourton.....1 E2
Boveridge.....190 B1
Bovington Camp.....139 D6
Bowden.....9 E4
Bowridge Hill.....6 B4
Boys Hill.....195 E5
Bradford Abbas.....28 D1
Bradford Peverell.....106 F6
Bradpole.....69 A1
Bramblecombe.....209 C4
Branksome.....120 F5
Branksome Park.....120 F1
Bransgore.....93 B8
Braytown.....140 A1
Briantspuddle.....112 B7
Bridge.....202 C8
Bridport.....100 B6
Broadmayne.....136 A1
Broadoak.....67 D5
Broad Oak.....197 D7
Broadshard.....191 F5
Broadstone.....87 B3
Broadwey.....152 A4
Broadwindsor.....203 F5
Brockhampton Green.....196 C1
Broom Hill.....51 D2
Bryanston.....212 A3
Brympton D'Evercy.....26 B3
Buckhorn Weston.....9 B6
Buckland Newton.....208 A7
Buckland Ripers.....151 D1
Bugley.....10 A6
Burleston.....78 F1
Burstock.....203 D6
Burton
  Christchurch.....92 D2
  Dorchester.....107 F4
  Mere.....3 D5
  Yeovil.....193 C8
Burton Bradstock.....128 B8
Bushey.....162 D3

C

Camel Green.....42 D6
Camesworth.....68 F7
Canford Cliffs.....147 E8
Canford Heath.....87 E1
Canford Magna.....60 A1
Cann.....24 A7
Cann Common.....24 D7
Castle.....202 A4
Castle Park.....134 D7
Castletown.....181 C1
Catherston Leweston.....65 C1
Cattistock.....206 C2
Cerne Abbas.....207 E4
Chalbury.....201 C1
Chalbury Common.....201 D1
Chaldon Herring or East Chaldon.....156 C3
Chalmington.....206 C3
Chard Junction.....202 B7
Charing Cross.....42 A5
Charlestown.....166 E2
Charlton Down.....75 D3
Charlton Marshall.....211 D6
Charlton on the Hill.....211 C7
Charminster
  Bournemouth.....90 C2
  Dorchester.....107 E5
Charmouth.....97 B7
Charnage.....3 F4
Chedington.....204 E8
Cheselbourne.....209 B2
Chesil.....186 E8
Chetnole.....194 D2
Chettle.....200 B8
Chickerell.....166 C5
Chideock.....99 A6
Chilbridge.....58 E7
Chilcombe.....102 D3
Child Okeford.....198 B7
Chilfrome.....206 B1
Chilson Common.....202 A7
Chilton Cantelo.....14 A8
Christchurch.....124 D5
Church Knowle.....176 C8
Clapgate.....50 E2
Clapton.....191 C1
Clifton Maybank.....194 A8
Closworth.....193 F5
Cobb.....96 B4
Cobley.....189 D7
Cocknowle.....161 A1
Coldharbour.....166 E7
Cold Harbour.....142 A8
Colehill.....60 B8
Colesbook.....5 E4
Combe Almer.....84 D7
Compton Abbas.....24 A2
Compton Valence.....104 E7
Coneygar.....100 D7
Coombe
  Axminster.....65 B7
  Crewkerne.....191 B4
  Shaftesbury.....13 E2
Coombe Keynes.....158 A5
Coombses.....202 B8
Corfe Castle.....177 B8
Corfe Mullen.....86 C6
Corscombe.....205 A8
Coryates.....150 F7
Cosmore.....207 E8
Court Orchard.....100 C8
Cowgrove.....58 D4
Crab Orchard.....45 B2
Cranborne.....40 B7
Creech.....160 D3
Creekmoor.....118 F8
Crendell.....41 B7
Crewkerne.....191 E5
Cripplestyle.....41 B5
Crooked Withies.....51 F7
Cross Lanes.....209 A5
Crossways.....137 E5
Crouch Hill.....196 A5
Crow.....55 E4
Cruxton.....73 A5
Cucklington.....4 B4

D

Daggons.....41 E5
Damerham.....190 F2
Dean.....188 E2
Deanend.....188 E4
Deanland.....189 A5
Dean Park.....122 A4
Dewlands Common.....44 F6
Dewlish.....209 C1
Dinnington.....191 B8
Dorchester.....107 C2
Dottery.....68 B3
Downton.....127 F7
Drimpton.....203 D8
Drive End.....194 A2
Droop.....197 A3
Dudsbury.....61 C1
Duntish.....196 A1
Durweston.....198 E3

E

East Bloxworth.....82 E1
East Brook.....59 C5
East Burton.....139 E2
East Chelborough.....205 D8
East Chinnock.....192 E8
East Coker.....193 D7
East Compton.....24 A2
East Creech.....160 F2
East End.....58 E1
East Fleet.....166 B5
East Holme.....159 E8
East Holton.....117 A3
East Howe.....89 C3
East Knighton.....157 A8
East Lulworth.....173 D8
East Martin.....190 C6
East Melbury.....24 D5
East Morden.....83 D4
Easton.....187 B4
East Orchard.....36 E8
East Parley.....90 B8
East Pulham.....196 D4
East Stoke.....140 F1
East Stour.....10 E3
East Stour Common.....11 A3
Ebblake.....45 F4
Eccliffe.....10 D7
Edmondsham.....40 C3
Ellingham.....47 B5
Elm Hill.....7 B1
Elwell.....152 B6
Enmore Green.....12 D3
Ensbury.....89 F6
Ensbury Park.....89 C2
Evershot.....206 A7

F

Fairmile.....91 F1
Farnham.....188 C2
Farrington.....37 A3
Ferndown.....61 B5
Fiddleford.....197 F8
Fifehead Magdalen.....20 F7
Fifehead Neville.....197 C5
Fifehead St Quintin.....197 B5
Filford.....67 E7
Fleet.....166 A5
Folke.....195 D8
Folly.....208 D6

Fontmell Magna 37 F7
Fontmell Parva 36 D2
Fordingbridge 43 B8
Forston. 75 B4
Fortuneswell. 186 E7
Foxholes 120 A6
Frampton 73 F3
Friars Cliff 125 D7
Frogham 43 F7
Frome St Quintin 206 D5
Furzebrook 161 A4
Furzehill. 50 E1

G

Gannetts 21 C4
Gasper 1 C7
Gaunt's Common. 51 B8
Giddy Green 139 E1
Gillingham 5 E1
Glanvilles Wootton . . . 195 E2
Goathill 31 D7
Godmanstone 75 A7
God's Blessing Green . . 51 C3
Godwinscroft 93 C5
Gold Hill 198 B8
Gore 14 E3
Gotham 41 A3
Grange 50 F2
Grange Estate 62 F8
Greenham 203 C7
Grimstone 74 B1
Grove 187 B6
Gussage All Saints 201 A6
Gussage St Andrew . . . 188 E1
Gussage St Michael . . . 200 F6
Guy's Marsh 23 B6

H

Haddon Hill. 90 E1
Hains 20 F4
Hale 4 A3
Halstock 193 C3
Ham Common 6 C1
Hamlet 194 D3
Hammoon 36 B2
Hampreston 60 E2
Hamworthy 118 C3
Hanford 198 D6
Happy Bottom 58 F1
Harbridge 43 B2
Harbridge Green 43 A2
Harcombe Bottom 64 A4
Hardington Mandeville . 193 A6
Hardington Moor 193 A7
Harman's Cross 177 F6
Hartgrove 22 F1
Haselbury Plucknett . . . 192 C6
Hawkchurch 202 B3
Haydon 31 C4
Haymoor Bottom. 87 F1
Haythorne 201 F2
Hazelbury Bryan 196 F3
Hemsworth 49 C8
Henbury 56 E1
Henley
  Buckland Newton . . . 208 A7
  Crewkerne 191 E2
Henstridge 19 A4
Henstridge Ash 19 A5
Henstridge Bowden 18 A6
Henstridge Marsh 19 E5
Hermitage 195 B2
Herston 178 F3
Hewish 191 D3
Hewood 202 C6
Highcliffe 125 E8
Higher Ansty 209 B6
Higher Bockhampton . . 109 A5
Higher Chalmington . . . 206 C4
Higher Eype 99 F5
Higher Halstock Leigh . 193 A2
Higher Kingcombe 205 E3
Higher Melcombe 208 F5
Higher Nyland 8 E1
Higher Row 51 F5
Higher Sandford 15 F5
Higher Totnell 194 F4
Higher Whatcombe 210 C5
Higher Woodsford 137 D7
Higher Wraxall 205 F4
Highlands 100 A4
Hightown 55 F6
Highwood 158 F8
Hilfield 207 A7
Hillbourne 87 A2
Hillbutts 58 F6
Hill View 209 D6
Hilton 209 D6
Hincknowle 69 B8
Hinton
  Christchurch 94 A3
  Yeovil 14 A6
Hinton Martell 201 B1
Hinton Parva 50 B5
Hinton St George 191 D7
Hinton St Mary 35 B4
Hogstock 200 B1
Holdenhurst 91 B3
Holditch 202 B5
Hollands 27 C7
Hollow Oak 113 B8
Holmebridge 141 E2
Holnest 195 C4

Holt 51 B4
Holt Heath 52 C6
Holton Heath 116 B3
Holt Wood 51 C8
Holway
  Chard 202 E6
  Sherborne 16 A5
Holwell
  Mere 3 C5
  Sturminster Newton . . 196 B5
Holywell
  Dorchester 206 C7
  Yeovil 193 C8
Hooke 205 C2
Hordle 95 F3
Horton 201 E2
Horton Common 44 F2
Horton Heath 44 C2
Hound Hill 58 E7
Houndstone 26 D6
Hummer 14 D4
Hungerford 43 F5
Huntingford 6 A8
Hurn 91 B2
Hursey 203 E5
Hurst 111 C1
Hyde
  Bridport 100 F5
  Fordingbridge 43 F6

I

Ibberton 197 D2
Ibsley 47 C7
Iford 123 D7
Ivy Cross 13 A4
Iwerne Courtney or
  Shroton 198 E7
Iwerne Minster 37 F1

J

Jumpers Common 91 E1

K

Kimmeridge 175 D4
Kingsbury Regis 17 D3
Kingsland 68 A7
King's Stag 196 D5
Kingston
  Corfe Castle 176 F3
  Ringwood 55 B1
  Sturminster Newton . . 197 A4
Kingston Maurward 108 F2
Kingston Russell 104 C3
Kington Magna 9 C3
Kinson 89 B5
Kitford 197 C3
Kit Hill 23 A4
Kittwhistle 203 A6
Knackers Hole 197 D6
Knapp Hill 7 C2
Knighton
  Poole 88 D8
  Yetminster 194 E6
Knob's Crook 44 B4
Knowlton 201 D4

L

Lake 118 D1
Lambrook 68 E5
Lambs' Green 58 F2
Lane End 113 C6
Lanehouse 166 F2
Langham 9 E8
Langton Herring 150 C2
Langton Long
  Blandford 212 F3
Langton Matravers 178 A3
Laymore 202 F7
Leigh
  Sherborne 194 E3
  Sturminster Newton . . 197 D3
  Wimborne Minster . . 59 F4
Leigh Park 59 E4
Lewcombe 193 E2
Lillington 194 F7
Lilliput 147 C8
Limpers Hill 3 D4
Littlebredy 131 E7
Little Canford 60 D4
Littledown 123 A7
Littlemoor 152 F3
Little Pamphill 58 F5
Littleton 211 C7
Littlewindsor 203 F7
Litte Woolgarston 177 D8
Litton Cheney 103 C1
Loders 69 D1
Lodmoor 167 E7
Long Bredy 103 F1
Longburton 195 C2
Long Crichel 200 E5
Long Cross 2 B5
Longfleet 119 D4
Longham 61 A1
Loscombe 69 E8
Lower Ansty 209 B6
Lower Blandford St
  Mary 212 E1
Lower Bockhampton . . . 109 A2

Lower Daggons 41 D8
Lower Eype 99 F3
Lower Halstock Leigh . . 193 B2
Lower Hamworthy 119 A1
Lower Holwell 40 F6
Lower Kingcombe 205 E1
Lower Mannington 52 C7
Lower Marsh 19 F6
Lower Nyland 19 F8
Lower Odcombe 26 A4
Lower Parkstone 120 B3
Lower Row 51 F7
Lower Strode 204 A2
Lower Turmer 46 F7
Lower Whatcombe 210 D4
Lower Wraxall 206 A3
Lower Zeals 2 D5
Lufton 26 B6
Lulworth Camp 173 A7
Lyatts 193 B6
Lydlinch 196 F8
Lyme Regis 96 D5
Lyon's Gate 207 D8
Lytchett Matravers 84 D4
Lytchett Minster 116 F7

M

Madjeston 10 F7
Maiden Newton 73 A8
Mangerton 69 B4
Mannington 52 C8
Manston 36 A3
Manswood 200 E3
Mapperton
  Beaminster 204 F2
  Spetisbury 211 D1
Mappowder 196 F1
Margaret Marsh 22 C2
Marnhull 20 F2
Marshalsea 202 F3
Marshwood 202 A8
Martin 190 B6
Martin Drove End 190 A8
Martinstown or Winterbourne
  St Martin 133 D6
Meerhay 204 D5
Melbury Abbas 24 C5
Melbury Bubb 194 C1
Melbury Osmond 194 A2
Melbury Sampford 206 A8
Melcombe Bingham . . . 209 A5
Melcombe Regis 167 E6
Melplash 204 D1
Mere 3 B5
Merley 59 D1
Merriott
  Beaminster 70 A4
  Crewkerne 191 E7
Merriottsford 191 E6
Merritown 90 E7
Middle Bockhampton . . 92 F6
Middle Chinnock 192 C8
Middlemarsh 195 D1
Milborne Port 17 C2
Milborne St Andrew 91 C8
Milborne Wick 17 B6
Miles Cross 99 E7
Milton Abbas 209 F4
Milton on Stour 5 B5
Minchington 188 D1
Minterne Magna 207 C7
Minterne Parva 207 D6
Misterton 192 A2
Mockbeggar 47 E7
Monkton Up Wimborne . 201 C8
Monkton Wyld 64 B5
Moorbath 67 C3
Moordown 90 A2
Moorside 21 D3
Moortown 55 D5
Morcombelake 66 B1
Moreton 138 E7
Mosterton 204 B8
Motcombe 12 B8
Mounters 20 E1
Mount Pleasant 86 C7
Muckleford 106 B7
Mudeford 125 A5
Mudford 14 A4
Muscliffe 90 C4

N

Nash 193 C8
Neacroft 93 B6
Netherbury 204 C2
Nether Cerne 207 E1
Nether Compton 28 F7
Netherhay 203 C8
Netherstoke 193 D3
Netherton 193 E6
Nettlecombe 70 B3
New Milton 94 E5
Newport 82 C2
New Swanage 179 B6
Newton 197 D8
Newton Peveril 56 B4
Newtown
  Beaminster 204 D5
  Corfe Mullen 86 D7
  Poole 120 B7
New Town
  Gillingham 9 C2

Milborne Port 17 B2
Pimperne 188 C2
Sixpenny Handley 188 F6
Verwood 201 A2
Yeovil 27 E6
Norden 161 C3
Northay 202 D3
North Bockhampton . . . 92 F7
Northbourne 89 E4
North Bowood 203 F2
Northbrook 78 B2
North Chideock 99 A8
North Coker 193 D8
North End
  Fordingbridge 190 D3
  Gillingham 7 A3
North Gorley 43 D3
North Kingston 55 E2
North Perrott 192 C4
North Poorton 205 B1
Northport 142 E5
North Poulner 47 F2
North Wootton 30 F2
Norwood 205 B8
Nottington 152 A2
Notton 73 B4

O

Oakdale 119 D6
Oakley 59 E2
Oathill 203 B8
Oborne 16 E2
Okeford Fitzpaine 197 F5
Orgarford 116 B6
Old Milton 94 E1
Old Town 119 C2
Osehill Green 195 E4
Osmington 154 A3
Osmington Mills 169 C7
Ossemsley 94 E8
Overcombe 168 A7
Over Compton 28 E7
Owermoigne 155 E7
Oxbridge 68 F8

P

Packers Hill 196 C5
Pallington 111 C3
Pamphill 58 E6
Park Gate 196 F2
Parkway 14 F7
Parley Green 90 C7
Peacemarsh 5 E3
Pear Ash 1 C4
Pendomer 193 B5
Pen Mill 28 A6
Penn 64 C3
Pensehwood 1 B4
Pentridge 189 E4
Perry Street 202 B8
Piddlehinton 76 F7
Piddletrenthide 208 A3
Pidney 196 F4
Pig Oak 51 A3
Pilford 60 A8
Pillwell 21 A3
Pilsdon 203 C2
Pimperne
  Blandford Forum . . . 199 D4
  Yeovil 194 A3
Pinehurst Park 53 A1
Pleck
  Marnhull 34 E8
  Sturminster Newton . . 196 B6
Pleck or Little Ansty . . . 209 C7
Plush 208 C5
Pokesdown 123 A4
Poole 119 B3
Poolestown 33 E5
Portway 156 F7
Post Green 116 F7
Poulner 55 F8
Powerstock 70 B5
Poxwell 154 E5
Poyntington 16 D4
Preston 168 B8
Preston Plucknett 26 F4
Puddletown 78 A1
Puddle Town 192 B5
Pulham 196 B3
Puncknowle 129 F6
Purewell 124 D7
Purse Caundle 32 B8
Purtington 191 A4
Putton 166 E5
Puxey 197 B7
Pymore 68 D1

Q

Queen Oak 2 A3

R

Radipole 167 B7
Rampisham 205 F5
Redbridge 138 B5
Redford 206 D8
Red Hill 89 F5
Redlands 152 B1
Rew 208 B8

Ridge . . . . 143 B
Rimpton . . . . 15 C
Ringwood . . . . 47 D
Rivers' Corner . . . . 197 C
Rixon . . . . 35 C
Rockford . . . . 47 E
Rodden . . . . 150 C
Rodgrove . . . . 8 E
Rodwell . . . . 167 D
Rolls Mill . . . . 197 C
Romford . . . . 44 E
Rook Street . . . . 3 A
Rossmore . . . . 120 E
Roundham . . . . 191 D
Rowlands . . . . 59 C
Rushton . . . . 141 B
Ryall . . . . 66 D
Ryme Intrinseca . . . . . . 194 D

S

St Andrew's Well . . . . . 100 C
St Ives . . . . 54 C
St James . . . . 12 E
St Leonards . . . . 54 A
Salwayash . . . . 68 B
Sandbanks . . . . 147 C
Sandford . . . . 142 F
Sandford Orcas . . . . 15 F
Sandhills
  Cattistock . . . . 206 B
  Sherborne . . . . 195 F
Sandpit . . . . 203 D
School House . . . . 202 D
Seaborough . . . . 191 E
Seatown . . . . 99 A
Sedgehill . . . . 7 F
Shaftesbury . . . . 12 E
Shaggs . . . . 158 C
Shapwick . . . . 56 C
Sharnhill Green . . . . 208 C
Sherborne . . . . 30 A
Sherford . . . . 115 D
Shillingstone . . . . 198 C
Shipton Gorge . . . . 101 C
Silkhay . . . . 204 B
Silton . . . . 5 A
Sitterton . . . . 80 F
Sixpenny Handley . . . . . 189 A
Skilling . . . . 100 B
Sleight . . . . 58 D
Slepe . . . . 115 F
Somerford . . . . 124 E
Sopley . . . . 92 B
South Bockhampton . . . 92 E
Southbourne . . . . 123 F
South Bowood . . . . 203 F
Southbrook . . . . 3 B
South Chard . . . . 202 A
South End . . . . 190 F
South Gorley . . . . 43 E
Southill . . . . 167 A
Southlands . . . . 180 E
Southover
  Burton Bradstock . . 128 B
  Dorchester . . . . 73 D
South Perrott . . . . 192 C
South Poorton . . . . 70 C
Southwell . . . . 186 F
Spetisbury . . . . 211 D
Springbourne . . . . 122 C
Spyway . . . . 102 D
Stafford's Green . . . . 16 A
Stalbridge . . . . 33 E
Stalbridge Weston . . . . . 33 A
Stallen . . . . 29 D
Stanbridge . . . . 59 D
Stanley Green . . . . 119 C
Stanpit . . . . 124 F
Stapehill . . . . 60 F
Steeple . . . . 175 C
Sterte . . . . 119 E
Stinsford . . . . 108 E
Stoborough . . . . 142 E
Stoborough Green . . . . 161 A
Stockwood . . . . 194 C
Stoford . . . . 193 E
Stoke Abbott . . . . 204 A
Stokeford . . . . 140 F
Stoke Wake . . . . 197 B
Stone
  Bridport . . . . 101 A
  Wimborne Minster . . 59 A
Stourpaine . . . . 198 F
Stour Provost . . . . 21 D
Stour Row . . . . 22 C
Stourton Caundle . . . . . 32 E
Stratton . . . . 106 E
Strouden . . . . 90 E
Stubhampton . . . . 199 E
Stuckton . . . . 43 E
Studland . . . . 164 D
Sturminster Marshall . . 56 F
Sturminster Newton . . . 35 A
Summerlands . . . . 26 F
Sutton Bingham . . . . . . 193 D
Sutton Holms . . . . 44 B
Sutton Poyntz . . . . 153 D
Sutton Waldron . . . . 37 E
Swanage . . . . 179 C
Swyre . . . . 129 D
Sydling St Nicholas . . . 207 A
Symondsbury . . . . 99 E
Synderford . . . . 202 F

T

adnoll.........138 C2
albot Heath........121 B7
albot Village.......89 C1
albot Woods........121 E7
arrant Crawford......211 E6
arrant Gunville.....199 F8
arrant Hinton......200 A6
arrant Keyneston....48 A5
arrant Launceston...200 B4
arrant Monkton....200 B3
arrant Rushton......48 B8
empleman's Ash....203 B3
he Borough......196 B6
he Causeway......3 C4
he Common......197 E5
he Mount......69 A6
horncombe......202 E6
horne Coffin......26 C8
hornford......194 D8
hornicombe......210 F6
hree Gates......195 A2
hree Legged Cross.....45 A1
hroop
  Bournemouth......90 E4
  Briantspuddle......112 D7
idpit......190 C6
iley......195 E1
illworth......202 A3
incleton......110 D4
iptoe......95 D8
odber......21 D4
ollard Farnham......188 B2
ollard Royal......188 B4
ollerford......72 E8
oller Fratrum......72 C7
oller Porcorum......71 E8
oller Whelme......205 B4

Tolpuddle......79 D2
Totnell......194 F3
Towns End......19 B3
Town's End......81 C3
Trent......14 E2
Trickett's Cross......61 F7
Tuckton......123 F5
Turlin Moor......118 B4
Turner......46 F8
Turners Puddle......112 D8
Turnworth......198 B2
Twyford......23 D2
Tyneham......174 C5

U

Ulwell......179 A6
Up Cerne......207 C5
Uphall......205 E5
Uploders......101 F8
Up Mudford......14 A2
Upper Parkstone......120 B5
Uppington......201 D1
Up Sydling......207 A4
Upton
  Poole......118 D7
  Preston......169 E8
Upwey......152 A6

V

Verwood......45 B6

W

Walditch......101 A6
Walkford......94 C1

Wallisdown......89 A2
Walton Elm......34 F8
Wareham......142 E5
Warmwell......137 A1
Warren......113 D3
Waterditch......93 B5
Waterloo......87 B1
Watton......100 B4
Wayford......191 B1
Waytown......68 E8
Well Bottom......39 D6
West Bay......100 C2
West Bexington......129 E2
Westbourne......121 C3
West Bourton......4 C7
West Chaldon......155 F2
West Chelborough......205 D8
West Chinnock......192 B8
West Cliff......121 C1
West Coker......193 A8
West Compton......71 E1
West End......29 E5
Westfields......196 D1
Westham......167 A3
West Holme......159 D8
West Howe......88 E4
West Hurn......90 F6
West Knighton......136 C3
West Lulworth......172 D6
West Melbury......24 A5
West Milton......69 E6
West Moors......53 B2
West Morden......83 B4
Weston
  Beaminster......204 F8
  Fortuneswell......186 E3
West Orchard......36 D6
West Parley......61 E1
West Pulham......196 A3
West Southbourne......123 D5

West Stafford......136 B8
West Stour......10 A2
Weymouth......167 E3
Whitchurch......19 A6
Whitchurch
  Canonicorum......66 A4
Whitcombe......135 F5
Whitecross......204 B2
White Cross......1 E5
Whitefield......83 A2
White Hill......3 C2
White Lackington......208 C1
Whitmore......44 B6
Wick......124 B4
Wigbeth......201 F2
Wimborne Minster......59 A6
Wimborne St Giles......201 D7
Winfrith Newburgh......156 F6
Winkton......92 C5
Winterborne Came......135 D5
Winterborne Clenston..210 D6
Winterborne
  Herringston......134 F5
Winterborne Houghton.210 B7
Winterborne Kingston..81 D8
Winterborne Monkton..134 C4
Winterborne Muston....82 A7
Winterborne Stickland..210 C7
Winterborne Tomson....82 D7
Winterborne
  Whitechurch......210 D3
Winterborne Zelston...82 F7
Winterbourne
  Steepleton......132 F8
Winton......121 F7
Winyard's Gap......192 E1
Witchampton......200 F1
Wolverton......2 B4
Wonston......196 F2

Woodbridge......23 B1
Woodcutts......188 D4
Woodlands......44 A6
Woodlands Common....44 C6
Woodrow......196 F4
Woodsford......110 D2
Woodville......21 F8
Woodyates......189 D6
Wool......140 B2
Woolbridge Heath......140 A6
Woolford's Water......208 A8
Woolgarston......177 F8
Woolland......197 C1
Woolminstone......191 B3
Woolsbridge......53 D7
Wooth......68 E3
Wootton......95 B8
Wootton Fitzpaine......65 B4
Worgret......142 B2
Worth Matravers......183 D7
Wych......100 E2
Wyke......5 D1
Wyke Regis......180 D7
Wynford Eagle......72 D4

Y

Yenston......18 E7
Yeovil......27 A4
Yetminster......194 D5
Yondover......101 D8

Z

Zeals......2 A4

Index of streets, hospitals, industrial estates, railway stations, schools, shopping centres, universities and places of interest

216 8th–Ash

8th August Rd BH20 . . . .**139** E7

A

Aaron Cl BH17 . . . . .119 F7
Abbey Cl 5 TA20 . . . . .202 A8
Abbey Ct 5 DT2 . . . . .207 D4
Abbey Gdns
  Cerne Abbas DT2. . . . . . . .207 D4
  Ferndown BH21. . . . . .60 D5
Abbey Hill Cl SO23. . . . . . .126 E8
Abbey Hill Rd SO23 . . . . . .126 E8
Abbey Mews 2 TA20. . . . .202 A8
Abbey Pas SO23 . . . . .126 E5
Abbey Prim Sch SP7 . . . . . . .12 D1
Abbey Rd
  Sherborne DT9 . . . . .30 B6
  West Moors BH22 . . . . .62 A8
  Yeovil BA21 . . . . .26 F6
Abbey St
  Cerne Abbas DT2. . . . . . . .207 D4
  Crewkerne TA18 . . . . .191 E4
  Hinton St George TA17 . . . .191 C7
Abbey View 4 DT11. . . . . .211 E5
Abbey Wlk SP7 . . . . .12 E2
Abbotsbury Castle (Hill Fort)
  DT3 . . . . .130 D2
Abbotsbury Hill DT3 . . . . . .130 D1
Abbotsbury La DT2 . . . . . . .130 F7
Abbotsbury Rd
  Corfe Mullen BH18 . . . . . . .86 F5
  Weymouth DT4 . . . . .167 B3
Abbotsbury Sub-Tropical
  Gdns DT3. . . . . .148 E7
Abbotsbury Swannery
  DT3 . . . . .149 B5
Abbots Cl BH23. . . . . .125 F7
Abbots Meade BA21 . . . . . . .26 F6
Abbots Quay 4 BH20 . . . . .142 E3
Abbots Row 1 SO22 . . . . . .126 D6
Abbots Way
  Sherborne DT9 . . . . .29 F5
  Yeovil BA21 . . . . .26 F7
Abbots Wlk DT2 . . . . .207 D4
Abbott Cl BH9 . . . . .122 A8
Abbott La TA16 . . . . .192 A8
Abbott Rd BH9 . . . . .122 A8
Abbotts Cl SO23 . . . . .126 E8
Abbotts Ct SO22 . . . . .126 D8
Abbotts Mdw BH16 . . . . . . .84 D3
Abbotts Rd SO23. . . . . .126 E8
Abbott St BH21. . . . . .58 D6
Abbotts Way BH22 . . . . .62 A8
Abbott's Way SP5 . . . . .5 F3
Abbott's Wootton La
  Marshwood DT6 . . . . .202 E1
  Whitchurch Canonicorum
  DT6 . . . . .65 D7
Alder Cross DT9 . . . . .14 F4
Abels La DT9 . . . . .14 E2
Aberdare Rd BH10 . . . . .89 E3
Abingdon Dr BH23 . . . . . . .126 C8
Abingdon Rd BH17. . . . . . . .119 D8
Abinger Rd BH7 . . . . .123 B6
Abney Rd BH10 . . . . .89 D3
Acacia Ave BH31. . . . . .45 E4
Acacia Cl DT4 . . . . .167 B6
Acacia Rd SO41. . . . . .95 F3
Acer Ave
  Bridport DT6 . . . . .100 F8
  2 Bridport DT6 . . . . .68 F1
Acer Dr BA21 . . . . .26 E7
Ackerman Rd DT1 . . . . .108 C1
Acland Rd
  Bournemouth BH9 . . . . . . .122 B8
  7 Dorchester DT1 . . . . . . .108 A2
Aconbury Ave 2 DT1 . . . . .107 C1
Acorn Ave BH15 . . . . .119 D2
Acorn Bsns Pk BH12 . . . . . .120 B8
Acorn Cl
  Christchurch BH23 . . . . . . .123 F8
  New Milton BH25. . . . . .95 C4
  St Leonards BH24 . . . . .54 A3
  Winchester SO22. . . . . .126 B8
Acorns The
  West Moors BH24 . . . . .62 B8
  Wimborne Minster BH21. . . .60 A4
Acorn Way BH31. . . . . .45 C6
Acreman Cl 1 DT2 . . . . . . .207 D4
Acreman Pl DT9 . . . . .30 B5
Acreman St
  Cerne Abbas DT2. . . . . . . .207 D4
  Sherborne DT9 . . . . .30 B6
Acres Ct 8 BA22 . . . . .193 F8
Acres Rd BH11. . . . . .89 B2
Acton Rd BH10 . . . . .89 B1
Adamsfield Gdns BH10. . . . .89 C2
Adastral Rd BH17 . . . . .119 F8
Adastral Sq BH17 . . . . .119 F8
Ad Astro Fst Sch BH17 . . . . .87 F1
Adber Cl 5 BH21 . . . . .212 D4
Addington Pl BH23 . . . . . . .124 D6
Addiscombe Rd BH23 . . . . .124 A7
Addison Cl
  Gillingham SP8 . . . . .6 A1
  Winchester SO22. . . . . .126 A3
Addison Sq BH24 . . . . .55 D7
Addlewell La BA20. . . . . .27 D4

Adelaide Cl BH23 . . . . .123 F8
Adelaide Cres DT4. . . . . . . .167 B3
Adelaide La 17 BH1. . . . . . .121 F3
Adeline Rd BH1,BH5. . . . . . .122 E4
Admirals Cl DT9 . . . . .30 D8
Admirals Way BH20 . . . . . . .142 E6
Admirals Wlk 13 BH2. . . . .121 D2
Admiralty Rd BH6. . . . . .123 F3
Admiralty St BH21 . . . . .60 E6
Aggis Farm Rd BH31. . . . . . .45 A6
Agglestone Rd BH19 . . . . . .164 B1
Aigburth Rd BH19 . . . . .178 F3
Airetons Cl BH18 . . . . .87 C3
Airfield Cl DT2. . . . . .137 D5
Airfield Ind Est
  Christchurch BH23 . . . . . . .124 F6
  Christchurch BH23 . . . . . . .125 A4
Airfield Rd BH23 . . . . .124 F6
Airfield Way BH23 . . . . .124 F7
Airlie Cnr SO22. . . . . .126 C4
Airlie Ct SO22 . . . . .126 C4
Airlie La SO22 . . . . .126 C4
Airlie Rd SO22 . . . . .126 C4
Airspeed Rd BH23 . . . . .125 B7
Akeman Cl BA21 . . . . .26 F7
Akeshill Cl BH25. . . . . .95 B5
Alamein Rd BH20 . . . . .139 F6
Alan Ct 10 BH23 . . . . .126 B7
Alastair Cl BA21 . . . . .27 B7
Alastair Dr BA21. . . . . .27 B7
Albany BH1. . . . . .122 C3
Albany Cl
  Old Milton BH25 . . . . .94 F1
  Sherborne DT9 . . . . .30 C8
Albany Ct 6 BH2 . . . . .121 F4
Albany Gdns BH15. . . . . .45 A1
Albany Gdns BH15. . . . . . . .118 F2
Albany Ho 17 BH13 . . . . . . .121 A4
Albany Pk BH7 . . . . .119 B8
Albany Rd DT4 . . . . .166 E4
Albemarle Rd BH3 . . . . .121 F7
Albert Cl BA21. . . . . .27 A7
Albert Ct SO23. . . . . .126 D7
Albert Rd
  Bournemouth BH1. . . . . . . .121 F3
  Corfe Mullen BH21 . . . . . . .86 D5
  Dorchester DT1 . . . . .107 F1
  Ferndown BH22. . . . . .61 D5
  New Milton BH25. . . . . .94 F2
  Poole BH12 . . . . .120 D6
Albert St
  Blandford Forum DT11 . . . .212 D4
  5 Radipole DT4 . . . . .167 D3
Albert Terr DT5 . . . . .186 E8
Albion Cl BH12 . . . . .120 B7
Albion Pl 4 SO23. . . . . .126 D6
Albion Rd BH23. . . . . .91 F1
Albion Way BH31. . . . . .44 F6
Alby Rd BH12. . . . . .120 F5
Alcester Rd BH12 . . . . .120 D6
Aldamond Ct DT3. . . . . .166 D4
Aldbury Ct BH25. . . . . .127 A7
Alderbury Cl 5 BH19 . . . . .178 F2
Alder Cl
  Burton BH23 . . . . .92 D1
  3 Sandford BH20 . . . . .116 A1
  Sturminster Newton DT10. . .35 C2
Alder Cres BH12 . . . . .120 F7
Alder Dr SP6 . . . . .42 B5
Alder Gr
  Crewkerne TA18 . . . . .191 F5
  Yeovil BA20 . . . . .27 A2
Alder Hills BH12 . . . . .121 A7
Alder Hills Ind Pk BH12 . . .121 A7
Alder Hills Nature Reserve
  BH12 . . . . .121 A7
Alderholt Pk SP6 . . . . .42 A7
Alderholt Sports Club
  SP6 . . . . .42 C5
Alder Hts BH12 . . . . .121 A7
Alderley Rd BH10 . . . . .89 D4
Alderney Ave BH10. . . . . . . .88 D1
Alderney Rbdt BH12 . . . . . . .88 D2
Alder Rd
  Poole BH12 . . . . .120 F6
  Poole BH12 . . . . .121 A7
  Sturminster Newton DT10. . .35 C2
Aldis Gdns BH15. . . . . .118 C2
Aldondale Gdns BA20. . . . . .27 C3
Aldridge Rd
  Bournemouth BH10. . . . . . .89 C5
  Ferndown BH22. . . . . .61 E3
Aldridge Way BH22 . . . . .61 F3
Alexander Cl BH23. . . . . . . .124 E6
Alexandra Ct DT6 . . . . .100 C5
Alexandra Lodge 8 BH1 . . .122 A3
Alexandra Rd
  Bournemouth BH6 . . . . . . .123 C5
  Bridport DT6. . . . . .100 C6
  Dorchester DT1 . . . . .107 F1
  Poole BH15 . . . . .120 D5
  Radipole DT4 . . . . .167 D5
  Weymouth DT4 . . . . .166 E3
  Yeovil BA21 . . . . .27 F6
Alexandra St DT11 . . . . . . .212 D4
Alexandra Terr
  2 Dorchester DT1 . . . . . . .108 A2
  Winchester SO23. . . . . .126 D5
Alexandria Ct BH22 . . . . . . .61 E3
Alford Rd BH3 . . . . .121 D7
Alford Pl DT1 . . . . .108 B1
Alfred St DT1 . . . . .108 A1

Alfred St DT11 . . . . .212 D4
Alice in Wonderland Family
  Fun Park BH23 . . . . .90 E7
Alice Rd DT1 . . . . .107 E1
Alington 22 BH4 . . . . .121 C3
Alington Ave DT1 . . . . .135 C8
Alington Cl BH14 . . . . .147 C7
Alington Ho BH14. . . . . .147 C7
Alington Rd
  Bournemouth BH3. . . . . . . .122 A6
  Dorchester DT1 . . . . .108 B1
  Poole BH14 . . . . .147 C7
Alington St 4 DT1. . . . . . . .108 A2
Alington Terr 6 DT1 . . . . . .108 B2
Alipore Cl BH14. . . . . .120 D5
Alipore Hts BH14 . . . . .120 D3
Alisons The BH20 . . . . .139 E2
Alison Way 6 SO22 . . . . . . .126 D6
Allamanda Rd DT3 . . . . .152 E2
Allbery Gdns DT1 . . . . .168 A8
Allenby Rd BH17 . . . . .87 B2
Allenby Rd BH17 . . . . .87 B2
Allen Cl 8 DT11 . . . . .198 C7
Allen Ct BH21 . . . . .59 C5
Allen Rd BH21 . . . . .59 C4
Allens La BH16 . . . . .118 D5
Allens Rd
  Upton BH16 . . . . .117 F6
  Upton BH16 . . . . .118 D6
Allenview Rd BH21. . . . . .59 C5
Allingham Rd BA21 . . . . .27 E7
Allington Gdns 3 DT6 . . . . .100 B8
Allington Mead 3 DT6. . . . .100 C8
Allington Pk 2 DT6. . . . . . . .100 B7
All Saints CE Prim Sch
  SO23 . . . . .126 F4
All Saints Cl DT4. . . . . .180 D8
All Saints CE VC Prim Sch
  DT9 . . . . .196 A2
All Saints' Rd
  Dorchester DT1 . . . . .108 B2
  Weymouth DT4 . . . . .180 C8
Alma Rd
  Bournemouth BH9 . . . . . . .121 F7
  Bournemouth BH9 . . . . . . .122 A7
  Weymouth DT4 . . . . .167 C3
Almer Rd BH15 . . . . .118 E3
Almond Gr
  Bournemouth BH2 . . . . . . .120 D7
  Radipole DT4 . . . . .167 B6
Almshouses BH10. . . . . .89 C1
Alpha Ctr The BH7. . . . . . . .119 B7
Alpha House Gall DT9. . . . . .30 C5
Alpine Rd BH24 . . . . .54 E2
Alswitha Terr 3 SO23. . . . .126 E7
Alton Cl 3 SO23. . . . . .126 E8
Alton La DT2 . . . . .207 E4
Alton Mead La DT9 . . . . . . .194 E4
Alton Rd
  Bournemouth BH10 . . . . . . .89 B1
  Poole BH14 . . . . .120 C3
Alton Rd E BH14 . . . . .120 D3
Alum Chine Rd BH4. . . . . . . .121 B3
Alumdale Rd BH4 . . . . .121 B2
Alumhurst Rd BH4. . . . . . . .121 B2
Alvandi Gdns 2 BH25. . . . . .95 B3
Alverton Ave BH15. . . . . . . .119 F3
Alverton Hall 11 BH4 . . . . .121 C2
Alvington La BA22 . . . . .26 D4
Alyth Rd BH3 . . . . .121 D6
Amado Ho BH25 . . . . .95 A5
Ambassador Cl BH23 . . . . . .125 A6
Ambassador Ind Est
  BH23 . . . . .125 A6
Ambassador Trade Pk
  SP8. . . . . .20 C7
Amberley Cl BH23 . . . . .125 F8
Amberley Ct 10 BH1 . . . . . .122 A3
Amberley Ho BH22. . . . . .61 D7
Amber Rd BH21. . . . . .86 C4
Amberwood BH22 . . . . .61 E7
Amberwood Dr BH23 . . . . . .93 F2
Amberwood Gdns BH23 . . . .94 A2
Amberwood Ho BH23 . . . . . .94 A2
Ambleside
  Christchurch BH23 . . . . . . .91 E3
  Radipole DT4 . . . . .167 B7
Ambrose Cl DT9 . . . . .28 D2
Ambury La BH23 . . . . .124 F8
Amelia Cl DT5 . . . . .186 F8
Amen Cnr BH21 . . . . .201 B5
Amersham St 37 BH4 . . . . .121 C3
Amesbury Rd BH6 . . . . .123 C6
Amethyst Rd BH23 . . . . . . .124 F7
Ameysford Rd
  Ferndown BH22. . . . . .52 E1
  Ferndown BH22. . . . . .61 C7
Amiens Rd BH20 . . . . .139 E7
Amira Ct 2 BH2 . . . . .121 E3
Ammerham La TA20. . . . . . .202 D8
Ampfield Rd BH8. . . . . .90 D3
Amsterdam Sq BH23 . . . . . .124 D6
Ancaster Rd BH17 . . . . .178 F3
Anchor Cl
  Bournemouth BH11. . . . . . . .88 F6
  Christchurch BH23 . . . . . . .125 A5
Anchor Rd BH11. . . . . .88 F5
Ancrum Lo 15 BH4. . . . . . . .121 B3
Andbourne Ct BH6. . . . . . . .123 F3
Andover Cl BH23. . . . . .125 B7
Andover Gn BH20 . . . . .139 C6

Andover Rd SO23 . . . . .126 D8
Andover Road Ret Pk
  SO23 . . . . .126 D7
Andre Ct BH23. . . . . .126 B8
Andrew Cl DT11 . . . . .212 E5
Andrew La BH25. . . . . .95 D2
Andrews Cl BH11. . . . . .89 A3
Angel Cl DT3 . . . . .150 C1
Angeline Cl BH23 . . . . .125 F8
Angel La
  Barton on Sea BH25 . . . . . .127 D8
  Ferndown BH21. . . . . .61 B3
  Langton Herring DT3. . . . . .150 C2
  Mere BA12. . . . . .3 A5
Angel Mews BH5 . . . . .119 B2
Angers La DT10 . . . . .197 E2
Anglebury Ave 2 BH19 . . . .179 B4
Anglebury Bsns Pk BH20 . .142 E5
Anglewood Mans 2
  BH4 . . . . .121 C3
Anglo-European Coll of
  Chiropractic BH5. . . . . . . .123 A4
Angus Cl DT11 . . . . .212 E5
Anjou Cl BH11 . . . . .88 D5
Annadale Ct BH6. . . . . .123 D4
Anncott Cl BH16 . . . . .84 D3
Anne Cl
  Blandford Forum DT11 . . . .212 E4
  Christchurch BH23 . . . . . . .92 A1
Annerley Rd BH1 . . . . .122 C4
Annet Cl BH15 . . . . .118 E2
Anning Rd DT7 . . . . .96 C6
Annings La DT6. . . . . .101 E1
Anson Cl
  Christchurch BH23 . . . . . . .124 F6
  Ringwood BH24 . . . . .55 E8
Anstey Cl BH11 . . . . .89 A6
Anstey Rd BH11. . . . . .89 A5
Ansty La DT11 . . . . .79 C8
Antell's Way SP6. . . . . .42 C5
Antelope Wlk 13 DT1. . . . . .108 A2
Anthony's Ave BH14. . . . . . .120 C1
Antler Dr BH25 . . . . .94 E4
Anvil Cl 1 BH19 . . . . .178 E2
Anvil Cres BH18 . . . . .86 F5
Anvil Rd BH20 . . . . .199 D4
Aplands Cl 1 DT11 . . . . . . .198 B8
Apollo Cl
  Dorchester DT1 . . . . .134 F8
  Poole BH12 . . . . .120 D7
Apple Acre 1 DT11 . . . . . . .198 C7
Applebee Way 2 DT7. . . . . . .96 C6
Apple Gr BH13 . . . . .121 A4
Applefield Rd DT8 . . . . .203 C8
Apple Gr BH23 . . . . .91 E2
Appleslade Way BH25 . . . . . .95 B5
Appletree Cl
  Bournemouth BH6 . . . . . . .123 C5
  New Milton BH25. . . . . .95 A1
Apreece Rd BH9 . . . . .90 A1
Apsley Cres BH17 . . . . .87 C1
Apsley Ct 3 BH8 . . . . .122 A5
Aragon Cl DT4 . . . . .180 B8
Aragon Way BH9 . . . . .90 B4
Arbour Ct 20 SO22 . . . . . . .126 D6
Arbutus Cl DT1 . . . . .108 A1
Arcade BH4. . . . . .121 B3
Arcade The 14 BH1. . . . . . . .121 F3
Arcadia Ave BH8. . . . . .122 B7
Arcadia Rd BH23. . . . . .91 F1
Archbishop Wake CE Fst Sch
  DT11 . . . . .212 D4
Archdale Cl BH10. . . . . .89 D2
Archery La SO23 . . . . .126 D5
Archway Rd BH14. . . . . .120 C4
Arden Rd BH9 . . . . .89 F1
Arden Wlk BH25 . . . . .95 B2
Ardmore Rd BH14. . . . . .120 B4
Arena Bsns Ctr BH17. . . . . .119 B8
Argyle Rd
  Christchurch BH23 . . . . . . .124 D7
  Radipole DT4. . . . . .167 D6
  Swanage BH19 . . . . .179 B2
Argyll Mans 8 BH5. . . . . . . .122 E4
Argyll Rd
  Bournemouth BH5. . . . . . . .122 E4
  Poole BH12 . . . . .120 D6
Ariel Cl BH6 . . . . .124 B4
Ariel Dr BH6 . . . . .124 B4
Ark Dr BH22 . . . . .61 F3
Arlecks La 2 DT11 . . . . . . .199 D4
Arley Rd BH14 . . . . .120 B3
Arlington Ct BH23 . . . . .127 B8
Arlington Dr BH14 . . . . .167 A5
Arlington Cl BA21. . . . . .26 E7
Arlington Pl 3 SO23 . . . . . .126 E6
Armada Way DT1. . . . . .135 B8
Armoury Rd BA22 . . . . .26 C6
Armoury Rd BA22 . . . . .26 C6
Armstrong Rd DT6 . . . . .100 C8
Arne Ave BH12 . . . . .120 E7
Arne Cres BH12 . . . . .120 E7
Arne Rd BH20 . . . . .143 D1
Arne Reedbeds National
  Nature Reserve BH20. . . .144 E6

Arnewood Ct BH2. . . . . . . .121 E
Arnewood Gdns BA20. . . . . .27 E
Arnewood Rd BH6. . . . . . . .123 C
Arnewood Sch The BH25 . . .94 F
Arnold Cl BH22. . . . . .53 A
Arnold Rd BH22 . . . . .53 A
Arnolds Cl BH25 . . . . .126 F
Arran Way BH23 . . . . .94 E
Arras Cres BH20 . . . . .139 C
Arras Rd BH20 . . . . .139 D
Arrowfield DT6 . . . . .100 C
Arrow Field DT6. . . . . .100 C
Arrowsmith Ct BH18 . . . . . . .87 A
Arrowsmith La BH21. . . . . . .87 E
Arrowsmith Rd BH21. . . . . . .87 E
Arthur Cl BH2 . . . . .121 E
Arthur La 3 BH23 . . . . .124 A
Arthur Rd
  Christchurch BH23 . . . . . . .124 A
  Winchester SO23. . . . . .126 E
Artillery Rd BA22 . . . . .26 C
Artist Row DT5 . . . . .186 F
Arts Inst of Bournemouth
  The BH12 . . . . .121 C
Arun Cl 2 SP8 . . . . .5 F
Arundel Cl BH25. . . . . .94 B
Arundel Rd BA21 . . . . .28 A
Arundel Way BH23 . . . . . . .125 F
Aschan Rd BH8 . . . . .122 E
Ascot Rd BH18. . . . . .87 A
Ash Ave BH20 . . . . .116 B
Ashbarn Cres SO22 . . . . . . .126 C
Ashbourne Ct 1 BH1. . . . . .122 A
Ashbourne Rd BH5. . . . . . . .123 B
Ashbrook Wlk BH16. . . . . . .117 A
Ashburn Garth 2 BA21 . . . .55 F
Ashburton Gdns BH10. . . . . .89 D
Ash Cl
  Alderholt SP6. . . . . .42 C
  Sandford BH20 . . . . .143 A
  Shaftesbury SP7 . . . . .13 A
  Swanage BH19 . . . . .178 E
  Upton BH16. . . . . .118 B
Ashcombe La DT9 . . . . .31 D
Ashdene Cl DT2 . . . . .59 D
Ashdown
  8 Bournemouth BH2 . . . . .121 D
  Bournemouth BH2 . . . . . . .121 D
Ashdown Tech Coll BH17 . . .87 E
Ashdown Wlk BH25. . . . . . . .95 C
Ash End BA8 . . . . .19 A
Ashford Gr BA21. . . . . .27 D
Ashford Rd
  Bournemouth BH6 . . . . . . .123 D
  Fordingbridge SP6. . . . . . . .42 E
Ash Gr BH24. . . . . .55 E
Ashgrove 1 BA12 . . . . .3 B
Ash Hill DT2. . . . . .106 F
Ashington Gdns BH21. . . . . .86 F
Ashington La BA21 . . . . .59 A
Ashington Pk BH25. . . . . . . .95 B
Ashington St 3 DT1 . . . . . .107 D
Ash La DT6 . . . . .68 D
Ashland Ct TA18 . . . . .191 E
Ashlands CE VC Fst Sch
  TA18. . . . . .191 E
Ashlands Cl 1 TA18. . . . . . .191 F
Ashlands Mdw TA18. . . . . . .191 F
Ashlands Rd TA18. . . . . . . .191 F
Ashleigh Ave DT2. . . . . .72 F
Ashleigh Rise BH10. . . . . . . .89 D
Ashlet Gdns BH25. . . . . .95 D
Ashley Arnewood Ct 5
  BH25 . . . . .95 B
Ashley Cl
  Bournemouth BH1. . . . . . . .122 E
  Ringwood BH24 . . . . .55 F
Ashley Common Rd BH25 . . .95 C
Ashley Cross BH14 . . . . . . .120 A
Ashley Ct BH22 . . . . .62 A
Ashley Dr BH24 . . . . .46 E
Ashley Dr N BH24. . . . . .54 B
Ashley Dr S BH24 . . . . .54 B
Ashley Dr W BH24 . . . . .54 B
Ashley Fst Sch BH25. . . . . . .95 C
Ashley Jun Sch BH25,SO41. .95 C
Ashley Meads BH25 . . . . . . .95 D
Ashley Pk BH24 . . . . .54 C
Ashley Rd
  Bournemouth BH1. . . . . . . .122 E
  Dorchester DT1 . . . . .135 A
  Marnhull DT10 . . . . .21 A
  New Milton BH25. . . . . .95 D
  Poole BH14 . . . . .120 C
Ashley Wood Golf Club
  DT11 . . . . .199 E
Ashley Wood Rd DT11 . . . . .211 F
Ashling Cl BH8 . . . . .122 C
Ashling Cres BH8 . . . . .122 C
Ashmead
  Bournemouth BH4 . . . . . . .121 C
  Yeovil BA20. . . . . .26 E
Ashmeads Cl DT2 . . . . .59 C
Ashmeads Way BH21. . . . . . .86 E
Ashmore BH21. . . . . .59 D
Ashmore Ave
  Barton on Sea BH25 . . . . . .127 B

shmore Ave continued
Hamworthy BH15 . . . . . . .118 F1
shmore Bottom DT11 . . . .39 D1
shmore CI DT11 . . . . .212 D5
shmore Cres BH15 . . . . . .118 F1
shmore Gr BH23 . . . . .93 E1
shmore Rd 39 BH4 . . . . .121 C3
shmore Rd SO22 . . . . . . .126 B7
shridge Ave BH10 . . . . . . .89 D5
shridge Gdns BH10 . . . . . .89 D5
shridge Par 2 BH11 . . . . .89 D5
shstead Gdns BH8 . . . . . . .90 C3
shton Ct
  New Milton BH25 . . . . . . .95 B3
  Poole BH13 . . . . .121 A2
shton Rd
  Bournemouth BH9 . . . . . . .89 F2
  1 Weymouth DT4 . . . . . .167 C2
shtree CI BH23 . . . . .95 D2
sh Tree La 2 DT2 . . . . . . .78 B1
sh Tree La SP7 . . . . .24 D6
shurst Rd
  Bournemouth BH8 . . . . . . .90 D3
  Ferndown BH22 . . . . .53 A3
shwell Ct BH23 . . . . .91 F1
sh Wlk BA8 . . . . .19 A5
shwood Dr
  Broadstone BH18 . . . . . . .87 C4
  4 Yeovil without BA21 . . .28 A8
sker Gdns BH10 . . . . .100 D6
skwith CI DT9 . . . . .29 F5
spen Dr BH31 . . . . .45 D6
spen Gdns BH12 . . . . . . .120 F7
spen PI BH25 . . . . .95 B1
spen Rd
  Charminster DT2 . . . . . . .75 D3
  Poole BH12 . . . . .120 F7
spen Way
  10 Crewkerne TA18 . . . . .191 F5
  Poole BH12 . . . . .120 F7
squith CI BH23 . . . . .124 D6
ss Hill BH21 . . . . .201 B4
stbury Ave
  Poole BH12 . . . . .121 A8
  Poole BH13 . . . . .89 A1
ston Mead BH23 . . . . . . .91 E4
strid Way 3 DT4 . . . . . . .167 E4
Athelhampton House & Gdns
  DT2 . . . . .78 E1
thelhampton Rd DT2 . . . .78 E1
thelney Ct 7 BH1 . . . . . .122 B3
thelney Way BH21 . . . . . .26 F6
thelstan Rd
  Bournemouth BH6 . . . . . .123 E5
  2 Dorchester DT1 . . . . . .108 B1
thelstan Rd BH25 . . . . . .127 B8
tlantic Ct SO22 . . . . .126 A5
tlantic Rd BH19 . . . . .179 B1
trium The
  Ferndown BH22 . . . . .61 E7
  20 Winchester SO23 . . . .126 D6
ttisham La DT6 . . . . .203 B4
tkinson CI SP6 . . . . .42 B5
uburn Mans 5 BH13 . . . .121 B4
uckland Rd BH23 . . . . . . .125 C7
udemer Ct BH24 . . . . . . .55 E8
udrayton Ct 8 BH6 . . . . .123 E3
ugusta Ct DT5 . . . . .187 B5
ugustan Ct 1 DT1 . . . . . .134 F7
ugusta Rd DT5 . . . . .187 B6
usten Ave
  Bournemouth BH10 . . . . . .89 E6
  Winchester SO22 . . . . . . .126 A2
usten Ct SO23 . . . . .126 E8
usten Ct BH23 . . . . .125 B7
ustin Ave BH14 . . . . .120 B1
ustin CI DT1 . . . . .122 D5
ustralia Rd DT3 . . . . .166 E3
utumn CI BH22 . . . . .61 B7
utumn Copse BH25 . . . . . .95 D2
utumn Rd BH11 . . . . .88 D3
valanche Rd DT5 . . . . . . .186 E2
valon BH14 . . . . .147 C8
vebury Ave BH10 . . . . . . .89 E6
venue Ct BH13 . . . . .121 B3
venue La 12 BH2 . . . . . .121 E3
venue The
  Bournemouth BH2 . . . . . .121 E3
  Christchurch BH23 . . . . . .123 F7
  Christchurch BH23 . . . . . .124 A8
  Lyme Regis DT7 . . . . .96 B5
  New Milton BH25 . . . . . . .95 A3
  Radipole DT4 . . . . .167 D4
  Walkford BH23 . . . . .94 C2
  Wimborne Minster BH21 . .59 D4
  Winchester SO23 . . . . . . .126 C6
venue Sh Ctr The 14
  BH2 . . . . .121 E3
venue The
  Bournemouth BH9 . . . . . . .89 F1
  6 Crewkerne TA18 . . . . .192 A3
  Ferndown BH22 . . . . .53 A3
  Poole BH13 . . . . .121 A2
  Sherborne DT9 . . . . .30 C1
  West Moors BH24 . . . . . . .62 B8
  Yeovil BA21 . . . . .27 D6
viation Park W
  East Parley BH23 . . . . . . .90 C8
  Hurn BH23 . . . . .62 D1
vington Ct SO22 . . . . . . .126 A5
vlan Ct SO23 . . . . .126 D3
vocet CI
  Chickerell DT3 . . . . .166 D5
  2 Weymouth DT4 . . . . . .180 D6
von Ave BH24 . . . . .54 F3
von Bldgs BH23 . . . . .124 B7
vonbourne Sch BH7 . . . .123 A7
von Castle Dr BH24 . . . . .54 F3

Avon Castle Dr BH24 . . . . .54 F4
Avon CI
  Bournemouth BH8 . . . . . .122 D6
  Weymouth DT4 . . . . .166 E4
  Yeovil BA21 . . . . .27 F6
Avoncliffe Rd BH6 . . . . . .123 E3
Avon Cotts BH23 . . . . .92 C5
Avon Cswy BH23 . . . . .91 C7
Avon Ct
  Christchurch BH23 . . . . . .124 C6
  3 Poole BH13 . . . . .121 A4
Avondale Gdns SP8 . . . . . . .5 F3
Avon Dr BH20 . . . . .142 E5
Avon Farm Cotts BH23 . . .63 E3
Avon Farm Ctry Pk BH24 .54 D3
Avon Heath Ctry Pk (South
  Pk) BH24 . . . . .63 B8
Avon Ho BH2 . . . . .121 E2
Avon Mews BH4 . . . . .122 C6
Avon Pk BH24 . . . . .54 F6
Avon Rd
  Bournemouth BH8 . . . . . .122 C6
  Ferndown BH22 . . . . .53 A1
Avon Road E BH23 . . . . . .124 A8
Avon Road W BH23 . . . . . .123 F8
Avon Run Cl BH23 . . . . . .125 B5
Avon Run Rd BH23 . . . . . .125 B5
Avonsands BH17 . . . . .125 A5
Avon View Par BH23 . . . . .92 C3
Avon View Rd BH23 . . . . . .92 C3
Avon Wharf BH23 . . . . . . .124 C5
Award Rd
  Ferndown BH21 . . . . .60 F5
  Wimborne BH21 . . . . .61 A6
Axe La
  Broadwindsor DT8 . . . . . .203 C8
  West Crewkerne TA18 . . .191 C1
Axford Cl BH8 . . . . .90 D3
Axminster Rd DT6 . . . . . . .96 F8
Axnoller La DT8 . . . . .204 A8
Aylesbury Rd BH1 . . . . . . .122 E4
Aynsley Cl 3 DT4 . . . . . .167 C4
Aysha CI BH31 . . . . .95 B1
Azalea CI BH24 . . . . .54 C5
Aztec Ctr BH17 . . . . .119 D8
Azura CI BH23 . . . . .53 D6

B

Babwell Rd BA9 . . . . .4 B3
Babylon Hill DT9 . . . . .28 D5
Babylon View BA21 . . . . . .28 B7
Back Dro DT9 . . . . .194 E3
Back La
  Bere Regis BH20 . . . . .81 A3
  Bradford Abbas DT9 . . . . .28 D1
  5 Broadwindsor DT8 . . . .203 E6
  Cerne Abbas DT2 . . . . . .207 D4
  Chetnole DT9 . . . . .194 D8
  East Chinnock BA22 . . . . .192 E8
  East Coker BA22 . . . . . . .193 C7
  Evershot DT2 . . . . .206 A7
  Frome Vauchurch DT2 . . .72 F7
  Gillingham SP8 . . . . .5 D5
  Halstock BA22 . . . . .193 C3
  Hazelbury Bryan DT10 . . .197 A4
  Kington Magna SP8 . . . . . .9 C3
  North Perrott TA18 . . . . .192 C4
  4 Okeford Fitzpaine DT10 197 F5
  Rimpton BA22 . . . . .15 B8
  Sherborne DT9 . . . . .30 B6
  Sixpenny Handley SP5 . . .189 A4
  Sturminster Marshall BH21 .56 D5
  Swyre DT2 . . . . .129 D5
  Sydling St Nicholas DT2 . .207 A2
Back Rivers La DT6 . . . . . .100 D6
Back St
  Abbotsbury DT3 . . . . .149 B7
  East Stour SP8 . . . . .10 E3
  Portesham DT3 . . . . .132 A1
  Winchester SO23 . . . . . . .126 D2
Backwater DT2 . . . . .78 B2
Badbury CI BH18 . . . . .87 C3
Badbury Ct BH22 . . . . .61 F7
Badbury Dr DT11 . . . . . . .212 D5
Badbury Rings (Hill Fort)
  DT11 . . . . .49 A2
Badbury View Rd BH21 . . .59 D5
Badbury View Rd BH21 . . .86 D8
Baden Cl BH25 . . . . .95 B1
Baden-Powell & St Peter's
  CE Mid Sch BH14 . . . . . .120 B3
Bader Rd BH17 . . . . .119 E8
Badger Mts BA22 . . . . .26 D5
Badger La DT2 . . . . .209 A5
Badgers Ct BH24 . . . . .54 B5
Badgers Copse BH25 . . . . .95 C6
Badgers Way DT10 . . . . . . .35 B2
Badgers Wlk BH31 . . . . . . .45 E7
Badger Sett DT11 . . . . . . .212 C6
Badgers Wlk BH24 . . . . . . .54 B5
Badgers Way BH19 . . . . . . .179 F5
Badlake DT2 . . . . .103 C2
Bagman's La BH21 . . . . . . .201 E3
Bagwood Rd DT11 . . . . . . .81 C7
Bailey CI
  New Milton BH25 . . . . . . .95 D4
  Winchester SO22 . . . . . . .126 B4
Bailey Cres BH15 . . . . . . .119 C5
Bailey Ct BH23 . . . . .123 F7
Bailey Hall BH23 . . . . .123 F7
Bailey Ridge DT9 . . . . .195 A4
Bailey Ridge La DT9 . . . . .194 F4
Bailey's Dro BH20 . . . . . . .139 F2
Baileys Hill BH21 . . . . . . .201 D6

Bailie Gate Ind Est BH21 . .56 E3
Baiter Gdns BH15 . . . . . . .119 C1
Bakehouse La BH9 . . . . . .191 F7
Bakehouse La 1 DT9 . . . . .28 D1
Baker Rd BH11 . . . . .89 A5
Bakers La 3 BH21 . . . . . . .201 D1
Bakers Farm Rd BH31 . . . .45 A7
Baker's Cross DT6 . . . . . . .65 D4
Bakers Paddock DT2 . . . .136 C2
Bakers Rd BH21 . . . . .86 D6
Balaclava Rd
  Bovington Camp BH20 . . .139 E7
  Fortuneswell DT5 . . . . . . .181 D1
Balcombe Rd BH13 . . . . . .121 A3
Baldwin CI BH22 . . . . .61 F8
Balena CI BH17 . . . . .119 A8
Balfour CI BH23 . . . . .125 D8
Balfour Rd BH9 . . . . .89 F1
Ballam CI BH14 . . . . .118 C7
Ballard CI
  Lytchett Matravers BH16 . .84 D4
  New Milton BH25 . . . . . . .95 B4
  Poole BH15 . . . . .119 D1
Ballard Coll BH25 . . . . . . .95 A4
Ballard Lee BH25 . . . . .179 C5
Ballard Rd
  Poole BH15 . . . . .119 C5
  Swanage BH19 . . . . .179 C5
Ballard Sch BH25 . . . . .95 A4
Ballard Way BH19 . . . . . . .179 C5
Ball's Hall BA22 . . . . .26 A7
Ball's La BH21 . . . . .56 D5
Balmer Rd DT2 . . . . .212 E6
Balmoor CI 5 BA12 . . . . . . .3 B3
Balmoral Ave BH8 . . . . . . .90 E1
Balmoral Cres DT1 . . . . . .135 C8
Balmoral Ct 3 BH23 . . . . .126 B7
Balmoral Ho BH2 . . . . . . .121 D3
Balmoral Rd
  Poole BH15 . . . . .120 C3
  Swanage BH19 . . . . .179 C5
Balmoral Wlk BH25 . . . . . .94 F3
Balston Rd BH14 . . . . .120 A6
Balston Terr BH15 . . . . . . .119 B2
Banbury Rd BH17 . . . . . . .119 C7
Bancroft Rd BH10 . . . . . . .89 E5
Bank Chambers BH14 . . . .120 E3
Bank CI BH23 . . . . .124 C6
Bankside No 3 SO22 . . . . .126 C6
Bankside Rd BH9 . . . . .90 A3
Banks Rd BH13 . . . . .147 C4
Banstead Rd BH18 . . . . . . .87 A5
Banton Shard DT6 . . . . . . .68 A5
Barberry Way BH31 . . . . . .45 E5
Barbers Gate 8 BH15 . . . .119 B1
Barbers Piles 9 BH15 . . . .119 B1
Barbers Wharf 8 BH15 . . .119 B1
Barclay Mans BH2 . . . . . . .121 F5
Barclay Rd BH7 . . . . .167 C3
Bardolfeston Village DT2 . .78 D2
Bar End Ind Est SO23 . . . .126 F3
Bar End Rd SO23 . . . . . . .126 F4
Barfield CI SO23 . . . . .126 F4
Bargates BH23 . . . . .124 B7
Barges CI DT2 . . . . .103 C2
Baring Rd
  Bournemouth BH6 . . . . . .124 A3
  Winchester SO23 . . . . . . .126 F5
Barlake Ct 5 DT1 . . . . . . .107 D1
Barlands CI
  Burton BH23 . . . . .92 C2
  Portland DT5 . . . . .186 E5
Barley CI DT1 . . . . .194 A2
Barleycroft Rd BH11 . . . . .86 E3
Barley Down Dr SO22 . . . .126 B2
Barleyfields 1 SP8 . . . . . . .5 F2
Barley Way DT1 . . . . .167 E1
Barlynch Ct 1 BA21 . . . . . .26 F6
Barnaby Mead SP8 . . . . . . .5 F2
Barnack Wlk DT11 . . . . . .212 C3
Barn CI
  8 Crewkerne TA18 . . . . .191 F5
  Upton BH16 . . . . .118 A7
Barn Cres 7 TA18 . . . . . . .191 E4
Barndale Dr BH20 . . . . . . .143 A1
Barnes CI
  Blandford Forum DT11 . . .212 E5
  Bournemouth BH10 . . . . . .89 D3
  Marnhull DT10 . . . . .21 A2
  Sturminster Newton DT10 .35 B1
  Winchester SO23 . . . . . . .126 D3
Barnes Cres
  Bournemouth BH10 . . . . . .89 D3
  Wimborne Minster BH21 . .59 E4
Barnes Cross DT9 . . . . . . .196 A6
Barnes Rd
  Bournemouth BH10 . . . . . .89 D3
  Wareham Town BH20 . . . .142 D2
Barnes Wallis CI DT1 . . . .166 F2
Barnes Way 5 DT1 . . . . . .108 B1
Barnet CI DT6 . . . . .97 B8
Barney's CI DT6 . . . . .97 B8
Barnfield BH23 . . . . .125 D8
Barnhaven CI DT6 . . . . . . .97 B8
Barnhill Rd BH20 . . . . .143 A1
Barn La TA18 . . . . .191 E6
Barn Rd BH18 . . . . .87 B3
Barnsfield Rd BH24 . . . . . .54 D7
Barnsley Dro BH21 . . . . . . .50 A3
Barns Rd BH20 . . . . .62 A6
Barnsome 2 BH2 . . . . .121 D4
Barons Rd BH11 . . . . .88 D6
Barrack La BH20 . . . . .55 F4
Barrack Rd
  Christchurch BH23 . . . . . .123 E8

Barrack Rd continued
  Christchurch BH23 . . . . . .124 A6
  Ferndown BH22 . . . . .62 A2
  Weymouth DT4 . . . . .167 E2
Barracks CI BA22 . . . . .26 D7
Barrack St BH15 . . . . .100 D7
Barrie Rd BH9 . . . . .89 F3
Bar La
  Burton Bradstock DT6 . . .128 A8
  Shipton Gorge DT6 . . . . .101 D4
Barrow Ct DT1 . . . . .134 E7
Barrow Dr BH8 . . . . .90 F2
Barrowfield CI DT6 . . . . . .128 A8
Barrowgate Rd BH8 . . . . . .90 D3
Barrowgate Way BH8 . . . . .90 D3
Barrow Hill
  Bere Regis BH20 . . . . .81 B3
  Stalbridge DT10 . . . . .33 C8
  Stourton Caundle DT10 . . .32 F2
Barrowland La DT2 . . . . . . .71 B5
Barrow Rd BH8 . . . . .90 F2
Barrow Rise DT1 . . . . .134 E7
Barrow Street La BA12 . . . . .3 F3
Barrow View BH22 . . . . . . .61 B6
Barrs Wood Dr BH25 . . . . .95 B4
Barrs Wood Rd BH25 . . . . .95 B4
Barrs La BA22 . . . . .192 F6
Barter Rd DT1 . . . . .121 A7
Barters La
  Broadstone BH18 . . . . . . .86 F3
  Donhead St Mary SP7 . . . .25 D8
Bartholomew La 7 SO23 . .126 D7
Bartlets CI DT2 . . . . .133 C6
Bartlett Dr BH7 . . . . .123 B8
Bartlets Pl DT2 . . . . .123 B8
Bartletts The 2 BA12 . . . . . .3 B4
Bartley Ct 2 BH21 . . . . . . .59 B5
Barton Chase BH25 . . . . . .126 F7
Barton CI
  Sturminster Newton
    DT10 . . . . .197 C8
  Toller Porcorum DT2 . . . . .71 D8
  West Stafford DT2 . . . . . .136 B8
Barton Common La
  BH25 . . . . .127 B8
Barton Common Rd
  BH25 . . . . .127 B8
Barton Court Ave BH25 . . .127 A8
Barton Court Rd BH25 . . . .95 A1
Barton Croft BH25 . . . . . . .127 A7
Barton Dr
  Barton on Sea BH25 . . . . .126 F8
  Overcombe/Preston DT3 . .153 B1
Barton Gdns DT9 . . . . .29 F6
Barton Gn BH25 . . . . .127 B6
Barton Hill
  Kington Magna SP8 . . . . . . .9 D4
  Melbury Osmond DT2 . . .194 A2
  Shaftesbury SP7 . . . . .12 E3
Barton Ho BH25 . . . . .126 F7
Barton La
  Barton on Sea BH25 . . . . .126 E8
  Mere BA12 . . . . .3 A5
Barton Lo BH12 . . . . .120 B6
Bartonside Rd BH25 . . . . .126 C7
Barton Wood Rd BH25 . . .126 F8
Barwick CP Sch BA22 . . . .193 E8
Basan Hill DT2 . . . . .78 D5
Bascott Cl BH11 . . . . .89 A1
Bascott Rd BH11 . . . . .89 A1
Bashley Common Rd
  BH25 . . . . .95 A1
Bashley Cross Rd BH25 . . .94 E5
Bashley Rd BH25 . . . . .95 A6
Bassett Rd BH12 . . . . .120 B6
Bat Alley DT10 . . . . .20 E1
Batchelor Cres BH11 . . . . .88 F3
Batchelor's La BH21 . . . . .201 D1
Batchpool La BA8 . . . . .8 A7
Batcombe CI BH11 . . . . . . .88 E3
Bath CI DT9 . . . . .194 F1
Bath Hill Ct 11 BH1 . . . . .122 A2
Bath Hill Rdbt BH1 . . . . . .122 A2
Bath Orch 6 DT6 . . . . .68 C1
Bath Rd
  Sturminster Newton DT10 . .35 B2
Bathsheba Terr 8 DT1 . . . .135 B8
Bath St DT4 . . . . .167 D2
Bathwell La DT9 . . . . .17 D2
Bats La DT1 . . . . .106 E1
Batstone Way BH22 . . . . . .61 B9
Batten CI BH23 . . . . .124 D7
Batteley Dro DT1 . . . . .41 B4
Battery Hill SO22 . . . . . . .126 A4
Battle Mead
  Corfe Castle BH20 . . . . . .177 A8
  Swanage BH19 . . . . .179 B4
Batts La DT6 . . . . .203 C2
Bauntons CI 1 DT9 . . . . . .17 C2
Bauntons Orch DT9 . . . . . .17 C2
Baverstock Rd BH12 . . . . .121 B8
Bayard Rd DT3 . . . . .152 E2
Bay CI
  Swanage BH19 . . . . .179 C5
  Three Legged Cross BH21 . .53 A8
  Upton BH16 . . . . .118 B5
Baycliffe Rd DT4 . . . . .167 B2
Bay Cres BH19 . . . . .179 B5

Baydon Cl DT3 . . . . .153 B1
Bay Fields SP8 . . . . .5 F2
Bayfran Way DT11 . . . . . .212 D4
Bay Hog La BH15 . . . . . . .119 B2
Bay La SP8 . . . . .9 A2
Baynard's Rd DT11 . . . . . .107 D1
Bay Rd SP5 . . . . .5 F2
Baytree Ho 24 SO23 . . . . .126 D6
Bay Tree Way BH23 . . . . . .93 D1
Bay View
  Bournemouth BH2 . . . . . .121 C2
  3 Swanage BH19 . . . . . .178 E2
Bayview Gdns BH2 . . . . . .121 C2
Bayview Mews BH2 . . . . . .121 C2
Bayview Rd DT7 . . . . .96 B6
Beach Ave BH25 . . . . .126 F7
Beach CI BH13 . . . . .147 G8
Beachcroft BH13 . . . . .121 A3
Beach Gdns BH19 . . . . . . .179 B3
Beach Rd
  Burton Bradstock DT6 . . .128 C2
  Poole BH13 . . . . .147 G8
  Studland BH19 . . . . .164 C2
  Upton BH16 . . . . .118 A6
Beach View BH13 . . . . . . .147 C4
Beachview CI 1 DT4 . . . . .180 B8
Beacon Dr BH23 . . . . .125 F7
Beacon Dr BH23 . . . . .125 F7
Beaconfield Rd BA20 . . . . .27 A1
Beacon Gdns BH18 . . . . . .86 E3
Beacon Hill La BH21 . . . . .86 B3
Beacon Park Cres BH16 . . .118 A8
Beacon Park Rd BH16 . . . .118 B7
Beacon Pk Cres BH16 . . . .117 C7
Beacon Rd
  Bournemouth BH2 . . . . . .121 F2
  Broadstone BH18 . . . . . . .86 E3
  Corfe Mullen BH18 . . . . . .85 F3
  Poole BH16 . . . . .118 B7
Beaconsfield Rd
  Christchurch BH23 . . . . . .124 B7
  Poole BH12 . . . . .120 D6
Beacon Way BH18 . . . . . . .86 E3
Beadon La TA16 . . . . .191 E7
Beaminster Mus DT8 . . . .204 D4
Beaminster Rd DT6 . . . . . .68 F1
Beaminster Sch DT8 . . . . .204 C5
Beamish Rd BH17 . . . . . . .119 F8
Bear Cross Ave BH11 . . . . .88 F6
Bear Cross Rdbt BH11 . . . .88 F6
Bearwood Prim Sch BH11 .88 E5
Beatty CI BH24 . . . . .55 E8
Beatty Rd BH9 . . . . .90 B1
Beauchamp PI BH23 . . . . .124 A7
Beauchamps Gdns BH7 . . .123 A8
Beaucroft La BH21 . . . . . . .59 E5
Beaucroft Rd BH21 . . . . . .59 E6
Beau Ct
  5 Bournemouth BH4 . . . .121 C3
  9 New Milton BH25 . . . . .95 A3
Beaufort CI BH23 . . . . . . .125 B7
Beaufort Dr BH21 . . . . . . .59 C5
Beaufort Ho 10 BH4 . . . . .121 C2
Beaufort Mews BH23 . . . . .59 B4
Beaufort Rd
  Bournemouth BH6 . . . . . .123 B4
  Winchester SO23 . . . . . . .126 D4
Beaufoy CI SP7 . . . . .13 A3
Beaufoys Ave BH22 . . . . . .61 D7
Beaufoys CI BH22 . . . . . . .61 C6
Beaufoys CI BH22 . . . . . . .61 C6
Beaulieu DT4 . . . . .167 A6
Beaulieu Ave BH23 . . . . . .123 E7
Beaulieu Dr BA21 . . . . .94 E3
Beaulieu Rd
  Bournemouth BH4 . . . . . .121 B1
  Christchurch BH23 . . . . . .123 E7
Beaumont Gn 1 SO23 . . . .126 D5
Beaumont Ave
  Bridport DT6 . . . . .100 D8
  Radipole DT4 . . . . .167 D6
Beaumont Rd BH13 . . . . . .147 F7
Beaver Ind Est BH23 . . . . .125 A4
Beccles CI BH15 . . . . .118 F2
Becher Rd BH14 . . . . .120 E3
Beckett CI DT11 . . . . .212 C2
Beckhampton Rd BH15 . . .118 E3
Becklands La DT6 . . . . .65 E4
Beckley Copse BH23 . . . . .94 A2
Becton La BH25 . . . . .127 B7
Becton Mead BH25 . . . . . . .95 B1
Bedale Way BH15 . . . . . . .119 F5
Bedford Cres BH7 . . . . . . .123 C7
Bedford PI DT10 . . . . .100 D7
Bedford Rd
  Weymouth DT4 . . . . .167 A3
  Yeovil BA21 . . . . .27 F8
Bedford Rd N BH12 . . . . . .88 C2
Bedford Rd S BH12 . . . . . .88 C2
Bedford Terr DT6 . . . . . . .100 D7
Beech Ave
  Bournemouth BH6 . . . . . .123 C4
  Christchurch BH23 . . . . . .123 D8
  Holton Heath BH20 . . . . .116 B3
Beechbank Ave BH17 . . . . .86 F1
Beech CI
  Alderholt SP6 . . . . .42 C5
  Broadmayne DT2 . . . . . . .136 B1
  Broadstone BH18 . . . . . . .86 E4
  1 Spetisbury DT11 . . . . .211 E5
  Verwood BH31 . . . . .45 A5
  West Lulworth BH20 . . . .172 D6

Beechcroft
Bournemouth BH1 . . . . .121 F5
Bournemouth BH1 . . . . .122 A5
Beechcroft La **1** BH24 . . .55 D8
Beechcroft Mews **2**
BH24 . . . . .55 D8
Beechcroft St Pauls Prim
Sch DT4 . . . . .167 C4
Beech Ct BH21 . . . . .59 E4
Beeches The
Bournemouth BH7 . . . . . . .123 A8
1 Shaftesbury SP7 . . . . . .12 E3
Wareham St Martin BH20 .143 A8
Beechey Ct **6** BH8 . . . . .122 A5
Beechey Rd BH8 . . . . .122 A5
Beechfield **42** BH4 . . . . . .121 C3
Beech La
Hawkchurch EX13 . . . . . . .202 B1
Netherbury DT8 . . . . .204 A3
St Leonards BH24 . . . . .54 A2
Beech Rd
Puddletown DT2 . . . . .78 B1
Puncknowle DT2 . . . . .129 E2
Radipole DT3 . . . . .152 B4
Beechwood BA20 . . . . .27 A2
Beechwood Ave
Bournemouth BH5 . . . . . . .122 F4
Bournemouth BH5 . . . . . . .123 A4
New Milton BH25 . . . . .94 F4
Beech Wood Cl BH18 . . .87 A3
Beechwood Ct BH2 . . . . . .121 E2
Beechwood Ct **5** TA18 . .191 F5
Beechwood Gdns BH5 . .123 A4
Beechwood Lo **1** BH4 . .121 C2
Beechwood Rd BH25 . . . . .53 B1
Beel Cl **2** DT5 . . . . .181 B1
Berne Ct **8** BH21 . . . . . . .59 E4
Beggar's La SO23 . . . . . . .126 F6
Belben Cl BH12 . . . . .88 D2
Belben Rd BH12 . . . . .88 C2
Belchalwell St DT11 . . . . .197 E4
Belfield Park Ave DT4 . .167 B1
Belfield Rd BH6 . . . . .124 A4
Belgrave DT4 . . . . .167 B6
Belgrave Ct BH1 . . . . .122 D3
Belgrave Pl **8** DT5 . . . . .186 F8
Belgrave Rd BH13 . . . . . . .121 A2
Bellbury Cl **1** DT2 . . . . . .78 B1
Bell Chase BA20 . . . . .26 F5
Belle Vue Cl DT4 . . . . . . .167 E2
Belle Vue Cl BH6 . . . . . . .123 D4
Belle Vue Cres BH6 . . . . .123 C4
Belle Vue Gdns **2** BH6 .123 F4
Belle Vue Mans **6** BH6 .123 D4
Belle Vue Rd
Bournemouth BH6 . . . . . . .123 E3
Poole BH14 . . . . .120 C3
Swanage BH19 . . . . .179 C1
Weymouth DT4 . . . . .167 D1
Belle Vue Terr **6** DT5 . .186 F7
Belle Vue Wlk BH22 . . . . .61 E2
Bellflower Cl BH23 . . . . . .125 B8
Bell Heather Cl BH16 . . . .118 B8
Bellman's Cross BA8 . . . . .19 C6
Bellows Cross BH21 . . . . . .40 D8
Bells Ho BH21 . . . . .59 D6
Bells La BA12 . . . . .2 A6
Bell's Orch La BH20 . . . . .142 E4
Bell St
Shaftesbury SP7 . . . . .12 E3
Swanage BH19 . . . . .178 F2
Belmont Ave BH8 . . . . .90 C2
Belmont Cl
Shaftesbury SP7 . . . . .12 F2
Verwood BH31 . . . . .45 C5
Belmont Rd
New Milton BH25 . . . . .95 C4
Poole BH14 . . . . .120 C5
Belmour Lo **38** BH4 . . . .121 C3
Belvedere Rd
Bournemouth BH3 . . . . . . .122 A6
Christchurch BH23 . . . . . .124 A7
3 Swanage BH19 . . . . . .179 C1
Yeovil BA21 . . . . .26 D8
Belvoir Pk **8** BH13 . . . . .121 B3
Bembury La DT9 . . . . .194 D8
Bemister Rd BH9 . . . . .122 A8
Benbow Cres BH12 . . . . . . .88 E1
Benbridge Ave BH11 . . . . .88 F5
Bendigo Rd BH23 . . . . . . .123 E8
Benellen Ave BH4 . . . . . . .121 C4
Benellen Gdns BH4 . . . . .121 C4
Benellen Rd BH4 . . . . .121 C5
Benellen Twrs **1** BH4 . .121 C4
Bengal Rd BH9 . . . . .121 E8
Beningfield Wood Nature
Reserve DT6 . . . . .69 F7
Benjamin Cl BH23 . . . . . .123 F7
Benjamin Rd BH11 . . . . . .121 C1
Benlease Way BH19 . . . . .178 E2
Benmoor Rd BH17 . . . . . .119 A8
Benmore Cl BH25 . . . . .95 C2
Benmore Rd BH9 . . . . .90 A2
Bennett Ho **4** BH4 . . . . .121 C4
Bennetts Hill La DT6 . . . .101 C2
Bennetts Water Gdns
DT3 . . . . .166 D4
Ben Nevis Rd DT4 . . . . . .167 C1
Bennion Rd BH10 . . . . .89 C3
Benridge Bsns Pk BH17 .119 B8
Benridge DT18 . . . . .87 A3
Benson Rd BH17 . . . . .119 D7

Bentley Rd BH9 . . . . .89 F3
Benville La DT2 . . . . .205 C6
Benville Rd DT4 . . . . .166 F2
Bere Cl
Poole BH17 . . . . .87 D2
Winchester SO22 . . . . .126 B8
Bere Down La BH20 . . . . . .80 F5
Bere La DT9 . . . . .195 F7
Bere Marsh DT11 . . . . . . .198 B7
Bere Rd
Northport BH20 . . . . .142 D5
Winterborne Kingston DT11 .81 E8
Bere Regis Bsns Pk BH20 .81 B2
Bere Regis Fst Sch BH20 .81 B1
Bere Regis Sports Club
BH20 . . . . .81 C3
Beresford Cl BH12 . . . . . .120 D6
Beresford Gdns BH23 . . .124 E6
Beresford Rd
Bournemouth BH5 . . . . . . .123 B4
Poole BH12 . . . . .120 D6
Bereweeke Ave SO22 . . . .126 C8
Bereweeke Cl SO22 . . . . .126 C8
Bereweeke Ho SO22 . . . .126 C7
Bereweeke Rd SO22 . . . .126 C7
Bereweeke Way SO22 . . .126 C8
Berkeley Ave BH12 . . . . . .120 D8
Berkeley Cl
1 Pimperne DT11 . . . . . .199 D4
Verwood BH31 . . . . .45 A7
Berkeley Ct DT6 . . . . .100 C6
Berkeley Rd
Bournemouth BH3 . . . . . . .121 E7
1 Pimperne DT11 . . . . . .199 D3
3 Yeovil BA20 . . . . .27 C4
Berkeley Rise **8** DT11 .199 D4
Berkley Manor **8** BH21 .121 A4
Bermuda Ct **5** BH23 . . .126 A7
Bernards Cl BH23 . . . . . . .123 E8
Berne Ct **8** BH21 . . . . . . .59 E4
Beron Ct BH15 . . . . .119 E4
Berrans Ave BH11 . . . . .89 B6
Berrans Ct BH11 . . . . .89 A6
Berry La EX13 . . . . .202 D3
Bertram Rd BH25 . . . . .95 C4
Berwick La DT6 . . . . .129 D6
Berwick Rd BH3 . . . . .121 E7
Bessborough Rd BH13 . .147 E7
Bessells La DT11 . . . . .198 D8
Bessemer Cl BH31 . . . . . . .45 E4
Bestwall Cres BH20 . . . . .142 F3
Bestwall Rd BH20 . . . . . . .142 F3
Bethany Ave BH10 . . . . . . .89 D2
Bethany Ct BH21 . . . . .121 A7
Bethany Ho BH1 . . . . .122 D5
Bethany Jun CE Sch
BH1 . . . . .122 D5
Bethia Cl BH8 . . . . .122 D6
Bethia Rd BH8 . . . . .122 D6
Bettiscombe Cl BH17 . . . .87 E2
Beverley Gdns BH10 . . . . .89 D3
Beverley Grange **50** BH4 .121 C3
Beverley Rd DT3 . . . . .152 D3
Bexington Cl BH11 . . . . . . .88 E3
Bickerley Gdns BH24 . . . . .55 B6
Bickerley Rd BH24 . . . . . . .55 B6
Bickerley Terr **8** BH24 . .55 B6
Bicknell Gdns BA21 . . . . . .27 D8
Bicknell Sch **6** BH21 . . .123 A7
Bicton Rd BH11 . . . . .89 B3
Biddlecome Orch **5**
DT6 . . . . .100 C8
Biddlesden Rd BA21 . . . . .26 E7
Big Ope DT5 . . . . .186 B4
Bilberry Cl **11** SO22 . . . .126 D6
Billingsmoor La **4** DT1 .107 C1
Bilshay La DT6 . . . . .68 A2
Bimport SP7 . . . . .12 D2
Bincleaves Rd DT4 . . . . . .167 D1
Bincombe Dr **2** TA18 . .191 F5
Bincombe Rise DT3 . . . . .152 E3
Bindbarrow Rd DT6 . . . . .128 C6
Bindells The DT3 . . . . .166 D5
Bindon Abbey BH20 . . . . .140 D2
Bindon Cl
Poole BH12 . . . . .120 E7
West Lulworth BH20 . . . . .172 E7
Bindon La BH20 . . . . .140 D3
Bindon Rd BH20 . . . . .172 C5
Bindon Way **3** BH20 . . .140 B2
Bingham Ave BH14 . . . . . .147 D8
Bingham Cl
Christchurch BH23 . . . . . .124 E7
Verwood BH31 . . . . .45 D4
Bingham Rd
Bournemouth BH9 . . . . . . .122 A7
Christchurch BH23 . . . . . .124 E7
Verwood BH31 . . . . .45 C4
Binghams Rd DT2 . . . . . . .137 D6
Binnegar La BH20 . . . . . . .141 C3
Binnie Rd BH12 . . . . .120 D6
Birch Ave
Beckley BH25 . . . . .94 D5
Blandford St Mary DT11 .212 D1
Burton BH23 . . . . .92 C3
Ferndown BH22 . . . . .61 F1
Holton Heath BH20 . . . . . .116 B3
Birch Cl
Corfe Mullen BH21 . . . . . . .86 D6
Poole BH14 . . . . .120 C3
St Leonards BH24 . . . . .53 F3
Birch Copse BH17 . . . . . . .119 A8
Birch Ct **3** SO22 . . . . . . .126 A4
Birchdale **6** BA20 . . . . . .26 F2
Birchdale BH21 . . . . .59 D5
Birch Dr BH8 . . . . .91 A2

Birchfield Prim Sch BA21 .27 F8
Birchfield Rd BA21 . . . . . . .27 F7
Birch Gr
Ferndown BH22 . . . . .52 F2
Old Milton BH25 . . . . .95 A1
Birch La
Puddletown DT2 . . . . .77 F3
Yetminster DT9 . . . . .194 C5
Birch Rd BH24 . . . . .54 D4
Birch Wlk BH21 . . . . .61 F3
Birchwood Cl BH23 . . . . . .125 E8
Birchwood Dr SP6 . . . . . . .42 C5
Birchwood Mews BH14. .120 D3
Birchwood Rd
Bournemouth BH4 . . . . . . .120 D3
Upton BH16 . . . . .118 B6
Bird's Cl **1** BH18 . . . . . . .191 E4
Birds Hill Gdns **1** BH15 .119 E3
Bird's Hill Rd BH15 . . . . . .119 E3
Birinus Rd SO23 . . . . .126 F7
Birkdale Cl BH18 . . . . .87 A5
Birkdale Rd BH18 . . . . .87 A5
Bishop Cl BH12 . . . . .121 C7
Bishop Ct BH24 . . . . .55 C7
Bishop of Winchester Comp
Sch The BH8 . . . . .90 D1
Bishop Rd BH9 . . . . .122 A8
Bishops Cl
Abbotsbury DT3 . . . . .149 B7
Bournemouth BH7 . . . . . . .122 F7
Mere BA12 . . . . .3 A6
Bishops Ct BH18 . . . . .87 A3
Bishop's La DT9 . . . . .28 D2
Bishop's Rd
Abbotsbury DT3 . . . . .149 C8
Portesham DT3 . . . . .131 D1
Bishops Row **9** DT9 . . .179 A2
Bitcham's Mead BH20 . . . .81 A2
Bitterne Way BH31 . . . . . . .45 C5
Blackberry La
Christchurch BH23 . . . . . .124 F6
Radipole DT3 . . . . .152 C2
Sherborne DT9 . . . . .30 A7
Blackbird Cl BH17 . . . . . . .118 E8
Blackbird Way BH23 . . . . .93 C8
Blackburn Rd BH12 . . . . . .120 B6
Blackers Hole (Cave)
BH19 . . . . .184 D6
Blackfield La DT2 . . . . .53 A3
Blackfield Rd BH8 . . . . .90 D3
Black Hill BH31 . . . . .45 C6
Blackhill Rd BH16 . . . . . . .116 D3
Blackhill Rd W BH16 . . . .116 D2
Black La DT11 . . . . .212 E4
Blacklands La DT11 . . . . .197 D3
Black Lawn SP8 . . . . .5 F4
Blackmoor La BH20 . . . . . .26 C5
Blackmoor Rd BA8 . . . . . . .19 A4
Black Moor Rd BH31 . . . . .45 C6
Blackmore Rd
Shaftesbury SP7 . . . . .13 A4
Stalbridge DT10 . . . . .33 D8
Blacknell Ind Est **30**
TA18 . . . . .191 F4
Blacknell La TA18 . . . . . . .191 F4
Blackney La DT6 . . . . .203 E2
Blacknor Rd DT5 . . . . .186 E3
Blackpool Cnr DT6 . . . . . .202 B1
Blackrow La DT10 . . . . . . .196 D7
Blacksmith DT11 . . . . .86 D5
Blacksmith's La DT9 . . . . .194 D8
Blacksmith's Piece DT2 .105 E1
Black Swan Bldgs **18**
SO22 . . . . .126 D6
Blackthorn Way
New Milton BH25 . . . . .95 D4
Verwood BH31 . . . . .45 D4
Blackwater BH23 . . . . .91 D4
Blackwater Dr DT1 . . . . . .107 E2
Blackwater Gr SP6 . . . . . . .42 A5
Blackwater La EX13 . . . . .202 C3
Bladen View DT11 . . . . . . .79 E8
Blagdon Cl DT2 . . . . .133 D6
Blagdon Rd DT1 . . . . .107 D1
Blair Ave BH14 . . . . .120 C4
Blair Cl BH25 . . . . .94 E3
Blake Dene Rd BH14 . . . .120 B1
Blake Hill Ave BH14 . . . . .120 B1
Blake Hill Cres BH14 . . . .120 C1
Blake Rd **22** TA18 . . . . . .191 F4
Blandford Cl BH15 . . . . . .118 F2
Blandford Hill
Milborne St Andrew DT11 . .79 E8
Winterborne Whitechurch
DT11 . . . . .210 C3
Blandford Hospl DT11 . . .212 C5
Blandford Hts Ind Est
DT11 . . . . .212 E6
Blandford L Ctr DT11 . . . .212 C4
Blandford Rd
Corfe Mullen BH21 . . . . . . .86 D8
Hamworthy BH16 . . . . . . .118 C4
Iwerne Minster DT11 . . . . .37 F2
Pamphill BH21 . . . . .58 D7
Shapwick DT11 . . . . .210 B8
Shillingstone DT11 . . . . . .198 B6
Sturminster Marshall BH21 .56 C4
Blandford Rd N
Lytchett Minster & Upton
BH16 . . . . .118 B7
Upton BH16 . . . . .118 B7
Upton BH16 . . . . .118 B7
Blandford St Mary CE VA Fst
Sch DT11 . . . . .212 D1
Blandford Sch The DT11 .212 C4

Blaney Way BH21 . . . . .86 C6
Blandford Adult Ed Office
DT11 . . . . .212 D3
Blashford Lakes Study Ctr
BH24 . . . . .47 C4
Bleak St BA9 . . . . .1 C3
Bleax Cl SP7 . . . . .22 E1
Bleke St SP8 . . . . .10 D6
Bleke St SP7 . . . . .12 E3
Blemheim Rd BH13 . . . . . .152 B1
Blenheim Cres SO41 . . . . .95 F4
Blenheim Ct
55 Christchurch BH23 . . .121 C3
Christchurch BH23 . . . . . .124 A8
Blenheim Dr BH23 . . . . . .125 B6
Blenheim Mews **6** BH4 .121 C4
Blenheim Rd BA21 . . . . . . .27 F7
Blind La
Berwick St John SP7 . . . . .188 B8
Evershot DT2 . . . . .206 B7
Ringwood SP6 . . . . .43 E1
Thorncombe TA20 . . . . . . .202 E6
Wimborne Minster BH21 . . .59 B5
Blind La Cl DT6 . . . . .68 F2
Blindmere Rd DT1 . . . . . . .186 E4
Blind St BH20 . . . . .81 B2
Bloody Shard Gate DT11 .188 A1
Bloomfield Dr BH9 . . . . . . .89 F2
Bloomfield Pl BH9 . . . . . . .89 F2
Bloxworth Rd
Poole BH12 . . . . .120 F8
Poole BH12 . . . . .121 A8
Blue Ball Hill SO23 . . . . . .126 F6
Bluebell Cl BH23 . . . . .125 B8
Bluebell La BH17 . . . . .86 F1
Bluebell Rd BH18 . . . . .87 B4
Blue Pool BH20 . . . . .161 A3
Bluff The BH10 . . . . .89 F4
Bluntshay La DT6 . . . . .66 E8
Blyford Cl BH23 . . . . .91 D4
Blythe Rd BH21 . . . . .86 D6
Blythswood Ct BH25 . . . . .126 F7
Boar St BA13 . . . . .3 A5
Bob Hann Cl BH12 . . . . . .120 D5
Bockhampton Cross
DT2 . . . . .109 A3
Bockhampton La DT2 . . .109 A3
Bockhampton Rd BH23 . . .92 C2
Bodkin La DT3 . . . . .168 A6
Bodley Rd BH13 . . . . .147 F7
Bodorgan Rd BH2 . . . . . . .121 F4
Bodowen Cl BH23 . . . . .92 D2
Bodowen Rd BH23 . . . . . . .92 D2
Bodsmarsh La DT10 . . . . . .21 E1
Bognor Rd BH18 . . . . .86 F4
Bohay's Dr DT4 . . . . .180 C7
Bokerley Ditch SP6 . . . . . .187 E4
Bokerley Junc SP5 . . . . . .189 E6
Boldre Cl
Barton on Sea BH25 . . . . .126 D8
Poole BH12 . . . . .120 C8
Boleyn Cres
Bournemouth BH9 . . . . . . .90 C4
Weymouth DT4 . . . . .180 E7
Bolton Cl BH6 . . . . .123 E3
Bolton Cres BH22 . . . . .62 A6
Bolton Ct BH6 . . . . .123 E3
Bolton Rd BH6 . . . . .123 E3
Bon Accord Rd BH19 . . . .179 B1
Bond Ave BH22 . . . . .52 F4
Bond Rd BH15 . . . . .119 F5
Bond St
Radipole DT4 . . . . .167 D3
4 Yeovil BA20 . . . . .27 D4
Yeovil BA22 . . . . .26 C5
Boney Rd BH20 . . . . .139 E7
Bonfields Ave BH19 . . . . .179 B4
Bonham La BA12 . . . . .1 E7
Bonham Rd BH9 . . . . .121 F7
Bonhole La DT6 . . . . .101 E4
Bonington Cl BH23 . . . . . .124 E8
Bonnett's La BH20 . . . . . .142 E4
Bonscombe La DT6 . . . . . .101 C5
Bonvils Rd BH19 . . . . .183 B7
Bookham La DT11 . . . . . . .208 B7
Boot La **7** DT9 . . . . .194 D8
Boozer Pit TA16 . . . . .191 F8
Border Dr BH16 . . . . .118 C5
Border Rd
Lytchett Minster & Upton
BH16 . . . . .117 E5
Upton BH16 . . . . .118 B7
Boreham Rd BH6 . . . . .123 D5
Borthwick Rd BH1 . . . . . . .122 E5
Boscobel Rd SO22 . . . . . .126 D7
Boscombe Cliff Rd BH5 . .122 F3
Boscombe Grove Rd
BH1 . . . . .122 D5
Boscombe Overcliff Dr
Bournemouth BH5 . . . . . . .122 F3
Bournemouth BH5 . . . . . . .123 A3
Boscombe Spa Rd BH5 . .122 D3
Bosley Cl BH23 . . . . .91 E2
Bosley Way BH23 . . . . .91 E2
Boston Lo **31** BH4 . . . . .121 C3
Boswell's Cl BH20 . . . . . . .81 B3
Bosworth Mews BH9 . . . . .90 B4
Bothen Dr DT6 . . . . .100 C6
Bottlebush La BH21 . . . . .189 E1
Bouch Rd BH20 . . . . .139 E5
Boulnois Ave BH14 . . . . . .120 C3
Boulton Cl DT4 . . . . .180 D8
Boundary Ave BA22 . . . . . .26 C7
Boundary Cl
Swanage BH19 . . . . .185 C8
Yeovil BA21 . . . . .27 A7

Boundary Dr BH21 . . . . . . .59 D6
Boundary La BH24 . . . . . . .53 F7
Boundary Rd
Bournemouth BH10 . . . . . .121 D8
Bournemouth BH10 . . . . . .121 D8
Yeovil BA22 . . . . .26 C5
Boundary Rdbt BH3,
BH11 . . . . .121 D8
Boundary View **1** DT11 .212 D4
Boundary Way BA22 . . . . . .26 C7
Bound La DT9 . . . . .194 F2
Bountys La BH12 . . . . .120 E5
Bourne Ave BH2 . . . . .121 E3
Bourne Cl BH2 . . . . .121 D3
Bourne Ct
1 Bournemouth BH2 . . . .121 F1
Wimborne Minster BH21 . . .59 D7
Bourne Dr BH20 . . . . .142 D6
Bourne Dro DT2 . . . . .76 F8
Bournemouth Aviation Mus
BH23 . . . . .91 A8
Bournemouth Central Bsns
Pk BH1 . . . . .122 C5
Bournemouth Ho **2**
BH1 . . . . .122 C4
Bournemouth Int Ctr
BH2 . . . . .121 F2
Bournemouth International
Airport BH23 . . . . .90 E8
Bournemouth Learning
Support Centre PRU
BH10 . . . . .89 D1
Bournemouth Memorial
Homes BH8 . . . . .90 F1
Bournemouth Nuffield
Derwent Suite BH7 . . . . . .91 B8
Bournemouth Nuffield Hospl
The BH8 . . . . .122 B4
Bournemouth & Poole Coll
Annexe The BH1. . . . . . . .122 A4
Bournemouth & Poole Coll
(Constitution Hill Campus)
The BH14 . . . . .119 F5
Bournemouth & Poole Coll
(North Road Campus) The
BH14 . . . . .119 C4
Bournemouth & Poole Coll
The BH1 . . . . .122 B3
Bournemouth Rd
Blandford Forum DT11 . . .212 D2
Charlton Marshall DT11. . .211 D6
Poole BH14 . . . . .120 F4
Bournemouth Sch BH8. . . .90 C1
Bournemouth Sch for Girls
BH8 . . . . .90 C2
Bournemouth Station Rdbt
BH8 . . . . .122 B4
Bournemouth Univ
(Lansdowne Campus)
BH1 . . . . .122 B3
Bournemouth Univ (Talbot
Campus) BH12 . . . . .121 C8
Bournemouth West Rdbt
BH2 . . . . .121 D3
Bourne Pines **4** BH2 . . .121 E3
Bourne Pk DT2 . . . . .77 B8
Bourne River Ct **9** BH1 .121 E4
Bourne Valley Bsns Pk
BH12 . . . . .121 A5
Bourne Valley Rd BH12. . .121 A5
Bourne Way SP8 . . . . .5 F3
Bournewood Dr BH4 . . . . .121 C4
Bourton Gdns BH7 . . . . . .123 B8
Bouverie Cl **7** BH25 . . . . .95 A1
Boveridge Gdns BH9 . . . . .90 B4
Boveridge House Sch
BH21 . . . . .190 B1
Bovington Cl BH17 . . . . . . .87 F1
Bovington Fst Sch BH20 .139 D6
Bovington La BH20 . . . . . .139 C5
Bovington Mid Sch
BH20 . . . . .140 A3
Bowden La
Henstridge BA8 . . . . .18 C5
Milborne Port DT9 . . . . . . .17 F5
Bowden Rd
Abbas & Templecombe
BA8 . . . . .18 B8
Poole BH12 . . . . .88 C2
Bowdens **6** DT6 . . . . .97 E5
Bowdown BH20 . . . . .204 B2
Bower Ct **8** DT6 . . . . .194 C5
Bower Rd BH8 . . . . .122 D8
Bowers Rd **4** DT5 . . . . . .186 E3
Bowerswain Hollow
BH21 . . . . .201 B5
Bowerwood Rd SP6 . . . . . .42 E8
Bowes La **1** BH18 . . . . . .204 A8
Bowleaze BA21 . . . . .26 F6
Bowleaze Coveway DT3 .168 A6
Bowling Green La SP5 . . .189 D5
Bown Hill DT5 . . . . .186 E1
Bow The **3** DT1 . . . . . . .108 A2
Box Cl BH17 . . . . .119 B7
Boyd Rd BH12 . . . . .118 F1
Boyle Cl DT10 . . . . .33 D8
Boyle's Hill DT11 . . . . .38 D1
Boys Hill Dro DT9 . . . . . . .195 D5
Boyte Rd **14** DT11 . . . . . .199 D4
Bozley Hill SP7 . . . . .24 A7

Brabazon Dr BH23 . . . .125 B7
Brabazon Rd BH21 . . . .59 F1
Brabourne Ave BH22 . . .61 C4
Brackenbury Inf Sch
  DT5 . . . . .186 E7
Bracken Cl BH24 . . . . . .53 F4
Bracken Cl [10] BH4 . . . .121 D4
Brackendale Cl BH21 . . .52 F8
Brackendale Rd BH8 . . .122 D8
Bracken Glen BH15 . . . .119 E5
Brackenhill BH13 . . . . .121 A1
Brackenhill Rd BH21 . . .60 A7
Bracken Lodge [3] BH6 . .123 F4
Bracken Rd
  Bournemouth BH6 . . . .123 C4
  Ferndown BH22 . . . . .61 C4
Brackens Way [2] BH13 . .147 F8
Bracken Way BH23 . . . .147 F8
Bracket's Coppice Nature
  Reserve BA22 . . . . . .193 A2
Bracklesham Pl BH25 . . .126 F7
Brackley Cl BH23 . . . . .91 A8
Bradburne Rd BH21 . . .121 E3
Bradbury Ho BH22 . . . . .61 D7
Bradford Rd
  Bournemouth BH9 . . . . .90 C4
  [1] Crewkerne TA18 . . .192 A3
  Sherborne DT9 . . . . . .29 E5
  Weymouth DT4 . . . . .167 B2
Bradley Peak SO22 . . . .126 A7
Bradpole Rd BH8 . . . . . .90 E1
Bradstock Cl BH12 . . . .120 F8
Braemar Ave BH6 . . . . .124 A4
Braemar Cl BH6 . . . . . .124 A4
Braemar Dr BH23 . . . . .93 F1
Braemar Rd DT1 . . . . .135 C8
Braemore Ct SO22 . . . .126 A5
Braeside Bsns Pk BH15 . .119 B4
Braeside Rd
  Ferndown BH22 . . . . . .53 B3
  St Leonards BH24 . . . . .54 A4
Bradley Rd BH2 . . . . . .121 E4
Brailswood Rd BH15 . . .119 E4
Braishfield Gdns BH8 . . .90 D2
Brakes Hill DT2 . . . . . .194 A2
Bramar Cl BH4 . . . . . . .121 C2
Bramble Cl SP6 . . . . . . .42 C5
Bramblecombe La DT11 .209 D4
Bramble Cl BH22 . . . . . .53 A2
Bramble Dr BH16 . . . . .100 D2
Bramble Dro DT2 . . . . .136 A2
Bramble La
  Haselbury Plucknett
    TA18 . . . . .192 C5
  Walkford BH23 . . . . . .94 B1
Brambling Cl DT3 . . . . .152 C4
Bramdon Cl [5] DT3 . . . .150 A8
Bramdon La DT3 . . . . .150 C6
Bramley Cl [6] TA18 . . .191 F5
Bramley Ct BH22 . . . . . .61 C6
Bramley Hill
  Bridport DT6 . . . . . . .100 E8
  Mere BA12 . . . . .2 F5
Bramley Rd
  Bournemouth BH10 . . . .89 C5
  Ferndown BH22 . . . . . .61 C6
Bramshaw Gdns BH8 . . .90 D3
Bramshaw Way BH25 . . .126 D8
Branders Cl BH6 . . . . . .124 A4
Branders La BH6 . . . . . .124 B5
Brandon Ct [6] BH12 . . .121 C4
Brandwood Ct [4] BH14. .120 A3
Brandy La [2] DT5 . . . . .186 E7
Brandy Row [1] DT5 . . . .186 E7
Branksea Ave BH15 . . . .118 E1
Branksea Cl BH15 . . . . .118 E1
Branksome Cl BH25 . . . .95 B2
Branksome Ct [4] BH17 . .147 F8
Branksome Dene Rd
  BH4 . . . . .121 B2
Branksome Heath Mid Sch
  BH12 . . . . .120 C6
Branksome Hill Rd BH4 . .121 B5
Branksome Sta BH12. . . .120 F4
Branksome Twrs BH13 . . .147 H8
Branksome Wood Gdns
  BH2 . . . . .121 C4
Branksome Wood Rd BH2.
  BH4 . . . . .121 C4
Branscombe Cl [1] DT5. . .186 E7
Bransford BA22 . . . . . .193 D3
Bransgore CE Prim Sch
  BH23 . . . . .93 C8
Brantwood Cl DT8 . . . . .204 C4
Branwell Cl BH23 . . . . . .92 A1
Brassey Cl BH9 . . . . . . .90 A1
Brassey Rd
  Bournemouth BH9 . . . . .90 A1
  Winchester SO22 . . . . .126 D7
Brassey Terr BH9 . . . . . .89 F1
Bratch La DT11 . . . . . .200 D1
Bratch Cl SP8 . . . . .1 E2
Breaches La BH20 . . . . .163 A2
Breach Field [4] BH20 . .140 A2
Breach La
  Kington Magna SP8 . . . . .9 C3
  Shaftesbury SP7 . . . . . .12 D2
Breamore Cl BH23 . . . . .94 E3
Brearley Ct BH23 . . . . .126 B8
Brecon Cl
  Bournemouth BH10 . . . .89 E6
  New Milton BH25 . . . . .95 C5
Bredy Cl BH17 . . . . .87 D1
Bredy La DT6 . . . . .101 F1

Bredy Rd DT6 . . . . .128 D7
Bremble Cl BH12 . . . . . .88 C2
Breston Cl [2] DT5 . . . . .186 E1
Brewers Quay Sh Village
  DT4 . . . . .167 E1
Brian Cl BH20 . . . . . . .143 A8
Briar Cl
  Christchurch BH23 . . . .124 F6
  Gillingham SP8 . . . . .5 E2
  Mudford SA21 . . . . . . .28 A8
  Poole BH15 . . . . .119 E5
  Radipole DT4 . . . . . . .167 A5
Briarfield [49] BH4 . . . .121 C3
Briars End DT2 . . . . . . .137 E6
Briars The [3] BA20. . . . .26 C7
Briarswood Rd BH16 . . .118 C7
Briar Way BH21 . . . . . . .60 C5
Brickfields Ind Est SP8. . .10 F8
Brickyard La
  Bourton SP8 . . . . .1 E1
  Corfe Mullen BH21 . . . .58 A1
  Ferndown BH22 . . . . . .61 A6
  Gillingham SP8 . . . . .1 E1
  Silton SP8 . . . . .4 E8
  Sturminster Newton DT10.197 A7
  Swanage BH19 . . . . . .179 A5
Brick Yd La [4] TA18. . . .191 F5
Bridewell Ct DT9 . . . . . .30 C5
Bridewell La SP7 . . . . . . .7 A4
Bridge App BH15 . . . . .119 B1
Bridge Cl SP8 . . . . .6 A1
Bridge Inn La DT3 . . . . .153 C1
Bridge Pl BH10 . . . . . . .89 D7
Bridge Rd DT6 . . . . .97 B8
Bridge St BH22 . . . . . . .53 A3
Bridge St
  Bourton SP8 . . . . .1 E2
  Christchurch BH23 . . . .124 C6
  [1] Lyme Regis DT7 . . . .96 C5
  Netherbury DT6 . . . . . .204 C2
  Sturminster Marshall BH21.196 D8
  Sturminster Newton DT10.197 D3
  [7] Winchester SO23 . . .126 F5
Bridges The BH24. . . . . .55 A7
Bridgewater Rd BH12 . . .120 D6
Bridlebank Way DT3 . . .152 B3
Bridle Cres BH16 . . . . . .118 D7
Bridle Cres DT6 . . . . . .123 D7
Bridle Way
  Barwick BA22 . . . . . . .193 E8
  Wimborne Minster BH21. .60 C6
Bridleways BH31 . . . . . .45 D4
Bridport Com Hospl DT6 .100 A8
Bridport FC DT6 . . . . . .100 C5
Bridport L Ctr DT6 . . . .100 C5
Bridport Rd
  Beaminster DT8 . . . . .204 D3
  Broadwindsor DT8. . . . .203 C8
  Dorchester DT1 . . . . . .107 C1
  Poole BH12 . . . . .120 F8
  Verwood BH31. . . . . . . .45 B6
Bridport & W Dorset Golf
  Club DT6 . . . . .100 D1
Brierley Ave BH22 . . . . .61 E1
Brierley Cl BH10 . . . . . .89 E5
Brierley Hay [9] DT9. . . .194 C5
Brierley Rd BH10 . . . . . .89 E4
Brigadier Cl [1] BA22. . . .26 C5
Brightlay La DT5 . . . . . .67 A1
Brightlands Ave BH6 . . .123 F5
Brightlay Rd BH15 . . . .119 E5
Brightsmead DT2 . . . . .209 B6
Brimclose Rd TA17 . . . .191 B7
Brimley Rd EX13 . . . . .202 A3
Brincombe Valley Prim Sch
  DT3 . . . . .152 E3
Brinscombe La [3] SP7 . . .13 A1
Brinsley Cl DT3 . . . . . . .35 A1
Brinsons Cl DT3 . . . . . . .92 C3
Brionne Way SP7 . . . . . .13 A3
Brisbane Rd
  Christchurch BH23 . . . . .91 E1
  Radipole DT3 . . . . . . .152 E2
Brister End DT9 . . . . . .194 C5
Bristol Cl DT9 . . . . .30 B7
Briston Cl [6] DT1 . . . . .107 C1
Britannia Cl BH12. . . . . .120 B7
Britannia Rd BH14 . . . .120 A3
Britannia Way
  Christchurch BH23 . . . .125 B7
  Dorchester DT1 . . . . . .134 E8
Britmore La SP7 . . . . . . .13 F8
Brit The [4] DT8 . . . . . .204 D4
Brit View Rd DT6 . . . . .100 B2
Britwell Dr BH20. . . . . .172 C4
Brixey Cl BH12 . . . . . . .120 C7
Brixey La BH12 . . . . . . .120 C7
Brixey's La BH21 . . . . .142 E4
Broadacres
  East Coker BA22 . . . . .193 C8
  Gillingham SP8 . . . . .5 F3
Broad Ave BH8 . . . . . . .122 D8
Broad Chalke Down
  SO22 . . . . .126 A2
Broad Cl DT11 . . . . .81 E8
Broadcroft Gdns DT5 . . .187 A4
Broadhill La SP6 . . . . . . .43 F8
Broadhurst Ave BH10 . . .89 E4
Broad La
  Poole BH15 . . . . .100 B5
  East Chinnock BA22 . . .192 E7
Broadlands [27] BH4 . . .121 C3
Broadlands Rd BH23 . . .123 F4
Broadlands Cl
  Bournemouth BH8 . . . . .90 D3
  Walkford BH23 . . . . . . .94 B2

Broadlands Rd DT3 . . . .152 B2
Broadleaze BA21 . . . . . .26 F6
Broadmayne Fst Sch
  DT2 . . . . .136 C3
Broadmayne Rd BH12 . .121 A8
Broadmead DT2 . . . . . .136 B2
Broadmead Ave DT6 . . .100 B7
Broadmead Cl [3] DT8. . .204 A8
Broadmeadow Rd DT4 . .180 D7
Broad Mead Rd BH21 . . .45 A1
Broadmoor Rd BH21. . . .86 C7
Broadoak Ave [2] DT6. . .204 A7
Broadoak Rd DT6 . . . . . .67 E1
Broad Rd BH19 . . . . . . .179 C2
Broad Robin SP8 . . . . . . .5 E3
Broadshard La BH24 . . . .47 C1
Broadshard Rd TA18 . . .191 F5
Broad St DT7 . . . . .96 C5
Broads The BH21 . . . . . .86 A5
Broadstone Fst Sch BH18 .87 B4
Broadstone La
  Hardington Mandeville
    BA22 . . . . .193 A6
  West Chinnock TA18 . . .192 C8
Broadstone Mid Sch
  BH18 . . . . .87 C5
Broadstone Way
  Bournemouth BH7. . . . . .86 F1
  Poole BH17 . . . . .119 B7
Broadwater Ave BH14 . .120 C2
Broadway
  Merriott TA16. . . . . . . .191 E7
  Southbourne BH6 . . . . .124 B3
Broadway Cl BH12 . . . . .121 A1
Broadway Gables BH14 . .120 E4
Broadway Gdns [6] BH21. .59 F4
Broadway Ho BH16 . . . . .87 A4
Broadway La
  Bournemouth BH8 . . . . .90 C4
  West Chinnock BA22 . . .192 D8
Broadway Mews BH14 . .119 F3
Broadway Pk [2] BH21. . .59 F4
Broadway The
  Bournemouth BH10 . . . .89 D7
  Winchester SO23. . . . . .126 C5
Broadwey DT3 . . . . . . .152 C4
Broadwindsor CE Prim Sch
  DT8 . . . . .203 E5
Broadwindsor Craft & Design
  Ctr DT8 . . . . .203 F5
Broadwindsor Rd DT8 . .204 B4
Broadwindsor Road Ind Est
  DT8 . . . . .204 B4
Brockenhurst Rd BH9 . . .90 B2
Brockhills La DT7 . . . . . .95 C6
Brockington La BH21 . . .201 C5
Brockley Rd BH10 . . . . . .89 E4
Brocks Pine BH24. . . . . .54 B3
Brockwood DT4 . . . . . . .53 F2
Brodham Way DT11 . . . .198 B5
Brog St BH21 . . . . .58 C1
Broke La DT9 . . . . .195 D6
Brombys The [11] BH15 . .119 C2
Bromley Ho BH12 . . . . .121 B5
Brompton Cl BH12. . . . .121 C3
Bronte Ave BH23. . . . . . .92 A1
Brook Ave BH25 . . . . . . .95 B4
Brook Ave N BH25 . . . . .95 B4
Brook Cl BH10 . . . . .89 C5
Brookdale Cl BH18. . . . . .87 A4
Brookdale Farm BH18. . . .87 A4
Brook Dr BH31 . . . . .45 D4
Brook Ho BH25 . . . . . . .95 B4
Brookhouse St [8] DT1 . .107 D1
Brook La
  Bransgore BH23 . . . . . .93 B7
  Corfe Mullen BH21 . . . .86 C6
  Henstridge BA8 . . . . . . .19 A4
  Woodlands BH21 . . . . . .44 B7
Brooklands
  Bournemouth BH4 . . . .121 B3
  Milborne St Andrew DT11. .79 E8
Brooklands Farm
  Conservation Ctr DT2 . . .75 B3
Brookland Way [4] BA8 . .19 A4
Brooklyn Cl BH25 . . . . . .94 F3
Brookmead Cl DT3. . . . .153 D2
Brook Rd
  Bournemouth BH10 . . . .89 C4
  Poole BH12 . . . . .120 F8
  Wimborne Minster BH21. .59 F4
Brook Road Depot BH21 .59 E3
Brooks Cl BH24 . . . . . . .55 D6
Brookside
  [8] Gillingham SP8 . . . . .5 F3
  Milborne Port DT9 . . . . .17 D1
  Ringwood SP6 . . . . .43 E2
  West Coker BA22 . . . . .193 A8
Brookside Cl [2] DT3 . . .153 C2
Brookside Park Homes
  BH21 . . . . .86 B4
Brookside Rd
  Bransgore BH23 . . . . . .93 A8
  Wimborne Minster BH21. .59 F4
Brooks Sh Ctr The SO23.126 E6
Brook St
  Milborne Port DT9 . . . . .17 D1
  Shipton Gorge DT6 . . . .101 D4
Brook Terr SP6 . . . . .43 B8
Brook Way BH22 . . . . . .61 C5
Broomfield Cl BH22. . . . .61 E6
Broomfield Dr SP6 . . . . .42 C5
Broom Hill DT2 . . . . . . .205 F5
Broom La BH6 . . . . .123 B4
Broom Rd BH12 . . . . . . .88 C1
Broom Road Bsns Pk
  BH12 . . . . .88 C1

Broughton Ave BH10. . . .89 E3
Broughton Cl BH10 . . . . .89 E3
Broughton Cres DT4 . . .180 C2
Broughtons Dr [2] BH21. .192 A3
Brownen Rd BH9 . . . . . .122 B8
Brownes Pl DT2 . . . . . . .73 F3
Browning Ave
  Bournemouth BH5 . . . .122 F4
  Bournemouth BH5 . . . .123 A4
Browning Dr SO22 . . . .126 B6
Browning Rd BH12. . . . .120 D6
Brownlow Cl [33] BH4 . .121 C3
Brownlow St DT4 . . . . .167 D4
Brown's Cres DT3. . . . . .166 B5
Brownsea Ave BH21. . . . .86 D6
Brownsea Cl BH25 . . . . .94 E3
Brownsea Island BH15 . .147 B8
Brownsea Island BH15 . .146 D4
Brownsea Island Nature
  Reserve BH15 . . . . . .145 E5
Brownsea Rd BH13 . . . .147 B3
Brownsea View Ave
  BH14 . . . . .120 C1
Brownsea View Cl BH14 .120 C1
Browns La BH6 . . . . . . .190 E3
Brown's La SP6 . . . . .10 F3
Brown St DT9 . . . . .196 A7
Brudenell Ave BH13. . . .147 D7
Brudenell Rd BH13. . . . .147 D6
Brunel Cl BH31 . . . . .45 D4
Brunel Dr DT3 . . . . . . .153 B1
Brune Way BH22 . . . . . .61 D3
Brunsell's Knap DT10 . . .33 A2
Brunstead Pl [8] BH12 . .121 B4
Brunstead Rd BH12 . . . .121 B4
Brunswick Sq BH20 . . . . .27 C4
Brushy Bush La SP5. . . .188 F3
Brutus Cl DT1 . . . . .134 E7
Bryanstone Rd BH3 . . . .121 E7
Bryanston Sch DT11. . . .212 A5
Bryanston St DT11 . . . .212 A2
Bryant Rd BH12 . . . . . . .121 A8
Bryants La DT11 . . . . . .180 B8
Brymer Rd DT2. . . . . . .110 B8
Brymers Ave [5] DT5 . . .186 F7
Brympton Ave BA22 . . . . .26 A3
Brympton Way BA20 . . . .26 E3
Brym Rd
  Sandford BH20 . . . . . .143 A8
  Weymouth DT4 . . . . . .167 B2
Bryony Cl BH18 . . . . . . .86 F3
Bryony Gdns DT9 . . . . . . .5 D2
Bub La BH23 . . . . .124 C6
Buccaneers Cl BH23 . . . .124 E6
Buccleuch Rd BH13. . . . .147 B3
Bucehayes Cl BH23 . . . .126 A8
Buchanan Ave BH7 . . . .122 E6
Buckbury Mews [13] DT1. .135 B8
Buckhill Cl [5] TA18 . . . .191 F3
Buckhorn Cl DT1 . . . . . .69 B8
Buckingham Cl
  [1] Christchurch BH23 . .126 A7
  Poole BH15 . . . . .119 D3
  BH1 . . . . .122 A3
Buckingham Mans [6]
  Gillingham SP8 . . . . .5 F1
  Poole BH12 . . . . .120 D7
Buckingham Wlk BH25 . . .94 E3
Buckingham Way DT11 . .135 C8
Buckland Gr BH23 . . . . .173 C3
Buckland Newton Prim Sch
  DT2 . . . . .208 A8
Buckland Rd
  Poole BH12 . . . . .120 C5
  Yeovil BA21 . . . . .28 A6
Buckland Terr BH12. . . . .120 C5
Buckle Pl BA22 . . . . .26 A4
Bucklers Mead [1] DT9 . .194 C5
Bucklers Mead Rd BA21. .27 E8
Bucklers Way BH8 . . . . . .90 D3
Buckthorn Cl BH17 . . . . .86 F1
Buddens La SP7 . . . . . . .23 E4
Buddens Mdw BH21 . . . .86 C4
Buddle Hill SP6. . . . . . . .43 E4
Buddleia Cl DT3 . . . . . .152 F2
Budmouth Ave DT3 . . . .168 A6
Budmouth Com Sports Ctr
  DT4 . . . . .166 E3
Budnouth Tech Coll
  DT4 . . . . .166 E3
Buffalo Mews BH15. . . . .119 B2
Buffetts Rd DT10 . . . . . .35 B2
Bugden's Copse Nature
  Reserve BH31. . . . . . . .45 B6
Bugdens La BH31. . . . . . .45 C6
Bugway La TA20 . . . . . .202 B8
Bulbury La BH16 . . . . . .115 F7
Bulbury Woods Golf Club
  BH16 . . . . .115 F8
Bull Bridge Mead [4] BH21 .193 D3
Bull Cl [2] DT2 . . . . . . .106 E8
Bull Dro SO23 . . . . .126 C5
Buller Ave BA22 . . . . . . .26 C5
Buller's Way DT3 . . . . . .148 E6
Bullfinch Cl BH17 . . . . . .86 F1
Bull Garden La DT10 . . . .35 C1
Bull La
  Maiden Newton DT2 . . . .72 F8
  Puncknowle DT2 . . . . .129 E6
Bullocks La DT11 . . . . . .197 A1
Bulls La [4] TA18 . . . . . .191 E4
Bumpers La DT5 . . . . . .187 B4
Bunford La BA20 . . . . . . .26 E4
Bunting Rd BH22 . . . . . .61 B8
Burbidge Cl BH16. . . . . . .84 C2
Burbitt La DT6. . . . . . . .101 C4

Burbridge Cl BH17 . . . .119 E8
Burcombe Rd BH10 . . . . .89 C5
Burdens [2] DT10. . . . . .197 A4
Burdock Cl BH23 . . . . . .93 B1
Bure Cl BH23 . . . . .125 B6
Bure Haven Dr BH23 . . .125 B6
Bure Homage Gdns
  . . . . .125 B6
Bure Homage La BH23 . .125 B6
Bure La BH23 . . . . .125 B6
Bure Rd BH23 . . . . .125 B6
Burford Cl BH23 . . . . . . .91 D1
Burford Ct [4] BH1 . . . .122 B3
Burges Cl BH21 . . . . . . .20 E4
Burgess Cl BH11 . . . . . . .88 F4
Burgess Field BH21 . . . . .44 C6
Burleigh Rd BH6. . . . . . .123 D5
Burleston Dro DT2 . . . . .78 F2
Burley Cl
  Barton on Sea BH25 . . .126 D8
  Verwood BH31. . . . . . . .45 A5
Burley Rd
  Bransgore BH23 . . . . . .93 A8
  Poole BH12 . . . . .120 C6
  Winkton BH23 . . . . . . .92 D6
Burling Terr [1] BH13 . . .121 A4
Burlington Arc [11] BH1. .121 F3
Burlington Rd BH10 . . . .179 C4
Burnaby Cl BH4 . . . . . . .121 C1
Burnaby Rd BH4. . . . . . .121 C1
Burnage Ct [2] BH13 . . . .147 F7
Burnbake Rd BH21 . . . . .45 B5
Burnbrae Rd BH22 . . . . .61 D1
Burn Cl BH31 . . . . .45 D4
Burnett Ave BH23 . . . . .123 E8
Burnett Cl SO22 . . . . . . .126 A8
Burnett Rd BH23 . . . . . .123 F7
Burngate Rd BH15 . . . . .118 E2
Burnham Dr BH8 . . . . . .122 C7
Burnham Rd BH23 . . . . .92 C2
Burnham's La BH19 . . . .178 D5
Burnleigh Gdns BH25 . . .95 C4
Burnside
  Christchurch BH23 . . . .125 D8
  Winterborne St Martin
    DT2 . . . . .133 C2
Burns Rd
  Bournemouth BH6 . . . .123 D7
  Northport BH20 . . . . . .142 D6
Burn View DT2 . . . . . . .107 F5
Burraton Sq [4] DT1. . . .107 D1
Burroughes Ave BA21. . . .27 A4
Burrows La BH31 . . . . . .45 B8
Burrywells DT2 . . . . . . .102 C4
Bursledon Ho [4] BH25. . .95 A2
Burstock Cl DT8 . . . . . .203 C7
Burtley Rd BH6 . . . . . . .124 B5
Burton Bradstock CE Prim
  Sch DT6 . . . . .128 C2
Burton CE Prim Sch BH23 .92 C3
Burton Cl
  Burton BH23 . . . . .92 C3
  Shaftesbury SP7 . . . . . .13 A3
  St Leonards BH24 . . . . .53 F5
  Wool BH20 . . . . .139 F2
Burtoncroft BH23 . . . . . .92 C3
Burton Cross BH20. . . . .139 E1
Burton Hall DT6 . . . . . . .92 C3
Burton Hall Pl BH23 . . . .92 D3
Burton La DT2 . . . . .92 D1
Burton La BA22 . . . . . . .193 C8
Burton Rd
  Abbotsbury DT3 . . . . . .148 D6
  Burton BH23 . . . . .100 E2
  Burton Bradstock DT6 . .128 B4
  Christchurch BH23 . . . .124 E7
  Poole BH13 . . . . .121 A3
  Puncknowle DT2 . . . . .129 E1
  Wool BH20 . . . . .139 F2
Burton St DT10. . . . . . . .20 E3
Burton Wood BH20 . . . . .139 F1
Burt's Hill BH21 . . . . . . .59 D7
Burt's La BH21. . . . . .52 C8
Burt's Pl [6] BH19 . . . . .179 C2
Bury Rd
  Poole BH13 . . . . .120 F1
  Poole BH13 . . . . .120 F2
Bushell Rd BH15 . . . . . .119 C7
Bushes Hill SP8 . . . . .5 A7
Bushes Rd DT11 . . . . . .199 A4
Bushey La BH20 . . . . . .162 D3
Bushmead Dr BH24 . . . . .54 A5
Bush Pk DT11 . . . . .81 E8
Bushfield Rd [4] TA18. . .191 E3
Busket La SO23 . . . . . . .126 E5
Bute Dr BH23 . . . . .126 B8
Butlers La BH24 . . . . . . .47 E1
Butt Cl DT2 . . . . .78 B1
Buttercup Cl [2] SP8 . . . . .5 D2
Buttercup Dr DT11. . . . . .93 B1
Buttercup La DT11 . . . . .212 E5
Buttercup Way DT6 . . . .100 D2
Butterwick Dro DT9 . . . .195 D6
Buttery The BH6 . . . . . .124 D7
Butt Farm Cl DT2 . . . . .105 D1
Butt La
  Bere Regis BH20 . . . . . .81 B3
  Whitchurch Canonicorum
    DT6 . . . . .66 D2
Butt La Hollow BH20 . . . .81 B4
Butts Cl
  Marnhull DT10. . . . . . . .20 F1
  Winchester SO22 . . . . .126 B7

Butts Cl continued
3 Winfrith Newburgh DT2 156 F6
Butts La SP8 .... 21 C7
Butts Mead 1 SP7.... 13 A1
Butts Pond Ind Pk DT10.... 35 B2
Butts Quarry La TA18.... 192 A4
Butts The
　12 Child Okeford DT11.... 198 C2
　Shaftesbury SP7 .... 12 C3
Buxton Cl 2 DT4.... 180 D8
Buxton Rd DT4 .... 180 D8
Byron Ave SO22.... 126 B6
Byron Ct BH22.... 61 D5
Byron Ho 1 BH25.... 95 A2
Byron Rd
　Barton on Sea BH25 .... 126 E8
　Bournemouth BH5.... 122 F3
　Wimborne Minster BH21....59 C6

C

Cabot Bsns Village BH17 119 D4
Cabot La BH17.... 119 B8
Cabot Way BH25.... 94 F3
Cachy Rd BH20.... 139 E7
Caddy La BA12 .... 2 F5
Cadhay Cl BH25 .... 94 E3
Cadley Cl DT11.... 212 D5
Cadnam Way BH6.... 90 D3
Cadogan Rd BH24 .... 55 D7
Caernarvon Cl 4 DT1.... 135 C8
Caesar Gn 2 DT1.... 134 E7
Caesar's Way BH18.... 86 E4
Caird Ave BH5.... 95 C2
Cairns Cl BH23.... 123 F8
Caister Cl DT2.... 61 C6
Calcraft Rd BH20.... 177 A8
Calder Rd BH17.... 119 F8
Caledonian Cl
　Christchurch BH23.... 125 B7
　Radipole DT4.... 167 D5
Caledon Rd BH14.... 120 E3
Cale Way SP8.... 5 D1
Caley Way DT6.... 69 A1
Calf Close La DT10.... 197 F8
Calfhay La DT9.... 194 E1
Calkin Cl BH23.... 92 A1
Calluna Rd BH12.... 120 B8
Callway La DT2.... 209 B2
Calmore Cl BH8.... 90 F3
Calves La SP7.... 12 B4
Calvin Rd BH9.... 121 F8
Camborne St BA21.... 28 A5
Camborne St BA21.... 28 A6
Cambridge Cl BA20.... 26 F5
Cambridge Gdns BH23.... 91 F2
Cambridge Rd
　Bournemouth BH1.... 121 D3
　Dorchester DT1.... 107 D1
　Weymouth DT4.... 166 E3
Cambridge Wlk 1 DT1.. 107 D1
Camden Cl BH9.... 90 B1
Camden Way DT1.... 134 F7
Came Down Cl DT3.... 152 C3
Came Down Golf Club
　DT2.... 134 F2
Camel Green Rd 3 SP6.. 42 D6
Camellia Cl BH21.... 45 A1
Camellia Gdns BH25.... 95 B2
Camelot Way SP8.... 5 D1
Cameron Rd BH23.... 124 D7
Camesworth La DT6.... 69 A7
Came View Cl DT1.... 135 C8
Came View Rd DT1.... 135 C8
Camilla Ct BH13.... 121 B2
Cammel Rd BH22.... 61 D2
Campbell Rd
　Bournemouth BH1.... 122 E5
　Burton BH23.... 92 C3
Campion Cl
　5 Gillingham SP8.... 5 D1
　Radipole DT4.... 167 E7
Campion Dr BA22.... 26 D5
Campion Gr BH23.... 124 F6
Campion Rd
　Chickerell DT4.... 180 B8
　West Coker BA22.... 26 C1
Canberra Cres DT3.... 152 E3
Canberra Rd
　Christchurch BH23.... 91 E1
　Radipole DT3.... 152 E1
Candys Cl BH21.... 58 E2
Candys La BH21.... 58 E2
Candy's La 8 DT11.... 198 B6
Canford Ave BH11.... 89 A2
Canford Bottom BH21.... 60 C6
Canford Bottom Rdbt
　BH21.... 60 C5
Canford Cliffs Ave BH14.. 120 C2
Canford Cliffs Rd BH13.. 120 E2
Canford Cres BH13.... 147 E7
Canford Ct BH13.... 147 E6
Canford Gdns BH11.... 89 A1
Canford Heath Fst & Mid
　Schs BH17.... 119 D7
Canford Heath Nature
　Reserve BH11.... 88 A4
Canford Heath Rd BH21.. 60 A1
Canford Magna BH21.... 60 C6
Canford Park Events Arena &
　Sports Gd BH21.... 88 B7
Canford Pl 2 BH13.... 147 F7
Canford Rd
　Bournemouth BH11.... 89 A1

Canford Rd continued
　Poole BH15.... 119 D4
Canford Sch BH21.... 60 B2
Canford Summer Sch of
　Music DT9.... 30 B6
Canford View Dr BH21.... 60 B6
Cann Hill SP7.... 24 A5
Cannings Ct La DT2.... 196 C3
Cannington Coll BA20.... 26 E5
Cannon Cl BH18.... 87 A1
Cannon Ct Mews 1 DT9.. 17 D1
Cannon Hill Gdns BH21.. 60 B7
Cannon Hill Rd BH21.... 60 A7
Canon St SO23.... 126 E5
Canteen Rd DT5.... 181 D1
Canterbury Cl
　Ferndown BH22.... 53 A1
　Weymouth DT4.... 166 F3
Canute Rd 5 SO23.... 126 F4
Capella Ct BH21.... 59 B8
Capesthorne DT3.... 125 B5
Caphays Dro DT9.... 195 E7
Capital Ho 2 SO22.... 126 D6
Capitol Cl DT1.... 134 E8
Capper Rd 2 BH20.... 139 E6
Capper Rd W BH20.... 139 E6
Capstan Field BH19.... 178 A2
Capstans The BH14.... 147 B8
Capstone Pl BH8.... 122 D6
Capstone Rd BH8.... 122 B6
Captains Cove BH15.... 118 E3
Carbery Ave BH6.... 123 D5
Carbery Gdns BH6.... 123 E5
Carbery La BH6.... 123 C4
Carbery Row 2 BH6.... 123 C4
Cardigan Rd
　Bournemouth BH9.... 121 F8
　Poole BH12.... 120 F4
Cards Mill La DT6.... 66 A7
Carey App BH20.... 142 D5
Carey Cl BH20.... 142 D5
Carey Rd
　Bournemouth BH9.... 89 F3
　Northport BH20.... 142 D5
Careys Rd BH8.... 90 D4
Carina Ct BH13.... 147 C3
Carisbrooke
　Poole BH13.... 147 E2
　Radipole DT4.... 167 B6
Carisbrooke Cres BH15.. 118 D3
Carisbrooke
　1 Christchurch BH23.... 126 B7
　New Milton BH25.... 94 F3
Carisbrooke Gdns BA20.. 27 B5
Carisbrooke Way BH23.. 93 E1
Carlinford 5 BH5.... 122 F3
Carlton Ave BH25.... 126 D8
Carlton Gr BH12.... 120 D5
Carlton Mount BH2.... 121 E2
Carlton Rd BH1.... 122 C4
Carlton Rd N DT4.... 167 D5
Carlton Rd S DT4.... 167 D5
Carlyle Rd BH6.... 123 D6
Carmel Cl BH15.... 118 D2
Carnarvon Rd 4 BH1.... 122 E4
Caroline Ave BH23.... 124 F6
Caroline Ave DT3.... 124 F6
Caroline Pl 5 DT4.... 167 D3
Caroline Rd BH11.... 89 B2
Carpenters Cl 3 DT2.... 106 E8
Carradale BH23.... 125 B8
Carraway La DT10.... 20 F1
Carrbridge Cl BH3.... 121 D7
Carrbridge Gdns BH3.... 121 D7
Carrbridge Rd BH3.... 121 D7
Carrick Cl DT1.... 135 C8
Carrick Way BH25.... 95 C2
Carrington La 4 BH20.... 180 D8
Carrion La 4 BH20.... 142 E4
Carroll Ave BH22.... 61 A4
Carroll Cl BH12.... 121 A6
Carsworth Way BH17.... 88 A2
Carter Cl DT11.... 212 E5
Carter Com Sch BH15.... 118 F2
Carters Ave BH15.... 118 D4
Carters La BA22.... 192 E8
Carter's La
　Chideock DT6.... 98 E8
　5 Poole BH15.... 119 C2
Cartref Cl BH11.... 45 B6
Cartwright Cl BH10.... 89 C4
Carvers Ind Est BH24.... 55 C7
Carvers La BH24.... 55 C7
Carysfort Rd BH1.... 122 D4
Caseberry Cl 7 BH1.... 107 D1
Cashmoor Cl BH12.... 120 F7
Caslake Cl BH24.... 55 D7
Cassel Ave BH13.... 121 B1
Casselles Ct 6 BH25.... 95 A2
Cassiobury Rd DT4.... 167 D4
Casterbridge Cl
　Pimperne DT11.... 212 F6
　4 Swanage BH19.... 178 E2
Casterbridge Ct 8 BH4.. 121 C3
Casterbridge Ind Est
　DT1.... 108 B2
Casterbridge Rd
　Dorchester DT1.... 135 D8
　Ferndown BH22.... 61 C3
Castle Ave
　Christchurch BH23.... 125 E8
　5 Okeford Fitzpaine DT11 197 F6
　Winchester SO23.... 126 D6
Castle Cl
　Cranborne BH21.... 40 B7
　Dorchester DT1.... 107 D1

Castle Court Prep Sch
　BH21.... 86 B7
Castle Ct 2 BH23.... 126 A7
Castledene Cres BH14.. 120 A2
Castle Farm Rd BH16.... 84 C4
Castle Gate Cl BH8.... 90 C2
Castle Hill
　Poole BH15.... 120 A4
　Winchester SO22.... 126 D6
Castle Hill Cl DT7.... 12 D3
Castle Hill Cres BA12.... 3 A6
Castle Hill La
　Cranborne BH21.... 40 B6
　Mere BA12.... 3 A5
Castle Hill Rd DT4.... 180 B8
Castle La
　Buckland Newton DT2.... 208 B8
　Okeford Fitzpaine DT11.. 197 F6
　Owermoigne DT2.... 155 D8
Castle Lane E BH7.... 123 C8
Castle La W BH9.... 90 C2
Castlemain Ave BH6.... 123 C5
Castlemaine Rd DT3.... 152 E2
Castleman Smith Cl
　DT11.... 212 E6
Castleman Way DT2.... 55 C6
Castlemews BH24.... 54 E5
Castle Par DT7.... 123 D7
Castlepoint
　Bournemouth BH8.... 90 E1
　Bournemouth BH8.... 90 E2
Castle Rd
　Bournemouth BH9.... 90 A1
　Fortuneswell DT5.... 181 A1
　Sherborne DT9.... 30 D7
Castle Sq DT6.... 100 C5
Castle St
　Christchurch BH23.... 124 B6
　Cranborne BH21.... 40 B7
　Mere BA12.... 3 A5
　Poole BH15.... 119 C1
Castleton TA18.... 192 C5
Castleton Ave BH10.... 89 D6
Castleton Rd DT9.... 30 D6
Castleton Waterwheel Mus
　DT9.... 30 D6
Castletown DT5.... 181 B1
Castle Town Way DT9.... 30 C8
Castle View Dr BH14.... 84 C1
Castlewood Rd DT4.... 54 F5
Catalina Cl BH23.... 125 A6
Catalina Dr BH15.... 119 E1
Caters Pl DT1.... 108 A2
Cathedral View 4 SO23.. 126 F4
Catherine Wheel Mus
　BH23.... 91 E3
Cathole Bridge Rd TA18.. 191 F3
Cat La DT10.... 33 A2
Caton Cl DT12.... 121 B8
Catsley La DT2.... 205 B6
Cattistock Rd
　Bournemouth BH8.... 90 E2
　Maiden Newton DT2.... 72 F8
Cauldon Ave BH19.... 179 B4
Cauldon Barn Rd BH19.. 179 B4
Cauldron Cres BH19.... 179 B4
Cauldron Mdws 3 BH19.. 179 B4
Caundle La
　Stalbridge DT10.... 33 A6
　Stourton Caundle DT10.... 32 E1
Causeway Cl BH20.... 142 D5
Causeway La DT8.... 203 A6
Causeway The
　Hazelbury Bryan DT10...196 F4
　Milborne St Andrew DT11..79 E8
Cavalcade of Costume Mus
　DT11.... 212 D4
Cavalier Cl BA21.... 27 F8
Cavalier Way BA21.... 27 F8
Cavan Cres BH17.... 87 F1
Cave Hole DT5.... 186 F11
Cavendish Cl 4 BH4.... 121 C3
Cavendish Hall BH1.... 122 A5
Cavendish Pl BH1.... 122 A5
Cavendish Rd
　Bournemouth BH1.... 121 F5
　Bournemouth BH1.... 122 A5
Caversham Cl BH15.... 118 E3
Cawdor Rd BH3.... 121 D7
Caxton Cl BH23.... 125 A7
Cecil Ave BH8.... 122 C8
Cecil Cl BH21.... 86 E6
Cecil Hill BH8.... 122 B8
Cecil Rd
　Bournemouth BH5.... 122 E4
　Poole BH12.... 120 B6
　Swanage BH19.... 179 A2
Cecil St BA20.... 27 D5
Cedar Ave
　Bournemouth BH10.... 89 D6
　Christchurch BH23.... 123 D8
　St Leonards BH24.... 53 F1
Cedar Cl
　Upton BH16.... 118 B8
　1 Wool BH20.... 140 A2
Cedar Ct BH4.... 121 B2
Cedar Dr
　2 Easton/Weston DT5...186 F1
　Overcombe/Preston DT3..168 B8
　Sandford BH20.... 116 A1
　Wimborne Minster BH21.. 60 A6
Cedar Gdns BH25.... 94 F1
Cedar Gr BA21.... 27 A6
Cedar Grange 18 BH13.. 121 A4
Cedar Manor BH4.... 121 C3

Cedar Rd
　Charminster DT2.... 75 D2
　Dorchester DT1.... 107 E2
Cedars The BH4.... 121 C4
Cedar Trad Pk BH21.... 60 F6
Cedar Way BH22.... 61 C8
Cedar Wlk SO22.... 126 C5
Celandine Cl
　Christchurch BH23.... 125 B8
　Radipole DT4.... 167 D6
Celandine Rd 3 BA22.... 26 C5
Cellars Farm Rd BH6.... 124 A3
Celtic Cres DT1.... 134 E7
Cemetery Ave BH15.... 119 F6
Cemetery Junc BH2.... 121 F5
Cemetery Rd
　2 Gillingham SP8.... 5 F2
　Portesham DT3.... 150 A8
　Wimborne Minster BH21.. 59 B5
Centenary Gdns BA8.... 19 A4
Centenary Rd DT11.... 124 B7
Centenary Way BH11.... 122 E5
Central Acre 13 BA20.... 27 C7
Central Ave
　Corfe Mullen BH21.... 86 D7
　Poole BH12.... 120 E6
Central Dr
　Bournemouth BH1.... 121 E5
　West Moors BH24.... 62 B8
Central Rd BA20.... 27 D5
Centre Pl BH24.... 55 B7
Centurion Rd DT11.... 199 E2
Century Pk BA20.... 27 A5
Cereleton Pk DT11.... 211 C6
Cerne Abbas DT3.... 121 A1
Cerne Abbas CE Fst Sch
　DT2.... 207 C4
Cerne Abbas Giant DT2.. 207 D4
Cerne Abbas Tithe Barn
　DT2.... 207 D4
Cerne Abbey DT2.... 207 D4
Cerne Ave BH11.... 88 B8
Cerne Cl BH9.... 90 B4
Chaddesley Glen BH13.. 147 E6
Chaddesley Grange
　BH13.... 147 E6
Chaddesley Pines BH13.. 147 E6
Chaddesley Wood Rd
　BH13.... 147 E6
Chafeys Ave BH15.... 167 A5
Chaffey Cl BH24.... 55 E8
Chaffeymoor Hill SP8.... 1 B1
Chaffinch Cl
　Broadstone BH17.... 86 F2
　New Milton BH25.... 94 F2
　Radipole DT3.... 152 D3
Chalbury Cl
　Overcombe/Preston
　DT3.... 168 A8
　Poole BH17.... 88 A2
Chalbury Cnr 2 BH11.... 88 A2
Chalbury (Hill Fort) DT3 153 A4
Chaldecott Gdns BH10.. 89 C4
Chaldon Rd BH17.... 87 F2
Chalfont Ave DT1.... 91 D3
Chalice Cl BH14.... 120 A4
Chalk Cl BH20.... 81 B1
Chalk Pit La
　Litton Cheney DT2.... 103 A2
　Wool BH20.... 139 F1
Chalk The 2 DT11.... 37 F1
Chalky Rd DT2.... 136 A1
Challacombe St DT1.... 107 B2
Challenger Way BA22.... 26 C6
Chalwell 1 DT11.... 198 C2
Chalwyn Ind Est BH15,
　BH12.... 120 A7
Chamberlaine Rd DT4.. 180 C8
Champernhayes La DT6.. 64 E5
Champions 18.... 204 C4
Chancery La DT6.... 100 D6
Chander Cl BH22.... 61 E4
Chandler Cl DT1.... 167 D8
Chandlers DT9.... 30 C7
Chandlers Cl BH7.... 123 B8
Chandos Ave BH12.... 120 C6
Channel Ct
　Barton on Sea BH25.... 126 E7
Channel View Rd DT5.. 186 F4
Channons Ct 4 DT1.... 108 A2
Chant Cl BH23.... 124 D7
Chantmarle La DT2.... 206 B5
Chantry La BH23.... 93 F1
Chantry La DT8.... 204 C5
Chantry Mead SO22.... 126 C2
Chantry St DT4.... 204 C2
Chantry The
　Bournemouth BH1.... 122 A4
　Mere BA12.... 3 A5
Chantry View BA22.... 193 D8
Chapel Cl
　Corfe Mullen BH21.... 86 D7
　Lugg Herring DT3.... 150 C1
Chapel Gate BH23.... 91 C7
Chapel Gdns DT11.... 212 E3
Chapelhay Hts 1 DT4.... 167 D2
Chapelhay St DT4.... 167 D2
Chapel Hill SP8.... 9 D2
Chapel La
　Bransgore BH23.... 93 A8
　Corfe Mullen BH21.... 86 D7
　Dinnington TA17.... 191 B8
　East Parley BH23.... 90 C8
　Henstridge BA8.... 18 E7
　Maiden Newton DT2.... 72 F8
　7 Milborne Port DT9.... 17 D2

Chapel La continued
　Osmington DT3.... 154 B1
　Pen Selwood BA9.... 1 C
　2 Pimperne DT11.... 199 D5
　Poole BH15.... 119 C
　Radipole DT3.... 152 C
　Wimborne Minster BH21.. 59 B
　Woodlands BH21.... 44 B
　7 Yetminster DT9.... 194 C
　Zennor BA12.... 1 E
Chapel Mdw 6 DT9.... 194 C5
Chapel Rd
　Poole BH14.... 120 A4
　Sturminster Newton DT10.. 197 A8
Chapel Rise BH24.... 54 F2
Chapel St
　Milborne St Andrew DT11.. 79 E
　Shipton Gorge DT6.... 101 D
Chapel View 6 DT2.... 78 B
Charberry Rise DT6.... 96 F
Charborough Cl BH16.... 84 C
Charborough House BH20 83 F
Charborough Rd BH20.. 83 F
Charborough Way 1
　BH21.... 56 D
Chard La
　Broadwindsor DT8.... 203 C
　Wayford TA18.... 191 B
Chard Rd
　Broadwindsor DT8.... 203 C
　Crewkerne TA18.... 191 D
Chards Mead Rd DT6.... 100 C
Chard St DT1.... 202 E
Charfield Cl SO22.... 126 C
Charing Cl 3 BH24.... 55 C
Charing Cross SP6.... 42 B
Charlecote Mews 14
　SO22.... 126 D
Charles Cl SO23.... 126 F
Charles Cres BH25.... 95 B
Charles Garrett Cl 3 SP7.. 12 F
Charles Gdns BH10.... 89 D
Charles Keightley Ct
　BH21.... 59 D
Charles Rd
　Burton Bradstock DT6.... 128 B
　Christchurch BH23.... 124 F
　Poole BH15.... 119 D
　Yeovil BA21.... 27 F
Charles's La BH24.... 55 E
Charles St
　Blandford Forum DT11.... 212 D
　Dorchester DT1.... 108 A
　Poole BH15.... 167 D
Charlotte Cl
　Charminster DT2.... 107 E
　Christchurch BH23.... 125 A
　3 New Milton BH25.... 95 A
　Poole BH17.... 121 C
Charlton Beeches DT11.. 211 C
Charlton Cl
　12 Crewkerne TA18.... 191 F
　Hordle SO41.... 95 F
Charlton La SP7.... 23 E
Charlton Manor 1 DT11. 211 D
Charlton Mead 6 DT11.. 211 D
Charlton The Pit La
　DT11.... 121 F
Charminster Ave
　Bournemouth BH9.... 122 B
　Bournemouth BH9.... 90 B
Charminster Cl BH8.... 90 B
Charminster Pl BH8.... 90 C
Charminster Rd
　Bournemouth BH8.... 122 B
　Bournemouth BH9.... 90 B
Charmouth Ct DT7.... 96 C
Charmouth Gr BH14.... 120 A
Charmouth Heritage Coast
　Ctr DT6.... 97 A
Charmouth Prim Sch DT6 97 A
Charmouth Rd DT7.... 96 C
Charnock Cl SO41.... 95 F
Charnwood Ave BH9.... 90 B
Charnwood Cl 1 BH22.... 53 A
Chartcombe BH13.... 147 E
Charter Rd BH11.... 88 D
Chartwell
　5 Poole BH13.... 121 B
　Radipole DT4.... 167 D
Chaseborough Sq 4
　DT1.... 107 D
Chase Cres SP5.... 188 E
Chaseside BH4.... 123 A
Chase The
　St Leonards BH24.... 54 F
　Verwood BH31.... 45 E
Chaston La DT2.... 208 C
Chatham Rd SO22.... 126 A
Chatsworth Rd
　Bournemouth BH8.... 122 C
　Poole BH14.... 120 B
　Yeovil BA21.... 27 F
Chatsworth Way BH25.. 94 F
Chaucer Cl BH21.... 59 C
Chaucer Rd BH13.... 147 E
Chaucombe Pl BH25.... 94 F
Chaundler Rd SO23.... 126 E
Cheam Rd BH18.... 86 F
Cheap St DT9.... 30 B
Checkridge La EX13.... 202 A
Cheddington Rd BH9.... 90 A
Chedington Cl BH17.... 87 E
Chedington Court Golf Club
　DT8.... 192 D
Chedington La DT8.... 204 B
Cheese La DT3.... 150 E

helmsford Rd BH16..... 118 A7
helmsford St DT4..... 167 D4
helston Ave BA21.....27 D7
heltenham Rd BH12... 120 C5
helwood Gate DT4..... 166 E3
hene Rd BH21.....59 D4
herford Rd BH11.....89 B2
herita Ct BH15..... 119 F6
heriton BH4..... 121 C2
heriton Ave BH7..... 123 C8
heriton Cl SO22..... 126 B7
heriton Rd SO22..... 126 C6
heriton Way BH21..... 59 C6
herrett Cl BH1.....88 F4
herries Dr BH9.....89 E2
herry Cl
  Poole BH14..... 120 B4
  Sandford BH20..... 143 B8
herry Cl BH5..... 120 B5
herryfields SP8.....5 F4
herry Gr BH22.....61 C6
herry Tree Cl 100 B8
herry Tree Cl BH24.....53 F3
herry Tree Ct
  9 Crewkerne TA18.....191 F5
  4 New Milton BH25..... 95 B1
herry Tree Dr
  Beckley BH25.....94 E5
  Yeovil BA21.....26 F2
hescombe Cl DT2..... 207 D3
hescombe La DT11..... 210 B3
heselbourne Villiage Sch
  DT2.....209 A3
heshire Dr BH8.....90 A1
hesil Beach DT3..... 149 C2
hesil Beach Holiday Village
  DT4.....180 C5
hesil Beach Visitor Ctr
  DT4.....180 D4
hesilborne Gr BH8.....90 D3
hesildene Rd BH8.....90 D3
hesildene Dr BH8.....90 D3
hesil Gdns BH12..... 120 B8
hesil Terr SO23..... 126 F5
hesil Terr SO23..... 126 F5
hesil View BH14..... 120 B4
hessel Ave BH5.....122 F4
hessels Cl BA22..... 193 B8
hester Cl DT1..... 135 C8
hesterfield Cl BH17..... 147 F8
hesterfield Ct BH1..... 122 C3
hester Rd
  Poole BH15..... 121 A2
  Winchester SO23..... 126 F6
hestnut Ave
  Barton on Sea BH25.....127 A8
  Bournemouth BH6..... 123 C4
  Christchurch BH23..... 123 D8
  Verwood BH24.....46 D6
hestnut Cl DT2..... 207 D3
hestnut Dr BA20.....27 B3
hestnut Gr
  Blandford Forum DT11 ..212 B4
  Ferndown BH21.....60 E6
hestnut Pl DT3..... 167 C7
hestnut Rd
  Bridport DT6..... 100 D4
  Charminster DT2.....75 D2
hestnut Way
  Burton BH23.....92 C3
  Dorchester DT1..... 107 D2
  Gillingham SP8.....5 D1
hetcombe Rd BA12.....3 B6
hetnole Cl BH17.....88 A1
hetnole Sta DT9..... 194 C2
hetwode Way BH17.....87 B2
heviot Court Flats
  BH23.....124 F8
heviots The BH14..... 120 C3
heviot Way BH31.....45 E5
hewton Common Rd
  BH23.....126 B8
hewton Farm Rd BH23..94 C1
hewton Lodge BH23..... 126 B8
hewton Mews BH23.....94 A2
hewton Way BH23.....94 B1
heyne Cl **1** DT5..... 186 E1
heyne Gdns BH4..... 121 C2
hichester Rd **8** BH24.....47 E1
hichester Way BH23.....125 A5
hichester Wlk SO23.....59 E1
hickerell Cl BH9.....90 B3
hickerell Hill DT3..... 166 B6
hickerell Prim Sch
  DT3.....166 D5
hickerell Rd DT3..... 166 D4
hick's Copse La DT2... 205 F6
hiddeock Cl BH12..... 120 E6
hiddeock Hill DT6.....98 E7
higwell Rd BH8.....90 B1
hilbolton Ave DT2..... 107 E2
hilbolton Ct SO22..... 126 A5
hilbury Gdns DT10..... 155 D7
hilcombe Cl DT6..... 102 D3
hilcombe Hts SO23.....19 C7
hilcombe La DT6..... 102 D3
hilcombe Rd BH6..... 123 B5
hilday La DT8..... 203 C6
hilfrome Cl BH17.....87 C1

Chilfrome La
  Chilfrome DT2.....206 B1
  Maiden Newton DT2....72 E8
Chiltern Cl
  Old Milton BH25.....94 F1
  Poole BH4..... 121 B5
Chiltern Ct **5** BH23.....124 F8
Chiltern Dr
  Barton on Sea BH25.....126 E8
  Verwood BH31.....45 B6
Chilton Gr BA21.....27 C7
Chimes The BH4..... 121 C3
China La **1** DT11..... 199 F7
Chine Ct BH2..... 121 D2
Chine Crescent Rd BH2.. 121 D2
Chine Wlk BH2.....61 E1
Chinnock Hollow BA22..192 E8
Chippel La DT10.....20 F1
Chisels La BH23.....125 A6
Chislehurst **18** BH4..... 121 C3
Chiswell DT5..... 186 E8
Chiswell Rd BH17.....87 D1
Chitten Hill DT2..... 115 C7
Chivrick Cl DT10.....35 C3
Chloe Gdns DT2..... 120 D7
Chowins Rd **18** TA18..... 191 F4
Chris Cres BH16..... 118 C7
Christchurch Bay Rd
  BH25.....126 F7
Christchurch By-Pass
  BH23.....124 D8
Christchurch Castle
  BH23.....124 B6
Christchurch Gdns **1**
  SO23.....126 D3
Christchurch Hospl
  BH23.....123 F8
Christchurch Jun Sch
  BH23.....124 A7
Christchurch Prim Sch
  BH23.....124 C7
Christchurch Priory
  BH23.....124 C6
Christchurch Rd
  Barton on Sea BH25.....126 D8
  Bournemouth BH1,BH7.. 122 D4
  Bournemouth BH7..... 123 B6
  Ferndown BH22.....61 C1
  Hurn BH23.....91 C5
  Ringwood BH24.....55 C4
  Winchester SO23..... 126 D3
  Winchester SO23..... 126 D5
Christchurch Sta BH23...124 A7
Christopher Cl BA20.....27 A5
Christopher Cres BH15..119 C6
Christ's Hospital **13**
  SO23.....126 D5
Christ the King RC Prim Sch
  BH11.....89 A5
Christy's Gdns **2** DT5.....12 F3
Christy's La **5** DT5.....12 F3
Church Acre **3** DT1....108 B2
Church Cl
  Beer Hackett DT9.....194 D6
  2 Bourton SP8.....1 D1
  Bridport DT6.....69 A1
  Chetnole DT9..... 194 D3
  9 Dorchester DT1..... 108 A2
  Fontmell Magna SP7.....37 F7
  Longburton DT9..... 195 B7
  Stour Provost SP7.....22 C7
  5 Swanage BH19..... 179 B2
  Todber DT10..... 21 D4
Church Gn
  Buckhorn Weston SP8..... 9 B6
  2 Wareham BH20.....142 E3
Church Hill
  Bishop's Caundle DT9 ..196 A8
  Dinnington TA17..... 191 B7
  Iwerne Minster DT11.....37 F2
  Kington Magna SP8.....9 D3
  Langton Herring DT3..... 150 C1
  Marnhull DT10..... 21 A3
  Milborne St Andrew DT11...79 E7
  Piddlehinton DT2.....76 F7
  Shaftesbury SP7.....12 D3
  Stalbridge DT10.....19 C1
  2 Swanage BH19..... 179 B2
  West Stour SP8.....10 A3
  Woodlands BH21.....44 B7
Church Hill La DT2..... 104 D7
Church Hill View DT11..207 A2
Churchill Cl
  Alderholt SP6.....42 A5
  Sturminster Marshall BH21..56 D4
  4 Weymouth BH4..... 180 C8
Churchill Cres BH12..... 120 C6
Churchill Ct BH15.....94 F2
Churchill Dro BH21.....40 E7
Churchill Rd BH12..... 120 C5
Churchill Rd
  Blandford Forum DT11 ..212 D4
  Bournemouth BH1..... 122 E5
  Bovington Camp DT2.....139 C7
  Poole BH12..... 120 C6
  Wimborne Minster BH21...59 E3
Church Knap DT4..... 180 C8
Church Knowle Animal
  Sanctuary BH20.....176 B7

Church La
  Barwick BA22..... 193 E8
  Bere Regis BH20.....81 B2
  1 Blandford Forum DT11. 212 D3
  Charlton Marshall DT11.. 211 C6
  Chickerell DT3..... 151 D2
  Christchurch BH23..... 124 B6
  Coombe Keynes BH20..... 158 A5
  Crewkerne TA18..... 192 A3
  Damerham SP6..... 190 F2
  Easton/Weston DT5..... 186 F1
  East Orchard SP7.....36 F7
  Ferndown BH22.....89 F7
  Frampton DT2.....73 F3
  Godmanstone DT2.....75 B7
  Haselbury Plucknett TA18 192 C5
  Leigh DT9..... 194 E3
  Margaret Marsh SP7.....22 C2
  Old Milton BH25.....94 F1
  Osmington DT3..... 154 A1
  Overcombe/Preston DT3.. 169 A8
  Owermoigne DT2.....155 D7
  Piddletrenthide DT2..... 208 B3
  Portesham DT3..... 150 A8
  Rimpton BA22.....28 B7
  Shaftesbury SP7.....12 E2
  Stinsford DT2..... 108 E3
  Stour Provost SP8.....21 C7
  2 Sturminster Newton
    DT10.....197 D8
  Sutton Waldron DT11.....37 E4
  Sydling St Nicholas DT2 ..207 A2
  Wareham BH20.....142 F3
  Wool BH20.....140 B2
Churchmoor Rd BH21.....60 A5
Church Ope DT5..... 187 B3
Church Path
  2 Crewkerne TA18..... 191 F6
  Litton Cheney DT2..... 103 C2
  Yeovil BA20.....27 D5
Church Rd
  Bournemouth BH6..... 123 F4
  Bradford Abbas DT9.....28 D1
  Durweston DT11..... 198 E3
  Ferndown BH22.....61 C5
  Iwerne Minster DT11.....37 F1
  Maiden Newton DT2.....72 F8
  Overcombe/Preston DT3.. 168 D8
  Pimperne DT11..... 199 D5
  Poole BH14..... 120 A4
  5 Shillingstone DT11....198 B6
  Silton SP8.....2 A1
  Studland BH19..... 164 D2
  Thornford DT9..... 194 D8
  Three Legged Cross BH21..45 A1
  West Lulworth BH20..... 172 C6
Church Row DT11..... 209 C6
Church St
  Bridport DT6..... 100 D6
  Burton Bradstock DT6.....128 B8
  Christchurch BH23..... 124 B6
  Cranborne BH21.....40 A7
  Dewlish DT2..... 209 C1
  7 Dorchester DT1..... 108 A2
  Fontmell Magna SP7.....37 F7
  Fordingbridge SP6.....43 A8
  Henstridge BA8.....19 A4
  Hinton St George TA17 ..191 C7
  Kington Magna SP8.....9 C3
  Lyme Regis DT7.....96 C5
  Mere BA12.....3 A5
  Merriott TA16..... 191 F7
  Milborne Port DT9.....17 D2
  Poole BH15..... 119 B1
  Puncknowle DT2..... 129 C6
  Shapwick DT11.....56 B8
  Sturminster Marshall BH21..56 D4
  Sturminster Newton DT10....35 B1
  Upwey DT3..... 152 A7
  Wareham BH20.....142 E3
  2 West Coker BA22..... 193 A8
  West Stour SP8.....10 A3
  6 Wimborne Minster BH21..59 B5
  Winterborne Kingston DT11.81 E8
  Yeovil BA20.....27 D5
Church Track SP8.....5 E1
Church View SP8.....5 E1
Churchward Ave DT3..... 153 B1
Churchwell **3** DT7.....28 D1
Churchwell St DT9.....28 D1
Church Wlk
  Littlebredy DT2..... 131 D7
  Motcombe SP7.....12 C8
  Okeford Fitzpaine DT11...197 E4
Chur La BA21..... 193 A8
Churlands Cl BA22..... 193 A8
Chydyck Rd DT2..... 156 C3
Cinnamon La **7** BH15.....119 B1
Circle The
  3 Bournemouth BH9.....90 A4
  Poole BH13..... 147 F7
City Bsns Ctr SO23..... 126 E6
City Rd SO23..... 126 E6
Claire Ct **6** BH4..... 121 C3
Clammer Hill La TA18... 191 F4
Clanfield DT9.....29 F4
Clap La SP5..... 188 B4
Clappentail La DT7..... 96 A5
Clappentail Pk DT7.....96 A5
Clapton Court Gdns
  TA18.....191 D1
Clapton Rd TA18..... 191 D3
Clare Ave DT4..... 166 E2
Claremont Ave
  Bournemouth BH9.....90 B2
  Gillingham SP8.....5 F3

Claremont Gdns DT6..... 100 D8
Claremont Rd
  Bournemouth BH9.....90 B2
  Bridport DT6..... 100 D8
Clarence Cl **2** DT5..... 186 F4
Clarence Ct BA20.....27 C5
Clarence Park Rd BH1.. 123 A6
Clarence Pl BH23..... 123 F8
Clarence Rd
  Dorchester DT1..... 134 F8
  Easton/Weston DT5..... 186 F4
  3 Poole BH14..... 120 A3
  Weymouth DT4..... 166 F1
Clarence St BA20.....27 C4
Clarence Terr **4** BA20.....27 D4
Clarendon Ave DT3..... 152 C1
Clarendon Cl
  Broadstone BH18.....87 A4
  Gillingham SP8.....5 D2
Clarendon Ct **3** BH2.. 121 D2
Clarendon Rd
  Bournemouth BH4..... 121 D3
  Broadstone BH18.....86 F4
  Christchurch BH23..... 124 A7
Clarkham Cross BA22... 193 E2
Clarks Cl BA22..... 193 D2
Clark's Cl BH24.....55 C7
Clark's La **3** TA18..... 192 A3
Clatcombe La DT9.....15 F3
Claudius Cl DT1..... 134 E2
Clausentum Rd SO23.. 126 D3
Clay Castle TA18..... 192 C5
Clay Castle La **5** TA18.. 192 C5
Clayesmore Prep Sch
  DT11.....37 E2
Clayesmore Sch DT11.....37 E2
Clayford Ave BH22.....61 B7
Clayford Cl **1** BH17.....87 D2
Clay La
  Beaminster DT8..... 204 C4
  Puncknowle DT2..... 129 F4
Claylake Dr BH31.....45 C5
Claylands La DT1..... 204 A3
Clay Pigeon Raceway
  DT2.....206 E5
Claypits La
  Beer Hackett DT9..... 194 D6
  Winfrith Newburgh DT2.. 157 A6
Clayton Cl
  Radipole DT3..... 152 D3
  Yeovil BA22.....27 A5
Clearmount Rd DT4..... 180 E8
Cleasby Grange **2** BH5..122 F3
Cleeve Ho BH5..... 126 F7
Cleeves Cl BH12.....88 D2
Clematis Cl BH23..... 125 C8
Clement Mews BH4..... 121 B3
Clements La BH15..... 186 E8
Clement's La BA12.....3 A5
Clenston Rd DT11..... 210 C7
Cleveland Ave DT4..... 167 D7
Cleveland Cl BH20..... 126 D7
Cleveland Ct **4** BH2.. 121 D2
Cleveland Gdns BH1.. 122 C5
Cleverlawns DT3..... 148 F7
Cleves Cl DT4..... 180 E7
Cleve The BA21.....26 E6
Cliff Ave BH19..... 179 C4
Cliff Cres BH23..... 126 F7
Cliff Dr
  Christchurch BH23..... 125 C6
  Poole BH13..... 147 E6
Cliffe Rd BH23..... 126 E7
Clifford Rd BH9.....90 A1
Cliff Rd DT6..... 128 B7
Cliff Way DT5..... 186 D1
Cliff Wlk **11** BH4..... 121 C2
Clift La DT2..... 205 D1
Clifton Cl
  Swanage BH19..... 179 C4
  Yeovil BA21.....28 A6
Clifton Ct
  1 Bournemouth BH7.....122 F4
  Hamworthy BH15..... 118 D4
  3 New Milton BH25.....95 A1
Clifton Gdns BH22.....61 C4
Clifton Hill
  Clifton Maybank SP7..... 193 E8
  Winchester SO23..... 126 D6
Clifton Lodge No 1 **18**
  SO22.....126 A6
Clifton Lodge No 2 **19**
  SO22.....126 A6
Clifton Pl **1** DT4..... 167 D3
Clifton Rd
  Bournemouth BH6..... 123 D3
  Clifton Maybank SP7..... 194 B8
  Poole BH14..... 120 E2
  Swanage BH19..... 179 B4
  Winchester SO23..... 126 D6
Clifton Terr SO22..... 126 D6
Clifton View **3** BA22.. 193 F8
Clingan Rd BH6..... 123 D7
Clinton Cl BH23.....94 B2
Clive Ct **2** BH4..... 121 C3
Cliveden Cl BH17.....61 C7
Clive Rd
  Bournemouth BH9.....89 F1
  Christchurch BH23.....93 E2
Clivia Cl DT3..... 152 E2
Cloisters The
  3 Christchurch BH23...124 B6
  2 Ringwood BH24.....55 B6
Close Dr **8** TA18..... 192 A3
Close The
  Barton on Sea BH25.....127 B8
  Blandford Forum DT11 ..212 D3

Che–Col **221**

Close The continued
  Broadstone BH18.....86 E3
  Charlton Marshall DT11... 211 D6
  8 Merriott TA16..... 191 F7
  12 Pimperne DT11..... 199 D4
  Ringwood BH24.....55 B7
  St Leonards BH24.....54 C4
Clouds Hill BH20..... 143 C2
Clough's Rd BH24.....55 D7
Clovens Rd DT5..... 186 F7
Clover Cl BH23..... 125 B8
Clover Ct BH25.....95 C4
Clover Dr BH17.....86 F1
Cloverfields SP7.....12 E4
Clovermead DT9..... 194 B6
Clovers The BH12..... 121 A8
Clovers Wlk **5** BA20.....27 C4
Clowes Ave BH6..... 124 B3
Clump Farm Ind Est
  DT11.....212 D6
Clump Hill BH21.....44 C1
Cluny Cres BH19..... 179 C2
Clyde Rd BH17.....87 B2
Clyffe View DT2..... 137 D6
Clyppetts **2** DT11.....81 E8
Coach House Mews BH2..61 F2
Coach House Pl BH1.... 122 A5
Coach Rd
  1 Stourpaine DT11..... 198 F4
  Winterborne St Giles BH21.. 201 C7
Coach Rd The DT7.....64 A2
Coastguard Cotts BH25..126 E8
Coastguard Rd
  5 Fortuneswell DT5..... 186 F8
  Langton Herring DT3..... 150 B1
Coastguard Way BH23 ..124 F5
Cobbett Cl SO22..... 126 A3
Cobb Rd DT7.....96 B4
Cobbs La BH15..... 119 C6
Cobb's Rd BH21.....59 E6
Cobham Dr DT4..... 166 F3
Cobham Rd
  Blandford Forum DT11 ..212 E6
  Bournemouth BH9.....90 A3
  Ferndown BH21.....61 A8
  Ferndown Town BH22.....52 D1
Cobham Way BH21.....59 E1
Cobley Cl SP5..... 189 D6
Coburg Rd DT1..... 107 E1
Cockerell Cl BH21.....59 F1
Cocklands DT1..... 107 C6
Cockles La DT4..... 167 A1
Cockpit Hill DT6..... 203 C4
Codge La DT2..... 205 E5
Cod La BA22..... 192 D7
Codogan Rd **3** BH1.....122 B3
Cogdean Cl BH21.....86 E8
Cogdean Ct BH17.....87 D2
Cogdean Way BH21.....86 E8
Cogdean Wlk BH21.....86 E8
Coker Cl SO22..... 126 C6
Coker Hill La BA22..... 192 F8
Coker Hill La BA22..... 193 A7
Colber Medieval Village of
  DT10.....34 F1
Colborne Ave BH21.....59 F6
Colborne Cl BH15..... 119 D5
Colbourne Cl BH23.....93 A8
Colbourne Ct **7** SO23..126 E8
Coldharbour SP8.....5 E2
Cold Harbour
  Milborne Port DT9.....17 D2
  Sherborne DT9.....30 C7
Cold Harbour Bsns Pk
  DT9.....30 B8
Cold Harbour La BA22 ..192 F6
Colebrook Pl SO23..... 126 C5
Colehill Cres BH9.....90 B3
Colehill Dro DT2..... 156 D6
Colehill Fst Sch BH21.....60 B7
Colehill La
  Colehill BH21.....59 F8
  Holt BH21.....51 C1
  Wimborne Minster BH21...60 A8
Colehill Rd BH20.....83 F6
Coleman Rd BH11.....89 A3
Colemere Gdns BH23 ..125 C8
Colemore Rd BH7..... 123 C7
Coleridge Gn BH23..... 124 F8
Cole St La BH11.....11 B6
Coles Ave BH15..... 118 E2
Coles Cl DT1.....35 C1
Cole's Cross BH21..... 203 A5
Coles Gdns BH15..... 118 C2
Coles La
  Milborne St Andrew
    DT11.....209 F1
  Yetminster DT9..... 194 B6
Cole's La SP7.....12 A1
Colin Cl BH21.....86 D5
Collarway La BA22..... 192 F8
College BA22..... 192 E8
College Cl SO22..... 126 A3
College Ct **3** BH1..... 122 C3
College Gn BA11..... 193 A8
College Rd
  Blandford Camp DT11 ..199 D8
  Bournemouth BH5..... 123 A4
  Ringwood BH24.....55 C7
College St SO23..... 126 E5
College Wlk SO23..... 126 E5
Collett Cl DT1..... 153 B1
Colletts Ct BH21.....177 A7
Collier's La BH20..... 139 F1
Collingbourne Ave BH6..123 D7

Collingwood Cl **7** DT11. 199 D4
Collingwood Rd BH21......53 A6
Collins La
 Ringwood BH24..........55 C7
 Weymouth DT4.........180 C7
Colliton St DT1.........108 A2
Coll of Air Traffic Control
 BH23..................90 F7
Collwood Cl BH5.......119 C7
Collyer's Rise SP7......37 F6
Colman Ct BH1........122 C3
Colmer Rd BA21........27 D5
Cologne Rd BH20......140 A6
Colonnade Rd **3** BH5..123 A5
Colonnade Road W **2**
 BH5..................123 A5
Colson Cl BH23........126 F6
Colson Rd SO23.......126 F6
Colt Cl BH21...........60 B6
Columbian Way BH10...89 C2
Columbia Rd BH10......89 D2
Columbia Trees La BH10..89 C1
Columbine Cl BH23......93 B1
Colville Cl **4** BH5....123 A5
Colville Rd **5** BH5...123 A5
Colway Cl DT7.........96 B7
Colway La DT7.........96 B6
Colwell Sln Ctr DT4...167 D3
Combe Hill
 Milborne Port DT9......17 B3
 Templecombe BA8......18 E8
Comber Rd **1** BH9....90 A3
Combe Way DT2.......137 C5
Comet Cl DT4..........166 F1
Comet Way BH23.......125 A6
Comley Rd BH9.........89 F2
Commercial Rd
 Bournemouth BH1.......121 E3
 Poole BH14...........120 A4
 Radipole DT4.........167 D2
 Swanage BH19.........179 C2
Common Dro
 6 Child Okeford DT11...198 C8
 Farnham DT11.........188 B3
Common Hill DT8........203 E5
Common La
 4 Blandford Forum
  DT11...............212 D3
 Burton Bradstock DT6...128 C7
 East Stour SP8..........11 A3
 Halstock BA22.........193 D2
 Hardington Mandeville
  BA22...............193 A6
 Haselbury Plucknett TA18.192 D5
 Henstridge BA8.........18 F8
 Kington Magna SP8......9 C1
 Marnhull DT10..........34 D8
 Ryme Intrinseca DT9....194 B5
 Sturminster Newton DT10.197 D8
 Toller Porcorum DT2....205 D2
Common Mead Ave SP8...5 D1
Common Mead La SP8....5 D1
Common Rd SP5........188 F4
Common The
 Evershot DT2.........206 A4
 Hazelbury Bryan DT10..196 E5
 Moreton DT2..........138 C8
Common Water La DT8..203 F5
Compton Abbas Airfield
 SP5..................24 E2
Compton Acres Gdns
 BH13.................114 A4
Compton Ave BH14.....120 D1
Compton Beeches BH24..54 C5
Compton Cl
 Verwood BH31..........45 B6
 3 Yeovil BA21.........28 A8
Compton Cres BH22.....53 C1
Compton Ct
 4 Bournemouth BH6...123 F4
 Poole BH14...........120 D3
Compton Dr BH14......120 C2
Compton Gdns BH14....120 C2
Compton Lo **26** BH6...121 C3
Compton Rd
 New Milton BH25........95 A2
 Over Compton DT9......28 C5
 Winchester SO23......126 D5
Concorde Cl DT4.......166 F1
Condor Cl BH21.........53 D6
Coneygar Cl DT6.......100 D8
Coneygar La
 Bridport DT6..........100 D8
 Ferndown BH22.........61 B3
Coney Gn **18** SO23...126 E8
Conifer Ave BH14......120 B2
Conifer Cl
 Christchurch BH23......91 D3
 Ferndown BH22........61 F1
 St Leonards BH24......53 F4
 Winchester SO22......126 D2
Conifers **4** BH21....121 B3
Conifers Prim Sch DT4..167 A3
Coniston Ave BH11......88 F6
Coniston Cl BH31.......45 A5
Coniston Cres DT3.....167 C7
Coniston Gdns BA21....27 B7
Coniston Rd BH4.......54 C6
Connaught Cl BH25......94 E1
Connaught Cres BH12..120 E6
Connaught Gdns DT4...167 B1
Connaught Rd
 Bournemouth BH5......123 B5

Connaught Rd continued
 2 Weymouth DT4......180 E8
Connell Rd BH15.......119 C5
Conniger La BH20......142 F3
Conservatory The **8**
 SO23.................126 F5
Consort Cl DT1.........120 C5
Consort Ho BH22.......61 D6
Constable Cl
 Ferndown BH22........61 C4
 Yeovil BA21...........28 A8
Constable's Gate **10**
 SO23.................126 D5
Constitution Hill Gdns
 BH14.................120 A5
Constitution Hill Rd
 BH14.................120 A5
Convent Meadow Mobile
 Home Site BH23......124 C5
Conway Cl DT4..........95 B3
Conway Ct **10** BH25...95 B3
Conway Dr DT2.........136 B2
Conways Dr BH14......120 A4
Conway Wlk **7** DT1...135 C8
Cook Cl BH24...........55 E8
Cooke Gdns DT1.......120 F6
Cooke Rd BH12........120 F6
Cook Row BH21.........59 B4
Cooks La DT9...........30 B5
Cook's La DT10.........33 C3
Cookswell **11** DT11..198 B6
Coolhurst BH14.......147 C7
Coombe DT9.............30 A7
Coombe Ave
 Bournemouth BH10......89 E3
 Radipole DT4.........167 E6
Coombe Cl BA21........27 C8
Coombe Gdns BH10.....89 E2
Coombe Heath Nature
 Reserve BH20.........158 E6
Coombe Hill BH19.....178 C2
Coombe La
 Castleton DT9.........15 D1
 Stoke Abbott DT8......203 E3
Coombe Rd
 Dinnington TA17......191 B7
 Puddletown DT2........78 B1
 5 Shillingstone DT11..198 B5
 Winterborne Steepleton
  DT2................105 E1
Coombe St La BA21....127 C8
Coombes Cl DT21......123 A8
Coombe St
 Lyme Regis DT7........96 C5
 Pen Selwood BA9.......1 D3
Coombe Valley Rd DT3..153 A2
Coombe Wr La DT8.....203 B6
Cooper Dean Dr BH8....90 F1
Cooper Dean Rdbt The BH7.
 ....91 A1
Cooper Gdns **2** DT11..198 B8
Cooper's Cl **2** BH20..142 E4
Coopers Cl DT6.......100 D3
Coopers La BH31........45 B8
Copeland Dr BH14.....120 B2
Copper Beech Cl BH13..121 A4
Copper Beeches **2** BH2..121 F4
Copper Beech Gdns BH10.89 D2
Coppercourt Leaze **5**
 BH21.................59 C4
Coppers Ct SP6........42 C6
Coppice Ave BH22.....126 F4
Coppice Cl
 New Milton BH25........95 D4
 St Leonards BH24......54 B4
 West Coker BA20.......26 F2
 Winchester SO22......126 A7
Coppice The
 Chickerell DT3.......166 E5
 Christchurch BH23....125 B6
Coppice View BH10.....89 E3
Copse Cl BH25.........95 E3
Copse Cl BH14........119 F3
Copse Hill DT10......197 E7
Copse Rd
 Brympton BA22........26 D7
 New Milton BH25........95 B2
 Verwood BH31..........45 B6
Copse The BH24........62 C8
Copse Way BH23......123 E8
Copsewood Ave BH8.....90 E1
Copythorne Cl BH8......90 D2
Coral Ct **3** BH14.....121 A4
Coram Ave DT7.........96 B4
Coram Cl **3** SO23...126 E8
Corbar Rd BH23.......123 E8
Corbiere Ave BH12......88 D1
Corbin Way DT6........62 A6
Corbon Rd BH25........95 D3
Cordery Gdns SP8......5 F3
Cordova Gdns DT6....100 D7
Corfe Castle Fst Sch
 BH20................161 F1
Corfe Castle Model Village &
 Gdns BH20...........177 A8
Corfe Castle Mus **3**
 BH20................162 A1
Corfe Castle Sta BH20.162 A2
Corfe Hall Cl BH21......58 E1
Corfe Hills Sch BH18....86 F6
Corfe Lodge Rd BH18..86 D3
Corfe Mews BH15.....119 D4
Corfe Mullen Mdw Nature
 Reserve BH21..........85 D6

Corfe Rd
 Arne BH20.............160 F8
 Radipole DT3.........167 B8
 Stoborough Green BH20..142 E1
Corfe View Rd
 Corfe Mullen BH21......86 C5
 Poole BH18............86 C5
Corfe Way BH18.........86 E3
Corfu BH15.............147 E6
Corhampton Rd BH6....123 C6
Cornelia Cres BH12....121 A6
Corner Cl DT11.........21 B3
Corner La SP7...........7 C2
Corner The
 1 Iwerne Courtney or Shroton
  DT11...............198 C7
 Winchester SO23......126 C7
Cornerways Ct **3** BH25..95 B3
Cornes Cl SO23........126 B5
Cornflower Ct DT3.....152 F2
Cornflower Dr BH23....125 C8
Cornford Hill DT9.....196 A6
Cornford Way BH23....125 D8
Cornhill DT9...........30 A6
Cornhill Way DT3.....153 C2
Cornish Gdns BH10.....89 D1
Cornmarket Cl **7** BH21..59 B5
Cornpits La SP6.......190 E2
Cornwall Cl DT4.......167 A3
Cornwall Rd
 2 Dorchester DT1....107 F2
 2 Swanage BH19......179 C2
Coronation Ave
 Bournemouth BH9.......89 F2
 Upton BH16...........118 B7
 Yeovil BA21...........27 A7
Coronation Cl BH31.....45 B7
Coronation Rd
 Bridport DT6.........100 C5
 1 Fortuneswell DT5...186 F8
 Gillingham SP8.........5 E2
 Radipole DT4.........167 C7
 Verwood BH31..........45 B7
Corporation Rd
 Bournemouth BH1......122 C5
 Weymouth DT4........167 B3
Corpus Christi RC Prim Sch
 BH5..................123 A5
Corscombe Cl
 Poole BH17...........121 C3
 Radipole DT4.........167 D3
Corscombe **20** BH4...121 C2
Corton Cl **1** BA21.....28 A8
Cortry Cl BH12.........121 C2
Cossack La **2** SO23..126 E6
Cossack Lane Ho **26**
 SO23.................126 E6
Cossins La **1** TA18...191 F4
Cotes Ave BH11........120 A5
Cotes Ct BH14.........120 A5
Cothayes Dro DT2.....209 A6
Cotlands Rd BH1......122 B4
Cotswold Cl BH31......45 B6
Cotswold Ct **6** BH24...124 F8
Cottage Cl BH14.......140 A2
Cottage Gdns BH12....120 F5
Cottage Mews **2** BH4..55 B7
Cotton Cl BH18.........86 F5
Council Hos BH23......63 F2
Counter Cl DT11.......212 F5
Countess Cl BH21......87 E8
Countess Gdns BH21..122 F8
County Gates La **18** BH4..121 B4
County Hall DT1.......107 F2
County Mus DT1.......108 A2
County Records Office
 DT1..................107 F2
Court Ash BA20.........27 D5
Courtauld Dr DT4......180 D8
Court Barton
 3 Crewkerne TA18...191 E4
 Easton/Weston BH4....186 E4
Court Cl
 Bridport DT6..........68 F1
 3 Christchurch BH23..124 E7
Courtenay Cl BH20....142 F6
Courtenay Dr BH23....125 D8
Courtenay Rd BH14....120 B4
Court Gdns BA21........27 A8
Court Hill
 Corscombe DT2.......205 B8
 Damerham SP6.........190 F2
Courthill Fst Sch BH14..120 D4
Courthill Rd BH14.....120 D4
Court La
 Corscombe DT2.......205 B8
 Milborne Port DT9......17 C3
 5 Stofold BA22......193 F8
Courtlands Rd DT3.....167 E3
Courtleigh Manor **6**
 BH15.................122 C4
Courtney Cl DT11......198 E8
Courtney Pl BH21......86 C5
Court Orchard Rd DT6..100 C8
Court Rd
 Bournemouth BH9.......90 B1
 Radipole DT3.........152 B2
 Wimborne Minster BH21..60 A1
Covena Rd BH23........86 E6
Coventry Cl BH31.......45 C3
Coventry Cres BH17.....87 A1
Coventry Ct **6** SO23..126 E8
Cove Rd BH10..........89 B4
Cove Row **5** DT4.....167 E2

Cove St DT4...........167 E2
Cowards La DT3.......149 A7
Cow Down Rd DT4.....202 C8
Cowdray Ho **22** SO23..126 D6
Cowdray Gdns BH6......90 F2
Cow Dro BH20..........81 C2
Cowdrys Field **2** BH21..59 B6
Cowell Dr BH17.......123 B8
Cowen Cl TA18........191 F3
Cowgrove Rd BH21......58 F5
Cow La
 Long Bredy DT2.......103 C1
 Swanage BH20........179 A2
 Wareham BH20........142 E3
Cowlease **1** BH19....179 C2
Cowlease Rd DT2......133 D6
Cowleaze Rd DT20....136 B1
Cowley Cl **2** DT11...107 E1
Cowley Rd BH17.......119 D8
Cowleys Rd BH23.......92 C2
Cowper Ave BH25.......95 A1
Cowper Rd BH9.........89 F2
Cowpitts La BH24.......47 F2
Cowslip Rd BH18.......86 A2
Cox Ave BH9...........90 B4
Cox Cl BH21............90 B4
Cox Hill DT10..........34 D7
Cox's La
 Litton Cheney DT2....103 B1
 Long Bredy DT2.......130 D8
Coxstone La BH24.......55 B6
Coy Pond Rd BH12....121 B5
Crabbswood La SO41....95 E8
Crab La BA12...........2 B6
Crab Orchard Way BH25..45 A2
Crabton Close Rd BH5..122 F4
Crabtree Cl BH23.......92 C2
Crack La BH19.........178 C3
Crackmore DT9.........17 C1
Craigmoor Ave BH8.....90 F1
Craigmoor Cl BH8......90 F1
Craigmoor Way BH8.....90 E2
Craigside Rd BH24......53 F4
Craigwood Dr DT2......61 E4
Cranborne CE VA Fst Sch
 BH21.................40 B7
Cranborne Ct
 17 Bournemouth BH4...121 C3
 Bournemouth BH9......122 B8
Cranborne Dr **1** SP7...12 F4
Cranborne Manor BH21..40 A7
Cranborne Mid Sch BH21..40 B8
Cranborne Pl BH25.....123 A7
Cranborne Rd
 Alderholt SP6..........41 C5
 Bournemouth BH2......121 C2
 Hinton Parva BH21.....50 C5
 Swanage BH19.........179 B7
 Wimborne Minster BH21..59 C7
Cranbourne Ct BH17.....88 A2
Cranbrook Mews BH12..120 B6
Cranbrook Rd BH12....120 B6
Crane Cl BH31...........45 A7
Crane Dr BH31..........45 A6
Cranemoor Cl BH23.....93 E2
Cranemoor Ct BH23.....93 E2
Cranemoor Gdns BH23..93 F2
Cranes Mdw DT2......208 A8
Cranes Mews BH15....119 D3
Cranesmoor Cl BH20..139 C6
Crane St BH21..........40 B7
Crane Valley Golf Club
 BH21.................44 D6
Crane Way BH21.........53 D6
Cranfield Ave BH21......59 D5
Cranford Ave DT4.....167 E5
Cranleigh Cl BH6......123 E5
Cranleigh Gdns BH6...123 E5
Cranleigh Rd BH6......123 E5
Cranmer Rd BH21.....121 F8
Cransley Ct
 Bournemouth BH4......121 C2
 4 Wimborne Minster BH21..121 C2
Crantock Gr BH8........90 F2
Cranwell Cl BH11........88 E4
Cranworth Rd SO22...126 D7
Crate Hill DT10.......197 C5
Crate La SP7...........7 F5
Crawford Bridge DT11..211 E5
Crawford Down Rd **4**
 DT11.................199 E2
Crawford Pk DT11.....211 E4
Creasey Rd BH11.......89 A5
Creech Grange DT2...160 C1
Creech Rd BH12.......120 E6
Creech Way DT3.......167 B8
Creedy Dr BH23........91 F6
Creekmoor La BH17....119 A8
Crescent Ct
 Barton on Sea BH25...126 F2
 4 Bournemouth BH2...121 D2
Crescent Dr BH25.....126 F7
Crescent Rd
 Bournemouth BH2......121 E3
 Poole BH14...........120 A4
 Verwood BH31..........45 B6
 Wimborne Minster BH21..59 C4
Crescent St DT4.......167 E3
Crescent The
 Barton on Sea BH25...126 D8
 3 Bournemouth BH8...123 A3
 West Moors BH24......62 B8
 4 Yeovil BA21.........27 B7
Crescent Wlk BH22....61 E2
Cresta Gdns BH22.....61 E2
Crest Rd BH12........120 C6

Crewkerne Bsns Pk The **28**
 TA18.................191 F
Crewkerne Hospl TA18..191 E
Crewkerne Mus & Heritage
 Ctr TA18.............191 E
Crewkerne Sta TA18...192 A
Cribb Cl BH17..........119 E
Crichel House BH21....201 A3
Cricket La BH21........200 F7
Cricket Chambers BH1..122 A4
Cricket Cl BH23.......124 F5
Crimea Rd BH9.........121 F2
Cringle Ave BH6.......124 A4
Crispin Cl BH23.......125 F8
Crispstead La SO23....126 D1
Criterion Arc **18** BH1...121 C5
Crockford Cl BH21......95 B5
Crock La DT6..........100 E6
Crofton Cl BH21........27 D7
Crofton Pk BH23.......27 D5
Crofton Rd BA21........27 D5
Croft Rd
 Bournemouth BH9.......89 F2
 Bransgore BH23........93 B6
 Christchurch BH23....124 F7
 Easton/Weston BH4....186 E4
 Poole BH12...........120 E6
 Ringwood BH24.........47 E1
Croft The
 Wareham BH20........142 F4
 3 Yeovil BA20........26 E2
Cromer Gdns BH12.....120 F5
Cromer Rd
 Bournemouth BH8.......90 B2
 Poole BH12...........120 F5
Cromwell Pl **2** BH15..123 B5
Cromwell Rd
 Bournemouth BH5......123 A5
 Dorchester BH21......135 A8
 Poole BH15...........120 D5
 Weymouth DT4........167 B3
 4 Wimborne Minster BH21..59 D4
 Winchester SO22......126 C4
 Yeovil BA21...........27 F6
Crooked La BA9.........4 C3
Crooked Oak Hill DT6...204 D1
Crookhays SP7.........12 F4
Crook Hill DT6........204 D1
Cropmead Ind Est **29**
 TA18.................191 F4
Crosby Rd BH4.........121 A2
Crossfields DT9.........28 B1
Cross & Hand Stone DT2..206 F6
Cross Keys Pas **6** SO23..126 C5
Cross La BH23..........91 A6
Crossmead Ave BH25...95 A2
Cross Rd
 Bradford Abbas DT9....28 D2
 Swanage DT4.........180 E8
Cross St SO23.........126 D6
Cross The
 2 Bradford Abbas DT9...28 D1
 Child Okeford DT11...198 C7
 1 Okeford Fitzpaine DT11..197 F5
 Shillingstone DT11...198 B4
 3 Wool BH20.........140 B2
Crosstree Cl DT2......136 B1
Crossway **2** DT4....199 E3
Cross Way
 Bradford Abbas DT9....28 D1
 Christchurch BH23......91 D1
Crossways **13** TA20..202 A8
Crossways The BH16...118 C7
Croucher's Croft SO22..126 A7
Crouch La DT9.........196 A6
Crow Arch La **1** BH24..55 E6
Crow Arch Lane Ind Est
 BH24.................55 E6
Crowder Terr SO22....126 D5
Crowe Hill Ct **2** BH15..119 E4
Crow La BH24..........55 D6
Crown Cl BH12........120 C5
Crown Ct
 Milborne St Andrew DT11..79 E8
 4 Wimborne Minster BH21..59 B5
Crown Farm Terr DT5...187 A5
Crown Mead BH21.......59 C4
Crown Rd DT10.........21 A2
Crown Yd **2** DT2....156 F6
Crowthorne La DT7....208 A7
Crumpets Dr BH16......84 B3
Crumplers Cl BH16......84 B3
Crusader Cl **3** BH4...121 B4
Crusader Rd BH11......88 D4
Cruxton Farm Ctyd BH21..73 A6
Cruxton La DT2.........73 A6
Cucklington Gdns BH9...90 B4
Cuckoo Hill DT9......194 B4
Cuckoo La
 Broadwindsor TA20...202 F7
 Hilton DT11..........209 C2
 Stinsford DT2........109 A6
Cuckoo Rd BH12.......120 A8
Cudnell Ave BH11......88 E4
Cuffnells Cl BH24......54 C8
Cul-De-Sac BH25......126 C8
Culford Cl BH8.........90 F2
Culford Ct **1** BH8...122 A5
Cull Cl BH22...........61 F2
Culliford Cres BH17.....87 E2
Culliford Rd BH19.....179 A8
Culliford Rd N **6** DT1..135 B8
Culliford Rd S **11** DT1..135 A8
Culliford Way DT1.....152 E3

Cull La BH25 . . . . .95 B5
Cull Peppers Dish (Sink Hole) DT2 . . . . .112 A6
Cullwood La BH25 . . . . . . .95 B5
Culverhayes Cl 5 BH21 . .59 B6
Culverhayes PI BH21 . . . .59 B6
Culverlake La EX13 . . . .202 D3
Culver Mews BH23 . . . . .126 E5
Culver Rd
 New Milton BH25 . . . . . . .94 F2
 Winchester SO23 . . . . . .126 D4
Culvers Cl DT9 . . . . .30 A6
Culvers La SP8 . . . . .5 C1
Culvervell Gdns 4
 SO23 . . . . .126 D5
Cumberland Dr BH14 . . .166 F4
Cumnor Rd BH1 . . . . . . .122 A3
Cunnage La BA12 . . . . .3 C5
Cunningham Cl
 BH11 . . . . .89 A3
 Bovington Camp BH20 . .139 F2
 Christchurch BH23 . . . . .125 A6
 4 Ringwood BH24 . . . . .55 E8
 8 Weymouth DT4 . . . . .180 B8
Cunningham Cres BH11 . .89 B3
Cunningham Ct BH21 . . . .59 B6
Cunningham PI BH11 . . . .89 A3
Cunnington Cl DT1 . . . . .134 E7
Curlew Cl
 1 Chickerell DT3 . . . . .166 D5
 Ferndown BH22 . . . . .61 B7
Curlew Rd
 Bournemouth BH8 . . . . . .90 D2
 Christchurch BH23 . . . . .125 A6
Curlews The BH31 . . . . . .45 C5
Curlieu Rd BH15 . . . . . . .119 E6
Curriott Hill 19 TA18 . . .191 E3
Curriott Hill Rd 9 TA18 .191 E4
Curry Hole La DT2 . . . . .193 D2
Curtis Ct DT9 . . . . .196 A8
Curtis Rd BH12 . . . . .120 C5
Curzon Ct 46 BH4 . . . . .121 C3
Curzon Rd
 Bournemouth BH1 . . . . .122 D6
 Poole BH14 . . . . .120 A3
Curzon Way BH23 . . . . . .125 D8
Custard Hill BH21 . . . . . .201 B5
Custom House Quay
 DT4 . . . . .167 D2
Cuthburga Rd BH21 . . . . .59 C4
Cuthbury Cl BH21 . . . . . . .59 A4
Cuthbury Gdns BH21 . . . .59 A5
Cutler Cl
 New Milton BH25 . . . . . . .95 C3
 Poole BH12 . . . . .121 C7
Cutlers PI BH21 . . . . .60 A5
Cutt Mill La DT10 . . . . . . .34 F6
Cynthia Cl BH12 . . . . . . .120 B7
Cynthia Ho BH12 . . . . . .120 B7
Cynthia Rd BH12 . . . . . .120 B7
Cypress Dr BA20 . . . . .27 A2
Cypress Rd DT2 . . . . .75 D3
Cypress Way 1 SP8 . . . . . .5 F2
Cyril Rd BH8 . . . . .122 C6

D

Dacombe Cl BH16 . . . . . .118 C7
Dacombe Dr
 Upton BH16 . . . . .117 E7
 Upton BH16 . . . . .118 C7
Daggons Rd SP6 . . . . .41 A6
Dagmar Rd DT1 . . . . . . .107 F1
Dahlia Cl DT3 . . . . .152 F2
Dahlia Ct BH19 . . . . .131 E6
Dairy Cl
 Christchurch BH23 . . . . .124 D7
 Corfe Mullen BH21 . . . . .86 B4
Dairy Field DT11 . . . . . . .212 E6
Daisy Cl BH15 . . . . .119 D6
Dakota Cl BH23 . . . . . . .125 B7
Dale Ave DT4 . . . . .167 D6
Dale Cl BH15 . . . . .119 F6
Daler Ct 1 BH20 . . . . . .142 F3
Dale Rd BH15 . . . . .119 F6
Dales Dr BH21 . . . . .60 B5
Dales La BH23 . . . . .90 E7
Dale Valley Rd BH15 . . . .119 F7
Dalewood Ave BH11 . . . . .88 E5
Dalkeith Arc BH1 . . . . . .121 F3
Dalkeith Rd
 Corfe Mullen BH21 . . . . .86 D4
 Poole BH13 . . . . .121 A1
Dalling Rd BH12 . . . . . . .121 A5
Dalmeny Rd BH6 . . . . . . .124 A3
Dalwoods DT9 . . . . .30 B5
Dalzell 10 SO23 . . . . . . .126 E8
Damerham Rd BH8 . . . . . .90 D3
Damers Fst Sch DT1 . . . .107 F1
Damer's Rd DT1 . . . . . . .107 D1
Damory Court St DT11 . .212 D4
Damory Ct 2 DT11 . . . . .212 D4
Damory St 2 DT11 . . . . .212 D4
Dampier PI 2 BA21 . . . . .27 E5
Dampier St 3 BA21 . . . . .27 E5
Danecourt Cl BH14 . . . . .119 F4
Danecourt Rd BH14 . . . . .119 F4
Danecrest Rd SO41 . . . . . .95 F3
Dane Ct BH14 . . . . .120 A4
Dane Dr BH22 . . . . .61 E3
Danehurst New Rd SO41 . .95 C8
Danemark Ct 5 SO22 . . .126 E6
Danesbury Ave BH6 . . . .123 F4
Danesbury Mdws BH25 . . .95 C5
Danes Cl BH25 . . . . .127 A7

Danes Rd 4 SO23 . . . . .126 E7
Danestead Ho 3 BH25 . . .95 A3
Daneswood Rd BH25 . . . .95 C3
Daniel Dr BH20 . . . . .142 D5
Daniel Gdns 3 BH15 . . . .119 C1
Danielsfield Rd BA20 . . . .27 B2
Dansie Cl BH14 . . . . .120 B4
Darby La 6 DT6 . . . . . . .128 B8
Darby's Cl BH15 . . . . . . .119 D6
Darby's Cnr BH17 . . . . . .87 C2
Darby's La BH15 . . . . . . .119 D6
Darby's La N BH17 . . . . .119 D8
Dark La BH19 . . . . .179 A6
Dark La
 Fifehead Neville DT10 . . .197 C6
 Hinton BH21 . . . . .94 A4
 Mere BA12 . . . . .3 A5
 Sandford Orcas DT9 . . . . .15 D6
 Tincleton DT2 . . . . .110 D5
 Witchampton BH21 . . . .200 F7
Darknoll La DT11 . . . . . .197 E6
Darley Rd BH22 . . . . .61 C3
Darracott Rd BH5 . . . . . .123 E5
Darrian Ct BH14 . . . . . . .118 E7
Darwin Ave BH23 . . . . . . .91 E1
Darwin Cl DT3 . . . . .152 D3
Darwin Ct 4 BH13 . . . . .121 A4
Dashwood Cl DT10 . . . . . .35 C2
Davenant Cl 5 SP8 . . . . . .5 E1
Davenport Cl BH16 . . . . .118 C7
David Cowan Ho 23
 SO23 . . . . .126 D6
David La 3 BH24 . . . . . . .54 E5
David Way
 Poole BH15 . . . . .118 D2
 Upton BH15 . . . . .117 F2
Davis Ct BH12 . . . . .120 E5
Davis Field BH21 . . . . . . .94 F2
Davis Gdns DT11 . . . . . .212 E6
Davis Rd BH12 . . . . .120 E5
Dawkins Bsns Ctr BH15 .118 D3
Dawkins Rd BH15 . . . . . .118 D3
Dawkins Way BH25 . . . . . .95 A2
Dawlish Cres DT4 . . . . . .180 D7
Dawn Cl BH10 . . . . .89 C2
Dawn Gdns SO22 . . . . . .126 A4
Dawn Ave BH12 . . . . .89 B2
Daylesford Cl BH14 . . . . .120 A2
Day's Cl BH21 . . . . .59 D4
Day's Rd BH19 . . . . .178 E2
Daytona BH14 . . . . .147 C7
Deacon Gdns BH11 . . . . .89 A5
Deacon Rd BH11 . . . . . . .89 A5
Dean Cl
 Hamworthy BH15 . . . . . .118 E3
 Winchester SO22 . . . . . .126 A8
Dean Court (Bournemouth FC) Ltd 122 F6
Deane Ave SP8 . . . . .5 E1
Deane Way 5 TA20 . . . .202 A8
Dean La SP5 . . . . .188 F6
Dean La DT9 . . . . .188 F6
Dean Park Cres BH1 . . . .121 F3
Dean Park Rd BH1 . . . . .121 F4
Deans Court La BH21 . . . .59 C4
Deanscroft Rd BH10 . . . . .89 E4
Deans Dro BH16 . . . . . . .84 D2
Deans Gr BH21 . . . . .59 D7
Deansleigh Cl 6 DT3 . . .168 B8
Deansleigh Rd BH7 . . . . .91 B1
Dean's Rd 6 BH5 . . . . . .123 B5
Deans The BH1 . . . . .121 F4
Dean Swift Cres BH14 . . .147 C8
Dear Hay La BH15 . . . . . .119 C2
Decies Rd BH14 . . . . . . .120 B5
De Courtenai Cl BH11 . . . .88 E5
Deepdene La BH11 . . . . . .88 E5
Deep Ford La DT9 . . . . . .194 D3
Deer La DT9 . . . . .194 C3
Deerleap Way BH25 . . . . .95 B5
Deer Park Cl BH25 . . . . . .94 F4
De Haviland Cl BH21 . . . .59 F2
De Haviland Ho BH23 . . .125 A6
De Haviland Way BH21 . .125 A6
Delamere Gdns BH10 . . . .89 E3
Delft Mews BH23 . . . . . .124 D6
Delhi Cl BH14 . . . . .120 D3
Delhi Rd BH9 . . . . .187 A4
Delia Rd BH9 . . . . .89 F2
Delilah Rd BH15 . . . . . . .118 D2
De Lisle Rd BH3 . . . . . . .121 F7
Delkeith Ct BH22 . . . . . . .61 D4
Dell Cl BH18 . . . . .86 E4
Dell The BH23 . . . . .126 C8
Delph Rd BH21 . . . . .87 D8
Delph Woods Woodland Trail
 BH18,BH21 . . . . .87 C7
Delta Cl BH23 . . . . .125 A7
De Lunn Bldgs 8 SO23 .126 E8
De Mauley Cl BH13 . . . . .147 E8
De Mauley Rd BH13 . . . .147 E8
De Montfort Rd BH9 . . . . .89 F1
De Moulham Rd BH19 . . .179 B4
Denby Rd BH15 . . . . .119 E4
Dene Cl BH24 . . . . .55 B8
Denecote Lodge BH13 . . .147 H8
Denes Ave BA12 . . . . .3 A6
Dene The BH13 . . . . .121 A2
Denewood Cl BH7 . . . . . . .87 C1
Dene Wlk BH22 . . . . .61 E1
Denewood Copse BH22 . . .52 F4
Denewood Rd
 Bournemouth BH4 . . . . .121 B3
 Ferndown BH22 . . . . .61 D6
Denhall Cl DT10 . . . . .35 A2
Denham Cl
 Poole BH17 . . . . .87 E3

Denham Cl continued
 Winchester SO23 . . . . . .126 D8
Denham Dr
 Cann SP7 . . . . .23 A5
 Christchurch BH23 . . . . . .93 F1
Denhay La DT6 . . . . .127 B5
Denholm Cl BH24 . . . . . . .47 E1
Denison Rd BH17 . . . . . . .87 C1
Denmark La BH15 . . . . . .119 D3
Denmark Rd
 Bournemouth BH9 . . . . . .89 F1
 Poole BH15 . . . . .119 D3
Denmark Terr BH1 . . . . . .122 B4
Denmead BH6 . . . . .123 D7
Denmead Rd
 Corfe Mullen BH21 . . . . .86 C5
 Weymouth DT4 . . . . . . .167 B2
Dennison Ave BH23 . . . . .124 F7
Denzil Cl 3 BA22 . . . . . .193 A8
Derby Rd BH1 . . . . .122 C4
Derby St DT4 . . . . .167 D4
De Redvers Rd BH14 . . . .120 C2
Dereham Way BH12 . . . . .120 F6
Derritt La BH23 . . . . .92 D8
Derrybrian Gdns BH25 . . .95 A2
Derwent Cl
 Bournemouth BH9 . . . . . .90 A2
 Ferndown BH22 . . . . .62 A6
Derwent Gdns BA21 . . . . .27 F6
Derwent Rd
 New Milton BH25 . . . . . . .95 B5
 Weymouth DT4 . . . . . . .180 D6
Derwentwater Rd BH21 . . .59 C2
Derwent Way 3 BH21 . . . .26 E6
Deverel Cl BH12 . . . . . . .124 A8
Deverel Rd DT2 . . . . .75 D2
Devonedge La DT6 . . . . . .97 B8
Dewey La
 Christchurch BH23 . . . . .123 E8
 Poole BH15 . . . . .119 E5
 Weymouth DT4 . . . . . . .167 B4
Deweys La 8 DT4 . . . . . . .55 B7
Dewey's Way SP8 . . . . . . .5 F2
Dewlands Orch DT9 . . . .194 E3
Dewlands Rd BH31 . . . . . .44 F6
Dewlands Way BH31 . . . . .45 A6
Dewlish Cl BH17 . . . . .88 A2
Diamond Cl SP6 . . . . .43 A8
Diana Cl
 Dorchester DT1 . . . . . . .134 F7
Diana Ct 7 BH23 . . . . . .126 A7
Diana Way BH21 . . . . .86 F2
Dibbles La BA22 . . . . . . .193 A8
Dibden Cl BH8 . . . . .90 D3
Dickens Rd BH4 . . . . . . .121 B2
Dick o' Th' Banks Cl DT2 137 D6
Dick o' Th' Banks Rd
 DT2 . . . . .137 D6
Didcot Rd BH17 . . . . . . .119 D7
Digby Rd DT9 . . . . .30 B5
Diggory Cres DT1 . . . . . .135 B8
Dillons Gdns BH16 . . . . . .84 C2
Dilly La BH25 . . . . .127 A7
Diments Gdns 2 DT6 . . .100 C8
Dinah's Hollow SP7 . . . . . .24 C6
Dingle Rd BH5 . . . . .123 B4
Dingley Rd BH15 . . . . . . .119 D8
Dinham Ct BH20 . . . . . . .142 D5
Dinham Rd BH25 . . . . . . .95 A1
Dinhay DT10 . . . . .20 E4
Dinosaur Experience The
 SP7 . . . . .177 F1
Dinosaur Mus DT1 . . . . .108 A2
Diprose Rd BH12 . . . . . . .86 E7
Discovery Court Bsns Ctr
 BH12 . . . . .88 E2
Discovery (Interactive Science Ctr) DT4 . . . . .167 E1
Disraeli Rd BH23 . . . . . .124 D6
Dock Rd DT5 . . . . .181 C2
Doctor Roberts Cl DT6 . .100 C5
Dodham Cres BA20 . . . . . .27 B4
Dodhams Farm Cl BH21 . .86 F1
Doe Copse Way BH25 . . . .94 A4
Does La BH31 . . . . .44 F6
Dogbury Gate DT2 . . . . .207 C8
Dogdean BH21 . . . . .59 C8
Dogwood Rd BH18 . . . . . .86 E2
Doiberg Rd N BH12 . . . . .88 D2
Doiberg Rd S BH12 . . . . .88 D2
Dollings The 1 BH20 . . . .177 A7
Dollin's La 2 BH20 . . . . .142 E4
Dolmans Hill BH10 . . . . . .88 A1
Dolphin Ave BH10 . . . . . .89 E5
Dolphin Cl 2 BH17 . . . . . .96 C5
Dolphin Ctr 3 BH13 . . . .121 B2
Dolphin La SP8 . . . . .5 E4
Dolphin Mans BH25 . . . . .94 B8
Dolphin Quays 10 BH15 .119 C1
Dome Alley SO23 . . . . . .126 E4
Dominion Cntr BH11 . . . . .88 E3
Dominion Rd BH11 . . . . . .88 E3
Domum Rd SO23 . . . . . .126 F4
Doncaster Rd DT4 . . . . . .180 B8
Donhead Hollow SP7 . . . . .25 D7
Donkey La
 Bere Regis BH20 . . . . . .113 B6
 Bridport DT6 . . . . .100 B6
 5 Burton Bradstock DT6 128 B8
Donnelly Rd BH6 . . . . . .123 F5
Donnington Ct 2 SO23 . .126 E7
Donnington Dr BH23 . . . .125 B7
Donoughmore Rd 1
 BH1 . . . . .122 E4

Dorcester Mkt DT1 . . . . .108 A1
Dorchester Adult Ed Ctr
 DT1 . . . . .108 B1
Dorchester Gdns BH15 . .119 E5
Dorchester Hill
 Blandford Forum DT11 . .212 C2
 Milborne St Andrew DT11 . .79 E8
 Winterborne Whitechurch
 DT11 . . . . .210 C2
Dorchester Mans BH1 . . .122 D3
Dorchester Mid Sch DT1 134 E8
Dorchester Prep Sch
 DT1 . . . . .108 B1
Dorchester Rd
 Askerswell DT2 . . . . . . .103 A4
 Bincombe DT3 . . . . .134 C1
 Cerne Abbas DT2 . . . . . .207 D4
 Closworth BA22 . . . . . . .193 F6
 Loders DT6 . . . . .101 C6
 Maiden Newton DT2 . . . . .73 A7
 Poole BH15 . . . . .119 E6
 Radipole DT3 . . . . .152 B2
 Stratton DT2 . . . . .106 C8
 Sydling St Nicholas DT2 .207 A2
 Tolpuddle DT2 . . . . .79 B2
 Upton BH16 . . . . .118 A7
 Wool BH20 . . . . .139 E1
 Yeovil BA20 . . . . .27 C2
Dorchester South Sta
 DT1 . . . . .108 A1
Dorchester Town Football
 Club DT2 . . . . .134 B5
Dorchester W Sta DT1 . . .107 F1
Dore Cl BA21 . . . . .26 E7
Dormers The BH25 . . . . . .94 F1
Dornie Rd BH13 . . . . . . .147 E7
Dorset Ave BH22 . . . . . . .61 D3
Dorset Cl BH22 . . . . .61 D3
Dorset Fire & Rescue Service
 HQ DT1 . . . . .108 A3
Dorset Grange BH23 . . . .123 F7
Dorset Heavy Horse Mus
 DT1 . . . . .40 F2
Dorset Ho BH1 . . . . .121 A2
Dorset Lake Ave BH14 . . .147 B8
Dorset Lake Manor
 BH14 . . . . .120 A2
Dorset Police HQ DT2 . . .139 D2
Dorset Rd
 Bournemouth BH4 . . . . .121 C5
 Christchurch BH23 . . . . .124 F8
Dorset St DT11 . . . . .212 D4
Dorset Teddy Bear Mus
 DT1 . . . . .108 A2
Dorset Terr 8 DT4 . . . . .167 D2
Dorset Way BH17 . . . . . .119 E7
Dottery Rd DT6 . . . . .99 A7
Double Comm DT6 . . . . . .99 A7
Douglas Ave BH23 . . . . . .124 A6
Douglas Cl BH12 . . . . . . .120 E5
Douglas Mews
 Bournemouth BH6 . . . . .123 D5
 Upton BH16 . . . . .118 C8
Douglas Rd
 Bournemouth BH6 . . . . .123 E4
 Poole BH12 . . . . .120 E5
 Weymouth DT4 . . . . . . .180 B6
Doulton Cl 5 DT4 . . . . . .167 C3
Doulton Gdns BH14 . . . . .120 B2
Doussie Cl BH16 . . . . . . .118 B8
Dover Cl BH13 . . . . .121 A3
Dover Rd
 Poole BH13 . . . . .121 A3
 Weymouth DT4 . . . . . . .180 D6
Dover St SP7 . . . . .21 F5
Doveshill Cres BH10 . . . . .89 D3
Doveshill Gdns BH10 . . . .89 D3
Doveshill Mobile Home Pk
 BH10 . . . . .89 D3
Doves The DT3 . . . . .152 D3
Dowlands Cl BH10 . . . . . .89 D4
Dowlands Rd BH10 . . . . . .89 D4
Dowman PI DT4 . . . . . . .180 D5
Downash La EX13 . . . . . .202 B3
Downclose 2 DT4 . . . . . .180 D7
Downclose La TA18 . . . . .192 C4
Down End DT2 . . . . .107 E6
Downes St DT6 . . . . .100 E5
Downey Cl BH11 . . . . .88 F2
Down House La DT6 . . . . .99 F7
Down La
 Folke DT9 . . . . .195 D8
 Trent DT9 . . . . .14 F2
Downlands CE Fst Sch
 DT11 . . . . .199 F3
Downlands PI BH17 . . . . .119 F3
Downleaze 1 BA20 . . . . . .26 F2
Down Lodge Cl SP6 . . . . .42 C6
Down Rd
 8 Pimperne DT11 . . . . .199 D4
 Weymouth DT4 . . . . . . .167 C1
Downside
 Blandford Forum DT11 . .212 E4
 Charmouth DT6 . . . . .89 C2
 Mere BA12 . . . . .3 A6
Downside La DT11 . . . . . .107 C1
Downside Cl DT9 . . . . . . .194 C5
Down's La DT9 . . . . .194 A5
Downsview Dr SP8 . . . . . . .5 F3
Downton Cl BH8 . . . . .90 D3
Downton La SO41 . . . . . .95 C4
Downview Rd SP6 . . . . . .190 B6
Down Wood Rd 2 DT11 .199 E2
Doyne Rd BH12 . . . . .120 E6
Dozens Cnr TA17 . . . . . .191 A7
Dragons Hill DT7 . . . . . . .96 C7

Dragoon Way BH23 . . . . .123 F7
Drake Ave DT3 . . . . .166 D5
Drake Cl
 Christchurch BH23 . . . . .124 F6
 New Milton BH25 . . . . . . .94 F3
 Ringwood BH24 . . . . .47 E1
Drake Ct BH15 . . . . .119 C1
Drake Rd BH15 . . . . .119 C1
Drakes Cres 6 TA20 . . . .202 A8
Drake's La DT12 . . . . . . .208 F3
Drakes Mdw BA22 . . . . . .193 C7
Drakes Rd BH22 . . . . .61 F3
Draper Rd
 Bournemouth BH10 . . . . .89 A4
 Christchurch BH23 . . . . .124 F7
Drax Ave BH20 . . . . .142 E5
Draycott Rd BH10 . . . . . . .89 D2
Drayton St SO22 . . . . . . .126 A4
Dreadnought Trad Est
 DT6 . . . . .100 B6
Dreswick Cl BH23 . . . . . .91 D4
Drew Cl
 Bridport DT6 . . . . .68 F1
 Poole BH12 . . . . .121 C7
Drew Grange BH15 . . . . .118 E4
Drewitt Ind Est BH11 . . . .88 E3
Drew's Cl DT10 . . . . .19 C1
Drift Rd DT2 . . . . .72 F8
Drift The TA20 . . . . .202 B8
Drive The
 Poole BH13 . . . . .120 D5
 Poole BH13 . . . . .147 F8
Drones La SP7 . . . . .23 D2
Drove Cl DT10 . . . . .32 F3
Drove La DT9 . . . . .36 F6
Drove Rd DT10 . . . . .32 F3
Droves The 188 E4
Drove The
 Arne BH20 . . . . .160 F8
 Shapwick DT11 . . . . .56 F7
 Thornford DT9 . . . . .194 D8
 Winfrith Newburgh DT2 . .156 E8
Droveway La BA21 . . . . . .14 A5
Droxford Rd BH6 . . . . . . .123 B6
Druce La DT2 . . . . .77 F3
Druids Cl BH22 . . . . .61 D2
Druitt Rd BH23 . . . . .124 F8
Drum La DT10 . . . . .196 F3
Drummond Cl SO22 . . . . .126 C3
Drummond Rd
 Bournemouth BH1 . . . . .122 D4
 Swanage BH19 . . . . . . .179 C1
Drury La DT6 . . . . .204 C2
Drury Rd BH4 . . . . .121 B2
Dryden Cl BH24 . . . . .54 A5
Dry La SP8 . . . . .5 C1
Duart Ct BH25 . . . . .95 C3
Duchy Cl DT1 . . . . .135 C8
Ducking Stool La BH23 . .124 D6
Duck Island La BH24 . . . . .55 B6
Duck La
 Bournemouth BH11 . . . . .88 F4
 Stalbridge DT10 . . . . .19 C1
Duckpool La TA18 . . . . . .192 B8
Duck St
 Bridport DT6 . . . . .100 E4
 Cattistock DT2 . . . . .206 C2
 Cerne Abbas DT2 . . . . . .207 D4
 Chideock DT6 . . . . .99 A6
 Child Okeford DT11 . . . .198 C5
 Hilton DT11 . . . . .209 D5
 Symondsbury DT6 . . . . . .99 F7
 Winterborne Kingston DT11 .81 E7
 Wool BH20 . . . . .140 B1
Dudley Ave SO41 . . . . . . .95 F3
Dudley Gdns BH10 . . . . . .89 D5
Dudley PI 3 BH25 . . . . . .95 B1
Dudley Rd BH10 . . . . .89 D5
Dudmoor Farm Rd BH23 . .91 F4
Dudmoor La BH23 . . . . . .91 F3
Dudsbury Ave BH22 . . . . .61 D4
Dudsbury Cres BH22 . . . . .61 E4
Dudsbury Gdns BH22 . . . .89 E8
Dudsbury Rd BH22 . . . . . .61 D1
Dudsway Ct BH22 . . . . . . .61 D4
Dugberry Hill DT6 . . . . . . .70 B6
Dugdell Cl BH22 . . . . .61 F6
Duke's Ave DT1 . . . . . . .108 B1
Dukes Cl
 Bournemouth BH6 . . . . .123 D6
 Martinstown DT2 . . . . . .133 C6
Dukes Dr BH11 . . . . .88 E5
Dukesfield BH23 . . . . .91 D2
Dullar La
 Lytchett Matravers BH20 . .84 B6
 Sturminster Marshall BH21 . .56 C2
Dulsie Rd BH3 . . . . .121 C7
Dumbarton Rd DT4 . . . . .180 D6
Dummer Mews 5 SO23 .126 D5
Dumpton Sch BH21 . . . . . .59 D8
Dunbar Cres BH23 . . . . . .93 F2
Dunbar Rd BH3 . . . . .121 E6
Dunbury Fst Sch
 Winterborne Stickland
 DT11 . . . . .210 C7
 Winterborne Whitechurch
 DT11 . . . . .210 C3
Dunbury La DT11 . . . . . .209 F6
Duncan Cres BH20 . . . . .139 F6
Duncan PI BH20 . . . . . . .139 F6
Duncan Rd BH25 . . . . . . .95 D4
Duncliff Ct DT3 . . . . .194 D3
Duncliffe Cl DT10 . . . . . . .33 E8
Duncliff View SP8 . . . . . . .10 E3
Duncliff Rd BH6 . . . . . . .124 A4

Duncombe Dr BH24 . . . . **46** E3
Dundas Rd BH17 . . . . **119** E8
Dundee Rd DT4 . . . . **180** D6
Dune Crest BH13 . . . . **147** C3
Dunedin Cl BH22 . . . . **61** B3
Dunedin Dr BH22 . . . . **61** B3
Dunedin Gdns BH22 . . . . . . **61** B3
Dunedin Gr BH23 . . . . **125** C7
Dunford Cl
 Barton on Sea BH25 . . . . . **126** E8
 Old Milton BH25 . . . . **94** E1
Dunford Pl ⊞ BH19 . . . . . . **179** B2
Dunford Rd BH12 . . . . **120** D5
Dunkeld Rd BH3 . . . . **121** E6
Dunlin Cl BH23 . . . . **125** B5
Dunnock Cl DT2 . . . . **61** B8
Dunn's La
 Iwerne Minster DT11 . . . . . **37** F2
 Silton SP8 . . . . **2** A1
Dunsham La TA18 . . . . . . **191** C2
Dunspit La DT11 . . . . **188** B1
Dunstans La BH15 . . . . . . **120** A6
Dunyeats Rd BH18 . . . . **87** B4
Dunyeats Rdbt BH18 . . . . . . **87** D5
Duplock Ho BH25 . . . . **95** A3
D'Urberville Cl ▲ DT1 . . . . **134** F7
D'Urberville Dr BH19 . . . . **179** B4
Durdells Ave BH11 . . . . **89** A5
Durdells Gdns BH11 . . . . . . **89** A5
Durland Cl BH25 . . . . **95** A1
Durley Chine Ct 12 BH2 . . **121** D2
Durley Chine Rd BH2 . . . . **121** D2
Durley Chine S BH2 5 . . . **121** D2
Durley Gdns BH2 . . . . **121** D2
Durley Rd BH2 . . . . **121** E2
Durley Rdbt BH2 . . . . **121** E2
Durlston Court Sch
 BH25 . . . . **127** A8
Durlston Cres BH23 . . . . **91** D4
Durlston Cty Pk BH19 . . . . **185** B7
Durlston Rd
 Poole BH14 . . . . **120** C2
 Swanage BH19 . . . . **179** C1
Durnford Dro BH19 . . . . . . **178** B1
Durngate Pl SO23 . . . . **126** F6
Durngate St DT1 . . . . **108** A2
Durngate Terr 5 SO23 . . **126** F6
Durnover Ct DT1 . . . . **108** B2
Durrant Cl ▲ DT10 . . . . . . **197** D8
Durrant Rd DT9 . . . . **30** B5
Durrant Rd
 Bournemouth BH2 . . . . **121** E4
 Poole BH14 . . . . **120** C3
Durrington Pl BH7 . . . . **123** B6
Durrington Rd BH7 . . . . **123** B7
Durweston CE Fst Sch
 DT11 . . . . **198** F3
Durweston Cl BH9 . . . . **90** B3
Dyke Head DT1 . . . . **195** B6
Dymewood Rd DT1 . . . . **53** A7
Dyson Dr SO23 . . . . **126** E8

E

Eadon Cl DT3 . . . . **168** A7
Eagle Cl 8 SO23 . . . . **126** D6
Eagle House Gdns DT11 . **212** C4
Eagle Rd BH13 . . . . **121** A4
Eagle Rise BH8 . . . . **90** D1
Eaglhurst 5 BH13 . . . . . . **121** A4
Earle Cl 1 BH1 . . . . **108** B1
Earle Rd BH4 . . . . **121** C1
Earle St BA20 . . . . **27** C2
Earlham Dr BH14 . . . . **120** C4
Earls Cl DT9 . . . . **30** C7
Earlsdon Way BH23 . . . . . . **125** F8
Earlswood 16 BH4 . . . . . . **121** C2
Earlswood Dr SP6 . . . . **42** B5
Earlswood Pk BH25 . . . . **95** C4
Earthpits La SP5 . . . . **189** E4
Eastacre SO22 . . . . **126** C7
East Ave
 Barton on Sea BH25 . . . . . **126** C7
 Bournemouth BH3 . . . . **121** D6
East Avenue Rdbt BH3 . **121** C6
East Borough 5 BH21 . . . . **59** B5
Eastbrook Row BH11 . . . . . . **59** C4
East Burton Rd BH20 . . . . **139** F2
Eastbury Ct BH23 . . . . **124** F4
East Cl BH25 . . . . **126** D8
East Cliff
 Bournemouth BH2 . . . . **121** F4
 Lyme Regis DT7 . . . . **96** C5
East Cliff Way BH23 . . . . . . **125** C7
East Coker Prim Sch
 BA22 . . . . **193** D2
East Coker Rd BA20 . . . . **27** B1
Eastcott Cl BH7 . . . . **123** A8
East Dorset Trade Pk
 BH21 . . . . **60** F6
Eastdown Ave DT3 . . . . . . **167** F8
Eastdown Gdns 3 BH3 . . **168** A6
East Dr BH24 . . . . **62** B7
East Dro BH19 . . . . **178** B2
Easter Rd BH9 . . . . **90** A2
East Farm La DT2 . . . . **105** D7
Eastfield ▲ DT9 . . . . **194** D8
Eastfield Ct BH24 . . . . **55** E7
Eastfield La
 North Perrott TA18 . . . . **192** C4
 Ringwood BH24 . . . . **55** E7
 West Chinnock BA22 . . . . **192** D8
Eastgate St SO23 . . . . **126** F5

Easthams Rd TA18 . . . . . . **191** F4
Easthay La TA20 . . . . **202** D4
East Hill
 Charminster DT2 . . . . **107** D6
 Evershot DT2 . . . . **206** A7
 Winchester SO23 . . . . **126** F4
East Howe La BH10 . . . . **89** C4
East Knighton La DT2 . . . **157** A7
East La TA18 . . . . **192** B8
Eastlake Ave BH1 . . . . **120** C6
Eastland Rd BA21 . . . . **27** C5
Eastlands
 New Milton BH25 . . . . **95** B1
 10 Yetminster DT9 . . . . . . **194** C5
Eastleaze Rd DT11 . . . . . . **212** D6
East Mill La DT9 . . . . **30** C6
East Morden Dro BH20 . . **83** D6
Easton Hollow SP5 . . . . . . **188** B7
Easton La DT5 . . . . **187** A5
Easton Sq DT5 . . . . **187** A5
Easton St DT5 . . . . **187** A4
Eastop La DT10 . . . . **33** B5
East Overcliff Dr BH1 . . . **122** C3
East Quay 11 BH15 . . . . . . **119** C1
East Quay Rd BH15 . . . . . . **119** C1
East Rd DT6 . . . . **100** E6
East St
 Beaminster DT8 . . . . **204** D4
 Blandford Forum DT11 . . **212** D3
 ▲ Bourton SP8 . . . . **1** E1
 Bridport DT6 . . . . **100** D6
 Chickerell DT3 . . . . **166** C6
 Corfe Castle BH20 . . . . . . **162** A1
 Crewkerne TA18 . . . . **191** F4
 Fortuneswell DT5 . . . . **186** F7
 Milborne Port DT9 . . . . **17** D2
 North Perrott TA18 . . . . . . **192** C4
 Poole BH15 . . . . **119** C1
 Radipole DT4 . . . . **167** E2
 Sydling St Nicholas DT2 . **207** A2
 Wareham BH20 . . . . **142** E3
 West Coker BA22 . . . . **193** A8
 9 Winterborne Kingston
  DT11 . . . . **81** E8
East Stoke Fen Nature
 Reserve BH20 . . . . **140** E2
East View Rd BH24 . . . . **55** D7
Eastville BA21 . . . . **27** E5
East Walls BH20 . . . . **142** F3
East Way
 Bournemouth BH8 . . . . **90** C1
 Corfe Mullen BH21 . . . . **86** D5
East Weare Rd DT5 . . . . . . **181** B1
Eastwell La DT10 . . . . **35** A8
Eastwood Ave BH22 . . . . **61** E6
Eastworth Rd BH31 . . . . **45** E7
East Wyld Rd DT4 . . . . **167** A3
Eaton Rd BH13 . . . . **121** A1
Ebblake Ind Est BH31 . . . . **45** E4
Ebden Rd SO23 . . . . **126** F6
Ebenezer La 6 BH24 . . . . . . **55** B7
Ebor Cl BH22 . . . . **61** E2
Ebor Rd
 Poole BH12 . . . . **120** D6
 Weymouth DT4 . . . . **180** C8
Ebury St 7 BH21 . . . . **121** C3
Eccles Rd BH15 . . . . **119** A2
Eddison Ave DT1 . . . . **108** C1
Eddy Green Rd BH16 . . . . . . **84** B2
Eden Ct
 9 Bournemouth BH1 . . **122** B3
 1 Bournemouth BH4 . . **121** C2
Eden Gr BH21 . . . . **59** D3
Edenhurst 12 BH4 . . . . . . **121** C3
Edgar Rd SO23 . . . . **126** D4
Edgarton Rd BH17 . . . . **87** D3
Edgar Villas SO23 . . . . **126** D4
Edgehill Rd
 Bournemouth BH9 . . . . **121** E8
 Bournemouth BH9 . . . . **89** F1
 Bridport DT6 . . . . **100** B5
Edgemoor Rd BH22 . . . . **53** C1
Edifred Rd BH9 . . . . **90** A4
Edinburgh Ho ▲ SO22 . . **126** D6
Edington Rd BH23 . . . . **126** E7
Edith Ct 2 SP8 . . . . **6** C1
Edmondsham Ho 16 BH21 **121** E3
Edmondsham House & Gdns
 BH21 . . . . **40** C4
Edmondsham Rd BH31 . . **45** A7
Edmunds Cl 3 BH24 . . . . . . **55** A1
Edward Cl BA22 . . . . **26** D6
Edward Cres BH24 . . . . . . **142** E4
Edward May Ct BH11 . . . . . . **89** A4
Edward Rd
 Bournemouth BH9 . . . . **89** B3
 Christchurch BH23 . . . . . . **124** F8
 Dorchester DT1 . . . . **107** F1
 Poole BH14 . . . . **120** C5
 Winchester SO23 . . . . **126** D3
 5 Christchurch BH23 . . **124** A8
Edward St
 Blandford Forum DT11 . **212** D4
 ▲ Radipole DT4 . . . . **167** D4
Edwina Cl DT3 . . . . **47** E1
Edwina Dr BH17 . . . . **87** B2
Egbert Rd SO23 . . . . **126** E7
Egdon Cl
 Bere Regis BH20 . . . . **81** B2
 Ferndown BH22 . . . . **61** B3
Egdon Ct BH16 . . . . **118** B7
Egdon Dr BH21 . . . . **87** B8
Egdon Glen DT2 . . . . **137** E6
Egdon Rd
 Dorchester DT1 . . . . **135** B7

Egdon Rd continued
 Northport BH20 . . . . **142** D5
Egerton Cl BH8 . . . . **122** D6
Egerton Gdns BH8 . . . . . . **122** D6
Egerton Rd BH8 . . . . **122** D6
Eggardon Cl 5 DT8 . . . . . . **204** C4
Eggardon Hill (Fort) DT6 . **71** A2
Egmont Cl BH24 . . . . **54** E2
Egmont Dr BH24 . . . . **54** F2
Egmont Gdns BH24 . . . . . . **54** F2
Egmont Rd BH16 . . . . **118** B4
Elbury View SP7 . . . . **37** E7
Elderberry La 8 BH23 . . **124** F6
Elder Cl SO22 . . . . **126** A2
Elder Rd BH20 . . . . **81** A2
Eldon Ave BH25 . . . . **126** E8
Eldon Cl BH25 . . . . **126** E8
Eldon Ct 5 BH14 . . . . **120** A4
Eldon Pl BH4 . . . . **89** E1
Eldon Rd BH9 . . . . **89** E1
Eldons Dro BH16 . . . . **84** C3
Eldon Terr 5 BH19 . . . . . . **179** B2
Eldridge Cl 3 DT1 . . . . . . **134** F7
Eleanor Cl BH25 . . . . **94** F1
Eleanor Dr BH11 . . . . **88** D5
Eleanor Gdns BH23 . . . . . . **123** E8
Elfin Dr BH22 . . . . **61** C7
Elgar Rd BH10 . . . . **89** B4
Elgin Rd
 Bournemouth BH4 . . . . **121** D6
 Poole BH14 . . . . **120** C2
Elijah Cl BH15 . . . . **118** E2
Eliot Ho 8 BH25 . . . . **95** A2
Eliotts Dr BA21 . . . . **27** A7
Elizabeth Ave
 Bridport DT6 . . . . **100** C5
 Christchurch BH23 . . . . . . **123** F8
Elizabeth Cl 1 DT7 . . . . . . **96** C6
Elizabeth Cl
 1 Bournemouth BH2 . . **122** B3
 Ferndown BH22 . . . . **61** D6
 83 New Milton BH25 . . . . . . **95** B2
Elizabeth Gdns BH23 . . . **125** D7
Elizabeth Pl DT1 . . . . **107** D1
Elizabeth Rd
 Blandford Forum DT11 . **212** E5
 Poole BH15 . . . . **119** D3
 Upton BH16 . . . . **118** C7
 Wimborne Minster BH21 . **59** C5
Elizabeth Way DT3 . . . . . . **166** E3
Ellerslie Cl DT2 . . . . **107** E6
Ellesdon Rd **97** B8
Ellesfield Dr BH22 . . . . **61** C2
Elles Rd BH20 . . . . **139** D7
Ellingham Dr BH24 . . . . **46** E4
Ellingham Dro BH24 . . . . . . **47** E5
Ellingham Rd BH24 . . . . . . **126** D8
Elliott Rd BH11 . . . . **88** F3
Elliott's Hill BA22 . . . . **192** D7
Elm Ave
 Christchurch BH23 . . . . **91** E1
 Holton Heath BH20 . . . . . . **116** B3
 New Milton BH25 . . . . **95** A2
Elm Cl
 Motcombe SP7 . . . . **7** B1
 Overcombe/Preston DT3 . **168** A6
 Sturminster Newton DT10 . **35** C1
Elm Cres 5 New Milton BH25 . . . . . . **95** A2
Elm Ct
 New Milton BH25 . . . . **95** A2
 Winchester SO23 . . . . **126** C6
Elmes Rd BH9 . . . . **89** F2
Elmgate Dr
 Bournemouth BH7 . . . . **122** F7
Elm Gdns BH4 . . . . **121** C5
Elmhurst Ave BH22 . . . . **61** F5
Elmhurst Rd
 Bournemouth BH11 . . . . . . **89** A5
 Ferndown BH22 . . . . **53** B1
Elmhurst Way BH22 . . . . **53** B1
Elm La DT2 . . . . **25** E7
Elmleigh BA21 . . . . **26** D2
Elmore Dr BH24 . . . . **54** A6
Elm Rd SO22 . . . . **126** C6
Elmrise Prim Sch BH11 . **89** A4
Elms Ave BH14 . . . . **120** A1
Elms Cl BH14 . . . . **120** A1
Elmstead Rd BH13 . . . . . . **147** F8
Elm Way BH6 . . . . **123** E7
Elm Tree Wlk BH22 . . . . **89** E8
Elmwood Way BH23 . . . . . . **126** A7
Elphinstone Rd BH23 . . . . **94** B1
Elsdon's La DT6 . . . . **64** B4
Elston Medieval Village of
 DT2 . . . . **207** A3
Eltham Cl BH7 . . . . **123** B8
Elvastone St DT4 . . . . **107** C1
Elveroakes Way DT4 . . . . **180** C6
Elvin Cl SO41 . . . . **95** F3
Elwell DT6 . . . . **100** E5
Elwell Manor Gdns DT5 **157** D1
Elwell St DT3 . . . . **166** F3
Elwood Cl DT2 . . . . **142** F8
Elwyn Rd BH1 . . . . **122** C5
Elysium St DT2 . . . . **25** E7
Elziver Cl DT3 . . . . **166** D5
Embankment Way BH24 . **55** D6
Emberley Cl BH22 . . . . **62** A6
Emerald Cl BH24 . . . . **54** A6
Emerson Cl 12 BH15 . . . . **119** C2
Emerson Rd
 Poole BH15 . . . . **119** D2
 Weymouth DT4 . . . . **167** B2
Emily Cl BH23 . . . . **92** A1
Emily Ct BH15 . . . . **120** E5
Emley La 1 BH21 . . . . **201** C1
Emmadale Rd DT4 . . . . . . **167** B3

Emmanuel CE VC Mid Sch
 The BH31 . . . . **45** A4
Emminster Cl DT3 . . . . . . **168** A8
Empool Cl DT2 . . . . **137** D5
Emsbury Rd DT10 . . . . **35** C3
Encombe Cl BH12 . . . . **120** F8
Encombe Rd BH20 . . . . . . **142** D3
Endeavour Ind Pk BH24 . **55** D6
Endfield Cl BH23 . . . . **91** F1
Endfield Rd
 Bournemouth BH9 . . . . **90** A2
 Christchurch BH23 . . . . . . **119** F1
Enfield Ave BH15 . . . . **119** E6
Enfield Cres BH15 . . . . **119** E6
Enfield Rd BH15 . . . . **119** E6
Englands Way BH11 . . . . . . **88** D4
English Cl 15 BH2 . . . . . . **121** D4
Enkworth Rd DT3 . . . . **168** A7
Ensbury Ave BH10 . . . . **89** D1
Ensbury Cl BH10 . . . . **89** D1
Ensbury Dro BH16 . . . . **84** C3
Ensbury Park Rd BH9 . . . . **89** E2
Enterprise Way BH23 . . . . **90** C8
Epiphany CE Prim Sch The
 BH9 . . . . **90** B4
Erica Dr BH17 . . . . **86** D6
Ericksen Rd BH11 . . . . **89** C3
Erinbank Mans BH1 . . . . . . **122** B3
Erin Rd BH20 . . . . **139** E7
Ermine St BA21 . . . . **26** F7
Erpingham Rd BH12 . . . . . . **121** A1
Erskine Rd SO22 . . . . **126** C5
Esmonde Way BH17 . . . . . . **119** F8
Esplanade
 Bridport DT6 . . . . **100** B1
 Poole BH13 . . . . **147** F7
 Portland DT5 . . . . **186** E8
 Radipole DT4 . . . . **167** E2
Essex Ave BH23 . . . . **91** F1
Essex Rd BH17 . . . . **167** C3
Ethelbert Rd BH21 . . . . **59** D4
Eton Gdns BH4 . . . . **121** C4
Eton Mans 2 BH4 . . . . . . **123** E3
Ettrick Rd BH13 . . . . **121** A1
Eucalyptus Ave BH24 . . . . **54** C2
Euston Gr BH24 . . . . **55** C6
Evans Cl
 Bournemouth BH11 . . . . . . **88** F1
 St Leonards BH24 . . . . **54** A6
Evelyn Mews 1 BH9 . . . . . . **89** F1
Evelyn Rd BH9 . . . . **90** A2
Evening Glade BH22 . . . . . . **61** E4
Eventide Homes BH8 . . . . **90** E2
Everdene Cl DT2 . . . . **61** C2
Everdene Dr BH22 . . . . **61** C2
Everdene Dr DT4 . . . . **135** B8
Everest Rd
 Christchurch BH23 . . . . . . **124** E8
 Weymouth DT4 . . . . **180** B8
Everetts La 1 DT11 . . . . . . **198** B5
Everglades Cl BH22 . . . . **61** A7
Evergreen Cl DT11 . . . . **53** A8
Evergreens BH24 . . . . **54** A6
Evering Ave BH12 . . . . **88** D1
Evering Gdns BH12 . . . . **88** C1
Everon Gdns BH25 . . . . **95** B5
Evershot Rd BH8 . . . . **90** E2
Eversley Cl SO22 . . . . **126** B3
Everton Rd 3 BA20 . . . . . . **27** C4
Evesham Ave BA21 . . . . **26** E6
Evesham Cl BH7 . . . . **123** B8
Evesham Cl BH13 . . . . **121** A1
Exbourne Manor BH1 . . . **122** C3
Exbury Dr BH11 . . . . **88** F5
Excelsior Rd BH14 . . . . **120** A2
Exeter Cres 5 BH23 . . . . . . **121** F3
Exeter La BH2 . . . . **121** F2
Exeter Park Mans BH2 . . **121** F2
Exeter Rd
 Bournemouth BH2 . . . . **121** F3
 4 Swanage BH19 . . . . . . **179** C1
Exton Rd BH6 . . . . **123** D7
Eynon Mews DT4 . . . . **54** B6
Eype Down Rd DT6 . . . . **99** E5

F

Fabers Yd 12 SO22 . . . . . . **126** D6
Factory Hill BH21 . . . . **1** F3
Factory La
 Buckland Newton DT2 . . **207** F8
 Tatworth & Forton TA20 . **202** A8
Factory Rd BH16 . . . . **118** C6
Fairclose DT1 . . . . **167** B1
Faircourt 8 BH25 . . . . **95** B3
Faircross Ave DT4 . . . . **167** C1
Fairey Cl SP8 . . . . **5** F3
Fairey Cres SP8 . . . . **5** F3
Faira 1 DT6 . . . . **99** A6
Fairfield
 Christchurch BH23 . . . . . . **124** E8
 Crewkerne TA18 . . . . **191** E4
 Sherborne DT9 . . . . **30** B7
Fairfield Bglws DT11 . . . . **212** D5
Fairfield Cl
 Christchurch BH23 . . . . . . **124** B7
 9 Okeford Fitzpaine DT11 **197** F6
 Wimborne Minster BH21 . **59** F5
Fairfield Hts DT9 . . . . **30** B7
Fairfield Pk DT7 . . . . **96** C6
Fairfield Rd

Fairfield Rd continued
 2 Dorchester DT1 . . . . . . **107** F1
 Iwerne Courtney or Shroton
  DT11 . . . . **198** E7
 Wimborne Minster BH21 . **59** F4
 Winchester SO22 . . . . **126** D7
Fairhaven Ct 3 BH5 . . . . . . **122** E4
Fairhouse Rd BA22 . . . . . . **193** E8
Fairies Dr BH22 . . . . **61** F3
Fairlawn SP7 . . . . **13** A2
Fairlawn BH22 . . . . **61** D5
Fairlawn Ho 9 SO22 . . . . **126** D5
Fair Lea BH22 . . . . **121** E2
Fair Lea **47** E1
Fairlie BH24 . . . . **47** D1
Fairlight La SO41 . . . . **95** D8
Fairmead Rd BA21 . . . . **27** E8
Fairmead Sch BA21 . . . . **27** E8
Fairmile Par BH23 . . . . **91** F1
Fairmile Rd BH23 . . . . **91** F1
Fair Mile Rd DT11 . . . . **210** F8
Fairoak Way 8 DT6 . . . . . . **204** A7
Fairthorn Ct 3 BH2 . . . . . . **121** F4
Fairview Cres BH18 . . . . **87** A5
Fairview Dr BH18 . . . . **87** A5
Fairview Pk BH14 . . . . **47** A5
Fairview Rd
 Broadstone BH18 . . . . **87** A5
 Weymouth DT4 . . . . **180** D7
Fairway Dr
 Christchurch BH23 . . . . . . **123** F6
 Wareham Town BH20 . . **142** C6
Fairway Rd BH14 . . . . **147** C8
Fairways BH22 . . . . **61** F6
Fairway The BH25 . . . . **127** B7
Fairway View BA21 . . . . **27** F6
Fairwinds BH13 . . . . **147** B3
Fairwood Rd BH31 . . . . **45** E5
Fairy Bridge Wlk 1 SP8 . . **5** F3
Falcon Dr BH23 . . . . **125** A5
Falconer Dr BH15 . . . . **118** E4
Falcon View SO22 . . . . **126** A2
Falkland Sq 2 BH15 . . . . **119** C2
Fallow Field SO22 . . . . **126** B2
Fallows The BH25 . . . . **95** B5
Fancy Rd BH12 . . . . **120** B8
Fancy's Ct BH25 . . . . **187** A4
Fancy's Row BH20 . . . . . . **116** B4
Fantley La SP8 . . . . **2** B1
Farcroft Rd BH12 . . . . **120** B6
Far Ends 4 BH14 . . . . **120** B4
Farfrae Cres DT1 . . . . **135** B8
Faringdon Ct 17 SO23 . . **126** E8
Farm Cl
 Radipole DT4 . . . . **167** A5
 Ringwood BH24 . . . . **55** C8
Farm Ct BH21 . . . . **59** C5
Farmdene Cl BH23 . . . . **125** D8
Farmer Palmer's Farm Pk
 BH16 . . . . **116** B5
Farmers Wlk 1 BH21 . . . . **59** B6
Farm La
 Christchurch BH23 . . . . . . **125** A5
 West Lulworth BH20 . . . . **172** C6
Farm La N BH25 . . . . **127** A8
Farm La S BH25 . . . . **127** A8
Farm Rd
 Bradford Abbas DT9 . . . . . . **28** C2
 Ferndown BH22 . . . . **52** F2
Farnham Rd BH12 . . . . **121** A7
Farriers Cl BH21 . . . . **59** A4
Farrington Cl 2 DT1 . . . . **134** F7
Farrington
 24 Bournemouth BH4 . . **121** C2
 Farr's Orch 5 TA16 . . . . **191** F7
Farthings (The 13 BH1)**122** A3
Farwell Cl BH23 . . . . **92** C3
Farwell Rd BH12 . . . . **120** E6
Faversham
 Bournemouth BH2 . . . . **121** D2
 Poole BH14 . . . . **167** A6
Fawcett Rd BH25 . . . . **94** F2
Fawley Gn BH8 . . . . **90** D3
Fawn Gdns BH25 . . . . **95** B4
Fellowsmead DT10 . . . . **20** F2
Felton Cres BH14 . . . . **119** F5
Felton Ct BH14 . . . . **119** F5
Fenleigh Cl BH25 . . . . **95** B1
Fennel Rd 5 BA12 . . . . **3** B6
Fennel Way BA21 . . . . **5** F3
Fenton Rd BH6 . . . . **123** C5
Fenway Cl DT1 . . . . **108** C1
Fenwick Ct BH8 . . . . **122** B5
Fern Bank
 Bournemouth BH4 . . . . **121** F3
 Three Legged Cross BH21 . **53** A7
Fern Barrow BH12 . . . . **121** A2
Fern Brook La SP8 . . . . **6** B1
Fern Cl
 Alderholt SP6 . . . . **42** C5
 Burton BH23 . . . . **92** C2
Ferncroft Gdns BH10 . . . . **89** D5
Ferncroft Rd BH10 . . . . **89** D5
Ferndale Gdns BA21 . . . . **27** A6
Ferndale Rd
 New Milton BH25 . . . . **95** A6
 Radipole DT4 . . . . **167** D6
Ferndown Forest Golf Club
 BH22 . . . . **52** E1
Ferndown Fst Sch BH22 . **61** C5
Ferndown Ind Est BH21 . **60** F7
Ferndown Mid Sch BH22 . **61** C5
Ferndown Rd DT1 . . . . **53** C7
Ferndown Upper Sch
 BH22 . . . . **61** C4
Ferne Hollow SP5 . . . . **188** A8

Ferney Way SP5 188 C4
Fernglade BH25 95 A3
Fernheath Cl BH11 89 A3
Fernheath Rd BH11 89 A3
Fern Hill SP8 11 A3
Fernhill Ave DT4 167 D6
Fernhill Cl BH17 88 A2
Fernhill Flats 6 BH2 121 F3
Fernhill Gate BH25 95 A5
Fernhill La BH25 95 A4
Fernhill Rd BH25 95 A3
Fernlea BH23 124 D6
Fernlea Ave BH22 61 D4
Fernlea Cl
Ferndown BH22 61 D4
St Leonards BH24 54 A4
Fernlea Gdns BH22 61 D4
Fernside Ave BH14 119 F4
Fernside Bsns Pk BH22 61 A7
Fernside Ct BH15 119 E4
Fernside Rd
Bournemouth BH9 121 E8
Ferndown BH22 53 A2
Poole BH15 119 E4
Fernway Cl BH21 60 B4
Fernwood Cl BH24 54 D5
Ferris Ave BH8 90 D2
Ferris Cl BH8 90 D2
Ferris Pl BH8 90 D2
Ferrymans Way 5 DT4 180 D5
Ferry Rd
Bournemouth BH6 123 F3
Poole BH15 119 B1
Poole BH19 147 A1
Studland BH19 164 C3
Ferry Way BH13 147 B3
Feversham Ave BH8 90 E1
Fiddleford Manor DT10 197 F8
Field Barn Dr DT4 167 B5
Field Cl DT10 35 C2
Fieldfare Cl DT3 152 D3
Fielding Rd BA21 27 E6
Fieldings The SP8 10 D3
Field La
Gillingham SP8 5 B4
Kington Magna SP8 9 D2
Pen Selwood BA9 1 B3
Field Pl
Barton on Sea BH25 126 D8
Verwood BH31 45 A7
Fields Barn DT2 156 E5
Field's Cl 1 DT11 210 C3
Fields Oak DT11 212 D4
Fields The BA12 3 B6
Field View Rd 2 DT11 212 D4
Fieldway BH24 55 D8
Field Way
Christchurch BH23 93 D1
Corfe Mullen BH21 86 E8
Fifehead Hill SP8 20 F7
Fifehead Wood Nature Reserve SP8 20 E8
Filbridge Rise DT10 35 C2
Filford La DT6 67 E8
Filleul Rd BH20 115 F1
Fillybrook Bsns Pk SP8 9 B5
Finches The DT3 152 C3
Finchfield Ave BH11 88 F6
Findlay Pl BH19 178 F3
Fineshade 7 BH13 147 F7
Fippenny Hollow 3 DT11 197 F5
Fir Ave
Holton Heath BH20 116 B3
New Milton BH25 95 B2
Firbank Rd BH9 122 B8
Firch La DT6 101 B6
Fir Cl BH22 53 A3
Fir Dr DT3 153 C1
Firecrest Cl DT3 152 C4
Firmain Rd BH12 88 D1
Firs Glen Rd
Bournemouth BH9 121 E8
Ferndown BH22 53 A2
Verwood BH31 45 B5
Firshill BH23 125 E8
Firside Rd BH21 86 C4
Firs La BH14 147 B8
First Cliff Wlk 1 DT6 100 B2
Firs The
Bournemouth BH1 122 A4
Winchester SO22 126 C7
First Marine Ave BH25 126 F7
Firsway BH16 118 C7
Fir Tree Cl
Dorchester DT1 107 D2
Netherbury DT6 68 B6
St Leonards BH24 53 F2
Firtree Cres SO41 95 F3
Fir Tree Hill SP6 42 C6
Fir Tree La BH23 93 D1
Fir Vale Rd BH1 121 F3
Fisherbridge Rd DT3 168 C8
Fisherman's Ave BH5 123 B4
Fisherman's Bank BH23 124 E5
Fishermans Cl DT3 166 D6
Fishermans Rd BH15 119 C1
Fisherman's Wlk BH5 123 B4
Fishers Cl DT9 14 E2
Fisher's Cl DT11 212 D3
Fisher's La TA17 191 A7
Fishers Pl DT2 170 A7
Fisherway La TA19 191 A5
Fishey La SP7 36 E5
Fishpond Bottom Rd DT6 202 D1
Fishweir Fields 1 DT6 68 F1
Fishweir La DT6 68 F1
Fitzharris Ave BH9 122 A7
Fitzmaurice Rd BH23 123 E8
Fitzpain Cl BH22 61 D2
Fitzpain Rd BH22 61 D2
Fitzwilliam Cl BH11 88 E5
Fitzworth Ave BH16 118 C4
Five Acres DT6 97 A7
Five Bridges Rd SO23 126 C1
Fiveways Specl Sch BA21 27 F6
Flaghead BH13 147 E6
Flaghead Chine Rd BH13 147 E6
Flaghead Rd BH13 147 E7
Flambard Ave BH23 92 A1
Flambard Rd BH14 120 C2
Flanders Cl DT10 21 A2
Flaxfield Dr 15 TA18 191 F4
Flax La DT9 28 F7
Flax Way BA21 26 E6
Flazen Cl BH11 88 D3
Fleet Ct DT3 166 E3
Fleet Rd DT3 166 A5
Fleetsbridge Bsns Ctr BH17 119 B7
Fleet's Cnr BH17 119 B7
Fleets Est BH15 119 B6
Fleets La BH15 119 C6
Fleetspoint Bsns Ctr BH15 119 B5
Fleet St DT8 204 D4
Fleet View DT4 180 C7
Fleetwood Ct BH15 119 C7
Fletcher Cl BH10 89 D3
Fletcher Rd BH10 89 D3
Flood La DT6 100 D4
Floral Farm BH21 60 A2
Florence Rd
Bournemouth BH5 122 F4
Dorchester DT1 134 E8
Poole BH14 120 D4
Floriston Gdns BH25 95 D3
Flower Ct BH21 59 D3
Flowers Dro BH16 84 D4
Flushing Mdw BA21 28 A5
Folke La DT9 31 A1
Folly Farm La BH24 54 E6
Folly Fields BA21 27 D7
Folly La
Blandford St Mary DT11 212 C1
Gillingham SP8 10 D5
Kington Magna SP8 9 E4
Nether Compton DT9 28 F8
Wareham BH20 142 E4
Wool BH20 140 A2
Folly Mill Gdns DT6 100 D6
Folly Mill La DT6 100 D6
Folly The DT2 207 D4
Font La BA22 193 B7
Fontmell Down Nature Reserve SP5 24 D1
Fontmell Rd BH18 87 C3
Font Villas BA22 193 B7
Footners La BH23 92 C2
Foot's Hill SP7 24 B7
Ford Cl BH22 61 F7
Ford Down La DT2 208 A7
Forde Abbey & Gdns TA20 202 C8
Forde Pk BA21 26 E7
Fordhay BA22 192 E7
Fordingbridge Rd SP6 42 C7
Fordington Ave SO22 126 C6
Fordington Gdns 3 DT1 108 B1
Fordington Gn 5 DT1 108 B2
Fordington Rd SO22 126 C7
Ford La
Corscombe DT2 205 B7
Ferndown BH22 62 A7
Forehill Cl DT3 168 B8
Foreland Cl BH23 91 D4
Foreland Rd BH16 118 C4
Fore St
Evershot DT2 206 A7
Thorncombe TA20 202 E6
Forest Cl
Christchurch BH23 93 D1
Verwood BH24 45 F4
Forest Ct BH25 95 B2
Forest Ct Hills 3 BH24 55 F6
Forest Edge BH25 95 C4
Forest Edge Dr BH24 53 F5
Forest Edge Rd BH20 142 F7
Forest Hill BA20 27 A2
Forest Ho 14 BH1 122 A3
Forest La
Corfe Castle BH20 162 F1
Verwood BH31 45 A7
Forestlake Ave BH24 55 F6
Forest Links Rd BH21 52 D1
Forest Oak Dr BH25 95 A5
Fore Store St TA20 202 A8
Forest Pines BH25 95 A4
Forest Rd
Ferndown BH22 53 B3
Poole BH13 121 A2
Forest Rise BH23 93 D2
Forestside Gdns BH24 47 E1
Forestside The BH31 45 F5
Forest View
Beckley BH25 94 D5
Crossways DT2 137 D6
Forest View Cl BH9 90 A2
Forest View Dr BH21 61 A5
Forest View Rd BH9 90 A3
Forest Way
Christchurch BH23 93 D1
Ferndown BH21 61 A5
Forge End 2 SP8 10 D2
Forge La
East Chinnock BA22 192 E8
Verwood BH31 44 F5
Zeale SP8 1 F3
Forsters La DT6 69 A1
Forsyth Gdns BH10 89 C1
Fort Cumberland Cl BH15 118 D2
Fortescue Rd
Bournemouth BH3 122 A6
Poole BH12 120 D6
Forton Cl BH10 89 E4
Fortress Gn 5 DT1 134 E7
Fortuneswell DT5 186 E8
Forty Foot Way DT6 100 B2
Forum Gn 1 DT1 134 E7
Forum Sch The DT11 198 B6
Fosse Cl BA21 26 F7
Fosse Gn 7 DT1 134 E7
Fossett Way 4 DT4 180 B8
Fosse Way 1 BA21 26 F7
Foss Orch DT6 99 A6
Foss Way TA17 191 C8
Fosters Hill DT9 196 B5
Fosters Mdws 2 DT11 210 C3
Fosters Spring 1 BH16 84 D2
Foundry Cl DT6 100 A7
Foundry Knapp DT6 100 A7
Foundry La DT6 100 C6
Foundry Sq 13 TA18 191 F4
Fountain Ct BH13 121 B2
Fountain Mead 3 SP7 12 F4
Fountain Rdbt BH23 124 B6
Fountains Cl BA21 26 E7
Fountain Way BH23 124 B6
Fouracre Cl DT6 100 D8
Four Acres DT5 186 E3
Fourgates Rd 1 DT1 107 E1
Fourth Cliff Wlk DT6 100 B2
Four Wells Rd BH21 60 A7
Foxbury BH20 139 C7
Foxbury Rd
St Leonards BH24 54 B1
St Leonards BH24 62 F8
Fox Cl DT6 69 A1
Foxcote 1 BA20 26 E2
Foxcote Gdns BH25 94 F3
Foxcroft Dr BH21 60 B5
Foxdale Ct 17 BH2 121 E3
Foxes Cl BH31 45 B5
Foxglove Cl
Christchurch BH23 125 C8
Gillingham SP8 5 E2
Foxglove Pl BH25 95 D4
Foxgloves BH16 118 B7
Foxglove Way
Bridport DT6 100 D3
Radipole DT3 152 F2
Yeovil BA22 26 C5
Foxhill Cl 8 BH19 179 A2
Foxhills BH31 45 D6
Foxhills Cres BH16 84 D3
Foxhills Dr BH16 84 D3
Foxhills La BH16 84 D1
Foxhills Rd BH16 84 D3
Foxholes 1 BH6 123 F4
Foxholes Rd
Bournemouth BH6 123 F4
Poole BH15 119 F6
Fox La
Wimborne Minster BH21 60 C5
Winchester SO22 126 A3
Fox La Terr DT10 35 B1
Fox Mdws 16 TA18 191 F5
Foxs Cl DT9 196 B5
Foxwell La TA18 192 C7
Foxwood Ave BH23 124 F5
Foyle Hill SP7 12 C1
Framerville Rd BH20 139 E7
Frampton Cl BH25 95 C5
Frampton Pl BH24 55 C7
Frampton Rd
Bournemouth BH9 122 A8
16 Pimperne DT11 199 D4
Francesca Ct 5 BH23 124 E7
Francesca Grange 4 BH23 124 E7
Francesca Lo 1 BH23 124 E6
Frances Ct 7 BH23 126 B7
Frances Rd BH1 122 C4
Frances Sheldon Ct SO22 126 C5
Franchise St DT4 167 D2
Francis Ave BH11 88 D3
Francis Avenue Ind Est BH11 88 D3
Francis Rd
Poole BH12 120 E5
Weymouth DT4 167 B2
Frankland Cres BH14 120 E3
Franklin Cl DT4 167 B2
Franklin Rd
Bournemouth BH9 90 A3
New Milton BH25 95 C4
Weymouth DT4 167 B3
Franklyn Cl BH16 118 B7
Frankston Rd BH6 123 C4
Franks Way BH12 120 B7
Frank Wareham Cottage Homes The BH9 90 A4
Fraser Ave DT4 166 F1
Fraser Ct BH25 94 F3
Fraser Rd BH12 120 F8
Freame Way SP8 5 D1
Freda Rd BH23 123 F6
Frederica Rd BH9 121 E8
Freedom Ave BA21 27 A6
Freemans Cl BH21 60 B6
Freemans La BH21 60 B5
Freemantle Rd DT4 166 F1
Freesia Cl DT3 152 E2
Fremington Ct 6 BH25 95 B3
French Hill La SP7 23 F4
French Mill La SP7 23 F7
French Mill Rise SP7 12 F1
French Rd BH17 87 B1
French's Farm Rd
Upton BH16 117 B7
Upton BH16 118 A7
Frensham Cl BH10 89 E3
Freshwater Cl 4 DT5 186 E1
Freshwater Dr BH15 118 D3
Freshwater Rd BH23 125 C6
Friars Ave BA21 26 F6
Friars Cl 2 DT1 135 C8
Friarsgate SO23 126 E6
Friars Gate BH23 125 C6
Friars Moor DT10 35 C1
Friars Rd BH23 125 B6
Friars Wlk BH25 127 A8
Friar Waddon Rd DT3 151 F8
Friary Gdns 7 SO23 126 D5
Friary Hill DT1 108 A2
Friary La DT1 108 A2
Friday's Heron BH21 40 B7
Frinton Ct 2 BH14 120 A4
Fritham Gdns BH8 90 D3
Frizzel's Hill DT10 196 F4
Frobisher Ave BH12 88 F1
Frobisher Cl
Christchurch BH23 124 F6
3 Ringwood BH24 47 E1
Frogham Hill SP6 43 F6
Frog La
Dinnington TA17 191 B8
Fordingbridge SP6 43 A7
Iwerne Courtney or Shroton DT11 198 F7
Motcombe SP7 12 C7
Frogmore La DT2 71 E8
Frome Ave BH20 139 F2
Frome La DT2 72 F7
Frome Rd BH20 142 D3
Frome Terr DT1 108 A2
Frome Valley Rd DT2 137 C6
Frome View
Bradford Peverell DT2 107 A6
Maiden Newton DT2 73 A8
Front La BH21 56 D5
Front St
East Stour SP8 10 F3
Portesham DT3 132 A1
Froom's La BH20 81 C1
Frost Rd BH11 88 F3
Froud Way BH21 86 C4
Froxfield Rd DT11 212 D5
Fryer Cl BH11 89 B5
Fryers Copse BH21 60 C6
Fryers Rd BH21 53 A8
Frys Cl BH16 84 C4
Fry's Cl DT3 150 A8
Fry's La DT2 75 A7
Fudge Hill DT2 205 A8
Fulbrooks Cl DT6 100 C7
Fulbrooks La DT6 100 C7
Fulcrum Ctr The BH12 88 C2
Fulflood Ct 2 SO22 126 C6
Fulmar Rd BH23 125 A5
Fulwood Ave BH11 88 E5
Furge Gr BA8 19 A4
Furge La BA8 19 A3
Furland Rd 6 TA18 191 F4
Furlands DT5 186 F3
Furley Cl 8 SO23 126 F6
Furlong La DT9 17 B3
Furlong Mews 3 BH24 55 B7
Furlong Sh Ctr BH24 55 B8
Furlongs The DT9 30 B7
Furlong The BH24 55 B7
Furnell Rd BH15 119 D1
Furzebrook Cl BH17 87 E3
Furzebrook Rd BH20 161 A4
Furze Croft BH25 95 A2
Furzehill
Colehill BH21 59 C8
Holt BH21 50 F1
Furze Hill Dr BH14 120 C1
Furzelands Rd BH21 53 A8
Furze The 2 BA20 26 E2
Furzey Rd BH16 118 B6
Furzy Cl DT3 168 B7

G

Gablehurst BH16 118 C7
Gabriel Gn 1 DT1 135 B8
Gadbridge Ct 14 BH4 121 C2
Gainsborough DT9 17 C2
Gainsborough Ave BH25 95 B5
Gainsborough Ct 4 BH5 123 B5
Gainsborough Dr DT9 29 E5
Gainsborough Hill DT9 30 C4
Gainsborough Ho BH25 127 A6
Gainsborough Rd
Bournemouth BH7 122 F7
St Leonards BH24 54 A5
Gainsborough Way BA21 28 A8
Gale Cres DT6 100 C5
Gales Hill DT2 207 E7
Gallop's La BH20 83 C2
Gallop Way BH12 121 C7
Galloway Rd BH15 118 D4
Gallows Cnr
Iwerne Courtney or Shroton DT11 36 F1
Gallows Cnr *continued*
Milton Abbas DT11 209 D3
Gallows Dr BH22 61 E1
Gallows Hill
Arne BH20 161 C4
Owermoigne DT2 155 D6
Gallwey Rd DT4 180 C7
Galton Ave BH23 123 F6
Gannetts Pk BH19 179 B3
Garden Cl
Bridport DT6 100 D7
Litton Cheney DT2 103 B2
New Milton BH25 95 A1
Garden Ct BH1 122 D6
Garden Ho 6 BH1 122 B3
Garden La
St Leonards BH24 54 A3
25 Winchester SO23 126 E6
Gardens Cres BH14 147 B8
Gardens Ct 5 BH15 119 E3
Gardenside 1 DT6 97 A7
Gardens Rd BH14 147 B8
Garden Wlk BH22 61 E7
Gardner Ct BH23 123 E8
Gardner Rd
Christchurch BH23 123 E8
Ringwood BH24 55 D6
Garfield Ave
Bournemouth BH1 122 D5
Dorchester DT1 134 E8
Garland Cres DT1 135 B8
Garland Rd BH15 119 D4
Garlands La DT11 197 D4
Garnier Rd SO23 126 E3
Garrett Rd BA20 26 F3
Garsdale Cl BH11 89 A6
Gar St SO23 126 D5
Garston Hill DT3 166 C6
Garston Wood Nature Reserve SP5 189 B6
Gartells 1 DT10 197 A4
Garth Cl BH24 53 F4
Garth Rd BH9 90 A1
Gascoigne's La SP7 23 E8
Gascoyne La DT2 107 B6
Gashay La EX13 202 E3
Gas House Hill DT9 30 C5
Gas La TA17 191 C7
Gasper St BA12 1 C6
Gassons La DT6 66 A4
Gate Cl EX13 202 A3
Gatemore Rd DT2 138 E1
Gateway The BH13 120 F4
Gaydon Rise BH11 88 E4
Gaza Rd BH20 139 D7
Gazelle Rd BA20 26 F3
Geelong Cl DT3 152 E2
General Johnson Ct 4 SO22 126 A4
Geneva Ave BH6 123 D5
Gent Cl DT11 212 E5
George Eyston Dr SO22 126 B4
George Rdbt The BH15 119 C3
Georges Cl DT6 97 B8
Georges Mews BH21 86 D7
George Smith Way BA22 26 C6
George St
Bridport DT6 100 C2
Sherborne DT9 30 B6
Georgian Cl BH24 55 C8
Georgian Way BH10 89 F4
Georgina Cl BH12 121 C8
Georgina Talbot Ho BH12 121 B8
Gerald Rd BH3 122 A6
Germaine Cl BH23 125 F8
Gervis Cres BH14 120 A4
Gervis Pl BH1 121 F3
Gervis Rd BH1 122 B3
Giant's Grave DT2 209 A4
Gibbs Gn BH16 84 D2
Gibbs La DT6 66 C1
Gibbs Marsh Trading Est DT10 20 A4
Gibson Rd BH17 119 E7
Giddy Gn La BH20 139 E2
Giddy Gn Rd BH20 139 E2
Giddylake BH21 59 D6
Gifle View 2 DT9 194 D8
Gigg La SP8 8 E4
Gilbert Cl SP6 42 D6
Gilbert Rd
Bournemouth BH8 122 D6
Swanage BH19 179 B2
Giles Cl DT2 107 A6
Giles's La
Bishop's Caundle DT9 196 A7
Morden BH20 83 D3
Gillam Rd BH10 89 D5
Gillett Rd BH12 121 C7
Gillingham Adult Ed Ctr
Gillingham SP8 5 F2
Shaftesbury SP7 12 D3
Gillingham Cl BH9 90 C4
Gillingham L Ctr SP8 6 A2
Gillingham Mus SP8 5 F1
Gillingham Prim Sch SP8 5 F2
Gillingham Sch SP8 6 A2
Gillingham Sta SP8 5 F1
Gillion Ct 2 BH23 124 E6
Gipsy La DT6 68 E1
Gipsy's Dro DT10 197 C7
Girt La DT2 205 F7
Glacis DT5 187 A7
Gladdis Rd BH11 88 F3

Gladelands Cl BH18.......86 E4
Gladelands Pk BH22.......61 F7
Gladelands Way BH18.....86 E4
Glade The
  Christchurch BH23.........91 E1
  St Leonards BH24.........54 A5
Gladiator Gn **3** DT1....134 E7
Gladstone Cl
  Bridport DT6.............100 E7
  Christchurch BH23........124 D6
  2 Radipole DT3.........152 E2
Gladstone Rd
  Bournemouth BH7.........122 F5
  Poole BH12..............120 C5
Gladstone Rd E BH7......122 F5
Gladstone Rd W BH1.....122 E5
Gladstone St SO23.......126 D6
Glamis Ave BH10..........89 E5
Glastonbury Ct BA21......26 F6
Gleadowe Ave BH23......124 A6
Glebe Cl
  Abbotsbury DT3..........149 C7
  Bridport DT6............100 D5
  Maiden Newton DT2.......72 F8
  Overcombe/Preston DT3..169 A8
  8 Thornford DT9........194 D8
  Weymouth DT4...........167 C1
Glebe Ct **4** DT11.........37 F1
Glebefields DT2..........106 F7
Glebeford Cl DT2.........155 E7
Glebe Gdns SP7............12 B8
Glebeland Cl DT2.........136 A7
Glebeland La DT6..........65 F7
Glebelands **8** TA16......191 F7
Glebe Rd BH16.............84 C1
Glebe The
  3 Durweston DT11......198 E3
  1 Iwerne Courtney or Shroton
    DT11..................198 F7
  2 Iwerne Minster DT11....37 F1
Glebe Way DT2...........136 C3
Glenair Ave BH14.........120 A3
Glenair Cres BH14........120 A3
Glenair Rd BH14..........120 A3
Glen Ave DT4..............167 C2
Glenavon BH25............95 C2
Glenavon Rd BH23.........93 F1
Glen Cl BH25.............126 D8
Glencoe Rd
  Bournemouth BH7.........122 F7
  Poole BH12..............120 D5
Glendale Ave BH22........61 E6
Glendale Cl
  Christchurch BH23........91 D3
  Wimborne Minster BH21...59 C5
Glendale Ct BH23.........91 D3
Glendale Rd BH6.........124 A4
Glendinning Ave DT4.....167 D5
Glendon Ave BH10.........89 C6
Glendrive BH25...........126 C8
Gleneagles
  Christchurch BH23.......123 F6
  Poole BH13.............121 B2
Gleneagles Ave BH14.....120 D2
Gleneagles Cl BH22.......61 A6
Glenferness Ave BH4.....121 D5
Glen Fern Rd BH1........122 A3
Glengariff Rd BH14.......120 C2
Glengarry BH25............95 C2
Glengarry Way BH23......125 C6
Glenives Cl BH24..........54 B4
Glenmeadows Dr BH10....89 B5
Glenmoor Cl BH10.........89 D1
Glenmoor Rd
  Bournemouth BH9.........121 E8
  Ferndown BH22...........61 D3
Glenmoor Sch BH10.......89 D1
Glenmore Rd BH14........167 B4
Glenmount Dr BH14......120 B4
Glenmore Way DT3.......166 D4
Glen Rd
  Bournemouth BH5.........122 F4
  Poole BH14.............120 B4
Glenroyd Gdns BH6.......123 E4
Glenside BH23,BH25......126 B7
Glen Spey BH25............95 D2
Glen The
  Poole BH12..............120 D6
  Poole, Canford Cliffs BH13.147 E8
Glenthorne Ave BA21......27 D7
Glenville Cl BH23..........94 B2
Glenville Gdns BH10.......89 C2
Glenville Rd
  Bournemouth BH10........89 C2
  Walkford BH23...........94 B2
  Yeovil BA21..............27 F6
Glenwood Cl BH22.........53 A2
Glenwood La BH22.........53 A2
Glenwood Rd
  Ferndown BH22..........53 A2
  Verwood BH31...........45 A5
Glenwood Way **2** BH22..53 A2
Glissons BH22.............61 A2
Globe Cl **8** BH19.......178 F2
Globe La BH15...........119 C2
Globe Orch TA18.........192 C6
Gloucester Cl DT3........166 E3
Gloucester Mews DT4....167 D3
Gloucester Rd
  Bournemouth BH7.........122 F5
  3 Dorchester DT1......107 E1
  Poole BH12.............120 E5
Glovers Cl **2** BH18......17 D2
Glovers Walk Sh Ctr BA20 27 E4

Glovers Wlk **10** BA20....27 D4
Glue Hill DT10...........197 C8
Glyde Path Rd DT1.......108 A2
Glyn Pl SP7...............24 D6
Glynville Cl BH21..........60 A7
Glynville Ct BH21.........60 A7
Glynville Rd BH21.........60 A7
Goathill Rd
  Goathill DT9.............31 D6
  Milborne Port DT9........17 C1
Goathorn Cl BH16.........118 D4
Godlingston Manor
  BH19..................178 E5
Godmanston Cl BH17......88 A1
God's Blessing La BH21....51 B3
Godshill Cl BH8...........90 D3
Godson Ho **27** SO23....126 E6
Goldcrest Cl DT3.........152 C4
Goldcroft BA21............27 D5
Goldcroft Ave DT4.......167 C5
Goldcroft Rd DT4........167 C6
Golden Gates BH13.......147 B3
Golden Hill DT10..........32 F2
Goldenleas Ct BH11.......88 D3
Goldenleas Dr BH11.......88 D3
Golden Sands BH21.......147 B3
Goldensteps Pool & L Ctr
  BA20...................27 C3
Goldfinch Cl BH25.........94 F2
Goldfinch Rd BH17.......118 E8
Gold Hill
  Child Okeford DT11......198 B8
  Shaftesbury SP7...........12 E2
Golding's La DT9..........17 C1
Gold St DT10..............33 C8
Golf Links Rd
  Broadstone BH18.........87 B5
  Ferndown BH22...........61 E4
Goliath Rd BH15..........118 D2
Good Rd BH12............120 C7
Goodwin's La BH20........83 D2
Goosacre La BA22........26 C1
Gooseberry La **7** BH24...55 B7
Goose Hill DT3...........149 F7
Gordon Cres **1** DT4....166 F2
Gordon Ct **7** BH4......121 C4
Gordon Mount BH23......126 B8
Gordon Rd
  Bournemouth BH1.........122 D4
  Christchurch BH23........126 A8
  Poole BH15.............121 A5
  6 Swanage BH19.......179 A2
  Wimborne Minster BH21...59 E4
Gordon Rd S BH12........121 A5
Gordon's La DT9..........195 A8
Gordon Watson Ho
  SO23..................126 D3
Gordon Way BH21.........92 D1
Gore Cross DT6............92 E7
Gore Cross Bsns Pk DT6...68 E2
Gore Cross Way **5** DT6..68 F1
Gore Grange BH20........94 F2
Gore La DT6...............68 F2
Gore Rd BH25..............94 E2
Gore Rd Ind Est BH25.....94 E2
Gorey Rd BH12............88 D1
Goring Field SO22.......126 A7
Gorleston Rd BH12.......120 F5
Gorley Lynch SP6..........43 F4
Gorley Rd BH24............47 E1
Gorse Cl
  New Milton BH25..........95 D4
  St Leonards BH24.........53 F4
Gorsecliff Cl **1** BH5....122 D4
Gorsecliff Rd BH10........89 D1
Gorsefield Rd BH25........95 B4
Gorse Hill Cl BH15.......119 F5
Gorse Hill Cres BH15.....119 F5
Gorse Hill Rd BH15......119 F5
Gorse Knoll Dr BH31......45 A7
Gorse La BH16............118 D7
Gorseland Ct BH22.........61 E3
Gorse Rd
  Corfe Mullen BH21........86 C5
  Poole BH15..............85 E5
Gort Rd
  Bournemouth BH11........89 B3
  Poole BH17..............87 A1
Gosling Cl **1** DT4......119 F7
Goss Pl **2** DT4.........167 C4
Gough Cl **1** TA16......191 F7
Gough Cres BH17..........87 B2
Goughs Cl DT14...........35 A1
Gould's Hill
  Upwey DT3.............152 A7
  Winterborne St Martin
    DT2..................133 F3
Goulds Hill Cl DT3.......152 A7
Gover Cl BH20............143 B1
Gower Rd SP7.............13 A2
Grace Darling Ho BH15...119 D1
Grafton Ave DT4.........167 A6
Grafton Cl
  Bournemouth BH3.........122 A7
  Christchurch BH23.......124 D6
Grafton Rd
  Bournemouth BH3.........122 A6
  Winchester SO23.........126 D4
Grammar School La BH1...59 E4
Granby Cl DT14..........166 F3
Granby Ind Est DT14.....166 E4
Granby Rd BH9............90 A4
Granby Way DT14.........166 E4
Grand Ave BH6...........123 C4
Grand Par **13** BH15....119 B1

Grange BH21................50 E1
Grange Arch (Folly)
  BH20..................175 C8
Grange Cl SO23...........126 C2
Grangecroft Rd **3** DT5..186 E3
Grange Ct **5** BH21.....122 B3
Grange Gdns BH12........120 E8
Grange Hill BH20.........160 C1
Grange La DT8...........203 D5
Grange Pk **1** DT9......194 D8
Grange Rd
  Bournemouth BH6.........123 D3
  Broadstone BH18.........87 A4
  Christchurch BH23........125 B7
  Church Knowle BH20.....160 D4
  Radipole DT14...........167 E5
  St Leonards BH24.........53 F2
  Winchester SO23.........126 C1
Grange Road Bsns Ctr
  BH23..................125 A7
Grange Sch The BH23....124 E7
Grangewood Hall BH21....59 D5
Grans Barrow (Long Barrow)
  SP6...................190 E6
Grantham Rd BH1.........122 E5
Grantley Rd **3** BH5.....122 F4
Grant's Ave BH1..........122 D6
Grants Cl BH1............122 E6
Granville Gdns **2** SP7...12 F3
Granville Pl
  9 Bournemouth BH1....121 F3
  Winchester SO23.........126 F4
Granville Rd
  Bournemouth BH5.........123 A5
  Poole BH13.............147 B3
  Radipole DT3............167 C6
Granville Way DT9.........30 C8
Grasmere Cl BH23.........91 D3
Grasmere Gdns BH25......95 B5
Grasmere Rd
  Bournemouth BH5.........123 A4
  Poole BH13.............147 B3
Grass Royal BA21..........27 E6
Grass Royal Jun Sch
  BA21...................27 E6
Gravel Hill BH17,BH18,
  BH21...................87 D5
Gravel La
  Charlton Marshall DT11...211 C7
  Ringwood BH24...........55 C8
Gray Cl BH17.............119 F8
Graycot Cl BH10..........89 C5
Grays Cl SP7.............167 B6
Gray's Yd **5** BH15......119 C1
Great Cnr BA21............26 E6
Great Dorset Maize Maze &
  Farm Pk The DT3........150 B4
Great Down La DT10.......21 B4
Great Gd SP7..............13 A4
Great George St DT4.....167 D3
Great Head La DT2........206 F7
Great Hill BA9.............1 B3
Great La SP7..............12 F2
Great Minster St **2**
  SO23..................126 E5
Great Owens Dr DT10....142 D6
Great Pit La BA22.........15 B5
Great Western Rd DT1...108 A1
Great Western Terr
  Radipole DT4............167 D6
  Yeovil BA21..............27 F5
Greaves Cl BH10..........89 C3
Grebe Cl
  Broadstone BH17.........118 E8
  2 Chickerell DT3......166 D5
  Christchurch BH23.......125 A6
Greenacre
  Barton on Sea BH25......127 A8
  Charminster DT2.........107 E6
Greenacre Cl BH16.......118 C6
Greenacres
  Bournemouth BH4.........121 C3
  Puddletown DT2...........78 A1
Greenacres Cl BH23......124 F7
Greenacres Rd BH10......89 E6
Green Acres Cl BH24......54 F5
Green Bottom BH21........60 A7
Green Cl
  Bere Regis BH20..........81 B1
  2 Bradpole DT6.......100 F8
  Charlton Marshall DT11...211 D6
  Poole BH15.............119 D1
  Sturminster Newton DT10..35 C2
Greenclose La BH21........59 D4
Green Dr La BH21..........42 D6
Greenfield Gdns BH25....127 B8
Greenfield Rd
  3 Charlton Marshall
    DT11.................211 D6
  Poole BH15.............119 E7
Greenfields **1** BH21....120 F7
Greenfinch Cl BH17........86 F1
Greenford CE Prim Sch
  DT2....................72 E8
Greenford La
  Compton Valence DT2....104 C8
  Maiden Newton DT2.......72 D4
Green Gdns BH15.........119 D1
Greenham La TA18.......203 B7
Greenham Yd TA18.......203 B7
Greenhayes
  Broadstone BH18.........87 C2
  Charmouth DT6............96 F7
  2 Okeford Fitzpaine DT11 197 F5
Greenhays Rise BH21......59 C5

Greenhill
  Blandford Forum DT11....212 D5
  Radipole DT4............167 E5
  Sherborne DT9............30 B6
Greenhill Ave SO22......126 C6
Greenhill Cl
  Wimborne Minster BH21...59 D6
  Winchester SO22.........126 C6
Greenhill La BH21.........59 D6
Greenhill Rd
  Wimborne Minster BH21...59 D6
  Winchester SO22.........126 B6
  Yeovil BA21..............27 E7
Greenhill Terr
  4 Fortuneswell DT5...186 F8
  Winchester SO22.........126 C6
Greenings Ct **7** DT1....108 B2
Green Jacket Cl SO22....126 C3
Green La
  Ashmore SP5..............39 C8
  Barton on Sea BH25......127 B8
  Bournemouth BH10.........89 D3
  Bradpole DT6............101 A7
  Bridport DT6............100 E5
  Chickerell DT3..........166 E5
  Crossways DT3...........137 D6
  East Chinnock BA22......192 E8
  Ferndown BH22...........61 A1
  Hooke DT8...............205 C2
  Kington Magna SP8.........9 C3
  Ossemsley BH25...........94 E8
  Ringwood BH24............55 D3
  Ringwood BH24............55 D7
  Sixpenny Handley SP5....188 E4
  Stour Provost SP7........22 D4
  Sturminster Marshall DT11..56 B5
  Tatworth & Forton TA20...202 A7
  West Coker BA22.........193 B8
  Weymouth DT4...........180 E8
Green Loaning BH23......124 F5
Green Mead BA21..........26 E6
Green Park Cl SO23.......126 C3
Green Pk Knapp DT6.......65 B2
Green Pk BH1............122 D3
Green Rd
  Bournemouth BH9.........122 A8
  Poole BH15.............119 D1
Greens Cross Dr **4** DT8.204 C4
Greenside Cl BH25.......127 B6
Greensleeves Ave BH18....87 B6
Greensome Dr BH22........61 F6
Green St TA17............191 D7
Green The
  Burton BH23..............92 D2
  3 Hazelbury Bryan DT10.197 A4
  Mappowder DT10.........196 E1
  Puddletown DT2...........78 B1
  Sherborne DT9............30 B6
  Stratton DT2............106 D8
Greenway
  10 Child Okeford DT11..198 C7
  Lyme Regis DT7............96 A5
Greenway Cl DT3.........167 C8
Greenway Cres BH16.....118 A7
Greenway La DT11........198 B7
Greenway Rd DT3.........152 C1
Greenways
  Christchurch BH23........125 F8
  Easton/Weston DT5......186 F3
Greenways Ave BH8.........90 C3
Greenways Ct BH22........61 E3
Greenwood Ave
  Ferndown BH22...........61 E6
  Poole BH14.............147 C8
Greenwood Copse BH24....54 B4
Greenwood Rd
  Bournemouth BH9.........121 E8
  Yeovil BA21..............26 F7
Greenwoods **6** BH25....95 B1
Greenwood Way BH24.....54 B4
Grenfell Rd BH9...........89 F3
Grenville Cl BH24.........47 E1
Grenville Ct
  1 Bournemouth BH4....121 D4
  10 Poole BH15........119 C2
Grenville Rd BH9..........59 D4
Gresham Rd BH9...........90 E1
Grexy Cross DT2.........205 E7
Greyfriars **2** SO23.....126 E5
Greyhound Yd DT1........207 A2
Grey Mare & Her Colts (Long
  Barrow) DT3............131 C3
Greys Rd **7** TA16......191 F7
Greystoke Ave BH11.......88 F5
Greystones Cl DT2.......137 D6
Gribb View TA20.........202 E6
Griffin Cl BH21..........119 D3
Griffiths Gdns BH10.......89 B5
Grim's Ditch SP5.........189 D7
Grimsey La SP8............4 F8
Grosvenor Cl BH24........53 F5
Grosvenor Cres DT1......135 A8
Grosvenor Ct
  8 Bournemouth BH1....122 B3
  15 Poole BH15........119 C2
  Christchurch BH23.......126 B8
Grosvenor Gdns BH1......122 C4
Grosvenor Ho **6** BH4...121 C4
Grosvenor Lo **8** BH4...121 C3
Grosvenor Pines **13** BH4 121 C3
Grosvenor Rd
  Bournemouth BH4.........121 C3
  Dorchester DT1..........135 A8
  Easton/Weston DT5......167 D6
  Shaftesbury SP7..........12 F4
  Stalbridge DT10..........33 C8

Grosvenor Rd continued
  Swanage BH19...........179 C1
Grove Ave
  Radipole DT4............167 D6
  Yeovil BA20..............27 B5
Grove Gdns BH25.........127 A3
Grove Inf Sch DT5.......187 C6
Grove La
  Abbotsbury DT3.........149 B6
  Bothenhampton DT6.....101 B6
  Portesham DT3..........150 C5
  Stalbridge DT10..........33 C8
Grove La Cl DT10..........33 C3
Grove Orch **3** DT6....128 B8
Grove Rd
  Barton on Sea BH25......127 A3
  Bournemouth BH1.........122 B3
  Burton Bradstock DT6....128 B8
  Easton/Weston DT5......187 B5
  Poole BH12.............120 D6
  Wimborne Minster BH21...59 D6
Grove Rd E BH23.........124 A8
Grove Road W BH23......123 F8
Grove The
  Bournemouth BH9.........89 F3
  Bournemouth BH9.........90 A4
  Christchurch BH23........91 E1
  Dorchester DT1..........107 F2
  Stour Provost SP7........22 D4
  Verwood BH31............61 C4
Grove Trading Est The
  DT1....................107 F1
Grower Gdns BH11.........89 A4
Grugs La BH21.............40 A3
Gryphon L Ctr DT9........30 C8
Gryphon Sch The DT9.....30 B8
Guard Ave BA22...........26 D6
Guernsey Rd BH12.........88 D3
Guernsey St **2** DT5....186 F2
Guest Ave BH12..........121 A6
Guest Cl BH12............121 A6
Guest Rd BH16...........118 B3
Guildford Ct **8** BH4....121 C4
Guildhall Ct BH15........119 B2
Guildhall Mus BH15......119 B2
Guildhill Rd BH6.........123 E4
Guinevere Cl BA21........26 F7
Gulliver Cl BH14.........147 C6
Gulliver's Ct **6** BH21....59 C5
Gullivers Orch **1** DT6...101 D4
Gulway Mead **7** TA20..202 A8
Gundry La DT6...........100 C6
Gundry Moor Trading Est
  BH21...................53 B6
Gundry Rd DT6...........100 F2
Gunners La BA22..........26 C5
Gunn La **3** DT11.......198 B5
Gunville Cres BH9.........90 B3
Gunville Down Rd DT11...199 F4
Gunville La
  East Coker BA22.........193 B3
  Hermitage DT2..........195 C2
Gunville Rd DT11.........199 F4
Gurjun Cl BH16...........118 A8
Gurkha Mus The SO23....126 D5
Gurney Rd BH21...........86 E6
Gussage Rd BH12.........120 F6
Gwenlyn Rd
  Upton BH16.............117 E6
  Upton BH16.............118 C6
Gwynne Rd BH12.........120 E5
Gyllas Way SP8...........5 F4
Gypshayes BH19.........178 B2
Gypsy La
  Easton/Weston DT5......186 F3
  Ringwood BH24...........55 D8
  2 Weymouth DT4......167 C2

H

Haarlem Mews BH23......124 D7
Hackney DT2.............205 A4
Haddon Rd BH18.........122 D6
Haddon La DT10...........19 E2
Haddons Dr BH21..........52 F6
Hadley Way BH18..........86 E3
Hadow Rd BH10............89 C3
Hadrian Cl BH21..........61 D2
Hadrian Way BH21........86 E8
Hahnemann Rd BH2......121 E2
Haig Ave BH13...........120 E3
Haimes La SP7............12 E3
Hainault Dr BH31..........45 C4
Haines La DT8...........203 A5
Hains La DT10.............20 E5
Haking Rd BH23..........124 D2
Halcyon Ct BH15.........119 C6
Hale Ave BH25............95 B2
Hale Gdns BH25...........95 B2
Hales Mdw BA21..........14 A3
Halewood Way BH23......123 F6
Half Acres DT9...........30 A5
Half Hide Down SP5......188 B3
Half Moon St DT9.........30 B2
Halfpenny La SP5..........37 C2
Halifax Way DT3.........125 B7
Hallet Ct DT11............96 B6
Hallet Gdns BA20........27 C4
Hall Rd BH11.............88 F3
Halls Cnr BH16............84 C1
Halls Rd BH16.............84 B1

Hall & Woodhouse Brewery Visitor Ctr DT11 212 D2
Halsey Gn DT2 196 B3
Halstock Cl 1 DT3 153 C2
Halstock Cres BH17 87 D2
Halter Path BH15 118 E3
Halter Rise BH21 60 C6
Halton Cl BH23 93 B8
Halves Cotts BH20 177 A7
Halves La BA22 193 B8
Hambledon Cl
Blandford Forum DT11 212 E4
Todber DT10 21 D4
Hambledon Gdns
Blandford Forum DT11 212 E4
Bournemouth BH6 123 C6
Hambledon Hill National Nature Reserve DT11 198 D7
Hambledon Rd
Bournemouth BH7 123 B7
Bournemouth,West Southbourne BH6 123 C6
Hambledon View DT10 35 C2
Hamble Rd BH15 120 A6
Hamblin Way BH8 90 E2
Hambro Rd DT5 186 F7
Hamcroft DT5 186 F4
Hamilton Bsns Pk BH25 94 E2
Hamilton Cl
Bournemouth BH1 122 D5
Christchurch BH23 124 F4
Hamworthy BH15 118 E2
Radipole DT3 152 E2
Hamilton Cres BH15 118 E2
Hamilton Ct
1 Bournemouth BH8 122 B5
1 Wimborne Minster BH21 59 B5
Hamilton Mews BH23 93 B8
Hamilton Rd
Bournemouth BH1 122 D4
Corfe Mullen BH21 86 E5
Hamworthy BH15 118 E2
Hamilton Way BH25 94 E2
Ham La
1 Gillingham SP8 6 B1
Hampreston BH21 60 E3
Marnhull DT10 20 D4
Trent DT9 15 A2
Wimborne Minster BH21 60 C5
Hamlands DT2 105 E1
Ham Mdw DT10 20 D4
Hammett Cl DT2 79 D1
Hammond Ave DT4 167 A6
Hammonds Mead DT6 97 A7
Hammond St DT10 196 E1
Hampden La BH6 123 B5
Hampreston CE Fst Sch BH21 60 E3
Hampshire Cl BH23 91 F2
Hampshire Ct 3 BH2 121 F3
Hampshire Hatches La BH24 55 B4
Hampshire Ho 2 BH2 121 F3
Hampshire Rd DT4 166 F4
Hampton DT3 132 A1
Hampton Cl 8 BA22 193 F8
Hampton Ct 5 BH2 121 D4
Hampton Dr BH24 47 D1
Hampton La SO22 126 A7
Hamworthy Fst Sch BH15 118 F1
Hamworthy LODGE BH15 118 F2
Hamworthy Mid Sch BH15 118 F1
Hamworthy Sta BH16 118 D4
Hanbury Rd 7 BH19 179 A2
Handley Ct BH24 55 B7
Handley Lodge 2 BH12 120 F7
Hands La DT3 149 B7
Handy Villas 22 SO23 126 E6
Hanford Sch DT11 198 D6
Hanham Ct BH12 121 B8
Hanham Rd
Corfe Mullen BH21 86 D5
Wimborne Minster BH21 59 C5
Hankinson Rd BH9 122 A8
Hanlon Cl BH11 89 B4
Hannam's Cl BH16 84 D3
Hannington Pl BH7 123 A5
Hannington Rd BH7 123 A5
Hanover Cl DT10 35 A2
Hanover Ct DT11 212 C4
Hanover Gn BH17 119 F7
Hanover Ho BH15 119 D3
Hanover La SP8 5 D1
Hanover Lodge SO23 126 D4
Hanover Rd DT4 167 D5
Happy Island Way DT6 100 F7
Harbeck Rd BH8 90 C3
Harbour BA21 26 E5
Harbour Cl BH13 147 D6
Harbour Cres BH23 124 E5
Harbour Ct
Barton on Sea BH25 126 E7
Christchurch BH23 124 E6
Poole BH13 147 E6
Harbour Hill DT3 166 F8
Harbour Hill Cres BH15 119 E5
Harbour Hill Rd BH15 119 E5
Harbour Hospl The BH15 119 D3
Harbour Lights BH15 119 E4
Harbour Prospect BH14 147 C8
Harbour Rd
Bournemouth BH6 124 A3
Sherborne DT9 30 C7
Harbour View Cl BH14 120 A5
Harbour View Ct BH23 124 B5
Harbour View Rd
Fortuneswell DT5 186 F8
Poole BH14 120 A5
Harbour Watch BH14 147 C7
Harbour Way DT9 30 B7
Harbridge Dro BH24 42 E3
Harbridge Sch BH24 46 F8
Harcombe Cl BH17 87 E3
Harcombe Rd DT7 64 A3
Harcourt Mews 6 BH5 123 A5
Harcourt Rd BH5 123 A5
Harding's La SP8 6 A1
Hardwick St 2 DT4 167 E4
Hardy Ave DT4 167 B2
Hardy Cl
2 Beaminster DT8 204 D4
Ferndown BH22 53 B1
Marnhull DT10 21 A3
Martinstown DT2 133 D6
New Milton BH25 94 F3
Hardy Cres
Stalbridge DT10 33 D8
Wimborne Minster BH21 59 D4
Hardy Ct 23 TA18 191 F3
Hardy Mon DT2 132 C4
Hardy Rd
Bridport DT6 100 E7
Ferndown BH22 53 B1
Poole BH14 120 D4
Wareham BH20 142 D2
Hardy's Birthplace DT2 109 B5
Hardy's La DT8 203 D6
Hare La
Cranborne BH21 40 F5
New Milton BH25,SO41 95 E3
Hares Gn BH7 123 A8
Harewood Ave
Bournemouth BH7 122 F7
Bournemouth BH7 123 A6
Harewood Cres BH7 122 F8
Harewood Gdns BH7 122 F7
Harewood Pl BH7 123 B6
Harewood Rd DT1 107 C1
Harford Rd BH12 120 C8
Hargrove La DT10 33 F4
Harkwood Dr BH15 118 E4
Harland Rd BH6 124 A3
Harleston Villas 5 BH21 59 D4
Harley Gap BH21 201 B8
Harley La BH21 201 A5
Harman's Cross Sta BH19 177 E5
Harness Cl BH21 60 B6
Harper Rd 21 TA18 191 F4
Harpitts La SP8 9 E4
Harpway La BH23 92 C6
Harraby Gn BH18 87 A3
Harrier Dr BH21 59 D2
Harriers Cl BH23 125 D8
Harrington Ct BH23 125 F7
Harrison Ave BH1 122 D6
Harrison Cl BH23 92 C3
Harrison Way BH22 53 A3
Harris Way BH25 95 B6
Harrow Cl BH23 93 B7
Harrow Down SO22 126 B2
Harrow Rd BH23 93 B6
Harry Barrow Cl 1 BH24 55 C6
Harry Lodge's La SP8 5 A1
Hart Cl BH25 94 F4
Hartfoot Cl DT2 209 B5
Hartfoot La DT2 209 B5
Harting Rd BH6 123 D7
Hartland Moor National Nature Reserve BH20 161 E7
Hartlebury Terr 2 DT4 167 D2
Hartley St DT2 195 B1
Hartmoor Hill SP8 9 D5
Hartnell Ct BH21 86 D5
Hartsbourne Dr BH7 123 B8
Hart's La
Holt BH21 51 C3
Nether Compton DT9 29 B6
Harvest Cl SO22 126 B2
Harvey Rd
Bournemouth BH5 123 A5
Oakley BH21 87 E8
Harveys Cl DT2 73 A8
Harwell Rd BH17 119 D7
Harwood Ct BH25 94 F3
Haselbury Plucknett VC Fst Sch TA18 192 C5
Haskells Rd BH12 120 B7
Haslemere Ave BH23 126 A8
Haslemere Pl BH23 126 A8
Hasler Rd BH17 87 D2
Haslop Rd BH21 60 A7
Hastings Rd
Bournemouth BH8 90 F2
Poole BH17 87 B2
Hatch Pond Rd BH17 119 C8
Hatfield Ct BH25 94 E3
Hatfield Gdns BH7 123 B8
Hathaway Rd BH6 123 D4
Hatherden Ave BH14 119 F5
Hatherley Rd SO22 126 D7
Hathermead Gdns BA21 27 F7
Havelins DT11 198 E4
Havelock Rd BH12 121 A5
Havelock Way BH23 93 D2
Haven Cotts BH23 125 A4
Haven Ct BH13 147 B3
Haven Gdns BH25 95 B2
Havenhurst BH13 147 E6
Haven Rd
Corfe Mullen BH21 86 C6
Poole BH13 147 E7
Haverstock Rd BH9 90 B2
Haviland Mews BH7 122 F5
Haviland Rd
Bournemouth BH7 122 F5
Ferndown BH21 61 A7
Haviland Rd E BH7 122 F5
Haviland Rd W BH1 122 F5
Hawden Rd BH11 89 A1
Hawkchurch Gdns BH17 87 E2
Hawkchurch Prim Sch EX13 202 B3
Hawkchurch Rd EX13 202 B3
Hawk Cl BH21 60 A7
Hawkcombe La SP7 23 E1
Hawker Cl BH21 59 F1
Hawker's La SP7 22 B8
Hawkesdene SP7 12 F1
Hawkesdene La SP7 12 F2
Hawkesworth Cl DT3 153 B1
Hawkins Cl 2 BH24 47 E1
Hawkins Rd BH12 88 F1
Hawkins Way BA21 26 E6
Hawkmoor Hill EX13 202 E2
Hawkwood Rd BH1,BH5 122 F4
Haworth Cl BH23 92 A1
Hawthorn Ave SP8 5 E2
Hawthorn Cl
5 Dorchester DT1 107 E2
New Milton BH25 95 C4
Radipole DT4 167 A6
1 Shaftesbury SP7 13 A4
Hawthorn Dr BH17 86 F1
Hawthorne Cl 15 TA18 191 F5
Hawthorne Rd DT1 107 E2
Hawthorn Rd
Bournemouth BH9 121 F8
Burton BH23 92 E4
Charminster DT2 75 D2
Yeovil BA21 27 F7
Hawthorns The
Christchurch BH23 124 F6
Stalbridge DT10 33 E7
Haxen La TA17 191 A8
Haycock Way 2 BH21 56 D4
Haycombe 4 DT11 198 E3
Haycrafts La BH19 177 E3
Haydon Hill Nature Reserve DT2 75 B1
Haydon Hollow DT9 31 C5
Haydon La
Frome St Quintin DT2 206 D7
Lydlinch DT10 197 A6
Haydon Rd BH13 121 B1
Haye Cl DT7 96 A6
Haye La DT7 96 A6
Hayes Ave BH7 122 E6
Hayes Cl BH21 60 A4
Hayes La BH21 60 B5
Hayes The 3 DT8 203 E5
Hayeswood Fst Sch BH21 60 B6
Hayeswood Rd BH21 60 A6
Haylands DT5 186 F3
Haymoor Ave DT3 167 F8
Haymoor Mid Sch BH17 87 E1
Haymoor Rd BH15 120 A7
Haynes Ave BH15 119 D4
Haysoms Cl BH25 95 B1
Hayters Way SP6 42 C6
Hayward Cres BH31 45 A5
Hayward La DT11 198 B7
Haywards Ave DT3 167 D7
Haywards Farm Cl BH31 45 A5
Haywards La
Child Okeford DT11 198 C7
Corfe Mullen BH21 86 C7
Hayward Way BH31 44 F5
Hazelbury Bryan Com Prim Sch DT10 197 A3
Hazel Cl
Alderholt SP6 42 C5
Christchurch BH23 93 C1
Hazel Ct
Bournemouth BH9 90 C4
1 New Milton BH25 95 B1
Winchester SO22 126 A8
Hazeldown Ave DT3 167 F8
Hazel Dr
Ferndown BH22 61 D8
2 Overcombe/Preston DT3 153 B2
Hazel Gr SO22 126 B3
Hazel La DT2 129 E7
Hazell Ave BH10 89 B2
Hazelton Cl BH7 123 A8
Hazel View 11 TA18 191 F5
Hazelwood Ave BH25 94 F4
Hazelwood Dr BH31 45 D4
Hazlebury Rd BH17 119 A7
Hazlemere Dr BH24 54 A3
Hazzard's Hill BA12 3 B5
Headinglea 9 BH13 121 B3
Head La SP8 10 D3
Headland Cl 3 DT5 186 E1
Headlands Bsns Pk BH24 47 C2
Headless Cross BH10 89 D5
Heads Farm Cl BH10 89 E5
Head's La BH10 89 E5
Headstock Rd TA20 202 B7
Headswell Ave BH10 89 E4
Headswell Cres BH10 89 E4
Headswell Gdns BH10 89 E4
Heanor Cl BH10 89 C2
Heath Ave BH15 119 D6
Heath Cl
Bovington Camp BH20 139 C7
Wimborne Minster BH21 60 B7
Heathcote Cl DT1 108 B1
Heathcote Ct 2 BH7 122 F4
Heathcote Rd BH5,BH7 122 F4
Heatherbank Rd BH4 121 C3
Heatherbrae La BH16 118 B6
Heather Cl
Bournemouth BH8 90 D4
Corfe Mullen BH21 86 E6
St Leonards BH24 54 A3
Walkford BH23 94 A2
Heatherdell
Upton BH16 117 D6
Upton BH16 118 B6
Heatherdown Rd 1 BH22 53 C1
Heatherdown Way 2 BH22 53 C1
Heather Dr BH22 61 D7
Heather Fields 2 SP8 5 F4
Heatherlands Fst Sch BH12 120 E5
Heatherlands Rise BH12 120 D5
Heatherlea Rd BH6 123 D4
Heather Lo 1 BH25 95 A3
Heather Rd
Bournemouth BH10 89 D3
Yeovil BA21 27 E7
Heather View Rd BH12 120 F7
Heather Way
Ferndown BH22 61 D7
Yeovil BA22 26 C5
Heath Farm Cl BH22 61 C3
Heath Farm Rd BH22 61 C3
Heath Farm Way BH22 61 C3
Heathfield Ave BH12 121 A8
Heathfield Rd BH22 53 C1
Heathfields Way SP7 12 F4
Heathfield Way BH22 53 B1
Heath Green Rd BH19 164 B1
Heathland Cl DT2 137 D5
Heathlands Ave BH22 61 D2
Heathlands Cl
Burton BH23 92 C3
Verwood BH31 45 C6
Heathlands Prim Sch BH11 89 A3
Heath Rd
Hordle SO41 95 F3
St Leonards BH24 53 F4
Walkford BH23 94 B1
Heathwood Ave BH25 126 E8
Heathwood Rd
Bournemouth BH9 121 E8
Weymouth DT4 167 B4
Heathy Cl BH25 126 F8
Heaton Rd BH10 89 B2
Heavytree Rd BH14 120 B4
Heber's La TA17 191 A5
Heckford La BH15 119 D3
Heckford Rd
Corfe Mullen BH21 86 C5
Poole BH15 119 D4
Hectors Way DT11 212 C1
Heddington Dr DT11 212 C5
Hedgerley BH25 127 B8
Heights App BH16 118 C7
Heights Rd BH16 118 C8
Helena Rd BA20 26 F1
Helen La 2 DT4 167 E2
Helic Ho 2 BH21 59 C5
Hell Cnr DT2 194 D1
Hell La DT6 99 A8
Hell Stone (Long Barrow) DT3 132 A2
Helston Cl DT3 132 A1
Helyar Rd BH8 90 F2
Hembury Rd DT2 102 C7
Hemlet's Cl DT6 68 F1
Hemsbach Ct 1 BH20 142 E3
Henbest Cl BH21 60 C5
Henbury Cl
Corfe Mullen BH21 86 D6
Poole BH17 88 A2
Henbury Rise BH21 86 D6
Henbury View Fst Sch
Corfe Mullen BH21 86 C6
Poole BH21 85 E6
Henbury View Rd BH21 86 D6
Henchard Cl BH22 61 C2
Hendford 6 BA20 27 D4
Hendford Gdns BH10 89 D2
Hendford Gr BA20 27 C4
Hendford Hill BA20 27 B3
Hendford Rd BH10 89 D2
Hendrie Cl BH19 178 F2
Hengistbury Head Nature Reserve BH6 124 E2
Hengistbury Head Nature Trail BH6 124 C3
Hengistbury Rd
Barton on Sea BH25 126 E8
Bournemouth BH6 124 A3
Hengist Cvn Pk BH6 124 B4
Hengist Rd BH1 122 D4
Henhayes La 3 TA18 191 F4
Henley Gdns BH7 123 A7
Henley View 7 TA18 191 F3
Henning's Park Rd BH15 119 E5
Henning Way DT9 17 D3
Henry Cl DT4 180 E7
Henry's Way DT7 96 C6
Henstridge Trad Est BA8 20 A5
Henville Rd 6 BH8 122 C5
Herbert Ave BH12 120 D7
Herbert Ct BH12 120 D7
Herbert Hospl BH4 121 B2
Herberton Rd BH6 123 C5
Herbert Rd
New Milton BH25 95 B3
Poole BH4 121 B2
Herblay Cl BA21 28 A6
Herbury La DT9 194 D4
Hercules Rd BH15 118 D3
Hereford Cres DT4 167 A3
Hereford Rd DT4 167 A3
Heritage Ct BH13 147 F7
Hermitage Ct 8 DT1 107 C1
Hermitage La DT2 195 B1
Hermitage Rd BH14 120 A5
Hermitage St TA18 191 F4
Hermitage The BH14 120 A5
Herm Rd BH12 88 D1
Heron Cl
3 Chickerell DT3 166 D5
Overcombe/Preston DT3 168 A6
Heron Court Rd BH3,BH9 122 A7
Heron Dr BH21 60 A8
Herrington Rd DT1 135 A7
Herrison Rd DT2 75 E2
Herstone Cl BH17 87 F1
Herston Halt Sta BH19 178 E3
Hertford Ct 6 BH23 126 B7
Hertford Rd BA21 28 A8
Hesketh Cl BH24 54 C5
Hessary St 9 DT1 107 C1
Hestan Cl BH23 91 D4
Heston Way BH22 52 F3
Hetherly Rd DT3 167 C7
Hewish La TA18 191 D3
Hewitt Rd BH15 118 E4
Hewlett's Dro DT10 197 C7
Heysham Rd BH18 87 A3
Heytesbury Rd BH6 123 D5
Hibbard Ct BH10 89 D1
Hibberds Field BH21 40 B7
Hibberd Way BH10 89 D1
Hibbs Cl
Northport BH20 142 E5
Upton BH16 118 C7
Hickes Cl BH11 88 F4
Hickory Cl
1 Upton BH16 117 C8
Upton BH16 118 A8
Highacres DT6 69 D1
Highbridge Rd BH14 120 C3
High Brow BH22 61 D5
Highbury Cl BH25 95 B2
High Cl BH21 56 D4
Highcliffe Castle BH23 125 E7
Highcliffe Cnr BH23 126 B8
Highcliffe Rd
Christchurch BH23 125 C7
1 Swanage BH19 179 C4
Winchester SO23 126 F4
Highcliffe St Mark's Prim Sch BH23 93 F1
Highcliffe Sch BH23 93 D1
Highcliff Rd DT7 96 A5
Highdown DT3 167 F8
Highdown Ave DT1 107 D1
Higher Barn Cl SP7 24 C6
Higher Beadon TA16 191 E7
Higher Blandford Rd
Corfe Mullen BH18,BH21 86 F6
Shaftesbury SP7 13 A1
Higher Bullen BA22 193 F8
Higher Cheap St DT9 30 B6
Higher Coombses TA20 202 A8
Higher Day's Rd BH19 178 E2
Higher Dro DT2 205 F2
Higher Easthams La TA18 192 A5
Higher End DT3 166 C5
Higher Eype Rd DT6 99 F5
Higher Filbank BH20 177 A7
Higher Gdns BH20 177 A8
Higher Gunville 5 DT9 17 D2
Higher Kingsbury DT9 17 D3
Higher Kingsbury Cl DT9 17 C3
Higher Kingston BA21 27 D5
Higher Merley La BH21 86 E8
Higher Ream BA21 26 E6
Higher St La DT8 205 C3
Higher Sea La DT6 97 A8
Higher Shaftesbury Rd DT11 212 D8
Higher St
Bridport DT6 69 A1
Iwerne Minster DT11 37 F2
Lillington DT9 194 F7
Merriott TA16 191 F8
Morden BH20 83 D4
Okeford Fitzpaine DT11 197 F5
West Chinnock TA18 192 B8
Higher Westbury DT9 28 D1
High E St DT1 108 A2
Highfield Ave BH24 55 C8
Highfield Cl
Charminster DT2 107 D7
Corfe Mullen BH21 86 E5
Highfield Dr BH24 47 C1
Highfield Gdns 1 DT6 204 C2
Highfield Ho 3 BH14 120 B4
Highfield Rd
Bournemouth BH9 89 E2
Corfe Mullen BH21 86 E5
Ferndown BH22 53 A4
Ringwood BH24 55 C8
Yeovil BA21 27 E6
Highfields
Blandford Forum DT11 212 E4
West Chinnock TA18 192 B8
Highfield Terr 1 SO22 126 D5
Highgate La DT2 136 D6
Highgrove SP8 5 F4
Highgrove Cl 5 DT1 135 B8
High Howe Cl BH11 88 E4

High Howe Gdns BH11 . . . . .88 E4
High Howe La BH11 . . . . .88 E4
Highland Ave BH23 . . . . .94 B1
Highland Rd
 Poole BH14 . . . . .120 B5
 Weymouth DT4 . . . . .167 C3
 Wimborne Minster BH21 . . . .59 D6
Highlands Cres BH10 . . . . . . .89 C4
Highlands Rd BH25 . . . . .127 A8
Highland View Cl BH21 . . . . .59 D5
High Lea BA21 . . . . .27 D8
High Marryats BH25 . . . . . . .127 A7
High Mead BA22 . . . . .61 A2
High Mead La BH22 . . . . .61 A1
Highmoor Cl
 Corfe Mullen BH21 . . . . .86 D5
 Poole BH21 . . . . .120 B3
Highmoor Rd
 Bournemouth BH11 . . . . .89 A1
 Corfe Mullen BH21 . . . . .86 D5
 Poole BH11 . . . . .120 B3
 Poole BH21 . . . . .85 F5
High Oaks Gdns BH11 . . . . . .88 E4
High Park Rd BH18 . . . . .86 E4
High Pines BH23 . . . . .125 D7
High St Cl DT20 . . . . .140 A2
High St Fordington DT1 . . . .108 B2
High St N BH15 . . . . .119 D3
High St
 Ashmore SP5 . . . . .39 C8
 1 Broadwindsor DT8 . . . .203 E5
 Burton Bradstock DT6 . . . . .128 B7
 Child Okeford DT11 . . . . . . .198 C7
 Christchurch BH23 . . . . .124 B6
 Corscombe DT2 . . . . .205 A8
 Cranborne BH21 . . . . .40 A7
 Damerham SP6 . . . . .190 F3
 East Chinnock BA22 . . . . . . .192 E8
 3 Easton/Weston DT5 . . .186 F1
 Fortuneswell DT5 . . . . .186 E7
 Gillingham SP8 . . . . .5 F2
 Hardington Mandeville
  BA22 . . . . .193 A6
 Henstridge BA8 . . . . .19 A4
 Hinton St George TA17 . . . .191 C7
 Lytchett Matravers BH16 . . . .84 C3
 Milborne Port DT9 . . . . .17 D2
 Piddlehinton DT2 . . . . .76 E8
 Poole BH15 . . . . .119 C2
 Puddletown DT2 . . . . .78 B1
 Rimpton BA22 . . . . .15 B8
 Ringwood BH24 . . . . .155 B7
 Shaftesbury SP7 . . . . .12 E2
 Shapwick DT11 . . . . .48 C1
 Sixpenny Handley SP5 . . . . .189 A4
 Spetisbury DT11 . . . . .211 E5
 Stalbridge DT10 . . . . .33 C8
 St Leonards BH24 . . . . .54 A6
 Stourton with Gasper BA12 . . .1 E8
 Sturminster Marshall BH21 . . .56 D4
 Swanage BH19 . . . . .178 B2
 Sydling St Nicholas DT2 . . . .207 A2
 Tarrant Monkton DT11 . . . . .200 B3
 Thorncombe TA20 . . . . .202 E5
 Toller Porcorum DT2 . . . . . . .71 D8
 Weymouth DT4 . . . . .180 C7
 Wimborne Minster BH21 . . . .59 B4
 Winchester SO23 . . . . .126 D6
 Winchester SO23 . . . . .126 E5
 Winchester SO23 . . . . .126 F5
 Winfrith Newburgh DT2 . . . .156 F5
 Wool BH20 . . . . .140 B2
 Yeovil BA20 . . . . .27 D4
 Yetminster DT9 . . . . .174 C5
 Zeale SP8 . . . . .1 F3
Hightown Gdns BH24 . . . . . .55 D6
Hightown Ind Est BH24 . . . . .55 D6
Hightown Rd BH24 . . . . .55 C6
High Trees
 Broadmayne DT2 . . . . .136 C1
 Poole BH13 . . . . .147 G8
Hightrees Ave BH8 . . . . .90 F1
High Trees Dr SO22 . . . . . . .126 C8
High Trees Wlk BH21 . . . . . . .61 D7
Highview Cl BH23 . . . . .91 E3
Highview Gdns BH22 . . . . . .120 C7
High Way BH18 . . . . .86 F3
Highwood Cl SP6 . . . . .41 F6
Highwood La BH24 . . . . .47 E4
Highwood Rd BH14 . . . . . . .120 E4
High W St
 Dorchester DT1 . . . . .108 A2
 Weymouth DT4 . . . . .167 D2
Hilary Rd DT4 . . . . .87 C1
Hilcot Way DT11 . . . . .212 D5
Hilda Rd BH12 . . . . .120 E7
Hiley Rd BH15 . . . . .119 C6
Hilfield La DT2 . . . . .194 F1
Hillard Ct **7** BH20 . . . . . . .142 E3
Hillary Rd BH23 . . . . .124 E8
Hillborne Gdns **1** BA21 . . . .26 E6
Hillbourne Com Fst & Mid
 Schs BH17 . . . . .87 B2
Hillbourne Rd
 Poole BH17 . . . . .87 A2
 1 Weymouth DT4 . . . . . .180 D7
Hill Brow DT9 . . . . .29 F4
Hillbrow Rd BH6 . . . . .123 B6
Hillbury Rd SP6 . . . . .42 D6
Hill Cl
 Bransgore BH23 . . . . .93 A8
 5 Bridport DT6 . . . . . . .100 B2
Hillcrest Ave BH22 . . . . .61 C8

Hillcrest Cl
 Bournemouth BH9 . . . . .90 A3
 Sturminster Newton DT10 . .197 C8
Hillcrest Hospl BH10 . . . . . . .89 D1
Hillcrest Rd
 Bournemouth BH9 . . . . .90 A3
 Corfe Mullen BH21 . . . . .86 C5
 Poole BH12 . . . . .120 A5
 Weymouth DT4 . . . . .180 C7
Hill Crest Rd BA21 . . . . .27 E6
Hillfield Cl DT3 . . . . .152 B4
Hillfort Cl DT11 . . . . .134 E7
Hillfort Mews **6** DT1 . . . . .134 E7
Hillgrove Ave BA20 . . . . .27 B2
Hill House Cl DT11 . . . . .30 C7
Hillier Way SO23 . . . . .126 E8
Hillingdon DT6 . . . . .100 E8
Hillingdon Ct BA14 . . . . .26 E6
Hilling La DT2 . . . . .208 A7
Hill La
 Bransgore BH23 . . . . .93 A8
 Burton BH23 . . . . .92 F2
Hillman Rd BH14 . . . . .120 D5
Hillmeadow BH31 . . . . .45 C4
Hill Rd
 Blandford Forum DT11 . . . .212 E6
 Lyme Regis DT7 . . . . .96 B5
 Swanage BH19 . . . . .179 B5
Hill Rise DT6 . . . . .100 B2
Hill Rise Rd DT7 . . . . .96 B5
Hillsea Rd BH19 . . . . .179 A2
Hillside Cl
 Mere BA12 . . . . .2 E5
 Winchester SO22 . . . . .126 A8
Hillside Dr BH23 . . . . .91 D3
Hillside Fst Sch BH31 . . . . . . .45 B7
Hillside Gdns BH21 . . . . .86 C4
Hillside Mews
 Corfe Mullen BH21 . . . . .86 C4
 2 Poole BH21 . . . . .85 E4
Hillside Rd
 1 Blandford Camp
  DT11 . . . . .199 E3
 Corfe Mullen BH21 . . . . .86 C5
 Poole BH12 . . . . .88 F1
 Verwood BH31 . . . . .45 C7
 Woodlands BH21 . . . . .44 C6
 3 Wool BH20 . . . . .141 A4
Hillside Terr **4** BA20 . . . . . .27 E5
Hillside View **2** BH21 . . . .193 F8
Hill St BH15 . . . . .119 C2
Hill Terr BH21 . . . . .60 A2
Hilltop Cl BH22 . . . . .61 B7
Hilltop Rd
 Corfe Mullen BH21 . . . . .86 E5
 Ferndown BH22 . . . . .61 B7
Hillview DT6 . . . . .68 F1
Hill View
 Bishop's Caundle DT9 . . . . .196 A7
 Charminster DT2 . . . . .107 C6
 5 Hazelbury Bryan DT10 .197 A4
 Maiden Newton DT2 . . . . . . .73 A7
 Mudford BA21 . . . . .14 A3
 Overcombe/Preston DT3 . . .169 A8
 Yeovil BA20 . . . . .27 E5
Hill View Cl BH21 . . . . .192 B7
Hillview Est **1** DT4 . . . . . .100 C8
Hill View Prim Sch BH10 . . . .89 E3
Hillview Rd
 Bournemouth BH10 . . . . . . .89 D3
 Swanage BH19 . . . . .179 A2
Hill View Rd BH22 . . . . .61 C7
Hill Way BH24 . . . . .54 A5
Hilmar Dr SP8 . . . . .5 E2
Hiltom Rd BH24 . . . . .55 D7
Hilton Cl BH15 . . . . .120 A5
Hilton Rd BH25 . . . . .95 B4
Hilton Rd Cl DT11 . . . . .79 E8
Hinchliffe Cl BH15 . . . . .118 F2
Hinchliffe Rd BH15 . . . . . . .118 F2
Hine Cl SP8 . . . . .11 B8
Hine's Mead La DT2 . . . . . . .103 C1
Hington La DT11 . . . . .198 B6
Hingston La DT16 . . . . .204 B2
Hintock St DT1 . . . . .107 D1
Hinton Admiral Mews
 BH23 . . . . .93 E2
Hinton Admiral Sta BH23 . . . .93 E2
Hinton Cl
 Blandford Forum DT11 . . . .212 D5
 Hinton St George TA17 . . . .191 C7
Hinton Cross BA22 . . . . .14 B5
Hinton La DT10 . . . . .35 C7
Hinton Rd
 Bournemouth BH1 . . . . .121 F3
 West Crewkerne TA18 . . . . .191 E5
Hinton St George Prim Sch
 TA17 . . . . .191 C7
Hinton St Mary Roman Villa
 DT10 . . . . .35 B4
Hinton View DT10 . . . . .35 B2
Hinton Wood Rd BH1 . . . . . .122 A2
Hinton Wood Ave BH23 . . . . .93 E1
Hintonwood La BH23 . . . . . . .93 E2
Hitchen **5** TA16 . . . . .191 F7
Hive Cl DT6 . . . . .128 C7
Hive Gdns BH13 . . . . .147 D6
Hobart Rd BH25 . . . . .94 F2
Hobbs Pk BH24 . . . . .54 B4
Hobbs Rd BH12 . . . . .120 C8
Hobgoblin DT11 . . . . .37 F1
Hoburne Cvn Pk BH23 . . . . .125 C8
Hoburne Gdns BH23 . . . . . . .93 C1
Hoburne La BH23 . . . . .125 C8
Hoburne Rd BH19 . . . . .179 A2
Hodder's La DT7 . . . . .64 A2

Hod Dr DT11 . . . . .198 E5
Hodges Cl BH17 . . . . .119 E7
Hod Hill (Hill Fort & Roman
 Fort) DT11 . . . . .198 E5
Hod View **2** DT11 . . . . . . .198 F4
Hodway La DT11 . . . . .198 D5
Hogarth Way BH8 . . . . .91 A2
Hog Cliff National Nature
 Reserve DT2 . . . . .73 D7
Hogshill St DT8 . . . . .204 C4
Hogue Ave BH10 . . . . .89 D5
Holbaek Cl DT11 . . . . .135 B7
Holburne Naish BH25 . . . . . .126 D8
Holbury Cl BH8 . . . . .90 E3
Holcombe Cl DT3 . . . . .168 D8
Holcombe Mead DT7 . . . . . .208 A6
Holcombe Rd BH12 . . . . .118 B6
Holdenhurst Ave BH7 . . . . . .123 C7
Holdenhurst Rd
 Bournemouth BH8 . . . . . . .122 C5
 Bournemouth, Holdenhurst
  BH8 . . . . .91 B3
Holditch Ct La TA20 . . . . . . .202 A5
Holditch La TA20 . . . . .202 A5
Holdscroft La DT11 . . . . .202 E1
Holebrook La DT10 . . . . .196 F7
Hole House La DT10 . . . . . . .197 D8
Holes Bay North Rdbt
 BH17 . . . . .119 A6
Holes Bay Rd BH15 . . . . . . .119 B4
Holes Bay Rd BH15 . . . . . . .119 B4
Holes Bay Rdbt BH15 . . . . . .119 B5
Holes Cl SO41 . . . . .95 F4
Holland Rd DT4 . . . . .167 C3
Hollands Cl BH20 . . . . .176 F8
Hollands Mead Ave DT2 . . . .155 D7
Hollands Wood Dr BH25 . . . .95 B5
Holland Way
 Blandford Forum DT11 . . . .212 D5
 Corfe Mullen BH21 . . . . .86 F5
Holland Way Ind Pk
 DT11 . . . . .212 E6
Hollenden **3** BH13 . . . . . .121 A4
Holleys Cl **4** TA20 . . . . . .191 E2
Hollies The
 3 Crewkerne TA18 . . . . .191 E3
 Yeovil BA21 . . . . .27 E7
Hollis Way BA22 . . . . .193 D3
Holloway Ave BH11 . . . . .88 F5
Holloway La DT11 . . . . .198 C5
Holloway Rd DT11 . . . . .108 B2
Hollow Hill DT2 . . . . .108 F4
Hollow La TA17 . . . . .191 B7
Hollow Oak BH20 . . . . .113 B8
Hollow Oak Rd BH20 . . . . . .142 E1
Hollow The
 Affpuddle DT2 . . . . .112 B6
 Child Okeford DT11 . . . . . . .198 C8
 4 Sixpenny Handley SP5 .189 A4
Hollow Way DT6 . . . . .100 D4
Holly Cl
 3 Dorchester DT1 . . . . . .107 E2
 Ferndown BH22 . . . . .52 F2
 7 Sandford BH20 . . . . . .116 A1
 St Leonards BH24 . . . . .53 F4
 Upton BH16 . . . . .118 A7
Holly Ct BH15 . . . . .119 D4
Holly Gdns BH23 . . . . .92 D1
Holly Gr
 Merriott TA16 . . . . .191 F5
 Verwood BH31 . . . . .45 A5
Holly Green Rise BH11 . . . . . .88 E4
Holly Hedge La BH17 . . . . . .119 C8
Holly La
 Broadwindsor DT8 . . . . . . .203 D8
 New Milton BH25 . . . . .95 C4
 Walkford BH23 . . . . .94 C2
Holly Lo **3** BH23 . . . . .121 A4
Holly Mdws SO22 . . . . .126 A8
Hollymoor Cl **3** BH20 . . . .204 D4
Hollymoor Common La
 DT8 . . . . .192 D7
Hollymoor Gdns **7** BH20 . .204 D4
Hollymoor La DT8 . . . . .192 D7
Holly Rd BH14 . . . . .167 C3
Holm Ct BH24 . . . . .47 E1
Holmead Wlk DT1 . . . . .107 D1
Holme Cl DT3 . . . . .167 B8
Holme La
 East Holme BH20 . . . . .160 B7
 East Stoke BH20 . . . . .141 A1
Holmes Rd BH23 . . . . .126 B8
Holmes Rd BH19 . . . . .178 E2
Holmfield Ave BH7 . . . . .123 C7
Holm Hill La BH23,BH25 . . . .94 B7
Holmhurst Ave BH23 . . . . . . .93 F1
Holmlea Cl **1** DT11 . . . . . .212 E5
Holm Oak Cl BH31 . . . . .45 A8
Holmwood Garth **1** BH24 .54 E6
Holnest Rd BH17 . . . . .87 D1
Holten's La BA22 . . . . .192 E6
Holt Heath Ind Est
 BH23 . . . . .116 D2
Holton Heath Sta BH16 . . . .116 D1
Holton Rd BH16 . . . . .116 D2
Holt Pl BH21 . . . . .61 F7
Holt Rd
 Holt BH21 . . . . .51 D5

Holt Rd continued
 Horton BH21 . . . . .52 F8
 Poole BH12 . . . . .120 F6
 Wool BH20 . . . . .139 D6
Holway Cl BH21 . . . . .202 A8
Holway La DT2 . . . . .206 A5
Holway Woods Nature
 Reserve DT9 . . . . .16 A5
Howell Dro DT9 . . . . .195 F5
Howell Rd DT10 . . . . .196 C5
Howorth Cl BH11 . . . . .88 E3
Howroyd Cl BH17 . . . . .119 A8
Holy Trinity CE Inf Sch **1**
 DT4 . . . . .167 C1
Holy Trinity CE Jun Sch
 DT4 . . . . .167 C1
Holy Trinity CE VA Prim Sch
 BA20 . . . . .27 A3
Holywell Cl BH17 . . . . .87 D3
Homecliffe Ho BH23 . . . . . . .126 B8
Homecorfe Ho BH18 . . . . . . .87 B5
Homedale Ho BH2 . . . . .121 F5
Home Ho BH15 . . . . .119 D3
Home Dr BA21 . . . . .27 A6
Home Farm BH25 . . . . .127 E8
Home Farm Cl DT6 . . . . .101 E8
Home Farm La BA22 . . . . . . .15 A8
Home Farm Way
 Shipton Gorge DT6 . . . . . . .101 D3
 Verwood BH31 . . . . .45 A7
Homefield
 6 Child Okeford DT11 . . .198 C7
 Mere BA12 . . . . .2 F5
 Milborne St Andrew DT11 . . .79 F7
 Shaftesbury SP7 . . . . .12 F4
Homefield Ho **7** BH25 . . . . .95 A2
Homefield Ind Prep Sch
 BH6 . . . . .123 F5
Homelake Ho BH14 . . . . . . .120 B3
Homelands Est BH23 . . . . . .123 F6
Homelands Ho BH22 . . . . . . .61 D5
Homeleigh Ho **5** BH8 . . . .122 A5
Homelife Ho BH23 . . . . .122 A2
Homemill Ho **8** BH25 . . . . .95 A3
Homeoaks Ho BH2 . . . . .121 F5
Home Rd BH11 . . . . .89 B6
Homerise Ho **1** SO23 . . . .126 E6
Homeside Rd BH9 . . . . .90 A2
Homestour Ho **1** BH23 . . .124 A6
Homeview Ho BH15 . . . . . . .119 B3
Homewood Cl BH25 . . . . .95 C3
Honeybourne Cres BH6 . . . .124 A4
Honeybrook Victorian Farm
 & Ctry Pk BH21 . . . . .50 D2
Honeycombe Rise DT9 . . . . .29 F4
Honeyfields **8** SP8 . . . . .5 F4
Honeymead La DT10 . . . . . . .35 B2
Honeysuckle Cl
 Radipole DT3 . . . . .152 F2
 Winchester SO22 . . . . .126 C2
Honeysuckle Gdns **2**
 DT11 . . . . .198 B5
Honeysuckle La **1** BH17 . . .86 F1
Honeysuckle Way BH23 . . . .125 B8
Honeywood Ho BH14 . . . . . .147 C7
Hood Cl BH10 . . . . .89 B1
Hood Cres BH10 . . . . .89 B1
Hooke Cl BH17 . . . . .88 A2
Hooke Ct Sch DT8 . . . . .205 B3
Hooper's La
 Barwick BA22 . . . . .193 F7
 Puncknowle DT2 . . . . .129 F6
Hop Cl
 Upton BH16 . . . . .117 B7
 Upton BH16 . . . . .118 A7
Hope Bottom DT6 . . . . .204 C2
Hope Cl DT2 . . . . .137 D5
Hope Cross DT9 . . . . .9 A6
Hopegood Cl **4** DT11 . . . .211 D6
Hope Sq **9** DT4 . . . . .167 E1
Hope Terr DT1 . . . . .133 D6
Hopkins Cl BH8 . . . . .91 A2
Hopmans Cl BH16 . . . . .116 A4
Hopsfield DT11 . . . . .79 E8
Horace Rd **2** BH5 . . . . . . .122 E4
Hornbeam Cl DT4 . . . . .167 B6
Hornbeam Rd DT2 . . . . .75 D3
Hornbeam Sq BH15 . . . . . . .119 D2
Hornbeam Way BH21 . . . . . . .59 E5
Horncastles La DT9 . . . . .29 F6
Horning Rd BH12 . . . . .120 F5
Hornpark Quarry Ind Est
 DT8 . . . . .204 A5
Horn Pk DT8 . . . . .204 B5
Horsa Cl BH6 . . . . .123 E4
Horsa Cl BH6 . . . . .123 E4
Horsa Rd BH6 . . . . .123 E4
Horsecastles DT9 . . . . .30 A5
Horsecliffe La BH19 . . . . . . .179 C3
Horsefields SP8 . . . . .5 E4
Horshill La DT8 . . . . .204 A3
Horseponds SP7 . . . . .12 D3
Horseshoe Cl BH21 . . . . .60 B6
Horseshoe Common Rdbt
 BH1 . . . . .121 F3
Horseshoe Cl **1** BH21 . . . .121 E4
Horseshoe Rd BH20 . . . . . . .202 D7
Horseshoe The BH13 . . . . . .147 C4
Horsey Knap DT2 . . . . .205 E7
Horsey La
 East Chelborough DT2 . . . .205 E7
 Yeovil BA21 . . . . .27 C4
Horsford St DT4 . . . . .167 E1
Horsham Ave BH10 . . . . .89 C6
Horton Cl
 Bournemouth BH9 . . . . .90 C3
 Yeovil BA21 . . . . .26 F6

Horton Ho BH22 . . . . .61 F2
Horton Rd
 Horton BH21 . . . . .44 D2
 St Leonards BH24 . . . . .54 C8
 St Leonards & St Ives BH24 .53 E4
 Woodlands BH21 . . . . .201 F1
Horton Twr (Folly) BH21 . . . .44 F5
Horton Way BH31 . . . . .44 F8
Horyford Cl **8** BH23 . . . . .153 C2
Hosey Rd DT10 . . . . .35 C3
Hosker Rd BH5 . . . . .123 B5
Hospital La
 Allington DT6 . . . . .100 B8
 Sherborne DT9 . . . . .30 A5
Hotton Heath National
 Nature Reserve BH16 . . . . .116 F3
Houlton Rd BH15 . . . . .119 E6
Hound St DT9 . . . . .30 B6
Houndstone Cl BA22 . . . . . . .26 E5
Houndstone Ct **2** BA22 . . .26 C5
Hounds Way BH21 . . . . .60 B5
Hounslow Cl BH15 . . . . .118 F7
Howard Cl
 Bothenhampton DT6 . . . . . .101 A3
 Christchurch BH23 . . . . . . .124 F6
 Weymouth DT4 . . . . .180 A7
Howard Rd
 Bournemouth BH8 . . . . . . .122 C5
 Bridport DT6 . . . . .100 F6
 4 Swanage BH19 . . . . . .179 A2
 Verwood BH31 . . . . .45 B6
 Yeovil BA21 . . . . .28 A6
Howard's La BH20 . . . . .142 E3
Howarth Cl **1** BH23 . . . . . .128 B8
Howe Cl
 Christchurch BH23 . . . . . . .124 F5
 New Milton BH25 . . . . .94 F3
Howe La BH31 . . . . .45 A5
Howell Ho BH21 . . . . .59 F7
Howe's Eype La DT6 . . . . .99 E5
Howeth Cl BH10 . . . . .89 D3
Howeth Rd BH10 . . . . .89 C6
Howton Cl BH10 . . . . .89 C5
Howton Rd BH10 . . . . .89 C5
Hoxley Rd BH10 . . . . .89 C8
Hoyal Rd BH15 . . . . .118 D3
Hubert Rd SO23 . . . . .126 C2
Hudson Cl
 Poole BH12 . . . . .88 C2
 Ringwood BH24 . . . . .55 E8
Hughes Bsns Ctr BH23 . . . . .125 A7
Huish BA20 . . . . .27 C4
Huish CP Sch BA20 . . . . .27 C4
Huish La DT9 . . . . .31 E6
Hull Cres BH11 . . . . .88 A6
Hull Rd BH11 . . . . .88 A6
Hull Way BH11 . . . . .88 A6
Humber Chase BH20 . . . . . .142 C5
Humber Rd BH22 . . . . .62 A6
Humpy La DT9 . . . . .31 B1
Hundred Stone BA21 . . . . . . .27 D8
Hundredstone Cl BA21 . . . . .27 D8
Hungerford Hill SP6 . . . . . . .43 D6
Hungerford Rd BH8 . . . . .90 D3
Hunger Hill BH15 . . . . .119 C2
Hunter Cl
 Christchurch BH23 . . . . . . .125 A1
 Wimborne Minster BH21 . . . .60 C6
Hunters Cl BH31 . . . . .45 E5
Hunters Mead SP7 . . . . .7 B8
Huntfield Rd BH9 . . . . .90 B2
Huntick Est BH16 . . . . .84 D3
Huntick Rd BH16 . . . . .84 D3
Huntingdon Dr BH21 . . . . . . .59 E1
Huntingdon Gdns BH23 . . . . .92 A2
Huntley Down DT11 . . . . . . .209 F3
Huntly Rd BH3 . . . . .121 D2
Hurn Rd
 Blandford Forum DT11 . . . .212 E4
 Christchurch BH23 . . . . . . .124 F8
 Poole BH15 . . . . .119 E4
Hunt's Hill DT10 . . . . .21 E4
Hunts Mead DT9 . . . . .31 E6
Hurdle Way BH9 . . . . .90 B5
Hurdles The BH22 . . . . .123 E8
Hurn Cl BH24 . . . . .54 F7
Hurn Court La BH23 . . . . .90 F6
Hurn La BH24 . . . . .91 A4
Hurn Rd
 Christchurch BH23 . . . . .91 D3
 St Leonards & St Ives BH24 .54 F4
Hurn Way BH23 . . . . .91 D3
Hurricane Cl DT2 . . . . .137 D6
Hursley Cl BH7 . . . . .123 C8
Hurstbourne Ave BH23 . . . . .93 E1
Hurst Cl
 Barton on Sea BH25 . . . . . .126 D8
 Walkford BH23 . . . . .94 C2
Hurst Ct **1** BH23 . . . . .126 A2
Hurstdene Rd BH8 . . . . .90 E2
Hurst Hill BH14 . . . . .147 C5
Hurst Rd
 Moreton DT2 . . . . .111 C3
 Ringwood BH24 . . . . .155 A7
Hussar Cl DT2 . . . . .123 F2
Hussey Cl **2** SO23 . . . . . . .126 E6
Hussey's DT10 . . . . .20 F4
Hutchins Cl DT1 . . . . .134 E2
Hut Gate TA13 . . . . .192 A8
Hyacinth Cl BH17 . . . . .106 A3
Hybris Bsns Pk DT2 . . . . . . .137 B8
Hyde Abbey Rd SO23 . . . . . .126 E6
Hyde CE Prim Sch SP6 . . . . .43 F7
Hyde Church Path **6**
 SO23 . . . . .126 E6
Hyde Cl SO23 . . . . .126 E6

Hyde Ct BA21 . . . . 26 E6
Hyde Gate 10 SO23 . . . . . . 126 E7
Hyde Gdns 6 DT11 . . . . . 199 D4
Hyde House Gdns 5
SO23 . . . . 126 E7
Hyde La SP6 . . . . 43 E6
Hyde Lodge SO23 . . . . . . 126 D7
Hyde Rd
Bournemouth BH10 . . . . . . 89 C5
Gillingham SP8 . . . . 5 E3
Wool BH20 . . . . 140 A2
Hydes La DT10 . . . . 196 D7
Hyde St SO23 . . . . 126 E7
Hyde The
New Milton BH25 . . . . 94 E4
Swanage BH19 . . . . 178 C2
Hynesbury Rd BH23 . . . . 125 C6
Hythe Rd BH15 . . . . 120 A7
Hythe The DT3 . . . . 166 D5

I

Ibbertson Cl BH8 . . . . 90 C1
Ibbertson Rd BH8 . . . . 90 F2
Ibbertson Way BH8 . . . . . . 90 F2
Ibbett Rd BH10 . . . . 89 C3
Ibsley Cl BH8 . . . . 122 C6
Ibsley Dro BH24 . . . . 43 D1
Icen La
Bincombe DT3 . . . . 152 C4
Shipton Gorge DT6 . . . . . 101 E4
Icen Rd DT3 . . . . 167 C7
Icen Way DT1 . . . . 108 A2
Idsleigh Rd
Bournemouth BH3 . . . . . . 121 F6
Bournemouth BH3 . . . . . . 122 A6
Iford Bridge Home Pk
BH6 . . . . 123 D7
Iford Gdns BH7 . . . . 123 C7
Iford La BH6 . . . . 123 E6
Ilchester Rd
Weymouth DT4 . . . . 167 C3
Yeovil BA21 . . . . 27 B7
Ilford Cl BH6 . . . . 123 F5
Ilminster Rd BH19 . . . . . . 179 B2
Islington House DT1 . . . . . 78 C1
Isington Rd DT2 . . . . 109 F4
Iver Dr BH23 . . . . 125 F8
Imber Rd SP7 . . . . 13 A3
Imbrecourt BH13 . . . . 147 E7
Imperial Ct 4 BH13 . . . . 147 F7
Incline Rd DT5 . . . . 187 B6
Ingarth 7 BH6 . . . . 123 E3
Inglegreen Cl BH25 . . . . . 94 F7
Inglesham Way BH15 . . . . 118 E4
Inglewood Ave BH8 . . . . . 90 F1
Inglewood Dr BH25 . . . . . 95 B2
Ingram Wlk 1 BA21 . . . . . 59 D4
Ingworth Rd BH12 . . . . . . 121 A5
Inmosthay DT5 . . . . 187 A5
Inner Breakwater Rd
DT5 . . . . 181 D1
Insley Cres BH18 . . . . 86 E5
Institute Rd BH19 . . . . . . 179 C2
Inveravon BH23 . . . . 124 F4
Inverclyde Ho BH14 . . . . 120 B4
Inverclyde Rd BH14 . . . . 120 C4
Inverleigh Rd BH6 . . . . . . 123 C6
Inverness Rd BH13 . . . . . 147 E7
Ipswich Rd BH12 . . . . 121 B4
Iris Gdns 6 SP8 . . . . 5 E1
Iris Rd BH9 . . . . 89 F1
Irvine Rd BH23 . . . . 124 E8
Irving La BH6 . . . . 123 D5
Irving Rd BH6 . . . . 123 D5
Isaacs Cl BH13 . . . . 121 B7
Island View Ave BH23 . . . 125 B5
Island View Rd BH25 . . . . 126 C7
Isle of Purbeck Golf Club
BH19 . . . . 178 E3
Isle Rd DT5 . . . . 186 E3
Isles La BA22 . . . . 193 D6
Itchen Ct 3 SO23 . . . . . . 126 F6
Ivamy Pl BH11 . . . . 88 F2
Ivel Cl DT1 . . . . 135 B8
Ivel Ct BA20 . . . . 27 E4
Ivelway 14 TA18 . . . . 191 F4
Ivor Rd
Corfe Mullen BH21 . . . . . . 86 D4
Poole BH15 . . . . 119 A1
Ivy Cl
4 Gillingham SP8 . . . . 5 D2
St Leonards BH24 . . . . 53 F4
Winchester SO22 . . . . . . 126 C3
Ivy La BH24 . . . . 47 D4
Ivy Mead BA12 . . . . 3 B5
Ivy Rd BH21 . . . . 87 D8
Iwerne Cl BH9 . . . . 90 B4

J

Jacey Ho 6 BH1 . . . . 122 A3
Jacklin Ct BH18 . . . . 87 B5
Jack Paul Cl BA12 . . . . 3 A6
Jack's Hedge Cnr BH21 . 189 F2
Jackson Gdns BH12 . . . . . 120 C6
Jackson Rd BH12 . . . . 120 C6
Jack the Treacle Eater
(Folly) BA22 . . . . 27 E1
Jacmar Ct 8 BH23 . . . . . . 93 F8
Jacobean Cl BH23 . . . . 94 B1
Jacobs Ladder 2 BH23 . . 198 C7
Jacobs Rd BH15 . . . . 118 E2
Jacqueline Rd BH12 . . . . 120 C7
James Cl DT11 . . . . 212 F5
James Cross La BH21 . . . 201 A6

James Day Mead 2
BH19 . . . . 179 B5
Jameson Rd BH9 . . . . 89 F1
James Rd
Dorchester DT1 . . . . 134 E8
Poole BH12 . . . . 121 A5
James St DT4 . . . . 167 D2
Janred Ct BH25 . . . . 126 E7
Jarvis Cl DT10 . . . . 33 D7
Jarvis Way DT10 . . . . 33 D8
Jasmine Cl
Crewkerne TA18 . . . . 191 F5
Yeovil BA22 . . . . 26 D5
Jasmine Way 2 DT4 . . . . 180 B8
Jaundrells Cl BH25 . . . . . . 95 C3
Jay's Ct BH23 . . . . 126 B8
Jeanneau Cl 4 SP7 . . . . . 12 F3
Jefferson Ave BH1 . . . . . . 122 D6
Jellicoe Cl BH14 . . . . 119 F5
Jellicoe Dr BH23 . . . . 124 F6
Jenner Cl BH31 . . . . 45 A7
Jenner Way DT3 . . . . 152 D3
Jennings Rd BH14 . . . . . . 120 C2
Jennys La BH16 . . . . 84 B4
Jephcote Rd BH11 . . . . 88 F4
Jeremy Cl 1 BH20 . . . . . 140 B2
Jersey Cl BH12 . . . . 88 D1
Jersey Rd BH12 . . . . 88 D1
Jesmond Ave BH23 . . . . . 125 F8
Jesop Cl 8 SP8 . . . . 5 E1
Jessica Ave BH31 . . . . 44 F7
Jessopp Ave DT6 . . . . 100 F7
Jessopp Cl BH10 . . . . 89 F4
Jessopp Ho 6 BH21 . . . . . 59 C5
Jessopp Rd BH21 . . . . 60 B6
Jesty's Ave DT3 . . . . 152 C4
Jewell Rd BH8 . . . . 91 A2
Jewry St SO23 . . . . 126 E6
Jimmy Brown Ave BH21 . . . 93 A5
Jock's Hill DT2 . . . . 78 E6
Johnson Rd BH21 . . . . 61 A8
Johnson's Ctyd DT9 . . . . . 30 C5
Johns Rd BH20 . . . . 142 D5
Johnston Rd BH23 . . . . . 124 E6
Johnston Rd BH15 . . . . . 119 D7
Jolliffe Ave BH15 . . . . . . 119 D4
Jolliffe Rd BH15 . . . . 119 D4
Jopps Cnr BH23 . . . . 92 C4
Jordan Hill Roman Temple
DT3 . . . . 152 E8
Jordan Way 3 DT3 . . . . . 152 C4
Joshua Cl BH15 . . . . 118 E2
Journeys End DT6 . . . . . . 100 B6
Jowitt Dr BH25 . . . . 94 F2
Joyce Dickson Cl 2
BH24 . . . . 55 D6
Joys Rd BH21 . . . . 53 A8
Juan's La SP8 . . . . 9 D2
Jubilee Cl
Corfe Mullen BH21 . . . . . . 86 E7
Radipole DT4 . . . . 167 D4
Ringwood BH24 . . . . 55 E8
Jubilee Cres BH12 . . . . . . 120 D5
Jubilee Ent Ctr DT4 . . . . 167 D4
Jubilee Gdns
Bournemouth BH10 . . . . . 89 D2
3 Corfe Castle BH20 . . . 177 A7
Jubilee Rd
Bournemouth BH10 . . . . . 89 D2
Poole BH12 . . . . 120 D5
Swanage BH19 . . . . 178 F2
Jubilee Trail DT2 . . . . . . 135 C4
Jubilee Way DT11 . . . . . . 212 C5
Julia Cl BH23 . . . . 125 F8
Julian's Rd BH21 . . . . 59 A4
Jumpers Ave BH23 . . . . . 123 E8
Jumpers Rd BH23 . . . . . . 123 F8
Junction Rd
Bournemouth BH9 . . . . . 121 F8
Hamworthy BH16 . . . . . . 118 D4
Juniper Cl
Ferndown BH22 . . . . 61 C8
Three Legged Cross BH21 . 53 A8
Winchester SO22 . . . . . . 126 B3
Yeovil BA20 . . . . 27 B3
Juniper Flats BH23 . . . . . 123 E8
Juniper Gdns 7 SP8 . . . . . 5 E1
Juniper Way DT3 . . . . . . 152 C3
Jupiter Way BH21 . . . . 86 E8
Justin Bsns Pk BH20 . . . . 142 F5
Justin Gdns BH10 . . . . 89 E4

K

Kamptee Copse BH25 . . . . 95 B6
Kangaw Pl BH15 . . . . 118 D2
Katherine Chance Cl
BH23 . . . . 92 C3
Katterns Cl BH23 . . . . 91 E2
Kay Cl BH23 . . . . 124 E6
Kayes Cl DT4 . . . . 180 C8
Keable Rd BH21 . . . . 60 B7
Keats Ho 1 BH25 . . . . 95 A1
Keble St SO22 . . . . 126 A4
Keble Cl BH10 . . . . 89 D6
Keeble Cres BH10 . . . . 89 D6
Keeble Rd BH10 . . . . 89 D6
Keepers La BH21 . . . . 60 F4
Keep Military Mus The
DT1 . . . . 107 F2
Keighley Ave BH18 . . . . . . 86 F1
Keith Rd BH3 . . . . 121 D7
Kellaway Ct 10 DT4 . . . . 167 E2
Kellaway Rd BH17 . . . . . . 119 F8

Kellaway Terr DT4 . . . . . . 167 C3
Kelly Cl BH17 . . . . 119 F8
Kelsall Gdns BH25 . . . . . . 95 A3
Kemp Rd BH9 . . . . 121 F8
Kempston Rd DT4 . . . . . . 167 D1
Kemp Welch Ct BH12 . . . 121 B8
Kendalls La SP8 . . . . 5 E5
Kenilworth DT4 . . . . 167 B6
Kenilworth Cl DT4 . . . . . . 95 B3
Kenilworth Ct
2 Christchurch BH23 . . . 124 A7
1 Poole BH13 . . . . 147 F8
9 Winchester SO23 . . . . 126 E8
Kenmoor Cl DT3 . . . . 167 F8
Kenmore Dr BA21 . . . . 27 D6
Kennard Ct BH25 . . . . 94 F3
Kennard Rd BH25 . . . . 94 F3
Kennart Rd BH17 . . . . 119 B7
Kennel La DT2 . . . . 206 C2
Kennels La DT9 . . . . 195 E2
Kenneth Ct 9 BH25 . . . . . 126 B7
Kennington Rd BH17 . . . . 119 D8
Kennington Way BH17 . . 142 E4
Ken Rd BH6 . . . . 123 E4
Kensington Ct 14 BH13 . 121 B3
Kensington Dr 1 BA21 . . 27 B6
Kensington Wlk 6 DT1 . 135 C8
Kent Cl DT4 . . . . 166 F3
Kent Ho 82 BH4 . . . . 121 C3
Kentisworth Rd DT10 . . . . 20 F1
Kent La BH24 . . . . 43 A1
Kent Rd
Poole BH12 . . . . 120 E6
10 Tatworth TA20 . . . . . 202 A8
Kents La 1 TA20 . . . . 202 A8
Kenwyn Rd DT6 . . . . 100 E7
Kenyon Cl BH15 . . . . 119 E7
Kenyon Rd BH15 . . . . 119 E7
Keppel Ct BH24 . . . . 55 D7
Kerley Rd BH2 . . . . 121 E2
Kernells Ct 2 BH4 . . . . . . 121 B4
Kerrfield SO22 . . . . 126 B5
Kerrfield Mews SO22 . . . 126 B5
Kestrel Cl
Ferndown BH22 . . . . 61 B7
Upton BH16 . . . . 118 B8
Winchester SO22 . . . . . . 126 B2
Kestrel Dr BH23 . . . . 84 C6
Kestrel Dr BH23 . . . . 55 C8
Kestrel View DT15 . . . . . 152 C3
Kestrel Way SP6 . . . . 42 F5
Keswick Ct BH25 . . . . 95 B5
Keswick Rd
Bournemouth BH5 . . . . . 122 F4
Bournemouth BH3 . . . . . 123 A4
New Milton BH25 . . . . 95 B5
Keswick Way BH31 . . . . . . 45 A5
Keverstone Ct BH1 . . . . . 122 D3
Keyes Cl
Christchurch BH23 . . . . . 124 F6
Poole BH12 . . . . 120 B8
Keynston Down Rd 7
DT11 . . . . 199 E2
Keysworth Ave BH25 . . . 126 F8
Keysworth Dr BH20 . . . . 143 A8
Keysworth Rd BH16 . . . . 118 C4
Khartoum Rd DT4 . . . . . . 180 B8
Khyber Rd BH12 . . . . 120 D5
Kiddles BA21 . . . . 27 C5
Kidmore Cl 2 DT6 . . . . . . 97 A7
Killicks Hill DT6 . . . . 186 F7
Killock 6 BH13 . . . . 147 F7
Kilmarnock Rd BH9 . . . . . 89 F1
Kilmington Way BH23 . . . 125 F8
Kiln Cl BH21 . . . . 86 C4
Kiln Way BH31 . . . . 45 C4
Kilwood Coppice & Meadows
Nature Reserve BH20 . . 161 B2
Kimberley Cl
Christchurch BH23 . . . . . 123 F8
1 Radipole DT3 . . . . 152 E2
Kimberley Rd
Bournemouth BH6 . . . . . 123 C5
Poole BH14 . . . . 120 B1
Kimmeridge Ave BH12 . . 120 C8
Kimmeridge Cl DT3 . . . . 167 B8
Kine Bush La SP8 . . . . 10 C3
King Alfred Pl SO23 . . . . 126 E8
King Alfred's Way SP7 . . . 12 F3
King Alfred Terr 3
SO23 . . . . 126 E7
King Arthur Dr BA21 . . . . 26 F7
King Charles Way DT1 . . 100 F7
King Cl BH24 . . . . 54 B4
Kingcombe Cross Roads
DT2 . . . . 205 E3
Kingcombe La DT2 . . . . . 205 E3
Kingcombe Meadows Nature
Reserve DT2 . . . . 205 D2
Kingcup Cl BH18 . . . . 86 E2
King Down Dro BH21 . . . . 49 C3
King Down Rd DT11 . . . . 199 F3
King Edmund Ct SP8 . . . . . 5 F2
King Edward Ave BH9 . . . . 90 A2
King Edward Ct BH9 . . . . . 90 A2
King Edward's Dr DT11 . 209 F5
Kingfisher Cl
Bournemouth BH6 . . . . . 123 E6
Ferndown BH22 . . . . 53 B2
1 Weymouth DT4 . . . . . 180 B8
Kingfisher Park Homes 3
BH10 . . . . 89 F4
Kingfishers 4 BH23 . . . . 124 A5
Kingfishers The BH31 . . . . 45 C5

Kingfisher Way
Christchurch BH23 . . . . . 125 A5
Ringwood BH24 . . . . 47 D1
King George Ave BH9 . . . . 89 F2
King George Mobile Home
Pk BH25 . . . . 94 F1
King George St 7 BA20 . . 27 D4
King George V Rd BH20 . 139 E7
King Harold Ct SO23 . . . 126 D4
King John Ave BH11 . . . . . 88 D5
King John Cl BH11 . . . . . . 88 D6
King John Rd BH11 . . . . . . 88 D6
Kingland Cres 4 BH15 . . 119 C2
Kingland Rd BH15 . . . . . . 119 D2
King Richard Dr BH11 . . . 88 D5
Kings Arms La BH24 . . . . . 55 B7
Kings Arms Row BH24 . . . 55 B7
Kings Ave
Poole BH14 . . . . 120 D2
Winchester SO22 . . . . . . 126 C3
King's Ave BH23 . . . . 123 F6
Kingsbere Ave BH10 . . . . . 89 B2
Kingsbere Cres DT1 . . . . 135 A7
Kingsbere Gdns BH23 . . 126 A8
Kingsbere Rd SP7 . . . . 13 C4
Kingsbere Rd
Overcombe/Preston
DT3 . . . . 168 A7
Poole BH15 . . . . 119 E5
Kingsbridge Rd BH14 . . . 120 C3
Kingsbury's La BH24 . . . . . 55 B7
Kings Cl
Ferndown BH22 . . . . 53 A1
Longburton DT9 . . . . 195 B8
Poole BH15 . . . . 119 D5
Kingscourt Cl 2 SP8 . . . . . 6 B1
Kingscourt Rd SP8 . . . . 6 B1
Kings Cres DT9 . . . . 30 E7
King's Cres BH14 . . . . 120 E2
King's Ct Pal SP8 . . . . 6 B1
Kingsdale Rd 9 SO22 . . . 126 D6
Kingsfield BH24 . . . . 55 B6
Kingsgate 8 BH13 . . . . . . 121 B3
Kingsgate Rd SO23 . . . . . 126 D4
Kingsgate St SO23 . . . . . 126 E4
Kings Grange 11 BH4 . . . 121 D2
Kings Head Yd 1 SO23 . . 126 E5
Kings High Sch BH10 . . . . 89 C3
Kings Hill 2 SP7 . . . . 12 E3
Kings La BH21 . . . . 201 F4
King's La DT6 . . . . 70 D5
Kingsland Ct BH13 . . . . . 147 F7
Kingsleigh Prim Sch
BH10 . . . . 89 C3
Kingsley Ave BH6 . . . . . . 124 A4
Kingsley Cl BH6 . . . . 124 A4
Kingsley Paddock DT2 . . . 72 F7
Kingsley Pl SO22 . . . . 126 C3
Kingsman La SP7 . . . . 12 E2
Kings Mead DT2 . . . . 78 B1
Kingsmead Ct 6 BH21 . . . 59 B5
Kingsmead Rd BH17 . . . . 119 C7
Kings Park Com Hospl
BH7 . . . . 122 F5
King's Park Dr BH7,BH1 . 122 F6
King's Park Prim Sch
BH1 . . . . 122 E5
King's Park Rd BH7 . . . . . 122 E6
King's Pitt 3 DT1 . . . . . . 107 C1
Kings Rd
Dorchester DT1 . . . . 108 B1
New Milton BH25 . . . . 95 C3
Radipole DT4 . . . . 167 C2
Sherborne DT9 . . . . 30 B7
Winchester SO22 . . . . . . 126 A4
King's Rd
Blandford Forum DT11 . . 212 E5
Bournemouth BH3 . . . . . 122 A7
Thornford DT9 . . . . 194 D7
Kings Rd E BH19 . . . . 179 B2
Kings Rd W BH19 . . . . . . 179 A2
Kings Row 3 SO22 . . . . . 126 D5
King's Royal Hussars Mus
The SO23 . . . . 126 D5
King's St BH21 . . . . 56 F5
King St
Bridport DT6 . . . . 100 D6
Fortuneswell DT5 . . . . . . 186 F7
Radipole DT4 . . . . 167 D4
Wimborne Minster BH21 . . 59 D4
Yeovil BA21 . . . . 27 C6
Kingsthorn Rd 1 DT1 . . . 107 C2
Kingston BA20 . . . . 27 C5
Kingston Cl DT11 . . . . . . 212 C5
Kingston Hill BH20 . . . . . 176 F4
Kingston La DT10 . . . . . . 196 F4
Kingston Lacy House
BH21 . . . . 58 B7
Kingston Maurward Coll
DT2 . . . . 108 F3
Kingston Maurward Gdns &
Animal Pk DT2 . . . . . . 108 A3
Kingston Rd BH15 . . . . . . 119 D4
Kingston View BA21 . . . . . 27 D6
Kingsway
Ferndown BH22 . . . . 61 B8
Lyme Regis DT7 . . . . 96 C6
Kingsway Cl BH23 . . . . 91 F1
Kingswell Cl BH10 . . . . . . 89 D2
Kingswell Gdns BH10 . . . . 89 B2
Kingswell Rd BH10 . . . . . . 89 C2
King's Wlk 8 SO23 . . . . . 126 E5
Kingswood 15 BH4 . . . . . 121 C2
Kingswood Cl BH23 . . . . . 91 F1
Kingswood Rd 6 TA18 . . 191 F3

Kinross Rd BH3 . . . . 121 E6
Kinsbourne Ave BH10 . . . . 89 D2
Kinson Ave BH15 . . . . 120 A7
Kinson Gr BH10 . . . . 89 C6
Kinson Park Rd BH10 . . . . 89 D6
Kinson Pottery Ind Est
BH14 . . . . 120 A6
Kinson Prim Sch BH11 . . . 89 B5
Kinson Rd BH10 . . . . 89 C3
Kiosks The 9 BH15 . . . . . 119 C1
Kipling Rd BH14 . . . . 120 B5
Kirby Cl BH15 . . . . 119 F6
Kirby Way BH6 . . . . 123 E4
Kirkham Ave BH23 . . . . . . 92 C3
Kirkleton Ave DT4 . . . . . . 167 D5
Kirkway BH18 . . . . 87 B4
Kitchener Cres BH17 . . . . . 87 B3
Kitchener Rd DT4 . . . . . . 167 B3
Kite's Nest La SP8 . . . . 1 E1
Kitford La DT11 . . . . 197 C3
Kithill TA18 . . . . 191 F3
Kit La DT2 . . . . 155 D7
Kitscroft Rd BH10 . . . . 89 C5
Kitt Hill DT9 . . . . 30 A6
Kittiwake Cl BH6 . . . . 123 D6
Kiwi Cl BH15 . . . . 119 E3
Knacker's Hole La TA20 . 202 F4
Knap Barrow (Long Barrow)
SP6 . . . . 190 D6
Knapp Cl BH23 . . . . 124 A8
Knapp Mill Ave BH23 . . . 124 A8
Knapps DT11 . . . . 198 B6
Knapp The
Chickerell DT3 . . . . 166 C6
Fontmell Magna SP7 . . . . 37 F6
Hilton DT11 . . . . 209 D8
Shaftesbury SP7 . . . . 12 D3
Knapwater Wlk 12 DT1 . 135 B8
Knight Cl SO23 . . . . 126 E8
Knighton Heath Cl BH11 . . 88 E4
Knighton Heath Ind Est
BH11 . . . . 88 E2
Knighton Heath Rd BH11 . 88 E4
Knighton House Sch
DT11 . . . . 198 E3
Knighton La
Bournemouth BH21 . . . . . 88 D7
Broadmayne DT2 . . . . . . 136 C2
Knighton Pk BH25 . . . . . . 126 E8
Knightsbridge Ct BH2 . . . 121 E2
Knights Cl 1 DT11 . . . . . 212 D2
Knightsdale Rd DT4 . . . . 167 B2
Knightsdale Road Swimming
Pool DT4 . . . . 167 B2
Knights Rd BH11 . . . . 88 D1
Knightstone Ct 2 BH20 . 142 F3
Knightstone Rise DT6 . . . . 68 C3
Knightwood Cl BH23 . . . . 125 D8
Knobcrook Rd 3 BH21 . . . 59 B6
Knole Ct BH11 . . . . 122 C4
Knole Gdns BH11 . . . . . . 122 C4
Knole Rd BH11 . . . . 122 C4
Knoll Gdns
Ferndown BH21 . . . . 60 F4
St Leonards BH24 . . . . 54 B4
Knoll La BH21 . . . . 86 B2
Knoll Manor BH21 . . . . . . 121 F5
Knoll Pl BH25 . . . . 95 B2
Knoll Rise 3 . . . . 152 E2
Knollsea Cl 1 DT11 . . . . . 179 C1
Knotts Paddock DT9 . . . . . 30 C6
Knowle Cross DT8 . . . . . . 203 D6
Knowle Hill BH20 . . . . . . 140 A1
Knowle La TA18 . . . . 191 F1
Knowles Cl BH23 . . . . 124 E8
Knowle Wood Knap 1
BH20 . . . . 140 A1
Knowl La BH20 . . . . 101 D7
Knowlton Church BH21 . . 201 D5
Knowlton Circles BH21 . . 201 D5
Knowlton Gdns BH9 . . . . . 90 B3
Knowlton Rd BH17 . . . . . . 87 F2
Knyeton Rd BH1 . . . . 122 B4
Knyveton Rd BH1 . . . . . . 122 C4
Kynegils Rd SO22 . . . . . . 126 B8
Kyrchil La BH21 . . . . 59 F5
Kyrchil Way BH21 . . . . 59 F7

L

Labrador Dr BH15 . . . . . . 119 D1
Laburnum Way SP8 . . . . . . 5 E5
Laburnum Cl
Ferndown BH22 . . . . 61 B6
Radipole DT22 . . . . 167 B6
1 Sandford BH20 . . . . . . 116 A1
Verwood BH31 . . . . 45 E5
Laburnum Cres 13 TA18 . 191 F5
Laburnum Ho 8 BH10 . . . 89 F4
Laburnum Rd DT2 . . . . 75 D3
Laburnum Way BA20 . . . . 26 F2
Lacey Cres BH15 . . . . 120 A8
Lackington Dro DT2 . . . . 208 B1
Lacy Cl BH21 . . . . 59 C6
Lacy Dr BH21 . . . . 59 C6
Lady Baden Powell Way
DT11 . . . . 212 E6
Lady Caroline's Dr DT11 . 210 D7
Lady Mead 3 DT5 . . . . . . 187 A4
Lady St Mary CE Fst Sch The
BH20 . . . . 142 D3
Ladysmith Cl BH23 . . . . . 124 E7
Lagado Cl BH14 . . . . 147 C8

Lagland Ct 14 BH15 .... 119 C2
Lagland St BH15 .... 119 C2
Lagoon Cl BH14 .... 147 B8
Lagoon Rd BH14 .... 147 B8
Laidlaw Cl DT1 .... 121 B8
Lainston Cl SO22 .... 126 A8
Lake Ave BH15 .... 118 D1
Lake Cres BH15 .... 118 E3
Lake Dr
  Hamworthy BH15 .... 118 D1
  Poole BH15 .... 118 D2
  Upton BH15 .... 117 F1
Lake Farm Cl BH22 .... 89 B8
Lakefields BA22 .... 193 B7
Lakegate La DT9 .... 194 A5
Lake Grove Rd BH25 .... 95 A4
Lake La DT1 .... 100 D4
Lake Rd
  Bournemouth BH11 .... 89 C6
  Hamworthy BH15 .... 118 E2
  Verwood BH31 .... 45 C4
Lakeside BH24 .... 55 E6
Lakeside Gdns DT3 .... 167 B7
Lakeside Pines BH25 .... 95 A4
Lakeside Rd BH13 .... 121 A1
Lakeview Dr BH24 .... 55 E6
Lake View Manor BH25 .... 95 A3
Lakewood Rd BH23 .... 93 F1
Lambert Cl 4 DT9 .... 17 C2
Lambert's Castle (Fort)
  DT6 .... 202 E2
Lambourne CT TA18 .... 191 F5
Lamb Plot DT9 .... 194 D2
Lambs Cl BH17 .... 87 C1
Lambsfield DT9 .... 30 C7
Lambsgreen La BH21 .... 58 F2
Lambs La BH21 .... 56 D3
Lammas Cl SP8 .... 5 F3
Lampton Cl BH20 .... 139 F2
Lampton Gdns 9 BH9 .... 89 F1
Lanark Cl BH15 .... 118 E2
Lancaster Cl
  Christchurch BH23 .... 125 C7
  Corfe Mullen BH18 .... 86 F5
Lancaster Dr
  Corfe Mullen BH18 .... 86 F5
  Verwood BH31 .... 45 A5
Lancaster Rd
  Dorchester DT1 .... 108 B1
  Ferndown BH22 .... 61 A8
  Radipole DT3 .... 152 B1
Lancer Cl BH23 .... 125 C7
Lanchards La DT11 .... 198 B6
Lanchards La DT11 .... 198 B5
Lander Cl BH15 .... 119 D1
Landers Reach 3 BH16 .... 84 D2
Landford Rd BH8 .... 90 D2
Landford Way BH8 .... 90 D2
Landscombe Vale DT2 .... 208 A8
Landseer Rd 3 BH4 .... 121 C3
Landshire La
  Fifehead Magdalen SP8 .... 20 C5
  Stalbridge BA8 .... 19 D3
Lane Cl DT11 .... 212 F6
Lane End DT11 .... 79 F7
Lanehouse Rocks Rd 1
  DT4 .... 180 C8
Lane Lowther Gdns The 4
  BH8 .... 122 C5
Lane-side SP7 .... 12 F4
Lanes The BH20 .... 95 A5
Lane The BH20 .... 176 F4
Langdon Cl BH14 .... 120 D4
Langdon La
  Beaminster DT8 .... 204 E4
  Chideock DT6 .... 98 E2
Langdon Rd BH14 .... 120 D4
Langdons DT9 .... 30 C7
Langdons Way 1 TA20 .... 202 A8
Langfords La 2 SP7 .... 12 D2
Langham Ct BH23 .... 91 F1
Langham La SP8 .... 4 F1
Langley Chase BH24 .... 54 B5
Langley Rd
  Christchurch BH23 .... 93 E1
  Poole BH14 .... 120 F4
Langmead Rd 3 TA18 .... 191 F3
Langmead Rd TA18 .... 191 F3
Langmead Sq 1 TA18 .... 191 F3
Langmoor La EX13 .... 202 A2
Lang Rd TA18 .... 191 E3
Langside Ave BH12 .... 121 A8
Langside Sch BH12 .... 121 A8
Langton Ave DT4 .... 180 C6
Langton Cl
  Barton on Sea BH25 .... 127 B8
  Winchester SO22 .... 126 C7
Langton Cres DT11 .... 212 E3
Langton Matravers Mus
  BH19 .... 178 B3
Langton Rd
  Blandford Forum DT11 .... 212 D3
  Bournemouth BH7 .... 122 F5
Lankhills Rd SO23 .... 126 E2
Lansdell Ct BH15 .... 119 E3
Lansdowne Ave SO23 .... 126 D3
Lansdowne Cres BH1 .... 122 B3
Lansdowne Ct 3 SO23 .... 126 D3
Lansdowne Gdns BH1 .... 122 A4
Lansdowne Rd
  Bournemouth BH1 .... 122 A5
  Bridport DT6 .... 100 D4
Lansdowne Rdbt The
  BH1 .... 122 A3
Lansdowne Sq DT4 .... 167 C1

Lantern Ct SO23 .... 126 C4
Lapwing Rd BH21 .... 60 A7
Lara Cl BH8 .... 90 D3
Larch Cl
  Broadstone BH17 .... 86 E1
  Hordle SO41 .... 95 F3
  Sandford BH20 .... 143 B8
  St Leonards BH24 .... 54 C1
Larch Way BH22 .... 61 C7
Larcombe La DT6 .... 69 D5
Larkhill Rd BA21 .... 27 A6
Lark Hill Rise SO22 .... 126 B2
Lark Rd BH24 .... 125 A6
Larks Cl BH22 .... 61 B7
Larksfield Ave BH9 .... 90 C3
Larkshill Cl BH25 .... 95 B4
Larks Mdw DT10 .... 33 E8
Larksmead DT11 .... 212 E5
Larkspur Cl DT4 .... 167 E6
Larkspur Cres BA21 .... 26 F7
Larks Rise BH22 .... 61 B7
Larmer Tree Gdns SP5 .... 188 E4
Lascelles Ct 3 BH7 .... 123 B6
Lascelles Rd BH7 .... 123 B6
Latch Farm Ave BH23 .... 124 A8
Latimer Rd BH9 .... 121 F8
Latimers BH23 .... 93 F1
Launches The BH20 .... 172 C6
Laundry La 3 SP7 .... 12 D2
Laurel Ave BH20 .... 116 B2
Laurel Cl
  1 Bridport DT6 .... 100 B8
  Christchurch BH23 .... 93 D1
  Corfe Mullen BH21 .... 86 D6
  Hordle SO41 .... 95 E4
  St Leonards BH24 .... 54 A4
  West Coker BA22 .... 193 B8
Laurel Dr BH18 .... 87 C4
Laurel Gdns BH18 .... 87 C4
Laurel La BH24 .... 54 A3
Laurels The
  Broadstone BH18 .... 87 B4
  17 Crewkerne TA18 .... 191 F5
  Ferndown BH22 .... 61 C7
  8 Gillingham SP8 .... 5 E1
  2 Iwerne Courtney or Shroton
    DT11 .... 198 E7
Lavender Cl BH31 .... 45 E5
Lavender Rd
  Bournemouth BH8 .... 90 D4
  Hordle SO41 .... 95 E3
Lavender Villas BH23 .... 126 A8
Lavender Way BH18 .... 86 D3
Lavender Wlk BH8 .... 90 D4
Laver's La TA20 .... 202 C6
Laverstock 8 BH15 .... 122 F3
Lavinia Rd BH12 .... 120 C7
Lawford Rd 90 A4
Lawn Ct 13 BH2 .... 121 D4
Lawn Ho 24 SO23 .... 126 E6
Lawns Cl BH21 .... 60 C6
Lawns Rd BH21 .... 60 B6
Lawn St SO23 .... 126 E6
Lawns The
  Charmouth DT6 .... 97 B7
  Christchurch BH23 .... 126 B8
Lawn View BH25 .... 94 D5
Lawrence Cl BH8 .... 122 C6
Lawrence Dr
  Crossways DT2 .... 137 D5
  Poole BH12 .... 120 E1
Lawrence La
  Hyde BH20 .... 43 D4
  Witchampton BH21 .... 201 A2
Lawrence of Arabia's Cottage
  BH20 .... 112 C2
Lawrence of Arabia's Grave
  DT2 .... 138 E7
Lawrence Rd BH24 .... 47 E2
Lawrence Way 4 SO23 .... 126 E8
Lawson Rd BH12 .... 120 B6
Layard Dr BH21 .... 59 D1
Laymoor La BH21 .... 60 D5
Layton Ct BH12 .... 120 D5
Layton La SP7 .... 12 E2
Layton Rd BH12 .... 120 D5
Lea Cl BA21 .... 27 D8
Leamington Rd
  Bournemouth BH9 .... 122 A7
  Weymouth DT4 .... 166 F2
Leaphill Rd BH7 .... 123 B6
Lea Rd DT4 .... 180 B8
Learoyd Rd BH17 .... 119 E7
Lea The BH31 .... 45 C5
Lea Way BH11 .... 88 E6
Lea La BA21 .... 28 A4
Lecher La DT8 .... 192 B1
Lechlade Gdns BH7 .... 123 B8
Ledbury Rd BH23 .... 124 F5
Leddington Way SP8 .... 5 E4
Ledgard Cl BH14 .... 120 B4
Lee Ct DT6 .... 61 D4
Leedam Rd BH10 .... 89 D4
Leeds Cres DT4 .... 166 F2
Lee La DT6 .... 101 A7
Lees Cl BH23 .... 91 D4
Leeson Cl 2 BH19 .... 178 F2
Leeson Dr BH22 .... 61 B8
Leeson House Field Studies
  Ctr BH19 .... 178 C2
Leeson Rd BH7 .... 123 C8
Leet Cl 11 DT5 .... 181 B1
Leet Dr DT9 .... 29 F4
Legg La BH21 .... 59 D4
Legion Cl
  Dorchester DT1 .... 134 C7
  Hamworthy BH15 .... 118 C2

Legion Rd
  Hamworthy BH15 .... 118 E2
  Yeovil BA21 .... 27 B6
Leicester Rd BH13 .... 120 F3
Leigham Vale Rd BH6 .... 123 D4
Leigh Cl DT1 .... 59 E4
Leigh Comm BH21 .... 59 E5
Leigh Gdns BH21 .... 59 D4
Leigh La
  Halstock BA22 .... 193 C3
  Ibberton DT11 .... 197 D3
  Wimborne Minster BH21 .... 59 F5
Leigh Rd
  New Milton BH25 .... 95 A3
  Wimborne Minster BH21 .... 59 E4
  Wimborne Minster BH21 .... 60 A4
Leighton La 8 BH21 .... 121 D4
Le Neubourg Way SP8 .... 5 F1
Lennox St DT4 .... 167 D4
Lentham Cl BH17 .... 87 D1
Lenthay Cl DT9 .... 29 F4
Lenthay Rd DT9 .... 29 F4
Lent Hill Ct SO22 .... 126 B4
Le Patourel Cl BH23 .... 124 F7
Lerrett Cl DT3 .... 166 D6
Leslie Rd
  Bournemouth BH9 .... 121 F7
  Poole BH14 .... 120 B4
Lessingham Ave DT4 .... 180 C6
Letton Cl DT11 .... 212 F6
Leven Ave BH4 .... 121 D5
Leven Cl BH4 .... 121 D5
Leven Cl BH4 .... 121 D4
Levet's La 4 BH15 .... 119 B1
Lewell Way DT2 .... 136 C3
Lewens Cl DT11 .... 211 C4
Lewens La BH21 .... 59 C4
Lewesdon Cl 6 DT8 .... 204 C4
Lewesdon Dr BH18 .... 86 F4
Lewesdon Hill DT8 .... 203 E4
Leybourne Ave BH10 .... 89 D4
Leybourne Cl BH10 .... 89 C5
Leydene Ave BH8 .... 90 F1
Leydene Cl BH8 .... 90 F1
Leyland Rd BH12 .... 88 E2
Leyside BH23 .... 124 F6
Leyton Conyers 11 BH13 .... 147 F7
Liberty Cl BH13 .... 53 D6
Liberty Ct BH23 .... 123 F7
Liberty's Raptor & Reptile Ctr
  BA22 .... 55 E5
Library Mews BH12 .... 121 A8
Library Rd
  Bournemouth BH9 .... 89 F1
  Ferndown BH22 .... 61 D5
  Poole BH12 .... 120 E5
Lichfield Rd DT4 .... 167 A2
Liddington Cres DT11 .... 212 D5
Liddon Hill TA18 .... 191 C5
Liederbach Dr BH31 .... 45 E3
Lighthouse Rd BH19 .... 185 C7
Lights Cl BH23 .... 124 B7
Lilac Cl BH20 .... 142 D2
Lilliput CE Fst Sch BH14 .... 147 C8
Lilliput Ct BH14 .... 120 B3
Lilliput Rd BH14 .... 147 D8
Limber Rd BA22 .... 26 C6
Lime Cl
  Dorchester DT1 .... 134 F8
  Poole BH15 .... 119 F6
Lime Hill DT6 .... 70 B7
Lime Kiln BA21 .... 26 E5
Lime Kiln La 8 BH21 .... 186 E2
Lime Kiln Rd BH16 .... 84 C4
Limerick Cl 3 DT9 .... 17 C2
Limes The SP7 .... 12 E8
Lime Tree Ave BA20 .... 27 A2
Lime Tree Cl SP6 .... 42 B6
Limited Rd BH9 .... 90 A1
Lin Brook Dr BH24 .... 47 E2
Linclieth Rd 3 BH20 .... 140 A2
Lincoln Ave
  Bournemouth BH1 .... 122 D5
  Christchurch BH23 .... 91 F2
Lincoln Rd
  Poole BH12 .... 120 D7
  2 Weymouth DT4 .... 166 F2
Lindbergh Rd BH21 .... 61 A8
Linden Ave DT1 .... 108 A1
Linden Cl BH22 .... 61 D1
Linden Gdns BH24 .... 55 B8
Linden Pk SP7 .... 13 A2
Linden Rd
  Bournemouth BH9 .... 90 A3
  Ferndown BH22 .... 61 D1
  Poole BH12 .... 120 D7
  Swanage BH19 .... 179 A2
  Yeovil BA20 .... 27 B5
Lindens The BH23 .... 92 D3
Lindford Rd BH24 .... 47 F1
Lindlar Cl SP7 .... 12 F4
Lindsay Cl 11 BH13 .... 121 A4
Lindsay Manor 11 BH13 .... 121 A4
Lindsay Pk 13 BH13 .... 121 A4
Lindsay Rd
  Poole BH13 .... 120 F4
  Poole BH13 .... 121 A4
Lindum Ct 3 BH13 .... 121 A4
Linen Yard The 27 TA18 .... 191 F4
Lineside BH24 .... 124 C8
Linford Cl BH25 .... 95 B4
Linford Rd BH24 .... 47 F2
Lingdale Rd BH6 .... 123 D6
Lingfield Ave BA21 .... 27 F7
Lingfield Grange 11
  BH13 .... 121 B3
Ling Rd BH11 .... 88 B1
Lington Cl DT2 .... 137 D6

Lingwood Ave BH23 .... 124 F6
Linhorns La BH25 .... 95 A5
Linkhay 12 TA20 .... 202 A8
Linkhay Cl 11 TA20 .... 202 A8
Link Rd BH24 .... 47 E1
Link Rise BH21 .... 86 E6
Links Dr BH23 .... 91 D1
Linkside Ave BH7 .... 122 F8
Links Rd
  Poole BH14 .... 120 D2
  Weymouth DT4 .... 167 B4
  Winchester SO22 .... 126 B7
Links View Ave BH14 .... 120 C2
Linmead Dr BH11 .... 89 A6
Linnet Cl
  Radipole DT3 .... 152 C4
  Ringwood BH24 .... 55 C6
Linnet La BH25 .... 94 F3
Linnet Rd BH17 .... 205 D5
Linnet Rd BH17 .... 118 F8
Linsay Rd BH20 .... 139 E5
Lintern La SP8 .... 11 A5
Linthorpe Rd BH15 .... 119 E4
Linton Lawns BH21 .... 62 E3
Linwood Rd BH9 .... 122 B7
Linwood School BH9 .... 122 B7
Lionheart Cl BH11 .... 88 D5
Lions Hall 4 SO22 .... 126 D5
Lions Hill Way BH24 .... 53 E4
Lions La BH24 .... 53 F4
Lions Wood BH24 .... 54 A4
Liscombe Cl DT1 .... 107 D2
Lisle Cl SO22 .... 126 C4
Lissenden 1 BH13 .... 121 B3
Litchford Rd BH25 .... 95 B4
Little Barrs Dr BH25 .... 95 A4
Little Britain DT1 .... 108 C1
Little Content La SP7 .... 12 F3
Littlecroft Ave BH9 .... 90 B3
Little Croft Rd BH12 .... 120 B6
Little Ct
  Poole BH14 .... 147 C3
  Poole, Canford Cliffs BH13 .... 147 F8
Little Dewlands BH31 .... 44 F6
Littledown SP7 .... 12 F5
Littledown Ave BH7 .... 122 F7
Littledown Dr BH7 .... 122 F7
Little England DT11 .... 79 E7
Littlefield DT9 .... 29 F4
Littlefield La 13 SP5 .... 189 A4
Little Forest Mans 12
  BH1 .... 122 E4
Little Forest Rd BH4 .... 121 E5
Little Fosters BH13 .... 147 E6
Little Lane DT11 .... 198 A6
Little Lonnen
  Colehill BH21 .... 59 F8
  Wimborne Minster BH21 .... 60 A8
Littlemead
  Broadmayne DT2 .... 136 B1
  Radipole DT3 .... 152 B3
Littlemead Cl BH17 .... 119 A7
Littlemill La SP6 .... 190 F3
Little Minster St SO23 .... 126 E5
Littlemoor Ave BH11 .... 88 D4
Littlemoor Rd
  Overcombe/Preston
    DT3 .... 168 A8
  Radipole DT3 .... 152 C4
Litteton Dro DT11 .... 211 B6
Littletowns DT11 .... 212 D6
Littleview Rd DT4 .... 166 F2
Litton Hill DT2 .... 103 B2
Litton La
  Askerswell DT2 .... 102 E5
  Litton Cheney DT2 .... 103 B1
  Puncknowle DT2 .... 129 F7
Liverpool Rd 3 DT4 .... 166 F2
Livingstone Rd
  Bournemouth BH5 .... 123 B5
  Christchurch BH23 .... 124 D7
  Poole BH12 .... 120 C6
  Wimborne Minster BH21 .... 59 E4
Llewellin Cl
  8 Upton BH16 .... 117 E7
  Upton BH16 .... 118 C7
Llewelyn Cl BH16 .... 118 C7
Loaders Cl BH9 .... 122 A8
Load La DT2 .... 194 F1
Locarno Rd BH19 .... 179 B2
Lockeridge Cl DT11 .... 212 C5
Lockett's La DT2 .... 207 F7
Locks La
  Glanvilles Wootton DT9 .... 195 E3
  Loders DT6 .... 101 F6
  Stratton DT2 .... 106 E8
Locksley Cl BH22 .... 61 C3
Locks Piece 15 BH20 .... 140 A2
Lockwood Terr SP8 .... 11 B8
Lockyers Cl DT11 .... 61 F6
Lockyers Mid Sch BH21 .... 86 D8
Lockyers Rd BH21 .... 86 E8
Lockyer's Way BH21 .... 84 D3
Loders CE Prim Sch DT6 .... 69 C1
Loders Cl BH17 .... 87 D3
Loders La DT6 .... 101 E4
Lodge Cl BH14 .... 120 C4
Lodge La DT11 .... 100 B7
Lodge Rd
  Christchurch BH23 .... 123 D8
  Holt BH21 .... 51 B6
Lodge The BH2 .... 121 E4

Lodge Way DT4 .... 180 D8
Lodmoor Ave DT3 .... 167 D2
Lodmoor Ctry Pk DT3 .... 167 F4
Loewy Cres BH12 .... 88 D2
Lombard Ave BH6 .... 123 D5
Lombardy Cl BH31 .... 45 D5
Lomer La SP6 .... 42 E4
Lomond Dr DT4 .... 167 C1
London Cl
  1 Dorchester DT1 .... 108 B2
  Piddlehinton DT2 .... 76 F7
London La BH23 .... 63 F2
London Rd
  Dorchester DT1 .... 108 B2
  Milborne Port DT9 .... 17 E1
London Row DT2 .... 76 F7
Lone Pine Dr BH22 .... 61 E3
Lone Pine Pk BH22 .... 61 F3
Lone Pine Way BH22 .... 61 F3
Long Acre DT5 .... 187 A4
Longacre Dr BH22 .... 61 E3
Long Ash La
  Frampton DT2 .... 74 A3
  Frome St Quintin DT2 .... 206 D6
Longbarrow Cl BH8 .... 91 A1
Long Barrow La DT8 .... 204 B3
Long Bredy Hut La DT2 .... 103 F2
Longbury Hill La SP8 .... 5 B4
Long Cl
  Winchester SO23 .... 126 C3
  Yeovil BA21 .... 26 E5
Longcroft Rd
  Weymouth DT4 .... 167 B3
  Yeovil BA21 .... 27 D6
Long Cross SP7 .... 12 E8
Longdown Rd DT9 .... 194 D7
Long Entry DT7 .... 96 C5
Longespee Rd BH21 .... 87 E8
Longfield Dr
  Bournemouth BH11 .... 89 A6
  Ferndown BH22 .... 89 A8
Longfield Rd BH7 .... 167 D1
Longfleet CE Comb Sch
  BH15 .... 119 D4
Longfleet Rd BH15 .... 119 E4
Longford Rd DT9 .... 194 D7
Longforward Hill TA17 .... 191 A8
Longforward La TA17 .... 191 B8
Long Furlong La BA22 .... 193 C8
Longham Bsns Ctr BH22 .... 61 B2
Longhayes Ave BH21 .... 86 D8
Long Hall BA12 .... 2 F5
Long La
  Bothenhampton DT6 .... 100 F4
  Burton SP8 .... 1 B1
  Cann SP7 .... 24 A7
  Colehill BH21 .... 51 B1
  Colehill BH21 .... 59 E8
  Cucklington BA9 .... 4 A1
  Puddletown DT2 .... 78 B2
  Ringwood BH24 .... 55 C4
  Whitechurch Canonicorum
    DT6 .... 65 C4
Longlands La BA22 .... 193 C4
Longland's La
  Littlebredy DT2 .... 133 F7
  Winterbourne Abbas DT2 .... 105 B1
Longleat Gdns BH25 .... 94 E3
Longman's Rd BH21 .... 201 A3
Long Mdw DT9 .... 195 A2
Longmead SP7 .... 12 F3
Long Mead BA21 .... 26 E5
Longmead Ind Est SP7 .... 12 F3
Longmeadow Rd BH17 .... 118 E8
Longmeadow Sch BH17 .... 119 D7
Long's La DT6 .... 100 E7
Longspee Sch BH17 .... 119 D7
Long St
  Cerne Abbas DT2 .... 207 D4
  Sherborne DT9 .... 30 C6
Longstone Cl DT5 .... 186 C1
Lonnen Rd
  Wimborne Minster BH21 .... 51 D1
  Wimborne Minster BH21 .... 60 A8
Lonnen Wood Cl BH21 .... 60 A8
Lonsdale Rd BH3 .... 121 F6
Looke La DT2 .... 129 F6
Lopen Rd TA17 .... 191 D8
Loraine Ave BH23 .... 126 A8
Lord Cl BH17 .... 119 F7
Lordsmead Rd BA22 .... 3 B4
Lorne Park Rd BH1 .... 122 A3
Lorne Rd DT1 .... 107 E1
Lornton Wlk 10 DT1 .... 133 B5
Lorton La DT3 .... 152 B3
Lorton Mdws Nature Reserve
  DT3 .... 152 E2
Loscombe Nature Reserve
  DT6 .... 204 F1
Lotmoor Hill SP8 .... 10 C2
Louise Rd DT1 .... 108 B1
Louse La DT11 .... 211 E4
Louviers Rd DT4 .... 152 E6
Lovage Way 6 BA12 .... 3 F8
Love La
  Marnhull DT10 .... 21 A4
  Shaftesbury SP7 .... 12 D2
Lovelands DT2 .... 193 A1
Lovells Mead DT10 .... 20 E3
Loveridge La 16 TA20 .... 202 A8
Loverley La BH21 .... 50 A4
Lovers La SP6 .... 41 C5
Lowden Cl SO22 .... 126 B2
Lower Acreman St DT9 .... 30 B3
Lower Beadon TA16 .... 191 E7
Lower Blandford Rd
  Broadstone BH18 .... 87 B3

ower Blandford Rd continued
Cann SP7.........................24 A7
ower Blandford La DT9....16 E3
ower Brook St SO23.......126 E6
ower Catherston Rd DT6 65 B1
ower Comm La BH21.........53 C7
ower Comm Rd BH21........36 D1
ower Coombess TA20....202 A8
ower E Coker Rd BA20.....27 B1
ower Fairmead Rd BA21. 27 F8
ower Golf Links Rd BH18 87 D5
ower Gunville ■ DT9........17 D2
ower Hillside Rd BH20...140 A1
ower Kingsbury DT9..........17 D3
ower North Rd SP5...........188 C5
ower Odcombe BA22........26 A4
ower Putton La DT3........166 D6
ower Rd
 Stalbridge DT10...............33 E7
 Toller Porcorum DT2........71 E8
ower Ream BA21.................54 D2
ower St Alban St ■
 DT4.............................167 D2
ower St Edmund St ■
 DT4.............................167 D2
ower Sch La ■ DT11....212 C1
ower Sea La DT6................97 A7
ower South Rd SP5........188 C4
ower St
 Lillington DT9................194 F7
 Merriott TA16.................191 F7
 Morden BA20....................83 C2
 Okeford Fitzpaine DT11..197 F6
 West Chinnock TA18.......192 B8
 Witchampton BH21.........200 F1
ower Stanmore La
 SO23.............................126 C3
ower Stepens SH19.........178 C2
ower Townsend DT6......128 B8
ower Turners Barn La
 BA20.................................27 B1
ower Walditch La DT6....100 F6
ower Way DT3................166 D6
ower Wraxhill Rd BA21....54 A3
owesmore Ct BH14.......120 C4
ow's Hill La DT9..............29 C5
owther Gdns ■ BH8.....122 C5
owther Rd
 Bournemouth BH8..........122 B6
 Yeovil BA21.......................28 A7
ox La SP7..........................11 E4
oyd-Lindsay Sq SO22..126 B8
ubbecke Way DT1.........108 C1
Lucas Rd
 Poole BH15...................119 B1
 Poole, Upper Parkstone
 BH12.............................120 C6
Lucerne Ave BH10............89 D2
Lucetta La DT1................135 B8
Luckham Cl BH9................90 B2
Luckham Gdns BH9..........90 C2
Luckham Pl BH9................90 B2
Luckham Rd BH9...............90 B2
Luckham Rd E BH9............90 B2
Ludbourne Rd DT9...........30 C5
Ludlow Rd DT4................166 F2
Ludney La TA17...............191 A7
Lufton Manor Coll BA22...26 B7
Lufton Trad Est BA22.......26 C7
Lufton Way BA22...............26 D6
Lugger Cl DT3.................166 C6
Luke St SP7....................188 B8
Lulworth Ave BH15........118 E1
Lulworth Castle BH20....158 C1
Lulworth Cl BH15............118 E1
Lulworth Cres BH15........118 E1
Lulworth Ct BH15...........118 E1
Lulworth Her Ctr BH20...172 C5
Lulworth Rd BH20...........140 B1
Lumber La BH21..............201 C5
Lumby Dr BH24..................55 D8
Lumby Drive Pk BH24........55 D8
Lupin Way BA22.................26 D5
Lurmer St SP7...................37 F6
Luscombe Rd BH14.........120 C2
Luther Rd BH9.................121 F8
Luton Down Rd ■ DT11.199 E2
Luton Dro DT11...............200 A2
Lyatts Hill BA22...............193 A6
Lych Gate Ct BH24............55 E6
Lyde La BA21.....................28 B6
Lyde Rd BA21.....................27 F5
Lydford Gdns BH11...........89 A2
Lydford Rd BH11................89 A2
Lydfords La SP8..................5 D2
Lydgate St ■ DT1...........107 C1
Lydlinch Cl BH22...............61 D1
Lydwell Cl
 Bournemouth BH11...........88 F5
 Poole BH17....................180 E8
Lyell Rd BH12..................120 C6
Lyewater TA18................191 E4
Lym Cl DT7.........................96 C5
Lyme Cres BH23..............125 F8
Lyme Rd
 Crewkerne TA18............191 E3
 Lyme Regis DT7................96 A7
Lyme Regis Golf Club
 DT7.................................96 D8
Lyme Regis L Ctr DT7......96 B5
Lyme Regis Marine Aquarium
 DT5.................................96 C4
Lymes ■ DT4...................180 C8
Lymington Rd
 Christchurch BH23..........125 F7
 New Milton BH25..............95 C1
Lynch Cl
 Mere BA12...........................3 B5

Lynch Cl continued
 Milborne St Andrew DT11...79 D8
 Winchester SO22............126 C8
Lynch La
 Hardington Mandeville
 BA22.............................193 A6
 Weymouth DT4...............166 F2
Lynch La Ind Est DT4.....166 F2
Lynch Rd DT4.................166 F2
Lyndale Rd DT4..............180 D6
Lyndhurst Rd
 Bransgore BH23...............93 D6
 Christchurch BH23............93 D2
Lyndon Cl BH23................91 F1
Lynes La BH24...................55 B7
Lynford Ave SO22...........126 C8
Lynford Way SO22..........126 C8
Lynmoor Rd DT4.............167 E6
Lynn Rd BH17....................87 F1
Lynric Cl BH25................127 A7
Lynton Cres BH23.............91 D3
Lynwood Cl BH22.............61 D7
Lynwood Ct DT4..............126 D8
Lynwood Dr BH21.............87 E8
Lynx Trad Est BA20...........26 F3
Lynx West Trading Est
 BA20.................................26 E3
Lyon Ave BH10..................95 B3
Lyon Rd BH12....................88 E2
Lysander Cl BH23............125 C7
Lysander Rd BA20.............26 F3
Lystra Rd BH9....................90 A3
Lytchett Dr BH18...............86 F2
Lytchett La BH20.............140 A4
Lytchett Matravers Prim Sch
 BH16.................................84 C2
Lytchett Minster Sch
 BH16.............................116 F8
Lytchett Way BH16..........118 B6
Lytham Rd BH18................87 A3
Lytton Rd BH1,BH8.........122 C5

M

Mabey Ave BH10...............89 D2
MacAndrew Rd BH13.......147 F7
MacAulay Rd DT4..............87 A4
McCreery Rd DT9..............30 A7
McIntyre Rd BH23.............91 A8
McKay Way DT4..............166 E2
McKinley Rd BH4.............121 C2
Macklin Ho ■ SO22.......126 D6
MacLaren Rd BH9.............89 F3
Maclean Rd BH11.............88 F3
Macville Ave BH20...........140 B1
McWilliam Cl DT4............121 C8
McWilliam Rd ■ BH9.......90 A2
Madeira Rd
 Bournemouth BH1...........122 A4
 Poole BH15....................120 D5
Madeline Cl BH12............120 B7
Madeline Cres BH12........120 B7
Madison Ave DT1...............88 A4
Maen Gdns DT1...............108 B1
Magdalen Hill SO23........126 F5
Magdalen La
 Bridport DT6....................100 B6
 Christchurch BH23..........124 A6
Magdalen Mews ■
 SO23.............................126 F5
Magiston St DT1.............106 D8
Magna Cl
 Bournemouth BH11...........88 F6
 Yeovil BA21.......................27 F8
Magna Gdns BH11.............88 F6
Magna Rd BH11.................88 C7
Magnolia Cl
 Bournemouth BH6..........124 A5
 ■ Radipole DT3............152 E2
 Verwood BH31..................45 E4
Magnolia Dr DT2...............75 E3
Magnolia Ho ■ BH4..........89 F4
Magpie Cl BH8...................90 C3
Magpie Gr SH7..................94 F2
Mag's Barrow BH22...........61 E2
Maiden Beech Mid Sch
 TA18..............................191 E3
Maiden Castle (Hill Fort)
 DT2.................................134 B6
Maiden Castle Rd DT2....134 B7
Maiden Newton Sta DT2...73 A8
Maiden St ■ DT4.............167 C2
Maidment Cl BH11............88 E4
Maincombe Cl ■ TA18...191 E3
Main Rd
 Fortuneswell DT5...........181 C1
 Tolpuddle DT2...................79 D1
 West Lulworth BH20.......172 C4
Main St
 Bridport DT6...................100 E4
 Broadmayne DT2............136 B2
 Chideock DT6....................99 A6
 Iwerne Courtney or Shroton
 DT11.............................198 F7
Maitlands The ■ DT1.....121 D2
Majorca Mans ■ BH1.....121 E1
Major's Comm ■ DT1....208 A7
Malan Cl BH17................119 E8
Malcomb Cl BH6.............124 A3
Mallams DT5...................186 E7
Mallard Bldgs ■ BH25....95 A3
Mallard Cl
 Bournemouth BH8............90 C1
 Christchurch BH23..........125 A6
Mallard Rd
 Bournemouth BH8............90 D1
 Wimborne Minster BH21...60 A7

Mallards Gn DT2.............133 F7
Mallory Cl BH23..............124 F8
Mallow Cl
 Broadstone BH18.............86 E3
 Christchurch BH23.........125 C8
Mallows The BH25.............95 A5
Malmesbury Ct BH4........122 C6
Malmesbury Gdns SO22 126 B8
Malmesbury Park Pl ■
 BH8.................................122 B5
Malmesbury Park Prim Sch
 BH8.................................122 B5
Malmesbury Park Rd
 BH8.................................122 B6
Malmesbury Rd BH24.......54 A3
Malmesbury Way BH21.....26 C6
Malmsbury Cl ■ BH23....124 A5
Maloren Way BH23............53 C1
Malta Cl ■ DT1...............107 C2
Malthouse ■ BH15.........119 C2
Malthouse La DT9.............14 F2
Malthouse Mdw DT3.......149 F8
Maltings The
 Blandford Forum DT11....212 C2
 ■ Cerne Abbas DT2......207 D4
 ■ Poole BH15................119 E3
 Weymouth DT4...............167 D1
Malvern Cl BH9.................90 A3
Malvern Ct
 ■ Bournemouth BH9.......90 A2
 ■ Christchurch BH23.....124 F8
Malvern Rd BH9................90 A3
Malvern Terr DT4.............167 B2
Mampitts La SP7...............13 A2
Mampitts Rd SP7..............13 A2
Mandalay Cl DT4...............45 A5
Mandale Cl BH11..............89 A4
Mandale Rd BH11.............88 F3
Mandeville Cl DT4...........180 B8
Mandeville Rd DT4..........180 B8
Mandeville Stoke La DT6..66 B7
Mangerton La DT6.............69 A3
Mangerton Water Mill
 DT6...................................69 C4
Mangle Cew/Sh Ret Le ■
 SP1.................................191 C5
Mannington Hall ■ BH4..121 C2
Manning Ave BH23............93 C1
Manningford Rd DT11.....212 D5
Mannings Heath Rd BH12 288 B1
Mannings Heath Rdbt
 BH17.................................88 B2
Mannings Heath Ret Pk
 BH12...............................120 A8
Mannington Pl ■ BH2....121 E3
Mannington Way BH22.....52 F2
Manor Ave
 Lyme Regis DT7................96 B6
 Poole BH12.......................88 C1
Manor Cl
 Ringwood BH24................55 C8
 Verwood BH31..................45 B6
Manor Ct
 ■ Merriott TA16............191 F7
 West Coker BA22...........193 B8
Manor Dr
 Bradford Abbas DT9........28 C2
 Dewlish DT2....................209 C1
 Ferndown BH22................61 E5
 ■ Portesham DT3..........150 A8
 South Perrott DT8.........192 C1
 Stratton DT2...................106 B3
 Templecombe BA8............18 D8
 ■ Winchester SO23.......126 F6
Manor Farm Cl
 Litton Cheney DT2...........103 C2
 Old Milton BH25...............94 F1
Manor Farm Ct DT3.........133 D6
Manor Farm Rd
 Bere Regis BH20..............81 B2
 Bournemouth BH10..........89 D7
Manor Farmyard BH8.......91 B3
Manor Fields DT6............100 C6
Manor Gdns
 ■ Beaminster DT8.........204 C4
 ■ Ringwood BH24..........55 B8
 Verwood BH31..................45 B6
Manor Gr DT2..................133 D6
Manor Ho BH16.................87 A4
Manor La
 Bradford Peverell DT2.....106 F5
 Verwood BH31..................45 B5
Manor Park CE Fst Sch
 DT1.................................135 B8
Manor Pk BH15...............119 B5
Manor Rd
 Bournemouth BH1...........122 C3
 Christchurch BH23..........124 A6
 Dorchester DT1...............135 A8
 Gussage St Michael BH21.200 F6
 Mere BA12...........................2 F7
 Milborne Port DT9............17 C3
 New Milton BH25..............95 B3
 Radipole DT3...................167 B8
 Ringwood BH24................55 C7
 Stourpaine DT11.............198 F14
 Studland BH19.................164 D2
 Swanage BH19................179 B2
 Verwood BH31..................45 B4
 Yeovil BA20.......................27 C4
Manorside Comb Sch
 BH12...............................88 D1
Manor St BA22................193 B8
Manor Vale ■ DT8..........204 A8
Manor View TA18............191 E3
Manor Way BH31...............45 B7
Mansard Ct BH13.............147 B3

Manscombe Abbey DT6...66 B2
Mansel Cl BH12...............121 C2
Mansel Rd BH14.............120 C4
Mansfield Cl
 Ferndown BH22................61 D2
 Poole BH14....................120 C4
Mansfield Rd
 Bournemouth BH9............89 E1
 Poole BH14....................120 C4
 Ringwood BH24................55 B7
Manshay La DT6.............203 A1
Manston Rd DT10..............35 C2
Manton Cl BH11..............118 E3
Manton Rd BH15............118 E3
Manton Rd BH17............118 E3
Manwell Dr BH19............179 A1
Manwell Rd BH19............179 B1
Manwell's La ■ BH19.....179 B2
Maple Cl
 Barton on Sea BH25........127 B7
 Christchurch BH23..........125 F7
 ■ Overcombe/Preston
 DT3.................................153 B2
 Sandford BH20................143 A8
 Shaftesbury SP7...............12 F4
Maple Dr
 ■ Crewkerne TA18........191 F5
 Ferndown BH22................61 C8
 Yeovil BA20.......................27 B3
Maple Gdns DT6.............100 D5
Maple Lo BH16................118 C7
Maple Rd
 Bournemouth BH9..........121 F8
 Charminster DT2...............75 D2
 Poole BH15....................119 D3
Maple Way SP8...................5 D1
Mapperton Cl BH17..........87 F2
Mapperton Mill BH17.......87 F2
Mapperton House & Gdns
 DT8.................................204 F2
Mapperton La DT6............69 B8
Mappowder Ct DT10.......208 F8
Marabout La DT4.............124 D7
Marchwood Rd BH10........89 C3
Margards La BH31.............45 A5
Margaret Pl BH11............107 E1
Marian Cl BH21..................86 C4
Marianne Rd
 Poole BH12....................121 C8
 Wimborne Minster BH21...60 A7
Marian Rd
 Corfe Mullen BH21............86 C4
 Poole BH11.......................85 E4
Marie Cl BH12.................120 D7
Marie Rd BH11................107 E1
Marina Cl
 ■ Bournemouth BH5.....122 E4
 Christchurch BH23..........126 A7
Marina Dr BH14..............120 D7
Marina Gdns DT4.............167 B1
Marina The BH1..............122 E3
Marina Twrs ■ BH5........122 E3
Marina View ■ BH23......124 A5
Marine Dr BH25...............126 D7
Marine Dr E BH25............126 D7
Marine Drive W BH25......126 C7
Marine Par DT7.................96 B4
Marine Point BH25..........126 F7
Marine Prospect BH25....126 F7
Marine Rd BH6................123 D3
Mariners Cl BH23............125 A6
Mariners Ct BH19............179 B6
Mariners Reach BH25......127 A6
Mariners Way DT3...........166 D6
Market Cl BH15...............119 C2
Market Pl
 Blandford Forum DT11....212 D3
 Ringwood BH24................55 B7
 Sturminster Newton DT10...35 B1
Markets La BH25.............101 E3
Market St
 Abbotsbury DT3..............149 B7
 Poole BH15....................119 B2
 Radipole DT3...................167 D2
 Winchester SO23............126 E5
 Yeovil BA20.......................27 D5
Market Way BH21..............59 D4
Markham Ave
 Bournemouth BH10..........89 D7
 Weymouth DT4...............167 B2
Markham Cl BH10..............89 D6
Markham Rd BH9............122 A8
Mark's La BH21..................95 A6
Marks Rd BH9....................89 F3
Marlborough Ave DT4.....186 F2
Marlborough Ct
 ■ Bournemouth BH4.....121 C3
 ■ Wimborne Minster BH21...59 D5
Marlborough Mans ■
 BH7.................................123 B6
Marlborough Pines ■
 BH4.................................121 C3
Marlborough Rd
 Bournemouth BH4..........121 C3
 Poole BH14....................120 C4
 Yeovil BA21.......................27 A7
Marler Ho ■ BH4............121 B4
Marley Ave BH25...............94 F3
Marley Cl
 New Milton BH25..............93 F3
 Overcombe/Preston DT3..153 C1
Marline Rd BH14.............120 D5
Marl La DT11.....................28 C1

Low–May 231

Marlott Rd
 Gillingham SP8....................5 E4
 Poole BH15....................119 C5
Marlow Dr BH23................91 E3
Marlow Rd DT14..............167 D1
Marlpit Dr BH23................94 A2
Marlpit La BH25................95 A8
Marmion Gn BH23...........124 F7
Marnhull Rd
 Hinton St Mary DT10........35 A5
 Poole BH15....................119 C5
Marnhull Rise SO22.........126 A5
Marpet Cl BH11..................88 F6
Marquis Cl DT4................166 F2
Marquis Way DT4..............88 D5
Marriage La DT10..............35 A6
Marrowbone La DT6........100 E4
Marryat Cl
 Christchurch BH23..........126 B7
 New Milton BH25..............94 F3
Marryat Rd BH23...............94 F3
Marshall Row ■ BH19.....179 C1
Marshallsay Rd DT3.........166 D6
Marshal Rd BH17...............87 B1
Marsh Athletics Ctr The
 DT4.................................167 B2
Marshfield BH21................59 F7
Marsh Gate DT6..............100 D3
Marsh La
 Christchurch BH23............91 F2
 Hazelbury Bryan DT10....196 F2
 Henstridge BA8.................19 D5
 Ibberton DT11................197 D3
 Pen Selwood BA9................1 A4
 Upton BH16.....................118 A7
 Wincanton BA9....................8 E8
 Winterborne Kingston DT11 81 F7
 Yeovil BA21.......................27 B7
Marshlands DT3...............124 D6
Marsh Rd DT4..................167 C2
Marsh The DT9................194 E3
Marsh Way
 ■ Pimperne DT11..........199 D4
 Swanage BH19................178 F3
Marshwood Ave DT4.........87 F3
Marshwood CE Prim Sch
 DT6.................................202 F2
Marshwood Rd ■ DT11..135 B8
Marston Cl
 Blandford Forum DT11....212 D5
 New Milton BH25..............95 B5
Marston Gate ■ SO23....126 E6
Marston Gr BH23...............93 E1
Marston Rd
 New Milton BH25..............95 B5
 Poole BH15....................119 B2
 Sherborne DT9..................30 A1
Martel Cl DT12..................136 A1
Martello Ho ■ BH13.......147 F8
Martello Pk BH13............147 F7
Martello Rd BH13............120 F1
Martello Rd S BH13.........147 F8
Martello Twrs BH13.........147 F7
Martells The BH13...........127 B7
Martin Cl BH17................118 F8
Martindale Ave BH21........60 B5
Martin Down National Nature
 Reserve SP5.................189 F6
Martin Drove End SP6....190 A7
Martingale Cl BH14.........118 D7
Martins Cl BH21.................61 E7
Martinscroft Rd ■ BH23...61 E3
Martins Dr BH22................61 E7
Martins Hill Cl BH23..........92 B3
Martins Hill La BH23..........92 C1
Martin's La SP8...................5 C8
Martins Way BH22............61 E7
Martleaves Cl ■ DT4.......180 C8
Martyr Cl DT1..................134 E7
Marwell Ct BH7...............123 A7
Mary Cossins Cl DT1.......212 C5
Mary Gdns ■ DT11.........197 F6
Mary La DT12.....................52 F2
Maryland Rd BH16...........118 C4
Mary St BA21.....................27 D5
Maskew Cl DT3................166 D5
Mason's La DT6...............204 A4
Masters Ct BH4...............121 D3
Masterson Cl BH23..........124 D7
Matchams Cl BH24............63 B7
Matchams La BH23,BH24..63 B4
Matchams L Pk BH24.......54 D2
Materloh Cl BH23..............126 E6
Matlock Rd BH22...............61 C3
Matthews Rd BA21.............27 E5
Maudlin Cross TA20........202 E8
Maudlin La TA20..............202 F8
Maud Rd DT1...................107 F1
Maumbury Rd DT11.........107 F1
Maumbury Rings DT1......135 A8
Maundeville Cres BH23...123 E8
Maundeville Rd BH23......123 E8
Maunsell Ave DT3............153 B1
Maureen Cl BH12.............120 B8
Maurice Rd BH8.................90 B1
Mavis Rd BH9.....................90 B1
Maxwell Rd
 Bournemouth BH9..........122 A7
 Broadstone BH18..............86 E3
 Poole BH13....................147 F7
Maycroft Rd DT4.............167 D1
Mayfair BH1.....................121 C2
Mayfair Ct BH11..............121 B2
Mayfair Gdns BH11............89 A4

Mayfield DT2 . . . . .133 E7
Mayfield Ave BH14. . . . . .120 E3
Mayfield Cl
  Ferndown BH22. . . . . .61 C6
  Radipole DT4. . . . . .167 A6
Mayfield Dr BH22. . . . . .61 C6
Mayfield Rd
  Bournemouth BH9. . . . . .90 A2
  Yeovil BA21 . . . . .27 F6
Mayfield Way BH22 . . . . . . .61 C6
Mayford Rd BH12 . . . . . . .121 B6
May Gdns
  Bournemouth BH11. . . . . . . .88 E4
  Walkford BH23 . . . . .94 B2
May Gr DT11 . . . . .211 D6
May La DT11 . . . . .199 D7
Maylyn Rd
  Beacon Hill BH16. . . . . .86 A2
  Lytchett Minster & Upton
    BH16. . . . . .85 B2
May Terrace Gdns DT3 . .166 D6
May Tree Cl SO22 . . . . . . .126 A2
Mead Ave BA22 . . . . .26 D6
Mead Bower DT5 . . . . . . .186 E1
Mead Cl BH18 . . . . .87 A1
Mead Fields DT6. . . . . . . .100 B8
Mead La
  Allington DT6. . . . . .100 A8
  Gussage All Saints BH21. . .201 A5
Meadowbank BH16 . . . . . .118 C8
Meadow Bottom DT2 . . .106 D8
Meadow Cl
  Bransgore BH23 . . . . .93 A8
  1 Cattistock DT2 . . . . . . .206 C2
  Chickerell DT3 . . . . .166 C5
  Ferndown BH21. . . . . .61 D1
  Henstridge BA8 . . . . .19 A5
  Ringwood BH24 . . . . .55 D8
  Sopley BH23 . . . . .92 B7
  Stalbridge DT10. . . . . .33 D8
Meadow Court Cl BH9 . . . .90 A3
Meadowcroft **4** SP8. . . . . .11 A8
Meadow Ct
  2 Bournemouth BH9 . . . . . .90 A3
  3 Wimborne Minster BH21 .59 D4
Meadow Farm La BH21 . . .86 D8
Meadow Gr BH31. . . . . .45 D5
Meadow La
  Burton BH23 . . . . .92 C2
  Wool BH20. . . . . .140 A2
Meadowland BH23 . . . . . .124 F6
Meadowlands DT6 . . . . . .100 D2
Meadow Rd
  5 Charlton Marshall
    DT11. . . . . .211 D6
  Langton Long Blandford
    DT11. . . . . .212 E3
  New Milton BH25. . . . . .95 B4
  Ringwood BH24 . . . . .55 D8
  Yeovil BA21 . . . . .27 F7
Meadow Rise BH18 . . . . . . .86 F5
Meadows Cl BH16 . . . . . . .118 C7
Meadows Dr
  8 Upton BH16 . . . . .117 E7
  Upton BH16 . . . . .118 C2
Meadowside **4** DT8 . . . .204 A7
Meadows The
  Bourton SP8 . . . . .1 F2
  3 Gillingham SP8. . . . . .11 A8
Meadowsweet Rd BH17 . .118 E8
Meadow Vale DT2. . . . . . .196 B3
Meadow View
  8 Blandford Forum
    DT11. . . . . .212 D3
  Bradford Peverell DT2. . . .107 A6
  Cattistock DT2 . . . . .206 B2
  Charminster DT2 . . . . .107 D6
  East Coker BA22 . . . . .193 C8
  7 Stofold BA22 . . . . .193 F8
Meadow View Cl BH20 . . .142 F3
Meadow View Rd
  Bournemouth BH11. . . . . . . .88 E4
  Radipole DT3. . . . . .152 C4
Meadow Way
  Barton on Sea BH25 . . . . . .127 A7
  Charmouth DT6 . . . . .97 B7
  Ringwood BH24 . . . . .55 D8
  Verwood BH31. . . . . .45 C4
  Winchester SO22. . . . . .126 A2
Mead Rd
  Corfe Castle BH20. . . . . . . .177 A7
  Radipole DT4. . . . . .167 A6
  Winchester SO23. . . . . .126 C2
Meads Cl DT2 . . . . .194 A2
Meads The DT7 . . . . .17 D2
Mead The BA8 . . . . .19 B3
Meadus's La BH20 . . . . . . .162 D3
Meadway **4** DT6 . . . . . . .100 B2
Meadway The BH23 . . . . . . .93 D2
Medbourne Cl DT11. . . . . .212 C5
Medina Way BH23 . . . . . . .125 C6
Medlar Cl BH23 . . . . .92 D1
Medway Dr DT3 . . . . .168 B8
Medway Rd BH22. . . . . .62 A6
Meech Cl DT10 . . . . .100 D4
Meech Way DT10 . . . . .75 E2
Meerhay La DT6 . . . . .65 A4
Meerhay Manor DT8 . . . . .204 D5
Meeting House La BH24. . .55 B7
Melancholy La BH20 . . . . .142 E1
Melbourne Rd
  Bournemouth BH8 . . . . . . .122 C6
  Christchurch BH23 . . . . .91 E1
Melbourne St DT1. . . . . . .167 B3
Melbury Abbas Mill SP7. . .24 B6

Melbury Ave BH12. . . . . . .120 E7
Melbury Cl BH22. . . . . .61 D4
Melbury House DT2. . . . . .194 A1
Melbury Pk DT2 . . . . .194 A1
Melbury Rd
  Weymouth DT4 . . . . .167 C3
  Yetminster DT9 . . . . .194 C5
Melbury Sq SP7. . . . . .24 C4
Melbury Way SP7. . . . . .13 A3
Melchester Cl **2** SP8 . . . . . .5 E4
Melcombe Ave DT4 . . . . . .167 E5
Melcombe Horsey DT2. . .208 F5
Melcombe Pl **1** DT4. . . . .167 E4
Melford Cl BH11. . . . . .122 A3
Mellstock Ave DT1 . . . . . .135 A7
Mellstock Cl DT11. . . . . . .212 F6
Mellstock Cres BH20. . . . .142 D5
Mellstock Rd BH15. . . . . . .119 D5
Melplash Ct DT6. . . . . .204 D1
Melrose Ct BH25. . . . . .95 C3
Melrose Rd BA21 . . . . .27 D6
Melstock Ave DT3 . . . . . . .168 A7
Melstock Rd DT3 . . . . .167 F7
Melton Cl
  Poole BH13. . . . . .120 F4
  14 Poole BH13 . . . . .121 A4
Melverley Gdns BH21 . . . . .59 D5
Melville Rd BH9 . . . . .121 E8
Melway Gdns **11** DT11. . .198 C2
Melway La DT11 . . . . .198 C7
Memorial Ave **19** TA18. . .191 F4
Memorial Rd BA22. . . . . . . .26 D6
Mendip Cl
  New Milton BH25. . . . . .95 B2
  Verwood BH31. . . . . .45 B5
Mendip Ct **8** BH23 . . . . . .124 F8
Mendip Rd BH31. . . . . .45 B6
Menin Rd BH20 . . . . .139 C6
Mentone Rd **2** BH14. . . .120 A3
Meon Ho SO23 . . . . .126 F4
Meon Rd BH7 . . . . .123 B7
Mercery Rd DT3 . . . . .166 F7
Merchants Pl **8** SO23. . . .126 E6
Mere By-pass BA12. . . . . . . .2 F6
Mere Castle BA12. . . . . .2 F6
Meredith Cl
  Christchurch BH23 . . . . . . .124 D7
  Halstock BA22 . . . . .193 C3
  Mere Sch BA12 . . . . .3 B5
Merevale Way BA21. . . . . . .26 E7
Meriden Cl BH13 . . . . .147 F7
Meriden Ct **11** SO23. . . . .126 E8
Meridians The BH23 . . . . .123 F6
Merino Way BH22. . . . . .53 B1
Merlewood Cl BH2 . . . . . .121 F4
Merlewood Ct **1** BH25. . . .95 B3
Merley Court Touring Pk
  BH21. . . . . .59 C1
Merley Dr BH23. . . . . .126 A8
Merley Fst Sch BH21. . . . . .59 D1
Merley Gdns BH21 . . . . . . .59 E1
Merley Ho BH21 . . . . .59 B1
Merley House Holiday Pk
  BH21. . . . . .59 B1
Merley House La BH21. . . .59 C1
Merley La BH21. . . . . .59 E1
Merley Park Rd
  Ashington BH21. . . . . .87 B8
  Corfe Mullen BH21. . . . . . . .86 F8
  Merley BH21 . . . . .59 C1
Merley Rd DT4 . . . . .180 D6
Merley Ways BH21 . . . . . . .59 D2
Merlin Ave N DT3. . . . . . . .152 B3
Merlin Ave S DT3. . . . . . . .152 B3
Merlin Cl BH24 . . . . .55 E6
Merlin Way BH23 . . . . .125 A6
Mermaid Ct **3** BH5. . . . . .122 E3
Mermond Pl BH19 . . . . . . .179 C2
Merredin Cl DT3 . . . . .152 D3
Merrefield Ave BH18 . . . . . .87 B5
Merrefield Cl BH18. . . . . . . .87 B6
Merrefield Dr BH18 . . . . . . .87 B6
Merrifield BH21. . . . . .59 E8
Merritt Fst Sch TA16. . . . .191 F7
Merritt Rd
  Hinton St George TA17 . . .191 D7
  Merriott TA18. . . . . .191 F6
Merritown La BH23 . . . . . . .90 D7
Merrivale Ave BH6. . . . . . .123 E5
Merrow Ave BH12. . . . . . . .121 B7
Merrow Chase **1** BH13 . .147 F7
Merryfield Cl
  Bransgore BH23 . . . . .93 A8
  Verwood BH31. . . . . .45 B7
Merryfield Ct BH10 . . . . . . .89 C4
Merryfield La BH10 . . . . . . .89 C4
Merryweather Est **5**
  BH22. . . . . .55 E8
Merton Cl
  2 Christchurch BH23. . . . .126 B7
  3 Poole BH15 . . . . .119 E4
Merville Gdns BH9. . . . . . .121 F8
Methuen Cl **2** BH8 . . . . . .122 C5
Methuen Rd
  Bournemouth BH8. . . . . . . .122 B5
  Poole BH17 . . . . .87 B2
Mews La SO22 . . . . .126 D5
Mews The
  Bournemouth BH21. . . . . . .121 D3
  Verwood BH31. . . . . .45 C4
Meyrick Cl BH23. . . . . .93 A7
Meyrick Park Cres BH3 . .121 F6
Meyrick Park Mans 7
  BH2. . . . . .121 F4
Meyrick Rd BH1 . . . . .122 B3
Michelgrove Rd BH5. . . . .122 E3
Michelmersh Gn BH8. . . . .90 D2
Mickleham Cl DT11. . . . . .121 B8

Middlebere Cres BH16 . . .118 C4
Middlebere Dr BH20 . . . . .142 D6
Middle Brook BH1. . . . . . . .89 A6
Middle Brook St SO23. . . .126 E6
Middle Farm Way DT1 . .107 D1
Middlefield BH20 . . . . .141 B3
Middlefield La TA13. . . . . .191 F8
Middle Field La DT9 . . . . . .15 D5
Middle Gn **8** DT8 . . . . . . .204 D4
Middlehill Dr BH21. . . . . . . .60 B6
Middlehill Rd BH21. . . . . . . .60 A6
Middle La
  Martin SP6. . . . . .190 A7
  Ringwood BH24 . . . . .55 C7
Middlemarsh St DT1. . . . .107 D1
Middle Path TA18 . . . . . . .191 E4
Middle Rd
  Bournemouth BH10. . . . . . . .89 C5
  Lytchett Matravers BH16 . . .84 B2
  Poole BH15 . . . . .119 E6
  Sturminster Marshall BH21. .56 E3
  Tiptoe SO41. . . . . .95 B8
  Winchester SO22. . . . . .126 C6
Middle St
  Bridport DT6. . . . . .69 A1
  Burton Bradstock DT6. . . . .128 B8
  Crewkerne TA18 . . . . .192 A3
  Dewlish DT2 . . . . .209 C1
  Rimpton BA22 . . . . .15 B8
  Yeovil BA20 . . . . .27 D4
Middleton Mews BH25. . . .94 F1
Middleton Rd
  Bournemouth BH9. . . . . .89 E2
  Ringwood BH24 . . . . .55 C8
Midland Rd BH9 . . . . .89 F1
Midleaze DT9. . . . . .209 E5
Midney La SP8 . . . . .4 B8
Midway Path BH13. . . . . . .147 C3
Midwood Ave BH8 . . . . .90 F1
Milborne Fst Sch DT11 . .120 E8
Milborne Fst Sch DT11. . . .79 E8
Milborne Port Prim Sch
  DT9 .17 D2
Milbourne Rd BH22. . . . . . .61 C6
Milburn Cl **3** BH4 . . . . . .121 C4
Milburn Rd **1** BH4 . . . . . .196 A7
Milburn Rd BH4. . . . . .121 B4
Mildenhall **5** BH2 . . . . . .121 D2
Midmay Ct **2** SO23 . . . . .126 F5
Midmay St SO23. . . . . .126 B3
Miles Ave BH20 . . . . .142 F8
Miles Gdns DT3 . . . . .152 B5
Milestone Rd BH15 . . . . . .119 D5
Milestone Way SP8 . . . . . . .5 D1
Milford Cl BH22 . . . . .53 E2
Milford Cl SP8. . . . . .5 D1
Milford Cty Jun Sch BA21 .27 D7
Milford Inf Sch BH11. . . . . .88 F5
Milford Ho SO23 . . . . .126 D3
Milford Rd
  Barton on Sea BH25 . . . . . .127 C7
  Dorchester DT1. . . . . .107 E1
  Yeovil BA21 . . . . .27 D6
Military La DT10 . . . . .197 A4
Milland Rd SO23. . . . . .126 F4
Millbank Ho **5** BA20. . . . . .59 C5
Millbrook Cl **2** DT11. . . . .198 C8
Millbrook Ct **3** DT11. . . .198 C8
Mill Cl BA22. . . . . .193 C8
Milldown CE Fst Sch
  DT11 . . . . .212 C5
Milldown CE Mid Sch
  DT11. . . . . .212 B5
Milldown Rd DT11 . . . . . . .212 B6
Mill End SP6. . . . . .190 F7
Miller Cl BH25 . . . . .95 C4
Miller Rd BH23 . . . . .124 D7
Millers Cl DT3 . . . . .153 C1
Miller's Cl DT1 . . . . .107 E3
Miller's Hill DT9 . . . . .17 A5
Miller's La
  Farnham DT11. . . . . .200 D8
  Sixpenny Handley DT11. . .188 D1
Millfield
  New Milton BH25. . . . . .94 E3
  Poole BH17 . . . . .119 A7
Mill Gn DT7 . . . . .96 C5
Mill Ham Island Nature
  Reserve DT11. . . . . .198 B7
Millhams Cl BH10 . . . . .89 B6
Millhams Dr BH10 . . . . .89 B6
Millhams Rd BH10 . . . . .89 B6
Millhams St BH23. . . . . . . .124 B6
Millhams Street N 2
  BH23 . . . . .124 B6
Mill Hill Cl BH14. . . . . .120 B3
Mill Hollow La SP7 . . . . . . .24 B6
Mill House Cider Mus
  DT2 . . . . .137 E3
Mill La
  Bourton SP8 . . . . .1 E2
  Bradford Abbas DT9 . . . . . . .28 D1
  Cann SP7 . . . . .24 A6
  Cattistock DT2 . . . . .206 B2
  4 Cerne Abbas DT2 . . . . .207 D4
  Charminster DT2 . . . . .107 D7
  Chetnole DT9 . . . . .194 D2
  Chideock DT6. . . . . .99 A4
  Christchurch BH23 . . . . . . .124 B6
  Cranborne BH21 . . . . .40 C6
  Crewkerne TA18 . . . . .191 F3
  Durweston DT11 . . . . .198 E3
  East Coker BA22 . . . . .193 C7
  Halstock BA22 . . . . .193 A2
  Hawkchurch EX13 . . . . . . .202 C3
  Hurn BH23. . . . . .91 B6
  Ibberton DT11. . . . . .197 D3

Mill La continued
  Kingstone TA17 . . . . .191 B8
  Lyme Regis DT7 . . . . .96 A7
  Lyme Regis DT7 . . . . .96 C5
  Marnhull DT10 . . . . .20 E4
  Mere BA12. . . . . .3 B5
  Misterton TA18 . . . . .192 B3
  Poole BH14 . . . . .120 B3
  Shapwick DT11 . . . . .56 E6
  Silton SP8 . . . . .1 F2
  Stour Provost SP8 . . . . .21 C7
  Stratton DT2 . . . . .106 E8
  Symondsbury DT6 . . . . .99 F8
  Trent DT9 . . . . .14 E1
  Wareham BH20. . . . . .142 E4
  West Coker BA22 . . . . .193 B8
  Wimborne Minster BH21 . . .59 C5
  Winterbourne Abbas DT2 . .132 F8
  Wootton Fitzpaine DT6 . . . .64 D4
  Yeovil BA20 . . . . .27 D4
  Yetminster DT9 . . . . .194 C5
Mill Rd BH23 . . . . .124 A8
Mill Rd N BH8 . . . . .90 D3
Mill Rd S BH8 . . . . .90 D2
Mill Rise SP8 . . . . .1 E2
Mills Rd DT3 . . . . .169 C8
Mill St
  Blandford Forum DT11 . . . .212 C3
  Burton Bradstock DT6. . . . .128 B7
  Dorchester DT1 . . . . .108 B2
  Fontmell Magna SP7 . . . . . .37 F6
  Puddletown DT2 . . . . .78 B1
  Radipole DT3 . . . . .152 B4
  Rimpton BA22 . . . . .15 B8
  Sleight BH21. . . . . .58 A1
Mills The BH12 . . . . .120 E7
Millstream Cl
  Poole BH17 . . . . .119 A7
  Wimborne Minster BH21. . . .59 C4
Millstream Trad Est BH24 .55 C5
Millyford Cl BH25 . . . . . . .126 D8
Milman Ct **2** SO23 . . . . . .126 B6
Milne Rd BH17 . . . . .87 B1
Milner Pl SO22 . . . . .126 C4
Milner Rd BH4 . . . . .121 C1
Milnthorpe La SO22. . . . . .126 C5
Milom La DT2 . . . . .110 C7
Milton Abbey Sch DT11 . .209 E5
Milton Bsns Ctr BH25 . . . .94 E2
Milton Cl
  Poole BH15 . . . . .120 D3
  Radipole DT4. . . . . .167 D6
  Yeovil BA21 . . . . .26 E6
Milton Cres DT3 . . . . .167 C6
Milton Ct BH22 . . . . .61 D5
Milton House BA21. . . . . . .14 B3
Milton La DT11 . . . . .198 D2
Milton Mead BH25 . . . . . . .94 F2
Milton Rd
  Bournemouth BH8. . . . . . . .122 A6
  Milborne St Andrew DT11. .79 E8
  Poole BH14 . . . . .120 D3
  Weymouth DT4 . . . . .167 C3
  Wimborne Minster BH21. . . .59 C6
Milton Terr DT4 . . . . .167 D6
Milton Villas BH8 . . . . .122 A5
Milvers La DT6 . . . . .101 B3
Milverton Cl BH23 . . . . .93 E1
Milverton Rd SO22. . . . . . .126 C6
Mimosa Ave BH6 . . . . .87 E8
Minden Way SO22 . . . . . . .126 A3
Minerva Cl DT1 . . . . .134 F8
Minstead Rd BH10. . . . . . . .89 F2
Minster La **3** SO23 . . . . .126 E5
Minster The BH21. . . . . .59 B4
Minster View BH21. . . . . . .59 C5
Minster Way BH16 . . . . . . .118 B7
Minterne Gdns DT2 . . . . . .207 D6
Minterne Grange BH14 . .147 C7
Minterne Rd
  Bournemouth BH9 . . . . .90 A2
  Christchurch BH23 . . . . . . .124 E5
  Poole BH14 . . . . .147 C7
Minters Ct **2B** SO23 . . . . .126 D6
Minton Mews BH21 . . . . . .121 F5
Minton Pl **1** DT1 . . . . . . .107 C4
Mission Hall La DT3 . . . . .153 D2
Mission St BH8 . . . . .122 A4
Mission Rd BH18 . . . . .87 A2
Misterton Sch TA18 . . . . .192 A2
Mistover Cl DT1 . . . . .135 A7
Mistover Rd BH20. . . . . . . .142 D5
Mitchell Cl BH25. . . . . .127 A7
Mitchell Rd
  Ferndown BH21. . . . . .61 A7
  Poole BH17 . . . . .119 F8
Mitchell St **1** DT4. . . . . . .167 E2
Mitchelmore Rd BA21. . . .27 D8
Mithras Cl DT11 . . . . .134 E8
Mitre Ct **5** BH23 . . . . . . .124 D7
Mixen La **15** DT1. . . . . . .135 B8
Miz Maze DT9 . . . . .15 A4
Moat Ct BH4 . . . . .121 C5
Moat La BH25 . . . . .126 F8
Moats Cotts DT2 . . . . .209 C1
Mockbeggar La BH24 . . . . .47 C7
Moffat Rd DT3 . . . . .166 D5
Mohune Way DT3 . . . . . . .166 D5
Mohuns Pk BA8 . . . . .25 D3
Molyneux Rd BH25. . . . . . .95 D3
Monaco Cl BH9 . . . . .122 B8
Monarch Cl **2B** BH4 . . . .121 C3
Monarch Way SO22 . . . . . .126 A4
Moneyfly Rd BH31. . . . . . . .45 D5
Monk Barton Cl BA21 . . . .26 E7

Monkey World Ape Rescue
  Ctr BH20. . . . . .140 B6
Monks Cl DT2 . . . . .62 A4
Monks Dale BA21 . . . . .26 F7
Monkshood Cl BH23 . . . . . .93 B7
Monks Rd SO23. . . . . .126 E6
Monks Way BH11 . . . . .88 D7
Monkswell Gn BH23 . . . . .124 D6
Monkton Cl BH22 . . . . .61 D6
Monkton Cres BH12. . . . . .120 E6
Monkton Down Rd 5
  DT11. . . . . .199 E2
Monkton Dro BH21. . . . . . .189 D1
Monkton Hill DT2 . . . . .134 E8
Monkton Wyld Cross DT6 .64 A4
Monkton Wyld La DT6 . . . .64 C5
Monkwood La DT6. . . . . . .203 E2
Monmouth Ave DT3. . . . . .167 D2
Monmouth Cl BH31 . . . . . . .45 C4
Monmouth Dr BH31. . . . . . .45 D4
Monmouth Rd
  Dorchester DT1. . . . . .108 B1
  Wareham BH20. . . . . .142 D1
  Yeovil BA21 . . . . .27 F1
Monmouth St **5** DT7 . . . . .96 C5
Monnington Dr DT1 . . . . .107 C2
Monsal Ave BH22 . . . . .61 B6
Mons The **16** SO23 . . . . .126 E5
Montacute Sch BH17. . . . . .87 C2
Montacute Way BH21 . . . . .87 E8
Montague Rd BH5 . . . . . . .123 B4
Montagu Pk BH23 . . . . . . .126 A3
Montagu Rd BH23 . . . . . . .126 B8
Monteray Dr SO41 . . . . .95 F4
Montgomery Ave BH11. . . .89 B2
Montgomery Cl SO22 . . . .126 A3
Montrose Cl
  1 Easton/Weston DT5. . . .186 F4
  Verwood BH31. . . . . .45 B6
Montrose Dr BH10 . . . . .89 B2
Monument La BH21. . . . . . .88 A8
Moonrakers Way BH23 . . . .93 E1
Moorcombe Dr DT2 . . . . . .153 B1
Moorcroft Ave BH23 . . . . . .92 C2
Moordown Ave DT3 . . . . .167 F6
Moordown Cl BH9 . . . . .89 F3
Moordown St John's CE Prim
  Sch BH9 . . . . .89 F1
Moore Ave BH11. . . . . .89 A4
Moore Cl BH25 . . . . .94 F1
Moorfield Gr BH9 . . . . .89 F1
Moorfield Rd DT5. . . . . . . .187 A4
Moorfields Rd BH13. . . . . .147 F6
Moorhaven BH22 . . . . .61 D6
Moorhills **2** BH21 . . . . . . .59 D4
Moorings Cl BH15 . . . . . . .118 F1
Moorings The **2** BH23 . . .124 A5
Moor La
  Broadwindsor DT8. . . . . . .203 B6
  Buckhorn Weston SP8. . . . . .4 D1
  East Coker BA22 . . . . .193 D2
  Hardington Mandeville
    BA22 . . . . .193 A2
  Sturminster Marshall BH21. .56 E3
Moorland Ave BH25. . . . . .126 F8
Moorland Cres BH16 . . . . .118 B2
Moorland Gate BH21 . . . . . .55 C5
Moorland Par BH16 . . . . . .118 B2
Moorland Rd BH16 . . . . . . .118 B2
Moorlands Coll BH23 . . . . .92 B6
Moorlands Rd
  Ferndown BH22. . . . . .53 A3
  Merriott TA18. . . . . .191 E6
  Verwood BH31. . . . . .45 B2
Moorlands Rise BH22 . . . . .53 A3
Moorland Way BH16 . . . . .118 B2
Moorlea **2** BH8 . . . . .122 B5
Moor Rd
  Broadstone BH18 . . . . .87 B5
  Swanage BH19 . . . . .179 B5
Moors Cl BH23 . . . . .91 B7
Moor Side BH24 . . . . .62 B8
Moorside Ave DT4 . . . . . . .167 E3
Moorside Cl BH11. . . . . .89 B3
Moorside Gdns BH11. . . . . .89 B3
Moorside Rd
  Bournemouth BH11. . . . . . . .89 A3
  Corfe Mullen BH21. . . . . . . .86 D5
  Ferndown BH22. . . . . .53 A2
Moors Valley Ctry Pk
  BH24. . . . . .46 B1
Moor The DT2 . . . . .78 B2
Moortown Dr
  Bournemouth BH21. . . . . . . .88 B8
  Wimborne Minster BH21. . . .60 B1
Moortown Farm BH21. . . . .88 B8
Moortown La BH24. . . . . . . .55 C4
Moortown La BH24. . . . . . . .55 C4
Moorvale Rd BH9 . . . . .90 A2
Moor View Rd BH15. . . . . .119 E6
Moorway La DT9. . . . . .15 C6
Morant Ct **4** BH25. . . . . . . .94 F1
Morant Rd BH24. . . . . .47 D1
Moreton **5** DT11. . . . . . . .107 C2
Moray Ct **3** BH21 . . . . . . .60 D5
Morden Ave BH20 . . . . .77 C7
Morden Bog National Nature
  Reserve BH20. . . . . .115 D2
Morden La BH20. . . . . .82 D3
Morden Park Cnr BH20 . .115 C4
Morden Rd
  Bournemouth BH9. . . . . .89 F2
  Wareham St Martin BH20. .115 C4
Morestead Rd SO23. . . . . .126 F1
Moreton Dr
  Moreton DT2 . . . . .138 F8
  Turners Puddle DT2. . . . . . .112 B2

Moreton House Gdns
DT2 .... 138 F7
Moreton Rd
Bournemouth BH9 .... 90 B4
Crossways DT2 .... 137 E5
Moreton Sta DT2 .... 137 F7
Morgan's La SP5 .... 189 E5
Moriconium Quay BH15 . 118 D1
Morington Ct 8 BH8 ... 122 A5
Morley Cl
Bournemouth BH5 ...... 123 A5
Burton BH23 .... 92 C3
Morley Rd BH5 .... 123 A5
Morley Way BH22 .... 61 F3
Mornington Dr SO22 ... 126 A8
Mornish Rd BH13 ...... 128 D7
Morrison Ave BH12 .... 120 F6
Morrison Rd BH19 ..... 179 A2
Morris Rd
Poole BH17 .... 119 D8
Wool BH20 .... 139 F6
Morston DT9 .... 194 D8
Mortain Cl DT11 ...... 212 D5
Mortimer Cl BH23 ..... 125 A6
Mortimer Rd BH8 .... 90 B1
Mossley Ave
Poole BH12 .... 121 A8
Bournemouth 89 A1
Moss Rd SO23 .... 126 F6
Mosterton Down La DT8 192 A1
Motcombe CE VA Prim Sch
SP7 .... 12 B7
Motcombe Park Sports Ctr
SP7 .... 12 B6
Motcombe Rd
Poole BH13 .... 121 A2
Shaftesbury SP7 .... 12 E3
Mountain Ash Rd 4 DT11 107 E2
Mount Ave BH25 .... 95 A1
Mountbatten Cl
Christchurch BH23 .... 125 A5
Weymouth DT4 .... 180 B8
Mountbatten Ct BH25 ... 94 F3
Mountbatten Dr BH22 ... 61 C5
Mountbatten Gdns BH8 .. 90 F2
Mountbatten Rd BH13 .. 121 B1
Mount Cl BH25 .... 95 A1
Mount Grace Dr BH11 .. 144 F7
Mount Heatherbank 7
BH1 .... 121 F3
Mount Joy DT6 .... 100 D3
Mountjoy Cl BH21 ...... 59 F2
Mountjoy Specl Sch
DT6 .... 100 D4
Mount Pleasant
BH16 .... 99 F3
Mount Pleasant
Bridport DT6 .... 100 C7
Christchurch BH23 .... 125 A5
East Lulworth BH20 ... 158 E1
Ringwood BH24 .... 55 C7
Wareham Town BH20 ... 142 E4
Yeovil BA21 .... 27 E5
Mount Pleasant Ave N
DT3 .... 167 B8
Mount Pleasant Ave S
DT3 .... 167 C7
Mount Pleasant Bsns Pk
DT3 .... 167 C8
Mount Pleasant Dr BH8 . 90 F1
Mount Pleasant La 3
BH19 .... 179 C2
Mount Pleasant Rd
BH15 .... 119 D3
Mount Rd
Bournemouth BH11 ..... 89 B4
Poole BH14 .... 120 B5
Mount Scar BH19 ...... 179 B1
Mount Skippet Way DT2 137 D5
Mount The
8 Blandford Forum
DT11 .... 212 D3
Ringwood BH24 .... 55 E8
Mower La DT11 .... 37 A5
Mowes La DT10 .... 34 F8
Mowleaze 1 BA22 ...... 193 F8
Mowlem Theatre BH19 . 179 C2
Moyles Court Sch BH24 . 47 E6
Moynton Cl DT2 .... 137 D6
Moynton Rd 5 DT11 ... 135 B8
Muchelney Way BA21 .. 26 E7
Muckleford Nature Reserve
DT2 .... 106 C7
Muddox Barrow La BH20 . 81 D5
Muddyford La DT6 ...... 98 D7
Mudeford Com Inf Sch
BH23 .... 124 C4
Mudeford Green Cl
BH23 .... 124 F5
Mudeford Jun Sch BH23 124 F4
Mudeford La BH23 ..... 124 F6
Mude Gdns BH23 ...... 125 A5
Mudford Rd BA21 ...... 27 D7
Mudros Rd DT11 ...... 199 E3
Mulberry Cl SP8 .... 5 F2
Mulberry Ct
4 Christchurch BH23 .. 124 A1
1 Sixpenny Handley SP5 189 B4
Mulberry Gdns
Charminster DT2 .... 75 D2
10 Crewkerne TA18 .... 191 F4
Fordingbridge SP6 ..... 43 A8
Mullins Cl DT12 ...... 121 C8
Munden's La DT9 .... 31 B1
Munster Rd BH14 ...... 120 D3
Murley Rd BH9 .... 122 A8
Murray-Smith Dr BA22 . 26 C6
Musbury Cl DT10 .... 20 E4

Musbury La DT10 .... 20 E4
Muscliffe Rd
Bournemouth BH9 ...... 90 B5
Muscliffe Rd
Bournemouth BH9 ..... 121 F8
Bournemouth BH9 ...... 89 F1
Muscliff Prim Sch BH9 . 90 C4
Musgrave Pl 4 DT4 .... 167 E4
Mus of Electricity BH23 124 B7
Mustons La DT11 ...... 82 A8
Mustons La 4 SP7 ..... 12 E3
Mutton St DT6 .... 203 A1
Myrtle Cl
10 Beaminster DT8 .... 204 C4
Hordle SO41 .... 95 F4
Myrtle Rd BH8 .... 122 C6

N

Nada Rd BH23 .... 93 D1
Nag's La TA18 .... 191 B1
Nairn Ct BH3 .... 121 E7
Nairn Rd
Bournemouth BH3 ..... 121 E6
Poole BH13 .... 147 E2
Naish Rd BH25 .... 126 E2
Nallers La DT2 .... 102 E6
Namu Rd BH9 .... 89 E1
Nansen Ave BH15 ..... 119 D5
Nantillo St 11 DT6 ... 107 D1
Napier Rd BH15 ...... 118 C3
Napiers Way DT11 ..... 37 E4
Narrow La BH24 .... 47 F1
Naseby Rd BH9 .... 90 A2
Nash La
Challington TA17 ..... 191 A6
Marnhull DT10 .... 21 A3
Marshwood DT6 .... 202 E2
Yeovil BA20 .... 26 F1
Nathan Cl BA20 .... 26 F2
Nathen Gdns BH15 .... 118 D3
Nations Rd SP8 .... 10 B6
Navarac Ct BH14 ...... 120 C3
Nea Cl BH23 .... 125 B8
Nea Dr BH24 .... 46 E4
Neal's La DT9 .... 194 D2
Nea Rd BH23 .... 125 E8
Neathem Rd BA21 ..... 27 E7
Neighbourhood Ctr BH17 87 E2
Nelson Cl BH23 .... 94 F3
Nelson Ct 13 BH15 ... 119 C2
Nelson Dr BH23 ...... 124 F6
Nelson Rd
Poole BH4,BH12 ...... 121 B4
Tarrant Monkton DT11 . 199 F3
Nether Abber Village
BA22 .... 14 D7
Netherby La DT4 ...... 204 A3
Nethercliffe Sch SO22 126 C2
Nethercoombe La DT9 . 30 A7
Netherhall Gdns BH4 . 121 C3
Netherhay La DT8 .... 203 C8
Nether Mead 1 DT1 ... 197 F6
Netherstoke La BA22 . 193 C3
Netherton La BA22 ... 193 F6
Netherton Rd
Weymouth DT4 .... 167 D1
Yeovil BA21 .... 27 F7
Netherton St 5 DT11 . 107 C1
Netherwood Pl DT11 .. 59 A5
Netley 3 BA21 .... 26 F5
Netley Cl BH15 ...... 120 A7
Netmead La 3 DT11 .. 198 B8
Nettlebed Nursery SP7 . 12 E3
Nettlecombe SP7 ...... 13 A3
Nettleton Cl DT11 .... 119 E7
New Barn Rd DT3 ..... 153 E6
Newberry Gdns 8 DT4 . 167 E2
Newberry Rd DT4 ..... 167 D2
Newberry La TA18 .... 192 A3
New Bond St DT6 ..... 167 D3
New Borough Rd DT11 . 59 D3
Newburgh St SO23 .... 126 D6
Newbury SP8 .... 6 A1
Newbury Dr BH10 ...... 89 D1
Newchester Cross TA16 191 E7
New Cl
Bourton SP8 .... 1 E2
Haselbury Plucknett TA18 192 B5
New Close Gdns DT4 .. 167 D1
New Combe La DT2 ... 108 E3
Newcombe Rd
Bournemouth BH6 ..... 123 E5
Ferndown BH22 .... 53 A3
New Cotts BH21 .... 60 E2
Newcroft Gdns BH23 .. 124 A8
Newcross DT9 .... 195 B8
New Cross Gate DT11 . 198 A2
New Cut BA12 .... 3 A6
Newell DT7 .... 30 A6
New Field La DT11 ... 198 D8
Newfield Rd DT11 .... 199 D8
New Fields Bsns Pk
BH17 .... 119 D8
Newfoundland Cl BH19 183 D8
Newfoundland Dr BH15 119 D2
Newfoundland Drive Rdbt
BH15 .... 119 D1
New Gd DT5 .... 187 A7
New Harbour Rd BH15 119 A1
New Harbour Rd S
Poole BH15 .... 146 B8
Poole BH15 .... 145 D8
New Harbour Road W
BH15 .... 119 A1
Newhaven DT2 .... 105 E1
New Inn St 2 DT6 .... 204 C1

New La
Bashley BH25 .... 94 F6
Cann SP7 .... 13 B1
Caundle Marsh DT9 ... 195 E8
Haselbury Plucknett TA18 192 C6
Morden BH20 .... 83 C3
Motcombe SP7 .... 12 B8
Stour Provost SP8 ..... 11 A3
Newland DT9 .... 30 C6
Newland Gdn DT9 ..... 30 C6
Newland La DT9 ...... 195 F3
Newlands Rd
Bournemouth BH7 ..... 123 A6
Christchurch BH23 .... 124 F7
New Milton BH25 ...... 95 B5
Newlands Way BH18 ... 86 D3
New Line DT6,DT1 .... 161 D3
Newlyn Way BH12 ..... 120 E7
Newman Cl 3 DT11 ... 212 C3
Newmans Cl
West Moors BH22 ...... 53 A5
West Moors Minster BH21 . 59 D3
Newman's La BH22 .... 52 E5
New Merrifield BH21 .. 59 F7
New Milton Inf Sch BH25 . 95 A1
New Milton Jun Sch
BH25 .... 95 A1
New Moors BH25 ...... 95 A3
Newmorton Rd BH9 ... 90 A4
New Orchard BH15 ... 119 B2
New Park BH10 .... 89 E3
New Park Rd BH6 .... 123 C4
Newport La BH20 ..... 82 C2
New Quay Rd BH15 ... 119 B1
New Rd
Arne BH20 .... 143 A1
Bournemouth BH10 .... 89 E7
Bourton SP8 .... 1 E3
Bovington Camp BH20 139 D7
Brympton BA22 .... 26 C5
Castleton DT9 .... 30 B4
Corfe Castle BH20 ... 162 E1
Ferndown BH22 .... 61 E3
Gillingham SP8 .... 6 A1
Haselbury Plucknett TA18 192 C6
Hinton St George TA17 191 C7
Loders DT6 .... 101 E7
Lytchett Minster & Upton
BH16 .... 116 F7
Poole BH12 .... 120 D6
Portesham DT3 .... 150 A8
Portland DT5 .... 186 F6
Radipole DT4 .... 167 D4
Ringwood BH24 .... 47 D8
Ringwood BH24 .... 55 C4
Shaftesbury SP7 .... 12 D3
Shapwick DT11 .... 198 D1
Stalbridge DT10 ...... 33 D8
Stoborough Green BH20 . 160 F8
Stofold BA22 .... 193 F8
Sturminster Newton DT10 . 197 D7
West Crewkerne TA18 . 191 B4
Weymouth DT4 .... 167 D2
Winsham TA20 .... 202 C8
Winterborne Stickland
DT11 .... 198 B1
Woodlands BH21 ...... 44 C7
Wool BH20 .... 139 F1
Zeale SP8 .... 2 A3
New St La
Loders DT6 .... 69 D1
Symondsbury DT6 ...... 99 F6
New St
2 Dorchester DT1 .... 108 A1
Easton/Weston DT5 ... 187 A4
North Perrott TA18 ... 192 C4
5 Poole BH15 .... 119 B1
Puddletown DT2 .... 78 B1
Radipole DT4 .... 167 E2
Ringwood BH24 .... 55 C6
Wareham BH20 .... 142 E3
Newstead Rd
Bournemouth BH6 ..... 123 D4
Weymouth DT4 .... 167 C2
Newton Cl
Gillingham SP8 .... 5 F1
Sturminster Newton DT10 . 197 D8
Newton Hill DT1 ..... 108 A1
Newton Pk DT2 .... 104 B1
Newton Manor Cl 2
BH19 .... 179 A2
Newton Morrell BH14 . 120 D3
Newton Rd
Barton on Sea BH25 ... 127 B8
Maiden Newton DT2 ... 73 A8
Poole BH14 .... 147 F8
Stofold BA22 .... 193 F8
Sturminster Marshall BH21 . 56 C4
Swanage BH19 .... 179 F1
Yeovil BA20 .... 27 E3
Newton Rise 4 BH19 .. 179 F2
Newton's Rd DT5 ..... 167 E1
Newton Surmaville BA20 . 27 F3
Newtown DT6 .... 204 C1
Newtown Bsns Ctr BH12 120 A1
Newtown Hill BH20 ... 157 F4
Newtown La
Corfe Mullen BH21 .... 86 D6
Ringwood BH24 .... 43 E1
Verwood BH31 .... 45 C5
Newtown Rd BH31 .... 45 C5
Nichola Cl DT12 ..... 120 B7
Nicholas Cl BH23 ..... 94 B2
Nicholas Gdns BH23 .. 89 C2
Nicholson Cl BH17 ... 119 E8
Nickel Cl SO23 ...... 126 F6
Nightingale Cl
Verwood BH31 .... 45 C5

Nightingale Cl continued
5 Winchester SO22 ... 126 A4
Nightingale Dr DT3 ... 152 C4
Nightjar Cl BH17 ..... 118 F9
Nimrod Way BH21 ..... 60 F6
Nine Stones (Stone Circle)
DT2 .... 105 C1
Noade St SP5 .... 25 C1
Noah Henville Cnr 4
DT11 .... 81 E8
Noake Rd DT9 .... 29 F5
Noble Cl BH11 .... 88 F1
Noel Rd BH10 .... 89 B2
Noel The BH25 .... 95 C3
Nonesuch Cl 8 DT1 .. 135 B8
Noon Gdns BH31 ...... 45 D6
Noon Hill Dr BH31 ... 45 D6
Noon Hill Rd BH31 ... 45 D6
Norburton DT6 .... 128 B8
Norcliffe Cl BH11 .... 89 B3
Norden Dr BH20 ...... 142 C6
Norden La DT2 .... 72 F8
Norden Sta BH20 ..... 161 F2
Nordon Rd DT11 ..... 212 D5
Nordons DT6 .... 100 E5
Norfolk Ave DT11 .... 91 F2
Norfolk Rd BH24 ..... 167 A4
Norleywood BH23 .... 125 F8
Norman Ave BH12 .... 121 A6
Norman Cl DT6 .... 100 F7
Normandy Dr BH23 ... 124 D7
Normandy Way
Bridport DT6 .... 100 D5
Dorchester DT1 ...... 107 E2
Hamworthy BH15 ..... 118 D2
Norman Gdns BH12 .. 121 A6
Normanhurst Ave BH8 90 E1
Norman Rd SO23 ..... 126 D4
Normanton Cl BH23 ... 91 F1
Norrie Cl BH24 .... 54 A4
Norris Gdns BH25 .... 95 A1
Norrish Rd BH12 ..... 120 C5
North Allington DT6 .. 100 C7
North Ave
Bournemouth BH10 .... 89 D6
Lyme Regis DT7 .... 96 B6
Northay La EX13 ..... 202 C3
North Bestwall Rd BH20 142 F4
Northbourne Ave BH10 89 D5
Northbourne Gdns BH10 89 E5
Northbourne Pl 3 BH10 89 D5
Northbourne Rdbt BH10 89 E5
North Bowood La DT6 203 F2
Northbrook Rd
Broadstone BH18 ...... 87 A2
Swanage BH19 .... 179 A5
Yeovil BA21 .... 27 E7
Northcote Rd BH1 .... 122 C4
North Cres DT4 .... 17 D4
North Cswy BH20 .... 142 E5
North Dr
Ossemsley BH25 ...... 94 E8
West Moors BH24 ..... 62 B8
North End DT9 .... 194 F3
North End La SP6 ..... 42 F4
Northernhay 1 DT1 .. 108 A2
Northey Rd BH6 ...... 123 E6
Northfield Rd BH24 ... 47 D1
Northgate Chambers 10
SO23 .... 126 E6
Northgate Lodge 2
SO23 .... 126 E6
North Gr 3 DT11 .... 199 E3
North Hill Rd
Burton Bradstock DT6 128 B8
Winchester SO22 ..... 126 D8
North Hill Cl SO22 ... 126 D7
North Hill Way DT6 .. 100 D4
North Instow BH19 ... 177 F5

North La
Hardington Mandeville
BA22 .... 193 A7
Nutheridge DT6 .... 27 D5
Northlands Dr SO23 .. 126 E8
Northleigh La BH21 ... 59 E6
North Lodge Rd BH14 120 E4
Northmead Dr BH17 .. 118 F8
Northmere Dr BH12 ... 120 F7
Northmere Rd BH12 .. 120 F7
North Mills Rd DT6 .. 100 C7
North Mills Trading Est
DT6 .... 100 D8
Northmoor Way BH20 142 D6
Northover Rd BH21 ... 61 F6
Northover Cl
Burton Bradstock DT6 128 C8
Puddletrenthide DT2 . 208 B2
Northover La SO41 ... 95 F7
North Perrott Rd TA18 192 C5
North Pk DT2 .... 73 F3
North Pl DT11 .... 212 D4
Northport Dr BH20 ... 142 E6
North Poulner Rd BH24 47 D2
North Quay DT4 ...... 167 D2
North Rd
Ashmore SP5 .... 25 C1
Bournemouth BH7 .... 122 E5
Chideock DT6 .... 99 A7
Mere BA12 .... 3 B4
Poole BH14 .... 120 A4
Sherborne DT9 .... 30 C7
Weymouth DT4 .... 180 B8
North Rew La DT2 .... 106 B1
Northshore BH13 ..... 147 C4
North Sq
Chickerell DT3 .... 166 C6
2 Dorchester DT1 .... 108 A2

North St
Beaminster DT8 ...... 204 C4
Bere Regis BH20 ...... 81 B2
Bradford Abbas DT9 ... 28 D2
Bridport DT6 .... 100 D7
Charminster DT2 ...... 75 D1
Crewkerne TA18 ..... 191 F5
Fontmell Magna SP7 .. 37 F2
Haselbury Plucknett TA18 . 192 C6
Langton Matravers BH19 178 A2
Mere BA12 .... 3 A5
Milborne Port DT9 ... 17 D2
Poole BH15 .... 119 C2
Wareham BH20 .... 142 E4
Winterborne Kingston DT11 81 E8
Winterborne Stickland
DT11 .... 210 C7
North Terr BA21 ...... 27 E6
North View SO22 .... 126 C6
North Walls
Wareham BH20 .... 142 D4
Winchester SO23 ..... 126 E6
Nortoft Rd BH8 ...... 122 B6
Norton Cl BH23 ...... 124 D7
Norton Gdns BH9 ..... 89 E1
Norton La DT11 ...... 198 D3
Norton Rd
Bournemouth BH9 .... 121 D8
Bournemouth 89 E1
Norton Way BH15 .... 119 A1
Norway Cl 3 BH9 .... 89 F1
Norway La DT8 ...... 203 F4
Norwich Ave BH2 .... 121 D3
Norwich Ave W BH2 .. 121 D3
Norwich Ct 5 BH2 ... 121 E3
Norwich Mans BH2 ... 121 D3
Norwich Rd
Bournemouth BH2 .... 121 E3
Weymouth DT4 .... 167 D3
Norwood Pl BH5 ..... 123 B5
Nothe Fort DT4 ...... 167 F2
Nothe Par DT4 .... 167 E2
Nottington La
Chickerell DT3 .... 151 C2
Radipole DT3 .... 152 A2
Noubele La BH24 ..... 55 F7
Noyce Gdns BH8 ...... 91 B2
Nuffield Ind Est BH17 119 D8
Nuffield Rd BH17 .... 119 D7
Nugent Rd BH6 ...... 124 A4
Nundico BH20 .... 142 E4
Nunnery Mead Nature
Reserve DT2 .... 73 D3
Nuns Rd SO23 .... 126 F2
Nuns Wlk SO23 ...... 126 F8
Nursery Gdns
Bridport DT6 .... 100 E7
3 Mere BA12 .... 3 A5
Winchester SO22 .... 126 B6
Nursery Rd
Blandford Forum DT11 212 D4
Bournemouth BH9 ..... 90 A3
Ringwood BH24 .... 55 C6
Yeovil BA20 .... 27 C3
Nursling Gn BH8 ..... 90 D2
Nutcombe Cl DT6 ..... 97 A8
Nutcrack La BH20 ... 142 F1
Nutgrove Ave DT4 ... 166 F1
Nuthatch Cl
Broadstone BH17 .... 118 F8
Ferndown BH22 .... 61 B8
Radipole DT3 .... 152 D3
Nutley Cl BH11 .... 88 F4
Nutley Way BH11 .... 88 F4
Nutmead Cl 4 DT11 .. 198 C8
Nyland La SP8 .... 8 D1

O

Oak Ave
Christchurch BH23 ... 123 D8
Holton Heath BH20 .. 116 B3
Oakbury Dr DT3 ...... 168 A7
Oak Cl
Corfe Mullen BH21 .... 86 C5
Ferndown BH22 .... 61 E1
Oakdale Rd BH15 .... 119 E6
Oakdale South Road Mid Sch
BH15 .... 119 C5
Oakdene Cl BH21 ..... 59 D5
Oakdene Rd BH20 ... 139 F1
Oak Dr BH15 .... 119 D2
Oakfield Rd BH15 .... 119 C6
Oakfield St DT11 .... 212 D4
Oakford Ct BH8 ...... 90 D3
Oak Gdns BH11 ...... 89 B1
Oakham Grange BH22 . 61 E5
Oakhurst BH23 .... 124 F7
Oakhurst Cl BH22 .... 53 B2
Oakhurst Fst Sch BH22 53 B2
Oakhurst La BH22 .... 53 B2
Oak La
Corscombe DT2 ...... 205 C6
Mere BA12 .... 3 B4
Ringwood BH24 .... 55 D8
Oaklands Cl
Verwood BH31 .... 45 A6
6 Winchester SO22 .. 126 A4
Oaklands Rd BA21 ... 27 F7
Oakland Wlk BH22 ... 61 F1
Oakleigh 8 BA20 ..... 26 F2
Oakleigh Way BH23 .. 125 F7
Oakley Gdns BH16 ... 118 A7

Oakley Hill BH21 . . . . .59 D2
Oakley La
  Farnham DT11 . . . . .188 C2
  Merley BH21 . . . . .59 E2
  Wimborne Minster BH21 . . .60 A2
Oakley Pl DT4 . . . . .167 D2
Oakley Rd BH21 . . . . .59 D2
Oakley Sh Ctr BH21 . . . . . . .59 E1
Oakley Straight BH21 . . . . . .59 E1
Oakmead Coll of Tech
  BH11 . . . . .88 E4
Oakmead Gdns BH11 . . . . . . .88 F4
Oakmead Rd BH17 . . . . .118 F7
Oak Mews BH12 . . . . .120 C5
Oak Rd
  Alderholt SP6. . . . . .42 B5
  Bournemouth BH8 . . . . .122 C6
  Charminster DT2 . . . . .75 D2
  New Milton BH25 . . . . .95 C3
  Upton BH16 . . . . .118 C6
Oaks Dr BH24 . . . . .53 F3
Oaks Mead BH31 . . . . .45 B6
Oaks The
  Gillingham SP8 . . . . .5 E1
  Verwood BH31 . . . . .45 A7
Oaktree Cl BH20 . . . . .142 E1
Oak Vale La BA8 . . . . .19 B4
Oak Way BA22 . . . . .26 C7
Oakwood
  Bournemouth BH3 . . . . .121 E7
  West Knighton DT2 . . . . . . .136 C3
Oakwood Ave BH25 . . . . .95 C4
Oakwood Cl BH9. . . . . .90 B2
Oakwood Ct BH25 . . . . .95 B3
Oakwood Dr 5 DT11. . . . . . .37 F1
Oakworde
  Bournemouth BH9 . . . . .90 B2
  Christchurch BH23 . . . . .93 E1
Oasis Mews BH16. . . . . .118 A7
Oasis The 12 BH13 . . . . . . .121 A4
Oates Rd BH9 . . . . .89 C1
Oathill La
  Broadwindsor TA18 . . . . . . .203 A7
  West Crewkerne TA18 . . . . .191 B1
Oban Rd BH3 . . . . .121 E7
Oborne Rd DT9 . . . . .30 D7
Oceanarium BH2 . . . . .121 F2
Ocean Hts 4 BH5 . . . . .122 F3
Octagon Theatre BA20 . . . . . .27 C4
Octavia Hill SO22 . . . . .126 B4
Odcombe Hollow BA22 . .192 E8
Oglander Rd SO23 . . . . .126 E6
Okeford Fitzpaine CE Prim
  Sch DT11 . . . . .197 F5
Okeford Rd BH18 . . . . .87 C2
OK Mobile Home Pk
  BH23 . . . . .125 B8
Old Bakery Cl 4 DT11 . . . . .199 D3
Old Bakery The 6 DT8 . . . . .203 E5
Old Barn Cl
  Christchurch BH23 . . . . .91 D2
  Ringwood BH24 . . . . .55 D7
Old Barn Rd BH21 . . . . .53 C5
Old Barn Way BA20 . . . . .27 A2
Old Bincombe La DT3 . . . . . .153 C2
Old Boundary Rd SP7 . . . . . .12 F2
Old Bound Rd BH16 . . . . . . .118 C6
Old Bowden Way DT9 . . . . . .17 D4
Old Brewery The 10
  BH15 . . . . .119 C2
Old Brickfields BH23 . . . . . .136 C3
Old Bridge Rd BH6. . . . . .123 D7
Old Castle Rd DT4 . . . . .180 E7
Old Chalk Pit BH20 . . . . .81 B1
Old Chapel Dr BH16. . . . . . . .84 C4
Old Christchurch La 12
  BH1 . . . . .121 F3
Old Christchurch Rd
  BH1 . . . . .121 F3
Old Church Rd DT6 . . . . .100 E4
Old Coach News BH14 . . . . .120 A4
Old Coastguard Rd BH13 .147 B4
Old Dairy Farm The
  DT10 . . . . .196 F3
Old Depot Rd SP8 . . . . .181 C1
Old Farm Cl BH24. . . . . .47 E2
Old Farm Ct DT11. . . . . .212 D6
Old Farm Gdns DT11 . . . . . .212 D6
Old Farm Rd BH15 . . . . .119 E6
Old Farm Way DT2 . . . . .137 D5
Old Forge Cl BH16 . . . . .116 F6
Old Forge Rd BH21 . . . . .60 F6
Old Furzebrook Rd BH20 .160 F8
Old Gdns SO22 . . . . .126 D8
Old Generator Ho The
  BH12 . . . . .121 A5
Old Granary Cl DT3 . . . . . . .153 C1
Old Ham La BH21 . . . . .60 D4
Old Highway Mews BH21 . .59 D4
Old Hillside Rd SO22 . . . . . .126 A8
Old Hitchen 4 TA16 . . . . . .191 F7
Old Hollow BA12 . . . . .3 B6
Old Kiln Rd
  Ridge BH20 . . . . .143 B1
  Upton BH16 . . . . .118 D6
Old Lifeboat House
  BH15 . . . . .119 C1
Old Lyme Hill DT6 . . . . .96 F8
Old Lyme Rd DT6 . . . . .96 F7
Old Malthouse Sch The
  BH19. . . . . .178 B2
Old Manor Cl BH21 . . . . .59 D4

Old Market Rd BH21 . . . . . . .86 A8
Old Mill La DT10. . . . . .21 A4
Old Mills DT2. . . . . .71 E8
Old Milton Gn BH25. . . . . . . .94 F1
Old Milton Rd BH25. . . . . . . .95 A2
Old Mkt Rd BH21 . . . . .85 B7
Old Mulberry Cl BH10. . . . . .89 A2
Old Oak Way DT11 . . . . . . .210 C3
Old Orchard BH15 . . . . .119 C1
Old Orchard Cl DT10 . . . . . .196 F8
Old Parish La DT4 . . . . .167 B3
Old Pines Ct BH22 . . . . .61 E4
Old Pound Cl BH20 . . . . .84 C3
Old Pound Ct 3 SP8. . . . . . . .1 D1
Old Priory Rd BH6 . . . . .123 F4
Old Rd
  Odcombe BA22 . . . . .26 A3
  Wimborne Minster BH21. . . .59 B5
Old Rd The DT9. . . . . .18 B2
Old Rectory Cl
  Charminster DT6 . . . . .97 A7
  Corfe Mullen BH21 . . . . .86 D8
Old Rectory La DT9 . . . . . . .195 E3
Old Ropewalk BH15 . . . . . . .119 A1
Old Rope Wlk The BH15 . .118 F1
Old St John's Mews BH9 . .89 F3
Old Sandpit La BH16. . . . . . .86 A2
Old Sawmill Cl BH31. . . . . . .45 A7
Old Sch Cl DT9 . . . . .31 B1
Old Sch La
  Hinton St Mary DT10 . . . . . . .35 A5
  Iwerne Minster DT11 . . . . . . .37 F1
Old School Cl
  Ferndown BH21 . . . . .61 C5
  Poole BH14 . . . . .120 A4
Old Sch Pl DT9 . . . . .30 A5
Old Sch Rd DT11 . . . . .56 E3
Old Stacks Gdns 1 BH24. .55 F6
Old Station App SO23 . . . . .126 F5
Old Station Gdns BA8 . . . . . .19 B5
Old Station Rd
  Radipole DT3 . . . . .152 B4
  4 Yeovil BA20 . . . . .27 C4
Old Station Way BA20. . . . . .27 C4
Old Town Mews 8
  BH15 . . . . .119 C2
Old Vicarage Cl BH10 . . . . . .89 C6
Old Vicarage Gdns DT7 . . . .96 B5
Old Wareham Rd
  Corfe Mullen BH16,BH21. . . .86 A3
  Poole BH12 . . . . .120 A7
Olga Rd DT1. . . . . .107 F1
Oliver's Battery Prim Sch
  SO22 . . . . .126 A1
Olivers Mead 1 DT11. . . . . .198 C8
Olivers Rd BH21 . . . . .60 A6
Olivers Way BH21. . . . . .60 A6
Onslow Gdns BH21 . . . . .59 D6
Onslow Ho BH21. . . . . .59 D6
Ophir Gdns BH8. . . . . .122 C5
Ophir Rd BH8 . . . . .122 B5
Oratory Gdns BH13 . . . . . . .147 F8
Orchard Ave
  Bridport DT6 . . . . .100 C8
  Poole BH14 . . . . .119 F2
Orchard Chase 2 DT11 . . .199 F7
Orchard Cl
  8 Charmouth DT6 . . . . .97 A7
  Cheselbourne DT2 . . . . .209 A3
  Christchurch BH23 . . . . .124 A6
  Corfe Mullen BH21 . . . . .86 D7
  Ferndown BH22 . . . . .61 C5
  Fontmell Magna SP7 . . . . . . .37 E6
  Lytchett Minster & Upton
    BH16 . . . . .116 F6
  6 Okeford Fitzpaine DT11 197 F6
  Ringwood BH24 . . . . .55 C8
  4 Stourpaine BH21 . . . . . . .198 F4
  Sturminster Newton DT10. .197 C8
  Sydling St Nicholas DT2 . . .207 A3
  4 West Coker BA22 . . . . . . .193 A8
Orchard Cres DT6 . . . . .100 C8
Orchard Ct BH31. . . . . .45 C5
Orchard Dr DT3. . . . . .168 B7
Orchard Gr BH25 . . . . .95 A1
Orchard Ho SO22 . . . . .126 C5
Orchard La
  Corfe Mullen BH21 . . . . .86 D7
  4 Crewkerne TA18 . . . . . . .191 F4
  Thorncombe TA20. . . . . . . .202 E6
  7 Winterborne Kingston
    DT11. . . . . .81 E8
Orchardleigh BA22. . . . . . . .192 E8
Orchard Leigh 2 BH25. . . . .95 A2
Orchard Mead
  Broadwindsor DT8 . . . . .203 E5
  8 Ringwood BH24 . . . . .55 B8
Orchard Mews
  2 Christchurch BH23. . . . . .124 A6
  7 Gillingham SP8 . . . . .5 D2
Orchard Rd
  Gillingham SP8 . . . . .5 E2
  Milborne Port DT9 . . . . .17 C2
Orchard St
  Blandford Forum DT11 . . . . .212 D4
  Bournemouth BH2. . . . . . . .121 E3
  Dorchester DT1 . . . . .108 A2
  Yeovil BA20 . . . . .27 B4
Orchard The
  Blandford Forum DT11 . . . . .212 C5
  Bournemouth BH11. . . . . . . .88 D6
  Bransgore BH23 . . . . .93 C8
  Hazelbury Bryan DT10. . . . .196 F3
  Radipole DT3 . . . . .152 B3
  2 Sixpenny Handley SP5 . . .189 B4

Orchard The continued
  Winfrith Newburgh DT2 . . . .156 F6
Orchard Way
  Misterton TA18 . . . . .192 A2
  2 Mosterton DT8 . . . . .204 A8
Orchard Wlk
  15 Bournemouth BH2 . . . . .121 E3
  Milborne Port DT9 . . . . .17 C2
  Winchester SO22. . . . . .126 B8
Orcheston Rd BH8 . . . . .122 C6
Orchid Way BH23 . . . . .124 C7
Orestes Gate BH23 . . . . . . .125 A5
Orford Cl BH23 . . . . .91 D4
Orford St DT2 . . . . .78 B1
Organford Rd BH16 . . . . . . .116 C4
Orion Rd DT4. . . . . .167 D1
Ormonde Rd BH13 . . . . .121 A2
Osborne Cl 5 DT11 . . . . . . .135 C8
Osborne Rd
  Bournemouth BH9 . . . . .121 E8
  New Milton BH25 . . . . .95 B3
  Poole BH14 . . . . .120 B5
  Swanage BH19 . . . . .179 B2
  Wimborne Minster BH21 . . . .59 D4
  Yeovil BA20 . . . . .27 C5
Osborne Sch SO23 . . . . .126 D7
Osborne Ho 4 BH25. . . . . . .95 A3
Osbourne Rd DT6. . . . . .100 D8
Osmay Rd BH19 . . . . .185 C8
Osmington Dro DT2. . . . . . .136 B1
Osmington White Horse
  DT3 . . . . .153 F5
Osprey Cl BH23 . . . . .125 A5
Osprey Quay Bsns
  Development DT5 . . . . .180 F1
Osprey Rd DT4 . . . . .180 D5
Ossemsley Manor Ho
  BH23 . . . . .94 D6
Ossemsley South Dr BH25 .94 F8
Osterley Cl BH23 . . . . .124 A8
Oswald Cl BH9 . . . . .89 E2
Oswald Rd BH9. . . . . .89 F2
Otterbourne La BH21 . . . . . .59 F2
Otter Cl
  Upton BH16. . . . . .118 A6
  Verwood BH31. . . . . .45 C5
Otter Rd BH15 . . . . .118 F2
Otters Wlk BH25 . . . . .95 C5
Ottery La DT9 . . . . .30 A5
Oval Gdn BH20 . . . . .160 F8
Oval The BH20. . . . . .172 F8
Overbury Cl DT4 . . . . .166 F2
Overbury Manor BH21. . . . .121 B5
Overbury Rd BH14 . . . . .120 A3
Overcliffe Mans BH1 . . . . . .122 C3
Overcombe BA8 . . . . .18 D8
Overcombe Cl BH17. . . . . . . .87 E2
Overcombe Dr DT3 . . . . . . .168 B7
Overlands Rd DT4 . . . . .180 B8
Over Links Dr BH14 . . . . . . .120 E3
Overton Cl DT7 . . . . .96 C7
Ovington Ave BH7 . . . . .123 C7
Ovington Gdns BH7 . . . . . . .123 C7
Owen's Rd DT7 . . . . .96 D5
Owermoigne CE Fst Sch
  DT2 . . . . .155 E7
Owlshotts BH13. . . . . .147 F7
Owls Rd
  Bournemouth BH5. . . . . . . .122 E3
  Verwood BH31. . . . . .45 C5
Ox Dro
  Berwick St John SP5 . . . . . .188 B7
  Bower Chalke SP5 . . . . .189 A8
Oxencroft 4 SP7 . . . . .12 F4
Oxen Rd 8 TA18. . . . . .191 F4
Oxey Cl BH25 . . . . .95 A1
Oxford Ave BH6 . . . . .123 B5
Oxford La BH11. . . . . .89 B6
Oxford Rd
  Bournemouth BH8. . . . . . . .122 C4
  Yeovil BA21 . . . . .28 B7
Oxhayes DT8. . . . . .203 C8
Ozone Terr DT7. . . . . .96 B4

P

Paceycombe Way DT1 . . .107 C2
Packers' Way 1 TA18 . . . . .192 B3
Paddington Cl BH11 . . . . .88 D4
Paddington Gr BH11 . . . . .88 D4
Paddock Cl
  Ferndown BH21 . . . . .61 A5
  Lytchett Matravers BH16 . . . .84 D4
  Poole BH12 . . . . .120 B7
  Shaftesbury SP7 . . . . .13 A2
  10 Sixpenny Handley SP5 . .189 A3
  St Leonards BH24 . . . . .54 B4
Paddock Gr BH31 . . . . .45 C5
Paddock's La DT6. . . . . .67 B8
Paddocks The
  Bournemouth BH10 . . . . .89 D4
  1 Iwerne Minster DT11 . . . . .37 F1
  Mere BA12. . . . . .3 A5
  5 Mosterton DT8. . . . . .204 A8
  Thornford DT9 . . . . .194 D8
Paddock The
  West Moors BH24 . . . . .62 C8
  Winterborne Kingston
Padfield Cl BH6. . . . . .123 E6
Padget Rd BH24 . . . . .47 E1
Padstow Pl SP6. . . . . .43 A8
Pageant Dr DT6 . . . . .30 B5
Pageants Cl DT6 . . . . .68 F1
Page Dr 1 DT5. . . . . .186 F1
Paget Cl BH21 . . . . .60 A7

Paget Rd BH11 . . . . .89 A4
Painters Field SO23 . . . . . .126 C2
Paisley Rd BH6 . . . . .123 C5
Palace Rd SP8 . . . . .6 A1
Palfrey Rd BH10 . . . . .89 D5
Palma Ct BH23 . . . . .126 A5
Palmer Pl BH25. . . . . .94 F2
Palmer Rd BH15 . . . . .119 C5
Palmers Brewery DT6. . . . .100 C5
Palmers La DT11. . . . . .211 D7
Palmers Orch BH8 . . . . .84 C3
Palmerston Ave BH21 . . . . .124 D6
Palmerston Cl BH16 . . . . . .118 D7
Palmerston Ct 2 SO23. . . .126 D5
Palmerston Rd
  Bournemouth BH1 . . . . .122 E5
  Poole BH14 . . . . .120 D4
  Upton BH16 . . . . .117 E7
  Upton BH16 . . . . .118 E8
Palm Hall Cl SO23 . . . . .126 F5
Pamphill CE Fst Sch BH21 .58 E5
Panorama Rd
  Poole BH13 . . . . .147 B3
  Swanage BH19 . . . . .179 A2
Pans Cnr BH22 . . . . .61 F3
Parade The
  4 Bournemouth BH6 . . . . . .123 C4
  New Milton BH25 . . . . .95 D3
  Old Milton BH25 . . . . .94 F1
  Poole BH17 . . . . .87 B1
Paradise La BH20 . . . . .83 C4
Paradise Rd BH21. . . . . .51 F7
Paradise St 18 BH15 . . . . .119 B1
Parchment St SO23 . . . . . . .126 E6
Parcroft Gdns BA20. . . . . . . .27 B5
Parcroft Jun Sch BA20 . . . . .27 B5
Pardys Hill BH21. . . . . .86 D8
Parfields BH23 . . . . .94 E3
Parham Cl BH25 . . . . .94 E3
Parham Rd BH10. . . . . .89 C2
Paris Ct SP5 . . . . .5 F1
Parish Mews 3 BH23. . . . . .92 A2
Parish Rd BH15 . . . . .119 E3
Park Ave
  Bournemouth BH10 . . . . .89 C6
  Winchester SO23. . . . . .126 C6
Park Cl
  Burton BH23 . . . . .92 C3
  New Milton BH25 . . . . .95 C5
  3 Stourpaine DT11 . . . . . . .198 F4
  Winchester SO23 . . . . .126 E8
Park Ct
  2 Poole BH13 . . . . .121 B3
  Winchester SO23 . . . . .126 D8
Park Dr
  Holton Heath BH20 . . . . . . .116 B3
  Verwood BH31. . . . . .45 A7
Parkelea 3 BH21 . . . . .56 D4
Parker Rd BH10. . . . . .89 C2
Parkers Cl BH24 . . . . .47 E1
Park Gate BH25 . . . . .95 A2
Park Gate Mews 7 BH21 .121 E4
Park Gdns
  Christchurch BH23 . . . . .124 C7
  Yeovil BA20 . . . . .27 C5
Park Gr DT10 . . . . .33 C8
Park Hill DT11 . . . . .212 D4
Park Homer Dr BH21. . . . . . .60 A6
Park Homer Rd BH21 . . . . . .59 F6
Park La
  Alderholt SP6. . . . . .42 B6
  Bournemouth BH10 . . . . .89 F4
  Cranborne BH21. . . . . .40 F2
  Glanvilles Wootton DT9. . . .195 F2
  Henstridge BA8 . . . . .19 B7
  Radipole DT4 . . . . .49 C3
  Shapwick DT11 . . . . .48 C1
  Thorncombe TA20 . . . . .202 D7
  Wayford TA18 . . . . .191 B1
  Wimborne Minster BH21. . . .59 C4
  Wimborne St Giles BH21. . .201 E7
  Woodlands BH21 . . . . .44 B6
Park Lake Rd BH15 . . . . . . .119 E2
Parkland Cl BH24 . . . . .45 F4
Parkland Dr BH25. . . . . .95 C5
Parkland Pl BH25 . . . . .95 A2
Parklands 1 BH4 . . . . .121 C3
Park Lands DT11 . . . . .212 C4
Park Mead Rd DT4 . . . . . . .180 C7
Park Pl BH14 . . . . .119 F4
Park Rd
  Blandford Forum DT11 . . . . .212 C4
  Bournemouth BH8 . . . . .122 A5
  Bridport DT6 . . . . .100 C7
  Easton/Weston DT5 . . . . . . .187 A4
  Henstridge BA8 . . . . .19 A4
  New Milton BH25 . . . . .95 C5
  Old Milton BH25 . . . . .94 F1
  Poole BH15,BH14 . . . . .119 F3
  Stalbridge DT10. . . . . .33 C8
  Swanage BH19 . . . . .179 C8
  Winchester SO22,SO23. . . .126 D6
  Yeovil BA20 . . . . .27 C5
Park Sch The BA20. . . . . . . .27 C5
Parkside
  Christchurch BH23 . . . . .93 D1
  Ringwood BH24 . . . . .55 D1
Parkside Gdns
  Bournemouth BH10 . . . . .89 E2
  Winchester SO22. . . . . .126 A8
Parkside Ind Est BH24 . . . . .55 C5
Parkside Rd BH14. . . . . .120 C4
Park's La DT2 . . . . .30 D7
Park St
  Radipole DT4 . . . . .167 D3
  Yeovil BA20 . . . . .27 D3

Parkstone Ave BH14 . . . . . .120 D4
Parkstone Gram Sch
  BH17 . . . . .87 B1
Parkstone Hts
  Poole BH14 . . . . .119 F5
  Poole BH14 . . . . .120 A5
Parkstone Rd BH15 . . . . . . .119 E3
Parkstone Sta BH14 . . . . . .120 B3
Park The
  Barton on Sea BH25 . . . . . .126 C7
  Wimborne Minster BH21. . . .60 A4
  Yeovil BA20 . . . . .27 C5
Parkview BH21 . . . . .121 E4
Park View
  Crewkerne TA18 . . . . .191 F3
  New Milton BH25 . . . . .95 A2
  7 Poole BH15 . . . . .119 C3
  Winchester SO22. . . . . .126 A8
Park View Ct BH8 . . . . .122 C7
Park View Mews BH25 . . . . .95 A2
Park Water La DT8. . . . . . . .203 C5
Parkway DT6. . . . . .97 B7
Park Way BH22 . . . . .53 A2
Parkway Dr BH8. . . . . .122 E5
Parkwood La 7 BH5. . . . . .123 D5
Parkwood Rd
  Bournemouth BH5 . . . . .123 A4
  Wimborne Minster BH21. . . .59 C4
Parley Cl BH22 . . . . .61 E1
Parley Cross BH22. . . . . .89 B7
Parley Fst Sch BH22 . . . . . . .61 D3
Parley Green La BH23 . . . . . .90 B7
Parley La BH23 . . . . .90 C7
Parley Rd BH9 . . . . .90 A2
Parliament Pl SO22 . . . . . . .126 A2
Parmiter Dr BH21 . . . . .59 E4
Parmiter Ho 6 SO23 . . . . . .126 F6
Parmiter Rd BH21 . . . . .59 E4
Parmiter Way BH21 . . . . .59 E4
Parnham House DT8 . . . . . .204 C3
Parrett & Axe CE Prim Sch
  DT8. . . . . .204 A7
Parrett Mead DT8. . . . . .192 C1
Parr Gr 5 DT11 . . . . .199 D4
Parr Ho 1 BH14 . . . . .120 A4
Parricks La EX13. . . . . .202 A3
Parr St BH14 . . . . .120 A4
Parsonage Barn La BH24. .55 C7
Parsonage Ct 8 BH8 . . . . .122 A5
Parsonage Hill BH21 . . . . . .201 D7
Parsonage Rd
  Bournemouth BH1 . . . . .122 A3
  Bridport DT6 . . . . .100 C8
  Bridport St SP7 . . . . .37 F6
Parsonage The 3 SP5 . . . .189 B4
Parsons Cl 1 BH21 . . . . . . .179 B5
Parsons La DT2 . . . . .102 C6
Parsons Pool 3 SP7 . . . . . .12 E3
Partridge Cl BH21 . . . . .120 C1
Partridge Dr BH21 . . . . .120 C1
Partridge Gn BH25 . . . . .95 B6
Partridge Wlk BH23 . . . . . . .120 B1
Partway DT10. . . . . .196 F3
Partway La
  Hardington Mandeville
    BA22. . . . . .192 F7
  Hazelbury Bryan DT10. . . . .196 F3
  Thorncombe TA20. . . . . . . .202 C6
Pascoe Cl BH14 . . . . .120 A4
Pasture Way DT6 . . . . .100 D5
Patchins Rd BH16. . . . . .118 B4
Patchins The BH14 . . . . . . .118 B4
Paternoster Ho 4 SO23. . .126 E5
Paternoster Row 5
  SO23. . . . . .126 E5
Patson Hill La DT9. . . . . .15 C2
Pattinson Cl BA21 . . . . .27 F6
Paulet Pl SO22 . . . . .126 C3
Paul's Mead DT5 . . . . .186 F7
Pauls Way DT2 . . . . .137 D6
Pauncefote Rd BH5 . . . . . . .123 A5
Pauntley Rd BH23 . . . . .124 E5
Pavan Gdns BH10. . . . . .89 C2
Pavilion The 23 BH4 . . . . . .121 C3
Pavilion Theatre DT4. . . . . .167 E3
Pavyotts La BA22 . . . . .193 E8
Payne Cl BH21 . . . . .53 A5
Payne Ct DT1 . . . . .76 C7
Peace Cl DT4 . . . . .93 A8
Peaceful La DT10 . . . . .76 F6
Peacemarsh Farm Cl 3
  SP8. .5 E4
Pear Ash La BA9 . . . . .1 C4
Pearce Ave BH14 . . . . .120 A3
Pearce Cl BH21 . . . . .120 A1
Pearce Rd BH16 . . . . .84 A8
Pearce-Smith Ct BH25 . . . .126 E7
Pear Cl BH12 . . . . .121 B4
Pearl Gdns BH10. . . . . .89 C4
Pearl Rd BH10 . . . . .89 C4
Pearson Ave BH14 . . . . .120 B5
Pearson Gdns BH10. . . . . . . .89 C4
Pear Tree Cl
  Alderholt SP6. . . . . .42 B5
  Bransgore BH23 . . . . .93 B8
Peascombe Nature Reserve
  DT6. . . . . .67 F2
Peatons La BH16 . . . . .84 B4
Peckham Ave DT5. . . . . .186 A1
Peddlars Wlk 4 BH24 . . . . . .55 B7
Peeks Mews BH14 . . . . .120 A3
Peel Cl
  Blandford Forum DT11 . . . . .212 D5
  Poole BH12 . . . . .120 C5
Peelers Ct DT6 . . . . .100 D7
Pegasus Cl
  Bournemouth BH11 . . . . . . .122 A5

Pegasus Ct continued
6 New Milton BH25 . . . . .95 A3
Pegasus Lodge BH22 . . . . .61 D5
Peggy's La TA18 . . . . .192 C5
Pelham 21 BH13 . . . . .121 A4
Pelham Cl DT13 . . . . .124 D6
Pelican Mead BH24 . . . . .55 E5
Pemberton Cl DT3 . . . . .152 D3
Pembroke Cl BA21 . . . . .28 A7
Pembroke Ct 4 BH23 . . . . . . .126 B7
Pembroke Rd
 Bournemouth BH4 . . . . .121 B2
 Poole BH12 . . . . .120 E5
Penbugle Yd 6 DT1 . . . . .107 D1
Pen Craig 8 BH13 . . . . .121 B3
Pendomer Rd BA22 . . . . .193 B5
Pendruffle La 12 DT1 . . . . . . .107 D1
Penelope Ct 3 BH23 . . . . .126 B7
Pengelly Ave BH10 . . . . .89 E5
Penhale Wlk 1 DT1 . . . . .107 D1
Peninsula Rd SO22 . . . . .126 C5
Peninsula Sq SO23 . . . . .126 D5
Pen Mill Hill BA9 . . . . .1 E3
Pen Mill Inf Sch BA21 . . . . .27 F6
Pen Mill Trading Est
 BA21 . . . . .28 B6
Penmore Rd DT9 . . . . .15 C5
Pennant Way BH23 . . . . .124 F7
Penn Cross DT6 . . . . .64 D1
Penn Hill BA20 . . . . .27 D4
Penn Hill Ave BH14 . . . . .120 D3
Penn Hill Pk BA20 . . . . .27 D4
Penn Hill View DT2 . . . . .106 D8
Pennine Ct 8 BH23 . . . . .124 F8
Pennine Way BH31 . . . . .45 B5
Pennington Cl BH22 . . . . .52 F1
Pennington Cres BH22 . . . . .52 F2
Pennington Ho 6 BH4 . . . . . .121 C2
Pennington Rd BH22 . . . . .52 F2
Penn La BA22 . . . . .193 A6
Pennsylvania Rd DT5 . . . . .187 B3
Penny Hedge BH25 . . . . .127 B8
Penny Plot DT7 . . . . .96 A6
Penny's Cnr SO41 . . . . .95 F4
Penny's Ct BH21 . . . . .61 D5
Penny's Mead BH21 . . . . .40 B7
Penny St
 Radipole DT4 . . . . .167 D4
 Sturminster Newton DT10 . . . . . .35 B1
Penny's Wlk BH22 . . . . .61 D5
Penny Way BH23 . . . . .125 C6
Pennywell Gdns BH25 . . . . .95 D4
Penrith Cl BH13 . . . . .45 A5
Penrith Rd BH5 . . . . .123 A4
Penrose Cl BH16 . . . . .84 C2
Penrose Rd BH22 . . . . .61 D6
Penton Ho 8 SO23 . . . . .126 F4
Pentons Hill SP6 . . . . .43 E6
Pentridge La DT10 . . . . .34 D4
Penwithen Sch DT2 . . . . .134 E5
Peppercorn Ct BH23 . . . . .124 E8
Pepper Hill DT11 . . . . .198 B5
Percy Gdns DT11 . . . . .212 D4
Percy Rd
 Bournemouth BH5 . . . . .122 F4
 Yeovil BA21 . . . . .27 F6
Peregrine Rd BH23 . . . . .125 A5
Pergin Cres BH17 . . . . .119 B7
Pergin Way BH17 . . . . .119 B7
Perrott Hill Sch TA18 . . . . .192 B4
Perryfield Gdns BH7 . . . . .123 B8
Perry Gdns BH15 . . . . .119 C1
Perry St BA20 . . . . .202 A7
Persley Rd BH10 . . . . .89 E4
Perth Cl BH23 . . . . .91 E1
Perth St DT4 . . . . .167 B3
Peter Grant Way BH21 . . . . .61 C5
Peters Cl BH16 . . . . .118 C6
Petersfield Pl BH7 . . . . .123 B7
Petersfield Rd BH7 . . . . .123 B8
Petersham La BH1 . . . . .51 A4
Petersham Rd BH17 . . . . .119 A8
Peters Rd BH22 . . . . .61 F3
Peter St 3 BA20 . . . . .27 D4
Peter Symonds Coll
 SO22 .126 D7
Petit Rd BH9 . . . . .90 A3
Petter's Way BA20 . . . . .27 D4
Pettitts Cl DT9 . . . . .28 C2
Pettridge La BA12 . . . . .3 A5
Pettycrate La DT6 . . . . .98 E5
Petwyn Cl BH22 . . . . .62 A6
Peverell Ave E DT1 . . . . .107 B2
Peverell Rd BH16 . . . . .118 B4
Peveril Cl BH24 . . . . .54 B6
Peveril Point Rd BH19 . . . . . . .179 D2
Peveril Rd BH19 . . . . .179 C1
Phelipps Rd
 Corfe Mullen BH21 . . . . .86 E6
 2 Poole BH21 . . . . .85 F6
Philip Green Meml Sch
 BH21 .190 C1
Philip Rd DT11 . . . . .212 E4
Phillips Rd DT10 . . . . .21 A2
Philpot Mus DT7 . . . . .96 C5
Phyldon Cl BH12 . . . . .120 B5
Phyldon Rd BH12 . . . . .120 B6
Piccadilly La DT11 . . . . .56 C8
Pickard Rd BH22 . . . . .62 B7
Pickering Cl BH18 . . . . .87 A2
Picket La DT8 . . . . .192 C1
Pickett La BA21 . . . . .27 C7
Picketts Cross DT2 . . . . .74 A4
Pickford Rd BH9 . . . . .89 E1
Piddlehinton Ent Pk DT2 . .77 A6
Piddle La DT2 . . . . .207 D3

Piddles Wood Nature
 Reserve DT10 . . . . .197 E7
Piddle Valley CE Fst Sch
 DT2 . . . . .208 B2
Pidney Hill DT10 . . . . .196 F3
Piece Rd DT9 . . . . .17 C3
Piece The 2 TA16 . . . . .191 F7
Pierston Fields SP8 . . . . .5 C6
Pigeon Cl
 Blandford Forum DT11 . . . . .212 D2
 Winfrith Newburgh DT2 . . . . . . .156 F5
Pig Hill BA22 . . . . .193 A7
Pig Shoot La BH23 . . . . .90 F5
Pikes La BH19 . . . . .183 C7
Pile La DT10 . . . . .32 F5
Pilford Heath Rd BH21 . . . . .60 B7
Pilford La BH21 . . . . .51 D2
Pilgrim Pk BH24 . . . . .55 E8
Pilgrim's Cl BH25 . . . . .95 C3
Pilgrims Gate SO22 . . . . .126 C7
Pilgrims Sch The SO23 . . . . . .126 C5
Pilgrims Way
 Poole BH17 . . . . .119 A7
 4 Radipole DT4 . . . . .167 E2
Pill Mdw SP8 . . . . .9 C3
Pilot Hight Rd BH11 . . . . .89 A4
Pilsdon Cl 7 DT8 . . . . .204 C4
Pilsdon Dr BH17 . . . . .87 E3
Pilsdon La DT6 . . . . .203 C3
Pilsdon Pen DT6 . . . . .203 C4
Pilwell DT10 . . . . .21 A3
Pimperleaze Rd BA12 . . . . .3 F1
Pimpern Cl BH17 . . . . .87 F2
Pimperne CE Fst Sch
 DT11 .199 D4
Pimpernel Cl 6 SP8 . . . . .5 D2
Pimperne Long Barrow
 DT11 .199 E5
Pineapple Bsns Pk DT6 . . . . . .68 D6
Pineapple La DT6 . . . . .68 C6
Pine Ave
 Bournemouth BH6 . . . . .123 C4
 Poole BH12 . . . . .120 F6
Pinebeach Ct BH13 . . . . .147 G8
Pine Cl
 Barton on Sea BH25 . . . . .126 E8
 Ferndown BH22 . . . . .61 C7
Pinecliffe Ave BH6 . . . . .123 C4
Pinecliffe Rd BH25 . . . . .126 C7
Pinecliff Rd BH13 . . . . .147 G8
Pine Cres
 Christchurch BH23 . . . . .125 E8
 Holton Heath BH20 . . . . .116 B3
Pine Dr
 Poole BH13 . . . . .120 F3
 Poole BH13 . . . . .121 A2
 St Leonards BH24 . . . . .54 B4
Pine End DT2 . . . . .61 F3
Pine Glen Ave BH22 . . . . .61 C8
Pine Grange 4 BH1 . . . . .122 A3
Pine Ho BH25 . . . . .95 A3
Pineholt Cl BH24 . . . . .54 C5
Pinehurst Ave BH23 . . . . .124 F5
Pinehurst Pk BH22 . . . . .61 F8
Pinehurst Rd BH22 . . . . .53 A1
Pine View Cl
 Upton BH16 . . . . .118 C6
 Verwood BH31 . . . . .44 F7
Pine View Rd BH31 . . . . .44 F7
Pine Wlk
 Lyme Regis DT7 . . . . .96 B4
 Verwood BH31 . . . . .45 D5
Pinewood Ave BH10 . . . . .89 D5
Pinewood Cl
 Bournemouth BH10 . . . . .89 D5
 Upton BH16 . . . . .118 A7
 Upton BH16 . . . . .94 A2
Pinewood Gdns BH22 . . . . .61 D7
Pinewood Rd
 Christchurch BH23 . . . . .93 F1
 Ferndown BH22 . . . . .61 C7
 Hordle SO41 . . . . .95 F3
 Poole BH13 . . . . .121 B1
 St Leonards BH24 . . . . .54 B4
 Upton BH16 . . . . .118 B7
Pinford La DT9 . . . . .30 E8
Pink Knoll Hollow DT9 . . . . . . .15 E8
Pinnacle The 7 BH41 . . . . . . .122 A3
Pipers Ash 2 BH24 . . . . .55 E8
Pipers Dr BH23 . . . . .125 A7
Pipit Cl DT3 . . . . .152 D3
Pippin Cl BH23 . . . . .91 E2
Pirates La DT4 . . . . .180 B7
Pitcher Cl 3 DT11 . . . . .81 E8
Pitchers DT6 . . . . .68 B6
Pitcote La 15 DT1 . . . . .107 D1
Pitfield Cnr BA22 . . . . .15 A6
Pit Hill TA17 . . . . .191 B7

Pitman's La DT6 . . . . .66 B1
Pit Rd TA17 . . . . .191 B7
Pitt Cl DT11 . . . . .212 C2
Pitthouse La BH23 . . . . .91 D8
Pitt La DT6 . . . . .65 E3
Pittmore Rd BH23 . . . . .92 C2
Pitt's Boro BH21 . . . . .49 E1
Pitts La
 Melbury Abbas SP7 . . . . .23 F5
 Sedgehill & Semley SP7 . . . . .7 C5
Pitts Orch DT10 . . . . .35 B1
Pitts Pl BH25 . . . . .95 D2
Pitwines Cl BH15 . . . . .119 C2
Pix Mead Gdns SP7 . . . . .13 A2
Placket La BA20 . . . . .27 A1
Plain The DT2 . . . . .109 A6
Plaisters La DT4 . . . . .180 E8
Plantagenet Chase BA20 . .27 A2
Plantagenet Cres BH11 . . . . . . .88 D5
Plantagenet Pk BA20 . . . . .27 A3
Plantagenet Way 8 SP8 . . . . . .5 D2
Plantation Cl DT7 . . . . .87 C1
Plantation Dr BH23 . . . . .94 A2
Plantation Rd BH17 . . . . .87 F3
Plant Park Rd BH24 . . . . .54 E2
Plassey Cl DT1 . . . . .107 E2
Plassey Cres BH10 . . . . .89 C5
Platts DT10 . . . . .196 F8
Playfield Cl 2 BA8 . . . . .19 A4
Playfields Dr BH12 . . . . .120 E6
Pleasance Way BH25 . . . . .94 F3
Pleck Hill DT10 . . . . .196 E3
Pleck La DT2 . . . . .209 B7
Plecy Cl BH22 . . . . .61 E2
Plemont Cl BH12 . . . . .88 E1
Plocks The DT11 . . . . .212 D3
Plot La DT9 . . . . .14 F1
Plott La BA8 . . . . .19 C5
Plough Est DT11 . . . . .212 D6
Plough Way SO22 . . . . .126 B2
Plover Cl 8 DT9 . . . . .17 C2
Plover Ct BA21 . . . . .26 F6
Plover Dr DT3 . . . . .166 D5
Plover Dr DT9 . . . . .17 C2
Plover Wlk 6 DT4 . . . . .180 D6
Plowman Cl DT10 . . . . .21 A3
Plucknett Row BA20 . . . . .26 E5
Plumbley Mdws 8 DT11 . . . .81 E8
Plumbtree Gdns BH15 . . . . . . .100 E5
Plumer Rd BH17 . . . . .87 A1
Plum Orch DT9 . . . . .28 F7
Podington Mdws DT3 . . . . . . .166 D5
Poets Way SO22 . . . . .126 A4
Point The BH15 . . . . .122 E3
Pokesdown Com Prim Sch
 BH5 . . . . .123 B5
Pokesdown Sta BH7 . . . . .123 A5
Polans DT9 . . . . .194 D2
Policemans La BH16 . . . . .117 B7
Pollards La DT2 . . . . .155 D7
Pomona Ct BH22 . . . . .61 A5
Pompey's Cnr BH21 . . . . .61 A4
Pompey's La BH22 . . . . .61 B2
Pond Cl
 Henstridge BA8 . . . . .19 A4
 New Milton BH25 . . . . .95 A3
Pond Head BH21 . . . . .51 C6
Pond Wlk DT10 . . . . .33 C8
Ponsonby Rd BH14 . . . . .120 D4
Pony Dr BH16 . . . . .118 D7
Poole Aquarium &
 Serpentarium BH15 . . . . . .119 C1
Poole Commerce Ctr
 BH12 .120 F5
Poole Gram Sch BH17 . . . . .87 D2
Poole High Sch BH15 . . . . .119 C4
Poole Hosp BH15 . . . . .119 D3
Poole Hospl BH15 . . . . .119 D3
Poole La BH11 . . . . .89 B5
Poole Rd
 Bournemouth BH4 . . . . .121 C3
 Lytchett Matravers BH16 . . . . . . .84 F5
 Poole BH13 . . . . .121 A4
 Sturminster Marshall BH21 . . . . . .56 D2
 Upton BH16 . . . . .118 D7
 Wimborne Minster BH21 . . . . . . .59 C4
Poole's Ct 4 DT7 . . . . .96 C5
Poole Sta BH15 . . . . .119 D3
Pool Lane Rdbt BH11 . . . . .88 E4
Poop Hill La TA18 . . . . .192 C8
Poorhouse La DT6 . . . . .66 C8
Pope's La DT9 . . . . .17 D2
Popes Rd BH15 . . . . .119 D6
Poplar Cl
 Bransgore BH23 . . . . .93 C8
 Christchurch BH23 . . . . .126 B8
 3 Poole BH15 . . . . .119 B1
 Radipole DT4 . . . . .167 A6
 Wimborne Minster BH21 . . . . . . .59 D5
Poplar Cres BH23 . . . . .55 D7
Poplar Dr BA21 . . . . .26 E7
Poplar Hill 1 DT11 . . . . .198 B6
Poplar La BH23 . . . . .93 C8
Poplar Rd BH25 . . . . .95 D4
Poplar Way BH24 . . . . .55 D7
Pople's Well TA18 . . . . .191 F4
Poppy Cl
 Christchurch BH23 . . . . .125 C8
 Upton BH16 . . . . .117 B7
 Yeovil BA22 . . . . .26 F5
Poppyfields SP8 . . . . .5 F4
Portadene 1 BH4 . . . . .121 D2
Portal Rd SO23 . . . . .126 F4
Portarlington Cl BH4 . . . . .121 D2
Portarlington Ct 14 BH4 . . . .121 C3
Portarlington Rd BH4 . . . . .121 C2
Portchester Ct 3 BH8 . . . . . . .122 B5

Portchester Pl BH8 . . . . .122 B5
Portchester Rd BH8 . . . . .122 A5
Portchester Sch BH7 . . . . .123 A7
Portelet Cl BH12 . . . . .88 C2
Porter Rd BH17 . . . . .119 B7
Porters La BH21 . . . . .60 C6
Portesham CE Prim Sch
 DT3 . . . . .150 A8
Portesham Gdns BH17 . . . . .90 B4
Portesham Way BH17 . . . . .87 E3
Portfield Cl BH23 . . . . .124 A7
Portfield Rd BH23 . . . . .124 A7
Portfield Sch
 Christchurch BH23 . . . . .124 A6
 East Parley BH23 . . . . .90 B8
Portiere Ho BH1 . . . . .89 A4
Port La DT6 . . . . .101 D3
Portland Beach Rd DT4 . . . . . .180 D8
Portland Bird Obsy DT5 . . . . .186 E10
Portland Castle DT5 . . . . .181 A1
Portland Cres DT4 . . . . .167 B2
Portland Ct DT7 . . . . .96 A5
Portland Hospl DT5 . . . . .181 B1
Portland Mus DT5 . . . . .187 B3
Portland Pl BH2 . . . . .121 F4
Portland Port DT5 . . . . .181 C2
Portland Rd
 Bournemouth BH9 . . . . .122 A8
 Weymouth DT4 . . . . .180 C7
Portman Cres BH5 . . . . .123 B4
Portman Ct BA22 . . . . .192 E8
Portman Dr 5 DT11 . . . . .198 C8
Portman Ho DT11 . . . . .212 C4
Portman Rd
 Bournemouth BH7 . . . . .122 F5
 11 Pimperne DT11 . . . . .199 D4
Portman Terr BH5 . . . . .123 B4
Portmore Ct BH18 . . . . .87 C6
Portmore Gdns DT4 . . . . .167 C1
Portnell's La BA12 . . . . .3 F4
Portreeve Dr BA21 . . . . .27 D6
Port Regis Sch SP7 . . . . .12 B5
Portswood Dr 2 BH10 . . . . . . .90 A4
Portway DT2 . . . . .102 C6
Portway BH23 . . . . .124 A6
Possessions Cnr SP5 . . . . .28 B3
Post Green Rd BH16 . . . . .116 F7
Post Office Bldgs BH9 . . . . . . .121 F8
Post Office La BH24 . . . . .54 C5
Post Office Rd
 18 Bournemouth BH1 . . . . .121 F3
 Gillingham SP8 . . . . .5 D6
Potterne Way BH21 . . . . .45 D4
Potterne Wood Cl BH31 . . . . . .45 E4
Potters Way BH14 . . . . .120 C2
Pottery Junc BH14 . . . . .120 E5
Pottery Lines BH20 . . . . .142 F7
Pottery Rd BH14 . . . . .120 B2
Poulner Hill BH24 . . . . .55 F8
Poulner Jun & Inf Sch
 BH24 . . . . .47 E2
Poulner Pk BH24 . . . . .47 E1
Poundbury Cres DT1 . . . . .107 A2
Poundbury Rd DT1 . . . . .107 A3
Poundbury Trad Est DT1 . . . .107 B2
Pound Cl
 Charminster DT2 . . . . .107 D6
 Poole BH15 . . . . .119 F5
 Ringwood BH24 . . . . .55 C8
 Stalbridge DT10 . . . . .33 C8
 Yeovil BA21 . . . . .27 C7
Pound Cottage Visitor Ctr
 DT2 . . . . .205 E2
Pound Hill
 Corscombe DT2 . . . . .205 B7
 Witchampton BH21 . . . . .200 F1
Pound La
 Bishop's Caundle DT9 . . . . .196 A7
 Burstock DT8 . . . . .203 D5
 1 Christchurch BH23 . . . . .124 B6
 Damerham SP6 . . . . .190 E3
 2 Dorchester DT1 . . . . .108 B2
 Gillingham SP8 . . . . .5 D2
 Okeford Fitzpaine DT11 . . . . . . .198 A5
 Poole BH15 . . . . .119 E5
 Shaftesbury SP7 . . . . .13 A2
 Wareham BH20 . . . . .142 E3
 Wootton Fitzpaine DT6 . . . . .64 B6
Pound Piece
 Easton/Weston DT5 . . . . .186 F4
 Maiden Newton DT2 . . . . .72 F8
Pound Rd
 Hawkchurch EX13 . . . . .202 C2
 Lyme Regis DT7 . . . . .96 B5
 Thornford DT9 . . . . .194 D8
Pound The BA12 . . . . .3 B5
Powell Rd BH14 . . . . .120 B3
Powell Theatre DT9 . . . . .30 B6
Powerscourt CE Prim Sch
 DT6 . . . . .70 A5
Powerstock Comm Nature
 Reserve DT6 . . . . .70 F6
Powis Cl BH25 . . . . .95 B3
Powys Cl BH14 . . . . .134 E8
Powys Gn DT9 . . . . .30 B7
Powyll Carn Circ DT2 . . . . .154 F2
Poxwell Dro DT2 . . . . .154 B4
Prankards Rd 3 DT2 . . . . .17 C2
Preetz Way DT11 . . . . .212 F6
Preston Cl BH16 . . . . .118 C7
Preston Ct BH20 . . . . .142 E5
Preston Cty Comp Sch
 BA21 . . . . .26 F1

Preston Gr BA20 . . . . .27 A5
Preston La BH23 . . . . .92 D3
Preston Rd
 Overcombe/Preston
 DT3 . . . . .153 C1
 Poole BH16 . . . . .119 C6
 Weymouth DT3 . . . . .167 F6
 Yeovil BA22 . . . . .26 C5
Preston VC Prim Sch
 BA21 . . . . .27 A5
Preston Way BH23 . . . . .125 D8
Preston Wildlife Gdn
 DT3 . . . . .152 D2
Prestwood Cl BH25 . . . . .94 F1
Pretoria Terr DT4 . . . . .167 C2
Priest La BH23 . . . . .92 B7
Priestlands DT9 . . . . .30 B7
Priestlands La DT9 . . . . .30 B7
Priestley Rd BH10 . . . . .89 B1
Priest's House Mus & Gdns
 BH21 . . . . .59 B4
Priest's Rd BH19 . . . . .179 A4
Priest's Way BH19 . . . . .178 F2
Prime La DT6 . . . . .65 F7
Primrose Cl 3 SP8 . . . . .5 D2
Primrose Gdns BH17 . . . . .86 F1
Primrose La BA21 . . . . .14 A1
Primrose Way
 Christchurch BH23 . . . . .125 C8
 Corfe Mullen BH21 . . . . .86 E7
Primula Cl DT3 . . . . .152 E2
Prince Of Wales Rd
 Bournemouth BH4 . . . . .121 C4
 Dorchester DT1 . . . . .108 A1
 3 Weymouth DT4 . . . . .167 C2
Prince of Wales Sch The
 DT1 . . . . .134 E8
Princes Cl 8 BH13 . . . . .121 A4
Princes Ct BH24 . . . . .61 D5
Prince's Dr DT4 . . . . .167 D6
Princes Pl SO22 . . . . .126 C3
Prince's Pl BH25 . . . . .95 C3
Princes Rd BH22 . . . . .61 D5
Princess Ave BH23 . . . . .124 B6
Princess Ct 11 SO23 . . . . .126 C6
Princess Rd
 Bournemouth BH4 . . . . .121 B4
 Bridport DT6 . . . . .100 C5
 Poole BH13 . . . . .121 A4
 Swanage BH19 . . . . .179 A2
Princes St BA20 . . . . .27 D4
Prince's St DT1 . . . . .108 A2
Pringles Cl BH22 . . . . .61 E5
Pringles Dr BH22 . . . . .61 E5
Prinstead Cl 13 SO23 . . . . . . .126 D6
Printers Row 17 SO23 . . . . . . .126 D6
Priors Barton SO23 . . . . .126 D3
Priors Cl BH23 . . . . .125 C7
Priors Cnr 2 BH21 . . . . .201 D1
Priors Rd BH17 . . . . .119 A8
Priors Wlk 3 BH21 . . . . .59 B5
Priory CE Prim Sch The
 BH23 . . . . .124 B6
Priory Cl BA20 . . . . .26 F1
Priory Gdns
 3 Pimperne DT11 . . . . .199 D3
 3 Spetisbury DT11 . . . . .211 E5
 West Moors BH22 . . . . .62 A8
 11 Winchester SO23 . . . . .126 A4
Priory Glade BA21 . . . . .26 E6
Priory Ho BH23 . . . . .124 C5
Priory Ind Pk BH23 . . . . .125 D8
Priory La DT6 . . . . .100 C6
Priory Quay BH23 . . . . .124 C5
Priory Rd
 Bournemouth BH2 . . . . .121 E2
 Portland DT5 . . . . .186 F6
 West Moors BH22 . . . . .62 A8
Priory View Ct 4 BH23 . . . . . .124 B6
Priory View Pl 3 BH9 . . . . .90 A3
Priory View Rd
 Bournemouth BH9 . . . . .90 A3
 Burton BH23 . . . . .92 C2
Privet Rd BH9 . . . . .121 F8
Promenade BH23 . . . . .125 B5
Prospect Cl 2 SP8 . . . . .6 A1
Prospect Cres BH19 . . . . .179 A3
Prospect Pl
 Mere BA12 . . . . .2 F5
 3 Weymouth DT4 . . . . .167 D2
Prospect Rd
 Dorchester DT1 . . . . .107 E2
 Lytchett Matravers BH16 . . . . . . .84 D3
Prosperous St 1 BH15 . . . . . . .119 C1
Prout Hill 9 DT6 . . . . .204 D4
Prunus Cl BH22 . . . . .61 B7
Prunus Dr BH22 . . . . .61 B7
Pryors Wlk 2 BH21 . . . . .84 D2
Pudbrook Rd 3 DT3 . . . . .17 D1
Puddledock La DT3 . . . . .153 C1
Puddletown CE Fst Sch
 DT2 . . . . .78 B1
Puddletown Cres BH17 . . . . .87 F2
Puddletown Rd
 Arne BH20 . . . . .142 A3
 Bere Regis BH20 . . . . .140 E7
 East Stoke BH20 . . . . .113 B1
Pugmill La DT13 . . . . .166 D5
Pullman Way BH24 . . . . .55 C6
Pulmans La 15 DT4 . . . . .167 B7
Purbeck Adult Ed Ctr
 BH20 . . . . .142 D3
Purbeck Ave BH15 . . . . .118 C1

Purbeck Cl
Loders DT6 .... 101 F8
Lytchett Matravers BH16 ... 84 D3
Upton BH16 .... 118 B7
Weymouth DT4 .... 167 B1
Purbeck Ct
Bournemouth BH5 .... 123 B3
3 Christchurch BH23 ..... 124 F8
Purbeck Dr BH31 .... 45 B5
Purbeck Gdns BH14 ...... 119 F5
Purbeck Hts BH14 ...... 120 B5
Purbeck Marine Wildlife Reserve BH20 .... 175 B2
Purbeck Rd
Barton on Sea BH25 ..... 126 D7
Bournemouth BH2 .... 121 E2
Lytchett Matravers BH16 ... 84 D4
Purbeck Sch The BH20 .. 142 C2
Purbeck Sports Ctr & Swimming Pool BH20 .. 142 C2
Purbeck Terr Rd BH19 ... 179 C1
Purbeck Toy & Musical Box Mus BH20 .... 144 C4
Purbeck View 9 BH19 ... 178 F2
Purbeck View Sch BH19 .. 179 B3
Purchase Rd BH12 ...... 121 C7
Purdy Ho BH11 .... 89 A4
Purewell BH23 .... 124 D6
Purewell Cl BH23 .... 124 E6
Purewell Cross BH23 ..... 124 E6
Purewell Cross Rd BH23 124 D7
Purewell Ct 2 BH23 ..... 124 E7
Purewell Rdbt BH23 ..... 124 E6
Purns Mill La SP8 .... 5 F5
Pussex La BH23 .... 91 A7
Putton La DT3 .... 166 D5
Putt's La DT9 .... 16 B8
Puxey La
Shillingstone DT11 .... 198 B5
Sturminster Newton DT10 .. 197 B7
Pye Cl BH21 .... 86 E7
Pye Cnr BH21 .... 59 B4
Pye La
Cranborne BH21 .... 41 A6
Tatworth & Forton TA20 .... 202 B8
Wimborne Minster BH21 .... 59 B4
Pymore La DT6 .... 68 C3
Pymore Rd DT6 .... 68 E1

Q

Quadrant Ctr The BH1 .... 121 F3
Quantock Ct 7 BH23 .... 124 F8
Quar Cl DT10 .... 196 E1
Quarr Dr DT9 .... 30 B8
Quarr Hill
Morden BH20 .... 83 C1
Wool BH20 .... 140 B1
Quarr La
Lytchett Matravers BH16 ... 84 A1
Sherborne DT9 .... 30 B8
Symondsbury DT6 .... 99 D6
Quarry Chase 4 BH4 ... 121 C3
Quarry Cl
2 Shipton Gorge DT6 .... 101 D4
Stour Provost SP8 .... 21 D8
Sturminster Newton DT10 .. 35 B2
3 Swanage BH19 .... 178 F2
Wimborne Minster BH21 .... 60 B7
Quarry Dr BH21 .... 60 B7
Quarry Fields Ind Est BA12 2 E5
Quarry La
Bothenhampton DT6 ...... 100 E4
Bradford Abbas DT9 ...... 28 C3
Longburton DT9 .... 195 B8
Melbury Abbas SP7 ...... 24 B5
Quarry Rd BH21 .... 60 B7
Quarterjack Mews 1
BH21 .... 59 C4
Quayle Dr BH11 .... 88 F6
Quay Point 8 BH15 ...... 119 C1
Quay Rd BH23 .... 124 B6
Quayside DT6 .... 100 C1
Quay The
Poole BH15 .... 119 C1
3 Wareham Town BH20 ... 142 E3
Quebec Pl 2 DT4 ...... 167 D3
Queen Anne Dr
Oakley BH21 .... 87 E8
Wimborne Minster BH21 .... 60 A1
Queen Eleanor Rd SP8 ...... 6 A1
Queen Elizabeth Ct BH21 .. 59 B4
Queen Elizabeth's Sch
BH21 .... 58 F6
Queen Mary Ave BH9 ..... 89 F2
Queen's Ave
Christchurch BH23 ...... 124 B5
Dorchester DT1 .... 134 E8
Queensbury Mans 9
BH1 .... 122 A3
Queens Cl BH22 .... 52 F1
Queen's Copse La BH21 ... 51 C8
Queens Ct
16 Bournemouth BH4 .... 121 D4
Bournemouth, Charminster
BH8 .... 122 B8
New Milton BH25 .... 95 D3
12 Winchester SO23 ..... 126 D5
Queens Gdns BH2 ...... 121 D4
Queens Gr
New Milton BH25 .... 95 C4
Pen Selwood BA9 .... 1 C3
Queensland Rd
Bournemouth BH5 ...... 123 A5
Queensland Rd *continued*
Weymouth DT4 .... 167 B3
Queensmead
Burton BH23 .... 92 A1
4 Wimborne Minster BH21 .59 C5
Queens Mead
8 Swanage BH19 .... 179 B2
Winchester SO22 .... 126 A4
Queen's Park Ave BH8 .. 122 D8
Queen's Park Gdns BH8 . 122 D7
Queen's Park Inf Sch BH8 90 C1
Queen's Park Jun Sch
BH8 .... 90 B1
Queen's Park Rd BH8 ... 122 D7
Queen's Park South Dr
BH8 .... 122 D7
Queen's Park West Dr
BH8 .... 122 D7
Queens Rd
Bradford Abbas DT9 ...... 28 D2
Bridport DT6 .... 100 C6
Ferndown BH22 .... 61 D7
Fortuneswell DT5 .... 186 E8
1 Mere BA12 .... 3 B6
Radipole DT3 .... 167 C7
Queen's Rd
Blandford Forum DT11 .... 212 E4
Bournemouth BH3 .... 121 D4
Christchurch BH23 .... 124 E6
Corfe Mullen BH21 .... 86 D5
Poole BH14 .... 120 D4
Swanage BH19 .... 179 B1
Winchester SO22 .... 126 B5
Queen St
Gillingham SP8 .... 5 F2
Radipole DT4 .... 167 E4
4 Yetminster DT9 .... 194 C5
Queensway
New Milton BH25 .... 94 E3
Ringwood BH24 .... 55 D7
Yeovil BA20 .... 27 C5
Queensway Pl BA20 ...... 27 C4
Queens Wlk
Charmouth DT6 .... 97 B7
Lyme Regis DT7 .... 96 B6
Queenswood Ave BH8 ..... 90 E1
Queenswood Dr BH22 ..... 61 D7
Queenwell DT6 .... 68 E1
Quibo La DT4 .... 167 A3
Quince La BH21 .... 59 E6
Quintin Cl BH23 .... 125 F8
Quomp The BH24 .... 55 C7

R

Rabin Hill DT10 .... 35 B2
Rabling La BH19 .... 179 B3
Rabling Rd BH19 .... 179 B3
Racedown Rd DT11 ...... 199 E3
Rachel Cl BH12 .... 120 C7
Radipole La
Radipole DT4 .... 167 A5
Weymouth DT4 .... 166 F4
Radipole Lake Visitor Ctr
DT4 .... 167 D4
Radipole Park Dr DT4 ... 167 C5
Radipole Prim Sch DT3 .. 167 B8
Radipole Rd BH17 .... 88 A2
Raglan Gdns BH11 .... 89 A2
Raglan Terr BA21 .... 27 A7
Railway Dr BH21 .... 56 D4
Railway Terr 4 SP8 .... 6 A1
Raleigh Cl
Christchurch BH23 ...... 124 F5
New Milton BH25 .... 94 F3
3 Ringwood BH24 .... 55 E8
Raleigh Rd
Poole BH12 .... 88 E1
Stalbridge DT10 .... 33 E8
Ralph Jessop Ct BH12 ... 120 D7
Ralph Rd BH21 .... 86 E7
Ram La DT11 .... 48 C1
Rampart Wlk 4 DT1 ..... 134 E7
Rampisham Hill DT8 ..... 205 C3
Ramsbury DT10 .... 196 D5
Ramsbury Cl DT11 ...... 212 D5
Ramsbury Ct DT11 ...... 212 C5
Ramsey Ct BH25 .... 94 F3
Ram's Hill DT10 .... 21 F2
Rances Way SO22 ...... 126 C3
Randall Cl DT3 .... 166 D5
Randalls Hill BH16 ...... 85 B1
Randolph Rd
2 Bournemouth BH1 ..... 122 E4
Poole BH14 .... 120 C5
Ranelagh Rd
Christchurch BH23 ...... 125 F7
Radipole DT4 .... 167 D4
Winchester SO23 .... 126 D4
Rare Breeds Ctr DT11 ... 209 D4
Rashley Rd DT3 .... 166 D5
Raspberry La SP7 .... 12 D2
Ratcliff's Gdn SP7 .... 12 D2
Ratleigh La DT9 .... 29 B6
Ravana Ct 4 BH8 ...... 122 A5
Ravenscourt Rd BH6 ..... 123 C5
Ravensdale Cl BH12 ..... 120 C6
Ravenshall 7 BH2 ...... 121 D2
Raven Way BH23 .... 125 A5
Ravine Ct BH13 .... 147 F7
Ravine Gdns 5 BH13 .... 147 F7
Ravine Rd
Bournemouth BH5 .... 123 B4
Poole BH13 .... 147 F8
Rawles Way DT6 .... 100 D7
Rawston Down Rd 6
DT11 .... 199 E2
Rax La DT6 .... 100 D7
Raymond Cl BH31 .... 45 D6
Raymond Rd DT4 .... 166 F2
Rayners Dr BH12 .... 120 D6
Rayscliff 21 BH4 .... 121 C2
Reap La DT5 .... 186 E2
Rebbeck Rd BH7 .... 123 A6
Reckleford BA20 .... 27 D5
Reckleford Inf Sch BA21 .. 27 E5
Recreation Rd BH12 ..... 120 E6
Rectory Ave BH21 .... 58 D1
Rectory Cl DT2 .... 136 B1
Rectory Gdns 2 DT11 .... 198 F7
Rectory La
Child Okeford DT11 ...... 198 C7
Hardington Mandeville
BA22 .... 193 A7
Puncknowle DT2 .... 129 E6
Studland BH19 .... 164 C2
West Stafford DT2 ...... 136 A8
Rectory Rd
Broadmayne DT2 .... 136 B2
Piddlehinton DT2 .... 76 E7
Poole BH15 .... 119 C6
Rectory Way DT4 ...... 167 C1
Redan Cl BH23 .... 125 F7
Redbreast Rd BH9 .... 90 A3
Redbreast Rd N BH9 ...... 90 A3
Redbridge La DT2 ...... 137 F5
Redbridge Rd DT2 ...... 137 F6
Redcliffe Cl BH23 .... 92 C3
Redcliffe Rd BH19 ...... 179 B5
Redcliff View DT4 ...... 167 E1
Redcotts La BH21 .... 59 B5
Redcotts Rd BH21 .... 59 B5
Red Deer Ct 4 SO22 .... 126 C6
Redgate Pk TA18 .... 191 E5
Redhill Ave BH9 .... 89 F3
Redhill Cl BH10 .... 89 E3
Redhill Cres BH9 .... 89 F3
Redhill Ct 1 BH10 ...... 90 A4
Redhill Dr BH10 .... 89 E3
Redhill Park Homes 1
BH10 .... 89 F4
Redhill Rdbt BH10 .... 89 F4
Redhoave Rd BH17 .... 87 E2
Redhole La DT9 .... 16 B2
Red Horn Cl BH16 ...... 118 C4
Red House Mus & Gdns
BH23 .... 124 B6
Red La
Corfe Mullen BH21 .... 86 A8
Seaborough DT8 .... 191 E1
Sixpenny Handley SP5 .... 189 A3
Todber DT10 .... 21 D4
Redlands
Christchurch BH23 ...... 125 A7
Poole BH12 .... 120 F5
Redlands La 7 DT8 ..... 203 F5
Red Lion Cl 3 DT10 .... 197 D8
Red Lion Yd DT11 .... 212 C3
Redmans La SP7 .... 24 B6
Redmans View BH31 ...... 45 A6
Red Oaks Cl BH22 .... 61 B7
Redpoll Cl 1 DT3 ...... 152 C4
Red Post
Bloxworth DT11 .... 82 C7
Poyntington DT9 .... 16 C4
Redsails BH13 .... 147 B3
Redshank Cl BH17 .... 86 F1
Redvers Rd BH23 .... 124 E7
Red Wing Rd DT9 .... 17 C2
Redwood Cl BH24 .... 55 D7
Redwood Dr BH22 .... 61 C8
Redwood Rd
Upton BH16 .... 118 A8
Yeovil BA21 .... 28 A8
Reedling Cl DT3 .... 152 C3
Reed View Cl DT4 ...... 167 A5
Reeves Orch BH21 .... 56 D5
Reforne DT5 .... 186 F4
Reforne Cl 1 DT5 ...... 187 A4
Regency Cres BH23 ...... 123 F8
Regency Ct 9 SP8 .... 5 D1
Regency Dr 7 DT3 ...... 152 C4
Regent Ct 13 SO23 ...... 126 E8
Regent Dr BH7 .... 122 F8
Regents The 2 BA21 ...... 26 E6
Regent Way BH23 .... 124 B6
Reid St BH23 .... 124 A8
Rempstone Rd
Oakley BH21 .... 87 D8
Swanage BH19 .... 179 B2
Rempstone Sh Arc 8
BH20 .... 142 E3
Remus Cl DT1 .... 134 E7
Renault Dr BH18 .... 87 A1
Rendalls Wlk DT6 .... 100 B6
Renfrew Cl DT1 .... 135 C8
Renscombe Rd BH19 ..... 183 B8
Restharrow BH1 .... 122 A4
Retreat Rd BH21 .... 59 D4
Revels Hill DT2 .... 207 E7
Rew La DT2 .... 208 A8
Rex La DT3 .... 166 D5
Rex's La BA22 .... 27 F1
Reynard Ct BH15 .... 119 F3
Reynards Way DT3 ...... 153 C1
Rhine Rd BH20 .... 139 E6
Rhode La DT7 .... 64 A1
Rhosewood Dr DT3 ...... 153 B1
Rhydderch Way 9 TA18 .. 191 F4
Ribble Cl BH18 .... 87 A2
Ribbonwood Hts BH14 ... 120 B4
Ricardo Cres BH23 ...... 125 A6
Rice Gdns BH16 .... 118 D4
Rice Terr BH16 .... 118 D4
Richard Cl
2 Upton BH16 .... 117 D8
Upton BH16 .... 118 B8
Richard Moss Ho 9
SO23 .... 126 E6
Richmond Cl DT9 .... 30 A5
Richmond Ct 7 BH25 ..... 95 A3
Richmond Gdns BH1 ..... 121 F3
Richmond Gn DT9 .... 30 A6
Richmond Hill BH2 ...... 121 F3
Richmond Hill Dr BH2 ... 121 F3
Richmond Ho 5 SO22 .. 126 D6
Richmond Park Ave BH8 122 C7
Richmond Park Cl BH8 .. 122 D6
Richmond Park Cres
BH8 .... 122 C7
Richmond Park Rd BH8 . 122 C7
Richmond Rd
4 Blandford Forum
DT11 .... 212 E5
Poole BH14 .... 120 C4
Sherborne DT9 .... 30 A5
Swanage BH19 .... 179 B2
Wimborne Minster BH21 .... 59 D4
Yeovil BA20 .... 27 C4
Richmond Rise BH8 ..... 122 D6
Richmond Way BA21 ...... 26 E6
Richmond Wood Rd
BH8 .... 122 C7
Ricketts La DT10 .... 35 B1
Rickhay Rise TA18 ...... 192 B8
Ridgeback La DT6 .... 69 E8
Ridge Dro DT10 .... 196 F5
Ridgefield Gdns BH23 ... 125 D8
Ridge La
Hazelbury Bryan DT10 .... 196 D5
West Coker BA22 .... 193 A8
Ridgemead 5 BA20 ...... 26 F2
Ridgemount Gdns BH15 .. 118 E3
Ridge The DT9 .... 16 E5
Ridge View DT10 .... 196 F8
Ridgeway
Bradpole DT6 .... 68 F1
Broadstone BH18 .... 87 B4
Corfe Mullen BH21 .... 86 D8
Ferndown BH22 .... 89 E8
Sherborne DT9 .... 29 F5
Winchester SO22 .... 126 A3
Ridge Way
Puddletown DT2 .... 76 F1
Shaftesbury SP7 .... 12 F4
Ridgeway La
Child Okeford DT11 ...... 198 C8
Hinton St Mary DT10 ...... 35 B4
Ridgeway Rd SP8 .... 5 E3
Ridgway TA18 .... 192 B8
Ridley Rd BH9 .... 121 F8
Ridout Cl BH10 .... 89 B1
Ridwood DT6 .... 99 A6
Rigg La DT9 .... 14 F2
Riggs Gdns BH11 .... 88 F2
Rigler Rd BH15 .... 119 A2
Rimbrow Cl DT3 .... 153 C1
Rimbury Way BH23 ...... 124 A8
Rimpton Hill BA22 .... 15 A7
Ring St DT10 .... 33 D8
Ringstead Cres DT3 ...... 168 B6
Rings The DT11 .... 79 F8
Ringwood Inf Sch BH24 ... 55 C7
Ringwood Jun Sch BH24 .. 55 C6
Ringwood La BH21 ...... 201 E7
Ringwood L Ctr BH24 ..... 55 C7
Ringwood Rd
Alderholt SP6 .... 42 C5
Bournemouth BH11 .... 88 E4
Bransgore BH23 .... 93 D5
Ferndown BH22 .... 61 C4
Fordingbridge SP6 .... 43 C5
Hyde SP6 .... 43 E4
Poole BH12 .... 120 B7
Sopley BH23 .... 92 A7
St Leonards BH24 .... 53 F2
Three Legged Cross BH21 ... 52 F8
Verwood BH31 .... 45 D6
Walkford BH23 .... 94 B1
West Moors BH22 .... 62 A8
Ringwood Rd Nature Reserve
BH11 .... 88 E5
Ringwood Road Ret Pk
BH11 .... 88 E3
Ringwood Sch BH24 ...... 55 C7
Ringwood Trad Est BH24 .. 55 C6
Rip Croft DT5 .... 186 E2
Ripley Ct BH22 .... 61 F7
Ripon Rd BH9 .... 90 A1
Ripp's La DT2 .... 207 F4
Rise The
Radipole DT4 .... 167 A5
Stratton DT2 .... 106 D8
Ritchie Pl BH22 .... 52 F3
Ritchie Rd
Bournemouth BH11 .... 89 B4
Yeovil BA22 .... 26 C5
River Cl BH21 .... 59 C6
Riverdale La BH23 ...... 124 A6
River La 2 DT11 .... 211 D6
Riverland Ct 4 BH23 ... 124 A6
Riverlea Rd BH23 ...... 124 A6
Rivermead Gdns BH23 .... 91 E2
River Pk BH6 .... 123 F6
Riversdale 8 BH21 ...... 59 C4
Riversdale Rd BH6 ...... 124 A4
Riversdene DT11 .... 48 A6
Riverside
3 Beaminster DT8 ...... 204 D4
4 Bournemouth BH10 ..... 89 F4
Ringwood BH24 .... 55 B6
Riverside Ave BH7 .... 91 C1
Riverside Cl 6 DT2 ..... 207 D4
Riverside Ct 7 BH4 ..... 121 D4
Riverside Ho 4 SO23 .... 126 F6
Riverside La BH6 .... 123 F5
Riverside Pk BH23 ...... 124 A5
Riverside Pk Ind Est BH21 59 D3
Riverside Rd
Blandford Forum DT11 ... 212 E3
Bournemouth BH6 .... 123 F5
Ferndown BH22 .... 52 F2
Riverslea Mews BH23 ... 124 D6
Rivers Mead DT10 .... 35 C2
Riversmeet Ct BH23 ...... 124 D6
Rivers Rd BA21 .... 27 F8
Rivervale DT6 .... 100 D8
River View SP8 .... 5 E2
River Way
Charmouth DT6 .... 97 B7
Christchurch BH23 .... 91 D2
Riviera 11 BH1 .... 122 B3
Riviera Ct
Bournemouth BH2 .... 121 D3
3 Poole BH13 .... 147 F7
Rixon Cl DT10 .... 35 C1
Rixon Hill DT10 .... 35 C1
R L Stevenson Ave BH4 .. 121 B3
RNLI Mus BH15 .... 119 C2
Roberts La
Poole BH17 .... 118 F7
Poole BH17 .... 119 A7
Robertson Rd BH20 ..... 139 D7
Roberts Pl DT1 .... 107 E1
Roberts Rd
Bournemouth BH7 .... 123 A6
Poole BH17 .... 87 B1
Robin Cl 2 DT3 .... 152 C4
Robin Cres BH25 .... 94 D5
Robin Gdns BH23 .... 124 A8
Robin Gr BH25 .... 94 F2
Robins Ct 7 BH21 .... 59 C4
Robins Garth DT1 .... 108 B1
Robins Gdn DT2 .... 209 A2
Robinson Hts DT10 .... 33 D8
Robins Way BH23 .... 125 B5
Robinswood Dr BH22 ..... 61 D7
Robsall Cl BH12 .... 120 E7
Robville Ct 3 BH7 ...... 123 B6
Rochester Rd BH11 .... 89 B4
Rockbourne Gdns BH25 . 126 D8
Rockbourne La SP6 ...... 190 F3
Rockford Cl BH6 .... 123 F3
Rockhampton Cl DT3 ... 152 D3
Rockley Mews BH15 ...... 118 E2
Rockley Pk Cvn Est BH15,
BH16 .... 118 B3
Rockley Rd BH15 .... 118 E1
Rocks La DT2 .... 206 A7
Rockway DT6 .... 101 C4
Rocky Knap DT3 .... 167 C7
Rodden Cl DT4 .... 180 C8
Rodden La DT3 .... 150 C5
Rodden Row DT3 .... 149 B7
Rodgett Cres BH20 ...... 142 F8
Rod Hill La DT2 .... 78 B1
Rodney Cl BH12 .... 121 A8
Rodney Ct
Christchurch BH23 ...... 125 A6
7 Poole BH15 .... 119 C1
Rodney Dr BH23 .... 124 F6
Rodway BH21 .... 59 C4
Rodwell Ave DT4 .... 167 D1
Rodwell Cl BH10 .... 89 C6
Rodwell Rd DT4 .... 167 D1
Rodwell St DT4 .... 167 D1
Roe Ave BA22 .... 26 C5
Roebuck Cl BH25 .... 95 B3
Roe La BA22 .... 15 B8
Roeshot Cres BH23 .... 93 E1
Roeshot Hill BH23 .... 93 C2
Roi-mar Home Pk BH8 .... 90 D4
Roke Rd BH20 .... 80 F4
Rolfe Cres DT3 .... 166 D6
Rolls Bridge La SP8 .... 5 E2
Rolls Bridge Way SP8 ...... 5 D2
Rolls Dr BH6 .... 124 B3
Rolls Mill Way DT10 ...... 197 C8
Roman Cl DT3 .... 167 C7
Roman Hill Trading Est
DT2 .... 154 D6
Roman Hts BH21 .... 86 E8
Roman Rd
Corfe Mullen BH18 .... 86 E5
Dorchester DT1 .... 134 F8
Osmington DT3 .... 154 A1
Radipole DT3 .... 167 C7
Romans' Rd SO23 .... 126 D4
Roman Way BH21 .... 58 C5
Romney Cl BH10 .... 89 E3
Romney Ct 51 BH4 ...... 121 C3
Romney Rd BH10 .... 89 E4
Romsey Rd
Winchester SO22 .... 126 A4
Yeovil BA21 .... 28 A7
Romulus Cl DT1 .... 134 E7
Ronald Bowker Ct 1
SO22 .... 126 C6
Rookery Cl SP8 .... 11 B8
Rookery La
Burstock DT8 .... 203 C6
Uplyme DT7 .... 64 A2
Rookery The DT2 ...... 130 F8
Rook Hill Rd BH23 ...... 125 B6
Rook La DT11 .... 210 C2
Rooks Down Rd SO22 .... 126 B3
Rook St BA12 .... 3 A4
Roosevelt Cres BH11 ...... 89 B6
Ropers La BH16 .... 118 D7
Roper's La BH20 .... 142 E4

Ropewalk Ho **7** SO23....126 E6
Rope Walks DT6..........100 C6
Roping Rd BA21...........27 C6
Ropley Rd BH7............123 C7
Rosamond Ave DT6......101 D4
Rosamund Ave BH21......59 E1
Roscrea Cl BH6..........124 B4
Roscrea Dr BH6.........124 B4
Rosebank La DT11.......212 F6
Rosebery Gdns **3** SP8....5 F3
Rosebery Ave BA21........27 F7
Rosebery Cl BH31.........45 E5
Rosebery Rd BH5.......123 A5
Rosebud Ave **1** BH9....90 A2
Rosecrae Cl BH25........94 F4
Rose Cres BH15.........119 F6
Rosecroft Rd DT4......166 F1
Rose Ct
 5 Gillingham SP8........6 A1
 Poole BH15............119 E3
Rosedale Cl **3** BH23...124 E6
Rose Farm Cl BH21.......61 B3
Rosefields **2** DT11....212 D2
Rose Gdns BH9...........90 A3
Rose Gdn The BH23......91 D1
Rose La
 1 Crewkerne TA18....191 E4
 Winsham TA20.........191 A4
Roselyn Cres DT9........31 B1
Rosemary Ct **8** BH23..126 B7
Rosemary Gdns BH21....120 B7
Rosemary La DT1........149 B2
Rosemary Rd BH12......120 C7
Rosemary St DT9.........17 C2
Rosemount Rd BH4......121 B2
Rose's La DT3...........150 C2
Rosewarne Ct **9** SO23..126 C7
Rosewood Gdns BH25....94 F4
Roslin Gdns BH3........121 D7
Roslin Rd BH3..........121 E7
Roslin Rd S BH3........121 E7
Ross Cl BH20...........139 F6
Ross Gdns BH11.........88 C5
Ross Glades BH3.......121 E6
Rossiters Quay BH15....124 C6
Rossley Cl BH23.........93 E2
Rossmore Com Coll
 BH12.................120 D8
Rossmore Par BH12....120 B8
Rossmore Rd BH12......120 D7
Ross Rd BH24............47 E1
Rotary Cl BH21..........59 F7
Rothbury Pk BH25.......95 B2
Rotherfield Rd
 Bournemouth BH5......123 B3
 Walkford BH23.........94 A1
Rotherham Rd DT5.....181 C1
Rothesay Dr BH23......125 E7
Rothesay Rd
 Bournemouth BH4.....121 C5
 Dorchester DT1.......135 A8
Rotterdam Dr BH24....126 D7
Rough Down La DT6.....65 B2
Rough Height BH19.....179 A4
Roumelia La BH1,BH5..122 E4
Roundham Gdns
 Bridport DT6..........100 D3
 Weymouth DT4.........167 A2
Roundhaye Gdns BH11...88 F6
Roundhaye Rd BH11.....88 F6
Roundhayes Cl DT4....167 A2
Roundways BH11.........88 F3
Rowan Cl
 Christchurch BH23....125 D8
 Radipole DT4.........167 A6
 Sandford BH20.......143 A8
 St Leonards & St Ives BH24..53 F4
Rowan Dr
 Broadstone BH17......86 E1
 Christchurch BH23....125 D8
 Verwood BH31.........45 D4
Rowan Way BA20.........27 A3
Rowbarrow Cl BH17......87 E2
Rowbarrow Hill DT9.....14 F4
Rowbarrow La BH17.....87 E2
Rowden Mill La DT10....32 E1
Rowe Gdns **8** BH11....120 F7
Rowena Rd BH6.........123 F5
Rowland Ave BH15.....119 E6
Rowlands Hill BH21.....59 D6
Rowlands Rd **5** DT11..198 F4
Rowls La BA9..............4 B3
Rownhams Rd BH8.......90 D3
Row The DT10...........35 A1
Roxborough **7** BH4....122 E1
Royal Arc **5** BH1......122 E4
Royal Bournemouth Gen
 Hospl The BH7.........91 B1
Royal Cl BA21............27 E6
Royal Greenjackets Mus
 SO23.................126 D5
Royal Hampshire Cty Hospl
 SO22.................126 C5
Royal Manor Sch The
 DT5.................186 F4
Royal Oak Rd BH10......89 C5
Royal Signals Mus DT1..199 E3
Royal Victoria Mews
 BH4.................121 D3
Royal Winchester Mews
 SO22.................126 A5
Roydon Cl SO22........126 C3
Royster Cl BH17.........87 F2
Royston Dr BH21.........59 D5
Royston D **7** BH25....127 B8
Rozelle Rd BH14........120 C4

Rozel Manor BH13......121 B2
Ruben Dr BH15.........118 D2
Rubens Cl BH15.........95 B3
Ruddock Cl BA22......193 B8
Ruddock Way BA21.....143 A8
Rue La DT9..............31 F4
Ruffield Cl SO22.......126 A8
Rufford Gdns BH6.....123 E5
Rugby Rd BH17........187 B3
Ruins La DT6............99 A6
Rundlestone Ct DT1...107 B2
Runnymede Ave BH11...88 C6
Runnymede Rd BA21....27 F8
Runton Rd BH12.......120 F5
Runway The BH23......125 B7
Rural La DT2.............73 F4
Ruscombe La DT6.......69 E6
Rushall La BH21........86 A5
Rushcombe Fst Sch
 Corfe Mullen BH21.....86 D5
 Poole BH21............85 F6
Rushcombe Way BH21...86 E6
Rushetts Cl **4** DT5...186 F1
Rushford Warren BH23..124 F5
Rushmere Rd BH6......123 D7
Rushmoor Cl BH23.....126 E6
Rushmore Fst Sch
 SP5.................188 C5
Rushton Cres BH3......121 F6
Ruskin Ave BH9..........90 B3
Russell Ave
 Swanage BH19........179 B1
 Winchester SO23.....126 A8
Russell Cl BH24.........47 E1
Russell Cotes Art Gall & Mus
 BH1.................122 A2
Russell Cotes Rd BH1..122 A2
Russell Ct **2** BH25....95 A3
Russell Dr
 Christchurch BH23....124 D6
 Swanage BH19........179 B1
Russell Gdns
 Hamworthy BH16.....118 C4
 St Leonards BH24.....54 D5
Russell Rd BH10.........89 C6
Russet Cl BH22..........61 D6
Russet Way BA20........26 F2
Rutland Manor **10** BH13..121 A4
Rutland Rd
 Bournemouth BH8.....122 B8
 Christchurch BH23.....91 F1
 Weymouth DT4.......167 B4
Ryall Rd
 Poole BH17............87 D1
 Whitechurch Canonicorum
 DT6.................66 D2
Ryall's La DT9 **3**...196 A7
Ryan Cl
 Ferndown BH22........61 C7
 Northport BH20......142 E5
Ryan Gdns
 Bournemouth BH11....89 B6
 Ferndown BH22........61 C7
Rydal Cl BH23..........91 D4
Rydal Ho **2** BH4....121 C2
Rydal Mews BH21.......59 D5
Ryecroft Ave BH11......88 E5
Ryefields Cl BA22......193 B8
Rye Gdns BA20..........26 F2
Rye Hill BH20............81 B1
Rye Hill Cl BH20.........81 B1
Rye Mead La DT4......180 C6
Rye Wr La TA18.......193 A1
Ryland's La DT11.......180 D8
Rymbury Rd DT3.......153 C1
Ryme Rd DT9.........194 B5

S

Sackmore Gn DT10......20 F3
Sackmore La DT10......20 F3
Sackville St DT11........81 B8
Sadborow La TA20....202 E5
Saddle Cl BH21..........60 C6
Saffron Ct BH11.........88 D3
Saffron Dr BH23.......125 B8
Saffron Way BH11........88 D3
St Alban's CE Comb Sch
 BH12.................121 A6
St Alban's Ave BH8....122 C7
St Alban's Cres BH8...122 B8
St Alban's Rd BH8.....122 B7
St Alban St DT4.......167 D2
St Aldhelm's BH14....120 F4
St Aldhelm's Cl BH13..120 F3
St Aldhelm's Pl BH13..120 F4
St Aldhelm's Rd
 Poole BH13...........120 F4
 Sherborne DT9.........30 B8
St Andrews **3** BH23..124 A6
St Andrews Ave DT3...167 D7
St Andrews CE Prim Sch
 Overcombe/Preston
 DT3.................153 A2
 Yetminster DT9......194 C6
St Andrews Cl **4** BH31..135 B8
St Andrews Cl DT9....194 E3
St Andrews Dr DT6......97 A8
St Andrews Ind Est DT6..100 B8
St Andrews Mdw DT7...96 B6
St Andrews Rd
 Broadstone BH18......87 A5
 Yeovil BA20............27 A5
St Andrews View SP7...37 E7
St Anne's Ave BH6....123 E5

St Annes Cl
 Cann SP7...............23 B6
 Winchester SO22.....126 A2
St Anne's Gdns BA21....27 A6
St Anne's Rd
 Upton BH16...........118 B7
 Weymouth DT4.......180 E7
St Ann's Cl **1** BH21..122 E5
St Ann's Hospl BH13...147 E6
St Anthony's Rd BH2..121 F5
St Antony's **3** BH4...121 D2
St Antony's Lewiston Sch
 DT9.................195 A7
St Aubyns Ct BH15....119 B3
St Augustines RC Prim Sch
 DT4.................167 B1
St Augustin's Rd DT4...167 B1
St Bartholomews CE Fst Sch
 11 BH18...........191 F4
St Bede CE Fst Sch
 SO23.................126 E6
St Bede's Ct **8** SO23..126 E7
St Brelades Ave BH12...88 D1
St Catherines BH21.....59 C4
St Catherines Chapel
 DT3.................124 A6
St Catherine's Cres **2**
 DT9...................30 A5
St Catherine's Par BH23..91 F1
St Catherines RC Prim Sch
 DT6.................100 D8
St Catherine's RC Prim Sch
 BH21.................60 B6
St Catherine's Rd
 Bournemouth BH6....123 F3
 Winchester SO23......91 D3
St Cecilia's Gdns DT6..100 D8
St Clair Rd BH13......147 F7
St Cleeve Way BH22....61 C3
St Clement's Gdns BH1..122 D5
St Clements Rd BH1...122 A7
St Clement's Rd BH1..122 D5
St Clement's & St John's CE
 Inf Sch BH1..........122 D5
St Clement Cl **2** SO23..126 D5
St Cross Cl **4** SO23...126 D5
St Cross Hospital SO23..126 D2
St Cross Mede SO23...126 C2
St Davids Cl **3** DT1..135 B8
St David's Cres BH23....27 D7
St David's Ct **3** BH1..122 C5
St David's Rd
 Upton BH16...........118 B7
 Weymouth DT4.......180 D7
St Denys **2** BH25.....95 B1
St Edmund St **6** DT4..167 D2
St Edwards **1** SP20...12 F3
St Edwards Cl BH20....177 A8
St Edward's RC/CE Sch
 BH15.................119 F7
St Faith's CE Prim Sch
 SO23.................126 D3
St Faith's Rd **1** SO23..126 D3
St George's Almshos **6**
 BH15.................119 B1
St George's Ave
 Bournemouth BH8....122 C8
 Poole BH18...........120 B8
 Radipole DT4........167 E6
 Yeovil BA21............27 D7
St Georges Ct DT11....108 D1
St George's Cl
 Bournemouth BH8....122 C8
 Christchurch BH23....125 D8
 Swanage BH19......178 B2
St Georges Ct BH22....61 C4
St George's Ct **1** BH1..122 E5
St George's Dr BH12..121 B8
St Georges Dr
 Bournemouth BH11....88 D3
 Bransgore BH23......93 B8
St George's Dr BH22....61 C4
St Georges Est **8** DT6..186 F4
St Georges Hill DT7....96 A6
St George's Ho **16** SO23..126 E6
St Georges St **5** DT6..186 F3
St Georges Mans **5** BH5..122 E4
St Georges Rd DT1....108 C1
St George's Rd
 Portland DT5.........186 F4
 Shaftesbury SP7.......12 F2
St George's Sch SP8.....1 D1
St George's St SO23...126 E6
St Gildas Cath Sch BA21..27 D5
St Giles CE
 Chideock DT6..........99 A7
 Winchester SO23.....126 E5
St Giles Hill SO23......126 F5
St Giles's House BH21..201 E6
St Gregory CE Prim Sch
 DT10..................20 F2
St Helen's Rd
 Dorchester DT1.......107 F2
 Sandford BH20.......143 A8
 Weymouth DT4.......166 F2
St Helier Ave DT3......152 B4
St Helier Rd DT4.........88 D1
St Ives End La BH24....55 B6
St Ives Pk BH24........121 F5
St Ives Pk BH24..........54 D5
St Ives Wood BH24......54 D5

St James CE Fst Sch
 Alderholt SP6..........42 C6
 Holt BH21.............51 A6
St James' CE Prim Sch
 BH7.................123 B6
St James Cl **3** BH23..124 A6
St James' La SO22,SO23..126 D5
Saint James Pk DT6....69 A1
St James Rd BH22.....61 A6
St James's BH5..........122 E3
St James Cl BA21.......26 F5
St James's Pk BA21....26 C5
St James's Sq BH15....123 A5
St James St SP7.........12 E2
St James' Terr SO22,
 SO23.................126 D5
St Johns CE Aided Prim Sch
 DT4.................167 B6
St Johns CE Fst Sch BH21..59 D4
St John's Cl BH21........59 D4
St John's Ct **4** BH1...122 E5
St John's Gdns **2** BH9..89 F1
St John's Hill
 Shaftesbury SP7.......12 D2
 Wareham BH20.......142 E3
 Wimborne Minster BH21..59 D5
St John's Hospital
 (Almshouses)(N) **1**
 SO23.................126 F5
St John's Hospital
 (Almshouses)(S) **3**
 SO23.................126 F5
St Johns Rd BH25........95 A7
St John's Rd
 Bournemouth BH5....122 E4
 Christchurch BH23....124 A6
 Poole BH15...........119 D4
 Winchester SO23.....126 F6
 Yeovil BA21............27 C7
St John's St SO23......126 F5
St Joseph's RC Comb Sch
 BH15.................120 E7
St Joseph's RC Prim Sch
 BH23.................125 A8
St Julien Cres BH23....152 B3
St Julien Rd **1** BH20..139 D7
St Just Cl BH22...........61 C3
St Juthware Cl BA22...193 C3
St Katharine's CE Prim Sch
 BH6.................124 B4
St Katherine's Ave DT6..100 E7
St Katherine's Dr DT6..100 E8
St Lawrence **4** DT6...128 B8
St Lawrence Cres SP7...12 F4
St Lawrence Rd DT3....152 C5
St Ledger's Hill BH8...122 D6
St Ledger's Rd BH8...122 D6
St Leonard's Ave DT11..212 E4
St Leonards Farm Pk
 BH22..................62 A8
St Leonards Mid Sch
 BH24.................53 E1
St Leonards Rd
 Bournemouth BH8....122 B6
 Weymouth DT4.......167 D1
St Leonards Way BH24...53 F5
St Luke's CE Prim Sch
 BH9.................121 F8
St Luke's Ct **3** DT6...100 B8
St Luke's Rd
 Bournemouth BH3....121 F7
 Weymouth DT4.......122 A7
St Maradox La BH9......89 F2
St Margarets Almshouses
 BH21..................59 A5
St Margaret's Ave BH23..124 B5
St Margarets Cl BH21....59 A5
St Margarets Hill BH21..59 A5
St Margaret's Rd
 Bournemouth BH10....89 C2
 Poole BH15...........119 D4
St Mark's CE Prim Sch
 BH10..................89 C1
St Marks CE VA Fst Sch
 BH19.................178 F2
St Mark's Rd BH11.....89 B3
St Martins Church DT11..212 B4
St Martins Cl DT12.....136 B2
St Martin's Cl
 1 Wareham BH20...142 E4
 Winchester SO23.....126 F6
St Martins Field DT2...133 D7
St Martin's La BH20...142 E4
St Martins Pre Sch TA18..191 E4
St Martins Rd BH16....118 A7
St Martin's Rd
 3 Fortuneswell DT5..186 F4
 Sandford BH20.......143 A8
 Shaftesbury SP7.......12 F2
 Winchester SO23.....180 E8
St Martin's Sq SP8......5 F2
St Martins Trad Pk SO23..126 F6
St Martins Way BA20....26 F2
St Mary CE Prim Sch
 DT10..................20 F2
St Mary CE Prim Sch DT9..28 D1
St Mary Magdalene
 Almshouses **4** SO23..126 F5
St Marys Cath Prim Sch
 DT1.................135 B8
St Marys CE Fst Sch
 Charminster DT2.....107 D6
 Ferndown BH22.......52 F3

St Marys CE Mid Sch
 DT2.................110 A8
St Marys CE Prim Sch
 DT8.................204 C4
St Marys Cl **3** BH23...93 C8
St Mary's Cl
 Northport BH20......142 C5
 3 Sixpenny Handley SP5..189 A4
 3 Winterborne Whitechurch
 DT11.................210 C3
St Mary's Cres BA21....27 C8
St Mary's Ct BH6.......123 E3
St Mary's Gdns **3** DT8..204 C4
St Mary's Maternity Hosp
 BH15.................119 D3
St Mary's Mews BH22...61 D4
St Mary's RC Comb Sch
 BH15.................119 E5
St Mary's RC Fst Sch
 Swanage BH19........179 B2
 Wool BH20............140 A2
St Mary's Rd
 Bournemouth BH1....122 D6
 Ferndown BH22........61 D5
 Poole BH15...........119 E4
 Sherborne DT9.........29 F5
St Marys Sta
 Bridport DT6.........100 C6
 Donhead St Mary SP7...13 D3
St Mary St
 7 Radipole DT4....167 D2
 Winchester SO22.....126 B3
St Mary the Virgin Prim Sch
 SO22..................11 B8
St Mary Well St **11** BH8..204 C4
St Mathews Rd SO22...126 B8
St Merrin's Cl BH23......89 C4
St Michaels DT7..........96 C6
St Michael's Ho BH2....121 D3
St Michael's Ave BA21...27 E7
St Michael's CE Mid Sch
 BH2...................59 E7
St Michaels CE Prim Sch
 BH2.................121 D3
St Michaels Cl
 Hamworthy BH15....118 E3
 Over Compton DT9....28 E7
 Verwood BH31.........45 B5
St Michaels Ct
 1 Bournemouth BH6..123 C4
 Weymouth DT4.......167 C1
St Michael's Gdns **8**
 SO23.................126 D5
St Michael's La DT6....100 C6
St Michael's Mews **9**
 BH2...................121 E3
St Michael's Pas SO23..126 E3
St Michael's Pl **1** BH2..121 E3
St Michaels Prim Sch
 DT7...................96 C6
St Michael's Rd BH31...45 B4
St Michael's Rd
 Bournemouth BH2....121 E3
 6 Wareham BH20...142 E3
 Winchester SO23.....126 D4
 Yeovil BA21............27 F6
St Michael's Rdbt BH2..121 D3
St Michaels Trading Est
 DT6.................100 C6
St Nicholas CE Prim Sch
 DT6.................198 C7
St Nicholas Cl
 1 Yeovil BA20........19 A4
 Winchester SO23......27 D4
St Nicholas Cl **5** DT11..198 C7
St Nicholas Gdns **7**
 DT11.................198 C7
St Nicholas & Lawrence CE
 Prim Sch DT3.........152 C2
St Nicholas St DT3.....167 D2
St Osmund Cl **3** SP7..194 C5
St Osmunds CE Mid Sch
 DT1.................135 B8
St Osmunds Com Sports Ctr
 DT1.................135 A8
St Patricks Ave DT4....166 F1
St Patricks Ind Est DT11..198 B6
St Patrick's Rd **2** BA21..26 F7
St Paul's Cl **1** SO22....30 C7
St Paul's Gdns **2** BH8..122 B4
St Paul's Hill SO22.....126 D6
St Pauls La BH8.........122 B4
St Pauls Pl BH8........126 D6
St Pauls Pl **28** BH8....122 B4
St Paul's Rd
 Bournemouth BH8....122 B4
 4 Fortuneswell DT5..186 F4
St Peter's Cl **1** DT11..199 E4
St Peters Ct **3** BH1....122 A3
St Peter's Ct **3** BH14..120 A4
St Peter's Gate **8** BH1..121 F3
St Peter's RC Comp Sch
 BH6.................123 F4
St Peter's Rd
 Bournemouth BH1....121 F3
 Parkstone BH14.......122 A3
 Poole BH14...........122 A3
St Peter's Rdbt BH1...122 A3
St Peter St SO23.......126 E6
St Peter's Wlk **8** BH1..121 F3
St Rayn Hill TA18......191 A4
St Richards Cl DT11...211 F7

St Rumbold's Rd SP7 ....12 F2
St Saviours Cl BH7 ......123 C7
St Stephen's Ct BH21 ...121 E4
St Stephens La BH31 ....45 C6
St Stephen's Rd
  Bournemouth BH2 ......121 E3
  ■ Dorchester SO22 .....126 B8
St Stephen's Way ₄ BH2 .121 F3
St Swithins Cl DT9 ......100 C7
St Swithins Cl DT9 ......30 C6
St Swithins Cl DT9 ......100 C7
St Swithin's Rd BH1 ....122 B4
St Swithin's Rdbt BH1 ..122 B3
St Swithin's Rd S BH1 ..122 B3
St Swithun St SO23 .....126 E5
St Thomas BH10 ....89 D2
St Thomas Cross ■ BA21 .27 E5
St Thomas Garnet's RC Sch
  BH5 ....123 A5
St Thomas Mews ₃ SO23 .126 D5
St Thomas Rd DT1 ......107 F2
St Thomas St
  Radipole DT4 ....167 D2
  Winchester SO23 ......126 D5
St Valerie Rd BH2 ....121 F5
St Vast's Rd BH19 ......179 C1
St Walburga's RC Prim Sch
  BH9 ....90 B1
St Winifred's Rd BH2 ...121 F5
Salcot Rd SO23 ....126 E8
Salerno Pl BH15 ....118 D2
Salisbury Cres DT11 ....212 D5
Salisbury Rd
  Blandford Forum DT11 .212 D4
  Bournemouth BH1 .....122 E4
  Burton BH23 ....92 D2
  Donhead St Mary SP7 ..13 D1
  Pimperne DT11 ....199 E4
  Poole BH14 ....120 C5
  Ringwood BH24 ....47 B7
  Ringwood SP6 ....43 C1
  Shaftesbury SP7 ......12 F2
  Sopley, Winton BH23 ..92 B5
  ₂ Swanage BH19 ......179 C1
  Weymouth DT4 ....167 C3
Salisbury St
  Blandford Forum DT11 .212 C3
  Cranborne BH21 ......40 A8
  Dorchester DT1 ....108 B2
  Marnhull DT10 ....21 B2
  Mere BA12 ....3 A5
  Shaftesbury SP7 ......12 F2
Sally Kings La SP7 ......12 D3
Sally Lovell's La SP8 ...18 E7
Salterns Ct BH14 ....147 B8
Salterns Point BH14 ....147 B8
Salterns Quay BH14 ....147 B8
Salterns Rd BH14 ......120 A3
Salterns Way BH14 .....147 B8
Salter Rd BH13 ....147 C3
Salthouse La BA20 .....27 C4
Saltings Rd BH16 ......118 B6
Salway Ash CE Prim Sch
  DT6 ....68 B8
Salway Dr DT6 ....68 B6
Samantha Cl BH10 .....89 E3
Samarate Way BA20 ....26 F5
Sammy Miller Motorcycle
  Mus BH25 ....94 E5
Samphire Cl DT4 ....167 D6
Samples Way BH17 ....119 F8
Samson Rd BH15 ......118 D2
Sannways Cl BA22 .....26 D5
Sancreed Rd BH12 .....120 E7
Sancroft Rd DT4 ....60 A1
Sandbanks Bsns Ctr
  BH13 ....147 B3
Sandbanks Rd
  Poole BH14 ....120 A2
  Poole BH15,BH14 ....119 F3
Sandbourne Ave DT11 ..212 E6
Sandbourne Cl ₆ BH19 .178 F2
Sandbourne Rd
  Bournemouth BH4 ....121 C1
  Overcombe/Preston DT3 .168 B7
Sandcotes Rd BH14 ...120 C3
Sanderling Cl ₄ DT3 ...152 C4
Sanderlings ₃ BH24 ...55 E6
Sanders Gn ₄ DT11 ...210 C3
Sandford Cl BH9 ....90 C3
Sandford Dr BH20 ....116 B2
Sandford La BH20 ....142 E5
Sandford Lane Ind Est
  BH20 ....142 F5
Sandford Mid Sch BH20 .116 A1
Sandford Orcas Manor
  House DT9 ....15 E6
Sandford Orcas Rd DT9 .15 F4
Sandford Rd
  Northport BH20 ......142 E5
  Sandford BH20 ......142 F7
  Wareham St Martin BH20 .116 B2
Sandford St Martin Fst Sch
  BH20 ....143 A8
Sandford Way BH18 ..86 F2
Sandhills Cl BH31 ....45 B7
Sandhills Cres BH20 ..139 E2
Sandhurst Dr BH21 ...53 C7
Sandhurst Rd BA20 ...27 B2
Sandilands Cl SP8 ....10 E3
Sandleheath Rd SP6 ..42 B7

Sandlewood Cl ₄ BA21 ..28 A8
Sandmartin Cl BH25 ...126 F7
Sandown Cl BA20 ......27 C5
Sandown Rd BH23 ....124 C6
Sandpiper Cl BH17 ....86 F1
Sandpiper Way DT4 ...180 D6
Sandringham Cl BH23 .90 B4
Sandringham Ct
  Bournemouth BH8 ...122 C6
  ■ Dorchester DT1 ....135 C8
Sandringham Gdns BH9 .90 B4
Sandringham Rd
  Poole BH14 ....120 C3
  Yeovil BA21 ....28 A6
Sandringham Sports Ctr
  DT1 ....108 B1
Sandroyd Sch SP5 ....188 C5
Sandsfoot Castle DT4 .180 E7
Sandy Cl BH21 ....60 A8
Sandy Hall La BH20 ..177 C8
Sandy Hole TA16 .....191 F8
Sandyhurst BH17 .....87 C1
Sandy La
  Bournemouth BH6 ...123 C5
  Christchurch BH23 ..91 E2
  Hilfield DT2 ....195 A1
  Lytchett Matravers BH16 .84 E6
  Minterne Magna DT2 .207 C7
  Pamphill BH21 ......58 B5
  St Leonards BH24 ...54 C5
  Upton BH16 ....118 B6
  Verwood BH21 ......45 A2
  Verwood BH31 ......45 C7
  Whitechurch Canonicorum
  DT6 ....65 A8
  Wimborne Minster BH21 .60 A8
Sandy Mead Rd BH8 ..90 F1
Sandy Plot BH23 .....94 A1
Sandy Way BH10 ....89 E4
San Remo Twrs ₄ BH5 .122 E3
Santoy BH13 ....147 D5
Sarah Ct BH7 ....123 B8
Sarah Sands Cl BH23 .124 D8
Sark Rd BH12 ....120 F7
Sarum Ave DT9 ......194 D8
Sarum Ave BH22 ....53 A4
Sarum Cl ₃ DT9 .....194 D8
Sarum Ct SO22 ......126 A5
Sarum Ct
  Poole BH14 ....120 C4
  Winchester SO22 ...126 B5
Sarum Road Hospl SO22 .126 A3
Sarum St ₂ BH15 ....119 B1
Saulfland Dr BH23 ...125 D8
Saulfland Ho BH23 ...125 D8
Saulfland Pl BH23 ...125 D8
Saville Ct BH21 ......59 D3
Sawyers La ₂ DT2 ...106 E8
Saxonbury Rd BH6 ...123 D6
Saxon Ct ₇ SO23 ....126 E6
Saxonford Rd BH23 ..125 C7
Saxon Hts BH6 ......123 E5
Saxonhurst Cl BH10 .89 E5
Saxonhurst Gdns BH10 .89 E4
Saxonhurst Rd BH10 .89 E4
Saxon King Gdns BH10 .124 B4
Saxon Mead Cl SP8 ..5 E3
Saxon Rd SO23 ....126 E6
Saxon Rise DT11 .....210 C7
Saxon Spur SP7 ......12 F4
Saxon Sq Sh Ctr BH23 .124 B6
Saxon Way SP6 ......42 C5
Scadden's Cnr DT6 ...66 B8
Scarf Rd BH17 ....119 F7
Schelin Way ₆ DT11 .198 B5
School Cl
  Chickerell DT3 ......166 D6
  ₄ Tarrant Gunville DT11 .199 F7
  Verwood BH31 ......45 C7
School Hill
  Chickerell DT3 ......166 D6
  Cucklington BA9 ....4 A3
  Powerstock DT6 ....70 B5
  South Perrott DT8 ..192 C1
School La
  Askerswell DT2 .....102 C7
  Blandford Forum DT11 .212 D2
  Bournemouth BH11 ..89 B6
  Broadwindsor DT8 ..203 B6
  Chetnole DT9 ....194 D3
  ■ Dorchester DT1 ...107 F2
  Gillingham SP8 .....6 A2
  ₄ Pimperne DT11 ..199 D4
  Poole BH11 ....119 C5
  Ringwood BH24 ....55 C7
  St Leonards BH24 ..54 C5
  Studland BH19 .....164 C1
  ₃ Tarrant Gunville DT11 .199 F7
  Tolier Porcorum DT2 .71 E8
  Verwood BH21 .....53 B7
  West Lulworth BH20 .172 D6
  Wimborne Minster BH21 .59 B5
  Winfrith Newburgh DT2 .158 F5
  Woodsford DT2 ....110 C1
School Rd
  ■ Bournemouth BH5 .5 F1
School St DT4 ....167 D3
Scimitar Rd BA22 ...26 D6
Scotchey Hill SP8 ...10 D1
Scotchey La SP8 ....10 F1
Scott Cl
  Poole BH12 ....88 F1
  Poole BH12 ....88 F1

Scott's Gn BH23 ....124 F5
Scotts Hill La BH23 ...124 D7
Scott's La DT6 ....64 A5
Scotts Way TA18 .....192 A8
Scouse La EX13 ......202 B2
Scutts Cl BH16 ....84 C4
Seabank Cl
  ₄ Bournemouth BH16 .117 C7
  Upton BH16 ....118 A7
Seaborough View TA18 .191 F3
Seaborne Pl ₅ BH25 ..123 B5
Seabourne Rd BH5 ...123 B5
Seacliff Ct BH6 ......123 D3
Seacombe Rd BH13 ..147 B3
Seacroft Ave BH25 ...126 E8
Seafield Cl BH25 .....126 F7
Seafield Dr BH6 .....123 E5
Seafield Rd
  Barton on Sea BH25 .126 E8
  Bournemouth BH6 ...123 D4
  Christchurch BH23 ..125 C7
Seagrim Rd BH8 .....90 C3
Seagull Rd BH8 ......90 C1
Sea La DT6 ....99 A5
Sea King Rd BH20 ...26 F3
Seamoor Cl DT3 .....167 F8
Seamoor La BH4 .....121 B3
Seamoor Rd BH4 ....121 B3
Sea Point ₈ BH13 ...147 F7
Sea Rd
  Barton on Sea BH25 .126 E8
  Bournemouth BH5 ...122 E4
  Bournemouth, Southbourne
  BH6 ....123 F3
Sea Rd N DT6 ....100 E7
Sea Rd S DT6 ....100 D5
Seaton Cl BH23 ......126 B8
Seaton Rd
  Christchurch BH23 ..126 B8
  Yeovil BA20 ....27 B4
Seatown Cl BH17 ....88 A1
Sea View ₆ BH25 ....186 F8
Seaview Rd
  Barton on Sea BH25 .126 D7
  Walkford BH23 .....94 C1
Sea View Rd
  Poole BH15 ....120 A6
  Upton BH16 ....118 A7
Sea Vixen Ind Est BH23 .125 A8
Seaward Ave
  Barton on Sea BH25 .126 F7
  Bournemouth BH6 ...123 B4
Seaward Gdns DT6 ..160 D8
Seaward Rd BH19 ...179 B4
Seaway BH25 ....125 C7
Seaway Ave BH23 ...125 C7
Second Cliff Wlk ₂ DT6 .100 B2
Second Marine Ave
  BH25 ....127 A6
Seddon Cl BH25 .....127 B8
Sedgefield Cl DT4 ...167 C3
Sedgemoor Cl BA21 .27 F6
Sedgley Rd BH9 .....121 E8
Seed Warehouse The ₃
  BH15 ....119 C1
Selborne Pl SO22 ...126 B3
Selby Cl BH18 ....87 A3
Seldown BH15 ......119 D3
Seldown Bridge BH15 .119 D3
Seldown La BH15 ...119 D3
Seldown Rd BH15 ...119 D2
Self Rd BH15 ....119 A2
Selfridge Ave BH6 ..123 D3
Selfridge Cl BH6 ....123 E3
Seliot Cl BH15 ......119 D5
Selkirk Cl BH21 .....59 C8
Selle Rd BH20 ....139 F6
Sellwood Way BH25 .126 D8
Selwood Cl DT10 ....35 C2
Selwood Pk BH10 ..89 C7
Selworthy Cl BH14 .120 A2
Selwyn Cl DT3 ......152 D3
Sentinal Ct BH15 ...119 A1
Sentry Rd BH19 .....179 C2
Sermon Rd SO22 ....126 A5
Serpentine Rd BH15 .119 C3
Sevenoaks Dr BH7 ..123 A8
Setley Gdns BH8 ....90 E3
Seven Acres ₅ DT5 ..186 E1
Seven Acres Rd BH31 .45 C3
Seven Ash Comm Rd
  DT9 ....195 B4
Seven Barrows Rd BH20 .142 B4
Sevenoaks Dr BH7 ..123 A8
Severalls Park Ave ₁₇
  TA18 ....191 F4
Severn Rd BH22 .....62 A5
Sewell Rd BH20 .....139 D7
Seymer Rd BH19 ....179 C2
Seymour Rd BH7 ....47 D1
Shadrack DT6 ....166 A3
Shadrack St ₈ DT6 ..204 C4
Shaftesbury Abbey Mus &
  Gdn SP7 ....12 E2
Shaftesbury Arts Ctr SP7 .12 E2
Shaftesbury Cl BH22 .53 B1
Shaftesbury Cl BH23 .121 F6
Shaftesbury L Ctr SP7 .12 E2
Shaftesbury Prim Sch
  SP7 ....13 A2
Shaftesbury Rd
  Bournemouth BH8 ...122 C6
  Child Okeford DT11 .198 C8
  Ferndown BH22 ....53 A1
  Gillingham SP8 .....11 C7
  Henstridge BA8 ....18 D6
  Kington Magna SP8 .20 A1

Shaftesbury Rd continued
  Mere BA12 ....3 B4
  Poole BH15 ....119 D3
Shaftesbury Sch SP7 .12 F1
Shaftesbury Town Mus
  ....12 E2
Shakespeare Rd
  Bournemouth BH6 ...123 D7
  Wimborne Minster BH21 .59 C6
Shamrock Ct ₂ BA21 .59 C4
Shapland Ave BH15 .88 E5
Shapwick Rd BH15 ..119 A1
Shard Cl BH31 ....45 C6
Sharlands Cl BH18 ..87 B3
Sharp Rd BH12 .....120 F8
Shaston Cl ₄ BH19 .178 F2
Shaston Cres DT11 .135 B7
Shaston Rd DT11 ...198 F4
Shatcombe La DT2 ..72 A3
Shatter's Hill DT10 .142 E4
Shave Cross DT6 ....203 C1
Shave Hill SP8 ......9 B7
Shave La
  Todber DT10 ....21 D5
  West Crewkerne TA18 .191 E3
Shaves La BH25 ....191 D5
Shaw Cl DT11 ......212 D5
Shaw Dr BH20 ......142 F8
Shawford Gdns BH8 .90 D2
Shawford Rd BH8 ..90 D3
Shaw Rd BH24 ......54 D5
Shear Plot DT6 .....99 F8
Shears Rd DT4 .....167 D7
Shearstones DT9 ...194 D5
Sheasby Cl ₉ SP5 ..189 A3
Shedbush La DT6 ...98 C8
Shedrick Hill TA20 .202 E8
Sheepcroft La BH21 .51 D3
Sheepdown Rd BH11 .107 C2
Sheephouse Dro BH21 .200 E2
Sheeplands La DT9 ..29 F6
Sheeplands The DT9 .29 F7
Sheep Market Hill ₂
  DT11 ....212 D3
Sheepspine La TA20 .202 C5
Sheepwash La
  Burstock DT8 ......203 D5
  Tatworth & Forton TA20 .202 A6
Shelbourne Cl BH8 .122 D6
Shelbourne Rd BH8 .122 D6
Sheldrake Rd BH23 .125 A5
Shell Bay Sailing Ctr
  ....147 A1
Shelley Cl
  Bournemouth BH1 ...122 E5
  Christchurch BH23 ..125 C7
  St Leonards BH24 ..54 A5
  Winchester SO22 ...126 A6
Shelley Ct
  ₁₀ Bournemouth BH4 .121 C3
  Ferndown BH22 ....61 D5
Shelley Gdns ₁ 122 E5
Shelley Hamlets BH23 .125 D7
Shelley Ho ₂ BH15 .125 D7
Shelley Rd
  Bournemouth BH1 ...122 E5
  Poole BH12 ....120 E6
Shelley Rd E BH7 ...122 F5
Shelton Rd BH6 .....123 C6
Shenstone Ct ₄ BH7 .95 A1
Shepherd Cl BH23 ..93 F1
Shepherds Croft DT5 .187 C5
Shepherds Hill BH24 .46 C6
Shepherd's Hill SP8 .9 C7
Shepherds La BH24 .46 C6
Shepherds Way
  Bournemouth BH7 ...123 A7
  West Lulworth BH20 .172 D6
Sheppards Field ₃ BH21 .59 B6
Sherborn Cres BH17 .88 A2
Sherborne Abbey DT9 .30 B6
Sherborne Abbey CE Prim
  Sch DT9 ....29 F4
Sherborne Cswy SP7 .11 E3
Sherborne Dr ₂ BH22 .61 D4
Sherborne Golf Club DT9 .16 A3
Sherborne Hill DT9 ..30 C3
Sherborne House DT9 .30 C5
Sherborne Mus DT9 .30 C5
Sherborne New Castle
  DT9 ....30 D5
Sherborne Prep Sch DT9 .30 C4
Sherborne Prim Sch DT9 .30 C7
Sherborne Rd
  Henstridge BA8 ....18 F4
  Milborne Port DT9 .17 C2
  Yeovil BA20 ....27 E5
Sherborne Sch DT9 .30 A6
Sherborne Sch for Girls
  DT9 ....30 A6
Sherborne Sta DT9 .30 B5
Sherborne La DT7 ..96 C5
Sherborne Old Castle
  DT9 ....30 D5
Sherborne Rd
  Frampton DT2 ......73 F3
  Winchester SO22 ...126 A3
Sheridan Cl
  Bournemouth BH9 ...90 A1
  Sheringham Rd BH12 .120 F5
Sherlands ₁ TA16 ...191 F7
Sherren Ave DT2 ....75 E2

Sherrin Cl BH15 ....119 D5
Sherwood Ave
  Ferndown BH22 ....61 C5
  Poole BH14 ....120 A3
Sherwood Cl BH23 ...123 F7
Sherwood Dr BH31 ..45 D6
Shetland View BH15 .45 C6
Shiller's La BH21 ....117 F8
Shillingstone CE Prim Sch
  DT11 ....198 B6
Shillingstone Dr BH9 .90 B3
Shillingstone Gdns ₃
  BH12 ....118 C2
Shillingstone La BH21 .198 A5
Shillito Rd BH12 ....120 E5
Ship Knapp DT6 .....98 B8
Shipney La DT10 ....118 C4
Shipstal Cl BH16 ....118 C4
Shipstal Nature Trail
  BH20 ....144 D3
Shipton La
  Burton Bradstock DT6 .101 E5
  Loders DT6 ....101 E5
Shipton Rd DT6 .....101 D3
Shirecroft Rd DT4 ...167 A3
Shiremoor Hill TA16 .191 F6
Shires Cl BH24 ......55 C4
Shires Copse BH6 ...123 E2
Shires Mead BH31 ..45 C6
Shirley Cl
  Ferndown BH22 ....53 A2
  Swanage BH19 .....178 F2
Shirley Rd
  Bournemouth BH9 ...90 A1
  Poole BH12 ....120 B6
  Upton BH16 ....118 C7
  Wareham BH20 .....142 D3
Shoe La DT6 ....100 F8
Shoot Hill TA17 .....191 C8
Shoplands DT6 .....203 C3
Shoreacres BH13 ...147 C3
Shore Ave BH16 ....118 C6
Shore Cl
  ₃ Upton BH16 .....117 E6
  Upton BH16 ....118 E5
Shoredown La DT9 ..17 C6
Shore Gdns BH16 ...118 C6
Shore La
  Lytchett Minster & Upton
  BH16 ....117 E5
  Upton BH16 ....118 E5
Short Cl
  Poole BH13 ....147 D5
  Poole BH13 ....147 D5
  Swanage BH19 .....179 C3
Short Cl BH12 ....121 A8
Short Cross DT12 ...206 C6
Shortedge DT10 ....35 C2
Shortlake La DT3 ...169 A8
Shortlands DT5 .....186 F3
Shortlands Rd DT3 .152 B5
Shortmarsh La TA18 .192 F4
Short Rd DT4 ....167 B3
Shorts Cl BH23 .....92 C1
Shortsford Ave DT12 .212 C3
Shottsford Cl ₇ BH19 .178 F2
Shottsford Rd BH15 .119 C5
Shreen Cl ₉ SP8 ....5 F3
Shreen Way SP8 ....5 F3
Shrewsbury Rd BA21 .26 D7
Shrubbery La DT4 ...180 C8
Shute La DT11 ......37 F1
Shute Lake La ₁₁ TA18 .191 F4
Shute's La SP8 .....9 C8
Sidings The DT9 ....194 C6
Sidmouth Rd DT7 ..96 A5
Sidney Gdns ₂ BH9 .90 B4
Sidney Smith Ct BH17 .87 E2
Silchester Cl BH17 .88 C6
Silchester Pl SO22 .126 B3
Silk House Barton DT10 .33 C8
Sillen La SP6 ....190 B6
Silton Rd SP8 ....5 F3
Silver Birch Cl BH13 .121 A4
Silver Bsns Pk BH23 .124 C7
Silverdale BH25 ....127 B7
Silverdale Cl BH18 .86 E4
Silverdale Cres ₂ SP6 .42 C6
Silver Hill SO23 ....126 E5
Silver St
  ₅ Christchurch BH23 .124 B5
  Crewkerne TA18 ...192 B3
  Lyme Regis DT7 ...96 B5
  Overcombe/Preston DT3 .153 D2
  ₂ Stofold BA22 .....193 F8
  Yeovil BA20 ....27 C5
Silver Way BH23 ...123 F7
Silverwood Cl
  Merley BH21 ....59 D2
  Winchester SO22 ...126 C3
Silwood Cl SO22 ...126 C3
Simmonds Cl BH15 .119 D5
Simonds Ct ₆ SO23 .126 E8
Simons Cl BH15 ....119 D5
Simsay Fields ₇ DT2 .207 D4
Sinclair Cl ₂ BH20 .89 C2
Singleton Dr BH10 .89 C2
Sir John Colfox Sch The
  ....68 C1
Sir Richard Hull Rd
  BH20 ....139 D6
Siskin Cl BH22 ......61 B7
Sitterton Cl BH20 ..81 A3
Sixpenny Cl BH12 ..120 F7
Sixpenny Handley Fst Sch
  SP5 ....189 A4

Six Ways Cross BH21 . . . . . 200 E3
Skilling Hill Rd DT6 . . . . . 100 C5
Skilling La DT6 . . . . . 100 B5
Skinner St BH15 . . . . . 119 C1
Skipton Cl BH18 . . . . . 87 A2
Slade La BA22 . . . . . 15 B6
Slader Bsns Pk BH17 . . . . 87 E1
Slades Farm Rd BH10 . . . . 89 D2
Slades Gn DT6 . . . . . 100 C5
Slades La BH10 . . . . . 121 C8
Slape Hill DT6 . . . . . 68 D8
Sleepbrook Cl BH31 . . . . . 45 A6
Sleepers Delle Gdns
SO22 . . . . . 126 C4
Sleeper's Hill SO22 . . . . 126 C4
Sleeper's Hill Gdns SO22 . 126 B4
Sleeper's Hill Ho SO22 . . 126 B4
Sleight Cl BA21 . . . . . 26 E6
Sleight La
Corfe Mullen BH21 . . . . 86 C8
Poole BH21 . . . . . 85 E8
Slepe Cres BH12 . . . . . 120 F8
Slinn Rd BH23 . . . . . 124 E7
Slip Way BH15 . . . . . 119 B2
Slodbrook La SP8 . . . . . 2 D1
Slopers Mead 2 DT11 . . 211 E5
Slough Dro DT2 . . . . . 205 E7
Slough La
Horton BH21 . . . . . 44 A2
Lytchett Minster & Upton
BH16 . . . . . 117 B6
Upton BH16 . . . . . 118 A6
Slyer's La
Puddletown DT2 . . . . 76 F1
Stinsford DT2 . . . . . 108 D6
Smacombe La DT6 . . . . 101 D4
Smallmouth Cl 4 DT4 . . 180 D5
Smishops La DT6 . . . . . 69 D1
Smithfield Pl BH9 . . . . . 89 F1
Smith's Hill TA18 . . . . 192 B8
Smith's La DT2 . . . . . 208 B3
Smithson Cl BH12 . . . . 121 C8
Smith's Terr BA21 . . . . 27 E6
Smithy La BH25 . . . . . 94 F6
Smokey Hole La DT1 . . 108 C1
Smugglers La BH21 . . . . 59 E7
Smugglers' La
Colehill BH21 . . . . . 50 F1
Stourpaine DT11 . . . . 199 A6
Smugglers La S BH23 . . 93 E1
Smugglers Reach BH23 . 93 E1
Smugglers Wood Rd
BH23 . . . . . 93 D1
Snag La DT11 . . . . . 79 E6
Snail's La BH24 . . . . . 47 D3
Snowdon Rd BH4 . . . . . 121 C4
Snow Down Rd 1 DT11 . 199 E2
Snowdrop Gdns BH23 . . 93 B1
Snow Hill BH20 . . . . . 81 B2
Snow Hill La BH20 . . . . 81 B2
Soberton Rd BH8 . . . . . 122 D6
Sodern La DT3 . . . . . 107 C7
Sodom La DT10 . . . . . 21 B3
Solar Ct BH13 . . . . . 121 A2
Soldiers Rd BH20 . . . . 161 C7
Soldier's Ring SP6 . . . . 190 D4
Solent Dr BH25 . . . . . 207 A7
Solent Lo S BH25 . . . . 95 A1
Solent Rd
Barton on Sea BH25 . . 126 D7
Bournemouth BH6 . . . . 124 A3
Swanage BH19 . . . . . 185 C8
Walkford BH23 . . . . . 94 B2
Solent View BH6 . . . . . 124 A3
Solly Cl BH12 . . . . . 120 E7
Solomon Way BH15 . . . . 118 D2
Somerby Rd BH15 . . . . 119 D6
Somerfields DT7 . . . . . 96 A5
Somerford Ave BH23 . . 125 A7
Somerford Bsns Pk
BH23 . . . . . 125 A7
Somerford Ct BH23 . . . 124 E7
Somerford Prim Com Sch
BH23 . . . . . 124 E7
Somerford Rd BH23 . . . 124 F7
Somerford Rdbt BH23 . . 125 A8
Somerford Way BH23 . . 124 E6
Somerleigh Rd DT1 . . . 108 A1
Somerley Pk BH24 . . . . 46 E5
Somerley Rd BH9 . . . . . 122 A8
Somerley View BH24 . . . 55 E8
Somers Cl SO22 . . . . . 126 B3
Somerset Cl SP8 . . . . . 5 E3
Somerset Rd
Bournemouth BH7 . . . 122 F5
Bournemouth BH7 . . . 123 A5
Christchurch BH23 . . . 123 E8
Weymouth DT4 . . . . . 167 A4
Somers Rd DT7 . . . . . 96 A5
Somerton Cl BH23 . . . . 95 D3
Somerville Rd BH25 . . . 94 F3
Somerville Rd
Bournemouth BH2 . . . 121 E5
Ringwood BH24 . . . . . 55 E8
Sonning Way BH8 . . . . 90 B2
Sopers La
Christchurch BH23 . . . 124 A6
Poole BH17 . . . . . 87 B1
Sopley Common Nature
Reserve BH23 . . . . . 91 C8
Sopley Farm Bldgs BH23 . 92 B5
Sopwith Cl BH23 . . . . 125 B6
Sopwith Cres
Merley BH21 . . . . . 59 E2
Merley BH21 . . . . . 59 F2
Sorrel Cl DT4 . . . . . 167 E6

Sorrel Gdns BH18 . . . . . 86 F2
Sorrell Ct BH23 . . . . . 125 B8
Sorrell Way BH23 . . . . 125 B8
Sorrel Way SP8 . . . . . 5 D2
Souter Way DT3 . . . . . 167 D8
Southampton Rd BH24 . . 55 D8
South Annings 2 DT6 . 128 B8
South Ave
Lyme Regis DT7 . . . . . 96 B6
New Milton BH25 . . . . 95 B2
Sherborne DT9 . . . . . 29 F4
Southbourne Coast Rd
BH6 . . . . . 123 E3
Southbourne Cross Roads 5
BH6 . . . . . 123 E3
Southbourne Gr BH6 . . . 123 C4
Southbourne Lane Central 6
BH6 . . . . . 123 D4
Southbourne Lane E 9
BH6 . . . . . 123 C4
Southbourne Lane W
BH6 . . . . . 123 B4
Southbourne Overcliff Dr
BH6 . . . . . 123 C3
Southbourne Rd BH6 . . . 123 C4
Southbourne Sands BH6 123 D3
Southbrook
Bere Regis BH20 . . . . 81 B2
Mere BA12 . . . . . 3 B6
Southbrook Cl BH17 . . . . 88 A2
Southbrook Gdns 2 BA12 . 3 B4
Southcliffe Rd
Barton on Sea BH25 . . 126 D7
Christchurch BH23 . . . 125 C6
South Cliff Rd
Bournemouth BH6 . . . 121 F2
Swanage BH19 . . . . . 179 C1
Southcote Rd BH1 . . . . 122 C4
South Cres DT11 . . . . . 199 E3
Southcroft Rd DT4 . . . . 166 F1
South Cswy BH20 . . . . 142 E2
South Ct DT9 . . . . . 29 F4
South Ct Ave DT1 . . . . 135 A8
Southdown Ave DT3 . . . 168 A6
Southdown Ct 1 BH23 . 124 F8
Southdown Rd DT4 . . . . 180 B8
Southdown Way BH22 . . 53 A1
South Dr
Cattistock DT2 . . . . . 206 C2
West Moors BH24 . . . . 62 B7
South Dro DT2 . . . . . 53 C1
Southernhay Rd BH31 . . 45 D6
Southern La
Barton on Sea BH25 . . 126 F8
Old Milton BH25 . . . . 94 F1
Southern Oaks BH25 . . . 94 F1
Southern Rd BH6 . . . . . 123 C4
Southey Rd BH23 . . . . 124 F7
South Farm Cl DT11 . . . 200 A6
Southfield Ave DT4 . . . 167 D6
Southfield Mews 4 BH24 . 55 C6
Southgate St SO23 . . . 126 D5
Southgate Villas SO23 . 126 D5
South Haven Cl BH16 . . 118 B3
South Lawns DT6 . . . . 100 D5
South Lawns Wlk BH25 . 94 F1
South Lodge BH24 . . . . 147 G7
South Mead BH20 . . . . 81 A2
Southmead Cres 20
TA18 . . . . . 191 F4
Southmead La BA8 . . . . 19 B3
South Mill La DT6 . . . . 100 D5
Southover DT6 . . . . . 128 B7
Southover Cl DT11 . . . . 212 D1
Southover La DT2 . . . . 79 C1
South Par DT3 . . . . . 167 E2
South Park Rd BH21 . . . 121 A8
South Poorton Nature
Reserve DT6 . . . . . 70 A8
South Rd
Bournemouth BH1 . . . 122 E5
Corfe Mullen BH21 . . . 86 E6
Poole BH15 . . . . . 119 C2
Swanage BH19 . . . . . 179 A2
Weymouth DT4 . . . . . 167 E3
South Road Comb Sch
BH15 . . . . . 119 C2
South Somerset Mus of
BA20 . . . . . 27 C4
South St
Arne DT6 . . . . . 142 E3
Bridport DT6 . . . . . 100 D6
Corfe Castle BH20 . . . 176 F3
Crewkerne TA18 . . . . 191 F4
Dorchester DT1 . . . . 108 A1
4 Gillingham SP8 . . . . 5 F1
Hinton St George TA17 . 191 D7

South St continued
Kington Magna SP8 . . . . . 9 C2
Leigh DT9 . . . . . 194 E3
Milborne Port DT9 . . . . 17 D2
Poole DT6 . . . . . 30 B5
Yeovil BA20 . . . . . 27 C4
South View
Bournemouth BH2 . . . 121 F5
Bradford Abbas DT9 . . . 28 D2
Piddletrenthide DT2 . . 208 C1
Winchester SO22 . . . . 126 C6
South View Park Homes
SO22 . . . . . 126 A1
South View Pl 10 BH2 . 121 E3
Southview Rd DT4 . . . . 167 B3
South View Rd
Christchurch BH23 . . . 124 A6
Poole BH12 . . . . . 17 C2
Southville BA21 . . . . . 27 E5
Southville Rd BH5 . . . . 123 B5
South Walks Rd DT1 . . 108 A1
South Way DT5 . . . . . 186 D1
South Way BA21 . . . . . 27 B7
Southway BA21 . . . . . 27 B7
Southway DT5 . . . . . 186 D1
Southwell 6 DT5 . . . . 186 D1
Southwell Prim Sch DT5 186 E1
Southwell Rd DT5 . . . . 187 A2
South Western Bsns Pk
DT9 . . . . . 30 B5
South Western Cres
BH14 . . . . . 120 B2
Southwick Pl BH6 . . . . 123 C7
Southwick Rd BH6 . . . . 123 C6
South Wlk DT6 . . . . . 100 C6
Southwood Ave
Bournemouth BH6 . . . 123 F7
Walkford BH23 . . . . . 94 B1
Southwood Cl
Ferndown BH22 . . . . 61 C6
Walkford BH23 . . . . . 94 A1
Southwoods BA20 . . . . 27 C3
Sovell Down Nature Reserve
BH21 . . . . . 201 A5
Sovereign Bsns Ctr
BH15 . . . . . 119 B6
Sovereign Cl BH7 . . . . 122 F8
Sovereign Ctr 6 BH1 . . 122 E4
Spa Ave DT3 . . . . . 167 C7
Spadger La BH21 . . . . 136 A8
Sparacre Gdns DT6 . . . 100 D7
Spa Rd DT3 . . . . . 167 B7
Sparkford Cl
Bournemouth BH7 . . . 123 B8
Winchester SO22 . . . . 126 C4
Sparkford Rd SO22 . . . 126 C5
Sparkford Croft SP8 . . . 11 B8
Sparrow Rd BA21 . . . . 27 D6
Sparrow La TA20 . . . . 202 B4
Specket La DT6 . . . . . 203 A5
Speckwell Dr BH23 . . . 125 B8
Speke Cl 10 TA16 . . . . 191 F7
Spence La DT6 . . . . . 64 F5
Spencer Ct 1 BH25 . . . 95 B2
Spencer Gdns 2 DT11 . 198 C5
Spencer Rd
Bournemouth BH1 . . . 122 C4
New Milton BH25 . . . . 95 B2
Poole BH13 . . . . . 147 F8
Spetisbury Fst Sch DT11 211 D5
Spetisbury Rings (Hill Fort)
DT11 . . . . . 211 E5
Spicer La BH11 . . . . . 88 A3
Spicers Ct 2 SO22 . . . . 126 C6
Spiller Rd DT3 . . . . . 166 D5
Spinacre BH23 . . . . . 127 B8
Spindle Cl BH18 . . . . . 86 F2
Spindlewood Cl 10 BH25 . 95 A1
Spingfield Rd BA22 . . . . 53 A1
Spinners' La DT6 . . . . 101 A6
Spinney Way 2 BA12 . . 3 B6
Spinney Cl 2 BH21 . . . . 52 E5
Spinneys La BH22 . . . . 61 C5
Spinney The
Broadmayne DT2 . . . 136 B1
Lytchett Matravers BH16 . 84 D2
Radipole DT3 . . . . . 152 B2
St Leonards BH24 . . . 54 B6
7 Yeovil BA20 . . . . . 27 C3
Spinney Way DT3 . . . . 95 B6
Spitfire Ct DT5 . . . . . 137 D5
Spittlefields BH24 . . . . 55 C7
Spittles La DT7 . . . . . 96 C6
Spread Eagle Hill SP7 . . 24 C3
Spring Ave DT4 . . . . . 167 D1
Springbank Rd BH7 . . . 123 B7
Springbourne Ct BH1 . . 122 D5
Springbourne Mews
BH1 . . . . . 122 C5
Spring Cl
1 Bridport DT6 . . . . . 68 F1
Verwood BH31 . . . . . 45 B5
Spring Ct BH12 . . . . . 120 D5
Springdale Ave DT6 . . . 86 F5
Springdale Fst Sch BH18 . 86 E4
Springdale Gr DT6 . . . . 86 E4
Springdale Rd BH18,BH21 . 86 E4
Springfield
3 East Chinnock BA22 . 192 F8
Punknowle DT6 . . . . . 91 D2
Springfield Ave
Bournemouth BH6 . . . 124 A4
Christchurch BH23 . . . 91 D2
Springfield Cl
2 Shaftesbury SP7 . . . 13 A4

Springfield Cl continued
Verwood BH31 . . . . . 45 B5
Springfield Cres
Poole BH14 . . . . . 120 B4
Radipole DT3 . . . . . 152 B3
8 Sherborne DT9 . . . . 30 A5
Springfield Gdns BH25 . 95 D2
Springfield Pl BA21 . . . 27 A7
Springfield Rd
Milborne Port DT9 . . . 17 D3
Poole BH14 . . . . . 120 A4
Radipole DT3 . . . . . 152 B3
4 Swanage BH19 . . . 179 B2
Verwood BH31 . . . . . 45 B5
Yeovil BA21 . . . . . 27 A7
Springfields
Alderholt SP6 . . . . . 51 B4
Stalbridge DT10 . . . . 33 E8
Spring Gdns
1 Fortuneswell DT5 . . 186 F7
Poole BH12 . . . . . 120 D5
West Knighton DT2 . . 136 C3
Weymouth DT4 . . . . . 167 B3
Spring Gr DT2 . . . . . 196 A1
Springham Wlk 18 DT1 . 107 D1
Springhill Gdns DT7 . . . 96 B6
Spring La
Longburton DT9 . . . . 195 B2
New Milton BH25 . . . . 95 D2
Sandford Orcas DT9 . . 15 F5
3 Yeovil BA21 . . . . . 167 D1
Spring Rd
Bournemouth BH1 . . . 122 C5
Weymouth DT4 . . . . . 167 D1
6 Weymouth DT4 . . . 167 E4
Spring St BH20 . . . . . 140 B2
Springvale Ave
Bournemouth BH7 . . . 122 F8
Bournemouth BH7 . . . 123 A8
Springwater Cl BH11 . . 89 A3
Springwater Ct BH23 . . 124 D6
Springwater Dr BH23 . . 124 D6
Springwater Rd BH11 . . 89 A3
Springwell Cl BH20 . . . 177 E6
Spruce Cl BH17 . . . . . 86 E1
Spur Cl BH1 . . . . . 60 C6
Spurgeon Rd BH7 . . . . 123 B6
Spur Hill Ave BH14 . . . 120 D3
Spur Rd BH14 . . . . . 120 D3
Spy Cl 6 BH16 . . . . . 84 D8
Spyway Rd DT11 . . . . 102 C7
Square Cl BH21 . . . . . 60 F3
Square The
Bournemouth BH2 . . . 121 F5
2 Cattistock DT2 . . . 206 C2
1 Corfe Castle BH20 . 162 A1
Cranborne BH21 . . . . 40 B7
4 Gillingham SP8 . . . . 5 F1
Langton Herring DT3 . . 150 C1
Mere BA12 . . . . . 3 A5
Milborne St Andrew DT11 . 79 E8
Powerstock DT6 . . . . 70 B4
Puddletown DT2 . . . . 78 B1
West Moors BH21 . . . . 62 B8
Wimborne Minster BH21 . 59 D3
Winchester SO23 . . . 126 E5
Squirrel's Cl BH21 . . . . 91 D2
Squirrel's Cnr BH21 . . . 189 D1
Squirrel Wlk BH31 . . . . 45 B5
Stables The BH23 . . . . 123 F7
Stacey Cl BH21 . . . . . 120 C7
Stacey Gdns BH8 . . . . 90 E2
Stadium Way BH15 . . . 119 C3
Stafford Cl DT11 . . . . 136 C4
Stafford Gdns DT2 . . . 136 A8
Stafford Rd
Bournemouth BH1 . . . 122 A4
Swanage BH19 . . . . . 179 C2
Stag Cl BH25 . . . . . 95 B4
Stagswood Rd BH11 . . 44 F6
Stainers Mead SP7 . . . 7 B1
Stainforth Cl DT4 . . . . 166 F3
Stake Ford Cross DT9 . 194 E4
Staker's Cross TA18 . . 191 B2
Staker's Cross La TA18 . 191 B2
Stakes La DT9 . . . . . 195 E6
Stalbridge CE Prim Sch
DT10 . . . . . 33 D8
Stalbridge Dr DT10 . . . 33 D8
Stalbridge Dr BH20 . . . 61 D4
Stalbridge La DT10 . . . 34 F2
Stalbridge Rd BH20 . . . 61 D4
Stalbridge Trad Est DT10 . 33 E8
Stalham Rd BH12 . . . . 120 F6
Stallards La DT7 . . . . . 96 B6
Stallon Cl DT2 . . . . . 136 A8
Stammery Hill EX13 . . 202 A1
Stanbarrow Cl BH20 . . . 81 A2
Standfast Wlk 16 DT1 . 135 B8
Standpitts La SP8 . . . . 5 F3
Stanfield Cl DT1 . . . . . 120 D7
Stanfield Rd
Bournemouth BH9 . . . 89 F2
Ferndown BH22 . . . . 61 C6
Poole BH12 . . . . . 120 D7
Stanier Rd DT3 . . . . . 153 B1
Staniforth Ct BH23 . . . 124 A8
Stanley Cl BH31 . . . . . 45 C5
Stanley Ct
Bournemouth BH1 . . . 122 C4
Poole BH15 . . . . . 119 C6
Stanley Green Cres
BH15 . . . . . 119 C6

Stanley Green Fst Sch
BH15 . . . . . 119 C6
Stanley Green Ind Est
BH15 . . . . . 119 B5
Stanley Green Rd
Poole BH15 . . . . . 119 C5
Poole BH15 . . . . . 119 C6
Stanley Pearce Ho BH17 . 87 C1
Stanley Pk (Cvn & Chalet
Site) BH25 . . . . . 95 C6
Stanley Rd
Bournemouth BH1 . . . 122 C5
Christchurch BH23 . . . 126 A8
Poole BH15 . . . . . 119 C1
Stanley St 1 DT4 . . . . 167 D4
Stanmore La SO22 . . . 126 B3
Stanmore Prim Sch
SO22 . . . . . 126 C3
Stannington Cl BH25 . . 95 B2
Stanpit BH23 . . . . . 124 E5
Stanstead Rd DT2 . . . . 23 A8
Stanton Cl DT1 . . . . . 212 D5
Stanton Lacy 12 BH13 . 147 F4
Stanton Rd BH10 . . . . 89 C2
Stapehill Cres BH21 . . . 60 C5
Stapehill Mus & Gdns
BH21 . . . . . 60 E5
Stapehill Rd BH21 . . . . 60 F4
Staple Close La BH15 . . 119 C6
Staple Cross BH23 . . . 124 E3
Staplecross La BH23 . . 124 D8
Stapleford Ave BH22 . . 61 F6
Staple Gdns SO23 . . . 126 D6
Staples Mdw 4 TA20 . . 202 A8
Staples Terr DT1 . . . . 96 C6
Star La
2 Ringwood BH24 . . . 55 B7
Whitechurch Canonicorum
DT6 . . . . . 98 D8
Starlight Farm Cl BH31 . 45 C7
Stars La BA20 . . . . . 27 D4
Station App
Broadstone BH18 . . . 87 A4
Dorchester DT1 . . . . 108 A1
Station Hill SO23 . . . . 126 D6
Station Rd 1 BH19 . . . 179 B2
Station Rd
Alderholt SP6 . . . . . 42 B6
Child Okeford DT11 . . 198 C7
Christchurch BH23 . . 124 A7
Christchurch, Highcliffe
BH23 . . . . . 93 E2
1 Easton/Weston DT5 . 187 A4
Ferndown BH22 . . . . 53 A2
Gillingham SP8 . . . . 5 F1
Henstridge BA8 . . . . 19 B5
Holton Heath BH20 . . 116 C3
Maiden Newton DT2 . . 72 F8
Milborne Port DT9 . . . 17 D4
Misterton TA18 . . . . 192 A3
New Milton BH25 . . . . 95 A2
Poole BH14 . . . . . 120 B4
Poole BH15 . . . . . 119 A1
Sherborne DT9 . . . . 30 D5
Stalbridge DT10 . . . . 19 D1
Sturminster Marshall BH21 . 186 E5
Sturminster Newton DT10 . 35 B1
Swanage BH19 . . . . . 179 B2
Tatworth & Forton TA20 . 202 A8
Verwood BH31 . . . . . 45 A7
Wareham St Martin BH16 . 116 C1
Wimborne Minster BH21 . 59 D3
32 Winchester SO23 . . 126 D6
Wool BH20 . . . . . 140 A2
Station Rd Ind Est
Gillingham SP8 . . . . 5 F1
Maiden Newton DT2 . . 72 F8
Station Terr BH21 . . . . 59 D4
Station Yd SP6 . . . . . 42 A6
Stavordale Rd DT4 . . . 167 C3
Stears La DT10 . . . . . 35 B5
Stedman Rd BH5 . . . . 123 B5
Steels La SP6 . . . . . 190 F2
Steel's La BA9 . . . . . 1 D4
Steel Well La BA8 . . . . 19 B4
Steepdene BH14 . . . . 120 B3
Steeple Cl
Poole BH17 . . . . . 87 D3
Radipole DT3 . . . . . 167 B8
Steepleton Rd BH18 . . . 87 C3
Steep St BA12 . . . . . 3 A6
Steer Rd BH23 . . . . . 124 B8
Stella Ct 18 BH23 . . . . 126 B7
Stem La BH25 . . . . . 94 F4
Stenhurst Rd BH15 . . . 119 C6
Stephen Langton Dr
BH11 . . . . . 88 D5
Stephen's Castle Nature
Reserve BH31 . . . . . 45 C8
Stephen's Reach BH16 . 118 D5
Steppes BH19 . . . . . 178 C2
Steppes Hill BH19 . . . . 178 C2
Step Terr SO22 . . . . . 126 C3
Sterte Ave BH15 . . . . 119 B4
Sterte Avenue W BH15 . 119 B4
Sterte Cl BH15 . . . . . 119 C4
Sterte Esp BH15 . . . . 119 C4
Sterte Ind Est BH15 . . . 119 B4
Sterte Rd BH15 . . . . . 119 C4
Stevens Cl 2 DT11 . . . 212 E5
Stevenson Cres BH14 . . 120 E3

Stevenson Rd BH6 . . . . 124 A3
Stevensons Cl 🖪 BH21 . . . 59 C4
Steward's La DT11 . . . . 56 B8
Stewart Cl 🖪 BH8 . . . . 122 C5
Stewart Rd BH8 . . . . 122 B6
Stewarts Way BH22 . . . . 61 E2
Stibles La DT11 . . . . 197 D3
Stiby Rd BA21 . . . . 27 A7
Sticklands VA Prim Sch
  DT2 . . . . 206 A7
Stileham Bank DT11 . . . . . . 79 E8
Stile La DT7 . . . . 96 B4
Stile Way DT2 . . . . 206 E6
Stillmore Rd BH11 . . . . 88 D3
Stinsford Cl BH9 . . . . 90 B4
Stinsford Hill DT2 . . . . 108 D1
Stinsford Rd BH17 . . . . 87 D1
Stinsford View DT1 . . . . . . 108 C1
Stirling Bsns Pk BH21 . . . . 60 F7
Stirling Cl BH21 . . . . 95 B3
Stirling Ct
  🖪 Bournemouth BH4 . . 121 C2
  🖪 New Milton BH25 . . . . 95 B3
Stirling Rd
  Bournemouth BH3 . . . . . 121 E7
  Radipole DT3 . . . . 167 C8
Stirling Way BH23 . . . . . . 125 B6
Stirrup Cl
  Upton BH16 . . . . 118 D7
  Wimborne Minster BH21. 60 C6
Stoborough CE Fst Sch
  BH20 . . . . 142 E1
Stoborough Cl DT3 . . . . . . 167 B8
Stoborough Dr BH18 . . . . . 87 A2
Stoborough Heath National
  Nature Reserve BH20. . . 143 B1
Stoborough Mdw BH20 . . 160 F8
Stockbridge Cl BH17 . . . . . . 88 B2
Stockbridge Rd SO22 . . . . 126 B7
Stockers Ave SO22 . . . . . . 126 B7
Stock Hill La DT9 . . . . 195 F4
Stock La SP8 . . . . 5 C8
Stockley Rd BH20 . . . . 142 D6
Stokehouse St DT1 . . . . . . 107 D1
Stoke La DT10 . . . . 196 F1
Stoke Mill La DT6. . . . . 67 A8
Stoke Rd
  Beaminster BH8. . . . . . . 204 C4
  Wareham DT4 . . . . 180 D7
Stokes Ave BH15. . . . . 119 D4
Stokes La DT10 . . . . 32 F3
Stoke Wood Rd
  Bournemouth BH3 . . . . . 121 F6
  Bournemouth BH3 . . . . . 121 F6
Stonebarrow La
  Charmouth DT6 . . . . 97 C7
  Hawkchurch EX13 . . . . . 202 D3
  Stanton St Gabriel DT6 . . 97 E7
Stonechat Cl
  Ferndown BH22. . . . . 61 B8
  🖪 Radipole DT3 . . . . . . 152 C4
Stonechat Ct BH23 . . . . . . 124 F7
Stonecrop Cl BH18. . . . . 86 E2
Stonedene DT9 . . . . 30 B8
Stone Gdns BH4 . . . . 91 A2
Stonehill Down Nature
  Reserve BH20. . . . . 160 E1
Stone La
  Wimborne Minster BH21. . 59 A6
  Yeovil BA21 . . . . 27 C8
Stone Lane Ind Est BH21 . . 59 B6
Stoneleigh 🖪 BH13 . . . . . . 147 F8
Stoneleigh Ave SO41. . . . . . 95 F4
Stoney Ct SO22 . . . . 126 C8
Stoney La
  East Coker BA22 . . . . . . 193 D6
  Winchester SO22 . . . . . . 126 C8
Stoneylawn DT10 . . . . 21 B2
Stoney Lawn DT11 . . . . 81 D8
Stonyacres DT9. . . . . 194 C6
Stony Down La DT6. . . . . 65 B4
Stony La
  Bishop's Caundle DT9 . 196 A8
  Burton BH23 . . . . 92 C2
  Christchurch BH23 . . . . . 124 C7
  Damerham SP6 . . . . 190 F4
  Holwell DT10 . . . . 196 C6
Stony Lane S BH23. . . . . . . 124 D6
Stopples La SO41 . . . . 95 F3
Stour La BH18 . . . . 87 B4
Stottingway St DT3 . . . . . . 152 B5
Stourbank Rd BH23 . . . . . . 124 A6
Stourcastle Cl 🖪 SP8 . . . . . 5 E4
Stour Cl
  🖪 East Stour SP8. . . . . . 10 D2
  Ferndown BH21. . . . . 60 D4
  🖪 Shillingstone DT11 . 198 C5
Stourcliffe Ave BH6. . . . . . 123 C4
Stourcroft Dr BH23 . . . . 91 E1
Stour Ct 🖪 BH13 . . . . 121 A4
Stour Dr BH20 . . . . 142 D6
Stourfield Inf & Jun Schs
  BH6 . . . . 123 D6
Stourfield Rd BH23 . . . . . . 123 B4
Stour Gdns SP8 . . . . 5 E1
Stour Hill SP8 . . . . 9 E1
Stour Hill Pk SP8 . . . . 9 E1
Stour Mdws SP8 . . . . 21 E8
Stour Rd BH23 . . . . 124 A5
Stourpaine Rd BH17 . . . . . . 87 D2
Stour Park Bsns Ctr
  DT11 . . . . 212 D2
Stour Pk
  Blandford Forum DT11. 212 D2

Stour Pk continued
  Bournemouth BH10. . . . . 89 E6
Stour Rd
  Blandford Forum DT11 . . 212 E3
  Bournemouth BH8. . . . . 122 D6
  Christchurch BH23 . . . . . 124 A6
Stour Rdbt BH23 . . . . 123 F5
Stourton Ct 🖂 BH4 . . . . . 121 C3
Stourton Way BA21 . . . . 26 E7
Stourvale Ave BH23 . . . . . 123 D8
Stourvale Pl 🖪 BH5 . . . . . 123 B5
Stourvale Rd BH6 . . . . 123 C6
Stour View Cl DT10 . . . . . . 35 B2
Stour View Gdns BH21. . . . 58 E1
Stour Way BH23 . . . . 91 D1
Stour Wlk
  Bournemouth BH8. . . . . . 90 D4
  Wimborne Minster BH21. 59 D3
Stourwood Ave BH6. . . . . . 123 D4
Stourwood Mans 🖪 BH6 123 C4
Stourwood Rd BH6 . . . . . . 123 D4
Stowcastle St 🖪 DT1 . . . 107 D1
Stowell Cres BH22 . . . . . . 142 D2
Stowell La 🖪 TA20 . . . . . 202 A8
Stower Provost Prim Sch
  SP8 . . . . 21 F8
Stowey St DT1 . . . . 107 C1
Straight La SP5 . . . . 188 E3
Straits BH15 . . . . 187 A4
Strand St BH15 . . . . 119 C1
Stratfield Pl BH25. . . . . 94 E3
Stratford Ct 🔟 SO23 . . . 126 E8
Stratford Rd BA21 . . . . 26 F5
Strathmore Dr BH31 . . . . . . 45 C6
Strathmore Rd BH9 . . . . 90 A4
Stratton Rd BH9 . . . . 90 C3
Streche Rd
  Swanage BH19 . . . . 179 C5
  Wareham BH20 . . . . 142 D3
Street La
  Longburton DT9 . . . . . . 195 C6
  Sedgehill & Semley SP7 . . 7 F4
Streets La BH24 . . . . 55 E4
Street The
  Charmouth DT6 . . . . 97 B8
  Moreton DT2 . . . . 138 E7
  Motcombe SP7. . . . . 7 B1
  Sutton Waldron DT11 . . . 37 D5
  Winterborne Zelston DT11. 82 F7
Streetway La DT2 . . . . 209 B3
Strete Mount 🖪 BH23. . . 124 E7
Stretton Ct BH14. . . . . 120 B4
Strides La BH24. . . . . 55 A7
Strode Gdns BH24 . . . . 54 D5
Strodes La DT2. . . . . 75 D2
Strongate La DT6 . . . . 68 A7
Stroud Cl BH21 . . . . 60 A6
Strouden Ave BH8 . . . . 122 C8
Strouden Rd BH9 . . . . 90 A1
Stroud Gdns BH23 . . . . . . 124 E6
Stroud La BH23 . . . . 124 E6
Stroudley Cres DT3 . . . . . . 153 C1
Stroud Park Ave BH23 . . . 124 E6
Struan Cl BH24. . . . . 54 C6
Struan Dr BH24. . . . . 54 C6
Struan Gdns BH24 . . . . 54 C6
Stuart Cl BH16. . . . . 118 B7
Stuart Cres SO22 . . . . 126 C3
Stuart La SP8. . . . . 5 D2
Stuart Rd BH23 . . . . 126 B8
Stuart Way DT10 . . . . 100 F7
Stubhampton Bottom
  DT11 . . . . 38 E5
Stuckton St SP6. . . . . 43 D8
Student Village BH12. . . . 121 D8
Studland Beach & Nature
  Reserve BH19. . . . . 164 C3
Studland Ct 🖂 BH4 . . . . . 121 C3
Studland & Godlington
  Heath National Nature
  Reserve BH19. . . . . 164 B6
Studland Rd BH4 . . . . 121 C1
Studland Way DT3 . . . . . . 167 B8
Studley Cl BH23 . . . . 126 C8
Studley Dr BH25 . . . . 126 D8
Sturminster L Ctr DT10 . . 35 B3
Sturminster Marshall Fst Sch
  BH21 . . . . 56 E4
Sturminster Newton High
  Sch DT10 . . . . 35 B3
Sturminster Newton Mus
  DT10 . . . . 35 B2
Sturminster Rd 🖪 BH9 . . . 90 B4
Sturt La BH20 . . . . 81 D4
Styles Cl 🖪 DT8 . . . . 204 C4
Styles La DT7 . . . . 78 B1
Sudan Rd DT4 . . . . 180 E8
Suffolk Ave BH23 . . . . 91 F2
Suffolk Cl BH21. . . . . 60 C6
Suffolk Rd BH2 . . . . 121 C3
Suffolk Rd S 🖪 BH2 . . . . 121 C3
Sugar Hill BH20 . . . . 114 B6
Summercroft Way 🖪
  BH22 . . . . 53 A3
Summerfield Cl BH23 . . . . . 92 C2
Summer Field Cl BH21 . . . . 60 A4
Summerfields
  Bournemouth BH7 . . . . . 122 F7
  Henstridge BA8 . . . . 19 B5
Summer Fields BH31. . . . . . 45 A4
Summer Hill TA17. . . . . . . 191 D7
Summerhill Rd DT7 . . . . . . 96 C6
Summer House Terr
  BA20 . . . . 27 D4
Summerhouse View BA21 . 27 D4
Summer La
  Evershot DT2 . . . . 206 A7
  Hinton St George TA17 . 191 D8

Summerlands
  Ferndown BH22. . . . . 61 D6
  Yeovil BA21 . . . . 27 A6
Summerlands Hospl BA21 27 B5
Summerleaze Pk BA20 . . . 27 A5
Summers Ave BH11. . . . . . . 89 B6
Summers La BH21 . . . . 92 D1
Summertrees Ct BH25 . . . . 95 D4
Sunbury Cl BH11. . . . . 89 A6
Sunbury Ct 🖂 BH4 . . . . . 121 C3
Sunderland Dr BH23 . . . . 125 B7
Sundew Cl
  Christchurch BH23 . . . . . . 93 C1
  New Milton BH25. . . . . . . 95 D4
Sundew Rd BH18 . . . . 86 E2
Sun La
  Piddletrenthide DT2 . . . 208 B1
  Whitechurch Canonicorum
    DT6. . . . . 98 D8
Sunningdale
  🐴 Bournemouth BH4 . . 121 C3
  Christchurch BH23 . . . . . 123 F6
  🐴 Poole BH15 . . . . 119 C3
Sunningdale Cl BH23. . . . . 89 C4
Sunningdale Gdns BH18. . 87 A5
Sunningdale Rd BA21 . . . . 27 E6
Sunningdale Rise DT3 . . . 153 B1
Sunninghill Prep Sch
  DT1 . . . . 108 A1
Sunnybank Cl DT1 . . . . 60 B6
Sunnybank Rd BH21. . . . . . 60 B6
Sunnybank Way BH21. . . . 60 B6
Sunnyfield Rd BH25 . . . . . 127 A8
Sunnyfields DT3 . . . . 153 C1
Sunny Hill Ct BH12 . . . . . . 120 D5
Sunnyhill Rd BH6. . . . . 123 C5
Sunny Hill Rd BH12 . . . . . 120 D5
Sunnylands Ave BH6. . . . . 123 F4
Sunnymoor Rd BH11. . . . . . 89 A1
Sunnyside
  Ridge BH20 . . . . 143 B1
  West Lulworth BH20 . . . 172 C6
Sunnyside Rd
  Poole BH12 . . . . 120 D6
  Weymouth DT4 . . . . 180 C7
Sunridge Cl
  Poole BH12 . . . . 121 A6
  Swanage BH19 . . . . 179 B1
Sunrise Bsns Pk DT11. . . 212 E7
Sunrise Ct DT1 . . . . 61 D5
Sunset Lo BH14. . . . . 121 A2
Surrey Cl
  Christchurch BH23 . . . . . . 91 F2
  Weymouth DT4 . . . . 166 F4
Surrey Gdns BH4 . . . . 121 C4
Surrey Lo 🖪 BH4. . . . . . . 121 C4
Surrey Rd
  Bournemouth BH4 . . . . . 121 D4
  Poole BH4,BH12 . . . . . . 121 B4
Surrey Rd S BH4 . . . . 121 D4
Sussex Cl BH9. . . . . 90 A4
Sussex Farm Way 🖪
  DT9 . . . . 194 C5
Sussex Rd SO23 . . . . 126 D6
Sutcliffe Ave DT4 . . . . 167 A6
Sutherland Ave BH18 . . . . . 86 E5
Suttil Cres DT6 . . . . 68 C2
Sutton Cl
  🖪 Gillingham SP8. . . . . . . 5 E1
  Overcombe/Preston DT3. 153 C2
  Poole BH17 . . . . 88 B2
Sutton Court Lawns DT3 153 C2
Sutton Cres BH23 . . . . . . 126 C8
Sutton Grange BA21 . . . . . 26 E6
Sutton Hill BA22 . . . . 193 D6
Sutton Holms Nature
  Reserve BH21. . . . . 40 B1
Sutton Pk DT3 . . . . 153 D1
Sutton Rd
  Bournemouth BH9 . . . . . . 90 B1
  Overcombe/Preston DT3. 153 C2
Swaffield Gdns 🖪 DT4. . 180 C8
Swainson Rd DT1 . . . . 199 E4
Swallow Cl BH17. . . . . 118 F4
Swallowcliffe Gdns BA20 . 27 A3
Swallowfields 🖪 SP8 . . . . . 5 F4
Swallow Way BH21. . . . . . . 60 A7
Swanage Fst Sch BH19. . 179 B1
Swanage Her Ctr BH19. . 179 C2
Swanage Hospl BH19 . . . 179 C2
Swanage Mid Sch BH19. 178 E3
Swanage Rd BH19 . . . . . . 164 C1
Swanage Rly BH20. . . . . . 177 D5
Swan Ct 🖪 BH23. . . . . 124 A5
Swan Dr BH23 . . . . 124 A5
Swan La TA18. . . . . 192 B5
Swan La
  Piddletrenthide DT2 . . . 208 B1
  Winchester SO23 . . . . . . 126 E6
Swan Mead BH24 . . . . 55 C3
Swanmore Cl BH7 . . . . . . 123 D7
Swanmore Rd BH7 . . . . . . 123 B7
Swansbury Dr BH8 . . . . 91 B2
Swan St BH21 . . . . 59 A7
Swan Theatre BA20 . . . . . . 27 D3
Sway Gdns BH8. . . . . 90 D2
Sway Rd BH25,SO41 . . . . . 95 C6
Sweep The BH20 . . . . 55 B7
Sweet Hill La DT5 . . . . 186 E1
Sweet Hill Rd DT5. . . . . . . 186 E1
Sweetmans Rd SP7 . . . . . . 12 F4
Swift Cl
  Broadstone BH17 . . . . . 118 F8
  Poole BH17 . . . . 87 F2
Swilletts La DT11. . . . . 203 D4
Swinton Ave BH20 . . . . . . 139 D7
Swordfish Dr BH23. . . . . . 125 B7

Swyre Rd DT2 . . . . 129 E3
Sycamore Ave BH20. . . . . 116 B3
Sycamore Cl
  Broadstone BH17 . . . . . . 86 F1
  Christchurch BH23 . . . . . 123 D8
  Sandford BH20 . . . . 143 B8
  🖪 Sixpenny Handley SP5 . 189 A4
Sycamore Dr
  🔟 Crewkerne TA18 . . . . . 191 F5
  Yeovil BA20 . . . . 27 B2
Sycamore Pl BH21. . . . . 60 D5
Sycamore Rd
  Hordle SO41 . . . . 95 F2
  Radipole DT3 . . . . 167 A6
Sycamore Way BH25 . . . . . 95 D1
Sydenham Cres BH20 . . . 139 F2
Sydenham Rd BH19 . . . . . 178 E2
Sydenham Way 🖪 DT1 . . 108 B1
Sydling Cl
  Cerne Abbas DT2. . . . . . 207 C3
  Yeovil BA21 . . . . 27 F6
Sydling Rd
  Cerne Abbas DT2. . . . . . 207 C3
  Yeovil BA21 . . . . 27 F6
Sydney Pl 🖪 SP8 . . . . 5 E1
Sydney Rd
  Broadstone BH18 . . . . . . 87 A3
  Christchurch BH23 . . . . . 91 E1
Sydney St DT4 . . . . 167 B3
Sylmor Gdns BH9. . . . . 90 A2
Sylvan Cl
  🖪 Gillingham SP8 . . . . 5 F3
  St Leonards BH24 . . . . . . 54 A2
Sylvan Fst Sch BH12 . . . . 120 B6
Sylvan Rd BH12 . . . . 120 B6
Sylvan Way SP8 . . . . 5 F3
Symes Cl TA18. . . . . 192 C4
Symes Rd BH15 . . . . 118 E4
Symondsbury CE Prim Sch
  DT6 . . . . 99 F8
Symonds Cl DT1. . . . . 167 D7
Symonds Rd SO23 . . . . . . 126 E5
Syward Cl DT1 . . . . 108 D1
Syward Rd DT1 . . . . 135 C8

T

Tabbit's Hill La BH20 . . . . 177 F6
Tabernacle La 🖪 BA20 . . . 27 C4
Tadden Cotts BH21. . . . . . . 58 D7
Tadden Wlk BH18 . . . . 86 F2
Tadnoll Nature Reserve
  DT2 . . . . 138 C3
Tail Mill La DT4 . . . . 199 E4
Tait Cl BH17 . . . . 119 E7
Talbot Ave BH3. . . . . 121 C8
Talbot Comb Sch BH12. . 121 B8
Talbot Ct BH9 . . . . 89 F1
Talbot Dr
  Christchurch BH23 . . . . . 93 F2
  Poole BH12 . . . . 121 B8
Talbothays Rd 🔟 DT11. . 135 B8
Talbot Heath Sch BH4. . . 121 C5
Talbot Hill Rd BH9. . . . . . 121 D8
Talbot House Prep Sch
  BH9 . . . . 121 E7
Talbot Manor BH11 . . . . . 121 D8
Talbot Mews BH11 . . . . . . 121 B8
Talbot Mews BH10 . . . . 89 B1
Talbot Rd
  Bournemouth BH9 . . . . . 121 D8
  Bournemouth BH9 . . . . . 121 D8
  Lyme Regis DT7 . . . . 96 B7
Tamar Cl BH20 . . . . 142 A5
Tamlin St BH20 . . . . 143 A8
Tamworth Rd BH7. . . . . . . 122 F5
Tanglewood Ct 🖪 BH25. 95 B3
Tanglewood Lo BH17. . . . 118 F8
Tangmere Cl BH23 . . . . . . 125 B6
Tangmere Pl BH21 . . . . . . 119 E7
Tan Howse Cl BH7 . . . . . . 123 B8
Tank Mus The BH20 . . . . . 139 D5
Tan La SP8 . . . . 2 A2
Tanner's La 🖪 BH20 . . . . 142 E3
Tanners La 🖪 SO23 . . . . . 126 E5
Tannery Rd DT6 . . . . 100 C5
Tansee Hill BH20 . . . . 200 D8
Tantinoby La BH20. . . . . . 142 E3
Tanyard
  Bournemouth BH9 . . . . . 206 A7
Tanyard La DT7 . . . . 12 D2
Tanzey La DT10 . . . . 21 B3
Taphouse La DT10 . . . . . . 203 B1
Tapper Ct BH21. . . . . 59 E4
Tark's Hill DT9 . . . . 194 C5
Tarn Dr BH17 . . . . 118 F8
Tarrant Cl BH17. . . . . 87 E2
Tarrant Dr BH20 . . . . 142 D6
Tarrant Dr BH9 . . . . 90 B3
Tarrants The 🔟 BH22 . . . 61 E3
Tarratt La BA20 . . . . 27 B1
Tarratt Rd BA20 . . . . 27 B1
Tasman Cl BH23 . . . . 125 B7
Tatnam Cres BH15 . . . . . . 119 C5
Tatnam Rd BH15 . . . . 119 C5
Tattershall Gdns 🖪 BH21. 56 D4
Taunton Rd BH9 . . . . 90 A1
Taverner Cl BH15 . . . . 119 D2
Taylor Dr BH8 . . . . 90 D4
Taylor's Bldgs 🖪 BH15 . 119 C1
Taylor's La
  Mappowder DT10 . . . . . 196 E1
  Whitechurch Canonicorum
    DT6. . . . . 98 B2
Taylor Way BH31. . . . . 45 C5
Teak Cl BH13 . . . . 147 H8
Teal Ave DT3 . . . . 166 D5

Teasel Way BH23 . . . . 53 A3
Tecan Way DT4 . . . . 166 F3
Technology Rd BH17. . . . 119 A4
Tedder Cl BH11 . . . . 88 D3
Tedder Gdns BH11. . . . . 88 D3
Tedder Rd BH11 . . . . 89 B3
Teeling Rd DT3 . . . . 167 D2
Teg Down Meads SO22. . 126 A7
Telegraph St DT11 . . . . . . 198 C5
Telford Cl DT3 . . . . 153 A2
Telford Rd BH21 . . . . 61 A8
Temple Cl BH11 . . . . 134 F8
Templecombe La SP8. . . . . 8 E5
Temple La BA8 . . . . 2 B7
Temple Mews BH1 . . . . . . 122 D6
Templer Cl BH11. . . . . 88 F1
Temple Trees 🖪 BH4. . . . 121 C2
Ten Acres SP7 . . . . 13 A3
Tennyson Rd
  Bournemouth BH9 . . . . . . 89 F2
  🖪 Poole BH14 . . . . 120 A3
  Weymouth DT4 . . . . 167 E2
  Wimborne Minster BH21. 59 C2
Tenon Ct BH23 . . . . 124 B7
Tensing Rd BH23 . . . . 124 B7
Terence Ave BH17 . . . . 87 C3
Terence Rd BH21. . . . . 86 C5
Termare Cl BA22. . . . . 26 D6
Terminus St 🖪 DT4 . . . . . 167 A4
Tern Ct BH6 . . . . 123 D6
Terrace La DT8 . . . . 204 C4
Terrace The DT2 . . . . 133 D7
Terracotta Warriors Mus
  DT1 . . . . 108 B2
Terrington Ave BH23 . . . . . 93 E1
Test Ho SO23 . . . . 126 F4
Tewkesbury 🖪 BA21 . . . . 126 F6
Thames Cl BH22 . . . . 61 C5
Thames Mews BH15 . . . . 119 B1
Thames St BH15 . . . . 119 B1
Thatcham Ct BA21 . . . . 27 B7
Thatcham Pk BA21 . . . . . . 27 B7
Thatched Ct BA21 . . . . 27 B7
Theobald Rd BH23 . . . . 91 A8
Thessaly Ct 🖪 BH5 . . . . . 122 F4
Thetchers Cl BH25 . . . . 95 A6
Thetford Rd BH12 . . . . 120 F5
Thickthorn Cross BH20. . 200 D7
Thickthorn La DT11 . . . . . 197 A2
Third Cliff Wlk 🖪 DT6 . . 100 B2
Thistlebarrow Rd BH7 . . . 122 E6
Thistle Cl BH23 . . . . 125 C8
Thomas Hardy Cl DT11. . . 35 B8
Thomas Hardy Dr SP7 . . . 13 A3
Thomas Hardye L Ctr
  DT1 . . . . 134 D8
Thomas Hardye The
  DT1 . . . . 134 E8
Thomas Lockyer Cl BH31. 45 C5
Thompson Cl
  Allington DT6. . . . . 100 B7
  Puddletown DT2 . . . . 78 A2
Thomson Dr 🔟 TA18. . . . 191 F4
Thoresby Ct BH25. . . . . 94 E3
Thornbury 🔟 BH4 . . . . . . 121 C3
Thornbury Rd BH6 . . . . . . 124 A4
Thorncombe Beacon DT6 . 99 D4
Thorncombe Cl
  Bournemouth BH9 . . . . . . 90 B4
  Poole BH17 . . . . 87 B4
Thorncombe Wood Nature
  Reserve DT2 . . . . 109 B5
Thorne Cl BH31 . . . . 45 A3
Thorne Gdns BA21 . . . . . . 26 E7
Thorne La BA21 . . . . 26 E7
Thorners CE Prim Sch
  DT2 . . . . 103 C1
Thornfield Dr BH23 . . . . . . 93 F1
Thornford CE Prim Sch
  DT9 . . . . 194 C0
Thornford Rd DT9 . . . . . . 194 C7
Thornford Sta DT9 . . . . . . 194 C7
Thornham Rd BH25. . . . . . . 95 A5
Thornhill Cl 🖪 DT11 . . . . 134 E7
Thornhill Cres DT4 . . . . 33 D8
Thornicks DT2 . . . . 72 A6
Thornley Rd BH10 . . . . 89 D4
Thornlow DT14 . . . . 108 B6
Thornton Prep Sch 🖪
  DT4 . . . . 167 C1
Thorn Rd BH21 . . . . 59 C4
Thornton Cl BH21 . . . . 86 C5
Thornton Rd BH21. . . . . . . 26 F8
Thorny La BA21 . . . . 26 E7
Thorogood Ct 🖪 BH15 . . 119 E4
Thrasher's La BH20. . . . . . 162 A3
Thread Mill La DT5 . . . . . . 68 D2
Three Acre Dr BH25. . . . . . 95 A3
Three Acre La BH19. . . . . 178 D2
Three Acres DT3 . . . . 207 A2
Three Corner Mead 🖪
  BA21 . . . . 26 C6
Three Cross Rd BH21 . . . . 53 A6
Three Lanes Way DT2. . . . 78 A2
Three Legged Cross Fst Sch
  BH21 . . . . 45 A1
Three Yards Cl DT5 . . . . . 186 F7
Thrift Cl DT10 . . . . 21 B3
Throop Cl BH8 . . . . 91 A2
Throop Hollow DT2 . . . . . 112 D6
Throop Rd
  Abbas & Templecombe BA8. . 8 A3
  Bournemouth BH8 . . . . . . 90 E4
  Bournemouth BH8 . . . . . . 91 A3
Throopside Ave BH9 . . . . . 90 D4
Thrush Rd BH12 . . . . 88 C1

hurmond Cres SO22 . . . . . 126 A4
hurmond Rd SO22 . . . . . . 126 A4
hursby Rd BH23 . . . . 93 F1
hurstin Way SP8 . . . . 5 F3
hwaite Rd DT2 . . . . 121 B5
demill Cl BH23 . . . . 124 A8
iffany Cl SO41 . . . . 95 F4
ilburg Rd BH23 . . . . 124 D7
ilbury Mead 2 BH20 . . . . 177 A7
iley Knap DT2 . . . . 195 E1
iller Gdns BH11 . . . . 89 A5
illycombe Rd DT5 . . . . . . 187 A4
illy Whim Caves BH19. . . 185 C6
illy Whim La DT1 . . . . . . 121 A1
imber Hill DT7 . . . . 59 F2
imewalk Journey DT4. . . 167 E1
imothy Cl BH10 . . . . 89 D5
incleton Cross DT2 . . . . . 110 D5
incleton Gdns BH9 . . . . . . 90 B4
inker's La
  Cucklington BA9 . . . . 4 B5
  Wareham BH20 . . . . 142 E4
inneys La DT9 . . . . 30 C6
in Pot La DT1 . . . . 212 D6
intagel Rd BA21 . . . . 26 F7
intern BA21 . . . . 26 E6
intern La 10 BH11 . . . . . . 107 C1
intinhull Rd BA21 . . . . 27 B4
iptoe Prim Sch SO41. . . . . 95 D8
ite Barn Mus BH19 . . . . . 179 B2
iverton Ct 24 BH4. . . . . . 121 C3
izard's Knap DT6 . . . . 66 B1
oby's Cl DT5 . . . . 186 F3
obys Cl SP7 . . . . 12 E3
odber Cl BH11 . . . . 88 D3
ollard Cl BH12 . . . . 120 D8
ollerdown Rd 4 DT4. . . . 166 F2
ollerford Rd BH17 . . . . 87 D2
oller La DT2 . . . . 206 A1
ollgate Pk SP7 . . . . 12 F5
ollgate Rd 3 SO23. . . . . 126 E7
olpuddle Gdns BH9 . . . . . . 90 B4
olstoi Rd BH14. . . . . 120 A6
omlins La SP8 . . . . 5 E2
omlins La Ind Est SP8. . . . . 5 E2
oms Field Rd BH19 . . . . . 178 B2
onge Rd BH11 . . . . 89 B6
oose The BA21 . . . . 26 E6
ophill Jun Sch DT5 . . . . . 187 A4
opiary The
  Poole BH14 . . . . 119 F5
  Poole BH15 . . . . 120 A5
op La
  Ringwood BH24 . . . . 55 C7
  Stourton with Gasper BA12. . . 1 D7
orbay Rd DT4 . . . . 120 C3
orre The BA21 . . . . 26 E6
orvain Rd BH14. . . . . 120 A5
otmel Rd BH17 . . . . 88 A2
ourney Rd BH11 . . . . 88 E6
out Hill
  East Stoke BH20 . . . . 140 B4
  Shaftesbury SP7 . . . . 12 D3
out Hill La DT2 . . . . 104 E6
ower Rd
  Bournemouth BH1. . . . . . 122 E5
  Poole BH13 . . . . 121 B2
  Winchester SO23 . . . . . . 126 D6
  Yeovil BA21 . . . . 27 D8
ower Rd W BH13 . . . . . . 121 A1
owers Farm BH21. . . . . . . 86 D7
ower St SO23 . . . . 126 D6
owers Way BH21. . . . . 86 D7
own Farm Pl 6 SP5 . . . . 189 B4
owngate Bridge BH23. . . . 124 C6
owngate Mews BH4. . . . . 55 C6
owngate Sh Ctr 1
  BH15 . . . . 119 C2
own Hall La BH19 . . . . . . 179 B2
ownsend BH21 . . . . 56 D4
ownsend Cl
  Bournemouth BH11 . . . . . . 89 B6
  Mere BA12. . . . . 1 C4
ownsend Gn BA8 . . . . 19 B4
ownsend La SP6. . . . . . . 190 A6
ownsend Mead BH20 . . . 177 A7
ownsend Nature Reserve
  BH19 . . . . 179 B1
ownsend Orch 14 BH20. . 191 F8
ownsend Prim Sch BH8 . .91 A2
ownsend Rd
  Corfe Castle BH20. . . . . . 177 A7
  Swanage BH19 . . . . 179 B1
ownsend Way DT6. . . . . . 66 F2
ownsville Rd BH9 . . . . 90 B2
ozer Cl BH11 . . . . 88 F2
racey Ct 8 BH23 . . . . . . 126 A7
radecroft DT5 . . . . 186 F6
radecroft Ind Est DT5. . . 186 F6
rafalgar Cl BH23 . . . . 124 F5
rafalgar Rd BH11 . . . . . . 121 F7
rafalgar St SO23 . . . . . . 126 D6

Treasury Ct 27 SO23 . . . . 126 D6
Treebys Cl BH23 . . . . 92 D1
Tree Hamlets BH16 . . . . . 118 C5
Treeside BH23 . . . . 93 C2
Treetops 9 BH13 . . . . 147 F7
Trefoil Way BH23 . . . . . . 125 C8
Tregonwell Ct 18 BH2 . . 121 E3
Tregonwell Rd BH2 . . . . . 121 E2
Trellech Cl 1 BA22 . . . . . . 26 E6
Treloen Ct 3 BH8. . . . . . . 122 A5
Trenchard Mdw BH16 . . . . 84 D3
Trenchard Way DT3. . . . . 166 D5
Trendle St DT9 . . . . 30 B5
Trent Cl
  Tolpuddle DT2 . . . . 79 D1
  Yeovil BA21 . . . . 28 A8
Trent Dr BH20 . . . . 142 D5
Trentham Ave BH7 . . . . . . 123 B8
Trentham Cl BH7 . . . . 123 B8
Trent Path La DT9 . . . . 29 E7
Trent Way BH22. . . . . 62 A6
Tresco Spinney BA21. . . . . 26 E6
Tresillian Cl BH23 . . . . 94 B2
Tresillian Way BH23 . . . . . 94 B2
Treves Rd DT1 . . . . 134 C8
Trevone 5 BH23 . . . . 95 B3
Triangle The
  Bournemouth BH2 . . . . . . 121 E3
  Upton BH16 . . . . 118 B7
Tricketts La BH22. . . . . 61 F6
Trigon Rd BH15. . . . . 119 D7
Trill La DT9. . . . . 194 B7
Trinidad 1 BH12 . . . . 120 C8
Trinidad Ho BH12 . . . . . . 120 C8
Trinity 2 BH1 . . . . 122 A3
Trinity CE VA Fst Sch
  BH31 . . . . 45 B8
Trinity Ct 10 DT4 . . . . . . 167 D2
Trinity Gdns 20 SO23 . . . 126 E6
Trinity House Lighthouse)
  DT5. . . . . 186 D9
Trinity Ind Est DT1 . . . . . . 59 E3
Trinity La BH20 . . . . 142 E3
Trinity Rd
  Bournemouth BH1 . . . . . . 122 A4
  Weymouth DT4 . . . . 167 D2
Trinity St
  Dorchester DT1 . . . . 108 A2
  7 Weymouth BH1 . . . . . . 167 E2
Trinity Terr DT1 . . . . 167 D2
Trinity Way DT6. . . . . 68 F1
Troak Cl BH23 . . . . 124 E8
Troon Rd BH18. . . . . 87 A5
Trotters La BH21. . . . . 60 B6
Troublefield Nature Reserve
  BH23 . . . . 91 A8
Trowbridge Ct 18 SO23. . 126 E6
Truman Rd BH11 . . . . 89 B6
Truscott Ave BH9 . . . . 90 A4
Trusthams 4 DT8. . . . . . . 203 F5
Trustin Cl 6 DT6 . . . . . . 100 C8
Trystworthy 3 BH2 . . . . . 121 E3
Tuckers Cl BH15. . . . . 118 F1
Tuckers Mill Cl BH20. . . . 160 F8
Tucks Cl BH23 . . . . 93 A8
Tuckton Cl BH6. . . . . 123 D4
Tuckton Rd
  Bournemouth,Southbourne
  BH6. . . . . 123 D5
  Bournemouth,West Southbourne
  BH6. . . . . 123 E4
Tuckton Rdbt BH6 . . . . . . 123 F5
TUC Mml Cottage &
  Tolpuddle Martyrs Mus)
  DT2 . . . . 79 B2
Tudor Arc Sh Ctr DT1 . . . 108 A1
Tudor Cl SP6 . . . . 42 C5
Tudor Ct
  Bournemouth BH1. . . . . . 122 A5
  Poole BH15 . . . . 119 E6
Tudor Gdns DT11 . . . . . . 212 E5
Tudor Rd BH18 . . . . 87 B4
Tulse Hill BA21. . . . . 1 F3
Tuncombe La TA18. . . . . . 191 D4
Tunnel Rd DT8. . . . . 204 C5
Turbary Cl BH12 . . . . 120 D8
Turbary Ct
  Bournemouth BH12. . . . . . 89 A1
  Ferndown BH22. . . . . 61 F6
  Upton BH15. . . . . 118 C8
Turbary Hts BH11. . . . . 88 F3
Turbary Park Ave BH11. . . 89 A2
Turbary Rd
  Ferndown BH22. . . . . 61 F6
  Poole BH12. . . . . 120 D8
Turbary Ret Pk BH11. . . . . 88 E3
Turberville Rd BH20. . . . . . 81 B2
Turbetts Cl BH16. . . . . 84 C4
Turf Croft Ct BH21 . . . . . . 94 B2
Turk's La BH14. . . . . 120 A1
Turlin Moor Com Fst Sch)
  BH16 . . . . 118 C4
Turlin Moor Com Mid Sch)
  BH16. . . . . 118 C4
Turlin Moor Mid Sch)
  BH16. . . . . 117 E4
Turlin Rd BH16 . . . . 118 C4
Turnberry Cl BH23. . . . . . 123 F6
Turner's Barn La BH21. . . . 27 B2
Turner's Cl 5 SP5 . . . . 5 E2
Turner's La
  Marshwood DT6 . . . . 202 E2
  Tarrant Monkton DT11 . . 200 B4
Turnpike Cl 2 TA18. . . . . 192 B3
Turnpike Gn 3 TA18. . . . 192 B3
Turnpike La DT11 . . . . . . 212 C1
Turnstone Cl BH23 . . . . . 152 D4
Turnworth Cl BH18. . . . . . . 87 C3

Turton St 3 DT4 . . . . . . 167 D3
Tut Hill DT9 . . . . 31 E1
Tweedale Rd BH9 . . . . 90 C3
Twemlow Ave BH14 . . . . 119 F3
Twin Oak Pk BH23 . . . . . . 92 D6
Twin Oaks Cl BH23 . . . . . . 87 A3
Twinways La DT6 . . . . 69 B8
Two Droves DT2 . . . . 109 F8
Two Elms BA22. . . . . 14 C8
Two Tower La BA20 . . . . . 27 D2
Twyford Cl BH8. . . . . 90 D3
Twyford Cl 3 SO23. . . . . 126 E8
Twyford Ho BH22 . . . . 61 F6
Twyford Rd BH17. . . . . 88 A2
Twynham Ave BH23 . . . . 124 A7
Twynham Rd BH23 . . . . . 124 A6
Twynham Sch BH23 . . . . 124 A6
Tyberton St 5 DT1 . . . . . 107 F1
Tynedale Cl BH9. . . . . 90 B4
Tyneham Ave BH12 . . . . 120 C8
Tyneham Cl
  Radipole DT3 . . . . 167 B8
  Sandford BH20 . . . . 143 A8
Tyneham Mus BH20 . . . . 174 C5
Tynham Cl DT3 . . . . 124 C6
Tyrrell Gdns BH8 . . . . 91 A2
Tytherley Gn BH8. . . . . . . 90 D2

U

Ubsdell Cl BH25. . . . . 95 A3
Uddens Dr
  Ferndown Town BH21. . . . 51 F1
  Wimborne Minster BH21 . . 60 D7
Uddens Trad Est BH21. . . . 60 E6
Ullswater Cres DT3 . . . . . 167 B7
Ullswater Rd BH21. . . . . . 59 C2
Ulwell Rd BH19 . . . . 179 C4
Umbers Hill 1 SP7 . . . . . 12 C3
Undercliff Dr
  Bournemouth BH1. . . . . . 121 F2
  Bournemouth BH2 . . . . . . 122 C2
Undercliff Rd BH5. . . . . . . 122 E3
Underdown Hollow DT9 . . 28 C8
Underhedge Gdns DT5 . . 186 E1
Underhill
  Mere BA12. . . . . 2 F5
  Pen Selwood BA9 . . . . 1 B2
Underhill Jun Sch DT5 . . 186 E7
Underwood Cl BH17 . . . . . 87 B1
Union St
  Winchester SO23. . . . . . 126 F6
  2 Yeovil BA20. . . . . 27 D4
Unity La 1 BH14 . . . . . . 192 A3
Univ Coll Winchester
  SO22 . . . . 126 C5
University Rdbt BH10 . . . 121 C8
Univ Southampton
  DT10 . . . . 197 D7
Uplands
  Bothenhampton DT6. . . . . 101 A6
  2 Yetminster BH19 . . . . 194 C5
Uplands Ave BH25 . . . . . 127 A8
Uplands Cl BH22. . . . . 62 A8
Uplands Gdns BH22. . . . . . 90 C2
Uplands Inf Sch
  BH8 . . . . 90 C2
Uplands Ind Pk DT11 . . . 212 D6
Uplands Rd
  Bournemouth BH8. . . . . . . 90 C2
  Ferndown BH22. . . . . 53 C1
Uplands Sch BH14 . . . . . 120 C3
Uplyme Cl BH17 . . . . 88 A2
Uplyme Rd DT7. . . . . 96 A6
Upper Brook St SO23 . . . 126 F6
Upper Fairfield Rd 3
  DT1. . . . . 107 F1
Upper Golf Links Rd BH18 87 F5
Upper Gordon Rd BH23 . . 94 A1
Upper High St SO23. . . . . 126 D6
Upper Hinton Rd BH1. . . . 121 F3
Upper Norwich Rd 6
  BH2 . . . . 121 E3
Upper N Rd SP5 . . . . 188 C5
Upper Rd BH25 . . . . 95 C5
Upper Sch La 1 DT11 . . . 212 C1
Upper St 4 DT11 . . . . . . 198 C7
Upper Terrace Rd BH1 . . 121 F3
Upper Water St 4 BA12 . . . 3 B5
Upper Westhill Rd DT7. . . 96 A5
Uppington Cl 8 BH21. . . 201 C1
Uppleby Rd BH12 . . . . . . 120 C6
Upton Cl BH16. . . . . 118 B7
Upton Cross Mobile Home Pk)
  8 Upton BH16. . . . . 117 E7
  Upton BH16. . . . . 118 C7
Upton Ctry Pk BH17 . . . . 118 C7
Upton Ctry Pk BH17 . . . . 118 C7
Upton Heath Est
  Upton BH16. . . . . 117 F7
  Upton BH16. . . . . 118 B7
Upton Ind Est
  Upton BH16. . . . . 117 F6
  Upton BH16. . . . . 118 A7
Upton Inf Sch BH16. . . . . 118 A7
Upton Jun Sch
  BH16. . . . . 117 C7
Upton Rd
  Bournemouth BH17. . . . . 118 F7
  Upton BH17. . . . . 118 F7
Upton Way BH18. . . . . 86 F3
Upway St 2 DT4 . . . . 167 D4
Upwey Ave BH15. . . . . . . 118 C3
Upwey Sta DT3. . . . . 152 C3
Utrecht Cl BH23 . . . . 124 D7

V

Vaggs La SO41. . . . . 95 E6
Vale Cl
  4 Crewkerne TA18. . . . . 191 F3
  Poole BH21 . . . . 120 E4
Vale Lodge BH1 . . . . 122 D5
Vale Mans 4 BH1 . . . . . . 122 D4
Vale Mead DT10 . . . . 196 F3
Valencia Cl BH23 . . . . 91 D4
Vale Rd
  Bournemouth BH1. . . . . . 122 D4
  Poole BH21 . . . . 120 E4
  Stalbridge DT10. . . . . 33 D8
  West Lulworth BH20 . . . . 172 E4
Vale St BH23 . . . . 28 A6
Vale St BA8 . . . . 19 A4
Vaiette Rd BH9 . . . . 90 A3
Vale View BA8 . . . . 19 A5
Vale View Pk SO41 . . . . . . 95 F7
Valiant Way BH23 . . . . . . 125 B7
Valley Bladen DT2 . . . . . . 112 A7
Valley Cl
  Christchurch BH23 . . . . . . 91 E3
  Overcombe/Preston DT3. . 153 D1
  Yeovil BA21 . . . . 27 D6
Valley Ct The SO22 . . . . . 126 B4
Valley of Stones National
  Nature Reserve DT2 . . . . 131 F4
Valley Rd
  Blandford Camp DT11. . . 199 E3
  Bournemouth BH8 . . . . 90 F3
  Bridport DT6 . . . . 100 D4
  2 Crewkerne TA18. . . . . 191 F3
  Langton Matravers BH20 . 187 A6
  Weston Matravers BH20 . . 177 D6
Valley The SO22. . . . . 126 B4
Valley View BH1 . . . . 121 B7
Vallis Cl BH15 . . . . 119 D1
Vanguard Ave DT4 . . . . . 166 F1
Vanguard Rd
  Bournemouth BH8. . . . . . . 90 E1
  6 Poole BH15 . . . . 119 C2
Vantage Way BH12. . . . . . 88 B2
Veals La DT10 . . . . 35 A5
Vearse Cl DT6 . . . . 100 B5
Vecta Cl BH23 . . . . 125 C6
Vectis Rd BH25 . . . . 95 A2
Velvet Lawn Rd BH25 . . . . 94 F4
Venator Pl DT1 . . . . 59 C6
Venn Hill TA20 . . . . 202 F6
Venning Ave BH11 . . . . . . 88 E5
Venn La
  Chideock DT6. . . . . 66 F2
  Stoke Abbott DT6 . . . . . . 203 D2
Venn The SP7. . . . . 12 E3
Ventnor Rd DT5 . . . . 186 F8
Ventry Cl BH13 . . . . 120 F4
Ventura Ctr The BH16 . . . 118 D6
Ventura Pl BH16 . . . . 118 D6
Verity Cres BH17 . . . . 88 A1
Verlands Rd BH21 . . . . . . 153 D1
Vermin La BH20 . . . . 83 B7
Vernalls Cl BH10 . . . . 89 D6
Vernalls Ct BH25. . . . . 95 C5
Vernalls Gdns BH10. . . . . . 89 D6
Vernalls Rd DT9 . . . . 30 B7
Verne Cl DT4 . . . . 167 C1
Verne Common Rd DT5 . . 186 F8
Verne Hill Rd DT5 . . . . . . 187 A7
Verne Rd
  Verwood BH31. . . . . 45 C5
  Weymouth DT4 . . . . 167 C1
Verne Way DT4 . . . . 167 C1
Verney Rd BH11 . . . . 89 B3
Verney Rd BH11 . . . . 89 A3
Vernham Rd SO22 . . . . . . 126 B5
Verno La BH23. . . . . 93 C1
Verona Ave BH6 . . . . 123 D5
Verriott's La DT6. . . . . 66 C1
Verulam Pl 8 BH1. . . . . . 121 F3
Verulam Rd BH14 . . . . . . 119 F4
Verwood CE Fst Sch
  BH31 . . . . 45 A5
Verwood Cres BH6. . . . . . 124 B4
Verwood Ind Est BH31 . . . 45 B6
Verwood L Ctr BH31 . . . . . 45 B6
Verwood Rd
  St Leonards & St Ives
    BH24. . . . . 46 C2
  Three Legged Cross BH21. . 45 B1
  Woodlands BH21. . . . . 47 D6
Verwood Sports Ctr BH31 45 C6
Vespasian Way DT1 . . . . 134 E2
Vetch Cl BH23 . . . . 125 C8
Vian Ct BH25 . . . . 94 F3
Vicarage Cl 8 BH20. . . . . 140 A1
Vicarage Cotts BH8 . . . . . 90 F3
Vicarage Ct 4 BH15 . . . . 100 C8
Vicarage La DT2 . . . . 107 E6
Vicarage Rd
  Bournemouth BH9 . . . . 89 E1
  Poole BH15 . . . . 100 F5
  Verwood BH31. . . . . 45 C5
Vicarage St 9 BA20 . . . . . 27 D4
Vicarage Way BH23 . . . . . 92 D2
Vickers Cl BH8. . . . . 91 B2
Vickery Way BH23 . . . . . 124 D7
Victoria Ave
  Bournemouth BH9. . . . . . . 89 E1
  Radipole DT3 . . . . 152 B5
  Swanage BH19 . . . . 179 A3
Victoria Ave Ind Est
  BH19. . . . . 178 F3

Victoria Cl
  Corfe Mullen BH21. . . . . . 86 D5
  Wool BH20. . . . . 139 D6
  Yeovil BA21 . . . . 27 F6
Victoria Cres BH12. . . . . . 120 D6
Victoria Gdns
  Ferndown BH22. . . . . 61 D6
  Ringwood BH24 . . . . 55 C6
Victoria Gr DT6 . . . . 100 D7
Victoria Ho 5 SO23. . . . . 126 D6
Victoria Hospl BH21 . . . . . 59 A5
Victoria Park Pl 4 BH9 . . . 89 F1
Victoria Park Rd BH9 . . . . 89 E1
Victoria Pl
  Bournemouth BH1,BH8 . . 122 C5
  Easton/Weston DT5 . . . . 187 A5
  Wimborne Minster BH21. . 59 B5
Victoria Rd
  Blandford Forum DT11 . . 212 D4
  Bournemouth BH1. . . . . . 122 C5
  Christchurch BH23 . . . . . 124 E5
  Ferndown BH22. . . . . 61 D6
  Easton/Weston DT5 . . . . 187 B5
  Gillingham SP8 . . . . 6 A1
  Poole BH12 . . . . 120 C6
  Swanage BH19 . . . . 179 A3
  Wimborne Minster BH21. . 59 B5
  Yeovil BA21 . . . . 27 F6
Victoria Sch BH13 . . . . . . 120 F4
Victoria Sq DT5. . . . . 186 E8
Victoria St
  Radipole DT4 . . . . 167 E4
  Shaftesbury SP7 . . . . 12 C3
Victor Jackson Ave DT1 . . 107 C1
Victory Cl BH21 . . . . 53 D6
Victory Rd DT5 . . . . 186 E8
View Rd DT7 . . . . 96 F5
Viewside Cl BH21 . . . . 86 C5
Viking Cl BH6 . . . . 124 A4
Viking Way
  Bournemouth BH6 . . . . . . 124 A4
  Christchurch BH23 . . . . . 125 A5
Village Rd BH23 . . . . 68 F1
Villas The BH25. . . . . 94 F3
Villette Cl BH23 . . . . 92 A1
Villiers Cl SO23 . . . . 126 D5
Vince Cl BH11 . . . . 89 B5
Vincent Pl BA20 . . . . 27 D5
Vincent Rd 1 BH25 . . . . . . 95 A2
Vine Cl BH7 . . . . 123 A7
Vine Cl BH7 . . . . 123 A7
Vine Farm Cl BH12. . . . . . 121 C8
Vine Farm Rd BH12 . . . . . 121 B8
Vine Hill BH21 . . . . 58 C1
Vineries Cl BH21 . . . . 59 F6
Vineries The BH25 . . . . 95 B2
Vineyard Cl BH16 . . . . 84 C3
Vinney Cross DT6 . . . . . . 102 A6
Vinneys Cl BH23 . . . . 92 C2
Violet Farm Cl BH21. . . . . 86 D8
Violet La BH25. . . . . 95 A4
Virginia Cl
  1 Henstridge BA8 . . . . . . 19 A4
  Poole BH12 . . . . 120 C7
Viscount Cl BH11. . . . . 88 D5
Viscount Ct BH11 . . . . 88 D5
Viscount Dr BH23 . . . . . . 125 B7
Viscount Rd DT4 . . . . 166 F1
Viscount Wlk BH11 . . . . . . 88 D5
Vista Marina BH14 . . . . . 147 D6
Vivian Pk BH19 . . . . 179 A4
Vixen Wlk BH25. . . . . 95 B5
Voss's La DT7 . . . . 206 B3
Vulcan Cl DT4 . . . . 166 F1
Vulcan Way BH23 . . . . . . 125 B7

W

Waddock Dro DT2 . . . . . . 111 E3
Waddon Hill (Roman Fort))
  DT2. . . . . 203 F4
Wadham Way DT6. . . . . . . 69 D2
Wadham Com Sch TA18 . 191 F5
Wadmore La BH14 . . . . . 164 C2
Wagtail Dr BH25 . . . . 94 F3
Wain Rd BH20 . . . . 139 D7
Wainwright Cl DT3. . . . . . 153 B1
Wakefield Ave BH10. . . . . . 89 E5
Wakeham DT5 . . . . 187 A4
Wakely Gdns BH11 . . . . . . 89 A5
Wakely Rd BH11 . . . . 89 B5
Walchren Pl BH15 . . . . . . 118 C3
Walcote Pl 30 SO23 . . . . 126 D6
Walcott Ave BH23 . . . . 91 F1
Walditch Gdns BH17 . . . . 100 F6
Walditch Rd DT6. . . . . 100 F6
Waldrens The 5 DT9 . . . . 194 D8
Wales St SO23. . . . . 126 F6
Walford Cl BH21 . . . . 59 C6
Walford Gdns BH21 . . . . . . 59 B6
Walford Mill Craft Ctr)
  BH21. . . . . 59 B6
Walker Cres DT4 . . . . 180 C6
Walkford La BH25. . . . . . . 94 C2
Walkford Rd BH23. . . . . . . 94 C2
Walkford Way BH23. . . . . . 94 B2
Walking Field La BH15 . . 119 C2
Walkwood Ave BH7 . . . . . 123 B8

Wallace Ct BH18..........87 A3
Wallace Rd BH18..........87 A3
Walliscott Rd BH11..........89 A1
Wallisdown Rd BH10...121 C8
Wallisdown Rdbt BH12...89 A1
Wallis Rd BH10..........89 B1
Wall La DT6..........203 D4
Wallsend Cl 5 DT5...186 E2
Walls View Rd BH20...142 D5
Walnut Ave DT1..........198 F1
Walnut Cl BH25..........94 F3
Walnut Gr SO22..........126 B7
Walnut Orch 3 DT3...150 A8
Walnut Rd BA12..........3 B4
Walnut Tree Field Nature
Reserve DT11..........56 D5
Walpole Rd
Bournemouth BH1..........122 C5
Winchester SO22..........126 A3
Walpole St DT4..........167 D4
Walrond Rd BH19..........179 B3
Walsford Rd DT4..........118 B8
Walsingham Dene BH7...122 F8
Walters Dr 13 DT11...199 D4
Waltham Rd BH7..........123 B6
Walton Elm Hill DT10...35 A8
Walton Pl SO22..........126 B3
Walton Rd
Bournemouth BH10..........89 C2
Poole BH15..........120 A6
Wanchard La DT2..........107 C7
Wanderwell DT6..........100 D3
Wanderwell Farm La
DT6..........100 D4
Wanstead Cl BH24...47 D1
Warbler Cl BH16..........118 B8
Warburton Rd BH17...119 E8
Wardcliffe Rd DT4...167 C3
Wareham Ct
Bournemouth BH7..........123 B6
Hamworthy BH15..........118 E2
Wareham Golf Club
BH20..........142 E6
Wareham Hospl BH20...142 D4
Wareham Mid Sch BH20 142 D3
Wareham Rd
Corfe Mullen BH21..........86 D5
Hawkchurch EX13..........202 B2
Lytchett Matravers BH16...84 D3
Lytchett Minster & Upton
BH16..........116 B6
Owermoigne DT2..........155 E7
Wareham St Martin BH16 116 D4
Warmwell DT2..........155 B7
Wareham Sta BH20...142 D5
Wareham Town Mus
BH20..........142 E3
Ware La DT7..........96 A4
Wares Cl 5 DT11...81 E8
Warland Way BH21...86 E7
Warmwell Cl
Bournemouth BH9..........90 B4
Poole BH17..........87 F2
Warmwell Dro DT2...154 D6
Warmwell Rd DT2...137 D5
Warne Hill DT6..........100 F7
Warner Ct 12 SO23...126 E8
Warnford Rd BH7..........123 B7
Warren Ave BH23..........124 F5
Warren Cl
St Leonards BH24..........54 F5
Weymouth DT4..........166 F2
Warren Dr BH24..........54 F5
Warren Edge Cl BH6...123 F3
Warren Edge Ct BH6...123 F3
Warren Edge Rd BH6...123 F3
Warren Hill DT2..........78 C7
Warren La BH24..........54 F5
Warren Rd
Bere Regis BH20..........113 C4
Bournemouth BH4..........121 B2
Poole BH14..........120 D4
Puddletown DT2..........78 B5
Warren Way BH16...116 D2
Warren Wlk BH22..........61 B7
Warrior Ave BA22..........26 C6
Warrior Rd BA22..........26 D6
Warwick Ave BH25..........95 B3
Warwick Cl 14 SO23...126 E8
Warwick Ct 13 SO23...126 E8
Warwick Pl 1 BH7...123 A5
Warwick Rd
Bournemouth BH7..........123 A5
Poole BH14..........120 C3
Washington Ave BH1...122 D6
Washpond La BH19...178 F5
Watcombe Rd BH6...123 D5
Water Cl SO23..........126 C5
Watercombe Hts BA20...26 F2
Watercombe La BA20...26 E3
Watercombe Pk BA20...26 F3
Waterditch Rd BH23...93 A4
Waterford Cl BH14...120 A2
Waterford Gdns BH23...126 A7
Waterford Lodge BH23...125 B6
Waterford Pl BH23...126 B6
Waterford Rd
Christchurch BH23..........126 B7
New Milton BH25..........95 C3
Waterfront Mus BH15...119 B1
Watergardens BH8..........122 A5
Water Hill DT10..........196 F3
Water La
Bournemouth BH6..........123 D7

Water La continued
Durweston DT11..........198 E3
Swyre DT8..........129 C8
Winchester SO23..........126 F5
Winfrith Newburgh DT2...156 F7
Winterborne Stickland
DT11..........210 B7
Water Lane Farm BH10...89 E6
Waterloo Ho BH17..........87 B1
Waterloo La
Silton SP8..........5 B7
Stourton Caundle DT10...33 A3
Waterloo Rd
Bournemouth BH9..........121 F7
Corfe Mullen BH21..........86 B5
Poole BH15..........119 C8
Waterloo Way 3 BA4...55 C6
Watermead
5 Christchurch BH23...124 A5
3 Tatworth TA20..........202 A8
Water Meadow La BH20 139 E2
Watermill Rd BH23...124 A8
Waterpot Hill DT6...204 C2
Waters Edge BH13...147 D6
Watership Dr BH24...55 F5
Waterside BH24..........47 D1
Watermead SO23..........126 D3
Watersmeet 5 SO23...126 F5
Watersmeet Ct SO23...124 B5
Water St
Berwick St John SP7...188 B8
Cranborne BH21..........40 B7
Mere BA12..........3 B5
Waterston Cl BH17..........87 D1
Waterston La DT7..........77 D3
Waterston Manor DT2...77 D3
Water Tower Rd BH18...87 C4
Watery La
Christchurch BH23..........125 A8
Donhead St Mary SP7...24 F8
Halstock BA22..........193 D2
Iwerne Minster DT11...37 F1
Lytchett Minster & Upton
BH16..........117 B7
Radipole DT12..........152 B4
Shaftesbury SP7..........12 E2
Studland BH19..........164 D1
Tincleton DT2..........110 D3
Upton BH16..........118 A7
West Crewkerne TA18...191 D2
Watford La DT16..........68 E2
Watkin Rd 1 BH5...122 F4
Watling St BA21..........26 F7
Watton Cl BH8..........91 A2
Watton Cross DT6...100 B5
Watton Gdns DT6...100 E8
Watton Pk DT6..........100 B5
Wavell Ave BH17..........87 A1
Wavell Rd BH11..........89 B4
Wavell Way SO22...126 A3
Wavendon Ave BH25...126 E8
Wavering La SP8..........5 C2
Waverley 14 BH4...121 C3
Waverley Cres BH15...119 D6
Waverley Ho BH25...95 B2
Waverley Rd
New Milton BH25..........95 B2
Radipole DT3..........167 C6
Wayclose La
Buckhorn Weston SP8...9 B8
Cucklington SP8..........4 B2
Wayford Hill TA18...191 B1
Wayground Rd BH21...58 E1
Wayman Rd BH21...86 E6
Wayne Rd BH12..........120 B6
Waynflete Pl SO22...126 A4
Wayside Rd
Bournemouth BH6..........123 E4
St Leonards BH24..........54 A1
St Leonards BH24..........62 F8
Waytown Cl BH17..........87 D1
Weare Cl DT5..........186 F7
Weatherbury Rd SP8...5 E3
Weatherbury Way DT1...135 A7
Weatherby Castle (Obelisk &
Hill Fort) BH21..........79 F5
Weavers Cl
Crewkerne TA18..........191 F4
Ferndown BH22..........53 A1
Webbers Cl BH20...176 F8
Webbers Piece DT2...206 C1
Webb La DT10..........196 E8
Webbs Cl BH24..........53 F6
Webb's Way BH11...88 F1
Webster Rd
Bournemouth BH9..........90 A3
Winchester SO22..........126 A7
Wedgewood Rd 4 DT4...167 C3
Wedgwood Dr BH14...120 A2
Weeke Manor Cl SO22...126 B8
Weeke Prim Sch SO22...126 B8
Weiner Cl DT11..........199 E2
Weir End Rd 2 DT1...107 C2
Weirs The 3 SO23...126 F4
Weir The DT1..........153 C1
Welbeck Rd BH21...86 C4
Weldon Ave BH11...88 E5
Welland Ct 10 DT1...107 D1
Welland Rd
Wimborne Minster BH21...59 D4
Yeovil BA21..........27 F7
Wellbridge Cl DT11...135 A7
Well Cl BH25..........94 F2
Wellesley Ave BH23...125 C7
Wellfield Hill EX13...202 E2

Wellfields Dr DT6..........100 F8
Wellington Ave BH23...125 C7
Wellington Ct
Bournemouth BH2..........121 D3
7 Bournemouth BH8...122 A5
New Milton BH25..........95 A3
Wellingtonia Gdns SO41...95 F4
Wellington Rd
Bournemouth BH8..........122 A5
Poole BH14..........120 C3
Well La
Poole BH15..........119 C4
Powerstock DT6..........70 B4
Shaftesbury SP7..........12 D3
Well Plot DT6..........101 D8
Wellstead Rd BH20...142 D6
Wendover Cl DT11...94 F1
Wendy Cres BH21...61 F3
Wenlock Ct 9 DT3...124 F8
Wentwood Gdns BH25...95 F2
Wentworth BH14..........147 C7
Wentworth Ave BH5...123 B4
Wentworth Cl
Broadstone BH18..........123 B3
Radipole DT3..........152 E2
Wentworth Ct
Bournemouth BH5..........123 A4
Christchurch BH23..........123 F6
Wentworth Dr
Broadstone BH18..........87 B5
Christchurch BH23..........123 F6
Wentworth Grange
Ferndown BH22..........61 D7
Winchester SO22..........126 C4
Wescott Way BH21...28 A7
Wescott Way BH11...88 E4
Wesley Cl
8 Bournemouth BH8...122 C5
Charmouth DT6..........97 B8
Wesley Grange 4B BH4...121 C3
Wesley Ho
Tricketts Cross BH22...61 F6
19 Winchester SO23...126 E6
Wesley Rd
Poole BH10..........120 C5
Wimborne Minster BH21...59 E5
Wessex Ave
New Milton BH25..........95 A2
4 Shillingstone DT11...198 B5
Wessex Cl BH23..........125 C7
Wessex Ct 22 SO23...126 D6
Wessex Dr
Bradford Abbas DT9...28 D1
Winchester SO22..........126 C8
Wessex Gate BH8..........55 D8
Wessex Gate BH8..........122 C6
Wessex Gate Ret Pk
BH15..........119 B6
Wessex Golf Ctr DT4...166 F5
Wessex Oval DT4...142 C5
Wessex Rd
Dorchester DT1..........107 D2
Poole BH14..........120 A3
Ringwood BH24..........55 D8
Stalbridge DT10..........33 E8
Yeovil BA21..........167 B3
Wessex Ridgeway DT11...39 C5
Wessex Trade Ctr BH12...120 A7
Wessex Way
Bournemouth BH2,BH4...121 C3
Bournemouth BH8..........122 C5
Dorchester DT1..........107 D2
Gillingham SP8..........5 E3
1 Swanage BH19...179 B4
West Allington DT6...100 B7
West Ave BH21..........53 A8
West Bay Cres DT4...180 C7
West Bay Rd DT6...100 D2
West Bexington Nature
Reserve DT2..........129 D2
West Borough BH21...59 B5
Westbourne Cl
Bournemouth BH4..........121 C3
Yeovil BA20..........27 A5
Westbourne Gate 13
BH4..........121 C3
Westbourne Gr BA20...27 A5
Westbourne Park Rd
BH4..........121 B2
Westbourne Rd DT4...167 D5
West Bourton Rd SP8...1 D1
Westbridge Pk DT9...29 F4
West Brook BH21...26 F6
Westbrook Cl BH10...89 D2
Westbrook Rd SP8...10 A8
Westbury
Bradford Abbas DT9...28 D2
Sherborne DT9..........30 B4
Westbury Cl
Barton on Sea BH25...127 B8
Bransgore BH23..........93 A7
Christchurch BH23..........93 F1
Westbury Rd 1 BH14...120 B4
Westbury Rd DT4...55 D7
Westby Rd BH5..........122 F3
West Chinnock Prim Sch
TA18..........192 B8
West Cl
Chickerell DT3..........166 C6
Verwood BH31..........44 F6
West Cliff 3 BH2...121 F4
West Cliff Cotts BH2...121 E2
West Cliff Ct 40 BH4...121 C3
West Cliff Gdns BH2...121 E2
West Cliff Ho 8 BH4...121 D2
Westcliff Mews BH2...121 E2
Westcliff Palms 18 BH4...121 C3
Westcliff Rd
Charmouth DT6..........96 F7

Westcliff Rd continued
Easton/Weston DT5...186 E3
West Cliff Rd
Bournemouth BH4..........121 C2
Bridport DT6..........100 B2
West Close Ho BH6...124 A4
West Coker Rd
East Coker BA20..........26 E1
Yeovil BA20..........27 A2
West Coker VC Prim Sch
BA22..........193 A8
Westcroft Par 7 BH25...95 B2
Westcroft Pk BH18...87 C4
Westdowne Cl DT4...167 A2
Westdown Rd BH11...89 A5
West Downs Student Village
SO22..........126 B5
West Dr
3 Swanage BH19...179 A2
West Moors BH24..........62 B8
West Durlston La BH19...179 B1
West End DT2..........206 C2
West End Terr SO23...126 C6
Westerhall Rd DT4...167 E5
Westerham Rd BH13...121 B3
Westerham Rd BH13...121 B3
Westerleigh 3 BH4...121 C2
Western Ave
Barton on Sea BH25...126 D8
Bournemouth BH10..........89 D4
Poole BH13..........120 F2
Western Gate SO22...26 D7
Western CE Prim Sch
SO22..........126 B6
Western Downland Prim Sch
SP6..........190 F2
Westergate 13 BH13...121 B3
Westerngate
Poole BH13..........121 A2
Poole, Canford Cliffs BH13 147 F8
Winchester SO22..........126 C6
Western St DT9..........28 D7
Westfield
2 Portesham DT3...150 A8
Sherborne DT9..........29 F4
10 Wimborne Minster BH21...59 B5
Westfield Ave BA21...27 A6
Westfield Cl BH21...59 B5
Westfield Com Sch BA21 27 A6
Westfield Cres BA21...27 B6
Westfield Ct BA12...1 F4
Westfield Gr BA21...27 B7
Westfield Inf Sch BA21...27 A6
Westfield Pl BA21...27 A7
Westfield Rd
Bournemouth BH6..........123 E4
Yeovil BA21..........27 A6
Westfields Tech Coll BA21 153 A1
West Gables Cl DT6...100 B7
Westgate SO23..........126 B3
Westgate Pk BH4..........126 B3
Westgate Sch The SO22...126 C7
Westham BH17..........87 E3
Westham Rd DT4...167 D3
Westhaven DT1..........167 A2
Westhaven Hospl DT4...167 A4
West Hayes SO22...126 B5
Westheath Rd BH18...87 B4
West Hendford BA20...27 C4
West Hill
Charminster DT2..........107 D6
Evershot DT2..........206 A7
Milborne Port DT9...17 D2
West Hill Cl 3 BH2...180 B8
West Hill Dr SO22...126 C6
West Hill Rd SO22...126 B6
West Hill Pl 8 BH2...121 E3
Westhill Rd DT4...180 C7
West Hill Rd
Bournemouth BH2..........121 D2
Lyme Regis DT7..........96 B5
West Howe Cl BH11...89 A4
West Howe Ind Est BH11...88 E3
West La
Arne BH20..........142 E1
Hazelbury Bryan DT10...196 E4
Melbury Abbas SP7...24 A3
Mosterton DT8..........204 A8
North Wootton DT9...31 A3
Westlake Cl DT3...152 B4
Westland Rd BA20...27 B4
Westlands Cl BH23...93 A8
Westlands Dr BH13...147 F8
Westleaze DT1..........107 E5
Westleaze Cl DT12...107 E5
Westley Cl SO22...126 B7
West Lulworth CE Fst Sch
BH20..........172 E6
West Mans 3 BH20...172 E6
West Mead DT6..........100 B7
West Mill Cres BH20...142 A7
West Mill La
Castleton DT9..........30 A3
Stalbridge DT10..........33 C7
West Mills Rd DT1...107 F2
Westminster BA20...26 D6
Westminster Cl 2 SP7...12 F4
Westminster Ho BH8...122 C6
Westminster Meml Hospl
SP7..........12 E2
Westminster Rd
Northport BH20..........142 C5
Poole BH13..........121 B1
Westminster Rd E BH13...121 B1
Westminster Rd Ind Est
BH20..........142 C5

Westminster St 10 BA20...27 D..
West Moors Mid Sch
BH22..........53 B..
West Moors Rd
Ferndown BH22..........61 D..
Three Legged Cross BH21...53 A..
West Moors Rd BH22...53 B..
Westmoreland Ct SO41...95 F..
Weston Dr BH11..........122 B..
Weston Hill SP8..........9 B..
Weston La
Closworth BA22..........193 E..
Corscombe DT2..........205 A..
Weston Rd
Colehill BH21..........59 F..
Easton/Weston DT5...186 F..
Weymouth DT4..........167 C..
Worth Matravers BH19...183 C..
Weston St
East Chinnock BA22...192 E..
Easton/Weston DT5...187 A..
West Overcliff Dr BH4...121 C..
Westover Hill DT6...64 F..
Westover La BH24...54 F..
Westover Rd
Bournemouth BH1..........121 F..
4 Dorchester DT1...107 B..
Westover Retail Pk BH9...90 A..
West Pk BA20..........27 B..
West Pk Dr SP6..........190 F..
West Pk La SP6..........190 F..
Westport Rd BH20...142 B..
West Quay Rd BH15...119 B..
Westray Hall BH1...121 E..
West Rd
Bournemouth BH5..........123 B..
Bransgore BH23..........93 A..
Symondsbury DT6...100 A..
Westridge 3 DT9...30 A..
West Row BH21..........59 B..
West Row Mews BH21...59 B..
West St
Abbas & Templecombe
BA8..........18 C..
5 Abbotsbury DT3...149 A..
Bere Regis BH20..........81 A..
Blandford Forum DT11...212 C..
Bridport DT6..........100 C..
Broadwindsor DT8...203 E..
Chickerell DT3..........166 C..
2 Corfe Castle BH20...162 A..
Corfe Castle BH20..........76 E..
Crewkerne TA18..........191 E..
Fontmell Magna SP7...37 E..
Hinton St George TA17...191 C..
Kington Magna SP8...9 C..
Poole BH15..........119 B..
Radipole DT4..........167 D..
Ringwood BH24..........55 B..
Shapwick DT11..........56 A..
Wareham BH20..........142 E..
Wimborne Minster BH21...59 B..
Winterborne Kingston DT11 81 D..
Winterborne Stickland
DT11..........210 C..
Yeovil BA20..........27 B..
West Station Terr BH4...121 D..
West Street Ct 8 BH21...59 B..
West Undercliff Prom
BH2..........121 D..
West View 3 SP7...37 E..
West View Rd
Christchurch BH23..........124 E..
Poole BH15..........119 C..
Westville BA21..........27 E..
West Walks Rd DT1...107 F..
West Walls BH20..........142 D..
West Way
Bournemouth BH9..........90 B..
Broadstone BH18..........86 F..
Easton/Weston DT5...186 E..
Winterborne Abbas DT2...105 D..
West Way Cl BH9...90 B..
West Ways BA22..........192 D..
Westwey Rd DT4...167 E..
West Wlk DT4..........100 B..
Westwoods & Dene Pk
BH25..........94 D..
West Wools DT5...186 E..
Wetherbury Cl DT11...212 C..
Wetherby
Broadstone BH18..........87 A..
Milborne St Andrew DT11...79 F..
Wet La BA12..........3 D..
Weyman's Ave BH10...89 C..
Weymans Dr BH10...89 C..
Weymouth Ave DT1...134 F..
Weymouth Bay Ave DT4...167 D..
Weymouth Coll DT4...167 E..
Weymouth Com Hospl
DT4..........167 E..
Weymouth Golf Club
DT4..........167 B..
Weymouth Marina DT4...167 D..
Weymouth Mus DT4...167 D..
Weymouth & Portland
Sailing Acad DT4...181 A..
Weymouth Rd
Dorchester DT1..........134 F..
Poole BH14..........120 C..
Weymouth Rugby Football
Club DT3..........167 E..
Weymouth Sealife Pk
DT4..........167 E..

Weymouth Sports Club DT3 . . . . .152 B1
Weymouth Sta DT4 . . . . . .167 D4
Weymouth Tennis Club DT4 . . . . .167 C5
Wey Valley Sch & Sports Coll The DT3 . . . . .152 C2
Weyview Cres DT3 . . . . . .152 B4
Wharf Cl BH12 . . . . .120 E6
Wharfdale Rd
  Bournemouth BH4 . . . . . .121 D4
  Poole BH12 . . . . .120 E6
Wharf Mill ■ SO23 . . . . . .126 F4
Wharf Mill ■ SO23 . . . . . .126 F4
Wharncliffe Cl BH23 . . . . .125 F7
Wharncliffe Gdns BH23 . .126 A7
Wharncliffe Rd
  Bournemouth BH5 . . . . . .122 D4
  Christchurch BH23 . . . . .126 A7
Whatcombe Rd DT11 . . . .210 D4
Whatleigh Cl BH15. . . . . .119 C1
Whatley La DT10. . . . . . . .202 C8
Wheat Cl ■ DT10. . . . . . . .197 A4
Wheatear Cl ■ DT3 . . . . . .152 C4
Wheat Farm La DT6 . . . . .166 D6
Wheathill La DT9 . . . . .17 D2
Wheathill La DT9 . . . . .17 E3
Wheathill Way DT9 . . . . . . .17 D2
Wheatland Cl SO22 . . . . .126 B3
Wheatlands DT5 . . . . .186 E1
Wheaton Grange ■ BH4 . . . . .121 D4
Wheaton Rd BH7 . . . . .123 A5
Wheatplot Park Homes ■ BH10 . . . . .89 F4
Wheelers La BH11 . . . . .88 D6
Wheel House La TA20 . . . .202 E7
Wheelwright's Cl SP5 . . . .189 A4
Whetham Mill La DT8 . . . .203 C6
Whetland's La DT6 . . . . . . .69 D1
Whimbrel Cl BH23 . . . . . .125 A6
Whincroft Cl DT22 . . . . . . .61 E7
Whincroft Dr BH22 . . . . . . .61 E6
Whitby Ave BH18 . . . . .87 A2
Whitby Cl BH23. . . . . .91 D4
Whitby Cres BH18 . . . . . . .87 A2
Whitchurch Ave BH18 . . . .87 C3
Whitchurch La BA8 . . . . . . .19 A6
Whitcombe Rd DT8 . . . . . .204 D3
Whitebeam Way BH31. . . . .45 D5
White Cl
  ■ Bridport DT6 . . . . .68 F1
  Poole BH15 . . . . .120 A7
Whitecliff DT11 . . . . .212 C4
Whitecliff Cres BH14 . . . .120 A2
Whitecliff Gdns DT11 . . . .212 C4
Whitecliff Rd
  Poole BH14 . . . . .119 F2
  Swanage BH19 . . . . .179 B5
Whitecross Cl BH17 . . . . . .87 E3
Whitecross Dr DT4. . . . . . .180 E8
White Farm Rd DT10 . . . .121 D8
Whitefield Dr SP8 . . . . .10 D3
Whitefield Rd
  New Milton BH25. . . . . . . .95 A2
  Poole BH14 . . . . .120 A2
Whitehall BH21. . . . . .128 B4
Whitehall Ct ■ TA18 . . . . .191 F5
White Hart Cl DT8 . . . . . .196 D5
Whitehart Fields ■ BH24 . . .55 E8
White Hart La SP7 . . . . .12 E2
Whitehayes Cl BH23 . . . . . .92 D2
Whitehayes Rd BH23 . . . . .92 C1
Whitehead Dr ■ DT4 . . . .180 D5
White Hill DT2. . . . . .110 A8
White Hill DT2. . . . . .79 C2
White Horse Dr
  Overcombe/Preston DT3. . . . . .153 C1
  Poole BH15 . . . . .119 C5
White Horse La
  Hinton St Mary DT10 . . . . .35 B5
  Overcombe/Preston DT3. .153 D2
White Horse Mews DT3 . .72 F8
White Horses BH25 . . . . .126 E7
White House La DT9 . . . . .195 A4
Whitehouse Rd DT1 . . . . . .59 D2
White Knights BH25 . . . . .126 C7
White La DT2. . . . . .205 D7
White Lane Cl DT10. . . . . . .35 B1
Whitelegg Way BH10. . . . . .89 F5
White Lovington BH21. . . . .81 B1
Whitemarsh ■ BA12. . . . . . .3 B4
White Mead BA21. . . . . .26 E6
White Mill DT11 . . . . .56 F6
White Mill Bridge BH21. . . .56 F5
White Pit DT11 . . . . .198 B5
White Pit La SP7 . . . . .24 D4
White Rd BA12 . . . . .3 B6
Whites Cl DT22 . . . . .76 E8
Whitesheets Prim Sch BA12 . . . . .2 A4
Whiteshute La SO23 . . . . .126 C3
White Way
  Buckland Newton DT2. . . .208 B6
  Litton Cheney DT2 . . . . . .103 C3
Whiteway Hill DT21. . . . . .201 B4
White Way La DT10 . . . . . . .21 E1
Whiteways BH21 . . . . .59 E6
Whitfield Pk BH24 . . . . .54 D5
Whitfield Rd DT11 . . . . . . .107 D1
Whithay La DT6. . . . . .68 B7
Whitingham La ■ BH5 . . .123 B5
Whitley Way BH25 . . . . .95 B5
Whitmore La BH21. . . . . . . .44 B7
Whitsbury Cl BH8. . . . . .90 D2
Whittle Rd BH21. . . . . .60 F7

Whittles Way BH15 . . . . . .119 B2
Whynot Way DT3 . . . . .166 D4
Wick 1 Ind Est BH25 . . . . . .94 E2
Wick 2 Ind Est BH25 . . . . . .94 E2
Wick Dr BH25. . . . . .94 E2
Wick Dr BH25. . . . . .94 E2
Wicket Rd BH10 . . . . .89 C5
Wicketsbeer Rd BA22 . . . .193 C6
Wick Farm BH6. . . . . .124 B5
Wickfield Ave BH23 . . . . . .124 B6
Wickfield Cl BH23 . . . . . . .124 B6
Wickford Ho BH23 . . . . . . .124 A6
Wickham Ct BH22. . . . . .61 C6
Wickham Dr BH21. . . . . .86 D4
Wickham Rd BH7 . . . . .123 A5
Wick Hill DT9. . . . . .17 B6
Wick La
  Bournemouth BH6. . . . . . .124 A5
  Christchurch BH23 . . . . .124 B6
Wicklea Rd BH6. . . . . .124 B4
Wickmeads Rd BH6 . . . . .124 B4
Wick Point Mews BH23 . .124 B5
Wick Rd DT9 . . . . .17 C4
Widdicombe Ave BH14. . . .120 E2
Wide St DT5. . . . . .186 F5
Widget Cl BH11. . . . . .89 B2
Widworthy Dr BH18. . . . . . .86 F5
Wightman's Orch DT12 . . .68 F2
Wight Wlk BH22 . . . . .61 E2
Wilberforce Cl ■ SO22 . . .126 A5
Wilderness The DT9. . . . . . .30 C6
Wilderton Rd
  Poole BH13 . . . . .120 F3
  Poole BH13 . . . . .121 A3
Wilderton Rd W BH13. . . .121 A4
Wildfell Cl BH23 . . . . .92 A1
Wildown Gdns BH6 . . . . . .124 A3
Wildown Rd BH6 . . . . .124 A3
Wilfred Rd BH5. . . . . .122 F4
Wilkinson Dr BH8. . . . . .91 B2
Wilkins Way BH15 . . . . . . .119 B2
Willett Rd BH21. . . . . .59 A2
William Barnes Prim Sch DT10 . . . . .197 D8
William Cl BH23 . . . . .94 A2
William Ct BH23 . . . . .126 B7
William Rd BH7. . . . . .122 F7
Williams Ave DT1. . . . . . . .180 C7
Williams Ave DT4. . . . . . . .180 C7
William's Ind Pk BH25. . . . .94 E2
William St DT5 . . . . .167 E4
Williams Way DT11 . . . . . .212 E6
Williford La DT12 . . . . .195 C2
Willis's La TA18 . . . . .192 B4
Willis Way BH15 . . . . .119 B6
Willoughby Cl ■ DT2 . . . . . .78 B1
Willow Cl
  Bournemouth BH8. . . . . . .121 B5
  St Leonards BH16 . . . . . . .53 F4
  Upton BH16 . . . . .118 D5
Willow Dr
  Holton Heath BH20 . . . . . .116 B2
  Overcombe/Preston DT3. .153 B2
Willow Ct BH7. . . . . .123 C6
Willowdene Cl BH23 . . . . . .95 C3
Willow Dr
  Christchurch BH6 . . . . . .124 A5
  Ringwood BH24 . . . . .55 C5
  Wimborne Minster BH21. . .60 C6
Willow Gr ■ DT8 . . . . .204 D4
Willow Lo BH4. . . . . .122 D4
Willow Mead BH8. . . . . .90 D4
Willow Pk BH14 . . . . .120 A3
Willow Pl BH23 . . . . .124 C6
Willow Rd BA21. . . . . .27 B6
Willows The BH25. . . . . . . .127 B8
Willow Tree Rise BH11 . . . .89 B3
Willow View
  Charminster DT2. . . . . .75 D3
  Hamworthy BH16 . . . . . . .118 C4
Willow Way
  Bridport DT6. . . . . .100 F7
  Christchurch BH23 . . . . .124 A5
  Ferndown BH22 . . . . .61 D7
  Motcombe SP7 . . . . .12 B8
  Northport BH20 . . . . .142 D5
Willow Wlk BH25 . . . . .127 B7
Wills Cl La DT22. . . . . .86 D4
Wills La DT22. . . . . .207 D4
Wills Rd
  Poole BH12 . . . . .120 F4
  Swanage BH19 . . . . .178 F2
Willwood Cl BH17. . . . . .87 E3
Wilmslow Rd DT11. . . . . . .166 D6
Wilmur Cres BH15 . . . . . . .119 C6
Wilson Rd BH11. . . . . .212 E4
Wilson Rd
  Bournemouth BH1. . . . . . .122 C6
  Dorchester DT1. . . . . .108 C1
  Poole BH14 . . . . .120 C4
Wilton Cl BH23 . . . . .91 D1
Wilton Dr DT4. . . . . .167 B1
Wilton Gdns BH25 . . . . .94 F3
Wilton Pl ■ BH23 . . . . . . .121 C2
Wilton Rd
  Bournemouth BH7 . . . . . .122 F5
  Yeovil BA21. . . . . .28 A8
Wiltshire Ave DT4. . . . . . . .167 A3
Wiltshire Cl SP8 . . . . .5 E3
Wiltshire Gdns BH23 . . . . .92 F8
Wiltshire Rd BH23. . . . . . . .92 F8
Wilverley Ave BH6 . . . . .90 F2
Wilverley Rd BH23 . . . . . .125 A7
Wilverly Gdns DT11. . . . . .212 E4
Wimborne Fst Sch BH21 . .59 B5
Wimborne Ho BH22 . . . . . .61 F1
Wimborne Minster Model Town & Gdns BH21. . . . . .59 B4

Wimborne Rd
  Blandford Forum DT11 . . . .212 E3
  Bournemouth BH11. . . . . . .89 C6
  Bournemouth BH9. . . . . . .121 F5
  Bournemouth BH9. . . . . . .121 F8
  East End BH21. . . . . .58 F1
  Langton Long Blandford DT11. . . . . .199 D1
  Lytchett Matravers BH16 . . .84 E4
  Poole BH15 . . . . .119 D4
  Poole BH15 . . . . .119 D6
  Tarrant Rushton DT11 . . . .48 A6
  Wimborne Minster DT11. . .59 E6
Wimborne Rd E
  Ferndown BH22. . . . . .61 B6
  Ferndown BH22. . . . . .61 E7
Wimborne Rd W
  Ferndown BH21. . . . . .60 E6
  Wimborne Minster BH21. . .60 B4
Wimborne St Giles CE VA Fst Sch BH21. . . . . .201 E7
Wimborne St BH21 . . . . . . .40 A7
Wimborough La BA22. . . .192 F7
Winbrook Fold ■ DT2. . . . . .6 B8
Winchelsea Specl Sch BH12. . . . . .88 D1
Winchester Cath SO23 . . .126 C5
Winchester Christian Sch SO22 . . . . .126 B3
Winchester City Mill SO23 . . . . .126 C5
Winchester Cl DT4 . . . . . . .166 F3
Winchester Coll SO23 . . . .126 C4
Winchester City Mus SO23 . . . . .126 E5
Winchester Gdns BA21. . . .27 E7
Winchester Pl ■ BH5 . . . .119 C2
Winchester Rd BH25 . . . . . .95 C4
Winchester Sch of Art SO23 . . . . .126 F6
Winchester Sta SO22 . . . .126 B5
Wincombe Bsns Pk SP7. . .13 A5
Wincombe Dr BH22. . . . . . .61 D3
Wincombe La SP7 . . . . .12 F3
Wincombe Pk SP7 . . . . .13 C5
Windermere Cl BH23 . . . . . .92 B2
Windermere Cres DT3. . . .167 B6
Windermere Rd BH3 . . . . .122 A7
Windgreen Est BH21 . . . . . .86 E7
Windham Mews BH1 . . . . .122 D5
Windham Rd BH1. . . . . . . .122 D5
Windmill Cl
  Shaftesbury SP7 . . . . .12 F4
  St Leonards BH24. . . . . . . .54 F4
Windmill La BH24 . . . . .54 F4
Windmill Rd DT11 . . . . . . .212 D3
Windmill Rise ■ TA18 . . . .191 F5
Windslade St ■ DT1. . . . . .107 D1
Windsor Cl
  Bovington Camp BH20. . . .139 E6
  Hordle SO41. . . . . .95 E4
  ■ Mosterton DT8. . . . . . .204 A7
  St Leonards BH24. . . . . . . .54 B5
Windsor Ct
  ■ Christchurch BH23. . . .126 A7
  Poole BH14 . . . . .120 B3
Windsor Ho ■ SO23 . . . . .126 F6
Windsor La SP8 . . . . .5 D1
Windsor Mans ■ BH1 . . . .123 E3
Windsor Rd
  Bournemouth BH5 . . . . . .122 E4
  Christchurch BH23 . . . . .123 E7
  Dorchester DT1. . . . . .107 E1
  Poole BH14 . . . . .120 B3
  Radipole DT3 . . . . .152 B4
Windsor Way SP6 . . . . .42 C6
Windwhistle Cnr SP7. . . . . .13 E4
Windy Cnr DT11 . . . . .200 C1
Wine St ■ BA20 . . . . .27 D4
Winfrith Cres BH14 . . . . . .120 E8
Winfrith Dro
  West Lulworth BH20. . . . . .172 E8
  Winfrith Newburgh DT2. . .156 F6
Winfrith Heath Nature Reserve DT2. . . . . .138 C2
Winfrith Newburgh CE Fst Sch DT2. . . . . .156 F6
Winfrith Tech Ctr DT2. . . .139 B2
Wingate Ave BA21. . . . . . . .27 C7
Wingfield Ave
  Christchurch BH23 . . . . . .93 D1
  Poole BH15 . . . . .119 D1
Wingfield Ct BH1 . . . . .122 C3
Wingfield Rd DT9. . . . . .30 A5
Wingreen Cl ■ DT3 . . . . . .153 B2
Win Green View SP7 . . . . . .13 A3
Winifred Rd BH15 . . . . . . .119 E5
Winkton Cl BH23. . . . . .92 C3
Winkton Gn BH23. . . . . .92 C5
Winkton Ho BH23. . . . . .92 C3
Winnards Cl BH22 . . . . .61 E2
Winniford Cl ■ DT6. . . . . . .99 A7
Winsford Cl BH23. . . . . .93 D1
Winsley Ave BH6. . . . . .123 C4
Winslow Rd DT3 . . . . .153 D1
Winspit Cl BH15 . . . . .118 C3
Winspit Rd BH19 . . . . .183 C7
Winston Ave BH12 . . . . . . .121 A6
Winston Cl
  ■ Christchurch BH23 . . . .124 A7
  ■ Old Milton BH25. . . . . . .95 A1
Winston Dr BA21. . . . . .27 B8
Winston Gdns BH12. . . . . .121 A6
Winston Par ■ BH12 . . . . .121 A6
Winston Pk BH12 . . . . .121 A6
Winston Rd BH9 . . . . .90 A3
Winston Way BH24. . . . . . . .55 D8

Winterborne La BH20 . . . . .82 F5
Winterbourne Cl BH15 . . .119 D4
Winterbourne Copse DT4 . . . . .180 D8
Winterborne Hospl DT1 . . . . .134 F7
Winterbourne Rd BH15. . .119 D5
Winterbourne Valley CE Fst Sch DT2 . . . . .105 D1
Winterhayes Cl BH17. . . . . .87 E3
Winter La DT9. . . . . .15 F5
Winters Cl ■ DT3 . . . . .150 A8
Winters La DT3 . . . . .150 A8
Winton Boys' Sch BH10. . .89 D1
Winton Cl SO22. . . . . .126 D8
Winton Prim Sch BH9. . . . .89 D2
Winton Way
  Bournemouth BH10. . . . . . .89 D1
  New Milton BH25. . . . . . . .95 B5
Winyards View TA18. . . . . .191 F3
Wisbech Way SO41 . . . . . . .95 F3
Wishart Gdns BH9 . . . . .90 B5
Wishay St ■ DT1 . . . . .107 D1
Wistaria Ho ■ BH4 . . . . . . .89 F4
Wisteria Cl BA22. . . . . .26 D5
Wisteria Dr BH31. . . . . .45 E4
Witcham La DT2 . . . . .205 F5
Witchampton CE Fst Sch BH21. . . . . .200 F1
Witchampton La BH21 . . . . .50 B8
Witchampton Rd BH18 . . . .86 F2
Witch Cl SP8 . . . . .10 D3
Witchers La SP8 . . . . .10 D3
Withermoor Rd BH9. . . . . .121 E8
Withies Croft DT5. . . . . . . .187 C5
Withingham Rd BH13 . . . .120 F3
Withybed La BA9 . . . . .4 C3
Witley BH14 . . . . .147 C2
Witney Rd BH17 . . . . .87 D1
Wittey's La TA20 . . . . .202 E8
Wivenhoe Ho BH22 . . . . . . .61 F6
Woburn Rd BA21 . . . . .28 A7
Woking Rd BH14. . . . . .120 C4
Wolfe Cl
  Christchurch BH23 . . . . .124 D7
  Winchester SO22. . . . . . .126 A3
Wollaston Ho BH1 . . . . . . .107 D5
Wollaston Rd
  Bournemouth BH6. . . . . . .123 F5
  Dorchester BH1. . . . . .108 A1
Wollaton Cres BH22. . . . . . .61 C3
Wollaton Rd BH22 . . . . .61 C3
Wollstonecraft Rd ■ BH5 . . . . .122 F3
Wolseley Rd BH12 . . . . . . .120 D6
Wolterton Rd BH12 . . . . . .121 A5
Wolverley Ct ■ BH4. . . . . .120 D6
Wolverton Rd BH7. . . . . . . .122 F5
Wolvesey Castle (Old Bishop's Palace) SO23. . .126 E5
Wolvesey Terr ■ SO23. . . .126 F4
Wonderholm Par BH11. . . . .89 B2
Woodacre Gdns BH22. . . . . .61 E4
Woodbury BH1 . . . . .122 A2
Woodbury Ave BH8 . . . . . . .90 F2
Woodbury Dro DT2 . . . . . .137 C6
Woodbury Hill (Hill Fort) BH20. . . . . .140 E6
Woodcocks Cres BH7 . . . .123 A8
Woodcote ■ BA20. . . . . .26 F2
Woodcote Dr BH16 . . . . . .118 B6
Woodcutts La BH21. . . . . . .50 D7
Woodfield Gdns BH23 . . . . .93 D1
Woodfield Rd BH11 . . . . . . .89 A5
Woodford Cl BH24. . . . . . . .55 D7
Woodford Rd BH1 . . . . . . .122 C4
Woodgreen Dr BH11 . . . . . .88 D4
Woodhayes BA8 . . . . .19 A3
Woodhayes Ave BH23 . . . . .93 E2
Woodhouse La EX13. . . . . .202 A1
Woodhouse Rd EX13 . . . . .202 A1
Wood La
  Bournemouth BH11. . . . . . .88 E6
  Broadwindsor DT8. . . . . .203 B7
  Hinton St Mary DT10 . . . . .35 A4
  Stalbridge DT10. . . . . .33 C7
  Symondsbury DT6. . . . . . .67 D5
Woodlake Cl BH17 . . . . .87 D1
Woodland Ave BH5 . . . . . .123 A4
Woodland Cl BH31 . . . . .45 A7
Woodland Ct BH7. . . . . . . .122 F5
Woodland Gr ■ BH20. . . . . .27 D4
Woodland Mans BH14. . . .120 B5
Woodlands
  Broadmayne DT2 . . . . . . .136 B1
  Hazelbury Bryan DT10. . . .196 F2
  ■ Poole BH13. . . . . .121 A4
Woodlands Cl BH23 . . . . . .118 F3
Woodlands Cl BH23 . . . . . . .93 A8
Woodlands Cres
  Dorchester DT1. . . . . .107 C2
  Hamworthy BH15 . . . . . . .118 F3
Woodlands Ct
  Poole BH12 . . . . .121 B5
  Winchester SO22. . . . . . .126 A8
  ■ Winchester SO23 . . . . .126 E7
Woodlands Dr BH20 . . . . .143 B8
Woodlands Manor BA12. . . .3 A3
Woodlands Mead DT10. . . .20 E4
Woodlands Rd
  Barton on Sea BH25 . . . . . .95 C1
  Mere BA12. . . . . .3 B2

Woodlands Rd Ind Est BA12. . . . . .3 B4
Woodlands Way
  New Milton BH25 . . . . .95 B5
  St Leonards BH24 . . . . . . .54 B4
Woodland Way BH23 . . . . .125 D8
Woodland Wlk
  Bournemouth BH5. . . . . . .123 A4
  Ferndown BH22. . . . . .61 F7
Wood Lawn Cl BH25 . . . . .126 F8
Woodlea Cl SO22 . . . . .126 C8
Woodleaze Cl BH18 . . . . . . .87 B6
Woodlinken Cl BH31 . . . . . .45 A4
Woodlinken Dr BH31. . . . . .45 A4
Woodlinken Way BH31. . . . .45 E4
Woodmead Rd DT7 . . . . . . .96 B5
Woodmill Cl DT10. . . . . .19 D1
Woodpecker Cl BH31. . . . . .45 B5
Woodpecker Dr BH17. . . . .118 F8
Woodpecker Mdw SP8 . . . .11 A8
Woodpeckers SO23 . . . . . .126 E8
Woodpeckers The DT3 . . .152 D4
Woodrising BH13 . . . . .147 B3
Woodroffe Mdw DT7. . . . . .96 A6
Woodroffe Sch The DT7. . .96 A6
Wood Row BH9. . . . . .90 E4
Woodruff Cl BH23 . . . . . . .125 C8
Woodsage Dr SP8 . . . . .5 D2
Woods Edge BH18 . . . . .87 A2
Woodsford Castle DT2 . . .110 B1
Woodsford Cl DT2 . . . . . . .137 D6
Woodsford Rd DT2 . . . . . .138 A7
Woodsford Rd DT2 . . . . . .137 D7
Woodside Cl BH22 . . . . .61 E6
Woodside Rd
  Bournemouth BH5. . . . . . .123 B4
  Ferndown BH22. . . . . .52 F4
  Ferndown BH22. . . . . .61 E6
  Poole BH14 . . . . .120 C3
Woodstock Cl BH14. . . . . .120 B2
Woodstock La BH24. . . . . . .55 C7
Woodstock Rd
  Burton BH23 . . . . .92 D2
  Poole BH14 . . . . .120 A2
  Yeovil BA21. . . . . .27 E7
Woodvale Rd BH9 . . . . . . .121 D8
Woodswater La ■ BH25 . .204 D4
Woodvale Gdns BH25 . . . . .95 C4
Wood View BH21. . . . . .60 A8
Woodward Pl DT4 . . . . . . .167 E6
Wooland Gdns DT4 . . . . . .180 C8
Woolands La SP7 . . . . .12 D4
Wool CE Fst Sch BH20 . . .140 B1
Woolcombe Rd DT5 . . . . . .186 E3
Woolcott La ■ SP8 . . . . .1 D1
Woolf Cl ■ SO22 . . . . .126 A4
Woolmer La BH24 . . . . .47 C2
Wool Rd BH12 . . . . .120 B8
Woolsbridge Ind Est
  BH21. . . . . .53 D6
Woolsbridge Rd BH24 . . . . .54 A4
Woolslope Cl BH22 . . . . . . .53 A1
Woolslope Gdns BH22 . . . .53 B1
Woolslope Rd BH22. . . . . . .53 A1
Wool Sta BH20 . . . . .140 B2
Woolven Cl BH14 . . . . .120 A5
Woolverston SO22 . . . . . . .126 A5
Wooperton St ■ DT4 . . . .167 D3
Wootton Cross BH25 . . . . . .65 C3
Wootton Gdns BH1 . . . . . .122 A3
Wootton Gr DT9 . . . . .30 B7
Wootton La BH25 . . . . .65 B4
Wootton Mount BH1 . . . . .122 A3
Wootton Rd BH25. . . . . .95 D7
Wootton Rough BH25. . . . . .95 B8
Worbarrow Gdns BH12 . . .120 C8
Wordsworth Ave BH8 . . . . .90 E1
Worgret Hill BH20 . . . . . . .141 F2
Worgret Rd
  Poole BH15 . . . . .119 D7
  Wareham BH20 . . . . .142 C3
Worrell Dr BH12 . . . . .120 B3
Worthington Cres BH14. . .120 A3
Worthy La SO23 . . . . .126 E7
Worthy Rd
  New Milton BH25. . . . . . . .95 A3
  Winchester SO23. . . . . . .126 E8
Wortley Rd BH23. . . . . .126 A7
Worwick Cl DT22 . . . . .106 E8
Wraxall Cl BH17 . . . . .87 D1
Wraxall La
  Chilfrome DT2. . . . . .206 B2
  Wraxall DT2. . . . . .206 A3
Wraxhill Rd BA20 . . . . .27 A1
Wren Cl
  Christchurch BH23 . . . . .125 B5
  New Milton BH25. . . . . . . .94 F2
  Ringwood BH24 . . . . .55 C6
  Winchester SO22. . . . . . .126 B3
Wren Cres BH12. . . . . .121 B5
Wren Gdns SP6. . . . . .42 D5
Wriggle River La DT2 . . . .194 E1
Writh Rd DT9. . . . . .31 C1
Wroxham Rd
  Poole BH12 . . . . .120 F5
  Poole BH12 . . . . .121 A5
Wyatts Cl BH21. . . . . .86 C6
Wyatts La BH21 . . . . .86 C6
Wyatt's La BH20 . . . . .142 F3
Wych Hill DT6. . . . . .100 D3
Wych Ridge DT6 . . . . .100 D3

Wychside Cl DT6 . . . . 100 D3
Wychwood **3B** BH4 . . . . . . 121 C3
Wychwood Cl BH2 . . . . 121 F4
Wychwood Dr BH2. . . . . . .121 F4
Wychwood Grange **1**
BH2 . . . . 121 F4
Wycliffe Rd BH9 . . . . .121 F8
Wydford Cl DT9. . . . . .29 F5
Wyelands Ave BH21 . . . . . .60 D5
Wykeham Cl BH17 . . . . . .119 E8
Wykeham Pl SO22 . . . . . . .126 B4
Wykeham Terr **7**
SO23 . . . . .126 F4
Wyke Mark SO22. . . . . 126 A8
Wyke Oliver Rd DT3. . . . . 153 A1
Wyke Prim Sch SP8. . . . . . .5 D1
Wyke Rd
Gillingham SP8 . . . . .5 E2
Weymouth DT4 . . . . .167 B1
Wyke Regis CE Jun Sch
DT4 . . . . 180 C7
Wyke Regis Com & Sports
Ctr DT4 . . . . 180 C6
Wyke Regis Inf Sch DT4. .180 B7
Wyke Sq **7** DT4 . . . . 180 C8
Wynchard Bank **1** DT11 .198 E3
Wyncombe Rd BH5 . . . . . .123 B5
Wyndham Cl BH23 . . . . . . .94 B2

Wyndham Rd
Poole BH14 . . . . .120 B3
Walkford BH23 . . . . .94 B2
Wyndham St BA20 . . . . . . .27 E5
Wyndham View BA21. . . . .27 F5
Wynford Rd
Bournemouth BH9 . . . . . . .90 B4
Poole BH14 . . . . .120 C4
Wynne Cl BH18 . . . . .86 F4
Wynnes Cl **4** DT9 . . . . . . .30 A5
Wynnes Rise DT9 . . . . . . .30 A5
Wynter Cl BH7. . . . . .122 F7
Wytch Pas BH20 . . . . 162 D8
Wyvern Cl
East Coker BA20 . . . . .26 E1
Poole BH12 . . . . .120 D7
Wyvern Ct **24** TA18 . . . . . 191 F4
Wyvern Rd **1** DT1 . . . . . . 107 E2
Wyvern Specl Sch DT4 . . 167 A2
Wyvern Way DT11. . . . . . . .212 E6

Y

Yalbury La DT2 . . . . 137 C6
Yalbury Wood SP8 . . . . .5 E3
Yard La DT6 . . . . 203 D2
Yarmouth Cl BH12 . . . . . . 121 A5
Yarmouth Rd
Poole BH12 . . . . .120 F6
Poole BH12 . . . . .121 A5

Yarnbarton **2** DT8 . . . . . .203 E5
Yarn Barton
10 Beaminster DT8. . . . . . 204 D4
5 Yeovil BA20. . . . . .27 C4
Yarrells Cl BH16 . . . . 118 C6
Yarrells Dr
Upton BH16 . . . . 117 D7
Upton BH16 . . . . 118 B7
Yarrells La BH16 . . . . 118 C6
Yarrells Prep Sch BH16 . 117 D7
Yarrells Sch BH16. . . . . . 118 B7
Yarrow Cl BH23 . . . . 125 B8
Yarrow Ct **1** SP8 . . . . .5 D2
Yarrow Rd BH12 . . . . 120 A8
Yearlings' Dro BH20. . . . . 113 A7
Yeates Rd DT5. . . . . .186 F6
Yeatman Hospl DT9 . . . . . .30 B6
Yeatmans Cl SP7 . . . . .12 D3
Yeatmans La SP7 . . . . .12 D3
Yeatmans Old Mill **10**
BH15 . . . . .119 B1
Yeatminster Rd BH17 . . . .87 F2
Yellowham Hill DT2. . . . . 109 C8
Yellow La DT6 . . . . .69 C2
Yelverton Rd **10** BH1. . . . 121 F3
Yenston Hill BA8. . . . . .18 E8
Yeolands Rd **5** DT5. . . . . 186 E3
Yeo L Pk BA20. . . . . .27 E4
Yeomans Ind Pk BH8. . . . . .90 F2
Yeomans Lodge **6** BH25. .95 B2
Yeomans Rd BH8 . . . . .90 E3

Yeomans Way BH8 . . . . . . .90 E2
Yeo Valley BA22. . . . . .27 F1
Yeovil Airfield BA20. . . . . .27 A4
Yeovil Coll BA21 . . . . .28 A6
Yeovil Coll IT Ctr BA20 . . .27 E4
Yeovil District Hospl
BA21 . . . . .27 C6
Yeovil Golf Club BA21. . . .28 A4
Yeovil Junction Sta
BA22 . . . . .28 A1
Yeovil Pen Mill Sta BA21 . .28 A5
Yeovil Rd
Crewkerne TA18 . . . . 192 A5
Halstock BA22. . . . . 193 D3
Sherborne DT9 . . . . .30 A6
Yeovil BA20 . . . . .27 B1
Yeovil Ski Activity Ctr
BA20 . . . . .27 E4
Yeovil Sports Club BA21. . .27 A7
Yerville Gdns SO41. . . . . . .95 F3
Yetminster Sta DT9 . . . . . 194 C5
Yew La BH25 . . . . .95 C4
Yews The BA12 . . . . .3 A6
Yewstock Specl Sch
DT10 . . . . .35 B2
Yew Tree Cl
Wimborne Minster BH21. . .59 D5
Yeovil BA20 . . . . .27 A2
Yew Tree Ct **5** BH25 . . . . .95 B1
Yew Tree La DT2 . . . . .106 F6
York Ave BH25 . . . . .95 B3

York Cl
Broadstone BH18 . . . . .87 A
Charminster DT2. . . . . . . .107 E
Christchurch BH23 . . . . . 123 F
York Ho **20** SO23. . . . . . .126 E
York Pl
Bournemouth BH7. . . . . . 123 A
7 New Milton BH25. . . . . .95 B
Yeovil BA20 . . . . .27 C
York Rd
Bournemouth BH1. . . . . . .122 B
Broadstone BH18 . . . . .87 A
Dorchester DT1. . . . . .108 E
York Terr **7** DT1. . . . . .135 E
Youngs Endowed Prim Sch
DT9 . . . . .14 E
Youngs Rd BH11 . . . . .89 A

Z

Zamek Cl BH11 . . . . .89 A
Zeals Green Dr BA12. . . . . .2 A
Zeals Rise BA12 . . . . .1 F
Zetland Ct BH4 . . . . .121 B
Zig Zag Hill SP7 . . . . .24 E
Zinnia Cl BH10. . . . . .89 E
Zoar La DT10 . . . . .197 B